MACROECONOMIC ANALYSIS

Second Edition

MACROECONOMIC ANALYSIS

ANALYSIS

Second Edition

EDWARD SHAPIRO
The University of Toledo

Under the Editorship of
WILLIAM J. BAUMOL
Princeton University

HARCOURT, BRACE & WORLD, INC.
New York   Chicago   San Francisco   Atlanta

To the Memory of My Father

ISBN: 0-15-551202-1

Library of Congress Catalog Card Number: 75-102871

Printed in the United States of America

FOREWORD TO
THE FIRST EDITION

The power of macroeconomic analysis as a basis for public policy seems to become ever clearer with the passage of time. Today no student can hope to understand the major public issues or the instruments that are available to deal with them unless he has a thorough grounding in the theory of macroeconomics.

In this volume Professor Shapiro has provided a painstaking exposition that takes the student step by step through the relevant materials, making it easy for him to grasp and retain their logic. Through the use of two-, three-, and four-sector models, Professor Shapiro suggests clearly how the complexity of the real world is likely to affect the abstract concepts, and yet, in doing so, he never loses his reader. With his clear presentation of the accounting framework, his constant provision of supporting empirical data, and his gradual approach to a high level of sophistication, he has written a textbook that should prove invaluable to the student and should constitute an important contribution to education in economics.

WILLIAM J. BAUMOL

Princeton, New Jersey

PREFACE

The objective of this second edition, like that of the first, is to provide a treatment of macroeconomic measurement, theory, and policy designed specifically for the student who starts with only the limited grasp of economic analysis secured in the customary year of introductory survey work. As in the first edition, the treatment provided here does not call on the student to bridge the huge gap between introductory economics and graduate level macroeconomics in the one-semester course usually devoted to the subject. It does, however, attempt to provide him with a solid grasp of what are generally recognized as the fundamentals of macroeconomic analysis.

It is my opinion that a brief, outline type of treatment is of little value to the typical student at this level and that it is worth taking the space and effort needed to spell out the fundamentals clearly and understandably. The favorable reception given to the first edition of this book suggests that many teachers agree. Although a number of changes have been made for the second edition, the rule followed in the first edition is unchanged: Each topic is developed in sufficient detail to be meaningful to the student.

One obvious problem presented by this approach is the tendency for a text that follows it to grow to unmanageable proportions before all the topics that appear to be fundamental at the intermediate level have been covered. Of course, there is ample room for difference of opinion as to what is and what is not "fundamental." One such difference of opinion has led to the first of the major changes in the second edition. At the time I wrote the first edition, I felt that national income accounting was little less fundamental than national income theory, and I attempted to develop the former in almost as thorough a fashion as the latter. However, most teachers of the course apparently feel that a brief coverage of accounting is adequate. The result has been a compromise between these points of view. A large part of the material on national income accounting has been rewritten for the present edition, the number of pages devoted to the subject has been reduced substantially, and even the number of chapters devoted to the subject has been reduced by one. The shortened treatment, however, remains much more than an outline and, I hope, succeeds in presenting national income accounting in a way that the student can understand and not merely memorize.

The next major revision is found in what is now Chapter 9. However much economists may differ as to what should be covered in the intermediate course, they will surely agree today that any discussion of the relationship between consumption and income requires analysis of the major income hypotheses. The chapter has therefore been reconstructed and expanded to include an equal treatment of the permanent income hypothesis, one that was unfortunately neglected in the first edition.

The section on the interaction of the multiplier and the acceleration principle, which was located in Chapter 14 in the first edition, has been relocated in what is, apart from this section, a completely new chapter called "Business Cycle Theory." A discussion of the acceleration principle itself, which is clearly in the area of investment, is provided, as it should be, in what is now Chapter 13 on investment demand, but the discussion of the interaction, which is just as clearly in the area of cycle theory, has been shifted to where it belongs—Chapter 20 on business cycle theory. This essentially new chapter also provides analyses of Schumpeter's innovation theory in its relation to the cycle and of Kaldor's model of the cycle. Following the discussion of the multiplier-accelerator interaction, the chapter examines Hicks's theory of the cycle, which is built on the interaction.

Another change that deserves to be called major is in Chapter 23 on economic growth theory. What was in the first edition essentially a presentation of the Domar model has now been expanded to provide an analysis of the difference between the Harrod and Domar versions of what is commonly described as the Harrod-Domar model. Much more important, however, is the addition in this chapter of a completely new part devoted to the neoclassical model, which has come to be a "must" in any coverage of growth theory. A fairly thorough development of a simple neoclassical growth model is provided.

Dozens of other minor changes have been made throughout the book. Some are a matter of recognizing recent policy developments, such as the demise of the wage-price guideposts and the growing popularity of Friedman's monetary "rule," while others have been made to recognize, although not always to incorporate, important recent developments in theory, such as an interest-elastic supply function for money in place of the traditional assumption of a perfectly inelastic function.

I hope, of course, that all the changes made have been for the better. Responsibility for the final product rests solely with me, but it should be noted that many of the changes, both major and minor, would not have been made except as a result of the numerous suggestions received from teachers over the past three years. To each of them I wish to express my thanks. Especially valuable in this regard have been the detailed reviews provided by Professors Joseph M. Perry of the University of Florida, Walter W. McMahon of the University of Illinois, Robert J. T. Emond of Denison University, and Bruce Gensemer of Kenyon College. My thanks also go to Professor William J. Baumol, who read the substantially revised and completely new sections of the manuscript and provided many helpful suggestions.

Edward Shapiro

CONTENTS

Part II
MACROECONOMIC THEORY: DETERMINATION
OF NATIONAL INCOME AND OUTPUT

Part III
CYCLES, GROWTH, AND STABILIZATION

MACROECONOMIC ANALYSIS

Second Edition

CHAPTER 1

THE BACKGROUND OF MACROECONOMIC THEORY

However we choose to define or delimit the area of study called economic theory, we today typically divide that area into two major branches, most commonly identified as *macroeconomics* and *microeconomics*. Numerous subdivisions are found under these headings, such as monetary theory, business-cycle theory, production theory, wage theory, and the like, but the initial broad separation is into macroeconomic and microeconomic theory.

There are several older terms sometimes used to identify these two branches, but these terms never became a part of the language of economics in the way that macroeconomics and microeconomics have in recent years. The main reason is that until the thirties, there was little need to distinguish the two branches of economic theory, for economists concentrated their attention almost exclusively on what came to be known as microeconomic theory. Macroeconomic theory was clearly the junior partner. A new interest in it, however, began in 1936, the year of the publication of John Maynard Keynes's *General Theory of Employment, Interest, and Money*,[1] the year of the beginning of a change so momentous that some choose to call it the "Keynesian Revolution." With the ferment begun by the ideas in Keynes's book, the economics profession's relative neglect of macroeconomic theory ended. Because a pair of terms was needed, the terms "macroeconomics" and "microeconomics" came to be generally used to distinguish the two major branches of economic theory.

[1] John Maynard Keynes, *General Theory of Employment, Interest, and Money*, Harcourt, Brace & World, 1936. This work will hereafter be referred to as *General Theory*.

MACROECONOMICS AND MICROECONOMICS

"The term 'macro-economics' applies to the study of relations between broad economic aggregates." [2] "Macroeconomic theory is the theory of income, employment, prices and money." [3] Macroeconomics is "that part of economics which studies the overall averages and aggregates of the system." [4] None of these, or any other short statement that could be given, satisfactorily specifies the meaning of the term, and the author of each of those given follows his short statement with several more sentences, paragraphs, or even pages in an attempt to give the term a clear meaning. While they differ somewhat in emphasis, all such explanations bring out the idea that macroeconomics deals with the functioning of the economy *as a whole*, including how the economy's total output of goods and services and its total employment of resources are determined and what causes these totals' to fluctuate. It seeks to explain why at some times as little as 3 percent of the labor force is unemployed and at other times as much as 7 percent or even more, and why at some times there is full utilization of the economy's productive capacity as measured by its workers, factories, equipment, and technological know-how and why at other times a good part of this capacity to produce goes to waste. It also seeks to explain why the total of goods and services produced grows at an average rate of 4 percent per year in one decade and at an average rate of 2 percent in another, and why in some time periods the price level rises sharply, while in others it remains stable or even falls. In short, macroeconomics attempts to answer the truly "big" questions of economic life—full employment or unemployment, capacity or undercapacity production, a satisfactory or unsatisfactory rate of growth, inflation or price-level stability.

In contrast, microeconomics is concerned, not with total output, total employment, or total spending for all goods and services combined, but with the output of particular goods and services by single firms or industries and with the spending on particular goods and services by single households or by households in single markets. The unit of study is the part rather than the whole. For example, microeconomics seeks to explain how the single firm decides the sale price for a particular product, what amount of output will maximize its profits, and how it determines the lowest cost combination of labor, materials, capital equipment, and other inputs with which to produce this output. It is also concerned with how the individual consumer determines the distribution of his total spending among the many products and services available to him so as to maximize his utility. In its approach, microeconomics takes essentially *as given* the total output, total employment, and total spending for all goods and

[2] R. G. D. Allen, *Macro-Economic Theory*, St. Martins, 1967, p. 1.
[3] J. M. Culbertson, *Macroeconomic Theory and Stabilization Policy*, McGraw-Hill, 1968, p. 7.
[4] K. E. Boulding, *Economic Analysis*, Vol. II, 4th ed., Harper & Row, 1966, p. 1.

services and proceeds to examine how output and employment are allocated among various individual industries and firms within industries and how the prices of the various products of these individual firms are established. Microeconomics asks how shifts in consumer spending from the product of one industry to that of another, or from the product of one firm within an industry to that of a competitor, will cause output and employment to be reallocated among different goods and services and among different industries and firms.

What microeconomics takes essentially *as given*—namely, the total output for the economy as a whole—is what macroeconomics takes as the prime *variable* whose size or value is to be determined. What macroeconomics takes *as given*—namely, the distribution of output, employment, and total spending among the particular goods and services of individual industries and firms—are all *variables* in microeconomics. In regard to prices, what microeconomics takes as given—namely, the general price level—macroeconomics takes as a variable; and what macroeconomics takes as given—namely, the relative prices or exchange ratios among individual goods and services—microeconomics takes as variables.

Although such a sharp distinction helps to clarify the essential differences, the preceding is admittedly a much sharper distinction than can legitimately be made. In practice, analysis of the economy is not conducted separately in two watertight compartments. As one analyzes macroeconomic variables and their relationships, he must also make allowance for changes in microeconomic variables that may have an impact on the macroeconomic variables and vice versa.[5] As one analyzes the economic processes that determine the nation's material well-being, he must consider both macroeconomic and microeconomic aspects. From the macroeconomic point of view, the nation's material well-being will be higher the closer the economy comes to *full utilization* of its total resources, taking as given the allocation, good to bad, of the amount of these resources that are actually employed in the production of the economy's output. From the microeconomic point of view, material well-being will be higher the closer the economy comes to *optimum allocation* of its resources, taking as given the degree of utilization, partial to full, of its total resources. Clearly, the basic macroeconomic and microeconomic goals are compatible; the maximum material well-being for the population as a whole, the attainment of which is the primary goal of both macroeconomic and microeconomic policy, can only be attained with both full utilization and optimum allocation of all available resources.

The distinction above between macroeconomics and microeconomics helps one account for the relatively recent shift of emphasis from the traditional concern with microeconomics to concern with the economy as a whole, a shift of emphasis that is generally recognized as a Keynesian phenomenon. Before the thirties, economists emphasized microeconomics as if by the default of

---

[5] For example, to the extent that labor's geographical immobility is such that workers fail to move from an area whose industry is declining to another whose industry is growing, total output and total employment may be less than they would be with less immobility.

macroeconomics, for at the time it seemed that there remained little more to say about macroeconomics.[6] The then accepted macroeconomic theory argued that total output was not really a variable but more in the nature of a constant in any short period, since its actual amount in any such period was simply whatever the fully employed economy could produce with the state of technology as then given. If this indeed were the case, the only relevant question would be whether these fully employed resources were being used to the best advantage—that is, whether they were optimally allocated among rival lines of production. The analysis of individual markets and their interrelationships required for an answer to this question falls clearly within the province of microeconomics.

Pre-Keynesian macroeconomic theory did recognize that total employment and total output could fall below the full-employment level, but such a situation was viewed as strictly temporary. It was argued that the automatic forces of competitive markets would carry employment and output back to the full-employment level in short order. As a consequence, departures from full employment did not generate widespread concern among economists, as long as economists believed that full employment was the normal situation to which the economy would automatically and promptly return. The fact that there were relatively few severe or prolonged depressions through at least the first half of the nineteenth century gave support to this belief. Lapses from full employment, being both infrequent and short-lived, could be easily explained away as exceptions to the full-employment rule.

Even though viewed as exceptions to the rule, the "panics," "crises," and "depressions" of the nineteenth century were nevertheless the subject of much study. David Ricardo wrote in 1817 of "revulsions in trade," and Mill in 1848 discussed "commercial crises" at length. However, the basic tenet underlying full employment as the norm went unchallenged by Ricardo, Mill, and others. On the contrary, they staunchly defended it against the attacks of what few dissenters there were. This basic tenet was that aggregate demand for goods and services could not, other than temporarily, fall short of the aggregate supply of goods and services. As long as aggregate demand could not fall short of aggregate supply, there was no barrier to the production of the aggregate supply that corresponded with full employment.

The handful of dissenters who attacked the rule that the economy automatically generated sufficient demand to absorb the supply produced under conditions of full employment failed, because none was able to buttress his attack with an alternative theory capable of supplanting the orthodox theory, which showed that aggregate demand could not be deficient. As James B. Conant has observed, "It takes a new conceptual scheme to cause the abandonment of an old one." [7] Before Keynes's there had been no alternative theory that could be made to stick. Thomas R. Malthus, a dissenter of the early

---

[6] John Stuart Mill, whose *Principles of Political Economy*, published in 1848, strongly influenced economic thinking during the latter half of the nineteenth century, had reached the same conclusion with respect to the theory of value, which is the essence of microeconomic theory. His conclusion was subsequently upset.

[7] *On Understanding Science*, Yale Univ. Press, 1947, p. 89.

nineteenth century, attacked the accepted theory unsuccessfully, for, in Keynes's words, "Since Malthus was unable to explain clearly (apart from an appeal to the facts of common observation) how and why effective demand could be deficient or excessive, he failed to furnish an alternative construction." [8] Although there were a number of other attacks on the classical orthodoxy during these many years, a really successful one did not come until over a hundred years after Malthus in the form of Keynes's *General Theory*. Keynes presented an alternative theory of the determination of employment and output that explained why the forces of a market economy did not assure that aggregate demand would automatically be that necessary for full employment. He maintained that the level of employment was a variable and that full employment was simply one possible level; an unlimited number of less-than-full-employment levels was also possible.

Keynes's *General Theory* offered an explanation of the economic disaster that the United States and many other countries suffered during the Great Depression, something the then existing body of theory was quite incapable of doing. The *General Theory* did not depend merely on "an appeal to the facts of common observation" to show that demand could be less than that needed for full employment; it supplied a theory to explain the facts, facts that were apparent to all in the early thirties. A "new" theory had come forth to deal with the reality of those depressed times.

During the decade following the appearance of the *General Theory*, economists addressed themselves to refining and building on the pioneer work of Keynes, to analyzing the complex economic processes that determine the actual level of employment—a level that the new theory showed could be one of full employment, one of severe unemployment, or any other level between these extremes. Keynesian theory was also applied during and after World War II to an analysis of inflation, a condition that was found to be closely connected with an economy at or near full employment. From such analysis came policy prescriptions designed to lift the system up to the full-employment level to which automatic forces might fail to carry it and to maintain this level without inflation. For these reasons macroeconomics rose through these years from relative obscurity to prominence.

MACROECONOMICS—CLASSICAL AND KEYNESIAN

Economic theory, as was noted, may be divided into macroeconomic and microeconomic theory; macroeconomic theory may in turn be divided into classical and Keynesian theory. But there is an all-important difference between these divisions, for whereas macro and micro theory are strictly *additive*, classical and Keynesian theory are largely *alternative*. One accepts macro and

[8] *General Theory*, p. 32. See Keynes's Chapter 23 for his review of the "dissenters," or "heretics," of their time who are identified as the precursors of his own theory.

micro theory as parts of a total; one accepts parts of Keynesian theory only by rejecting parts of classical macroeconomic theory. One does not argue the relative merits of micro and macro theory, for they are largely separate, noncompetitive branches of theory, both of which are necessary to a complete theory of the economy. One does, however, argue the relative merits of classical and Keynesian theory, for their basic postulates and conclusions are opposed.[9]

What is meant today by classical macroeconomic theory? Marx, who coined the term "classical," used it to cover the theories of David Ricardo, James Mill, and their predecessors. Keynes extended the term to include "the *followers* of Ricardo, those, that is to say, who adopted and perfected the theory of the Ricardian economics, including (for example) J. S. Mill, Marshall, Edgeworth, and Prof. Pigou." [10] This is now the generally accepted meaning of "classical" in its application to macroeconomic theory. It is theory not attributable to any one man but distilled from the writings of many men. What is more, the modern-day formulations of what is described as classical macroeconomic theory are nowhere to be found as such in the writings of the classical economists. These formulations had to be extracted from classical writings, since these writings did not specifically or systematically consider the basic questions raised by Keynes. Classical theory was not primarily concerned with the macroeconomic question of the level of employment because classical theory indicated a position of automatic full employment.

What is meant by Keynesian macroeconomic theory? Here Keynes himself may be singled out as the founding father. However, his role is only this, since a distinction must be made between "the economics of John Maynard Keynes" and "Keynesian economics." [11] The economics of Keynes, primarily his *General Theory*, is the foundation on which Keynesian economics has been constructed. Following the publication of his book, economists went through it line by line, accepting, correcting, and rejecting. What they have built on the foundation that remained is a massive structure known as Keynesian economics.

This serves only to distinguish classical theory and Keynesian theory on

---

[9] Microeconomic theory has also undergone drastic change since the thirties, but this was change of a nature distinctly different from that which occurred in macroeconomic theory. Before the thirties, the theory of the individual firm, a core of microeconomic theory, assumed that the firm was either a perfect competitor at the one extreme or a monopolist at the other extreme. Either the firm was only one of so large a number of competing firms all producing an identical product that the individual firm had no appreciable control over the price charged for its product, or else the firm was the only producer of a product with virtually complete control over the price of its product. During the thirties the theory of monopolistic competition, or imperfect competition, was introduced to cover the wide range of market situations between perfect competition at the one extreme and monopoly at the other, market situations in which an individual firm had limited but appreciable control over the price of its product. The introduction of monopolistic, or imperfect, competition *added* something sorely needed to the body of microeconomic theory; it did not supplant or replace existing microeconomic theory. In contrast, the introduction of Keynesian macroeconomic theory was offered not to fill a gap in classical theory but rather to supplant or replace parts of that theory.

[10] *General Theory*, p. 3.

[11] This distinction is the subject matter of a recent book, A. Leijonhufvud, *On Keynesian Economics and the Economics of Keynes*, Oxford Univ. Press, 1968.

the basis of a few of the principal names. The important distinction is, of course, on the basis of the actual content of the theories. What in Keynesian theory is really novel and different and what is merely an extension of classical ideas that were not spelled out by classical economists? What in classical theory was clearly wrong, at least when applied to the urbanized and industrialized economy of the twentieth-century world? These are extremely difficult questions that economists continue to debate. Still, what was advanced as "new" in the economics of Keynes and in the Keynesian economics that developed therefrom had an unprecedented impact on economic theory. The success of the Keynesian or "new" economics, as measured by its widespread acceptance, has few equals in the history of economic doctrine.[12]

This widespread acceptance of large parts of Keynesian economics over the past quarter-century has been equated with the widespread rejection of large parts of classical macroeconomics. This acceptance of a theory that showed that an economy may be in equilibrium with less than full employment amounted to a rejection of parts of classical theory that maintained that the only equilibrium position was the limiting one of full employment. This is the most fundamental of the differences in conclusions reached by the two theories.

The practical significance of this difference and what lies behind it cannot be exaggerated. For, once we accept the Keynesian argument—that left on its own the economy may not move toward or attain the position of full employment—the way is open to the use of policies, designed to achieve this objective, that were ruled out by the quite different argument of classical theory. The ultimate purpose of any economic theory is to contribute to a sound basis for policy actions, and the widespread acceptance of Keynesian theory over the past two decades has increasingly led to the adoption of policies suggested by that theory. As many economists are fond of pointing out, the massive federal tax cut of 1964 amounts to an acceptance of Keynesian theory by the U.S. Congress. However, to obtain any real understanding of the rationale of this and other policy actions, one must first gain an understanding of the essentials of Keynesian theory.

The main task of this book is the development of the essentials of the Keynesian theory of output and employment. It is this theory that has thoroughly dominated the past quarter-century of macroeconomic theorizing. It is a theory that started out as a revolution against the classical orthodoxy and ended up with such success that by the fifties it had in turn become a new orthodoxy. Like the classical theory before it, the Keynesian orthodoxy is not safe from attack. It is fair to say that some major portions of the classical orthodoxy have been permanently supplanted by Keynesian theory, but there are other portions of that classical orthodoxy that have emerged in modified form in recent years as the basis of an attack on the now well-established Keynesian theory. As we will see in a later chapter, a cornerstone of classical macroeconomics is the quantity theory of money, and the Keynesian success is

[12] It is interesting that the success of Keynes was perhaps equaled by that of Ricardo, whose economics Keynes attacked. As Keynes put it, "Ricardo conquered England as completely as the Holy Inquisition conquered Spain." *General Theory*, p. 32.

in large part a measure of the defeat of that theory. The attack on the Keynesian theory that is under way today involves a modified form of the old quantity theory, which goes under the name of the new quantity theory, a theory that has gained an appreciable number of influential supporters in the last five years. It has been in these last few years that this quantity theory has, so to speak, emerged, an accomplishment due largely to the intellectual leadership of Professor Milton Friedman of the University of Chicago. We will touch on this attack by Friedman and the quantity theorists at various points in this book, but the major focus throughout will be on Keynesian theory, which, so far at least, enjoys the support of a large majority of professional economists. What lies in the future is another matter. This brief look into the background of macro-economics has shown that it may, as a first step, be divided historically into two periods: before and after Keynes's *General Theory* of 1936. It may be that at some future date three periods will be required with the Keynesian period of 1936–? separating the old classical theory from what amounts to a new classical theory. As of the moment, however, an introduction to contemporary macroeconomic theory is essentially an introduction to Keynesian theory.

PART I

MACROECONOMIC
MEASUREMENT:
National Income
Accounting

CHAPTER 2

NATIONAL INCOME ACCOUNTING: TWO-SECTOR ECONOMY

Macroeconomic accounting and macroeconomic theory deal largely with the same variables, a number of which, such as income, output, and employment, were encountered in the first chapter. However, macroeconomic accounting deals with the accounting relationships, as opposed to the theoretical or functional relationships, that may be established among these variables. An accounting relationship is an identity—a relationship that is true by definition. For example, the balance-sheet identity is Assets $\equiv$ Liabilities $+$ Net Worth. A functional relationship, in contrast, is devised for explanatory purposes and may therefore be an oversimplification that is, at best, only approximately true.

For example, for any specified time period, personal saving is equal to disposable personal income less personal outlays. This is an accounting relationship and therefore completely valid by definition. In contrast, there can be only approximate validity in a functional relationship that asserts that, for any specified time period, personal saving "depends on" or "is determined by" or "is a function of" that period's disposable personal income. The functional relationship may or may not be true; whether or not it should be rejected as false can be decided only by empirical testing.

In this and the following three chapters we will be concerned almost exclusively with accounting relationships among variables.[1] The importance of the accounting relationships and the framework that is built from them will

[1] The relationships we will consider are those that make up national income accounting, the national economic accounting system that is relevant to our later analysis. We will not enter into other systems such as flow of funds, input-output tables, national balance sheets, and balance-of-payments accounts. See J. P. Lewis and R. C. Turner, *Business Conditions Analysis*, 2nd ed., McGraw-Hill, 1967, pp. 69–83, for a concise introduction to these systems and the references given there for detailed studies. For a comparison of the national income accounting systems of the major countries, see M. Yanovsky, *Social Accounting Systems*, Aldine, 1965.

become more apparent in Part II, which discusses functional relationships among these same variables. Suffice it to say at this stage that national income accounting provides a valuable foundation for the study of macroeconomic theory. This is especially true in light of the development of a comprehensive national income accounting framework, which gives us a systematic picture of the economic structure and process in terms of the interrelated flows of income and product, the basic variables of the economic process itself. In fact, one can learn a good deal about the economic process by studying this comprehensive accounting framework, even though it is essentially neutral in terms of macroeconomic theory.[2]

As developed for the U.S. economy by the Department of Commerce, this accounting framework (hereafter referred to as the *official accounts*) shows a degree of complexity that some might think approaches the complexity of the economy it describes. For that reason, before we consider the official accounts in Chapter 5, we will approach them step by step, in Chapters 2 through 4, through a series of hypothetical economies.

In this chapter, we will begin by considering the simplest of all possible economies, one far removed from the actual economy of the United States. The accounting framework for this economy is made up only of relationships among business firms and households and excludes relationships of these two groups with either the government or other economies. Such an economy may be described as a *two-sector economy*, composed of only a business sector and a household sector. In Chapter 3, government is admitted into the economy to produce a *three-sector economy*—business, household, and government. Finally, in Chapter 4, relationships between each of these sectors and other economies are admitted to produce the complete *four-sector economy*—business, households, government, and the rest-of-the-world.

In the accounting framework for the hypothetical four-sector economy, we will have a framework that, apart from a number of minor items, is essentially the same as the official one. To simplify the transition from our hypothetical economies to the actual economy, much of the terminology and classifications now used by the Department of Commerce will be introduced into the hypothetical economies at appropriate points. For the same reason, on the many occasions in which there are two or more possible procedures for handling a particular item (e.g., to include or exclude government interest from national income), the procedure followed in the hypothetical economies will be that followed in the official accounts. All that will remain, then, when we reach Chapter 5, will be to fit into the framework a number of minor items that we deliberately omitted in order to concentrate attention on the major items and relationships.

---

[2] Since the development of the accounting framework to its present advanced form progressed with and was influenced by Keynesian theory, it has been deliberately designed so as to be most useful in the study of macroeconomic problems undertaken with the set of tools provided by Keynesian theory. However, the framework itself is still based on a minimum number of theoretical preconceptions as to possible functional relationships among the variables of which it is composed.

These omissions in no sense make the earlier frameworks incorrect but only incomplete, if we take the official framework to be the "complete" one. In Chapter 5 these omissions will be made good.[3]

INCOME AND PRODUCT

Turning now to the first hypothetical economy, we can loosely define a fundamental accounting identity, which will apply in this economy in any time period, as

$$\text{Income} \equiv \text{Product} \equiv \text{Expenditures on product}$$

or, more formally,

$$\frac{\text{National}}{\text{income}} \equiv \frac{\text{Net national}}{\text{product}} \equiv \frac{\text{Expenditures on net national}}{\text{product}}$$

and also,

$$\frac{\text{National}}{\text{income}} + \text{Depreciation} \equiv \frac{\text{Gross national}}{\text{product}} \equiv \frac{\text{Expenditures on gross national}}{\text{product}}$$

The net version states that the dollar value of the economy's net production of final goods and services, or its net national product, for any time period is identical with expenditures on those final goods and services and with national income earned in the production of those final goods and services.[4] National

[3] Since our purpose in these chapters is to build the framework and describe the essentials of the methodology employed by the Department of Commerce, we may note here the official publications that provide a detailed treatment of material either lightly covered or excluded from these chapters.

The principal results of the latest periodic comprehensive revision of the national income and product accounts have been published in the *Survey of Current Business* for August 1965. This report contains a brief analysis of the various definitional changes and presents the basic income and product series for 1929–64 as modified by these changes. The definitional changes are the first that have been made since the last overhaul of the U.S. national accounts in 1958 and are quite limited. Most of the definitions underlying the U.S. income and product accounts remain as described in *National Income*, 1954 edition, and *U.S. Income and Output*, 1958, U.S. Department of Commerce. The Department proposes to publish some time in 1970 a detailed analysis of current definitions and methodology comparable to the preceding reports.

The detailed statistical series for 1929–65 are found in *The National Income and Product Accounts of the United States, 1929–1965, Statistical Tables*, U.S. Department of Commerce, 1966. The same series for each of the subsequent years are found in the July issues of the *Survey of Current Business*. Unless otherwise indicated, all national income and product figures for the U.S. economy given in this book are from these sources.

[4] The meaning of "final" goods and services will be explained below. For the moment, it is sufficient to note simply that the term excludes goods used up in the production of other goods. For example, a loaf of bread is a final good, but the flour that goes into making the bread is not, and neither is the wheat that goes into making the flour.

income is the sum of wages, rent, interest, and profits, or the sum of the earnings of the factors of production for the time period. For every dollar of final product, there is, on one side, a dollar of income earned in producing final product and, on the other side, a dollar of expenditures on final product. Since final product itself is a miscellaneous collection of all kinds of goods and services, its value can be expressed only in dollars. This dollar value is necessarily measured either by the amount of expenditures on it or by the amount of income earned by the factors of production in producing it. Each is equal to the other, and both are equal to—and therefore measures of—the value of the final product itself.

The measurement of net national product in terms of the economy's expenditures on final product yields a dollar figure based on the prices at which goods are sold in the market. The figure is obtained by adding up all the units of each final good and service sold, weighting each unit at the price at which it is sold. The measurement of net national product in terms of national income, or earnings of the factors of production, yields the same dollar figure in this hypothetical economy. Conceptually, it is a figure that would be secured by adding up all the units of each factor service supplied, weighting each unit at the price paid for, or the income earned by, that unit. The former approach is sometimes referred to as the value of net national product *measured at market prices*, and the latter as the value of net national product *measured at factor cost*. The former approaches final output in terms of the physical product itself and so carries the label of *national product;* the latter approaches final output in terms of the factor incomes that are earned in turning out the physical product and so carries the label of *national income*. The important point is that the value of final product is the same from either point of view, whether approached from the sales side as final output times output prices or from the income side as factor input times factor prices.

The gross version of the identity states that the dollar value of the economy's gross production of goods and services, or its gross national product, for any time period is identical with expenditures on those goods and services and identical with the sum of national income and depreciation. The gross version thus differs from the net in that it includes as part of product an amount of output excluded from the net version. Specifically, it includes, among other things, the economy's total output of new structures and producers' durable equipment produced during the period, while the net version deducts from this total an allowance for the amount of the total stock of structures and producers' durable equipment that was used up during the period in the process of producing that period's total output. This amount of product is measured by the depreciation allowances of business for the period, and so it is this amount that in effect is subtracted from both sides of the gross version of the identity to produce the net version.

On the income side of the gross version there is now a division of the gross income flow into the portion that constitutes factor earnings, or national income, and the portion that is, in effect, set aside in the depreciation reserves of business. An identity between expenditures on product and income is found in both versions, the essential difference being that the gross version involves a broader definition of product and, correspondingly, a broader definition of income, one in which national income is only a part of a now larger income flow.

In a two-sector economy, final product, whether defined in net or gross terms, is the sum of product produced by or originating in the business sector and the household sector. In practice, the amount originating in the household sector is relatively small, and for simplicity we will assume in this chapter that it is zero. Therefore, by measuring the amount of final product originating in the business sector, we will be measuring final product for the two-sector economy as a whole. From the fundamental identities set forth above, we may accordingly arrive at a figure for the economy's net national product by measuring those expenditures on goods and services purchased from business that are purchases of net final product or, alternatively, by measuring the amount of national income that originates in the business sector. Similarly, we may arrive at a figure for the economy's gross national product by measuring those expenditures on goods and services purchased from business that are purchases of gross national product or, alternatively, by measuring the sum of the amount of national income and depreciation allowances that originate in the business sector.

Most of the basic data required for this purpose are found in the ordinary profit-and-loss statements of business firms. It is through a combination, reorganization, and consolidation of these data that a business income-and-product account emerges, showing, on one side, the amount of product originating in business and, on the other side, the amount of income originating in business.

PRODUCT ORIGINATING IN THE SINGLE FIRM

We start off with a highly simplified Sales and Cost-of-Goods-Sold statement for a single firm, as shown in Table 2–1. The right-hand side of the account

TABLE 2–1

FIRM A
Sales and Cost-of-Goods-Sold Statement
January 1–December 31, 1970

Cost of goods sold		$205	Sales	$225
Purchases of goods and				
services from other firms	$80			
Wages and salaries	75			
Interest	20			
Depreciation	30			
Profit		20		
Total current costs				
plus profit		$225	Total sales receipts	$225

indicates the firm's total sales receipts of $225 for a particular time period. The left-hand side of the account indicates the allocation of these receipts. The costs chargeable against total sales are $205, so the residual is a profit of $20. If Cost of Goods Sold had been $40 larger than the figure shown, the residual would have been a loss of $20 rather than a profit of this amount. The profit or loss figure is whatever figure is required to make the allocations side balance with the receipts side.

Suppose we had statements like that of Table 2–1 for each of the firms in our two-sector economy. At first glance, it might seem that we could get a meaningful total for the economy's product simply by adding up the value of the goods sold or the sales receipts of all firms. There are several reasons why we cannot proceed in this way, the most obvious of which is the double counting involved. Table 2–1 shows that goods and services purchased from other firms at a cost of $80 were used up in the course of producing goods and services sold for $225. The firms from which Firm A purchased the $80 in goods and services show this same $80 among their sales. To include this same $80 as part of the output of Firm A clearly involves double counting of this $80. Beyond this, there may be triple and quadruple counting if behind these sales of $80 by other firms to Firm A are purchases by these other firms from still other firms of goods and services that are used up in producing the goods and services sold for $80. The very same good could be counted over and over as it passed through successive firms on its way to a final purchaser. If this were done, we would be counting and recounting what is known as *intermediate product*, or goods used up in the course of producing other goods. The total then derived by adding up the value of goods sold by all firms would in no sense be a meaningful total for the economy's output. To avoid any double counting, we must remove from the total of the value of goods sold by all firms the amount of goods that are intermediate in the production process. What then remains is a meaningful total for the economy's output that is known as *final product*.

A simple example will serve to illustrate this point. Let us take a loaf of bread that sells in a grocery store for 30¢. Assume that the amount of wheat embodied in this loaf of bread brought the farmer 6¢ when he sold it to a miller. After converting the wheat into flour, the miller sells the resulting amount of flour to a bakery for, say, 13¢. Next, the bakery uses the flour to produce a loaf of bread that is sold to a grocery store for 25¢. Finally, the grocery store takes a markup of 5¢ and sells the loaf of bread to a consumer for 30¢. If we sum the successive sales between firms and the final sale to the consumer, we have 6¢ + 13¢ + 25¢ + 30¢, or a total of 74¢, which has counted the original 6¢ worth of wheat four times. The figure we want is the value of the final product— this is the 30¢ expended by the final purchaser. This 30¢ counts the wheat only once. The concept can also be explained this way: if we assume that no materials are purchased by the farmer from other firms, the 6¢ he receives for the wheat represents the *value added* by the farmer at the first step of a productive process that terminates with the sale of the loaf of bread to a final purchaser. In the same way, the miller adds value of 7¢—the difference between the sale price of the flour, 13¢, and the 6¢ value of the wheat that was used up in the production of the flour. Next, the bakery adds value of 12¢, and finally the grocer adds value of 5¢.[5] The value of the final product, 30¢, is thus seen to be the sum of the amounts of value added at each stage in the production process: 30¢ = 6¢ + 7¢ + 12¢ + 5¢.

Although this illustration is oversimplified in its limitation to a single unit of a single commodity, we may take the total production of any firm at any stage in the production process and apply the same reasoning. For example, the bakery in the illustration may sell in a given time period $1,000 in bread and other bakery products. Its contribution to the economy's product, or its value added, will be $1,000 minus intermediate product—that is, minus the value of goods and services purchased from other firms that are used up in producing the output it sells for $1,000. In the same way, in Table 2–1, Firm A's contribution to production is measured by its value added, which is $145, or $225 − $80. We simply subtract from total sales the value of the goods and services purchased from other firms that were used up in producing the goods and services sold by Firm A during the period. This adjustment gives us a figure on the receipts side that measures the value of product originating in the firm. In the same way, subtracting the same amount of intermediate product on the allocations side leaves the items whose sum equals value added. In the present simplified statement, what remains on the allocations side as value added are the various factor earnings, including the residual figure for profit, plus one nonfactor charge against receipts—depreciation.

This approach to the measurement of product originating in the firm gives correct results as long as there is no change in the firm's inventories during the time period. Table 2–1 includes as costs only the current costs incurred in producing the goods and services *sold* during the period. However, the $80 of purchases from firms is not necessarily the total of purchases from other firms; it is the value of purchased goods and services that were used up in producing the goods and services sold during the period. Similarly, the figure for wages and salaries in Table 2–1 is not necessarily the total of wages and salaries paid; it is the amount chargeable against the sales for the period. The simplified statement does not show purchases from other firms, wages and salaries paid, and other factor charges that were incurred in the production of goods that were not sold but were instead added to inventories. In order to allow for this part of the firm's output, we must work with an expanded statement for the firm that includes the change in inventories.

Table 2–2 shows the modifications in the statement of Table 2–1 that result if the firm shows an increase in inventories of $15 during the period. To show the total production of the firm, this change in inventories is added to the total for sales given in Table 2–1. Total value of the firm's production is thus $240, or the sum of sales of $225 and the increase in inventories of $15. The same additional $15 is included on the allocations side, here assumed to be made up of an

---

[5] For simplicity, the illustration assumes that the only purchase a miller must make in producing flour is the purchase of wheat and, similarly, that the only purchase a bakery must make in producing bread is the purchase of flour. Dropping these assumptions greatly complicates the illustration but adds nothing to the principle involved.

TABLE 2–2

FIRM A
Production Statement
January 1–December 31, 1970

Purchases of goods and services from other firms	$ 90	Sales	$225
Wages and salaries	80	Change in inventories	15
Interest	20		
Depreciation	30		
Profit	20		
Charges against total value of production	$240	Total value of production	$240

additional $10 of purchases from other firms and an additional $5 in wages and salaries.[6]

Although the value of Firm A's production now appears to be $15 higher than the figure earlier derived from Table 2–1, its actual contribution to the economy's final product is only $5 greater than the earlier figure—against the $15 added to inventories, we now have the additional purchases of $10.[7] Since the product side now includes not only sales but also the change in inventories, to arrive at the value of the firm's contribution to production on the product side we must subtract not only purchased goods used up in producing the output *sold* but the total of *all* purchased goods, including those that are reflected in the change in inventories. Thus, in Table 2–2, subtracting the full $90 of purchases from both sides of the account is necessary to avoid double counting. What remains on the allocations side is value added of $150—a figure $5 higher than before, which reflects the additional $5 in wages and salaries paid by the firm. The same total of $150 is found on the product side after the corresponding subtraction from the total there.

The figure of $150 we have now arrived at may be described as the *gross* amount of national product originating with this firm for the period. It is called gross because no deduction was made for depreciation, the figure for which may be interpreted as the value of the amount of capital goods used up by the firm in

[6] Depending on the firm's inventory-valuation procedure, the same physical addition of goods to inventories might be valued at a higher or lower figure. For example, if these goods had been valued at $16 instead of $15, assuming as before that an additional $10 was spent for purchases of goods and services and an additional $5 for wages and salaries, the remaining $1 would appear as an additional $1 of profits. The other items on the allocations side—interest and depreciation, in this case—are in the nature of fixed costs and would remain unchanged during the period, whatever the total on the product side happened to be.

[7] Not all the $10 of purchases was necessarily used up during the period in producing whatever the firm produces. Some part could remain in the form in which it was purchased or in the form of goods in process. Whatever its form, however, it is valued on some basis and included in the figure for change in inventories.

producing its output for the period. In deriving the $150 figure from Table 2–2, we subtracted from both sides the total amount of purchases from other firms, but these purchases were restricted to services and to those goods that are treated as expenses by the firm. Such purchases may be described as purchases of *noncapital goods*. The firm also purchases goods of a durable type, described as *capital goods*, which are not *expensed* during the period but are *depreciated* over a number of periods. Because their full purchase price is not charged against the production of the accounting period during which they are acquired, such purchases do not appear in either of the statements above. What does appear in both is an entry for depreciation, which is the portion of the total cost of the firm's existing stock of capital goods that is charged against the particular period's production.

We earlier saw that the firm's purchases of noncapital goods and services had to be subtracted from the product side of its account to avoid double counting. During the course of the firm's productive activities, it also uses up capital goods, whether or not it buys any during the period, and a correct reckoning of the firm's contribution to the economy's product seems to call for a deduction of this amount as well. From this viewpoint, $150 (or $240 − $90) as the measure of the firm's contribution to the economy's product involves an overstatement of $30, which is the amount of the firm's depreciation for the period. If we deducted this $30, our final figure would be $120, which may be described as the *net* amount of national product originating with this firm for the period. Both the gross and net figures have their place, and both will appear in the accounting frameworks to be developed.

PRODUCT ORIGINATING IN THE BUSINESS SECTOR

In the actual procedure of estimating the amount of gross and net national product originating in business firms, national income accountants do not proceed on an individual-firm basis as was done here for the sake of illustration. They begin with combined data for all firms (or for large groups of firms, such as corporate and noncorporate) and, through a process of consolidation, estimate figures for gross national product and net national product originating in all firms (or, again, for large groups of firms).[8]

Account 1 of Table 2–3 is such a combined statement, each entry in which is the sum of the values for the corresponding entry in all the individual firm statements. All the individual statements, in the simple form of Table 2–2, will include the same entries except for the entry for profits. In the combined statement, the net income of all noncorporate firms appears as Proprietors'

[8] Recall that we are assuming in this chapter that all product and income originates in the business sector, so we may simply refer, in what follows, to gross national product instead of gross business product or gross product originating in business, and similarly for net national product and national income.

Income, and the net income of corporate firms as "corporate profits," broken down into the portion paid out in dividends and the portion retained.

Total sales in the combined account are broken down into sales to households and sales to business, with the latter broken down into sales that (from the viewpoint of the buyer) are purchases (1) of capital goods or (2) of services and noncapital goods. Since each firm shows only purchases of noncapital goods on its own statement, it necessarily follows in the combined statement that purchases of $300 on the allocations side must be identical with $300 in sales to business of noncapital goods on the product side. Furthermore, since these purchases are composed of goods and services either used up by the firms in producing the goods and services sold or else incorporated in the change in inventories, the amount involved, $300, must be subtracted from both sides to eliminate double counting. This adjustment yields a consolidated account, Account 2 of Table 2–3, whose total of $425 on the product side is equal to expenditures on gross national product and whose total on the allocations side, or what now may also be called the income side, is the sum of national income and depreciation.

Gross national product is defined to include the total purchases by business on capital account. However, as was noted in examining the production statement for Firm A by itself, a definition that includes in final product all the capital goods produced during the period is a definition that involves some double counting. Just as purchases of noncapital goods had to be deducted from both sides to avoid double counting, so, it may be argued, an amount of purchases of capital goods equal to the value of capital goods used up during the period must be deducted for the same reason. If the $45 of depreciation for all firms is taken as a measure of the value of capital goods used up during the period, this amount may be subtracted from both sides, reducing sales of capital goods to business from a gross figure of $60 to a net figure of $15. This adjustment yields Account 3 of Table 2–3, a consolidated account whose total of $380 on the product side is equal to net national product and whose same total on the allocation or income side is the sum of factor earnings or national income.

This brings us back to the fundamental accounting identities with which we began. In a two-sector economy, gross national product may be measured by the sum of national income and depreciation or by the sum of expenditures on goods and services that are included in the gross national product. In Account 2 of Table 2–3, depreciation is $45, and the sum of factor earnings or national income is $380, making a total of $425 on the income side of the account. On the product side of the account, what is a sale from the seller's viewpoint is, of course, an expenditure from the buyer's viewpoint. Thus, sales to households of $355 may also be described as personal consumption expenditures of this amount, and sales to business on capital account of $60 may also be described as fixed investment expenditures by business or simply fixed investment of this amount. The increase in inventories of $10 may also be viewed as a type of expenditure in which the business sector purchases from itself goods that are added to its inventories. Thus, the sum of expenditures on goods and services included in gross national product is $355 + $60 + $10; or, gross national

TABLE 2-3

ALL FIRMS COMBINED
Production Statement
(Account 1)

Purchases of goods and services		$300	Sales to households	$355
Wages and salaries		320	Sales to business of capital goods	60
Interest		35	Sales to business of services	
Depreciation		45	and noncapital goods	300
Proprietors' income		5	Change in inventories	10
Corporate profits		20		
Dividends	$15			
Undistributed profits	5			
Charges against total value of production		$725	Total value of production	$725

ALL FIRMS CONSOLIDATED
Business Income and Product Account—Gross Basis
(Account 2)

Wages and salaries		$320	Sales to households = personal consumption expenditures	$355
Interest		35		
Proprietors' income		5		
Corporate profits		20	Sales to business of capital goods = gross fixed investment	60
Dividends	$15			
Undistributed profits	5			
National income originating		$380	Change in inventories	10
Depreciation		45		
Charges against business gross product		$425	Business gross product	$425

product as measured by expenditures is $425. The same total for gross national product results from adding the items on either side of this account. For the fundamental identity for gross national product with which we started, we have the following figures:

National income					+ Depreci- ation	= Gross national product	=	Expenditures on gross national product		
Wages and salaries	+ Interest +	Proprie- tors' income	+	Corporate profits				Personal consumption + expenditures	Gross fixed investment	+ Change in inventories
$320 +	$35 +	$5	+	$20	+ $45	= $425	=	$355 +	$60	+ $10

TABLE 2–3   (continued)

ALL FIRMS CONSOLIDATED
Business Income and Product Account—Net Basis
(Account 3)

Wages and salaries		$320	Sales to households =	
Interest		35	personal consumption	
Proprietors' income		5	expenditures	$355
Corporate profits		20	Sales to business of capital	
Dividends	$15		goods less depreciation	
Undistributed profits	5		= net fixed investment	15
National income			Change in inventories	10
originating (= Net				
national product				
originating)		$380		
Charges against				
business net product		$380	Business net product	$380

For the two-sector economy, the identity in net terms states that national income is identical with expenditures on net national product. To move from the gross to the net national product identity simply involves eliminating the entry for depreciation on the income side and subtracting an equal amount from gross fixed investment on the product side. This leaves national income of $380 on the income side and personal consumption expenditures of $355, net fixed investment of $15, and the change in inventories of $10 on the product side, or $380 as the total of expenditures on net national product. For the fundamental identity for net national product with which we started, we thus have the following figures:

National income				= Net national = product	Expenditures on net national product		
Wages and + Interest + salaries	Proprietors' income	+	Corporate profits		Personal consumption + expenditures	Net fixed investment +	Change in inventories
$320 + $35 +	$5	+	$20	= $380 =	$355 +	$15 +	$10

Corresponding to each of the two definitions of product, we thus find an identity between the amount of expenditures on that product and the amount of income generated in the production of that product. In the case of gross national product, not all the income is made up of earnings of the factors, or national income; a part of that income flow is, in effect, set aside by business in depreciation reserves. Of the income flow that constitutes earnings of the factors, the larger part becomes income receipts of persons who have provided labor and property services to business. It may be noted that these income receipts in turn are the primary sources for financing the expenditures that appear on the product side of the business-sector account.

SECTOR ACCOUNTS IN THE TWO-SECTOR ECONOMY

As a final step, the complete set of accounting relationships in this simple two-sector system may be brought out by expanding Table 2–3 to include a sector account for households and a saving and investment account for the economy as a whole. Account 1 of Table 2–4 is basically the same as Account 2 of Table

TABLE 2–4

BUSINESS INCOME AND PRODUCT ACCOUNT
(Account 1)

Wages and salaries		$320	Personal consumption		
Interest		35	expenditures		$355
Proprietors' income		5	Gross private domestic		
Corporate profits		20	investment		70
Dividends	$15		Gross fixed investment	$60	
Undistributed profits	5		Change in inventories	10	
National income					
originating		$380			
Depreciation		45			
Charges against					
business gross					
product		$425	Business gross product		$425

PERSONAL INCOME AND OUTLAY ACCOUNT
(Account 2)

Personal consumption		Wages and salaries	$320
expenditures	$355	Interest	35
Personal saving	20	Proprietors' income	5
		Dividends	15
Personal outlay and			
saving	$375	Personal income	$375

GROSS SAVING AND INVESTMENT ACCOUNT
(Account 3)

Gross private domestic		Personal saving	$ 20
investment	$ 70	Undistributed profits	5
Gross fixed investment	$60	Depreciation	45
Change in inventories	10		
Gross investment	$ 70	Gross saving	$ 70

2–3. Account 2 of Table 2–4 is a household-sector account that shows on the right-hand side the income receipts of households, the total for which is known as *personal income*, and on the left-hand side the allocation of these receipts. In the present economy, which omits government and foreign transactions (and also assumes that no income originates in households), personal income originates in its entirety from payments made by business. All the wages and salaries, interest, and proprietors' income generated in the business sector passes on to households to become personal income. However, only that part of corporate profits paid out as dividends passes on to become personal income; the remainder, or undistributed corporate profits, is retained by business and, as will be explained below, is a part of gross business saving. The receipts side of the household-sector account accordingly shows personal income of $375, an amount $5 less than national income. Of this amount, persons devoted $355 to personal consumption expenditures as shown on the allocation side. (This is the same entry that appears on the product side of Account 1, the business-sector account.) The amount of personal income not devoted to personal consumption expenditures is personal saving, in the present case $20.

Account 3 of Table 2–4 introduces an accounting relationship not noted earlier but as fundamental as any in the accounting framework. This is *the identity between the economy's gross saving and its gross investment*. Account 3 is not a sector account—it does not indicate anything like receipts and allocations or product and income on its two sides. Rather, it summarizes the economy's transactions on capital account for the period and shows that, definitionally, for every dollar of investment in the economy there is a dollar of saving, and vice versa. *Investment* may be defined simply as the amount of the economy's *product* that is not consumed during the period, while the amount that is consumed is taken to be measured by personal consumption expenditures during the period. In the illustration, gross national product is $425, and personal consumption expenditures are $355. Unconsumed output, or gross investment, is then $70, the sum of gross fixed investment and the change in inventories.

Saving is defined in a manner parallel to the definition of investment: it is the amount of *income* not devoted to personal consumption expenditures. Since the size of the gross income flow is definitionally equal to the size of the gross national product, saving as the amount of gross national *income* not consumed is identical with investment as the amount of gross national *product* not consumed. Investment was seen to be $70 for the period, so saving must also be $70 for the period. It can be shown to be so, as follows: Of the gross income flow of $425, two parts, depreciation and undistributed profits, are the only ones retained by business. The sum of these two items, $50, equals gross business saving. The balance of the gross income flow of $375 passes on to households to become personal income. Of the $375 of personal income, $355 is devoted to personal consumption expenditures. The remainder of $20 is the saving of the household sector, or what is called *personal saving*. The sum of *gross business saving* of $50 and personal saving of $20 is accordingly $70, an amount equal to gross investment.

It is important to see that this identity between saving and investment holds under any and all circumstances. Suppose, for example, that the economy's output of final goods and services remains at $425 for the period, but that only $350 of the corresponding income flow is devoted to personal consumption expenditures. This means that $75 of the income flow is devoted to saving. It also means, perforce, that $75 of the economy's $425 worth of product is not consumed, since that much has not been matched by consumption expenditure. And, by definition, the amount of the economy's output that is not consumed is its investment. Investment is therefore $75 and equal to saving. If we varied the illustration in the other direction, with $360 of the income flow of $425 being devoted to consumption expenditures, by the same reasoning we find that investment will be $65, equal to saving of $65.

The derivation of the identity between gross saving and gross investment may be summarized in the steps shown in Table 2–5, which uses the appropriate

TABLE 2–5

National income			+ Depreciation	= Gross national product	=	Expenditures on gross national product			
$380			+ $45	= $425	=		$425		
Personal income	+	Undistributed profits	+ Depreciation	= Gross national product	= Personal consumption expenditures	+	Gross fixed investment	+	Change in inventories
$375	+	$5	+ $45	= $425	= $355	+	$60	+	$10
Personal consumption expenditures	+ Personal saving	+ Undistributed profits	+ Depreciation	= Gross national product	= Personal consumption expenditures	+	Gross fixed investment	+	Change in inventories
$355	+ $20	+ $5	+ $45	= $425	= $355	+	$60	+	$10

figures from Table 2–4. Canceling personal consumption expenditures from the income side leaves the amount of gross income not devoted to consumption expenditures, or the amount of gross saving; canceling personal consumption expenditures from the product side leaves the amount of gross product not consumed, or the amount of gross investment:

$$\underbrace{\begin{array}{ccccc} \text{Personal} & + & \text{Undistributed} & + & \text{Depreciation} \\ \text{saving} & & \text{profits} & & \\ \$20 & + & \$5 & + & \$45 \end{array}}_{\substack{\text{Gross saving} \\ \$70}} \equiv \underbrace{\begin{array}{ccc} \text{Gross fixed} & + & \text{Change in} \\ \text{investment} & & \text{inventories} \\ \$60 & + & \$10 \end{array}}_{\substack{\text{Gross investment} \\ \$70}}$$

The Gross Saving and Investment Account of Table 2–4 shows the same breakdown of gross saving and investment derived above. The totals on the two sides of the account or, what is the same thing, the two sides of the identity, will always be identical; the economy's gross saving and gross investment are definitionally the same dollar magnitudes.

It is now an easy matter to convert Table 2–4 from a gross to a net basis. For Account 1, we can use Account 3 of Table 2–3, instead of Account 2 of that table. This gives us the smaller *net* product of business, and the correspond-ingly smaller *net* income flow—both of which are less than the gross amounts by the $45 of depreciation. The household-sector account is unaffected, since the removal of $45 for depreciation from the gross income flow is the removal of a form of business saving, a part of the income flow that does not pass on to households. The saving and investment account will now be a *net* rather than a *gross* account. On the saving side will be the personal saving of $20 and the *net* saving of business of $5, equal to undistributed profits, giving a total for personal and net business saving of $25. On the investment side will be net fixed invest-ment of $15 (gross fixed investment of $60 less the $45 deduction for depreciation) plus the change in inventories of $10 as before. The total of net investment, $25, is identical with the total of net saving, $25.

Viewed in terms of the identity between saving and investment, we derive the *net* identity from the *gross* identity by simply deducting an amount equal to depreciation from both sides. On the investment side, we may first separate gross investment into net fixed investment and replacement investment. Then the deduction on the product side amounts to the exclusion of the amount of business spending that is for replacement of capital goods used up, the figure for depreciation being taken as the measure of the amount of capital goods used up. We start with the gross identity:

$$
\begin{array}{ccccccccc}
\text{Personal} & + & \begin{array}{c}\text{Undis-}\\\text{tributed}\end{array} & + & \text{Depreci-} & \equiv & \text{Replacement} & + & \text{Net fixed} & + & \text{Change in} \\
\text{saving} & & \text{profits} & & \text{ation} & & \text{investment} & & \text{investment} & & \text{inventories} \\
\$20 & + & \$5 & + & \$45 & = & \$45 & + & \$15 & + & \$10
\end{array}
$$

$$
\underbrace{\text{Gross saving}} \qquad \equiv \qquad \underbrace{\text{Gross investment}}
$$
$$
\$70 \qquad\qquad = \qquad\qquad \$70
$$

After subtracting the amount of depreciation from the saving side and its equivalent, replacement investment, from the investment side, we have:

$$
\begin{array}{ccccccc}
\text{Personal} & + & \text{Undistributed} & \equiv & \text{Net fixed} & + & \text{Change in} \\
\text{saving} & & \text{profits} & & \text{investment} & & \text{inventories} \\
\$20 & + & \$5 & = & \$15 & + & \$10
\end{array}
$$

$$
\underbrace{\text{Net saving}} \qquad \equiv \qquad \underbrace{\text{Net investment}}
$$
$$
\$25 \qquad\qquad = \qquad\qquad \$25
$$

CIRCULAR FLOW IN THE TWO-SECTOR ECONOMY

The production and sale of final product and the generation of income that accompanies these activities are processes that take place on a continuous, day-to-day basis. Table 2–4 presents figures that are accumulations of amounts over some accounting period, say a year. Thus, the figure for wages and salaries of $320 is a total for the year, but part of this total was paid out in the first week, part in the last week, and parts in the other fifty weeks of the year. Personal saving of $20 is a total for the year that is likewise composed of the amounts of saving during each shorter period into which the year may be divided. Similarly, for every item in Table 2–4, the figure is the cumulated total or the flow of this item over a time period here assumed to be one year.

As shown by the household-sector account, certain of these flows are combined to produce the aggregate flow known as *personal income*. Similarly, as shown by the business-sector account, certain of these flows are combined to produce the aggregate flow known as *business gross product*. The relationships among the aggregate flows of gross product, net product, national income, and personal income may be derived from a study of Table 2–4, but the flow nature of these same relationships may be seen more clearly by recasting the table into the circular-flow diagram of Figure 2–1. The diagrammatic presentation immediately focuses attention on a basic feature of the economy—the circular nature of the flow of payments from firms to households and of expenditures from households to firms. Thus, the upper loop of the figure shows a physical flow of productive services from households in exchange for a monetary flow of income from business in payment for these services; the lower loop, at the same time, shows a physical flow of consumer goods and services from firms in exchange for a monetary flow of expenditure from households. These two flows may also be viewed as one circular flow in real terms and one in monetary terms. The former is a clockwise flow of real productive services from households to firms and real goods and services from firms to households; the latter is a counterclockwise flow of monetary income from firms to households and monetary expenditure from households to firms.

Recall our assumption that all product is produced in the business sector, making gross product, net product, and national income originating in business the same as the economy's gross national product, net national product, and national income. Thus we see these three aggregates on the right-hand side of Figure 2–1, which shows firms. National income is equal to factor earnings, but the amount of these earnings paid out by firms is less than total factor earnings by the amount of undistributed corporate profits. National income is $380, but factor payments to persons are $375, the difference of $5 being the amount of national income retained by firms. In the present case, the only source of personal income is from factor payments by business, so we find the flow of factor payments from business reappearing on the left-hand, or households, side as an equal amount of personal income. Personal income is allocated to personal consumption expenditure, $355, and personal saving, $20, as shown in the lower loop of the figure.

In the present economy, national income and net national product are the same amount, the amount of factor income generated in producing the goods and services that constitute net national product being equal to the amount of expenditures on these goods and services. These expenditures are personal consumption expenditures and net business investment. With consumption expendi-

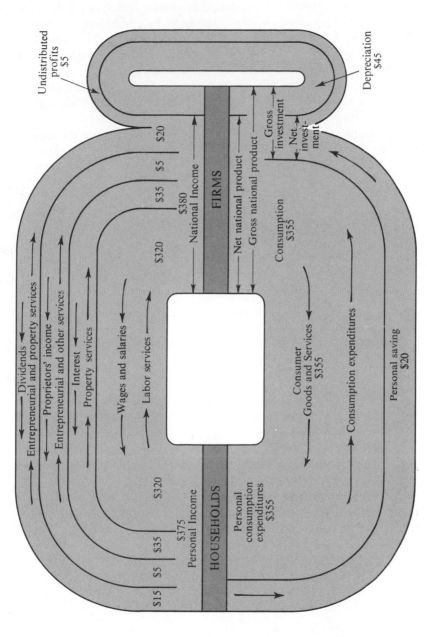

FIGURE 2–1 Circular Flow in the Two-Sector Economy

tures given as $355 and net national product as $380, net investment, as the part of net national product not consumed, is equal to $25. The identity between net investment and net saving is seen in the figure by combining personal saving of $20 coming out of households and net business saving of $5 for a total of $25, or an amount equal to net investment. The small loop on the right includes the $5 of undistributed corporate profits (net business saving) and suggests the sense in which this amount of saving that occurs within firms joins the flow of saving coming from households to make up a total of net saving definitionally equal to net investment.

Gross national product exceeds net national product by the amount of depreciation. Like undistributed corporate profits, depreciation is an amount of the gross income flow retained by business and appears together with undistributed corporate profits as the total of business saving in the small loop on the right-hand side of the figure. Given that gross investment is the part of gross national product not consumed, and given further that gross national product is $425 and that the amount of this consumed is $355, gross investment appears as $70. The identity between gross saving and gross investment is seen by combining the $20 of personal saving coming out of households with the gross business saving of $50 shown in the small loop for a total of $70, or an amount equal to gross investment.

The system of accounts developed in Table 2–4 and the representation of that system in Figure 2–1 has been limited to an economy made up of business firms and households only. In the next chapter the system of accounts and the circular-flow diagram of this chapter will be expanded to incorporate the government sector and to reflect the changes in the system that result from the inclusion of government transactions.

CHAPTER 3

NATIONAL INCOME
ACCOUNTING:
THREE-SECTOR ECONOMY

We first considered a two-sector economy in order to permit an analysis of the basic product and income, saving and investment relationships uncomplicated by government transactions. But an economy without government spending or taxation is a far cry from any real economy. In the United States today, every area of the private sector of the economy feels the impact of government transactions. Over the past decade, 21 percent of gross national product has consisted of government purchases of goods and services, and direct taxes on persons and corporations have amounted to over 15 percent of national income. With the addition of government transactions to our framework, all the identities developed earlier will have to be modified. None, however, need be rejected.

The structure of Table 3–1 parallels that of Table 2–4 but involves the addition of new entries in the various accounts as well as of entirely new accounts.[1] One of the new accounts, Account 3, is a consolidated statement of government receipts and expenditures, consolidated for the thousands of government units—federal, state, and local—that have the power to tax, spend, and incur debt. Intergovernmental transactions are canceled out in the consolidation, so the totals shown reflect only the position of the government sector relative to that of each of the other sectors of the economy. Any entry that appears as a receipt in one consolidated account must be an allocation of another (or in some cases the same) account, and vice versa. For each item included in government receipts, there is another account (or opposite side of the same account) in which that particular government receipt appears as an allocation in the form of a tax payment. Similarly, for each item included in government expenditures, there is another account (or opposite side of the same account) in which that particular

---

[1] Because of these additions, the dollar figures for the entries in Table 3–1 unavoidably differ from those for the same entries in Table 2–4. No direct comparison of dollar figures in these two tables is therefore possible.

TABLE 3-1   Accounts for Three-Sector Economy

BUSINESS SECTOR (Account 1)

Wages and salaries		$118	Personal consumption expenditures	
Employer contributions for social insurance		4	(or sales to households)	$155
Rent		5	Government purchases of goods and services	
Interest		8	(or sales to government)	30
Proprietors' income		25	Gross investment	40
Corporate profits		20	Change in inventories	$ 5
Profits tax	$10		Purchases of capital goods	35
Dividends	6			
Undistributed profits	4			
NATIONAL INCOME ORIGINATING WITH BUSINESS		$180		
Business transfer payments		1		
Indirect taxes		25		
Current surplus of government enterprises		1		
Less Subsidies		4		
NET NATIONAL PRODUCT ORIGINATING WITH BUSINESS		$203		
Capital consumption allowances (depreciation)		22		
GROSS NATIONAL PRODUCT ORIGINATING WITH BUSINESS		$225	GROSS NATIONAL PRODUCT OF BUSINESS	$225

HOUSEHOLD SECTOR (Account 2)

Personal taxes				$ 24	
Personal outlays				161	
Personal consumption expenditures			$160		
Purchases from business		$155			
Purchases from households		5			
Wages and salaries	$4				
Employer social insurance	1				
Interest paid by consumers		1			
Personal saving				15	
PERSONAL TAXES, OUTLAYS, AND SAVING				$200	

Wages and salaries				$141	
From business			$118		
From government			19		
From households			4		
Interest				13	
From business			$8		
From government			4		
From households			1		
Rental income of persons				5	
Income of unincorporated business				25	
Dividends				6	
Transfer payments				14	
From business			$ 1		
From government			13		
Less Personal contributions for social insurance				4	
PERSONAL INCOME				$200	

GOVERNMENT SECTOR (Account 3)

Purchases of goods and services			$50	
From business		$30		
From employees		20		
Wages and salaries	$19			
Social insurance contributions	1			
Transfer payments			13	
Net interest paid			4	
Subsidies less current surplus of government enterprises (4 − 1)			3	
Deficit			−1	
GOVERNMENT EXPENDITURES AND DEFICIT			$69	

Personal taxes			$24
Corporate profits taxes			10
Indirect taxes			25
Contributions for social insurance			10
Employer contributions		$6	
From business	$4		
From government	1		
From households	1		
Personal contributions		4	
GOVERNMENT RECEIPTS			$69

TABLE 3–1 (continued)

NATIONAL INCOME AND PRODUCT (Account 4)

Wages and salaries		$141	Gross national product originating with		
From business	$118		Business sector		$225
From government	19		Government sector		20
From households	4		Household sector		5
Employer contributions for social insurance		6			
Proprietors' income		25			
Corporate profits		20			
Profits tax	$10				
Dividends	6				
Undistributed profits	4				
Rent		5			
Interest		8			
NATIONAL INCOME		$205			
Business transfer payments		1			
Indirect business taxes		25			
Current surplus of government enterprises		1			
Less Subsidies		4			
NET NATIONAL PRODUCT		$228			
Capital consumption allowances (depreciation)		22			
GROSS NATIONAL PRODUCT		$250	GROSS NATIONAL PRODUCT		$250

GROSS SAVING AND INVESTMENT (Account 5)

Gross investment		$40	Personal saving		$15
Change in inventories	$ 5		Business saving		26
Purchases of capital goods	35		Capital consumption allowances (depreciation)	$22	
			Undistributed profits	4	
			Government saving		−1
GROSS INVESTMENT		$40	GROSS SAVING		$40

government expenditure appears as a receipt. If government expenditures are greater than tax receipts, there is a deficit; if they are less, there is a surplus. Unlike the other items in the government account, which lead to the business or household account, the deficit or surplus appears as government dissaving or saving in the gross saving and investment account (Account 5), which brings together all the economy's saving and investment.[2]

GOVERNMENT RECEIPTS

All government receipts may be treated as tax receipts if we include among tax receipts social-insurance contributions and incidental nontax revenue such as fines and license fees.[3] For present purposes, tax receipts may best be classified as of four types: personal taxes, corporate-profits taxes, social-insurance contributions, and indirect business taxes (including fines and license fees).

Each of these four types of taxes may be traced to the other sectors of the economy for which they are payments or allocations. Personal taxes ($24) are an allocation of the household sector; corporate-profits taxes ($10) and indirect taxes ($25) are allocations of the business sector; and social-insurance contributions ($10) are allocations of the business, government, and household sectors.[4] Wages and salaries paid by business, government, and household employers (total of $141) are shown inclusive of employee contributions but exclusive of employer contributions for social insurance. This total amount of wages and salaries is treated as if it passed on to households in its entirety. Then the amount of employee social-insurance contributions ($4) is subtracted from total receipts of households ($204), the remainder being called "personal income" ($200).

[2] If all government units consolidated show a deficit, the amount of the deficit or the amount borrowed may be shown in the government account on the receipts side as a plus item or on the expenditures side as a minus item. It will here be considered as a minus item on the expenditures side. A surplus accordingly will be considered as a plus item on the expenditures side.

[3] Government-producing enterprises, such as local water supply systems, are treated in the U.S. income and product accounts in much the same way as are private profit-making firms. Their receipts are primarily from sales of services rather than taxes, and for this reason they are included as a part of the business sector of the economy rather than a part of the government sector.

[4] Government receipts from social-insurance contributions in our hypothetical economy total $10: $4 is collected from the business sector as employer contributions, $1 from the government sector as employer contributions (the amount of $1 appears as both a receipt and an expenditure of government), $1 from the household sector as employer contributions, and the remaining $4 from households as employee contributions. Households and certain institutions included in the household sector employ persons and pay the employers' share of social-insurance contributions on wages and salaries of these employees. The figure here of $1 is disproportionate with wages and salaries paid but is used to avoid figures of less than $1.

GOVERNMENT EXPENDITURES

While many classifications of government expenditures are possible,[5] at this point the appropriate classification for national income purposes is simply (*a*) those expenditures for which government receives either goods or services (i.e., those that are matched by productive activity) and (*b*) those expenditures for which government receives neither goods nor services (i.e., those that are not matched by productive activity). In Table 3–1, government expenditures matched by productive activity are composed of goods and services purchased from business ($30) and services of labor purchased directly from government's own employees ($20). The balance of government expenditures ($20)—those not matched by productive activity—is composed of transfer payments ($13), subsidies less current surplus of government enterprises ($3),[6] and interest payments ($4).[7]

Government expenditures for goods and services cover goods from paper clips to aircraft carriers and services from those of a clerk to those of the President. In the United States, the bulk of these expenditures consists of payments to business firms for the goods and services purchased from them; the balance consists of wages and salaries paid directly to government employees. Just as business firms decide whether to "make or buy," within limits government decides which goods and services it will produce on its own and which ones it will purchase from business firms. For example, if a government agency needs 10,000 copies of a government report, the job can be handled either in the government's printing plant or by an outside printing firm. In either case, the cost to government will be included as part of government purchases of goods and services. If the reports are printed by the government, part of the total expenditure will be in the form of wages and salaries to government employees and part in the form of purchases of paper, ink, and other supplies from business firms. If they are printed by a private firm, the total government expenditure will

---

[5] The most familiar is by function: defense, general government, interest, education, etc., in the case of federal government.

[6] Subsidies of $4 less current surplus of government enterprises of $1. In the official accounts, only the difference is available, due to the fact that many subsidy programs are interwoven with the operations of government enterprises. An explanation of current surplus of government enterprises is provided later in this chapter.

[7] A question arises as to whether interest paid by government is a payment for a productive service. Net interest paid by business is plainly factor income to the lenders of funds. It is income received by them in exchange for a productive service (namely, the provision of funds to business) that contributes to additional production of goods and services and thereby produces additional income to business out of which the interest is paid. The major part of net interest paid by government is paid on debt incurred primarily to finance wars and the aftermath of wars. Since such debt cannot, in the ordinary sense of the word, be regarded as debt incurred for productive purposes, interest paid on such debt similarly cannot be regarded as a payment matched by productive activity. In the United States income and product statistics, interest paid by government is not viewed as a return to productive activity and is treated as the equivalent of a transfer payment.

be in the form of purchases from business firms. Therefore, in Account 3 of Table 3–1, of the total of government purchases of all kinds of goods and services ($50), part may be traced to the receipts side of the business sector (sales to government of $30), and part may be traced to the receipts side of the household sector (wages and salaries from government of $19 or, if employer contributions for social insurance on these wages and salaries are included, $20).

We have noted that government expenditures, other than for goods and services, consist of transfer payments ($13), subsidies less current surplus of government enterprises ($3), and interest payments ($4). Transfer payments to persons[8] include benefits paid under various social-insurance programs (old-age and survivors, unemployment, and railroad retirement insurance) and other programs such as direct relief and military pensions. Subsidies are monetary grants by government to business. Net interest is simply that paid on public debt less interest received by government. Each of these expenditures has one characteristic in common: The government receives no goods or services in exchange for them—no productive activity matches the expenditure.

Government transfer and interest payments are treated as receipts of the household sector. Although in reality a large portion of the interest payments on public debt is received by banks, insurance companies, and other firms, these interest payments are considered, in effect, to pass through business firms and to become, in their entirety, receipts of the household sector. Accordingly, the total of net interest paid by government appears directly as a receipt of this sector.

Sales to government appear on the receipts side of the consolidated business account, since the payment is received in return for goods and services produced for government. Government subsidies to business might also seem to belong on the receipts side of the business account. However, there is no productive activity to match the receipt of such subsidies, and their amount would have to be removed before the receipts side could be used as a measure of production originating in business. Therefore, government subsidies appear in Account 1 as a negative item on the allocations side. By appearing in this form, this placement also reflects the fact that the subsidies result in lower prices for the output of subsidized business and/or higher incomes to its owners and employees. That is, the increased receipts that subsidies would seem to represent are, in fact, balanced by lower receipts from sales (due to lower prices) or by larger total factor payments (ordinarily in the form of higher profits or higher wages and salaries) or by a combination of both.

---

[8] There are also foreign transfer payments made by government; these will be considered in the four-sector economy of Chapter 4.

GOVERNMENT PRODUCTION

In the two-sector economy, the question of production by government did not arise. All production originated in business firms.[9] As a result, measuring gross and net national product and national income originating with business firms was the same as measuring gross and net national product and national income for the economy as a whole. If government is now recognized as a producer, the measurement of income and product for the economy as a whole requires that income and product originating with government be added to that originating with business.

That government is a producer is readily seen if we include under government the many business-type agencies, such as the Post Office Department and publicly owned local transit and water-supply systems, whose costs are covered, at least to a substantial extent, by the sale of goods and services to their customers. For national income accounting purposes, the fact that these agencies are publicly rather than privately owned does not alter the fact that they are essentially business enterprises. Unlike private business enterprises, their survival does not depend on the earning of profits, but the business aspect of their operations is still paramount. These agencies, which are referred to as "government enterprises" in the U.S. income and product accounts, are treated as part of the business sector. Accordingly, the government sector is limited to those government agencies whose services are not or are only incidentally sold in the marketplace and whose expenses are covered almost entirely by taxes.

The government sector that emerges from this division is, for accounting purposes, similar to a mammoth household. Whatever it purchases from the business sector is final product in the same way that whatever the household sector purchases from the business sector is final product. If a city purchasing department buys 10,000 lead pencils, these pencils are final product just as they would be if purchased by households. The government sector does not resell what it purchases; therefore, what it purchases is not viewed as intermediate product. However, the same purchase of pencils by a business firm (either a private firm or a government enterprise) is clearly intermediate product, for the pencils will be used up in the course of producing the firm's output, and the cost of pencils will be charged against gross sales in order to arrive at that firm's final product.[10]

While these purchases by the government sector from the business sector are thus included as part of final product, they are clearly final product *produced*

---

[9] In the two-sector economy of Chapter 2, we assumed for simplicity that no production originates in the household sector. Actually, a relatively unimportant amount of production does originate in this sector and will be considered later in this chapter.

[10] Other things being equal, if the firm does not use up during the period all the pencils purchased, the remainder will appear as an increase in inventory and as such is part of the period's final product.

by the business sector. Does the government sector itself (distinguished from government enterprises) produce anything? Or does this sector merely tax and borrow on the one hand and spend on the other without producing anything in the process? What if government taxed and borrowed and spent the funds so raised entirely either on the purchase of goods and services produced by business firms or on transfer payments, subsidies, and interest? The former are goods and services produced by business, not by government. The latter involve no goods or services secured by government and, accordingly, no production on the part of either government or business. However, these two are not the only types of government expenditures; there remain government expenditures in the form of wages and salaries paid to employees. These employees are paid for the labor services they provide to government and thus to the public. The amount that they are paid may be taken as a measure of the amount of production these services represent.

Let us illustrate by returning to the 10,000 copies of a government report that could be printed in a government printing plant or by a private printing firm. In measuring the nation's net national product, the 10,000 copies of this report should be included at some dollar value in the economy's output of final goods and services, regardless of where they were produced. If the report is printed by a private firm, it is included in net national product, at the dollar amount paid by government to the printing firm, as product originating in the business sector. As a purchase by government, it is part of final product; as production of the business sector, it is part of final product originating in the business sector. If it is printed by government in its own printing plant, only part of its value will be made up of paper, ink, and other supplies that were purchased from business. The balance of its value will be the amount of wages and salaries paid by government to its employees for their labor services on this report. Assuming that the purchase price charged by a firm equals the cost to government if the report is produced in its own printing plant, the publication should enter the net national product at the same dollar value in either case. However, in the second case, it will appear in net national product at this dollar amount only if we include as part of net national product government expenditures for wages and salaries paid to its own employees as well as government purchases of materials from business. If we multiply this example a thousand-fold, not to include wages and salaries paid by government would result in a large but unreal increase in net national product any time government shifted work from its own employees to those of business firms. Conversely, the reverse shift would result in a large but unreal decrease in net national product. In short, not to include wages and salaries paid by government would be to understate the value of production in any period.

The same reasoning applies to whatever government acquires for its expenditures on goods and services, whether it be 10,000 copies of a report or some other good, or whether it be the provision to the public of the services of policemen and firemen, schoolteachers and research workers, doctors and lawyers or any of the hundreds of other services rendered by government employees. The contribution to production per time period of every government employee may be measured by the amount of his wages or salary for that time period. Thus, total production per time period by the government sector may be measured by government's expenditures for the services of its employees per time period. This, in effect, measures production originating in government on a cost basis, and the only cost of production included is labor cost. Otherwise viewed, government production or output is measured in terms of input, and the only input recognized is labor. In principle then, in the official income and product statistics, the value of government production is measured by the wages, salaries, and supplements thereto paid by government.

This method of measuring production in the government sector is seen to differ radically from the method described earlier for measuring production in the business sector. The measurement of production in the business sector can be approached conceptually from either the receipts or the allocations side of that sector's account. On the receipts side before consolidation, we found gross sales of goods and services to all sectors of the economy, including interfirm sales or sales within the business sector. After adjusting gross sales to show the amount of noncapital goods and capital goods used up in producing the gross amount of goods and services sold, and after further adjusting the receipts side to show any change in inventories, the remainder on the receipts, or sales, side is net production of final goods and services by the business sector.

A corresponding approach to a measure of government production on the receipts side is ruled out by the fact that government does not sell what it produces. For the business sector, the market prices at which final goods are sold dictate the dollar value at which these goods are to be included in the nation's final product. The government sector, however, does not sell but "gives away" practically all the goods and services it provides to the rest of the economy. It is true, of course, that, apart from a deficit, the services provided by each governmental unit are paid for through taxes; but taxes are not like prices, since there is no direct correspondence between the amount of product in the form of public services that a taxpayer receives and the amount of taxes that he pays. Even if there were a direct correspondence, the taxpayer is not given any real choice about how much he will pay in taxes or how much he will "purchase" in public services. Thus, the compulsory aspect of taxes paid to government, as compared with the volitional aspect of purchases made from business, rules out the possibility of measuring government production through government receipts in the way that production by business is measured through business receipts.[11]

[11] To illustrate further, assume that government receipts in the form of contributions for social insurance are doubled from $10 to $20 billion per year and are matched by an equal increase in government transfer payments per year. Despite the great increase in government receipts, this change does not affect government production at all. These dollars merely pass through government and are in no way related to production. In the same way, if an increase in tax receipts is matched by an equal increase in purchases of goods and services from the business sector, there is no change in government production. There may be additional production, but this is production of the business sector. Finally, suppose there is an increase in government receipts that is matched by an equal increase in government payrolls. In this event there is a matching increase in government receipts and government production, taking as the

If, then, government production must be measured from the expenditures or allocations side of the account, the measurement is necessarily in terms of factor cost and thus parallels the method followed in measuring business production from the allocations side of the business-sector account. The measurement task is more complex for the government sector, since differences of judgment can and do arise as to what items in government expenditures are to be included as factor cost. For example, as noted earlier, the United States accounts exclude net interest paid by government as a factor cost, whereas the reverse treatment is followed in the official accounts for some other countries. For our purposes, however, in measuring government production ($20 in Table 3–1), the method followed will be that found in the official accounts: Government production is valued at factor cost, and factor cost is equal to the compensation of government employees.

HOUSEHOLD PRODUCTION

The definition of production within the household sector is the same as that within the government sector.[12] Like the government sector, the household sector purchases goods and services from the business sector and directly from persons employed by the household sector. Again, following the procedure in the official accounts, the only direct purchases of factor services recognized in the household sector are purchases of labor services, and the amount of these services is measured by the wages and salaries paid to the sector's employees, including domestic servants of households and the employees of the various institutions and funds included in this sector. The sum of wages and salaries paid to its employees equals national income originating within this sector and is the measure of production within this sector.[13]

---

measure of government production its expenditures for wages and salaries. But even though this increase in government production may accompany an increase in government receipts, the two are in no fixed way tied together. With no fixed tie, there is no practical way of measuring government production from the receipts side of the government-sector account.

[12] The household sector is broader than the name suggests. In the official accounts it includes not only households in the ordinary sense of the word but also nongovernmental, nonprofit institutions, such as hospitals, churches, schools, clubs, and nongovernmental pension, health, and welfare funds.

[13] As in the case of interest paid by government, interest paid by consumers is not regarded as reflecting production in the household sector. Although this treatment is more controversial than the same treatment of government-paid interest, it is defended in part by the fact that, unlike interest paid by business, interest paid by consumers cannot be regarded as measuring the contribution of consumer capital to production. As in the case of government, debt resulting in interest payments may be incurred by consumers without a corresponding acquisition of capital assets. As noted above, the bulk of federal interest payments is the result of debt incurred during war, to which no acquisition of productive capital corresponds. Similarly, much of the interest paid by consumers results from loans for purposes other than the acquisi-

From Account 2 of Table 3–1, we see that the amount of production within this sector is $5. Households pay household employees $4 in wages and salaries, and they pay $1 in employer contributions for social insurance; $4 of these allocations appears as receipts of the same sector under wages and salaries, and the other $1 appears as a receipt of the government sector.

Here as with the government sector, to exclude the direct purchases of labor services by the household sector would be to understate the economy's total final product. For example, a householder may hire a business firm to wash the walls of his house, or he may give this task to a servant. In the former case, the expenditure for this service would appear as a sale to households by the business sector and as such would be part of final product originating in the business sector. If the same task were performed by a household servant (and, say, at the same cost), then unless the wages paid to the servant for this task appeared as factor income of the employee, final product for the economy as a whole would be lower than if the work were performed by a business firm. Since the very same production occurs in both cases, total wages and salaries paid to household employees must be included in final product to reflect the amount of services produced by these employees and the amount of income originating in the household sector.

Although interest paid by consumers is not regarded as a part of national income and product originating in the household sector, it is a part of personal outlays and appears under this heading on the allocations side of the household-sector account. This account shows interest paid by consumers of $1 and interest received of $13 ($8 from business, $4 from government, and $1 from house-holds). The $1 of interest from households on the receipts side is the same amount as the $1 of interest paid on the allocations side. The $8 of interest paid by business is part of national income originating with business and appears in its full amount as a receipt of households. The $4 of interest paid by government is excluded, for reasons already indicated, from national income originating with government but is part of the interest income of households. Thus, in the present three-sector economy, the interest component of national income for the economy as a whole is the $8 of interest that originates with business.

Since income and product originating with the household sector are defined as wages, salaries, and supplements paid by households, total income originating with this sector in Table 3–1 equals $5. In contrast to income originating in business ($180) and government ($20), the amount originating with households is, by present definition, a relatively small part of the total. But it could be many times larger under another definition—for example, if we included not only the wages and salaries actually paid to employees of this sector but also an imputed

---

tion of capital assets. This exclusion of interest does not, however, cover interest paid by consumers on mortgage debt, which continues to be regarded as a payment reflecting production. However, the purchase of residential structures by persons is treated in the official accounts as a business transaction, and the interest paid on the mortgage debt that results appears as net interest originating in the business sector. This will be explained in Chapter 5.

amount representing the wages and salaries that would be paid if housewives sold their services to the household instead of providing them free. Under present definitions, a wall-washing job in the home appears as part of gross national product whether it is done by a business firm or by a paid household employee. If it is done by the housewife herself, however, this output is not included as part of gross national product, despite the fact that the product in question is the same in all three cases.

The purpose of the present series of hypothetical economies is not to enter into these questions but to show the method by which an economy's income and product are measured with a given set of definitions of income and product. In Chapter 5 we will examine these actual definitions more closely to see exactly what is included and excluded from the income and product of each sector, and from this we will see what the resulting aggregates, such as national income and gross national product, seem to measure.

PRODUCTION FOR THE ECONOMY AS A WHOLE

We are now in a position to combine the income and product of the government and household sectors with that of the business sector to arrive at the national income and gross national product for the three-sector economy as a whole. The accounts of Table 3–1 are designed to trace the flows of income and product among the three sectors, so that the allocations of each sector are the receipts of other sectors and vice versa. On the basis of the data in these accounts, another set of accounts, Table 3–2, has been set up to focus attention specifically on the income and product originating with each of the three sectors. A comparison of Tables 3–1 and 3–2 will show that Accounts 1 and 4 of Table 3–2 merely repeat the same accounts of Table 3–1, for reasons that are explained below.

For the household and government sectors, net and gross national product originating with each equal national income originating with each. This follows from the definition of final product in each of these sectors as factor income directly generated by these sectors. In the business sector, however, as shown in Account 1 of Table 3–2, net and gross national product originating with business exceed factor income originating with business. This occurs because final product is valued at the market prices at which the sector's goods and services are sold, but not all the proceeds from the sale of output at market prices become national income or income of the factors of production. The principal additions to national income originating with the business sector that must be made in order to balance national income and gross national product originating with this sector are indirect business taxes and depreciation allowances, both of which have been considered earlier. Three other adjustments are needed, however, in order to account fully for the difference between national income and gross national product originating with this sector:

TABLE 3-2 Accounts for Income and Product Originating by Sector

CONSOLIDATED BUSINESS INCOME AND PRODUCT ACCOUNT (Account 1)

Wages and salaries		$118	Personal consumption expenditures	
Employer contributions for social insurance		4	(or sales to households)	$155
Rent		5	Government purchases of goods and services	
Interest		8	(or sales to government)	30
Proprietors' income		25	Gross investment	40
Corporate profits		20	Change in inventories	$ 5
Profits tax	$10		Purchases of capital goods	35
Dividends	6			
Undistributed profits	4			
NATIONAL INCOME ORIGINATING WITH BUSINESS		$180		
Business transfer payments		1		
Indirect taxes		25		
Current surplus of government enterprises		1		
Less Subsidies		4		
NET NATIONAL PRODUCT ORIGINATING WITH BUSINESS		$203		
Capital consumption allowances (depreciation)		22		
GROSS NATIONAL PRODUCT ORIGINATING WITH BUSINESS		$225	GROSS NATIONAL PRODUCT OF BUSINESS	$225

HOUSEHOLD INCOME AND PRODUCT ACCOUNT (Account 2)

Wages and salaries	$4		
Employer contributions for social insurance	1		
NATIONAL INCOME ORIGINATING WITH HOUSEHOLDS	$5	NET AND GROSS NATIONAL PRODUCT OF HOUSEHOLDS	$5

GOVERNMENT INCOME AND PRODUCT ACCOUNT (Account 3)

Wages and salaries	$19	
Employer contributions for social insurance	1	
NATIONAL INCOME ORIGINATING WITH GOVERNMENT	$20	NET AND GROSS NATIONAL PRODUCT OF GOVERNMENT $20

NATIONAL INCOME AND PRODUCT ACCOUNT (Account 4)

Wages and salaries		$141	Gross national product originating with
From business	$118		Business sector $225
From government	19		Government sector 20
From households	4		Household sector 5
Employer contributions for social insurance		6	
Proprietors' income		25	
Corporate profits		20	
Profits tax	$10		
Dividends	6		
Undistributed profits	4		
Rent		5	
Interest		8	
NATIONAL INCOME		$205	
Business transfer payments		1	
Indirect business taxes		25	
Current surplus of government enterprises		1	
Less Subsidies		4	
NET NATIONAL PRODUCT		$228	
Capital consumption allowances (depreciation)		22	
GROSS NATIONAL PRODUCT		$250	GROSS NATIONAL PRODUCT $250

1. Business transfer payments must be added.
2. Subsidies must be subtracted.
3. Current surplus of government enterprises must be added.[14]

Business transfer payments, like government transfer payments, are payments in exchange for which the payer receives no goods or services. In the business sector these transfer payments include gifts, prizes, and scholarships given by business to individuals, and also the bad debts of individuals to business. As such, these payments represent to the recipients not factor income but receipts for which no productive activity was involved. Although not factor payments, they are as much charges against business product as are wages and salaries or other factor costs. To omit them would produce a discrepancy between gross national product of business on the product side and the charges against gross national product of business on the income side. Yet to include them as factor income would falsely inflate the national income originating in the business sector. Hence, they are included as a charge against gross national product originating with business but excluded from national income originating with that sector. They appear as an item to be added to national income in going from national income to gross national product originating with the business sector.

Subsidies are similar to transfer payments in that no goods or services are provided to the payer of subsidies—that is, to government. They appear in the business sector as a negative item on the income side. As was noted earlier in the consolidation of the business-sector account, subsidies (which are actually a receipt of the business sector) are subtracted from both sides of the account, so that the total on the receipts side only reflects receipts from production. As a result of the receipt of subsidies, the prices of business output are lower, factor payments originating with business are higher, or some combination of both occurs. Let us assume the result is lower sale prices. Then subsidies as a negative item on the income side offset lower sale prices and so lower sale receipts on the product side. Alternatively, assume the result is higher factor incomes. Then subsidies as a negative item on the income side offset higher factor incomes on that same side, leaving sale receipts on the product side unchanged. On either assumption, if subsidies were not deducted on the income side, a discrepancy would result between the income and product sides of the account.

It will be recalled that government enterprises are included in the official accounts as part of the business sector. *Current surplus of government enterprises* is the difference between the receipts from their sales of final product and certain costs, thereby giving the term "surplus" the flavor of "profits," as that term is used in private business. As computed in the official accounts, however, depre-

---

[14] In the official accounts there is a fourth adjustment for the statistical discrepancy. The Commerce Department estimates the items on the income and the product side independently and terms the difference in the totals for the two sides the "statistical discrepancy." If the estimate for the income side exceeds that for the product side, the discrepancy appears as a negative item on the income side; if the other way around, it appears as a plus item on the income side. As a matter of practice, the discrepancy is shown on the income side. No such discrepancy, of course, appears in the accounts of our hypothetical economies.

ciation, interest, and taxes are not included among the costs of government enterprise, so that the residual "current surplus" is quite different from the related residual "profits" in private business.

Like private business, government enterprises sell goods and services in the marketplace, pay wages and salaries to employees, and buy goods and services from other firms. Consequently, their sales of final product appear as part of gross national product originating with the business sector, and their payments of wages and salaries appear as part of national income originating with the business sector. The difference between the value of their final product and wages and salaries paid is called *current surplus*, which may be positive or negative. Since this surplus is not recognized as profit, it is not factor income, and therefore is not part of national income. However, since surplus is the balancing item between sales of final product on the product side and charges against this product on the income side, the current surplus must be included somewhere. Accordingly, it is shown as an item to be added to national income to arrive at gross national product originating in the business sector.

Account 4 of Table 3–2 is obtained by adding Accounts 1, 2, and 3, which show gross national product and national income originating in the business, household, and government sectors of the economy, respectively. Thus, on the product side of Account 4 is shown the amount of gross national product originating with each of the three sectors, and on the income side the charges against this gross national product. These charges consist of the national income originating in all three sectors plus indirect taxes plus business transfer payments minus subsidies plus current surplus of government enterprises plus capital consumption or depreciation allowances of the business sector. Notice that in going from national income for the economy as a whole to its net and gross national product, the required adjustments are all found in the business sector account, or Account 1.

THREE MEASURES OF OUTPUT

Under our present system of national income accounting, there are three aggregate measures of the economy's output of goods and services: national income, net national product, and gross national product. *National income*, though it appears on the income side and not on the product side of the national income and product account, is nonetheless a measure of product. It is a measure of product with product valued at "factor cost," or in terms of the factor income earned (though not necessarily received) by the factors of production. As such, it is the narrowest measure. However, the proceeds from the sale of final goods and services at market prices are not matched by factor costs alone but by factor costs plus indirect taxes and business transfer payments and current surplus of government enterprises less subsidies. If we add all these elements, we get the broader measure of final output that is *net national product*. Although net national product is always greater than national income, they are both measurements of the same physical output, the difference being in the basis of measurement (i.e., in the valuation of output) and not in the thing being measured (i.e., the output itself). Finally, the proceeds from the sale of final goods and services at market prices can be taken to exclude or include the proceeds from the sale of capital goods for replacement purposes—that is, it can include among proceeds an amount equal to either net investment or gross investment—which leads to the distinction between net national product and *gross national product*. Recognizing gross investment as part of final product yields a larger total on the product side—larger by the excess of gross investment over net investment. A part of the proceeds from the sale of this larger product, exactly equal to the excess of gross over net investment, also appears as a charge on the income side in the form of capital consumption allowances. When capital consumption allowances are added to factor income plus other adjustments (indirect taxes plus business transfer payments plus current surplus of government enterprises less subsidies), the income side of the account exactly balances the product side, as shown in Account 4 of Table 3–2.

While national income and net national product are both measures of the *same* physical product, gross national product is a measure of a different and *larger* physical product, which includes the amount of capital goods used up during the period's production. If we subtract from gross national product the amount of capital goods used up during the period, we have net national product, which shows that net and gross national product measure two different physical amounts of output.[15] Viewed in this way, there are only two measures of the economy's output, a *net measure*, which at market price gives us net national product and at factor cost gives us national income, and a *gross measure*, which is gross national product.

The relationships among these several measures of output may be shown as below:[16]

GROSS NATIONAL PRODUCT		$250
Less	Capital consumption allowances	22
Equals	NET NATIONAL PRODUCT	$228
Less	Indirect business taxes	25
Less	Business transfer payments	1
Less	Current surplus of government enterprises	1
Plus	Subsidies	4
Equals	NATIONAL INCOME	$205

---

[15] Here it is assumed that capital consumption allowances accurately measure the amount of capital goods used up during the period; their failure to do so in the official accounts is discussed in Chapter 5.

[16] Notice that, apart from the reversal in order of entries, the presentation is the same as that on the allocations side of the national income and product account given as Account 4 of Tables 3–1 and 3–2. These tables work up to gross national product from national income, while the above works down from gross national product to national income. An entry added in one presentation is subtracted in the other.

PERSONAL INCOME

The format above, which is used in the official accounts to show the relationships among the three measures of output, leads directly to the derivation of another measure, *personal income*, which is defined as the current income of persons or households from all sources.[17] Unlike the other measures, personal income is not a measure of production, for it both excludes some items that are matched by productive activity and includes other items that are not. Thus, it includes both receipts for the productive services provided by persons and receipts, such as transfer payments, for which no productive services were provided by the recipients. Personal income is, therefore, derived from national income by subtracting from national income whatever parts of national income do not become receipts of persons and by adding to this remainder whatever receipts persons derive from sources not included in national income. The steps involved may be shown as follows:

NATIONAL	INCOME	$205
Less	Corporate profits	20
Less	Employer contributions for social insurance	6
Plus	Government transfer payments	13
Plus	Business transfer payments	1
Plus	Net interest paid by government	4
Plus	Interest paid by consumers	1
Plus	Dividends	6
Less	Employee contributions for social insurance	4
Equals	PERSONAL INCOME	$200

DISPOSABLE PERSONAL INCOME

Another aggregate measure is derived from personal income by deducting from that total the amount of personal income that is siphoned off by government in personal taxes. The remainder is *disposable personal income*, since it equals the amount available to persons to dispose of as they choose. The difference between this amount and the amount devoted to *personal saving* equals *personal outlays*. Personal outlays in turn, in the three-sector economy, are composed of personal consumption expenditures and interest paid by consumers as shown below:

[17] Income here includes more than actual cash receipts of persons; imputed or noncash receipts are also included. The role of imputations in the measures of production and in personal income is considered in Chapter 5.

PERSONAL INCOME			$200
Less	Personal taxes		24
Equals	DISPOSABLE PERSONAL INCOME		176
Less	Personal saving		15
Equals	PERSONAL OUTLAYS		$161
Personal consumption expenditures		$160	
Interest paid by consumers		1	

GROSS NATIONAL PRODUCT—FROM SECTOR OF ORIGIN TO SECTOR OF DEMAND

In measuring national income, net national product, and gross national product, we obtained each total by combining the national income or the net or gross national product originating in each of the three sectors. While such an arrangement answers the question of how much of the total national product was produced by each sector, it does not tell us how much of the product each sector secures for its own use. To learn this, we must turn to the expenditures of each sector on product. The aggregate of the expenditures of all sectors (including change in inventories as an expenditure) is necessarily the same magnitude as the aggregate of product originating in all sectors, since there is clearly an accounting identity between the total produced by all sectors and the total secured by all sectors. Table 3–3 shows how the presentation of gross national product by *sector of origin*, or sector of supply, may be rearranged to show the same total by type of expenditure, or what may be called *sector of demand*. The left-hand side of Table 3–3 corresponds with the product side of Account 4 of Table 3–2, although the order of entries has been changed to facilitate the present comparison.

Here we see that, from the point of view of gross national product by sector of supply or origin, government accounts for only $20. As a sector of demand it secures $50. The difference of $30 between what government produces directly and what it secures in total is the amount of goods and services produced by the business sector that is purchased by the government sector. The same reasoning applies to the $155 excess of household consumption ($160) over household production ($5). Since both the government and the household sectors secure more than they supply or produce, it follows that the business sector must supply more than it secures. This should not be taken to mean that households and government get something for nothing. Recall that gross national product originating in the business sector equals the sum of capital consumption allowances, indirect taxes plus minor adjustments, and national income originating in that sector. Most of the national income originating in the business sector becomes personal income of the household sector, and this enables households to purchase from business the bulk of its output. Similarly,

TABLE 3–3 Gross National Product by Sector of Origin and by Sector of Demand

SECTOR OF ORIGIN			SECTOR OF DEMAND		
Gross national product originating with government		$ 20	Government purchases of goods and services		$ 50
Wages, salaries, and supplements	$ 20		Services provided by government employees	$ 20	
Gross national product originating with business		225	Goods and services purchased from business	30	
Sales to government	30		Gross investment		40
Sales to business on capital account	35		Goods purchased from business on capital account	35	
Change in inventories	5		Change in inventories	5	
Sales to consumers	155		Personal consumption expenditures		160
Gross national product originating with households		5	Goods and services purchased from business	155	
Wages, salaries, and supplements	5		Services purchased from households	5	
GROSS NATIONAL PRODUCT		$250	GROSS NATIONAL PRODUCT		$250

a portion of the gross national product originating in business, mainly corporate profits taxes and indirect taxes, is a receipt of the government sector. These receipts, augmented by taxes on personal income, enable government to purchase a large part of business output. That portion of gross national product originating in the business sector that is not secured by either government or households remains in the business sector as unconsumed output, or gross investment.

FUNDAMENTAL IDENTITIES IN THE THREE-SECTOR ECONOMY

We have seen that in the absence of government, gross national product would be divided into consumption and gross investment. On the product side of the account, whatever is not consumed is gross investment, and, on the income side of the account, whatever is not consumed is gross saving. Gross saving is thus necessarily identical with gross investment.[18]

These relationships are modified by the introduction of government. On the product side, gross national product is split three ways because there are now three sectors that demand final goods and services: households, business, and government. Similarly, on the income side of the account, there is a three-way split, for income is now devoted to taxes as well as to consumption and saving.

In adding government demand to gross national product, only that part of government expenditures that goes toward the purchase of goods and services is included.[19] Therefore, in calculating gross national product, we exclude from government expenditures all transfer payments, interest payments, and subsidies minus current surplus of government enterprises. Since for every dollar on the product side there must be a dollar on the income side, we must similarly exclude from the income side an amount of taxes equal to these other government expenditures. In Account 3 of Table 3–1, government purchases of goods and services total $50, and this amount properly appears as part of gross national product. Other government expenditures total $20 and are not part of gross national product. Therefore, on the income side of the account, it is necessary to deduct $20 from gross tax receipts to yield net tax receipts. In effect, the $20 total of government transfers and related expenditures are negative taxes, for these government expenditures of $20 simply restore to the income side in redistributed form the very amount withdrawn from that side through taxes in the amount of $20.

---

[18] See Account 3 of Table 2–4.
[19] It will be recalled that gross national product as a measure of the value of final product can be obtained by summing up all expenditures on final product, including in expenditures on final product any change in inventories. To include government expenditures for other than final product is to overstate by that amount gross national product and to destroy its meaning as a measure of the value of final output of goods and services.

Thus, by taking taxes as net of these other government expenditures, we establish an identity between consumption (C), saving (S), and taxes (T) on the income side and consumption, investment (I), and government purchases of goods and services (G) on the product side, or

$$C + S + T \equiv C + I + G$$

In any given time period, the amount of government purchases of goods and services on the product side, or G, may be equal to, greater than, or less than the amount of taxes, T, on the income side. In other words, the government may show, respectively, a balanced budget, a deficit, or a surplus. Let us examine how each of these three possibilities affects the fundamental identity.

Balanced Budget

Assume the budget is balanced with total government expenditures of $69; purchases of goods and services are $50, other expenditures are $19, and total taxes are $69. Limiting expenditures to those for goods and services and adjusting taxes correspondingly to a net basis gives us a budget balanced with G of $50 and T of $50. Thus, the amount that government adds to the stream of spending for the period through its purchases of goods and services is exactly matched by the amount that it withdraws from the stream of income generated by the stream of spending on final goods and services.

The fundamental identity including government is $C + S + T \equiv C + I + G$. Since with a balanced budget $T = G$, it follows that $C + S \equiv C + I$ and, from this in turn, that $S \equiv I$. In other words, with a balanced budget, the identity between gross saving of the household and business sectors on the income side and gross investment of the business sector on the product side is just as it was in the two-sector economy. For every dollar of personal and business saving, S, there is a dollar of gross investment, I.

Deficit

For this case we can make use of the figures in Table 3–1, in which government shows a deficit. Here, total government expenditures of $70 exceed total taxes of $69, producing a deficit of $1. Government purchases of goods and services, G, are $50, and taxes on a net basis, T, are $49. There thus remains on the income side $1, which was put there by G but was not withdrawn by T. This remaining $1 on the income side is accounted for within the time period as $1 of additional S, or saving by persons and firms. Thus, we have:

$$C + S + T \equiv C + I + G$$
$$\$160 + \$41 + \$49 = \$160 + \$40 + \$50$$

and

$$S + T \equiv I + G$$
$$\$41 + \$49 = \$40 + \$50$$

Note that, with an unbalanced budget, the sum of personal and gross business saving, S, no longer equals gross investment, I, for S is $41 and I is $40. Yet it has been repeatedly emphasized that gross saving must equal gross investment as an unavoidable accounting identity, since investment is unconsumed product, saving is unconsumed income, and income equals the value of product. We must show that an unbalanced budget does not and cannot upset this fundamental identity.

Again in terms of the present set of figures, the sum of personal consumption expenditures, C ($160), and "public consumption expenditures," G ($50), measures total consumption of output in the economy.[20] Gross investment, I, ($40) is the unconsumed output of the economy. For every dollar of investment there must be a dollar of saving. Yet we have $41 of S and $40 of I. This extra dollar of S matches the government deficit of $1, and it is the deficit that produces this *apparent* inequality between saving and investment. Once the concept of government saving is introduced into our economy, we will see that the apparent inequality between saving and investment is just that—an *apparent* and not an actual inequality.

As in the household sector, where the difference between disposable personal income and personal outlays equals personal saving, in the government sector we find that the difference between net taxes and government purchases of goods and services equals *government saving*. If the household sector's personal outlays are greater than its disposable income, it "dissaves" to that extent, and personal saving for that period is negative. If the government spends more on goods and services than it collects in net taxes, it also dissaves to that extent, and government saving for the period is negative. Suppose, now, that we put together personal saving and gross business saving (composed of capital consumption allowances and undistributed profits) and call the total *gross private saving*, as distinct from government saving, which we will call *public saving*. Gross saving for the economy as a whole is then the sum of gross private saving (S) and public saving $(T - G)$, and it is this sum of $S + (T - G)$ that must equal gross investment. And it does. The sum of gross private saving ($41) and public saving $(-$1)$ is $40, and gross investment is also $40.

If we rearrange the fundamental identity as follows, we see that this is the case.

$$S + T \equiv I + G$$
$$\$41 + \$49 = \$40 + \$50$$

$$S + (T - G) \equiv I$$
$$\$41 + (\$49 - \$50) = \$40$$

---

[20] Government purchases of goods and services, like personal consumption expenditures, are all treated as if they were goods and services consumed, despite the fact that these purchases include long-lived goods such as buildings, dams, and ships. The same issue was faced earlier under personal consumption expenditures where purchases of cars, appliances, and other durable goods were treated as consumption expenditures in the same way that gasoline to power cars and electricity to power appliances were treated. This problem in the official accounts is considered in Chapter 5.

Looking back at Account 5 of Table 3–1, from which these figures were drawn, gives another view of the identity. For every dollar of *I* and *G* on the product side, there is a dollar of *either* *S* or *T* on the income side. *I* + *G* total $90; *S* + *T* total $90. If government withdraws less from the income stream through net taxes than it adds through its purchases of goods and services, the difference must appear in that time period as private saving and public dissaving.

Whatever the government deficit for any time period, there is necessarily an excess of private saving over investment in that period equal to the deficit. It then follows that government can, at least potentially, finance its deficit in any time period by borrowing an amount equal to the deficit from private saving, which will be larger than investment by the amount of the deficit. Alternatively, the government can finance its deficit by "printing" new money in the amount of the deficit. In this case, it pays for the excess of its expenditures over its taxes without borrowing from the public. But the amount of the deficit is still matched by an equal excess of private saving over investment. The difference is simply that in the case in which government borrows from the public, the public's saving is held in government securities, and in the case in which government finances its deficit with newly created money, the public's saving is held in the form of money. How the deficit is financed makes a great difference in other respects, especially in terms of the possible inflationary impact of the deficit, but, for the fundamental identity with which we are here concerned, either method gives the same result: *Gross private saving exceeds gross investment by the amount of the deficit*.

Surplus

In the case of a surplus, taxes withdraw from the stream of income generated by total spending on final product an amount greater than that which government purchases of goods and services contribute to this stream of income.

Let us assume an economy with a surplus of $1. Suppose government purchases of goods and services are $50 as before and net taxes are now $51. The identity reads:

$$C + S + T \equiv C + I + G$$
$$\$160 + \$39 + \$51 = \$160 + \$40 + \$50$$

The government surplus, or public saving, of $1 is necessarily offset by private saving, which is $1 *less* than it would otherwise be. For the economy, gross saving of $40 ($39 private and $1 public) is matched by gross investment of $40. Again, by dropping *C* from both sides and by rearranging the identity, we have:

$$S + (T - G) \equiv I$$
$$\$39 + (\$51 - \$50) = \$40$$

In this case, $1 more is withdrawn from the income side by government than is in effect placed on that side by government purchases of goods and services. This extra $1 is accounted for within the time period by a decrease of $1 in private saving. The economy's gross investment of $40 is matched dollar for dollar by gross saving. In the case of a surplus, part of the economy's saving is by government $(T - G)$, so private saving (S) is necessarily less than investment by the amount of government saving.

To summarize, for all three possible cases—balanced budget, deficit, or surplus—the economy's three sectors must collectively, in any time period, show an amount of saving (or unconsumed income) equal to that period's investment (or unconsumed product). The three cases differ only in that each gives a different distribution of the economy's gross saving between private and public saving. A government deficit must add to private saving an amount equal to the deficit, for government is withdrawing from the income side less than it places there through its purchases of goods and services on the product side. A government surplus must subtract from private saving an amount equal to the surplus, for government is withdrawing more from the income side than it places there through its purchases of goods and services on the product side. A surplus or deficit, in other words, so alters gross private saving in the given time period that private saving, when added to government saving or dissaving, yields a total equal to the period's gross investment.

CIRCULAR FLOW IN THE THREE-SECTOR ECONOMY

The circular flow of income and product for the three-sector economy is given in Figure 3–1. The dollar values shown are those in Table 3–1. The gross national product of $250 is broken down by sector of origin to the left of center and by sector of demand to the right of center. On the left of the figure we have a flow of income of $250, which results from the economy's flow of product for the period.[21] To this flow of income created by production is added a flow of income to which there corresponds no production—namely, an income flow of $20, which results from government transfer payments and related items. Since these items are not part of the economy's production, they appear at the very outer edge of the figure, separated from the economy's gross national product. In this broader sense, the economy's income totals $270, as seen at the far left of the figure. This total of $270 of income is disposed of by its recipients in three ways: Part is spent for consumer goods, $160; part is taken by government in taxes, $69; and the remainder is saved, $41.

In order to trace the fundamental identity between the total of C, S, and T on the left and the total of C, I, and G on the right, it is again necessary to put

---

[21] In the two-sector economy we assumed for simplicity that product originated only with the business sector. The circular flow, accordingly, was simply one of product from firms to households and of productive services from households to firms. In the present three-sector economy, we are allowing for the fact that production takes place in all three sectors, so a figure like Figure 2–1 is no longer appropriate to illustrate the circular flow.

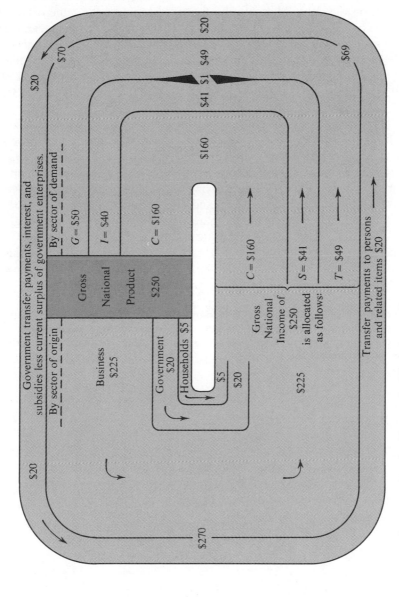

FIGURE 3-1 Circular Flow in the Three-Sector Economy

taxes on a net basis by subtracting $20 from taxes of $69.[22] This subtraction reduces taxes to $49, and the sum of C, S, and T to $250 on the left. This is matched by the $250 sum of C, I, and G, or gross national product by sector of demand, on the right. Alternatively, we could arrive at the same result in Figure 3–1 by ignoring altogether government transfer payments and related government expenditures as a source of income. This would limit income on the left to that earned in the course of production, or $250, and it would limit spending on the right to expenditures on final goods and services, or $250. This $250 may thus be split up into C, S, and T on the left, which matches the sum of C, I, and G on the right without any adjustment.

The circular flow for this three-sector economy shows a government deficit of $1 for the time period. As discussed earlier, this means that government purchases of goods and services, G of $50, exceed net taxes, T of $49, by $1, and this $1 is shown as $1 of private saving in excess of gross investment. Thus, Figure 3–1 shows a flow of private saving of $41 and of investment of $40 and a flow of net taxes of $49 ($69 − $20) and of government purchases of goods and services of $50. On the right of the figure a small channel appears through which $1 is diverted from the stream of private saving into the stream of taxes. To show the necessary balance between $S + T$ and $I + G$, one might think of this as $1 of private saving that was borrowed by government to finance the excess of its purchases of goods and services over its net tax receipts.

[22] As discussed earlier, this subtraction is to offset the subtraction of $20 from total government expenditures of $70, the latter being necessary to show only those government expenditures of $50 to which there corresponds production and which are therefore properly part of gross national product.

CHAPTER 4

NATIONAL INCOME
ACCOUNTING:
FOUR-SECTOR ECONOMY

An economy whose foreign transactions are excluded from analysis is termed a "closed" economy. By now including transactions with the "rest-of-the-world," we will have an "open" economy that includes all four of the sectors found in any actual economy.

The addition of the rest-of-the-world as the fourth and final sector now permits us to recognize that an actual economy's gross national product is not necessarily equal to the total of final goods and services secured by domestic consumers (as measured by personal consumption expenditures), by domestic government (as measured by government purchases of goods and services), and by domestic business (as measured by gross private domestic investment). If an economy for any time period shows net exports of goods and services, the amount of final goods and services *secured* by domestic consumers, government, and business is necessarily less than the amount domestically *produced*. If, however, the economy shows net imports, then domestic consumers, government, and business secure a total of final goods and services greater than that which was domestically produced during the time period. In either case, the open economy replaces with a four-way division the three-way division of gross national product found in a closed economy.

It also follows that in the four-sector economy any increase in net exports, *other things being equal*, produces an equal increase in the economy's gross national product for that period. If, during a given period, the total amount of final goods and services secured by consumers, government, and business remains unchanged and the excess of exports over imports grows or shrinks, then gross national product must also be larger or smaller than it was during the preceding period by the amount of this change.

In practice, for the economy of the United States, it makes little *quantitative* difference in gross national product whether we include or exclude net exports of goods and services. For 1968, with gross national product of $865.7 billion, net exports were $2.5 billion, or less than 1 percent. Since 1951, net exports have accounted for more than 1 percent of gross national product only in the years 1957, 1964, 1965. In contrast, government purchases of goods and services averaged about 20 percent of gross national product over these same years.

For this reason, the impact of actual changes in net exports on gross national product is small. A 100 percent change in the *net* exports of the United States would in itself change gross national product by less than 1 percent, disregarding the secondary effects induced by this change. But, whether the impact is large or small for the United States or any other economy, the income and product accounts for the economy are incomplete without their inclusion. In this brief chapter, we will outline the changes in the economy's income and product accounts that result from the inclusion of the economy's transactions with the rest-of-the-world.

NET FOREIGN INVESTMENT

Since an economy's income and product accounts measure, among other things, that economy's income and product, foreign transactions enter into its accounts only to the extent that they influence its income and product. The producing and consuming, saving and investing, and importing and exporting that take place in the rest-of-the-world have no effect on the accounts of the domestic economy, unless such activities involve transactions with the domestic economy. The introduction of the rest-of-the-world in no sense measures income or product in the rest-of-the-world; it shows only the effect on domestic income and product of transactions between the home economy and the rest-of-the-world.

It is true, of course, that whatever changes occur in the domestic economy's accounts through its foreign transactions must be matched by offsetting changes in the combined accounts of the rest-of-the-world, which record its transactions with the domestic economy. If we assume at this point that there are no transfer payments between countries, it turns out that a single item enters to balance the international books: *net foreign investment* (or disinvestment) by the domestic economy in the rest-of-the-world is matched by *net foreign disinvestment* (or investment) by the rest-of-the-world in the domestic economy.

An economy's net sales of goods and services to the rest-of-the-world are called "net foreign investment"; they are goods and services produced, but not secured, by the domestic economy's nationals. In this sense, net foreign investment is similar in nature to domestic investment as developed earlier for a closed economy. Investment there was simply defined as the difference between what was produced and what was consumed, or as the amount of unconsumed output. Now, when we distinguish between domestic investment and foreign investment, we find that the difference lies solely in the disposition of the economy's unconsumed output. Domestic investment is that part of unconsumed output that remains at home in the form of an addition to inventories or to the stock of capital goods; foreign investment is that part of unconsumed output that goes abroad, where, depending in part on the nature of the goods, it may be consumed, added to inventories, or added to the stock of capital goods of the rest-of-the-world.[1]

How net foreign investment fits into the accounts may be seen in general terms by expanding the fundamental identities developed for the three-sector economy. For that economy, the identity for gross national product was

$$C + S + T \equiv C + I + G$$

Total product by sector of demand was composed of goods and services consumed by households (C) or by government (G), or left unconsumed (I). Now, with the addition of the fourth sector, some portion of total domestic production is sold to the rest-of-the-world and is available neither for consumption by households or government nor for domestic investment. At the same time, some portion of the total amount of goods and services consumed by households and by government at home and some portion of the total amount of capital goods purchased and goods added to business inventories at home were not produced domestically but were purchased from the rest-of-the-world. Gross national product is accordingly equal to $C + I + G$ plus the excess of sales to foreigners over purchases from foreigners. This excess is termed *net foreign investment* and is designated I_f. Designating gross domestic investment I_d, we have the following identity for gross national product in the four-sector economy:

$$C + S + T \equiv C + I_d + I_f + G$$

Since net foreign investment, I_f, equals sales abroad less purchases abroad, we may also express the identity as follows:

$$C + S + T \equiv C + I_d + (S_a - P_a) + G$$

in which S_a designates sales abroad and P_a purchases abroad.

Both versions of this fundamental identity differ from the fundamental identity for the three-sector economy only in the breakdown on the product side. Unconsumed output in the three-sector economy was limited to gross domestic investment, whereas unconsumed output in the four-sector economy is the sum of gross domestic and net foreign investment.

---

[1] Net purchases from the rest-of-the-world are net foreign disinvestment to the domestic economy. If, however, the net purchases are not consumed but are added to inventories or to the stock of capital goods, domestic investment of the economy rises by the amount of its net foreign disinvestment, thus leaving the sum of domestic and net foreign investment unchanged. Similarly, net sales to the rest-of-the-world are net foreign investment. If, however, the amount of net sales represents a net withdrawal from the economy's inventories or stock of capital goods, domestic disinvestment offsets net foreign investment, thus leaving the sum of domestic and net foreign investment unchanged.

For the three-sector economy, we derived the identity between saving and investment from $C + S + T \equiv C + I + G$ by canceling the C's and rewriting to yield $S + (T - G) \equiv I$. Here the economy's gross saving (private saving of S and public saving of $T - G$), equals the economy's gross investment. Now, for the four-sector economy, gross saving remains the sum of private and public saving, but gross investment becomes the sum of gross domestic investment, I_d, and net foreign investment, I_f. The saving-investment identity now reads

$$S + (T - G) \equiv I_d + I_f$$

or

$$S + (T - G) \equiv I_d + (S_a - P_a)$$

since $(S_a - P_a)$ equals I_f.

FOREIGN TRANSFER PAYMENTS

The gross national product identity just developed for the four-sector economy includes under $C + I_d + (S_a - P_a) + G$ all the final goods and services produced during the period, but it does not accurately indicate the actual portion of final goods and services that was secured by the rest-of-the-world. This apparent contradiction results from the fact that the domestic economy's net foreign investment measures only the *net purchases* by the rest-of-the-world from the domestic economy. However, in addition to purchases, for which by definition payment is financed by the purchaser, goods and services are exported from the domestic economy for which payment is not so financed and which are thus not included in purchases. Yet the net amount of goods flowing from the domestic economy is part of that economy's gross national product, even though this net amount does not appear in full as net purchases by the rest-of-the-world. This difference must be included as part of gross national product and is so included under the headings of government purchases of goods and services and personal consumption expenditures.

For example, suppose that the federal government in a given year makes $2 billion in *grants* to other countries in the form of goods. This $2 billion would not appear as a part of net purchases from the United States, and therefore would not be included in net foreign investment, but would appear as a part of government purchases of goods and services, G. Similarly, suppose that in a given year persons give $1 billion in the form of goods to the rest-of-the-world. This, again, does not appear as part of net purchases from the United States, and therefore is not included in net foreign investment; rather, it appears as part of personal consumption expenditures, C.

If our purpose is only to measure the economy's income and product for the year, this procedure is altogether appropriate, for it does pick up all final goods and services. If we wish also, however, to measure the division of the gross national product into goods and services secured by the nationals of the domestic economy and goods and services secured by the rest-of-the-world, this procedure is not altogether appropriate.

In the years before World War II, this approach was not seriously inappropriate for the latter purpose, since in those years government grants were insignificant in comparison with what they have been since the war. In view of the postwar rise in government grants, the Commerce Department in 1958 introduced a revised treatment of foreign transactions to remove from government purchases and classify as foreign transfer payments an amount equal to net cash grants to the rest-of-the-world and thus to show this amount explicitly as part of foreign transactions. In the revisions introduced in 1965, government nonmilitary grants and personal remittances in cash and in kind have been accorded the same treatment.[2] In the household-sector account, a new entry, personal transfer payments to foreigners, appears, the amount of which is no longer included in personal consumption expenditures. Since, as a result of these changes, foreign transactions are no longer limited to *sales* and *purchases*, it is appropriate to use the broader terms, *exports* and *imports*. Although net exports (exports minus imports) now exceed net foreign investment, this causes no change in the magnitude of gross national product. The amount by which net exports $(X - M)$ exceed net foreign investment $(S_a - P_a)$ is exactly offset by a reduction in what otherwise would have been larger figures for G and C. The amount by which G is reduced is an amount called transfer payments from U.S. government to foreigners (net), and the amount by which C is reduced is an amount called personal transfer payments to foreigners (net).

FOREIGN TRANSACTIONS ACCOUNT

This treatment yields what is officially called the Foreign Transactions Account, shown as Table 4–1. In the present illustration, net exports are $5. Of this amount, $2 is accounted for by net foreign investment and the remaining $3 by foreign transfer payments, $2 from government and $1 from persons. From the point of view of the rest-of-the-world, $2 of the $5 of its net imports is accounted for by an excess of purchases from the domestic economy over sales to it and the remaining $3 by grants from domestic government and persons.

Included under imports and exports of goods and services are familiar items such as commodities of all kinds and "invisibles" such as shipping, banking, insurance services, and tourism, although this detail is not shown in the highly condensed Foreign Transactions Account. For national income purposes, the specific services described as factor services are separated out to determine the amount of national income originating in this sector. Income

---

[2] Military grants continue to be classified as government purchases of goods and services. Thus, it is the purchase of military equipment by the U.S. government that appears in the accounts rather than its subsequent transfer to foreign nations.

TABLE 4–1 **Foreign Transactions Account**

Exports of goods and services	$23	Imports of goods and services	$18
		Transfer payments from domestic government to foreigners (net)	2
		Personal transfer payments to foreigners (net)	1
		Net foreign investment	2
Receipts from foreigners	$23	Payments to foreigners	$23

earned for such services includes wages and salaries paid to nationals of the domestic economy who are employed either at home or abroad by foreign firms, governments, and institutions; interest and dividends received by nationals on holdings of securities issued by foreign companies and governments; and profits earned by foreign branches of domestic firms. The domestic economy also purchases such services from the rest-of-the-world and accordingly makes similar payments to the rest-of-the-world. If a breakdown of Table 4–1 showed $5 for factor services under Exports of Goods and Services and $1 for factor services under Imports of Goods and Services, on a net-basis, sale of factor services would amount to $4, and this would be the amount of the domestic economy's national income originating with the rest-of-the-world. National income, it will be recalled, is a measure of the earnings of the domestic economy's factors of production, and the net amount earned by these factors through providing such services to the rest-of-the-world is measured in this way and combined with the amounts earned by the factors from the other three sectors to yield the measure of the total national income for the economy.

It would now be possible to develop an entire set of accounts for the four-sector economy with all the detail given in Table 3–1 for the three-sector economy. However, we can by-pass this step and still see how each of the entries in the Foreign Transactions Account fits into the full set of accounts by simply indicating the counterentry for each as it would appear in the complete set of accounts.[3] Net exports of $5 in Table 4–1 has as its counterentry the same item on the product side of the National Income and Product Account. Net foreign investment has as its counterentry the same item under gross investment in the Gross Saving and Investment Account. Lastly, foreign transfer payments of government and of persons each has as its counterentry the same item on the allocations side of the government-sector and household-sector accounts.

The fundamental identities developed earlier in this chapter must be modified to allow for the introduction of foreign transfer payments. We had earlier the following for gross national product:

$$C + S + T \equiv C + I_d + I_f + G$$

or

$$C + S + T \equiv C + I_d + (S_a - P_a) + G$$

[3] These same entries may be traced in Table 5–1 (in the following chapter), which presents the full set of summary accounts with data for 1968 for the U.S. economy.

Designating transfer payments from domestic government to foreigners by R_{gf} and from persons to foreigners by R_{pf}, we now have the following for gross national product:

$$C + R_{pf} + S + T \equiv C + I_d + I_f + R_{gf} + R_{pf} + G$$

or

$$C + R_{pf} + S + T \equiv C + I_d + (X - M) + G$$

in which $(X - M)$ equals $I_f + R_{gf} + R_{pf}$

We had earlier the following identity for saving and investment:

$$S + (T - G) \equiv I_d + I_f$$

or

$$S + (T - G) \equiv I_d + (S_a - P_a)$$

Now, however, including foreign transfer payments by government and persons, we derive the following identity for saving and investment from the gross national product identity:

$$S + (T - G - R_{gf}) = I_d + I_f$$

The full series of fundamental identities developed through the successive economies may now be placed in order for comparison.

Economy	Gross National Product Identities	Saving and Investment Identities
Two-sector	$C + S \equiv C + I$	$S \equiv I$
Three-sector	$C + S + T \equiv C + I + G$	$S + (T - G) \equiv I$
Four-sector	$C + R_{pf} + S + T \equiv C + I_d + G + (X - M)$	$S + (T - G - R_{gf}) \equiv I_d + I_f$

In the two-sector economy, gross private saving was necessarily equal to gross domestic investment; there was neither public saving nor net foreign investment. In the three-sector economy, the sum of gross private saving and public saving was necessarily equal to gross domestic investment; there was no net foreign investment. Finally, in the four-sector economy, the sum of gross private saving (S) and public saving $(T - G - R_{gf})$ necessarily equals the sum of gross domestic investment and net foreign investment. Our final hypothetical economy has carried us to the point at which each class of saving and each class of investment found in the real world appears in the fundamental identities. However, from the two-sector to the four-sector economy, the principle is unchanged. In terms of gross national product, for every dollar of final product on the right there is a dollar of income on the left; in terms of saving and investment, for every dollar of final product on the right that is not consumed (i.e., for every dollar of investment), there is a dollar of income on the left not spent for public or private consumption (i.e., a dollar of saving).

CIRCULAR FLOW IN THE FOUR-SECTOR ECONOMY

The circular flow for an open economy, shown in Figure 4–1, contains only a few modifications of Figure 3–1, the flow for a closed economy. In the upper part of Figure 4–1, under gross national product *by sector of demand*, the rest-of-the-world appears as a fourth sector, with its demand measured by net exports ($5); under gross national product *by sector of origin*, the rest-of-the-world appears as a fourth sector, with income originating abroad measured by net factor income received by the domestic economy from the rest-of-the-world ($4).

The dollar figures in Figure 4–1 correspond with the following hypothetical figures for the basic identities in the four-sector economy.

The gross national product identity is:

$$C + R_{pf} + S + T \equiv C + I_d + (X - M) + G$$

or

$$
\begin{array}{c}
C\ +\ R_{pf} +\ S\ +\ T\ \equiv\ C\ +\ I_d\ +\ I_f\ +\ R_{pf} + R_{gf} +\ G \\
\$159 +\ \$1\ +\ \$41 + \$49\ =\ \$159 + \$36 + \$2\ +\ \$1\ +\ \$2\ + \$50
\end{array}
$$

The saving and investment identity is:

$$
\begin{array}{c}
S\ +\ (T\ -\ G\ -\ R_{gf}) \equiv\ I_d\ +\ I_f \\
\$41 + (\$49 - \$50 -\ \$2)\ =\ \$36 + \$2
\end{array}
$$

In Figure 4–1, GNP by sector of origin shows a flow of $250 of final goods and services, of which $221 is assumed to originate with business, $20 with government, $5 with households, and $4 with the rest-of-the-world. Corresponding to this flow of gross product is a flow of gross income, of which $159 is devoted to personal consumption expenditures, $41 to private saving, and $1 to personal transfer payments to foreigners and of which $49 is net taxes paid to government. In terms of demand for final goods and services, $159 of these goods and services is secured by households, $50 by government, $36 by business in the form of capital goods and additions to inventories, and $5 by the rest-of-the-world in the form of net exports from the domestic economy.

The essential difference between this circular flow and the flow for the three-sector economy lies in this breakdown of demand for final product. In the new flow we have the fourth sector of demand, net exports of $5, here shown divided into net foreign investment of $2, government transfer payments to foreigners of $2, and personal transfer payments to foreigners of $1. This division permits the further division within the diagram of the economy's gross investment of $38 into gross domestic investment of $36 and net foreign investment of $2. From the disposition of gross income, we find that gross private saving is $41, or $3 in excess of the sum of gross domestic and net foreign investment. At the same time, the sum of government purchases of goods and

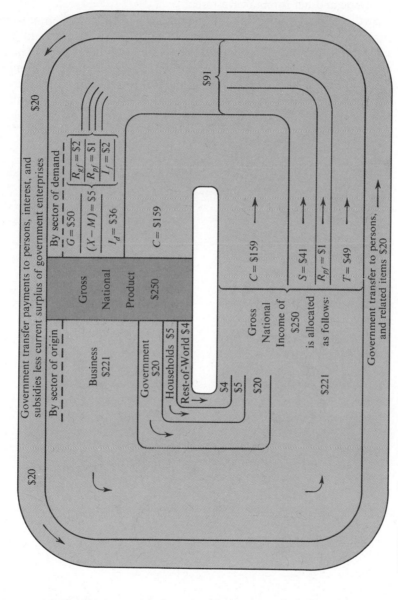

FIGURE 4–1 Circular Flow in the Four-Sector Economy

services and government transfer payments to foreigners is $52, or $3 greater than net tax receipts. The excess of private saving over gross investment thus equals government dissaving, or the deficit of $3. Gross saving, the sum of public saving of − $3 and private saving of $41, turns out to equal the sum of gross domestic and net foreign investment.

Apart from its hypothetical dollar amounts and the omission of some detail, Figure 4–1 gives one version of the circular flow of income and product for a real-world, four-sector economy. The step-by-step buildup of the circular flow process carried out through three successive hypothetical economies has brought us, in Figure 4–1, to the border of the real-world economy of the United States. In the next chapter, we will examine a more detailed circular flow diagram that describes the U.S. economy in terms of the complete official accounting framework, incorporating the actual figures recorded for the year 1968.

CHAPTER 5

THE NATIONAL INCOME
AND PRODUCT ACCOUNTS
OF THE UNITED STATES

Having worked through a series of increasingly complex accounting frameworks for hypothetical economies, we have only a short step to take from the last of these to the official accounting framework for the U.S. economy as constructed by the Department of Commerce. The first part of this chapter sets forth this framework and the circular flow and fundamental identities that emerge from it. The second part takes a brief look at the statistical record of national income and gross national product in the United States from 1929 to 1968. The last part examines a few of the many specific problems that, while ignored in the accounts of the hypothetical economies in the interest of simplicity, must be faced in the official accounts.

THE OFFICIAL ACCOUNTING FRAMEWORK

The complete official accounting framework of the United States, with data for the year 1968, is given in Table 5–1. There are several important differences between this framework and the frameworks developed earlier. First, there is no separate account for the business sector. The department's earlier six-account system was replaced in 1958 by a five-account system, which currently includes sector accounts for households (II), government (III), and rest-of-the-world or foreign transactions (IV), plus a national income and product account (I) and a gross saving and investment account (V). The elimination of the business-sector account sacrifices some detail, but since the national income and product account is not too different from the business-sector account,[1] the loss of detail is not great and is compensated for by the simplification of the system.

[1] Compare, for example, Accounts 1 and 4 of Table 3–1.

TABLE 5-1 Summary National Income and Product Accounts, 1968 (billions of dollars)

I. NATIONAL INCOME AND PRODUCT ACCOUNT

Item					Item				
1	Compensation of employees			$513.6	24 (C)	Personal consumption expenditures (II–3)			$536.6
2	Wages and salaries			465.0	25	Durable goods		$ 83.3	
3	Disbursements (II–7)		465.0		26	Nondurable goods		230.6	
4	Wage accruals less disbursements (V–4)				27	Services		222.8	
5	Supplements to wages and salaries			48.6	28 (I_d)	Gross private domestic investment (V–1)			126.3
6	Employer contributions for social insurance (III–14)	$24.4			29	Fixed investment		119.0	
7	Other labor income (II–8)	24.2			30	Nonresidential	$88.8		
8	Proprietors' income (II–9)			63.8	31	Structures	$29.3		
9	Rental income of persons (II–10)			21.2	32	Producers' durable equipment	59.5		
10	Corporate profits and inventory valuation adjustment			87.9	33	Residential structures		30.2	
11	Profits before tax			91.1	34	Change in business inventories		7.3	
12 (T_c)	Profits tax liability (III–11)		41.3		35 ($X - M$)	Net exports of goods and services			2.5
13	Profits after tax		49.8		36	Exports (IV–1)		50.6	
14	Dividends (II–11)	$23.1			37	Imports (IV–2)		48.1	
15 (S_u)	Undistributed profits (V–5)	26.7			38 (G)	Government purchases of goods and services (III–1)			200.3
16	Inventory valuation adjustment (V–6)			–3.2	39	Federal		99.5	
17	Net interest (II–13)			28.0	40	National defense	78.0		
18 (NI)	NATIONAL INCOME			$714.4	41	Other	21.5		
19 (R_b)	Business transfer payments (II–17)			3.4	42	State and local		100.7	
20 (T_i)	Indirect business tax and nontax liability (III–12)			77.9					
21 (R_s)	Less: Subsidies less current surplus of government enterprises (III–6)			.8					
22 (S_g)	Capital consumption allowances (V–7)			73.3					
23 (SD)	Statistical discrepancy (V–9)			–2.5					
	CHARGES AGAINST GROSS NATIONAL PRODUCT			$865.7		GROSS NATIONAL PRODUCT			$865.7

II. PERSONAL INCOME AND OUTLAY ACCOUNT

Item				Item				
1 (T_p)	Personal tax and nontax payments (III–10)		$ 97.9	7	Wage and salary disbursements (I–3)			$465.0
2 (PO)	Personal outlays		551.6	8	Other labor income (I–7)			24.2
3 (C)	Personal consumption expenditures (II–24)	$536.6		9	Proprietors' income (I–8)			63.8
4 (R_{pi})	Interest paid by consumers (II–15)	14.2		10	Rental income of persons (I–9)			21.2
5 (R_{pf})	Personal transfer payments to foreigners (net) (IV–4)	.8		11	Dividends (I–14)			23.1
6 (S_p)	Personal saving (V–3)		38.4	12	Personal interest income			54.1
				13	Net interest (I–17)	$28.0		
				14 (R_{gi})	Net interest paid by government (III–5)	11.9		
				15 (R_{pi})	Interest paid by consumers (II–4)	14.2		
				16	Transfer payments to persons			59.2
				17 (R_b)	From business (I–19)	3.4		
				18 (R_{gp})	From government (III–3)	55.8		
				19	Less: Personal contributions for social insurance (III–15)			22.6
	PERSONAL TAXES, OUTLAYS, AND SAVING		$687.9		PERSONAL INCOME			$687.9

III. GOVERNMENT RECEIPTS AND EXPENDITURES ACCOUNT

Item				Item			
1 (G)	Purchases of goods and services (I-38)		$200.3	10 (T_p)	Personal tax and nontax payments (II-1)		$ 97.9
2	Transfer payments		57.9	11 (T_c)	Corporate profits tax liability (I-12)		41.3
3 (R_pp)	To persons (II-18)	$55.8		12 (T_i)	Indirect business tax and nontax liability (I-20)		77.9
4 (R_gf)	To foreigners (net) (IV-3)	2.1		13 (T_s)	Contributions for social insurance		47.0
5 (R_gp)	Net interest paid (II-14)		11.9	14	Employer (I-6)	$24.4	
6 (R_s)	Subsidies less current surplus of government enterprises (I-21)		.8	15	Personal (II-19)	22.6	
7 (S_g)	Surplus or deficit (−), national income and product accounts (V-8)		−6.7				
8	Federal	−5.2					
9	State and local	−1.5					
	GOVERNMENT EXPENDITURES AND SURPLUS		$264.2		GOVERNMENT RECEIPTS		$264.2

IV. FOREIGN TRANSACTIONS ACCOUNT

Item			Item			
1	Exports of goods and services (I-36)	$50.6	2	Imports of goods and services (I-37)		$48.1
			3 (R_gf)	Transfer payments from U.S. government to foreigners (net) (III-4)		2.1
			4 (R_pf)	Personal transfer payments to foreigners (net) (II-5)		.8
			5 (I_f)	Net foreign investment (V-2)		−.3
	RECEIPTS FROM FOREIGNERS	$50.6		PAYMENTS TO FOREIGNERS		$50.6

V. GROSS SAVING AND INVESTMENT ACCOUNT

Item			Item		
1 (I_a)	Gross private domestic investment (I-28)	$126.3	3 (S_p)	Personal saving (II-6)	$38.4
2 (I_f)	Net foreign investment (IV-5)	−.3	4	Wage accruals less disbursements (I-4)	.0
			5 (S_u)	Undistributed corporate profits (I-15)	26.7
			6	Corporate inventory valuation adjustment (I-16)	−3.2
			7 (S_d)	Capital consumption allowances (I-22)	73.3
			8 (S_g)	Government surplus or deficit (−), national income and product accounts (III-7)	−6.7
			9 (SD)	Statistical discrepancy (I-23)	−2.5
	GROSS INVESTMENT	$126.0		GROSS SAVING AND STATISTICAL DISCREPANCY	$126.0

SOURCE: *Survey of Current Business*, U.S. Department of Commerce, July 1969, pp. 14–15. The symbols have been added by the author. Numbers in parentheses following entries indicate accounts and items of counter-entry in the accounts. Detail may not add to totals because of rounding.

Second, the official framework was revised in 1958 so that national income and gross national product no longer appear by sector of origin. From the data given in Table 5–1, it is not possible to break down national income of $714.4 billion or gross national product of $865.7 billion into the amounts originating in each of the four sectors of the economy.[2] Although this detail is given elsewhere in the department's statistical tables, from the summary shown in Table 5–1 all we can do is break down national income into types of income and gross national product into types of demand. Like the omission of the entire business-sector account, the omission of items showing the institutional origins of national income and gross national product on the income side of the sector accounts simplifies the accounts. It also focuses attention on the analytically more useful breakdown of gross national product by sector of demand, as found on the product side of the National Income and Product Account.

Apart from these differences in structure, Table 5–1 includes only a few minor items that were not encountered in previous tables. One of these is the statistical discrepancy, − $2.5 for 1968. This figure appears on the income side of Account I to balance off the difference between the department's estimates of gross national product, separately made on the product side and on the income side. For 1968, the estimated value of the items on the product side totaled $865.7, and the estimated value of the items on the income side totaled $868.2. Since the two sides are equal by definition, the discrepancy is clearly the result of errors in the estimates. The necessary balancing adjustment is made by subtracting $2.5 from the income side of the account. The other entries that were not discussed earlier are considered on pages 89–96.[3]

To understand fully the positioning of individual items and the overall organization of these items within the official five-account system, it is necessary

---

[2] Consider, for example, the third item in the first account, wage and salary disbursements of $465.0 billion. This represents the total amount of wages and salaries disbursed by business, government, households, and the rest-of-the-world. How it is broken down among these four sectors is not shown. The business-sector account is omitted altogether, and within the other three sectors no distinction is made between direct purchases of factor services, which are almost entirely wages and salaries, and purchases of final goods and other services. Whatever this amount is for each of these three sectors is included in personal consumption expenditures, government purchases of goods and services, and exports of goods and services, respectively, for the household, government, and rest-of-the-world sectors. Net interest of $28.0 billion also originates in part with business and in part with the rest-of-the-world (interest paid by government and by consumers is not part of national income). The balance of national income (proprietors' income, rental income of persons, and corporate profits) all originates with business. Similarly, the remaining charges against gross national product (Items 19–23) all originate with business and would be found in the omitted business-sector account.

[3] Note that certain items in Table 5–1 are designated by symbols; these will be used in the construction of identities later in this chapter. This system of symbols combines similar items under the same capital letter and uses subscripts to distinguish separate items in each class. Thus, transfer payments and other payments of a transfer nature are all designated by R. Business transfer payments are identified by subscript b, government transfer payments to persons by gp, government transfer payments to foreigners by gf, personal transfer payments to foreigners by pf, government interest payments by gi, personal interest payments by pi, and subsidies by s. Similarly for various types of taxes, T_i, T_c, T_p, and T_s, saving, S_p, S_u, S_d, and S_g, and investment, I_d and I_f.

to trace each item in the National Income and Product Account to its counter-entry in the other accounts and to fit each item and its counterentry into a picture of the circular-flow process. For example, take wage and salary disbursements of $465.0 billion, the first item in the National Income and Product Account for which there is a counterentry. The counterentry II–7 is wages and salaries of this amount received by the household sector as part of its personal income. We may say that personal income is the amount it is *in part* because wages and salaries are the amount they are. Since personal consumption expenditures depend *in part* on the amount of income persons receive and since that amount depends *in part* on wages and salaries received, we may say that personal consumption expenditures II–3 of $536.6 billion are the amount they are *in part* because wage and salary disbursements II–7 are the amount they are. Similarly, personal consumption expenditures II–3 may in turn be traced to the counter-entry, I–24. At this point we may say that wage and salary disbursements I–3, the starting point of our analysis, are *in part* the amount they are because personal consumption expenditures I–24 are the amount they are. Alternatively, we may backtrack to II–7 and follow a more complicated route, saying that personal tax payments II–1 of $97.9 billion are *in part* the amount they are because wage and salary disbursements II–7 are the amount they are. The entry for personal tax payments II–1 may in turn be traced to its counterentry, III–10, and, assuming that government purchases III–1 are not independent of tax receipts, we may say that government purchases of $200.3 billion are *in part* the amount they are because personal tax receipts III–10 are the amount they are. The entry for government purchases may in turn be traced to its counter-entry, I–38, and, at this point, we may say that wage and salary disbursements I–3, our original starting point, are *in part* the amount they are because government purchases I–38 are the amount they are. Another route would be to backtrack to II–7 and argue that personal saving II–6 is the amount it is *in part* because wage and salary disbursements II–7 are the amount they are, and then go on from there. In each case, we come full circle, tracing wage and salary disbursements I–3 all through the system, right back to the point at which we started, I–3. This may also be done for the other items in Account I. Tracing these flows item by item is one way of tying together the circular relationships among the individual items out of which the accounts are built.

Relation of Gross National Product to Other Aggregates

Tracing individual items through the accounts also reveals how each item fits into the various aggregates we have discussed.[4] In our illustration, wage and salary disbursements I–3, which are part of the aggregate national income, led to the counterentry of wage and salary disbursements II–7, which is part

---

[4] The term "aggregate" is used here to mean a combination of items that appear as separate items in Table 5–1. In a different sense, each of these items is itself an aggregate. Indirect taxes

of the aggregate personal income. Similarly, that part of national income that consists of undistributed profits, I–15, leads to the counterentry, V–5, which is part of the aggregate gross saving. That part of gross national product that consists of indirect business taxes, I–20, leads to the counterentry, III–12, which is part of the aggregate government receipts.

We may also trace the relationships among the aggregates themselves and see how one is derived from another by adding and subtracting individual items. Thus, as was examined in detail in Chapter 3,[5] we proceed from gross national product to personal income as follows (in billions of dollars):

	GROSS NATIONAL PRODUCT (GNP)	$865.7
Less	Capital consumption allowances (S_d)	73.3
Equals	NET NATIONAL PRODUCT (NNP)	$792.4
Less	Indirect business taxes (T_i)	77.9
	Business transfer payments (R_b)	3.4
	Statistical discrepancy (SD)	−2.5
Plus	Subsidies minus current surplus of government enterprises (R_s)	0.8
Equals	NATIONAL INCOME (NI)	$714.4
Less	Corporate profits taxes (T_c)	41.3
	Contributions for social insurance (T_s)	47.0
	Undistributed profits (S_u)	26.7
	Inventory valuation adjustment	−3.2
Plus	Government transfer payments to persons (R_{gp})	55.8
	Net interest paid by government (R_{gi})	11.9
	Interest paid by consumers (R_{pi})	14.2
	Business transfer payments (R_b)	3.4
Equals	PERSONAL INCOME (PI)	$687.9

From the aggregate personal income to the aggregate disposable personal income and last to personal consumption expenditures, the steps are as follows:

are an aggregate of state, local, and federal indirect taxes. Each of these in turn is an aggregate of sales taxes, property taxes, motor vehicle taxes, etc.

[5] See pp. 47–49. The presentation here differs from the earlier one by including the statistical discrepancy and inventory valuation adjustment. It also differs in the way it handles corporate profits in proceeding from national income to personal income. Instead of first subtracting the total of corporate profits from national income and then adding back that portion that becomes personal income—i.e., dividends—we here subtract from national income only the parts of corporate profits that do not become personal income—i.e., corporate-profits taxes and undistributed profits—thereby leaving the only part that becomes personal income—i.e., dividends. This alternative treatment shows explicitly the entries for corporate-profits taxes and undistributed profits, which entries are included in the circular-flow diagram of Figure 5–1.

PERSONAL INCOME (PI)		$687.9
Less	Personal tax payments (T_p)	97.9
Equals	DISPOSABLE PERSONAL INCOME (DPI)	$590.0
Less	Personal saving (S_p)	38.4
Equals	PERSONAL OUTLAYS (PO)	$551.6
Less	Interest paid by consumers (R_{pi})	14.2
	Personal transfer payments to foreigners (R_{pf})	0.8
Equals	Personal consumption expenditures (C)	$536.6

Here we see the relationships that exist among the aggregates. Although DPI is not specifically set forth in Table 5–1, it may be directly derived from Account II of that table.

United States Economy—Circular Flow and Fundamental Identities

The same relationships among the aggregates set forth above may also be shown as in Figure 5–1. Starting with GNP at the far left of the figure and following the central channel through to the far right, we see the various items that are deducted and added in moving from one aggregate to another. More importantly, the circular-flow process depicted here enables us to see the sense in which the total flow of spending on final product, which is equal to GNP, is matched by an equal flow of gross income, as well as the sense in which the portion of this gross income flow that is devoted to saving is matched by an equal portion of gross product devoted to investment.

Using the actual figures (in billions of dollars) for the United States economy in 1968, we have the following for the GNP identity:

$$C + R_{pf} + S + T \equiv GNP \equiv C + I_d + G + (X - M)$$
$$\$536.6 + \$0.8 + \$132.6 + \$195.7 = \$865.7 = \$536.6 + \$126.3 + \$200.3 + \$2.5$$

In the diagram, GNP of $865.7 on the product side is shown at the far left by total expenditures on final product by the four sectors of demand, $C + I_d + G + (X - M)$. The identity states that corresponding to the $865.7 on the product side, there must be on the income side an identical sum made up of $C + R_{pf} + S + T$. The income flow of $865.7 is split up into $C + R_{pf} + S + T$ as follows. Government extracts from the central flow of income a total of $264.2 ($T_i$ of $77.9, T_c of $41.3, T_s of $47.0, and T_p of $97.9), but it restores to this central flow a total of $68.5 ($R_s$ of $0.8, R_{gp} of $55.8, and R_{gi} of $11.9). Thus, we can say that government withdraws a *net* amount of $264.2 − $68.5, or $195.7, which equals net taxes, T. Next we must find how much of this gross income flow takes the form of private saving, S. The amount is readily identified by the downward diversions from the central income channel. Here we see that business saves $96.7 ($S_d$ of $73.3 and S_u of $23.4) [6] and that persons save $38.4 ($S_p$), making a total S of $135.1. We thus have a total of $S + T$ amounting to $330.8. A final minor diversion from the gross income flow is that for personal transfer payments to foreigners, R_{pf} of $0.8.[7] We then have a total of $S + T + R_{pf}$ of $135.1 + $195.7 + $0.8, or $331.6. What is left after these diversions is by definition C. Subtracting $331.6 from $865.7 leaves $534.1, which should be our figure for C in the identity. Looking at Figure 5–1, however, we see that C is $536.6. This difference is due to the statistical discrepancy (SD) of $-$2.5 for 1968, which represents the difference between the Commerce Department's estimates of GNP on the income and product sides of the National Income and Product Account. The discrepancy is treated in effect as an error in the estimate of the diversion into private saving, and the figure for private saving is adjusted accordingly. Therefore, we have $135.1 - $2.5, or $132.6, as the adjusted figure for private saving, S. The total of $S + T + R_{pf}$ thus becomes $132.6 + $195.7 + $0.8, or $329.1, which, when deducted from the gross income flow of $865.7, leaves the remainder, C, at $536.6, and the identity is satisfied.

The saving-investment identity, with data taken from Figure 5–1, is as follows:

$$S \quad + \quad (T \quad - \quad G \quad - \quad R_{gf}) \equiv \quad I_d \quad + \quad I_f$$
$$\$132.6 + (\$195.7 - \$200.3 - \$2.1) = \$126.3 + (-\$0.3)$$

In the GNP identity, neither gross saving (the sum of gross private and public saving) nor gross investment (the sum of gross private domestic and net foreign investment) appears explicitly. The saving-investment identity, however, expresses these factors explicitly in order to show that for every dollar of gross income *not* spent on the purchase of final goods and services by either government or households (i.e., gross saving) there is a dollar of final goods left unconsumed (i.e., gross investment). This is expressed by the identity given above, in which both sides (apart from a rounding error of $0.1) are equal to $126.0.

GROSS NATIONAL PRODUCT AND NATIONAL INCOME: THE 1929–68 STATISTICAL RECORD

The dollar amounts in Table 5–1 and Figure 5–1 are the actual amounts for the U.S. economy for the single year of 1968. Figures for this one year, of course,

---

[6] S_u of $23.4 includes the inventory valuation adjustment of $-$3.2.

[7] This diversion appears in Figure 5–1 as the small channel at the bottom of *PO*. The personal outlay for interest paid by consumers, which appears as the channel at the top of *PO*, is not a *net* diversion from the central income channel, for the part diverted from *PO* is offset by an equal amount added to *PI*. This is similar to the amount of taxes diverted to government that is offset by the return flow of government transfer payments to persons, government interest, and subsidies.

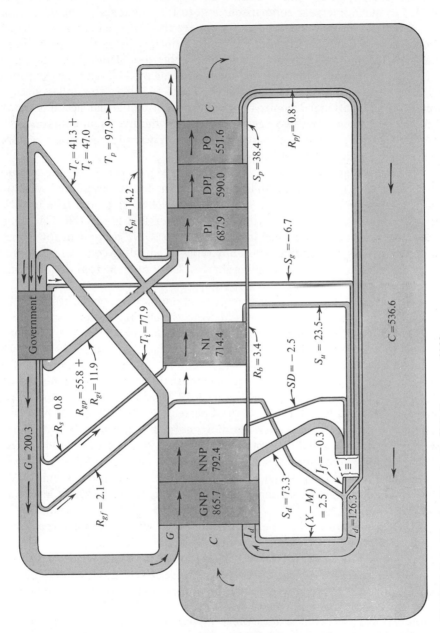

FIGURE 5–1 Circular Flow in the U.S. Economy, 1968

permit no comparisons other than those between the different flows for the year in question. Tables 5–2 and 5–3 have been added below to provide the data needed to make interyear comparisons and to trace changes in the magnitudes of a few basic income and product flows over the forty-year period ending in 1968. These two tables present data for the principal items that appear in the National Income and Product Account of Table 5–1. Thus, Table 5–2 gives the dollar amounts for the four major components of GNP and the percentage of GNP represented by each component. Table 5–3 gives the dollar amounts for GNP and national income, for the two main items that account for the difference between these two aggregates and for the five main components of national income; the second part of this table gives the percentage of GNP represented by each of these items.

In examining the composition of GNP as given in Table 5–2, one question of importance is the relative stability of each of the four types of final spending. Do some rise and fall closely in line with the cyclical rises and falls in GNP, or do they rise and fall proportionately more or less than GNP? A second question is the long-run change in the fraction of GNP accounted for by each of the four types of spending. Have any types of spending come to account for a gradually rising or gradually falling share of GNP over the four decades under observation? [8]

In terms of stability, the personal-consumption component heads the list, especially for the period since World War II. During these postwar years, consumption averaged 64 percent of GNP, varying from a low of 62.7 percent in 1952 to a high of 69.5 percent in 1947. The earlier years, from 1929 to 1945, included a decade of economic stagnation and a half-decade of war, and these unusual conditions gave rise to equally unusual but understandable results: During the thirties consumption averaged 77.2 percent of GNP, and during the years of World War II (1941–45) 55.4 percent of GNP. Based on the relative stability of this percentage over the more normal years since World War II, or the even greater stability over the years since 1953, one can perhaps expect consumption to account for a fairly steady 62 to 64 percent of GNP in the years ahead. Of course, a repetition of anything like the conditions from 1929 to 1945 would cause this percentage to move far away from the stable level it has recently held.

When we turn to the second question posed above, the forty-year record seems to show no trend in the percentage of GNP that takes the form of consumer goods and services. However, if we extend the record back before 1929 (not shown in Table 5–2), we discover that the relatively stable ratio of 62 to 64 percent in recent years is well below the approximately 75 percent figure that

---

[8] These questions could be more meaningfully investigated, if we were to break down each of the four major components of spending into its subcomponents as is done in the National Income and Product Account of Table 5–1. For example, if, instead of looking at personal consumption expenditures as a total, we looked separately at consumption expenditures for durable goods, nondurable goods, and services, we would give somewhat different answers to these questions. However, for the purpose of a brief look at the broad picture, we will limit ourselves to the four major types of spending.

obtained during the decade of the twenties. In part, this marked decline in the consumption percentage has been the result of a marked rise in the percentage of expenditures on final product accounted for by government purchases. The rise in the government's share in the last twenty-five years is to a significant degree the result of "hot" and "cold" war military expenditures, but it is also to a lesser degree the result of a shift from "private consumption" to "public consumption" that has gradually occurred since the twenties. A relatively larger share of total consumption has taken the form of publicly provided consumer goods and services, and a relatively smaller share has been composed of privately purchased consumer goods and services.

As compared with the years before 1930, the ratio of privately purchased consumer goods and services to GNP has now moved to a new lower plateau, at which it may remain or from which it may drift further downward. Those who argue that the public sector has been "starved" and that more of the economy's resources must be devoted to public programs in the fields of education, housing, health, worker retraining, pollution control, transportation, and the like, have suggested programs whose implementation would push the ratio of private consumption expenditures to GNP substantially below the fairly stable figure of recent years. Whether this will come to pass only the future will reveal.

It would, of course, be possible for the share of government purchases to grow at the expense of the share of gross private domestic investment, especially to the extent that such purchases were more in the nature of public investment expenditures than public consumption expenditures. However, to the extent that government expenditures are of an investment nature, they primarily involve investment of a type not undertaken on a large scale by the private sector and are thus more a supplement to private investment than a substitute for it. For example, government spending for education, health, and worker retraining involves "investment in people" and probably raises rather than lowers private investment spending for new plant and equipment.

Unlike the long-run movements noted in the percentages for government and consumption expenditures, the record of the past forty years indicates no similar trend in the percentage of GNP accounted for by gross private domestic investment. If we look only at relatively prosperous peacetime years, this percentage runs from 14 to 16. For example, the private investment percentage for the decade of the twenties, a relatively prosperous period, is not significantly different from that of the prosperous peacetime years of the fifties and sixties. The record thus suggests that the consumption percentage has gradually fallen, the government percentage has gradually risen, but the investment percentage has shown no similar trend.

In sharp contrast to the absence of a trend in the investment percentage is the considerable cyclical instability in this percentage. In the most extreme case, gross private domestic investment fell from a cyclical peak of 15.7 percent of GNP in 1929 to a cyclical low of 1.7 percent in 1932. Put differently, the share of GNP accounted for by investment expenditures in 1929 was almost ten times as large as the share accounted for in 1932. When read in this way, the other

TABLE 5–2 The Composition of Gross National Product, 1929–1968

Year	Gross National Product	Billions of Current Dollars Personal Consumption Expenditures	Gross Private Domestic Investment	Government Purchases of Goods and Services	Net Exports	Percent of Gross National Product Personal Consumption Expenditures	Gross Private Domestic Investment	Government Purchases of Goods and Services	Net Exports
1929	$103.1	$ 77.2	$16.2	$ 8.5	$ 1.1	74.9%	15.7%	8.2%	1.1%
1930	90.4	69.9	10.3	9.2	1.0	77.3	11.4	10.2	1.2
1931	75.8	60.5	5.6	9.2	0.5	79.8	7.4	12.1	0.7
1932	58.0	48.6	1.0	8.1	0.4	83.8	1.7	14.0	0.5
1933	55.6	45.8	1.4	8.0	0.4	82.4	2.5	14.4	0.7
1934	65.1	51.3	3.3	9.8	0.6	78.8	5.1	15.1	1.0
1935	72.2	55.7	6.4	10.0	0.1	77.1	8.9	13.8	0.2
1936	82.5	61.9	8.5	12.0	0.1	75.0	10.3	14.5	0.2
1937	90.4	66.5	11.8	11.9	0.3	73.6	13.1	13.2	0.1
1938	84.7	63.9	6.5	13.0	1.3	75.4	7.7	15.3	1.6
1939	90.5	66.8	9.3	13.3	1.1	73.8	10.3	14.6	1.2
1940	99.7	70.8	13.1	14.0	1.7	71.0	13.1	14.0	1.9
1941	124.5	80.6	17.9	24.8	1.3	64.7	14.4	19.9	1.0
1942	157.9	88.5	9.8	59.6	—	56.0	6.2	37.7	0
1943	191.6	99.3	5.7	88.6	−2.0	51.8	3.0	46.2	−1.0
1944	210.1	108.3	7.1	96.5	−1.8	51.5	3.4	45.9	−0.8

Year								
1945	$212.0	$119.7	$10.6	$82.3	$ −0.6	56.5%	5.0%	38.8%	−0.3%
1946	208.5	143.4	30.6	27.0	7.5	68.8	14.7	12.9	3.6
1947	231.3	160.7	34.0	25.1	11.5	69.5	14.7	10.9	4.9
1948	257.6	173.6	46.0	31.6	6.4	67.4	17.9	12.3	2.4
1949	256.5	176.8	35.7	37.8	6.1	68.9	14.0	14.7	2.4
1950	284.8	191.0	54.1	37.9	1.8	67.1	19.0	13.3	0.6
1951	328.4	206.3	59.3	59.1	3.7	62.8	18.1	18.0	1.1
1952	345.5	216.7	51.9	74.7	2.2	62.7	15.0	21.6	0.7
1953	364.6	230.0	52.6	81.6	0.4	63.1	14.4	22.4	0.1
1954	364.8	236.5	51.7	74.8	1.8	64.8	14.2	20.5	0.5
1955	398.0	254.4	67.4	74.2	2.0	63.9	16.9	18.6	0.6
1956	419.2	266.7	70.0	78.6	4.0	63.6	16.7	18.8	0.9
1957	441.1	281.4	67.8	86.1	5.7	63.8	15.4	19.5	1.3
1958	447.3	290.1	60.9	94.2	2.2	64.9	13.6	21.1	0.4
1959	483.6	311.2	75.3	97.0	0.1	64.3	15.6	20.1	0.0
1960	503.8	325.2	74.8	99.6	4.1	64.5	14.8	19.8	0.9
1961	520.1	335.2	71.7	107.6	5.6	64.4	13.8	20.7	1.1
1962	560.3	355.1	83.0	117.1	5.1	63.4	14.8	20.9	0.9
1963	590.5	375.0	87.1	122.5	6.0	63.5	14.8	20.7	1.0
1964	632.4	401.2	94.0	128.7	8.5	63.4	14.9	20.4	1.3
1965	684.9	432.8	108.1	137.0	6.9	63.2	15.8	20.0	1.0
1965	749.9	466.3	121.4	156.8	5.3	62.2	16.2	20.9	0.7
1967	793.5	492.3	116.0	180.1	5.2	62.0	14.6	22.7	0.7
1968	865.7	536.6	126.3	200.3	2.5	62.0	14.6	23.1	0.3

SOURCE: *The National Income and Product Accounts of the United States, 1929–65, Statistical Tables,* U.S. Department of Commerce, 1966, and *Survey of Current Business,* July 1969, U.S. Department of Commerce.

major shares stand out as much more stable cyclically. For example, over the same 1929–32 period, the consumption component showed a movement from 74.9 to 83.8 percent, little more than a 10-percent change in comparison with an almost 1,000-percent change for investment expenditures.

Although the investment percentage has clearly been the most unstable of the major components for the full forty-year period covered by Table 5–2, its instability in the last fifteen years of the period is minor in comparison to that of the preceding twenty-five years. For these last fifteen years, the percentage reached a high of 16.9 in the capital-spending boom year of 1955 and a low of 13.6 percent in the recession year of 1958. Finally, if we take only the eight years of economic expansion from 1961 through 1968, we find the figure varying over the very narrow range of 13.8 to 14.8 percent.

Focusing as we have on the percentage breakdown of GNP into the major types of spending tells us how the economic pie is split up, but it tells us nothing about the relationships between changes in the split of the pie from year to year and changes in the absolute size of the pie itself from year to year. A close examination of Table 5–2 shows that in those nonwar years in which gross private domestic investment dropped sharply (e.g., 1937–38 and 1948–49), the absolute size of GNP also dropped (or rose relatively little), and in the nonwar years in which gross private domestic investment rose sharply (e.g., 1949–50 and 1954–55), GNP itself showed relatively large increases. This suggests that in peacetime periods the explanation of major fluctuations in GNP is primarily a matter of explaining the fluctuations that occur in gross private domestic investment. In contrast, fluctuations in consumption expenditures do not appear to explain major fluctuations in GNP but are rather largely explained *by* fluctuations in GNP. Thus, we have the general relationship that as investment expenditures vary, GNP tends to vary in response, and as GNP varies, consumption expenditures tend to vary in response.[9] Apart from other qualifications, this general relationship, of course, applies only to peacetime periods. In war and early postwar years such as the period from 1941 to 1948, the fluctuations in GNP over the period as a whole are explained primarily by the massive expansion of government purchases during the war years and the contraction of such purchases immediately following the war.

Table 5–2 allows us to trace the shifting composition of GNP by types of expenditure; Table 5–3 allows us to do the same by income share. We saw

---

[9] Because of this relationship, the earlier comparison of changes in the percentage of GNP accounted for by investment understate the importance of fluctuations in investment as a cause of fluctuations in GNP. If an increase in investment changed GNP only by an amount equal to the increase in investment, investment as a percentage of the changed GNP figure would be larger than if the increase in investment changed GNP by an amount greater than the increase in investment. Since an increase in investment will raise GNP and since the rise in GNP raises consumption, the total increase in GNP is actually greater than just the increase in investment, and therefore investment as a percentage of GNP is smaller than it would otherwise be. The same is true for a decrease in investment. A given increase or decrease in investment as a percentage of GNP may thus appear as a very small change because a change in investment brings about a total rise or fall in GNP that is a multiple of the change in investment.

earlier that for every dollar of gross national product there is a dollar of gross income and that every dollar of gross income becomes a dollar either of factor income or of what may be called nonfactor income. The major types of non-factor income are capital consumption allowances and indirect business taxes. Apart from minor adjustments, the balance of gross income is the total of factor incomes, or the economy's national income. The last five columns of Table 5–3 show the breakdown of national income into its five major components.[10]

As was found for the composition of product, the depressed thirties, World War II, and the early postwar years show the most drastic changes in the composition of income. If we look at national income as a percentage of gross income, the record shows a drop from 84.2 in 1929 to 72.5 in 1933 and a rise in the war years and early postwar years to an average of about 86.[11] However, over the years since 1949, or the latter half of the forty-year period, national income constituted a fairly stable fraction of gross income, varying only between 81.9 and 84.8 percent. Thus, in each of these last twenty years, a little better than $4 out of every $5 of the gross income flow have been earnings of the factors of production.

When we look at the separate shares into which national income is divided, the breakdown by percentage of gross income suggests that the share making up compensation of employees has tended to rise over the years since 1929, while the share making up proprietors' income has tended to decline over the same four decades. The number of persons self-employed in proprietorships and partnerships has not grown as rapidly as the number of persons who work as employees, which has tended to shift a larger fraction of the gross income flow into the compensation-of-employees column and out of the proprietors'-income column. It should be noted that such a shift does not necessarily indicate a rise in labor's share of gross income, for a large but unknown part of proprietors' income is a labor return to the self-employed.

Apart from the moderate upward trend in the ratio for compensation of employees, this ratio on a year-to-year basis shows few large variations. The largest one-year variation is the jump from 54.0 percent in 1942 to 57.2 percent in 1943, a change primarily due to a return to a fully employed economy as the war machine reached high gear in 1943 and demanded all the labor it could get. Considerably larger year-to-year fluctuations are found in the ratio for pro-

[10] As GNP was broken down above only into its four major components, so we here have broken down gross income only into its seven major components, five of which add up to national income. Only a few illustrative conclusions will be drawn from this presentation. For a more refined look at the composition of income, we would want to break some of these components down into subcomponents, at least to the degree done in the National Income and Product Account of Table 5–1.

[11] During the years of the Great Depression, national income accounted for a smaller percentage of gross income than during any other period of the forty years covered. Despite the fact that the gross income flow shrank during these years, business accounting charges for depreciation and government indirect tax receipts hardly shrank at all; therefore, national income became a smaller percentage of the gross income flow. The very opposite occurred during the years of World War II. Depreciation and indirect tax receipts increased only moderately, while the gross income flow, because of the great increase in government purchases, rose sharply.

TABLE 5–3 The Composition of Gross Income, 1929–68

Billions of Current Dollars

Year	Gross Income	Capital Consumption Allowances	Indirect Business Taxes	National Income	Compensation of Employees	Propri- etors' Income	Rental Income of Persons	Corporate Profits*	Net Interest
1929	$103.1	$ 7.9	$ 7.0	$ 86.8	$ 51.1	$15.1	$ 5.4	$10.5	$4.7
1930	90.4	8.0	7.2	75.4	46.8	11.9	4.8	7.0	4.9
1931	75.8	7.9	6.9	59.7	39.8	9.2	3.8	2.0	4.9
1932	58.0	7.4	6.8	42.8	31.1	5.7	2.7	−1.3	4.6
1933	55.6	7.0	7.1	40.3	29.5	5.9	2.0	−1.2	4.1
1934	65.1	6.8	7.8	49.5	34.3	7.7	1.7	1.7	4.1
1935	72.2	6.9	8.2	57.2	37.3	10.8	1.7	3.4	4.1
1936	82.5	7.0	8.7	65.0	42.9	11.0	1.8	5.6	3.8
1937	90.4	7.2	9.2	73.6	47.9	13.2	2.1	6.8	3.7
1938	84.7	7.3	9.2	67.4	45.0	11.3	2.6	4.9	3.6
1939	90.5	7.3	9.4	72.6	48.1	11.8	2.7	6.3	3.5
1940	99.7	7.5	10.0	81.1	52.1	13.0	2.9	9.8	3.3
1941	124.5	8.2	11.3	104.2	64.8	17.5	3.5	15.2	3.2
1942	157.9	9.8	11.8	137.1	85.3	23.8	4.5	20.3	3.1
1943	191.6	10.2	12.7	170.3	109.5	28.6	5.1	24.4	2.7
1944	210.1	11.0	14.1	182.6	121.2	29.8	5.4	23.8	2.3

Year									
1945	$212.0	$11.3	$15.5	$181.5	$123.1	$31.4	$ 5.6	$19.2	$2.2
1946	208.5	9.9	17.1	181.9	117.9	36.5	6.6	19.3	1.5
1947	231.3	12.2	18.4	199.0	128.9	35.5	7.1	25.6	1.9
1948	257.6	14.5	20.1	224.2	141.1	40.2	8.0	33.0	1.8
1949	256.5	16.6	21.3	217.5	141.0	35.3	8.4	30.8	1.9
1950	284.8	18.3	23.3	241.1	154.6	37.5	9.4	37.7	2.0
1951	328.4	21.2	25.2	278.0	180.7	42.0	10.3	42.7	2.3
1952	345.5	23.2	27.6	291.4	195.3	42.1	11.5	39.9	2.6
1953	364.6	25.7	29.6	304.7	209.1	40.5	12.7	39.6	2.8
1954	364.8	28.1	29.5	303.1	208.0	40.0	13.6	38.0	3.6
1955	398.0	31.5	32.1	331.0	224.5	41.7	13.9	46.9	4.1
1956	419.2	34.1	34.9	350.8	243.1	42.7	14.3	46.1	4.6
1957	441.1	37.1	37.3	366.1	256.0	44.1	14.8	45.6	5.6
1958	447.3	38.9	38.5	367.8	257.8	46.6	15.4	41.1	6.8
1959	483.6	41.4	41.5	400.0	279.1	46.6	15.6	51.7	7.1
1960	503.8	43.4	45.2	414.5	294.2	46.2	15.8	49.9	8.4
1961	520.1	45.2	47.7	427.3	302.6	48.4	16.0	50.3	10.0
1962	560.3	50.0	51.5	457.7	323.6	50.1	16.7	55.7	11.6
1963	590.5	52.6	54.7	481.9	341.0	51.0	17.1	58.9	13.8
1964	632.4	56.1	58.4	518.1	365.7	52.3	18.0	66.3	15.8
1965	684.9	59.8	62.5	564.3	393.8	57.3	19.0	76.1	18.2
1966	749.9	63.9	65.7	620.6	435.5	61.3	20.0	82.4	21.4
1967	793.5	68.6	70.1	654.0	467.4	61.9	20.8	79.2	24.7
1968	865.7	73.3	77.9	714.4	513.5	63.8	21.2	87.9	28.0

TABLE 5-3 (Continued)

					Percentage of Gross Income				
Year	Gross Income	Capital Consumption Allowances	Indirect Business Taxes	National Income	Compensation of Employees	Propri- etors' Income	Rental Income of Persons	Corporate Profits*	Net Interest
1929	100.0%	7.7%	6.8%	84.2%	49.6%	14.6%	5.2%	10.2%	4.6%
1930	100.0	8.8	8.0	83.4	51.8	13.2	5.3	7.7	5.4
1931	100.0	10.4	9.1	78.7	52.5	12.1	5.0	2.6	6.5
1932	100.0	12.8	11.7	73.8	53.6	9.8	4.7	−2.2	7.9
1933	100.0	12.6	12.8	72.5	53.1	10.6	3.6	−2.2	7.4
1934	100.0	10.4	12.0	76.0	52.7	11.8	2.6	2.6	6.3
1935	100.0	9.6	11.4	79.2	51.7	15.0	2.4	4.7	5.7
1936	100.0	8.5	10.5	78.8	52.0	13.3	2.2	6.8	4.6
1937	100.0	8.7	11.2	81.4	53.0	14.6	2.3	7.5	4.1
1938	100.0	8.6	10.9	79.6	53.1	13.3	3.1	5.8	4.3
1939	100.0	8.1	10.4	80.2	53.1	13.1	3.0	7.0	3.9
1940	100.0	7.5	10.0	81.3	52.3	13.0	2.9	9.8	3.3
1941	100.0	6.6	9.1	83.7	52.0	14.1	2.8	12.2	2.6
1942	100.0	6.2	7.5	86.8	54.0	15.1	2.8	12.9	2.0
1943	100.0	5.3	6.6	88.9	57.2	14.9	2.7	12.7	1.4
1944	100.0	5.2	6.7	86.9	57.7	14.2	2.6	11.3	1.1
1945	100.0	5.3	7.3	85.7	58.1	14.8	2.6	9.1	1.0
1946	100.0	4.7	8.2	87.2	56.5	17.5	3.2	9.3	0.7
1947	100.0	5.3	8.0	86.0	55.7	15.3	3.1	11.1	0.8
1948	100.0	5.6	7.8	87.0	54.8	15.6	3.1	12.8	0.7
1949	100.0	6.5	8.3	84.8	55.0	13.8	3.3	12.0	0.7

1950	100.0%	6.4%	8.2%	84.7%	54.3%	13.2%	3.3%	13.2%	0.7%
1951	100.0	6.5	7.7	84.7	55.0	12.8	3.1	13.0	0.7
1952	100.0	6.7	8.0	84.3	56.5	12.2	3.3	11.5	0.7
1953	100.0	7.0	8.1	83.6	57.4	11.1	3.5	10.9	0.8
1954	100.0	7.7	8.1	83.1	57.0	11.0	3.7	10.4	1.0
1955	100.0	7.9	8.1	83.2	56.4	10.5	3.5	11.8	1.0
1956	100.0	8.1	8.3	83.7	58.0	10.2	3.4	11.0	1.1
1957	100.0	8.4	8.5	83.0	58.0	10.0	3.4	10.3	1.3
1958	100.0	8.7	8.6	82.2	57.6	10.4	3.4	9.2	1.5
1959	100.0	8.6	8.6	82.7	57.7	9.6	3.2	10.7	1.5
1960	100.0	8.6	9.0	82.3	58.4	9.2	3.1	9.9	1.7
1961	100.0	8.7	9.2	82.2	58.2	9.3	3.1	9.7	1.9
1962	100.0	8.9	9.2	81.7	57.8	8.9	3.0	9.9	2.1
1963	100.0	9.2	9.3	81.6	57.7	8.6	2.9	10.0	2.3
1964	100.0	8.9	9.2	81.9	57.8	8.3	2.8	10.5	2.5
1965	100.0	8.7	9.1	82.4	57.5	8.4	2.8	11.1	2.7
1966	100.0	8.5	8.8	82.8	58.1	8.2	2.7	11.0	2.9
1967	100.0	8.6	8.8	82.4	58.9	7.8	2.6	10.0	3.1
1968	100.0	8.5	9.0	82.5	59.3	7.4	2.4	10.2	3.2

SOURCE: *The National Income and Product Accounts of the United States, 1929–65, Statistical Tables*, U.S. Department of Commerce, 1966, and *Survey of Current Business*, July 1969, U.S. Department of Commerce.
* Includes inventory-valuation adjustment.

prietors' income, a reflection of the fact that this share contains a "profit" component that is a highly variable residual in proprietors' income.

The other major share of income is corporate profits. The forty-year record given here shows the pronounced cyclical instability in the percentage of gross income composed of corporate profits, but it shows no clear-cut trend in the size of this share for the period as a whole. In the prosperous year of 1929, corporate profits accounted for approximately $1 in every $10 of gross income, about the same as in the most recent decade in the table. However, on a cyclical basis, running down this column of percentages reveals an extreme drop from 10.1 in 1929 to *minus* 2.1 in 1933 and a rise to 7.4 in 1937. With the rapid expansion accompanying a shift to a war economy, the percentage jumped from 9.8 in 1940 to 12.8 in 1942 and then in 1945, at the end of the war, fell to 9.0. With the postwar boom, the percentage rose to 13.2 by 1950, the highest percentage for the forty-year period. Smaller variations characterize the years since 1950, but they are, on a relative basis, still far larger than those found in the other income shares for the same years.

If we now combine the few observations we have drawn from the data in the two tables, we discover that the most unstable share on the income side is corporate profits and the most unstable share on the product side is gross private domestic investment. This is not surprising, because the bulk of private investment is undertaken by corporations and because the level of corporate profits is an important factor influencing the level of plant and equipment expenditures by corporations. One may also argue that the relative stability of the compensation-of-employees share on the income side and the relative stability of personal consumption expenditures on the product side are associated in a similar way. The bulk of the amount included as compensation of employees reaches the hands of persons as disposable income and provides a large part of the income available for personal consumption expenditures. The link between these two shares on the opposite sides of the National Income and Product Account is probably considerably looser than that between corporate profits and gross private domestic investment. However, it appears to be sufficiently close to make us suspicious of any set of figures that shows pronounced instability in the share of national income made up of compensation of employees and an equally pronounced stability in the share of GNP made up of personal consumption expenditures.

Still other relationships would be revealed by a more detailed examination of the data in these two tables, but the several noted here suffice as illustrations. When we recognize that the presentation of the detailed historical record of the economy's income and product flows would require dozens of tables like the two we have been examining, we get an idea of the wealth of data now available on these flows and of the many quantitative relationships among them that thorough study has revealed. With these data fitted into the comprehensive national income accounting framework developed earlier, we have a systematic quantitative picture of the economic structure and process. From the brief look we have taken, it may be apparent that, by suitable organization of information, one can learn a great deal about the economic process itself from the actual year-to-year quantitative changes that occur in the various income and product flows.

PROBLEMS IN THE NATIONAL INCOME ACCOUNTS

In the hypothetical economies of Chapters 2–4, certain problems were ignored in order to simplify our development of the accounting frameworks and the relationships among the product and income flows out of which these frameworks were built. With the real-world economy of the United States, however, it is important to recognize that what is actually measured or, more correctly, estimated by the official income and product accounts depends on the way in which a number of special problems have been resolved by those who prepare the estimates. For many of these problems there is no clear solution, and national income experts differ as to what is the best compromise. In the remainder of this chapter we will touch only lightly on a few of the more important of these problems and the treatment given them in the official U.S. accounts.

Imputations

From the hypothetical two-sector economy to the actual U.S. economy, we have defined national product as the sum of expenditures for final product and national income as the sum of earnings of the factors of production. All income and product were implicitly assumed to take a monetary form. In the real-world economy, however, restricting income and product to those flows that take explicit monetary form clearly understates the economy's actual income and product. There are nonmonetary income and product flows that would escape inclusion unless certain imputed values were added to the accounts. The nature of these imputations can best be seen by describing a couple of those presently made in the preparation of the official income and product estimates.

Rental Value of Owner-Occupied Homes.   A person who rents a home to another earns gross rental income, which becomes net rental income after deduction of expenses.[12] To the tenant, rent paid for the home is an expenditure for the purchase of the services of property. It is part of personal consumption expenditures and therefore part of gross national product. For owner-occupied homes, however, there is in monetary terms neither net rental income as part of national income nor rent paid as part of gross national product. Since the same

---

[12] Net rental income of persons is limited to the rental income of persons *not* primarily engaged in the real estate business. Net rental income of those so engaged appears as proprietors' income and, in the case of corporations, as corporate profits.

real product is provided by a home, whether owner or tenant occupied, an imputation is made to provide consistent treatment in the accounts. It is assumed for accounting purposes that home ownership is a business in which the owner sells to himself as a tenant the services of the home. The amount of imputed rent is estimated as the sum for which the owner-occupied home could have been rented, and the imputed net rental income is estimated as that portion of the sum that would have accrued to the homeowner after deduction of all expenses. It is thus something like a profit that would be earned by a property owner whose ordinary business is the renting of residential property.

As a result of this imputation, personal consumption expenditure is increased on the product side of the National Income and Product Account by the imputed gross rental for owner-occupied homes. Net rental income of persons, indirect taxes (property taxes), net interest (on mortgages), capital consumption allowances (depreciation of owner-occupied homes), plus other adjustments add an equal amount on the income side of the account. Without this imputation, gross national product would vary in response to changes toward or away from home ownership. In any given time period, the larger the fraction of total housing that was tenant occupied, the larger gross national product would be. Similarly, gross national product would grow larger over successive time periods with a trend away from home ownership toward home rental. By making this imputation, such distortions in gross national product are avoided.

Wages and Salaries Paid in Kind.   Included under the heading Other Labor Income in Table 5–1 is an imputed amount for wages and salaries paid in kind. This simply acknowledges the fact that some compensation of employees takes the form of food and lodging provided by employers. No allowance for this labor income would be made in the national accounts if compensation of employees were limited only to monetary income. Accordingly, an estimate of wages and salaries paid in kind is made, and this amount is shown as a supplement to wages and salaries on the income side and as an increase in personal consumption expenditures on the product side. In effect, this accounting treatment assumes that the employer pays his employees the dollar value of the free food and lodging provided and that the employees in turn spend this amount to purchase the same food and lodging from the employer. The imputation thus adds an equal amount to gross national product in the form of personal consumption expenditures and to national income in the form of compensation of employees.

Other Imputations.   Several other imputations included in the official accounts are those made for food and fuel produced and consumed on farms, and for nonmonetary income and product flows arising from certain operations of commercial banks and financial intermediaries.[13]

[13] For a complete list of imputations and the estimated dollar amounts for each for 1929–65, see Table 7–3 of *The National Income and Product Accounts of the United States, 1929–1965, Statistical Tables,* U.S. Department of Commerce, 1966. For later years, see Table 7–3 of U.S. National Income and Product Accounts in the July issue of *Survey of Current Business,* U.S. Department of Commerce.

There are many other possible imputations that are not included in the official accounts. One of these is production in the form of housewives' services in their own homes. Because there is no statistically sound method of estimating the value of this production, there is no way of including it by imputation, and we must live with the paradox that results from its omission.[14] Thus, the housewife's output, which consists of cooking, washing, cleaning, child care, and other services, is all excluded from the national output. If, however, the housewife were to hire a woman who was previously employed in a factory to do the housework, and she took that woman's place in the factory, gross national product would show a net increase equal to the amount of the salary paid to the woman hired to perform the housework. Actual output is unchanged, but the estimate for gross national product is larger. The same paradox, of course, applies to work performed by the husband around the house: maintaining the grounds, painting the house, adding a room, or repairing an appliance. None of this production is included in gross national product, yet all of it would be included at the full price paid if a landscaper, painter, carpenter, or appliance repairman were hired to do the same work.[15]

With recognition of imputations, both those that are made and those that are not, comes recognition of the frequently overlooked fact that gross national product, as officially defined, is an amount that does not purport to be a measure of the economy's output in any all-inclusive sense. By the same token, national income does not purport to be a measure of factor earnings in any all-inclusive sense. Much is excluded from both income and product that would be included under broader definitions.

Intermediate and Final Product

The imputations made in the official accounts are designed to pick up the value of certain final goods and services that otherwise would not appear because they do not take monetary form. On the other hand, among those transactions that do take monetary form, the official accounts may pick up as final product certain goods and services that are really intermediate product. The problem of differentiating intermediate and final product, the complexities of which were completely ignored in the hypothetical economies, is one of the most difficult in the theory of national income accounting.

One very important aspect of this problem relates to government purchases of goods and services. By sector of demand, the official accounts show as government's share of gross national product an amount equal to its purchases of goods and services. For whatever purpose government expenditures may be made, so long as goods or services of some kind are received in exchange, these

---

[14] If it were included, it would appear as compensation of employees on the income side and as personal consumption expenditures on the product side.

[15] Only that part of production represented by the homeowner's labor services escapes inclusion; the grass seed, paint, lumber, and other materials are included in gross national product in both cases.

expenditures are treated as part of gross national product. Thus, expenditures for wages and salaries of employees who perform services such as police and fire protection, court operations, and tax enforcement and expenditures for such goods as traffic signs, aircraft carriers, and penitentiaries are all included in gross national product. Some economists argue that at least some purchases of goods and services by government, such as the examples just given, are actually intermediate to the production of final goods by other sectors, mainly the business sector, and should not be considered final product. Such expenditures are necessary simply to provide the conditions under which the business and other sectors can carry on their day-to-day productive activities. While there is the basis for a case here, the case virtually collapses when the problem of how to divide all government purchases into intermediate and final product on any such criterion is faced. On the grounds that so far there is no practical way of making such a division, the national income accountants simply include all government purchases as part of final product.

The same problem arises in classifying all purchases of consumer goods and services as final product. Expenditures by persons for food, clothing, transportation, medical care, and even recreation are in part necessary to the performance of their jobs as producers in the economy. Therefore, in a sense, at least some of these expenditures are really for intermediate product, but it is impossible to draw a line of separation. Therefore, in practice, all purchases of goods and services by persons are classified as final product in the official accounts.

We thus see that final product is not a definite quantity that lies plainly revealed, simply awaiting measurement by the technicians. On the contrary, it is whatever economists see it to be, and not all see it as the same thing. The technicians who are faced with the practical task of producing dollar estimates are forced to make compromises in order to obtain reasonable estimates, even though they recognize that part of what they report in the accounts as final product would really be intermediate product by a more ideal but statistically unmanageable definition.

Final Product—Consumption and Investment

Gross investment has been defined simply as unconsumed product, or the difference between gross national product and that part of the product that is secured by consumers and government. In 1968, with GNP of $865.7 billion, unconsumed product was equal to $126.0 billion ($I_d$ of $126.3 billion and I_f of $-0.3 billion); consumed product was equal to $739.7 billion ($C$ of $536.6 billion, G of $200.3 billion, R_{gf} of $2.1 billion, and R_{pf} of $0.8 billion). Putting aside the problem of estimating gross national product itself, let us examine the extent to which gross investment—the sum of gross private domestic and net foreign investment—accurately indicates the unconsumed portion of gross national product.

As will be seen in Chapter 22, one critical factor affecting the economy's potential for growth over future years is the share of its final product that is added to the economy's stock of capital goods in current years. The value of the official accounts is enhanced if that share—what is added to the capital stock—can be separated from the estimate of the flow of final product.

One aspect of this question was discussed in detail in Chapter 2: the fact that gross investment is not and does not purport to be an estimate of unconsumed product in a net sense. It does not deduct from the gross amount of capital goods produced the amount used up during the period, and thereby it plainly overstates the net amount of unconsumed product by the amount so used up. Accordingly, in the 1968 data we must deduct from gross investment of $126.3 billion the sum of $73.3 billion, which represents capital consumption. This gives us net investment of $53.0 billion. Correspondingly, the same $73.3 billion must be deducted from gross national product to yield net national product of $792.4 billion. Clearly, net investment is a conceptually superior measure of unconsumed product and net national product a conceptually superior measure of final product.

If this is the case, why are not net national product and net investment the commonly used measures? Here, again, statistical realities enter, and these are such as to make the estimate for capital consumption allowances one of the least reliable estimates in the official accounts. Ideally, this item would provide, in average prices for the time period in question, the dollar value of the actual physical amount of capital goods used up during that time period. However, the depreciation accounts of business firms, which are the principal sources of data for this estimate, do not measure the actual physical wear and tear of capital.[16] Since the capital consumption allowance figure in the official accounts is based on these unadjusted data, there is a possibility of sizable error in the estimate of net investment. The estimate for gross investment is not affected by the relatively unreliable estimate for capital consumption allowances, and, largely for this reason, gross national product has come to be emphasized as *the* measure of national product and gross investment as *the* measure of investment in the official accounts and in popular usage as well.

Quite apart from the difficulty of accurately deriving net investment from gross investment, or net national product from gross national product, there is the further problem that the definitions of these terms as they are used in the official accounts may understate both gross and net investment and thereby overstate the fraction of final product that is consumed. This situation follows from the fact that all purchases of goods by government, including public buildings, dams, and roads, are treated as if they were consumed in the year

[16] Because of the formidable statistical difficulties involved, no attempt is made by the Commerce Department to adjust business book values for depreciation to a figure that equals actual capital consumption measured in the period's average prices for capital goods. However, for that part of gross domestic investment made up of the change in inventories, an adjustment of business book values is made to convert the book value change into a physical volume change valued at average prices for the period. Although the statistical difficulties here are great too, failure to make this adjustment is more serious, and the need for the adjustment cannot be sidestepped by using a gross concept as in the case of fixed capital. This adjustment to inventory valuation will be discussed in the following section.

purchased. In contrast, the accounting treatment of purchases of durable goods by business allows for the fact that they are consumed only over a period of years by including them in gross investment. Thus, the purchase of a newly constructed office building by government becomes part of the economy's "consumed" output for the year, whereas the purchase of the same building by business becomes part of the "unconsumed" output, or gross investment, for the year.

Some economists argue that such government purchases should be treated the same way as business purchases of this type—that is, included as part of gross investment during the year purchased and depreciated over the number of years during which they render service. Thus, for each year, the value of services rendered would appear as imputed rental income. Such treatment has so far been ruled out of the official accounts on the grounds that, among other problems, there is no reliable basis for measuring depreciation of certain government property, like highways and dams, or for valuing the services rendered by such government property. In turn, there is then no reliable basis for estimating the imputed rental income flowing from such property.

This problem is treated in a different manner when it involves purchases of residential property by persons. The official accounts do recognize these purchases as part of the economy's unconsumed output, or gross investment,[17] because a value can be attached to the flow of services from purchases of new construction by persons. As was discussed in the section on imputations, a basis for estimating the imputed net rental income from owner-occupied homes is provided by the rental paid for similar tenant-occupied homes. Depreciation and other items may similarly be estimated on the basis of what is charged for these items on tenant-occupied property.

From this brief look at a few of the problems involved in the official division of national product into consumption and investment, it is clear that the division as made follows directly from the officially adopted set of definitions, which is but one of a number of possible sets of definitions. Just as the official definition of gross national product yields an estimate different from that which would follow from a different definition, so the division of product into consumption and investment is determined by the official definitions of consumption and investment.

Change in Inventories and the Inventory Valuation Adjustment

If during any year there is a change in the level of business inventories, then the economy's gross private domestic investment is greater or less than its purchases of new structures and producers' durable equipment for that year. For example, in the U.S. economy in 1958 the change in business inventories was − $1.5 billion, and new structures and producers' durable equipment were

---

[17] These purchases, it should be noted, are the only expenditure by persons that is classified in this fashion; all other expenditures by persons are assumed to be for goods and services that are consumed during the year acquired.

$62.4 billion. Accordingly gross private domestic investment was $60.9 billion. In 1968 the change in business inventories was $7.3 billion, new structures and producers' durable equipment were $119.0 billion, and gross private domestic investment was $126.3 billion.

Figures such as − $1.5 or $7.3 are the Commerce Department's estimates of the physical volume change in inventories for the year, valued at average prices paid for goods added to inventories during the year. This change may be larger or smaller than the book value change in inventories for the year as shown by the accounting data of business firms. The difference between the department's published figure and the figure derived from business accounting data is the *inventory valuation adjustment*. This adjustment, on the product side of the national income and product account, is designed to avoid understating or overstating the change in inventories and therefore to avoid understating or overstating gross domestic investment and gross national product; on the income side the adjustment avoids understating or overstating corporate profits and proprietors' income and therefore national income.

Although the department's methods of estimating the amount of the adjustment are very complicated, the meaning of the adjustment itself is fairly simple. Suppose, for example, that business book values show an increase in inventories of $3 billion during the year. This figure may be accompanied by an increase, no change, or even a decrease in the physical volume of inventories, since the book value change depends not only on the change in volume but also on changes over the year in the prices paid for inventories acquired. Assume that the change in inventories valued at average prices for the year is only $1 billion. The discrepancy between the two figures then follows from book values based on prices that are higher than average prices for the year. The Commerce Department would add an inventory valuation adjustment of − $2 billion to the book value figure of $3 billion, to give a net amount of $1 billion as the change in inventories valued at average prices for the year.

If prices were falling during the year, the discrepancy between the change in the book value of inventories and the change in inventories valued at average prices would be positive. The change in inventories might show a book value of − $2 billion, but a value at average prices over the year of $1 billion. Accordingly, the inventory valuation adjustment is $3 billion. Regardless of the direction of change in the physical volume of inventories, if prices have risen over the period, the inventory valuation adjustment will necessarily be negative, and if prices have fallen over the period, the adjustment will necessarily be positive.[18]

[18] For any time period, the size of the inventory valuation adjustment varies with the particular methods used by business in charging inventories against cost of goods sold. Under the more commonly used method [First-In, First-Out (FIFO)], inventories are charged against cost of goods sold in the order that inventories were acquired. Under another method [Last-In, First-Out (LIFO)], inventories are charged against cost of goods sold in reverse of the order that inventories were acquired. If both prices and the volume of inventories are rising, FIFO shows an inventory increase that reflects both the increase in volume and the higher prices paid for the last inventories acquired. For, with inventories carried in the books at original cost, FIFO includes the lower-cost inventories acquired earlier as a cost of goods sold during the period and includes the higher-cost inventories acquired later in the book value of in-

The inventory valuation adjustment does not appear explicitly on the product side of the National Income and Product Account; instead it is included in the published figure for the change in inventories. The adjustment does appear explicitly on the income side as an adjustment to corporate profits.[19] It follows from the identity between income and product that any adjustment on the product side must be balanced by an adjustment on the income side. That the adjustment on the income side should appear as an adjustment to corporate profits and proprietors' income follows from the fact that it is specifically these two types of income that would otherwise be either overstated or understated. Suppose that the inventory valuation adjustment were − $2 billion, indicating that $2 billion of the change in the book value of inventories was merely the result of valuation at prices higher than the period's average prices. This amounts to an understatement of $2 billion in the amount of noncapital goods used up by business during the period and therefore a $2 billion overstatement of the profits of business. The opposite would, of course, be true of an adjustment of $2 billion.

The inventory valuation adjustment in the official accounts varies from negligible to sizable amounts, depending primarily on the change in the physical volume of inventories and the change in prices at which these inventories are valued by business. For example, as a percentage of national income, it was a small fraction of 1 percent in each of the last few years, but it was 2 percent in 1950 and 3 percent in 1947. However, whether large or small, it is an item explicitly shown in the official framework, and some understanding of its nature is helpful to an understanding of the complete official framework.

Final Product—Current and Constant Dollars

Final product is equal to the sum of expenditures for those goods and services that are defined as final goods and services. In the preceding pages, we touched on a few of the many problems faced in deciding what goods and services are to be included in or excluded from final product. Once the definition is established, the economy's final product is simply measured by the expenditures made thereon. The total represents the dollar value of the output of final goods and services produced by the nation's economy, with each unit of final product valued at the actual market price paid for it.

---

ventories at the end of the period. The change in book values from the first to the end of the period, thereby, overstates the increase in volume, and a negative inventory valuation adjustment is required. If prices are falling and the volume of inventory is rising, the change in book values under FIFO understates the change in volume, and a positive inventory valuation adjustment is required. Whether prices are rising or falling, as long as volume is rising, LIFO results in neither overstatement nor understatement of the change in volume and no inventory valuation adjustment is required. However, under LIFO, if the volume is decreasing, the decrease is then being measured not in prices paid for those inventories acquired last but in prices paid for those inventories acquired earlier, and an adjustment is required.

[19] A small part of the total adjustment, not shown in Table 5–1, appears as an adjustment to proprietor's income.

Using this procedure in measuring final product, an increase or a decrease in the dollar value of final product from one year to the next will result from changes either in market prices paid, in the volume of goods and services purchased, or in both. The usual purpose of comparing figures for final product over time is to determine changes in the volume of goods and services, and, with qualifications, changes in the economic welfare of the economy. Yet, if the final product figures for each year are expressed in prices current in each year, such comparisons are practically ruled out. Plainly, we are faced with the task of eliminating from these figures the effects of price changes so as to reveal the actual volume changes over time.

One apparently easy method of accomplishing this might be to divide any year's final product, valued in that year's prices, by a price index such as the Consumer Price Index. By doing so one expresses the value of that year's final product as the dollar amount it would have been if prices had been the same as those in the base year of the index. For example, suppose that the Consumer Price Index, equal to 100 in the selected base year 1958, was 120 in the year 1968. This would indicate that consumer prices were 20 percent higher in 1968 than in 1958. Suppose further that 1958 final product valued in 1958 prices is $200 and 1968 final product valued in 1968 prices is $300. Since we know that prices have risen during these years, this increase of $100 in final product is clearly not altogether due to an increase in the volume of product. How do we determine what part of the increase is attributable to higher prices and what part to higher volume? One way of solving the problem is to divide 1968 final product valued in 1968 prices by the ratio of 1968 prices to 1958 prices.

$$\frac{\$300}{120/100} = \$300 \times \frac{100}{120} = \$250$$

This tells us that of the increase in final product of $100 measured in 1968 prices, half was due to an increase in volume and half to a rise in prices from 1958 to 1968. In other words, final product in 1968 valued in 1958 prices was $250. Final product for other years could be converted from prices current in each of those years to the prices in effect in the base year of 1958 in the same fashion, so that final product for each year would be expressed in "constant dollars of 1958 purchasing power," here measuring changes in the purchasing power of the dollar by the Consumer Price Index.[20]

---

[20] Designating final product by GNP, it follows that in any given year (g), GNP is that year's volume of output (O_g) multiplied by the prices paid for each unit of that output (P_g), or $GNP_g = O_g \times P_g$. Expressing prices of any given year as a percentage of prices in the base year gives us a price index in which base-year prices are equal to 100. In other words, the index number for any given year is P_g/P_b, where b designates the base year. Finally, the GNP figure for any given year, if divided by the price index of that year, may be converted into a figure for the output of the given year valued in base-year prices, as shown by the equation

$$\frac{GNP_g}{P_g/P_b} = \frac{O_g \times P_g}{P_g/P_b} = O_g \times P_g \frac{P_b}{P_g} = O_g \times P_b$$

Performing this operation for each given year yields a series of final figures for GNP in which output, O_g, is valued in base-year prices, P_b. Comparison of these adjusted GNP figures will presumably show only changes in volume, the effect of changes in prices having been eliminated.

In our numerical example, we may reliably conclude that the volume of final goods and services in 1968 was not 50 percent greater than that in 1958 ($300/$200 = 1.50). Can we also reliably conclude that it was 25 percent greater than that in 1958 ($250/$200 = 1.25), as indicated by the 1968 dollar value of $300 corrected to $250 by the Consumer Price Index? The answer is clearly no, for all that has been done is to adjust the 1968 market value of all kinds of diverse goods and services, including new factory buildings, aircraft carriers, machine tools, salaries of government employees, net exports, and everything else that is part of final product, by a single price index. This price index is at best appropriate only to that part of final product made up of the goods and services purchased by consumers. For the same reason, adjustment of 1968 final product by the Wholesale Price Index or any other single price index would be unreliable.

The fact that no single price index is appropriate suggests that one must break down final product as finely as possible and then adjust each such part by a price index appropriate to the goods and services included in it. This is essentially the procedure followed by the Commerce Department.[21] Thus, personal consumption expenditures are broken down into dozens of parts, and for each part a special price index is prepared if an acceptable one is not already available. A similar procedure is followed for government purchases of goods and services, gross domestic investment, and exports and imports. In each case the dollar value of each part for the given year is divided by its price index for that year; the resulting dollar values are added together, and the sum is taken as the given year's GNP valued in base-year prices.

This procedure is called "deflation" of GNP. The deflated GNP is termed GNP in "constant dollars" to distinguish it from undeflated GNP, which is in "current dollars." The use of the term "deflation" may be misleading, for to deflate GNP in current dollars to get GNP in constant dollars suggests that the constant dollar figure must be less than the current dollar figure. This, however, is true only in those years in which the prices of the goods and services comprising GNP are higher than those prices in the base year. For other years it is necessary, in effect, to "inflate" the current dollar figures to obtain the constant dollar figures. Nonetheless, by convention, the term deflation is applied in both cases.

Since prices in the years preceding 1958 were lower than those in 1958, the constant dollar figure for each such year is greater than the current dollar figure; since prices in the years following 1958 were higher than those in 1958, the constant dollar figure for each such year is less than the current dollar figure.

[21] Where there are ways of measuring directly the change in volume of a final good or service over time (e.g., in gross domestic investment, the number of freight cars of a given description purchased by railroads, or in government purchases of goods and services, the man-hours of labor, or the number of persons of a given class employed), the physical quantity purchased in any year multiplied by the base-year price per unit will equal the value of that final good or service for the given year in base-year prices. This technique by-passes the need for a price index. If data on volume are available, the department uses this method whenever it appears that by doing so it can obtain more accurate results.

The relationship between constant-dollar GNP and current-dollar GNP may be seen in Table 5–4, which gives GNP in current and constant dollars for selected years from 1929 to 1968.

TABLE 5–4   Gross National Product in Current and Constant (1958) Dollars, Selected Years 1929–68 (billions of dollars)

(1)	(2)	(3)	(4)
			Implicit Price Deflators
Year	Current Dollars	Constant Dollars	(1958 = 100)
1929	103.1	203.6	50.6
1933	55.6	141.5	39.3
1937	90.4	203.3	44.5
1939	90.5	209.4	43.2
1945	212.0	355.4	59.7
1948	257.6	323.7	79.6
1950	284.8	355.3	80.2
1954	364.8	407.0	89.6
1957	441.1	452.5	97.5
1958	447.3	447.3	100.0
1959	483.6	475.9	101.6
1960	503.8	487.8	103.3
1961	520.1	497.2	104.6
1962	560.3	529.8	105.8
1963	590.5	551.0	107.2
1964	632.4	581.1	108.8
1965	684.9	617.8	110.9
1966	749.9	658.1	113.9
1967	793.5	674.6	117.6
1968	865.7	707.6	122.3

SOURCE: *The National Income and Product Accounts of the United States, 1929–1965 Statistical Tables* and *Survey of Current Business*, July 1969, Tables 1.1, 1.2, and 8.1.

As a by-product of the department's deflation procedure, there emerge what are officially designated "implicit price deflators" for GNP. These are given in Column 4 of Table 5–4. For example, the deflator for 1968, 122.3, is "implicit" in the current and constant dollar figures for 1968 in that it is derived by dividing 865.7 by 707.6 and multiplying the quotient by 100. Column 4 turns out to be a price index but one quite different from the Consumer or Wholesale Price Index. Unlike the more specific coverage of other price indexes, the implicit price deflator covers all the varied goods and services included in the economy's GNP.

The department's deflation procedure yields more reliable results than those secured by any of the short-cut methods described earlier. Nevertheless, even though the official constant-dollar estimates are probably as accurate as present data and techniques can make them, some unknown error is unavoidably present in each estimate. In large part, this error results from the shortcomings of the price indexes themselves—for example, the problem of allowing in indexes for quality changes in the goods included and of adjusting for the appearance of new goods and disappearance of old. Whatever error may be present, these estimates still provide the most dependable indicator currently available for the actual changes over time in the physical volume of goods and services included in GNP.

PART II

MACROECONOMIC THEORY:
Determination of National Income and Output

CHAPTER 6

BASIC CONCEPTS

What determines the economy's real income or output of final goods and services in any year? This question, which is far less simple than it seems, defines one of the major tasks of macroeconomic theory and the one that will be our primary concern throughout Part II. It also leads logically to further questions: What determines the fluctuations in output from one year to the next (which is essentially the question of the business cycle)? What determines the rate at which output increases over a period of years (which is essentially the question of economic growth)? We will look into these additional questions in Part III.

The practical importance of the first question we raised cannot be exaggerated, for its answer provides in part the answer to the fundamental question of what determines the material well-being of the economy's population. A short-run goal of any economy is the production in each year of the maximum amount of goods and services possible with its currently available labor force, stock of plant and equipment, and technological know-how. An economy that managed to maintain such a maximum flow of output each year would thereby be providing its population with the highest per capita real income attainable each year. In an economy that failed to achieve this goal, the per capita real income of its citizens would be below what it could be; moreover, some people who wanted to work, and who could thereby increase aggregate output and per capita real income, would find themselves without jobs. When an economy fails in any period to produce actual output equal to its potential for that period, we cannot begin to explain its failure—or formulate a policy to remedy it—unless we can first explain what determines its actual output. In other words, whether actual output is at potential, just short of potential, or far below potential, we are at a loss to explain what we actually observe without a theory of what determines aggregate output.

If the economy's actual output in every year were equal or nearly equal to its potential for that year, however, the theory of the determination of aggregate output would be a far less important subject than it is. Attention would then focus primarily on growth theory, which attempts to explain the rate at which aggregate output grows over time. If that growth rate were, in turn, one that provided a very rapidly rising standard of living as well as uninterrupted full utilization of the labor force and other resources, neither the short-run theory of the determination of aggregate output nor the long-run theory of economic growth would be as important as they are. Unfortunately, instead of these ideal results, the actual record for the United States, as well as for other economies, shows sizable fluctuations in the level of output with attendant underutilization of labor and other resources and also, in some periods, a growth rate that has meant a slowly rising or even falling per capita real income. In view of this actual record, the short-run theory of income determination and the long-run theory of economic growth are addressed to subjects of anything but academic interest. They involve the problem of securing the highest possible standard of living for the nation's people, and there is probably no more important problem within the province of economics.

FROM MACROECONOMIC ACCOUNTING
TO MACROECONOMIC THEORY

Disconcerting as it may seem, the national income accounts do not provide the answer to what determines the economy's actual level of output in any period. They provide us with estimates of the economy's output for any time period, but they do not tell us what *determines* that output in any time period or what *determines* the changes that occur from one time period to another. For example, we may compare GNP in constant dollars for two years and label the difference the change in the economy's output from the first to the second year. Thus, for the U.S. economy in 1967 and 1968 we have the following figures in billions of 1958 dollars for the product side of the GNP identity:

$$\text{GNP} \equiv C + I_d + G + (X - M)$$

	GNP		C		I_d		G		$(X - M)$
1967	\$674.6	=	\$430.3	+	\$100.8	+	\$140.0	+	\$3.6
1968	\$707.6	=	\$452.6	+	\$105.7	+	\$148.4	+	\$0.9

The figure for GNP in 1968 is simply the official estimate of the final output flow for the year, and the figures for C, I_d, G, and $(X - M)$ are simply estimates of the composition of this total flow. GNP of \$707.6 billion was necessarily identical with the sum of its component parts, since it was derived by adding together these parts.[1] Although this is valuable for other purposes, it is nothing

---

[1] GNP may be broken down in other ways without altering this conclusion. For example, by major type of product we have durable goods of \$162.8 billion, nondurable goods of \$218.6 billion, services of \$259.9 billion, and structures of \$66.4 billion, all adding up to GNP of \$707.6 billion in 1968. In no sense, however, does this alternative breakdown—or any other— tell us what actually determined GNP in 1968.

more than an identity and as such is valueless as an explanation of *why* output was actually this amount in 1968.

What then did determine the economy's output in 1968 or in any other period we might choose to consider? As a first step toward any kind of an answer to what is a very complex question, we plainly have to discover the major variables that influence how much output the economy produces and to detect the relationships among these variables that give rise to the actual results we find in any period. In other words, as a first step we need a theory of income determination, which, in full-blown form, is a detailed analytical framework or model that expresses in the various relationships that make up that model how each variable is believed to be related to the other variables that have been identified as relevant to the problem. Such relationships are functional relationships in the sense that one variable in the relationship is believed to be a function of one or more other variables in a way specified by the particular theory that has been advanced. The relationship that makes aggregate consumption expenditures a function of disposable personal income is such a relationship; it expresses a theory, however simple, of the determination of aggregate consumption. It is only by devising theories, by hypothesizing functional relationships, that we can make any progress toward explaining the facts revealed, for example, by the data in the preceding identities. And devising theories, however indispensable in the process of explanation, is only a step in the process, for the theories devised may or may not be supportable. In order to decide which theories are to be at least tentatively retained and which are to be rejected, we must test theories against the "facts." Furthermore, a theory that is so supported is only provisionally accepted, for such support can never "prove" a theory. Sometimes we find a number of conflicting theories that receive equal support from the available data, and the question of which is the "true" theory remains at least temporarily unresolved.

We can bypass these and other complications that are faced in actually constructing and testing a detailed model, and still say something meaningful about what determines the economy's output by dropping down to the simplest possible model of Keynesian theory. In that theory the basic force determining aggregate output is aggregate demand, and the simplified model that emerges includes little more than a few functional relationships designed to explain in turn the determination of the level of each of the major components into which aggregate demand may be divided. There is a theory for aggregate consumption expenditure (the one noted above) and an equally simple theory for the other components. Nobody who seriously sets out to explain output determination limits himself to so crude a model, but even here we have a model that, despite its simplicity, takes us at least some distance toward answering the question we raised.

Unlike the simplest theoretical framework, no accounting framework, however elaborate, can in itself provide this answer we seek. Any such framework primarily provides facts, and facts do not speak for themselves. The accounting framework and the definitions of the items that comprise it are nonetheless essential as a setting within which may be developed the theoretical framework that will give us the answer. The more detailed the theoretical framework, the more detailed must be the accounting framework that supports it. If our purpose were only to develop the theory of the determination of income and output for a hypothetical two-sector economy, all we would need would be the simple accounting framework developed in Chapter 2. If our purpose were the more ambitious one of developing the theory for a three- or four-sector economy, we would need the more complex accounting frameworks developed in Chapters 3 and 4. If our purpose were to use the developed theory as the basis for policy, and such is the ultimate purpose of theory, we would need a real-world accounting framework such as that provided by the U.S. Department of Commerce. And, finally, if our purpose were to test the developed theory against the facts, and such is obviously desirable for any theory, again we would need a real-world accounting framework and the "facts" for the real world as provided in that framework. The relationships between the accounting framework and the theoretical framework present a question that will answer itself in the chapters that follow. We will see how macroeconomic theory, and especially the application of this theory to questions of policy, is intimately tied to macroeconomic accounting.

Before plunging into the development of macroeconomic theory, it will be helpful to examine a few of the basic concepts that run the full breadth of economic theory, such as stocks and flows, equilibrium and disequilibrium, and statics and dynamics. The presentation here is designed to provide only an elementary understanding of what are actually some of the most troublesome concepts in economic methods.[2] Furthermore, the meaning assigned here to each of these concepts is only one of the several meanings that economists have employed. Finally, the coverage in what follows is limited to the few concepts noted above; the many other concepts of narrower application may be more advantageously treated, where pertinent, in the chapters ahead.

STOCKS AND FLOWS[3]

The twin concepts of stocks and flows are not especially difficult to understand, but they can cause great difficulty if misunderstood or misused. To begin with, stocks and flows are both variables; they are quantities that may grow smaller or larger over time. The distinction between them is that a *stock* is a quantity measurable at a specified *point* in time and a *flow* is a quantity that can be measured only in terms of a specified *period* of time. For example, a gauge may indicate that the stock of water in a reservoir is 50 million gallons; the stock

[2] For an advanced discussion of these particular concepts, see J. R. Hicks, *Capital and Growth*, Oxford Univ. Press, 1965, Chs. 1–3 and 8.
[3] See also G. Ackley, *Macroeconomic Theory*, Macmillan, 1961, pp. 5–8, and W. S. Vickrey, *Metastatics and Macroeconomics*, Harcourt, Brace & World, 1964, pp. 116–17.

variable is 50 million gallons at this particular point in time. It would be meaningless to describe this as 50 million gallons a year, a month, a week, or a day. Another gauge may indicate that the flow of water into the reservoir amounted to 365 million gallons over the year then ended. Assuming that the flow was at a fixed rate over the year, this reading would also indicate that water had flowed in at a *rate* of 7 million gallons per week and 1 million gallons per day.

As another example, consider the total number of persons employed in the United States—this is a stock variable. In contrast, the number of persons who secure new jobs or leave employment are flow variables. The number employed is, say, 75 million at a point in time (on a particular day); it is nonsense to speak of the number employed as 75 million per year.[4] The number of persons who find employment may be, say, 100,000 for a given time period, the month of June. This is not 100,000 at a specific point in time, however.

Money is a stock, but the spending of money is a flow. To say simply that the stock of money is $200 billion has no meaning until we specify the point in time—for example, December 31, 1968—at which this amount was available.[5] Similarly, the statement that total spending for final output amounted to $866 billion is meaningless until we specify the time period, for example, the year 1968, during which this amount was spent. Here we can see the serious errors that can result from a failure to distinguish stocks from flows. Some people fail to make a distinction between the *amount* of money and the *spending* of money. They simply equate the two, perhaps because whatever money they get their hands on they promptly spend. From this error follows the more serious error of imagining an increase in the stock of money to be a certain means of producing an equal increase in the flow of spending. Far from being equal, however, the two can and at times do change in opposite directions to produce a combination of more money and less spending or less money and more spending. As soon as it is recognized that the variable money is a stock and the variable spending is a flow, there can be no equating of the two.[6]

There are dozens of other illustrations of the stock/flow distinction in any of the income and product tables of Part I. The word "flow" was used repeatedly in connection with the entries in these tables, and it should now be clear that

---

[4] We can and do say that employment or the number of persons employed *averaged* 75 million during the year, a figure derived by estimating employment at a number of specific points in time (e.g., the middle of each month during the year) and then computing the average value of these estimates. The average figure, no less than each of the twelve mid-month figures from which it was derived, is still a stock variable. This is not to be confused with the "unemployment rate," however, which is a *ratio* of two *stock* variables, the number unemployed divided by the number in the labor force.

[5] As in the case of employment, we can say that the stock of money averaged so many billions of dollars for the year, but again this average figure is a stock variable.

[6] The error of those who equate the two is, of course, their failure to allow for the velocity of money. Spending, a flow variable, divided by the money supply, a stock variable, equals velocity, a flow variable. Classical economists were never guilty of this error, but they seem to have made a related error on occasion by implicitly assuming velocity to be constant and therefore concluding that spending, though not equal to the stock of money, varied proportionately with changes in the stock of money. We will treat this topic in greater detail in Chapter 17, where classical theory is examined.

every entry there is without exception a dollar figure measuring a flow. Some of these figures, such as "change in business inventories," may at first glance appear to measure stocks. Notice, however, that the entry is not "inventories," which is clearly a stock, but rather "*change* in inventories," which is just as clearly a flow, for a change in any variable can only be measured over a period of time.

Some macroeconomic variables that have flow magnitudes also have a direct counterpart stock variable. However, others, such as imports and exports, wages and salaries, tax payments, social-security benefits, and dividends, are only flows; none has a direct stock counterpart as it is impossible to conceive of a "stock of imports" or a "stock of wages and salaries." Although such variables have no direct stock counterpart, flows of this type do indirectly affect the sizes of other stocks. Imports may affect the size of business inventories or the stock of capital goods; wage and salary receipts devoted to the purchase of newly produced houses may affect the stock of housing. In the case of some variables that have a direct counterpart in a stock variable, statistics on both the stock and the flow variable are unfortunately reported under headings that are practically the same. A person's saving is a flow ($25 for April), and his savings are a stock ($500 accumulated as of April 30); a firm's gross investment is a flow ($50,000 for April), and the *total invested*, or the dollar value of real capital accumulated, is a stock ($1 million as of April 30); the *change* in the nation's money supply is a flow ($1 billion increase during April), and the money supply is a stock ($195 billion as of April 30).

For those flow variables that have a direct stock counterpart, any change in the magnitude of the stock variable between two specified points in time must be the consequence of the magnitudes of its counterpart flow variables during the period.[7] Thus, the number of persons employed increases, decreases, or remains unchanged between two points in time, depending on the number of persons who secure employment and the number of persons who leave employment during the intervening period. The nation's stock of capital changes between two points in time depending on the inflow (the amount of gross investment or capital goods produced) and the outflow (the amount of capital goods consumed) during the intervening period.

Although it is necessarily true that a stock can change only as a result of flows, the magnitudes of the flows themselves may be determined in part by changes in the stock. The best example is the relationship between the stock of capital and the flow of investment. The stock of capital can increase only as a result of an excess of the flow of investment or of new capital goods produced over the flow of capital goods consumed. However, the flow of investment itself depends, among other things, on the size of the capital stock. In many theories of the business cycle, a critical factor in the explanation of business downturns is a decrease in the flow of investment, which is brought on by an "excessive"

[7] Since stocks and flows in macroeconomics are usually expressed in dollars, a change in a stock may occur with no change in the counterpart flows simply as a result of a revaluation of a given physical stock. Thus, the U.S. gold stock would increase in dollar value if there were a devaluation of the dollar, even if the inflow and outflow of gold were to leave the physical amount of gold unchanged.

stock of capital resulting from an earlier, prolonged upsurge in the flow of investment. This earlier upsurge in the flow of investment was usually brought on by a decrease in the stock of capital during the preceding depression, a period during which the flow of investment fell below that of the preceding period of prosperity. As is apparent, this process may continue ad infinitum and carry with it the endless sequence of ups and downs known as business cycles.

By definition, stocks can exert an influence on flows only if the time period is long enough to produce the required change in stocks. Where stocks are very large relative to flows, the changes in stocks resulting from flows are typically so small in the short-run period that stocks may be assumed to be constant in that period. Thus, to the extent that flows are influenced by changes in stocks, it follows that the flows will be uninfluenced by changes in stocks in the short-run. For example, if the net effect of the flows of gross investment and capital consumption is an increase in the stock of capital between January 1 and December 31 amounting to a fraction of 1 percent of the January 1 stock of capital, then the capital stock may be assumed to be approximately constant. Since it is approximately constant, it can have no significant effect on the flow of net investment in the following period.[8]

With respect to this relationship between the flow of investment and the stock of capital, we may define the short-run period as one in which changes in the stock of capital are too small to have an influence on the flow of investment and the long-run period as one in which such changes are large enough to have an influence on the flow of investment. In this sense, elementary macroeconomic theory is primarily short-run; it is essentially a study of relationships among flows in which the size of each flow in any time period is determined solely by the sizes of other flows. In the simplest formulation of Keynesian theory, the flow of consumer spending is determined by the flow of income, and the flow of income equals the flow of consumer spending plus the flow of investment spending. Although we are primarily concerned with elementary theory in this text, we will devote some attention to more advanced theory in which changes in such critical stocks as the stock of money and the stock of capital affect the all-important flows of income and product.

EQUILIBRIUM AND DISEQUILIBRIUM[9]

Equilibrium and its absence, disequilibrium, are concepts familiar in some degree to all students, whether from study of economics, other social or physical

[8] Among other things, this illustration glosses over the question of how investment is distributed by industry. If the increase should be concentrated in a few strategic industries, aggregate investment in the next year may be adversely affected by a small increase in the aggregate stock of capital this year. This might be the case if these industries discovered that they had over-expanded facilities relative to final demand for their products.

[9] For more on the meaning and types of equilibrium, see M. M. Bober, *Intermediate Price and Income Theory*, rev. ed., Norton, 1962, pp. 483–95. See also F. Machlup, "Equilibrium and

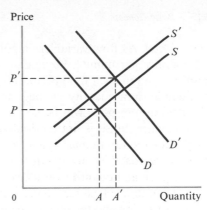

FIGURE 6-1 Supply of and Demand for a Commodity

sciences. The definition of equilibrium in the physical sciences as a state of balance between opposing forces or actions applies without modification in the field of economic theory. Disequilibrium in turn simply becomes the absence of a state of balance—a state in which opposing forces produce imbalance.

Since in economics we are continuously dealing with variables whose values change over time, the state of balance that defines equilibrium may perhaps be better expressed as a state of no change over time. This is not to say that economic equilibrium is a state of absolute rest, a motionless state in which no action takes place; rather, it is a state in which there is action but in which the action is of a repetitive nature as long as a given equilibrium position is maintained. Each time period exactly duplicates the preceding time period. This state of equilibrium results, even though the forces acting on the system are in a continuous state of change, as long as the net effect of these changing forces is such as not to disturb the established position of equilibrium.

Let us turn for a moment to microeconomic theory and consider the ordinary supply-demand analysis of price determination for a single commodity in which quantity supplied varies directly with price and quantity demanded varies inversely with price. Price per unit is determined by the opposing forces of supply and demand, opposing in the sense that an increase in supply tends to lower the price and an increase in demand tends to raise the price, with opposite tendencies following from opposite changes in supply and demand. In Figure 6-1, supply, S, and demand, D, are in equilibrium only at a price of OP and a quantity of OA. At any price higher or lower than OP, there is disequilibrium: At any price above OP there will be an excess of quantity supplied over quantity demanded, and at any price below OP an excess of quantity demanded over quantity supplied. In this particular model, in the event of disequilibrium, the opposing forces are such as to move price back to the equilibrium level of OP and quantity back to the equilibrium level of OA.

Supply and demand are functions that indicate the different quantities of a commodity that will be supplied and demanded at various prices *for a particular*

Disequilibrium: Misplaced Concreteness and Disguised Politics," *Economic Journal*, March 1958, pp. 1–24, reprinted in the author's *Essays in Economic Semantics*, Norton, 1967.

time period. As flow variables, supply and demand may be expressed in terms of quantity per minute, hour, day, week, or any other time period. If supply and demand in each time period are the same as in the preceding time period, the equilibrium quantity of the commodity purchased or sold will be *OA* and the equilibrium price will be *OP*, one time period after the other. The market is in balance, but it is not motionless, for sellers are continually bringing more of the commodity to market and buyers are continually taking more of it away. In other words, the market is in equilibrium; there is no change in the magnitude of the price and quantity variables.

Over time, of course, changes in supply and demand take place. Depending on the direction and the magnitude of the changes in supply or demand or both, equilibrium price and quantity may increase or decrease, with price and quantity changing in opposite directions or in the same direction. *S'* and *D'* in Figure 6–1 illustrate this last possibility. The new equilibrium price becomes *OP'*, and the new equilibrium quantity becomes *OA'*. As long as a supply curve sloping upward to the right intersects a demand curve sloping downward to the right, any possible change in supply and demand will define a new equilibrium price and a new equilibrium quantity at the point of intersection of the two curves.

In practice, the new equilibrium price and quantity are not instantaneously established. The process takes time, and during this time price and quantity are changing, and the market is by definition in disequilibrium. If the changes in supply and demand are frequent, sizable, or erratic, equilibrium may never be established. Before the market can reach that price-quantity combination that represents equilibrium for one set of supply and demand conditions, the supply and demand conditions change. In such a situation, the market is forever moving toward equilibrium, but equilibrium has become a shifting, evasive goal that always recedes before it can be reached. However, even for markets like this that are in continuous disequilibrium, the concept of equilibrium is a valuable tool of analysis. If at any point in time an equilibrium position exists, this at least tells us which way the system is going to move next, even though we know that before the system gets to the equilibrium position toward which it is momentarily headed it will be detoured by a change in the forces that change the equilibrium position.

Figure 6–1 was chosen to illustrate the concept of equilibrium because it is the simplest possible microeconomic model of a system with an equilibrium solution. This model contains only three variables—quantity of the commodity supplied, quantity of the commodity demanded, and price of the commodity—and only three relationships among these variables. Two are functional relationships: Quantity demanded is an inverse function of price, and quantity supplied is a direct function of price. The third relationship specifies the condition necessary for equilibrium: The quantity suppliers wish to sell must be equal to the quantity that demanders wish to purchase, or, in brief, supply must equal demand. All the variables other than price that influence the supply of and demand for the commodity, such as buyers' incomes, their tastes, the prices of other commodities, and the prices of inputs used in producing the commodity, are assumed to remain temporarily unchanged in order to focus attention on the way in which the equilibrium price is determined with given conditions of supply and demand.

There are macroeconomic models that are equally elementary but probably less familiar than the well-known model of commodity-price determination of Figure 6–1. The difference is in the variables that enter into the models. Quantity demanded, quantity supplied, and price are the variables in the model of market-price determination. The economy's aggregate output, aggregate consumption, and aggregate investment spending are the variables in one version of the two-sector Keynesian model. The model contains three relationships among these variables. Two are functional relationships: Aggregate consumption is a direct function of output or income; aggregate investment is (in one version) also a direct function of output or income. The third relationship specifies the condition necessary for equilibrium: The aggregate output that is being produced must be equal to the aggregate output that buyers wish to purchase for both consumption and investment purposes, or, in brief, aggregate output must be equal to aggregate demand.

Just as disequilibrium exists in the market for a single commodity whenever supply is not equal to demand, so disequilibrium exists in macroeconomic models whenever aggregate output is not equal to aggregate demand. In the market for a commodity, the price of the commodity adjusts upward or downward to bring quantity supplied and quantity demanded into equilibrium. In Keynesian theory, it is the level of aggregate output or income that adjusts upward or downward to bring aggregate output and aggregate demand into equilibrium. Furthermore, just as changes in supply of and demand for a commodity produce a new equilibrium price (or, under certain conditions, a state of continuous disequilibrium), so changes in consumption and investment propensities produce a new equilibrium output (or, under certain conditions, a state of continuous disequilibrium).

The idea of macroeconomic equilibrium may also be illustrated in a different way, through the concepts of stocks and flows examined in the previous section. Suppose water flowed into a reservoir at a rate of 100,000 gallons per day and out of the reservoir at a rate of 90,000 gallons per day. These flows would be described as equilibrium flows as long as they did not change in size from day to day or over the period of time considered relevant. This produces *flow* equilibrium, but it necessarily produces a disequilibrium in the *stock* of water. If the stock of water were measured at the same point in time each day, the gauge would show that the stock was growing by 10,000 gallons each day. Since the stock is changing, there is stock disequilibrium; since the flows are constant, there is flow equilibrium. Stock disequilibrium is thus logically consistent with flow equilibrium. Over time, however, a sufficient change in stock will begin to affect the previously constant flows. Unless the stock of water is to be permitted to overflow the banks of the reservoir, there must be a change either in the inflow (from 100,000 to 90,000 gallons per day) or in the outflow (from 90,000 to 100,000 gallons per day) or in both (to 95,000 gallons per day). If changes of this sort are made in the size of the flows, the system will be one in which both flows and stocks are in equilibrium.

An analogous situation is found in the flow of investment (capital goods produced), the flow of capital goods consumed, and the stock of capital goods. Gross investment at a constant rate of $95 billion per year and capital consumption at a constant rate of $55 billion per year define a flow equilibrium. These flows also define a stock disequilibrium in which the stock of capital increases every year by the amount of $40 billion.[10] This is one indication that the economy is a "growing" economy, if we measure economic "growth" by the accumulation of capital. In contrast, an economy in which there is equilibrium in both flows and stock, with, say, gross investment of $55 billion and capital consumption of $55 billion per year, is a "stationary" economy in which the stock of capital neither increases nor decreases over time.

Flow equilibrium may thus be described as short-run equilibrium, and both flow and stock equilibrium may be described as long-run equilibrium. Since stock equilibrium cannot exist without flow equilibrium, long-run equilibrium cannot exist without short-run equilibrium. In short-run equilibrium, we disregard the disequilibrating effects that flows produce on stocks and consider only the conditions necessary to achieve flow equilibrium. In long-run equilibrium, however, the countereffects produced on flows by disequilibrium in stocks must be recognized, and conditions for full equilibrium encompass those necessary for both flow and stock equilibrium.

An economic theory or model abstracts from the infinite complexity of the real world by establishing what are believed to be the significant relationships among a limited number of variables deemed relevant to the problem at hand. The concept of equilibrium is a valuable tool of theory because it identifies a position in which the values of the model's variables are in balance. This helps simplify the complexity of the real world, where these same variables may actually be in continuous short- and long-run disequilibrium. Disequilibrium is also a valuable tool of theory but in a different sense, for by simplifying less it more closely approximates economic reality. In fact, it may be said that short-run equilibrium analysis is a maximum in simplification and long-run disequilibrium analysis is a minimum in simplification. The more difficult branch of macroeconomic theory is therefore that which treats of systems in long-run disequilibrium by admitting into the analysis continuing changes in both flows and stocks.

At the end of the previous section we indicated that we would be primarily concerned with elementary macroeconomic theory in which changes in flows are considered but changes in stocks are not. For the same reason, the models we will consider will for the most part be those with an equilibrium solution. In other words, we will confine ourselves largely to short-run equilibrium models.

[10] This conclusion of a stock disequilibrium follows from the definition of disequilibrium as an *absolute* change in the variable. If investment, capital consumption, and the stock of capital grow at such rates that the *ratio* of stock of capital to the flow variables does not change period by period, then, although the stock of capital is changing in absolute terms, it is not changing relative to flows. From this emerges a different and more complex definition of equilibrium as constancy in the ratio of capital stock to the relevant flows. Under this definition then, what is disequilibrium in absolute terms may be equilibrium in relative terms. In this book equilibrium is a position of no change in absolute terms unless otherwise noted.

STATICS AND DYNAMICS[11]

We have noted that stocks and flows are the two types of variables found in economic models and that equilibrium and disequilibrium are the two possible positions of such models at any point in time. The actual position at any point in time is determined by the values attached to the variables that are parts of the model. Now let us examine briefly the two general methods employed in the construction and analysis of economic models—statics and dynamics.

These terms have been defined in somewhat different ways by different economists. One definition that conveys the meaning of dynamics in nontechnical language is offered by Professor Baumol: "Economic dynamics is the study of economic phenomena in relation to preceding and succeeding events."[12] Other definitions could be offered, but each in one way or another defines the essence of dynamics as the explicit recognition of time in the process of economic change.

In constructing formal models, one way of explicitly incorporating time into the model is to split up time into periods and to examine how what happens in one period is related to what happened in preceding periods and to what is expected to happen in succeeding periods. In other words, the variables in dynamic models are said to be "dated." In contrast, the variables in static models all pertain to the same period of time, and there is no need to bother with dating. By dating the variables in dynamic models, we can investigate such things as how the amount of goods that businessmen plan to purchase for inventory in a given period may depend on the amount of their sales in a previous period or on the amount of change in their sales between two previous periods. In turn, we can also investigate to what degree the sales volume in a previous period, or the change in sales between two periods, is influenced by the level of income of the economy in that previous period or by the change in the level of income between periods. In short, through this technique dynamic analysis is able to trace the changes in the values of the variables *over time*. The change in each variable from one period to the next is determined in a specified way by changes in the other variables included in the model.

Since statics ignores the passage of time, it is powerless to explain the *process* of change in a model. It can indicate the position of the model for a given period, but it cannot, except in a special case, tell exactly what the position will be in any other period. It is in the special case where the model is not changing at all but is simply repeating the same motion period after period that static analysis can reveal both where the system is in the present period and precisely

---

[11] For an introduction to the concepts of statics and dynamics with special reference to Keynes's *General Theory of Employment, Interest, and Money*, see A. H. Hansen, *A Guide to Keynes*, McGraw-Hill, 1953, pp. 44–54. See also J. R. Hicks, *Value and Capital*, Oxford Univ. Press, 1939, Ch. 9; P. A. Samuelson, *Foundations of Economic Analysis*, Harvard Univ. Press, 1947, pp. 311–17; and W. J. Baumol, *Economic Dynamics*, 2nd ed., Macmillan, 1959, Chs. 1 and 7.
[12] *Economic Dynamics*, p. 4.

where it will be in any future period—namely, exactly where it is in the present period. This special case is termed "stationary equilibrium," because the equilibrium position remains unchanged from one period to the next.

Pure static analysis is applicable only to a model in which a single, unshifting equilibrium position is established by the relationships among the variables. Applying statics to such a model in a period when it is in disequilibrium can only tell us for that particular period the values of the variables that are changing from that period to the next. Statics can explain *why* this is a disequilibrium, what relationship among the variables is necessary for equilibrium, and in what direction the system will next move. Given the fact that a single, unshifting equilibrium position exists, it may describe in general terms where the system must move to reach this predetermined equilibrium position. Statics cannot explain, however, the *actual* process, step by step or period by period, that the system follows over time in getting to that equilibrium position.

As the static method of analysis applies to models in equilibrium, the dynamic method of analysis applies to models in disequilibrium. Dynamics traces the process of change in the values of a model's variables over time, and a system in disequilibrium is, by definition, one whose variables are changing in value. Hence, to analyze a model in disequilibrium, we must use dynamics, the method that is capable of following the system from one point of disequilibrium to another toward an eventual equilibrium position or through an unending succession of disequilibrium positions.

To illustrate, let us return again to the supply-demand model discussed in the previous section. If for a given period the price-quantity combination is other than the equilibrium combination, price and quantity must change. Since we have assumed that there is an equilibrium position, the changes over time will be changes that are working toward this equilibrium price-quantity combination. Given the original supply and demand curves and assuming that the very process of working toward the indicated equilibrium of supply and demand will not cause a shift in either the supply or demand curves and therefore in the equilibrium position, static analysis can identify the equilibrium position and describe in general terms how the system will move to this position. If we were given more information about the way this market operates—much more than just the market's original supply and demand curves—dynamic analysis could be used to do what statics cannot. Dynamics could trace, period by period, the changes in the values of the variables as they moved through successive disequilibrium positions toward the single price-quantity equilibrium position.[13]

---

[13] This supply-demand model assumes for simplicity that the equilibrium price (*OP*) and quantity (*OA*) will be reached. However, it is possible that in any period purchases and sales made at prices other than the equilibrium price will cause shifts in the supply and demand curves in the next period. This means that transactions in the present period at disequilibrium prices can in the next period produce a change in the equilibrium price. Statics is forced to circumvent this problem in some way. One way is to assume that the original equilibrium price is "instantaneously" reached; another is to assume that all purchases and sales are tentative rather than final until the particular price at which there is equilibrium is arrived at by all buyers and sellers. The latter process is sometimes referred to as "recontract." Without such unrealistic assumptions, which statics is forced to make, purchases and sales made at dis-

Comparative Statics

We have noted that the static method is meaningful only when applied to models with equilibrium positions. We also know that the economic forces that determine the equilibrium position for a model may be expected to change over time so as to displace the original equilibrium and, under certain conditions, to lead to the establishment of a new equilibrium. Given an initial position of equilibrium and some specified changes in underlying forces, if it is possible to determine how these forces affect the position of the new equilibrium, one can compare the two equilibrium positions and explain the change between the two in terms of the changes in forces. It is the analysis of this particular kind of change, from one equilibrium position to another, that may be handled by the method of comparative statics.

Consider once again the supply-and-demand model given earlier. The original equilibrium is that defined by the intersection of the supply curve, *S*, and the demand curve, *D*. Suppose that changes in conditions external to the model, such as changes in income, or buyers' tastes, or prices of competing products, or prices of inputs used in production, cause the supply curve to shift to *S'* and the demand curve to shift to *D'*. Through the method of comparative statics, we can show the direction and the magnitude of the change in equilibrium price and quantity that follows from changes in the underlying forces that cause the shifts in the supply and demand curves. In our example, the changes in these forces are such as to raise equilibrium price from *OP* to *OP'* and equilibrium quantity from *OA* to *OA'*. Comparative statics can also tell us the magnitude and the direction of change in equilibrium price and quantity if the only shift that occurs is in the demand curve or in the supply curve. For example, if in our diagram a rise in consumer income were to shift the demand curve upward from *D* to *D'*, we could confidently predict that, with the supply curve, *S*, as shown, equilibrium price must rise. Thus, we have the comparative statics result that, with an upward-sloping supply curve, a rise in income that shifts the demand curve upward must raise equilibrium price.

We can conduct the same sort of analysis for changes in supply or demand other than those illustrated in the diagram. However, comparative statics is adequate for this task only when in each case a new equilibrium position succeeds the old. Comparative statics is inadequate for the task, when, as a result of changes in underlying economic forces, a system goes into a state of continuous disequilibrium. Furthermore, even if a new equilibrium does succeed the old, comparative statics is incapable of explaining the path followed by the system over time in getting from the old position of equilibrium to the new. In other words, comparative statics bridges the gap between equilibrium

---

equilibrium prices may set into motion a process that never reaches equilibrium, one disequilibrium price succeeding another. This might occur, for example, if a change in price in the present period gives rise to expectations among both buyers and sellers that there will be further price changes in the same direction during following periods. An analysis of a market such as this is possible only with the methods of dynamics.

positions in one instantaneous jump, but it tells us nothing about *how* we got from one equilibrium position to the other. In reality, since positions of disequilibrium are more the norm than the exception, we are likely to be more interested in the path followed between positions of equilibrium than in the positions of equilibrium themselves, and only dynamic analysis can handle this task.

To summarize the relationships between statics and dynamics and the concepts examined earlier in this chapter, the variables found in an economic model are either stocks or flows. Any given model may include only flow variables or both flow and stock variables. Certain relationships are postulated among these variables, such that the value of one variable is a function of the value of one or more of the other variables in the model. If all variables are considered in the same time period, the relationships are all *static;* if they cover different time periods, the relationships are *dynamic.* Thus, in the supply and demand model as presented, the relationships are static; all the variables are considered as of the same time period.

Any given set of relationships may or may not produce an equilibrium solution for the model. In the supply-and-demand model, equilibrium requires that quantity supplied be equal to quantity demanded. If there is a pair of values for these two variables that will equate the two, the price at which they are equal is the equilibrium price. If there is no such pair of values, there is no equilibrium price. The resultant model is a disequilibrium model in which the relationships between quantity supplied and quantity demanded must lead to constantly changing prices and quantities as transactions are carried through period after period at prices other than an equilibrium price.

If the model has an equilibrium solution, it may be analyzed by the static method. If it has no equilibrium solution, it can only be analyzed by the dynamic method. If the model is such that one equilibrium position, if upset by a change in some variable, will tend to be succeeded by a different equilibrium position in a manner that can be calculated from the change in the disturbing variable, the change from one equilibrium position to the next but not the actual path followed between equilibrium positions may be analyzed by the method of comparative statics.

CHAPTER 7

THE EQUILIBRIUM LEVEL
OF INCOME AND OUTPUT:
TWO-SECTOR ECONOMY

A basic proposition of Keynesian theory is that the equilibrium level of income and output depends on the economy's aggregate demand for output. If aggregate demand is not sufficient to call forth the level of output that requires the employment of all available workers for its production, unemployment results, and production of goods and services is below its potential. If aggregate demand is just sufficient, full employment results, and production is at full potential. If aggregate demand is excessive, inflation results as well as full employment and production at full potential. However, any level of output, ranging from that which calls for full employment of the labor force to that which imposes idleness on a large part of the labor force, is a possible equilibrium level. Given this wide range of possible equilibrium levels, the actual equilibrium level in any time period is determined by the aggregate demand for that period.

It must be emphasized that the concept of equilibrium carries with it no connotation of something "good" any more than the concept of disequilibrium carries with it the connotation of something "bad." For example, a system in disequilibrium but moving toward a higher equilibrium level of output and employment is preferable to a system that is firmly rooted at a lower equilibrium level of output.

In order to do one thing at a time, we will temporarily limit ourselves to the theory of the determination of the equilibrium level of income and output and will not ask whether the equilibrium level so determined is one of full employment, "a little" unemployment, or "severe" unemployment. We will also temporarily assume that changes in output and employment are proportionate to changes in income. Such a relationship between income and output is nothing more than the assumption of a constant price level.

Finally, we will limit this and the following six chapters to an economy in which there are only households and businesses. Government and the rest-of-the-world are assumed not to exist for the time being. Aggregate demand may thus be treated as the sum of consumption demand and private domestic investment demand. To explain what determines this aggregate demand in any time period, we must first develop the essentials of the theory of consumption demand. This is done in the section that follows. Then, by simply assuming investment demand to be constant at some fixed dollar amount, we can proceed without further delay to find the equilibrium level of income and output determined by the sum of consumption demand and investment demand so specified. In the following chapter, we trace the process by which changes in aggregate demand lead to changes in the equilibrium level of income and output. In Chapters 9 and 10 we expand the discussion of the theory of consumption demand of this chapter, and in Chapters 11 through 13 we develop the theory of investment demand to replace the temporary assumption of this chapter that investment demand is simply constant at some fixed dollar amount.

CONSUMPTION DEMAND AND THE CONSUMPTION FUNCTION

In any economy in which people have free choice, the total volume of personal consumption expenditures in any year is determined primarily by the amount of disposable income that people receive in that year. This proposition, simple in meaning and plausible in sound, is the cornerstone of the theory of consumption demand. In order to concentrate at first on this single most important determinant of consumption demand, the other less important determinants may be put aside for later consideration. What we are then assuming for the time being is that personal consumption expenditures are determined exclusively by the level of disposable personal income.

The Consumption Function

To consider how consumption expenditures are related to disposable income, we may begin by positing that consumption expenditures vary directly with disposable income. Second, we can be more specific and say something about how much such expenditures will vary as disposable income varies. Keynes did this in putting forth his "fundamental psychological law" that "men are disposed, as a rule and on the average, to increase their consumption as their income increases, but not by as much as the increase in their income." [1] In other words, as income increases consumers will spend part but not all the increase, for they will choose to save some part of it. Thus, the total increase in income will be accounted for by the sum of the increase in consumption expenditures and the increase in personal saving, if we simplify by assuming

[1] John Maynard Keynes, *General Theory of Employment, Interest, and Money*, Harcourt, Brace & World, 1936, p. 96.

that interest paid by consumers is zero. Finally, can we be still more specific on the nature of this relationship? Although Keynes placed great confidence in the correctness of his "fundamental psychological law," he advanced with less confidence the argument that a smaller *proportion* of income will be consumed (or a larger *proportion* of income will be saved) as income increases. If this is true, it means that not only will the absolute amount of saving increase with increases in income as indicated by the "fundamental psychological law," but that the ratio of saving to income will become greater with increases in income. Keynes felt that this was to be expected, *as a rule*, for, despite the fact that "the satisfaction of the immediate primary needs of a man and his family is usually a stronger motive than the motives toward accumulation," the latter "acquire effective sway when a margin of comfort has been established." [2]

It is this relationship between consumption and income advanced by Keynes that is employed in the simple theory of income determination to be developed in this and the following chapter.[3] We will, in other words, proceed on the assumption that the absolute level of consumption varies directly with the level of income and that the fraction of income consumed varies inversely with the level of income.

Theoretical and Empirical Consumption Functions. The relationship between consumption and income that emerges from these particular assumptions is referred to as a *theoretical consumption function*. As a tool of theory, a consumption function is somewhat analogous to an ordinary market-demand function for a single commodity, such as that in Figure 6–1. Just as a theoretical demand curve usually implies that the quantity of a commodity that will be purchased varies inversely with its price, all other things (including income) being unchanged, so the theoretical consumption function here employed holds that aggregate consumption varies directly but not proportionately with consumer *income*, all other things (including prices) being unchanged. The theoretical consumption function that we shall draw, like the theoretical demand function of Figure 6–1, is not derived from any actual statistical data. It is nothing more than an attempt to describe in general terms, on the basis of the assumptions stated above, a typical functional relationship between two variables, all other things being unchanged. Actually, for this purpose no explicit dollar amounts need be indicated; for example, they are not used in Figure 6–1.

A distinctly different type of consumption function, the historical or empirical consumption function, will be examined in Chapter 9. Here we may note that the simplest form of an empirical consumption function describes the statistics of income and consumption for each year over a period of years. Since these are recorded quantities, nothing can be assumed to have remained unchanged over the period of years involved. As a result, the actual level of

---

[2] *Ibid.*, p. 97.
[3] It may be noted here that the particular relationship between consumption and income advanced by Keynes is perhaps the first statement of what later came to be known as the absolute income theory or hypothesis. This theory, as well as the relative income and the permanent income theories, will be examined in Chapter 9.

consumption that accompanies the actual level of income for any year reflects every single factor that influenced consumption expenditures during that year, not just the year's disposable income. In fact, the nonincome factors may be such as to cause the actual level of consumption in any one year to rise above that of the preceding year, despite a fall in the actual level of disposable income. On the basis of income alone, a decrease in consumption would be expected between these two years, but what otherwise would have been a decrease was more than offset by these other factors that made for a net increase. We will note actual cases like this later, when we look into empirical consumption functions. However, for the present purpose of developing the simple theory of income determination, we need only the theoretical consumption function, which abstracts from all nonincome influences on consumption and posits a relationship between consumption and disposable income that satisfies certain assumptions.

The line labeled C in Figure 7–1, Part A, is one of many possible theoretical consumption functions that satisfy the specific assumptions stated above. The other line in Part A is a 45° guideline. Any point on this line is equidistant from the vertical and horizontal axes. For example, point K on the 45° line represents a value of income, or $Y = 160$, on the horizontal axis and an equal value on the vertical axis.

Since by definition any portion of disposable income that is not consumed must be saved, then, given the consumption function, the guideline, and the hypothetical amounts laid off on the axes, we can tell at a glance how people plan to allocate any given level of disposable income between spending and saving. For example, at $Y = 160$ (point M) total income is given by $MK = 160$. Since consumption is $ML = 140$, the balance of income, $MK - ML = 160 - 140$, must equal $LK = 20$. The specific consumption function in Figure 7–1 is drawn on the assumption that there is some level of income at which planned consumption is exactly equal to this income, which is referred to as the "break-even" level of income; this occurs at level 80, since the consumption function cuts the guideline at this level. At any higher level of income, people collectively feel well off enough to save some part of their aggregate income. Above the break-even level, therefore, the consumption function lies below the guideline, and the vertical distance between the two lines equals the amount of saving for that level of income. At any level of income below 80, people collectively spend more than their aggregate income. In this situation, the consumption function lies above the guideline and the vertical distance between the two lines equals the amount of dissaving, or the excess of consumption over income, at that level of income. At an income level of 40, the consumption function is 10 above the guideline; the excess of consumption over income is thus 10 at this income level.

Average Propensity to Consume.   The average consumption-income relationship is defined by the ratio C/Y for different levels of Y. For the function in Figure 7–1, at Y of 40, we have C of 50, so that $C/Y = 50/40$, or 1.25. At Y of 80, we have C of 80, so that $C/Y = 80/80$, or 1, the break-even ratio.

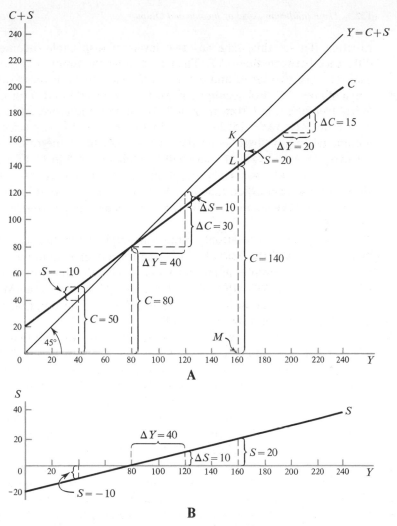

FIGURE 7–1   Consumption and Savings Functions

At Y of 160, we have C of 140, so that $C/Y = 140/160$, or 0.875. The C/Y ratio could be computed for any other level of Y in similar fashion. However, from what is given, it is apparent that the ratio of C to Y in this consumption function decreases steadily as income increases, and vice versa. In other words, C increases less than proportionately with increases in Y, and vice versa. The C/Y ratio, one of two basic ratios that may be derived from the consumption function, is known as the *average propensity to consume*, or the APC.

Marginal Propensity to Consume.   If we know the APC at all levels of disposable income, we know how each level of disposable income will be divided between consumption and saving. Suppose, however, we also want to know how any given *change* in the level of income will be divided between a *change* in consumption and a *change* in saving. The APC will not give us the answer directly, but the answer is given directly by the slope of the consumption function. To see this, take any two levels of disposable income and call the difference between them ΔY. Then determine the amount of consumption at each of these two levels and call the difference between these two amounts of consumption ΔC. For example, if we take Y of 200 and Y of 220, ΔY is 20. With Y of 200, C is 170; with Y of 220, C is 185; therefore, ΔC is 15. Expressed as a ratio, $\Delta C/\Delta Y = 15/20 = 3/4$. In Figure 7–1, for any selected change in income taken anywhere along the income axis, the same result will be found; for every change of 4 in Y there will be a change of 3 in C, or a constant ratio of $\Delta C/\Delta Y = 3/4$. Geometrically, it should be clear that this ratio equals the slope of the consumption function. $\Delta C/\Delta Y$, the second basic ratio derived from the consumption function, is known as the *marginal propensity to consume*, or the MPC.

Note, however, that only if the consumption function is a straight line as in Figure 7–1 will the MPC be the same for any change in income. Any other straight-line consumption function with a slope different from that in Figure 7–1 will indicate an MPC larger or smaller than 3/4, but again an MPC that is the same for any change in income. The slope of the consumption function is the geometric representation of the MPC.[4]

Up to this point, we have not considered any evidence that would indicate whether a consumption function of the type given in Figure 7–1 is a realistic description of the way that persons divide their income between consumption and saving at different levels of disposable income. We will turn to this question in Chapter 9, but at the moment all we have is the hypothesis that the consumption-income relationship exhibits certain properties that may be summarized as follows: The MPC is positive but less than one, this being Keynes's "fundamental psychological law." The MPC is the same for any change in income, this following from the assumption that the consumption function is a straight line. The APC is infinity at a zero level of income and declines steadily as income rises but is always greater than the MPC, this following from the previous assumptions plus the assumption that consumption remains positive no matter how low the level of income may fall.[5]

---

[4] If this is not apparent, keep the present straight-line consumption function anchored in its given position on the vertical axis and visually tilt it upward. The MPC will become greater than 3/4. Tilt is so that it becomes parallel with the guideline (which has a slope of 1) and the MPC becomes 1. Tilt it even more, and the MPC exceeds 1. Tilt the consumption function downward from its given position, and the MPC will become less than 3/4. Tilt it so that it becomes parallel with the horizontal axis, and the MPC becomes zero.

[5] Geometrically, the APC at any level of income is equal to the slope of a line from the origin to the point on the consumption function corresponding to that level of income. If such lines are drawn into Figure 7–1, it will be seen that the slopes of such lines start at infinity at zero income and fall steadily as income increases. Since the MPC equals the slope of the consumption function itself, any straight-line consumption function that cuts the vertical axis above the origin as in Figure 7–1 is a line whose constant slope is at all points less than the slope of a line from the origin to that point. In other words, for such a consumption function we have the property that $C/Y > \Delta C/\Delta Y$ at all levels of income. Note, however, that any straight-line consumption function that intersects the axes at the origin will be one for which $C/Y = \Delta C/\Delta Y$ at all levels of income. Finally, any straight-line consumption function that intersects the vertical axis below the origin will be one in which $C/Y < \Delta C/\Delta Y$ at all levels of income. For

The Consumption Function—Equations. Mathematically, the straight-line consumption function shown in Figure 7–1 may be described, in terms of its intercept with the vertical axis and its slope, with the aid of the simple equation of the straight line.[6] In the case of this consumption function, the intercept with the vertical axis indicates that C is 20 when Y is zero. For any level of income above zero, given the slope or the MPC as 3/4, C will be the 20 it would be at zero income *plus* 3/4 of the difference between zero income and any chosen level of income. This may be written in equation form as $C = 20 + \frac{3}{4}Y$. This theoretical consumption function may thus be thought of as the sum of two parts: an amount of consumption (20) that is independent of the level of income, since it is the amount found even at zero income, and an amount of consumption that depends on the level of income, since it rises and falls by a constant fraction (3/4) of any rise or fall in income.

This equation for the consumption function tells us everything that Figure 7–1 tells us. Just as we can find C for any level of Y by inspection in Figure 7–1, we can do the same by substituting any level of Y in the equation. Figure 7–1 shows that C is 80 when Y is 80, and the equation shows the same: $C = 20 + \frac{3}{4}(80) = 80$. Similarly, when Y is 160, the figure shows that C equals 140, and the equation shows the same: $C = 20 + \frac{3}{4}(160) = 140$. To find the APC or C/Y at any level of Y, we simply divide the original equation through by Y, or $C/Y = 20/Y + \frac{3}{4}Y/Y$, which equals $20/Y + 3/4$. When Y equals 80, $C/Y = 20/80 + 3/4 = 1$. When Y equals 160, $C/Y = 20/160 + 3/4 = 0.875$.

Since we will not restrict ourselves later to the consumption function with the intercept and slope of the function shown in Figure 7–1, a general equation for the linear consumption function may be given here: $C = C_a + cY$, in which the constant C_a is the amount of consumption when Y equals zero and the constant c is the slope of the function or the MPC. If we divide this equation through by Y, we derive the general equation for the APC: $C/Y = C_a/Y + c$. The hypothesis as to the way people divide their income between consumption and saving was summarized above as a set of properties. To satisfy these properties, it is required that the constant C_a be positive and that the constant c be positive but less than one. This may be verified by noting that if C_a is negative, the proportion of income consumed increases as income increases; if c is greater than one, the increase in consumption accompanying an increase in income exceeds the increase in income; and if c is negative, there is a decrease in consumption with an increase in income. All these possibilities conflict with the hypothesis.

---

nonlinear consumption functions, the relationships between C/Y and $\Delta C/\Delta Y$ are more complex.

[6] The standard linear equation is $y = a + bx$, where b is the slope of its graph and a is its y intercept (the value of y at the point where $x = 0$—that is, the point at which the graph cuts the y axis).

The Saving Function

Part B of Figure 7–1 shows the saving function that is the counterpart of the consumption function shown in Part A. In Part A the amount of saving at any level of income is the difference between the consumption function and the guideline. The saving function shown in Part B can therefore be directly derived from Part A.

When income is 80, we see in Part A that consumption is 80 and saving is 0; this is depicted in Part B by the intersection of the saving function with the horizontal axis at income of 80. When income is 40, consumption is 50, and saving is -10; the saving function lies 10 below the horizontal axis at income of 40. When income is 160, consumption is 140, and saving is 20; the saving function lies 20 above the horizontal axis at income of 160.

Average Propensity to Save.   The saving counterpart to the APC is the *average propensity to save*, or the APS. While the APC is the ratio of C to Y, the APS is the ratio of S to Y. Since Y itself is devoted to either C or S, it follows that the two ratios, C/Y and S/Y, must add up to one. Thus when Y is 40, C/Y is 50/40, or 1.25, and S/Y is $-10/40$, or -0.25. Similarly, when Y is 160, C/Y is 140/160, or 0.875, and S/Y is 20/160, or 0.125.

Marginal Propensity to Save.   There is also a saving counterpart to the MPC. If, instead of looking at the ratio of S to Y at any level of Y, we look at the ratio of the change in S to the change in Y for any change in Y, we have what is termed the *marginal propensity to save*, or the MPS. Given a change in Y, ΔY, then $\Delta S/\Delta Y$ is the ratio of the change in S to the change in Y, just as $\Delta C/\Delta Y$ is the ratio of the change in C to the change in Y. Since ΔY must be devoted to either ΔC or ΔS, the two ratios $\Delta C/\Delta Y$ and $\Delta S/\Delta Y$ must add up to one.

If the MPC is positive but less than one and is the same for any change in income, then it follows by subtraction, since MPS $= 1 -$ MPC, that the MPS must also be positive but less than one and that it must also be the same for any change in income. Furthermore, if the APC decreases steadily as income rises, then the APS must increase steadily as income rises, because these two ratios also add up to one at all levels of income. Finally, if the APC is always greater than the MPC, it follows that the APS is always less than the MPS.[7]

The Saving Function—Equations.   As was the case for a straight-line consumption function, so a straight-line saving function can be described, in terms of its vertical intercept and its slope, with the aid of the equation of the straight

---

[7] Earlier, in describing the relationship between APC and MPC, we saw that for a consumption function of the type given in Figure 7–1 APC $>$ MPC at all levels of income. Since APC $+$ APS $= 1$ and MPC $+$ MPS $= 1$, if APC $>$ MPC at all levels of income, it follows that MPS $>$ APS at all levels of income. For example, at $Y = 80$, APC $= 1$ and MPC $= 3/4$, while APS $= 0$ and MPS $= 1/4$. At Y of 160, APC $= 7/8$ and MPC $= 3/4$, while APS $= 1/8$ and MPS $= 1/4$.

line. The derivation of the equation for the saving function is analogous to that for the consumption function. When income is zero, saving is -20. For any level of income above zero, saving is -20 plus $1/4$ of the difference between zero income and any chosen level of income. Therefore, $S = -20 + \frac{1}{4}Y$. To derive the equation for the APS, or S/Y, we simply divide through by Y, which gives us $S/Y = -20/Y + \frac{1}{4}Y/Y$, or $S/Y = -20/Y + 1/4$.

The general equation for the linear consumption function was given as $C = C_a + cY$, so the general equation for the linear saving function may be given as $S = S_a + sY$, in which S_a equals the amount of saving at the theoretical zero level of income and s equals the marginal propensity to save.[8] If we divide this equation through by Y, we derive the general equation for the APS: $S/Y = S_a/Y + s$. The hypothesis as to the way that people divide their incomes between consumption and saving was summarized above with a set of properties. To satisfy these properties, it is required in the equation for the saving function, $S = S_a + sY$, that the value of S_a be negative and the value of s be positive but less than one. This may be verified by noting that if S_a is positive, the proportion of income saved decreases as income increases; if s is greater than one, the increase in saving accompanying any increase in income exceeds the increase in income; and if s is negative, there is a decrease in saving with an increase in income. All these possibilities conflict with the hypothesis.

DETERMINATION OF THE EQUILIBRIUM LEVEL OF INCOME AND OUTPUT

In a two-sector economy, final product is measured as the sum of consumption and investment expenditures. If investment expenditures are measured net of depreciation, the final product so measured is net national product. Since there is no government in this economy, national income equals net national product.[9] If we further assume that all firms are noncorporate, there are no undistributed profits, and personal income equals national income.[10] Again, since there is no government, there can be no taxes, and all personal income becomes disposable personal income. In this economy, disposable personal income equals net national product; every dollar spent during the time period for either consump-

---

[8] S_a equals $-C_a$, and s equals $1 - c$. This can be shown as follows: since $Y = C + S$, $S = Y - C$. Substituting $C_a + cY$ for C, we have $S = Y - (C_a + cY)$. From this, $S = Y - C_a - cY$, or $S = -C_a + Y - cY$, or $S = -C_a + Y(1 - c)$. Hence, since we have written $S = S_a + sY$, it follows that $S_a = -C_a$, and $s = 1 - c$ as was to be demonstrated.

[9] Strictly, this also requires that business transfer payments are zero, an assumption we make here.

[10] In a two-sector economy in which all firms are noncorporate, personal income would exceed national income by the amount of interest paid by consumers. The easiest way to avoid the complications this factor would otherwise bring into the analysis is to assume that interest paid by consumers is zero.

tion or net investment produces a dollar of disposable personal income. Disposable personal income must be devoted either to personal consumption expenditures or to personal saving.[11] Since disposable personal income equals net national product, personal saving (the amount of unconsumed disposable personal income) must then equal investment (the amount of unconsumed net national product).

If we measure the results for any time period in this economy, we have the following identities:

$$\text{Net National Product} \equiv C + I$$

$$\text{Disposable Personal Income} \equiv C + S$$

and

$$S \equiv I$$

Since net national product and disposable personal income are identical in this economy in any time period, we may refer to them interchangeably, disposable personal income being identical with the value of output and the value of output being identical with disposable personal income. If we designate both by Y, we may write:

$$Y \equiv C + I$$

$$Y \equiv C + S$$

and, as before,

$$S \equiv I$$

These are the fundamental accounting identities with which we will work in the two-sector economy. Note that these are the same identities developed in Chapter 2 and derived from Table 2–3. As identities, they are composed of the *realized* values for the variables for any time period. Thus, by our accounting definitions, realized saving is identical with realized investment. However, as we will see, realized investment may be greater or less than the amount of investment *planned* by businessmen, if the amount of investment planned by businessmen differs from the amount of saving planned by income recipients. In what follows we will use the terms *realized* and *planned* to make this distinc-

---

[11] Disposable personal income in a two-sector economy would be divided into personal saving and personal outlays and the latter into personal consumption expenditures and interest paid by consumers. Therefore, it could not be said that disposable personal income is devoted only to personal consumption expenditures and personal saving, unless interest paid by consumers happened to be zero. We have already decided to assume that it is zero. Note, however, for the relation between personal income, disposable personal income, and personal consumption expenditures, the result would be the same if we recognized interest paid by consumers to be the positive amount that it is. Since interest paid by consumers appears on both the outlay and income sides of the household account, we may for present purposes subtract it from both sides. This reduces personal income and disposable personal income by the amount of this interest and makes personal outlays identical with personal consumption expenditures. This in turn gives us the simpler identity, in which disposable personal income equals personal consumption expenditures and personal saving, that we may also get simply by assuming interest paid by persons to be zero.

tion. Later in the chapter we will turn to a more detailed examination of planned and realized investment.

Equilibrium Income and Output

What determines the economy's consumption and investment expenditures? According to the assumption we have worked with so far, disposable income is the sole determinant of consumption expenditures. What investment expenditures will be depends on factors yet to be considered. However, in order to get started, suppose that these factors are such that businessmen plan to spend a total of 20 (billion dollars) per time period for additions to plant and equipment and change in inventories. No matter how they may have arrived at these plans, all that is essential here is to assume for the time being that these plans are independent of the level of income. In other words, at all levels of income, planned investment expenditures are fixed at 20, or the investment function is simply $I = 20$.[12]

To determine aggregate demand, we must add together the consumption and investment functions. This is illustrated in Figure 7–2. Here the consumption function is the same as that shown in Figure 7–1, which indicates the amount of planned consumption at each level of income. In Figure 7–2 the investment function, which we have assumed is constant at 20 for all levels of income, is added to the consumption function. The resulting aggregate-demand function, $C + I$, is to be read as follows: If Y were 120, aggregate demand would be 130 (110 + 20), or, if Y were 160, aggregate demand would be 160 (140 + 20).

Given this aggregate-demand function, we can define the equilibrium level of income as that one particular level at which aggregate demand just equals aggregate output. In Figure 7–2, the equilibrium level is the income or output level of 160 and no other. Suppose that businessmen believe that during a given time period they can sell 160 in goods. They will then produce this amount of goods during the period, and disposable income will be 160.[13] With disposable income of 160, the consumption function in Figure 7–2 indicates that consumers will spend 140. Adding to this the 20 that businessmen will spend, we have aggregate demand of 160 when output is 160. *Businessmen produced aggregate output of 160 in the expectation that sales of output would total 160, and sales turned out to be exactly 160, so the plans of both sellers and buyers were realized.* Consumers with income of 160 purchase the 140 of consumer goods they plan to buy when income is 160; businessmen purchase the 20 of investment goods

[12] Although we are assuming for the time being that investment expenditures are not functionally related to any other variable, it is still convenient here to use the term "investment function" to parallel the term "consumption function." We will later examine the variety of factors that affect investment expenditures and will employ an "investment function" that makes investment explicitly dependent on such factors.

[13] Not all goods, of course, are produced for sale to consumers and to other firms. Parts of some firms' production may be intended as additions to their own inventories. Such output is viewed as if it were sales of goods by firms to themselves. Thus, some part of estimated sales of 160 is made up of planned "sales" by firms to themselves.

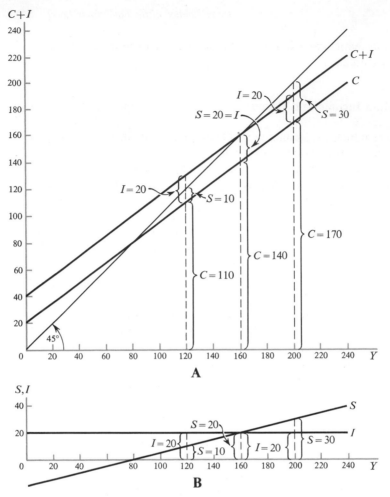

FIGURE 7–2 The Equilibrium Level of Income

they plan to buy. Both sectors purchase the amounts intended, and their purchases match exactly what businessmen intended to sell. In short, aggregate demand equals aggregate output—which is one way of stating the condition for equilibrium in the level of output.

In Part A of Figure 7–2, the aggregate-demand function, $C + I$, intersects the guideline at the equilibrium level of output. Aggregate output of 160, measured on the horizontal axis, is matched by an equal aggregate demand of 160 (140 + 20) on the vertical axis. Since any point on the guideline is equidistant from both axes, and since the condition for equilibrium in the level of output is that aggregate demand be equal to aggregate output, it follows that the equilibrium level of output must be that level of output at which the aggregate demand function intersects the guideline.

Equilibrium may also be defined as that level of output at which planned saving and planned investment are equal. Thus, in Parts A and B of Figure 7–2, at an income level of 160, planned saving is 20 since planned consumption is

140. Since planned investment is also 20, spending by businessmen for investment goods exactly offsets that portion of income that persons choose not to spend for consumer goods. When planned investment equals planned saving, aggregate demand or total spending for the period's aggregate output thus necessarily equals that aggregate output. In Part B planned saving and planned investment can be equal only at the intersection of the two curves. This intersection, which occurs at 160, accordingly represents the equilibrium level of income and output. Because we have assumed that planned investment is 20 at all levels of income, the investment curve appears as a horizontal line parallel with the income or output axis and 20 above it. The construction of the saving curve was explained earlier.

Equilibrium Income and Output—Equations

Taking as our condition for equilibrium the equality between aggregate demand and aggregate output, we may also determine this equilibrium income and output by solving the equation $Y = C + I$, in which C and I refer to *planned* consumption and *planned* investment. Solution of this equation gives that level of output at which planned spending by persons on consumption out of the income earned in producing that output will, when added to the planned spending on investment, be just sufficient to purchase the amount of output actually produced. The amount persons plan to spend on consumption at any possible level of income is given for our economy by the equation $C = 20 + \frac{3}{4}Y$. The amount businessmen plan to spend for investment is assumed to be fixed at 20 and is given by the equation: $I = 20$. This gives us the following three equations:

$$Y = C + I \qquad\qquad [1]$$
$$C = 20 + \frac{3}{4}Y \qquad\qquad [2]$$
$$I = 20 \qquad\qquad [3]$$

Substituting [2] and [3] in [1] and solving, we have

$$Y = 20 + \frac{3}{4}Y + 20$$

or

$$Y = 160$$

Alternatively, we may find the equilibrium level of output as that at which planned saving equals planned investment, or $S = I$. At this particular level of output, the amount *not* spent on *consumption* out of the income earned in producing that output will be exactly offset by an amount spent by businessmen for *investment*. The amount persons plan to save at any possible level of income is given by the equation: $S = -20 + \frac{1}{4}Y$. The amount businessmen plan to spend for investment is again assumed to be fixed at 20—that is, $I = 20$. Thus, we have the following three equations:

$$S = I \qquad [1]$$
$$S = -20 + \tfrac{1}{4}Y \qquad [2]$$
$$I = 20 \qquad [3]$$

Substituting [2] and [3] in [1] and solving for Y, we have

$$-20 + \tfrac{1}{4}Y = 20$$
$$Y = 160$$

This confirms that only when Y equals 160 will aggregate demand equal aggregate output and planned saving equal planned investment. With C, I, and S all referring to planned amounts, we may summarize as follows:

Output $\qquad Y = C + I$

$\qquad\qquad\qquad 160 = 20 + \tfrac{3}{4}(160) + 20$

Income $\qquad Y = C + S$

$\qquad\qquad\qquad 160 = 20 + \tfrac{3}{4}(160) + [-20 + \tfrac{1}{4}(160)]$

$\qquad\qquad\qquad S = I$

$\qquad -20 + \tfrac{1}{4}(160) = 20$

With the consumption function and investment function as given, we may further illustrate why 160 and only 160 is the equilibrium level of income and output by taking at random any other level of income and output and showing why it is necessarily a disequilibrium level.

Disequilibrium Income and Output

The actual level of output in any period is the result of the decisions of thousands of businessmen, and there is no reason to expect their collective decisions to be such as to result precisely in the equilibrium output. In our example, suppose these decisions are such as to result in output of 200. With an output of 200, disposable income will also be 200. The consumption function indicates that persons will now spend 170 on consumption. Adding planned investment of 20 to planned consumption of 170, we have an aggregate demand of 190 when output and income are 200. Aggregate demand is clearly insufficient to buy the amount of goods businessmen expected to sell. What is required for equilibrium with output of 200 is aggregate demand of 200; what is found is aggregate demand of 190, or a deficiency of 10.

This deficiency of aggregate demand is illustrated in Part A of Figure 7–2 by the difference in height between the aggregate demand function and the guideline. Instead of intersecting the guideline at 200, the aggregate demand function lies below the guideline at 200; the vertical distance between the two lines is the measure of the deficiency of aggregate demand. At this level of output, there is also necessarily disequilibrium between planned saving and planned investment; planned saving is 30 and planned investment is still the unvarying 20. Of the 200 of income earned in the course of producing 200 of output, the 30 that income receivers choose *not* to spend on consumer goods is greater than the 20 that businessmen choose to spend on investment goods. In Part B of Figure 7–2 the actual distance of the saving function above the investment function is the measure of the deficiency of aggregate demand at this level of output.

The equations also indicate that income and output of 200 is a disequilibrium level. Here we do not solve to find what level of Y is the equilibrium level but instead assume a given level of Y and find whether it is the equilibrium level. In the following set of equations, we know that the equilibrium level of Y must be that level of Y which satisfies Equation [2]. Equations [3] and [4] show that the equilibrium level could not be 200.

$$Y = C + I \qquad\qquad [1]$$

$$Y = 20 + \tfrac{3}{4}Y + 20 \qquad\qquad [2]$$

$$200 \neq 20 + \tfrac{3}{4}(200) + 20 \qquad\qquad [3]$$

$$200 \neq 170 + 20 \qquad\qquad [4]$$

In terms of saving and investment, the equilibrium level of Y is that level of Y that satisfies Equation [2] in the following set of equations. Could the equilibrium level be 200? Equations [3] and [4] show that it could not.

$$S = I \qquad\qquad [1]$$

$$-20 + \tfrac{1}{4}Y = 20 \qquad\qquad [2]$$

$$-20 + \tfrac{1}{4}(200) \neq 20 \qquad\qquad [3]$$

$$30 \neq 20 \qquad\qquad [4]$$

On our assumption that prices remain unchanged (there is no price-cutting by businessmen to move the surplus of goods), the deficiency of aggregate demand can mean only one thing: Business as a whole finds its inventories of goods 10 greater than it had planned.[14] If output is maintained at the 200 level period after period and the aggregate demand function remains as given, businessmen will experience an unplanned or involuntary addition of 10 to inventories in each period. Sooner or later, in order to get inventories down to a lower, desired level, businessmen will lay off workers and cut back output. This in turn will cause income to fall as fast as output. Once output and income are reduced to 160, equilibrium will be restored; aggregate demand will equal aggregate output, and planned saving will equal planned investment.

To consider another disequilibrium situation, suppose that businessmen

---

[14] Planned investment of 20 may include a planned increase in inventories. Perhaps plans call for 15 of net investment in plant and equipment and 5 in additional inventories. The result above would thus become an addition of 15 to plant and equipment and 15 to inventories, the planned addition of 5 plus the unplanned addition of 10.

err in the opposite direction and estimate that they can sell only 120 in output. If output is 120, income will be 120; if income is 120, planned consumption will be 110. Assuming an unvarying 20 of planned investment, aggregate demand will be 110 + 20, or 130, 10 in excess of aggregate output of 120. In Figure 7–2, with output at 120, the aggregate demand function at 130 is 10 above the guideline, and its vertical distance above the guideline is a measure of the excess in aggregate demand, just as its vertical distance below the guideline at output of 200 was a measure of the deficiency in aggregate demand. Planned saving is 10, and planned investment is 20. The 10 of income that income receivers choose *not* to spend for consumer goods is less than the 20 businessmen choose to spend for investment goods. The excess of planned investment over planned saving means that aggregate demand must be greater than aggregate output by the amount of this excess. In Part B the actual distance of the investment function above the saving function is the measure of the excess of aggregate demand at this level of output.

The equations also indicate that the income and output level of 120 is a disequilibrium level. The solution to Equation [2] would give us the equilibrium level, and Equations [3] and [4] show that this level could not be 120.

$$Y = C + I \tag{1}$$

$$Y = 20 + \tfrac{3}{4}Y + 20 \tag{2}$$

$$120 \neq 20 + \tfrac{3}{4}(120) + 20 \tag{3}$$

$$120 \neq 110 + 20 \tag{4}$$

Similarly, in terms of saving and investment, the solution to Equation [2] below would give us the equilibrium level. Again Equations [3] and [4] show that this equilibrium level could not be 120.

$$S = I \tag{1}$$

$$-20 + \tfrac{1}{4}Y = 20 \tag{2}$$

$$-20 + \tfrac{1}{4}(120) \neq 20 \tag{3}$$

$$10 \neq 20 \tag{4}$$

In each period during which output remains at 120 and demand at 130, there must be an unplanned decrease in inventories held by businessmen in the amount of 10.[15] Sooner or later, in order to stop this unplanned drain on inventories, businessmen will hire more workers and expand output. If they raise output to the 160 level, equilibrium will be restored.

---

[15] If plans had called for net investment of 10 in plant and equipment and 10 in inventories, per time period the addition to inventories would be 0. If plans had called for net investment of 20 in plant and equipment and no addition to inventories, per time period the results would be net investment of 20 in plant and equipment and −10 (a decrease) in inventories. In both cases, realized investment, or unconsumed output, (120 − 110) would be 10.

Investment—Planned Versus Realized

We have examined three levels of income and output for our simple economy, of which one (160) was the equilibrium level and the other two (120 and 200) disequilibrium levels. Since income and output are flows, these three levels must all be amounts corresponding to specific time periods. The national income accountant who seeks to measure income and output for these three time periods (the order of which here has no relevance) would summarize the data for the periods as follows:

	Realized	*Realized*	*Realized*
	$C + S \equiv Y \equiv C + I$		$S \equiv I$
Period A	$140 + 20 = 160 = 140 + 20$		$20 = 20$
Period B	$170 + 30 = 200 = 170 + 30$		$30 = 30$
Period C	$110 + 10 = 120 = 110 + 10$		$10 = 10$

Notice that the figures in the accountant's identities tell us nothing about the *planned* investment of businessmen and nothing about the equilibrium or disequilibrium of the economy at each of these income and output levels. The accountant's identities show only what income and output actually were, how the actual income was divided into realized consumption and realized saving, how the actual output was divided into realized consumption and realized investment, and, from these, the identity between realized saving and realized investment. Whether realized investment is equal to, less than, or greater than planned investment cannot be found from the accountant's identities.

Unlike the accountant, the economist seeks to determine at what level of output the economy will be in equilibrium. We assume that the economist knows the aggregate-demand function $(C + I)$ for the economy and therefore knows what planned consumption expenditures and planned investment expenditures will be at each level of income and output. In contrast to the accountant's identities, our economist uses a set of equations that show planned consumption and planned investment for the actual income and output levels in each of these time periods. Realized saving and realized investment for each period are repeated from above for easy reference.

	Planned	*Planned*	*Planned*	*Realized*
	$C + S = Y = C + I$		$S = I$	$S \equiv I$
Period A	$140 + 20 = 160 = 140 + 20$		$20 = 20$	$20 = 20$
Period B	$170 + 30 = 200 > 170 + 20$		$30 > 20$	$30 = 30$
Period C	$110 + 10 = 120 < 110 + 20$		$10 < 20$	$10 = 10$

Comparing the economist's equations with the accountant's identities, we find, as before, that only when income and output are 160 does planned investment of 20 correspond with realized investment. When income and output are

200, businessmen discover that, contrary to their plans for investment of 20, realized investment is 30: consumed output is 170, and unconsumed output of 30 equals realized investment. Similarly, when income and output are 120, businessmen discover, again contrary to their plans for investment of 20, that realized investment is 10: consumed output is 110, and unconsumed output of 10 equals realized investment. Since realized investment may be described as the sum of planned and unplanned investment, and since planned investment is the constant 20, the economist may also express this in equation form as follows:

	Planned Investment		Unplanned Investment		Realized Investment		Realized Saving
Period A	20	+	0	=	20	=	20
Period B	20	+	10	=	30	=	30
Period C	20	+	−10	=	10	=	10

In graphic form, the amounts of unplanned investment may be identified in both parts of Figure 7–2 as the difference between realized investment and planned investment at each of the three levels of income and output.[16] When unplanned investment is 10, the excess of realized investment over planned investment amounts to an unplanned increase in inventories of 10; some of the goods produced simply are not sold and remain in inventory, even though the producers do not want them to. When unplanned investment is −10, on the other hand, the excess of planned investment over realized investment amounts to an unplanned decrease in inventories of 10.

In short, if there is any unplanned investment, planned investment will not equal realized investment, and the economy will therefore be at a disequilibrium level of output. However, the identity between realized saving and realized investment is just as consistent with positive or negative unplanned investment as it is with zero unplanned investment.[17] The accounting identities, therefore, can tell us nothing about whether there is equilibrium or disequilibrium in a particular time period and, therefore, nothing about whether the level of income and output will rise or fall in succeeding time periods. To determine this we need equations that show the relation between planned saving and planned investment.

Hence we must work with definitions of saving and investment that at first appear to be contradictory. In the one definition, saving and investment (realized)

[16] Realized investment at any level of output is the difference between the *C* curve and the guideline in Part A and the difference between the horizontal axis and the *S* curve in Part B. Planned investment is the difference between the *C* curve and the *C* + *I* curve in Part A and the difference between the horizontal axis and the *I* curve in Part B.

[17] A discrepancy can appear only between planned investment and realized investment and not between planned saving and realized saving during a particular time period, because it has been implicitly assumed that income receivers succeed in saving the amount of income they plan to save at each level of income. One can drop this assumption and consider disequilibrium situations in which businessmen always succeed in investing the amount they plan to invest while income receivers fail to save the amount they plan to save at any given level of income. Disequilibrium will then appear as a result of planned saving being greater than or less than realized saving.

are necessarily equal in any time period; in the other definition they are not necessarily equal and in fact are typically unequal in any time period (planned). In the development of the national income accounts in Chapters 2–5, we used only the first definition of saving and investment and did not have to distinguish between planned and realized. From now on, however, they must be so distinguished. We must avoid saying in one breath that saving and investment can only be equal and that saving and investment can be unequal. We can, however, flatly and unambiguously say that realized saving and realized investment can only be equal and that planned saving and planned investment can be equal. Throughout the remainder of this book, all references to consumption, saving, and investment not specifically designated as realized quantities should be understood to be planned quantities.

CHAPTER 8

CHANGES IN THE EQUILIBRIUM LEVEL OF INCOME AND OUTPUT: THE MULTIPLIER

In the last chapter we saw that output may fluctuate above and below the equilibrium level as businessmen err in overproducing or underproducing, but the tendency is for output to move toward if not actually to attain that single equilibrium level determined by the given aggregate-demand function.

SHIFTS IN THE AGGREGATE DEMAND FUNCTION

From one time period to the next, it is not only possible but probable that the aggregate demand function itself will shift. In our two-sector economy, this function is the sum of the consumption function and the investment function. While it is possible for either or both of these functions to shift from one time period to the next, most observers agree that the consumption function is relatively stable and the investment function relatively unstable. The relative stability of the consumption function does not necessarily mean that the actual amount of consumption expenditures is relatively stable, since this amount will change with every change in the level of income. It means, however, that the amount of consumption expenditures *at any given level of income* is relatively stable and that an initial change in the level of income itself is typically the result of a shift in the investment function.[1] In terms of Figure 7–2, this means simply

---

[1] Given a stable consumption function of $C = 20 + \frac{3}{4}Y$, C can change only as a result of a change in Y. If Y were 100, C would be 95; if Y were 120, C would be 110. *Consumption expenditures* are not stable, for they change with the level of income; but the *consumption function* is, under these circumstances, perfectly stable. An unstable consumption function would show change in C with no change in Y, which could result only from a change in the value

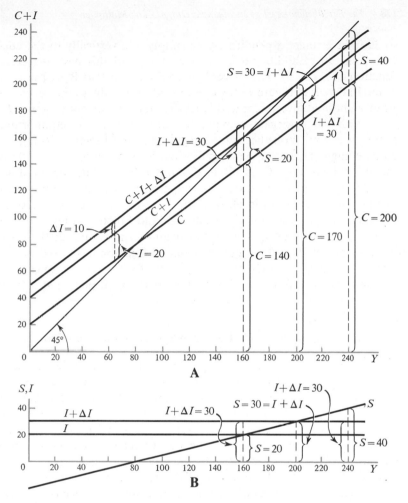

FIGURE 8–1 The Effect of a Change in Investment on the Equilibrium Level of Income

that the entire C curve does not bounce up and down over the short run. The $C + I$ curve does fluctuate over the short run, but this is due primarily to instability in the investment component rather than in the consumption component. For this reason, the analysis in this chapter will concentrate on changes in the equilibrium level of income that result from shifts in the investment function. It should be noted, however, that a parallel analysis applies to shifts in the consumption function.

To begin, assume that, due to an improvement in business expectations, investment expenditures rise permanently from 20 to 30 per time period, as before an amount that is the same at all levels of income. Figure 8-1 illustrates this shift in the investment function. The curves labeled C and $C + I$ are the same as those found in Part A of Figure 7–2. To indicate the increase from 20

---

of the constant 20 or of the constant 3/4. Thus, if Y is 120 and stays at 120, C can still change from one period to the next if the constant 20 rises to, say, 25.

to 30 in investment expenditures, we simply add vertically to the curve labeled $C + I$ the 10 of additional investment and label this new aggregate demand function $C + I + \Delta I$. The curves labeled S and I in Part B are the same as those found in Part B of Figure 7–2; we simply add vertically to the curve labeled I the 10 of additional investment and label this new investment function $I + \Delta I$.

With the aggregate demand function, $C + I$, the equilibrium level of output was 160. With the new aggregate demand function 10 higher than the old, we might expect the new equilibrium level of output to be 10 higher than the old, or an increase from 160 to 170. But 170 is not the new equilibrium level, for at 170 aggregate demand exceeds aggregate output and investment exceeds saving. The equilibrium level, therefore, must be greater than 170. Figure 8–1 reveals that, with the new aggregate demand function, only at output of 200 does aggregate output equal aggregate demand and saving equal investment. The upward shift of 10 in the aggregate demand function has raised the equilibrium level of output not merely by 10 but by 40, four times the upward shift in the aggregate demand function. This finding, perhaps surprising at first glance, will be explained fully in the following pages.

A Temporary Shift in the Aggregate-Demand Function

The new equilibrium level in Figure 8–1 was established as the aggregate demand function shifted from $C + I$ to the higher level of $C + I + \Delta I$. We have assumed that this is a permanent shift. However, to understand better the implications of a *permanent* shift, let us first examine the implications of a *temporary* shift in the function. Unlike the results shown in Figure 8–1, if the rise in investment is a temporary one, the rise in income and output will also be temporary. When investment subsequently drops back to its original level, income and output will also eventually drop back to their original level.

Changes in the level of income and output take place over time. To trace the process set into motion by a temporary increase in investment spending, we may split up the time interval required for the system to reestablish equilibrium into a series of shorter, numbered time periods. Let us assume that in Period 1 we have the original equilibrium position described in the previous chapter and shown in Figure 8–1; aggregate output is 160 and aggregate demand, the sum of consumption demand of 140 and investment demand of 20, is also 160. Then in Period 2 we upset this equilibrium by introducing an increase in investment demand of 10, or a rise in investment demand from 20 to 30. We assume that businessmen do not attempt to anticipate changes in the demand for their output but instead follow a simple rule of thumb of producing in each period an output equal to their sales in the preceding period. Given this behavior by businessmen, output in Period 2 will be equal to sales of Period 1; that is, output will be 160. Aggregate demand in Period 2, however, is found to be 170, for in this period we have the increase of 10 in investment demand. Inventories serve as a buffer —the *excess* of aggregate demand of 10 is absorbed in Period 2 by an unplanned decrease of inventories.

In Period 3 businessmen expand aggregate output to 170, the figure for total sales in Period 2. Output of 170 in Period 3 generates disposable income of 170 during this period. Given the consumption function, $C = 20 + \frac{3}{4}Y$, consumption demand in Period 3 will be 147.5 or 7.5 greater than in Period 2. If now in Period 3 investment demand drops back to its original level of 20 following its temporary rise to 30 in Period 2, we find in Period 3 consumption demand of 147.5 and investment demand of 20, or aggregate demand of 167.5. Since output in Period 3 is 170, there is in this period a *deficiency* of aggregate demand of 2.5, which is reflected in an unplanned increase in inventories. In Period 4 businessmen reduce aggregate output to 167.5, the total for sales in Period 3. This means a corresponding decline in income to 167.5, and the consumption function indicates that consumption in turn will be 145.6 in Period 4. Demand in Period 4 is accordingly this 145.6 plus 20 for investment or an aggregate of 165.6. Since output in Period 4 is 167.5, there is again a deficiency of demand, now equal to 1.9, which again is reflected in an unplanned increase in inventories. In Period 5 there is a further reduction in output and again a deficiency of demand but one smaller than that of Period 4. In this way, the level of output declines period by period until Period n, assumed to be the last period in what is actually an infinite number of periods. In Period n output is 160, income is correspondingly 160, consumption demand is 140, and investment demand is 20—or aggregate demand of 160 is equal to aggregate output of 160. The system has returned to the same equilibrium position from which we started in Period 1.

Table 8–1 gives the period-by-period detail of the process just described. In this table, C and I indicate the values for consumption and investment demand in the original equilibrium of Period 1. The change in consumption demand between Period 1 and any following period is shown by ΔC, and the change in investment demand between Period 1 and any following period is shown by ΔI. Total consumption demand in any period is then given by $C + \Delta C$, total investment demand by $I + \Delta I$, and aggregate demand by the sum of both. In the same way, Y indicates aggregate output in Period 1, ΔY the change in output between Period 1 and any other period, and $Y + \Delta Y$ the aggregate output for any period. The last two columns in the table show for each period *realized* investment, which equals saving, and *planned* investment. Planned investment for each period is the same as $I + \Delta I$. Realized investment or saving (or unconsumed output) in any period is the difference between that period's output and that period's consumption, or is equal to $(Y + \Delta Y) - (C + \Delta C)$.

In any time period, aggregate demand may be equal to, greater than, or less than aggregate output. To say the same thing in different words, in any time period planned investment may be equal to, greater than, or less than realized investment. The level of output is an equilibrium level in Period 1, for in this period we find aggregate demand of 160 just equal to aggregate output of 160 and planned investment of 20 just equal to realized investment of 20. The equilibrium of Period 1 is upset in Period 2 by the rise in planned investment, which is a rise in aggregate demand; and equilibrium is not restored until Period n, for in all intervening periods we find aggregate demand either greater than or less

TABLE 8-1 A Temporary (One-Period) Increase in Investment Demand

Period	$C + I + \Delta C + \Delta I =$	Aggregate Demand	$\geq \atop =\\ \leq$	Aggregate Output $=$	$Y + \Delta Y$	Investment Realized	Investment Planned
1	$140 + 20 + 0.0 + 0 =$	160.0	$=$	160.0 $=$	$160 + 0.0$	20.0	20
2	$140 + 20 + 0.0 + 10 =$	170.0	$>$	160.0 $=$	$160 + 0.0$	20.0	30
3	$140 + 20 + 7.5 + 0 =$	167.5	$<$	170.0 $=$	$160 + 10.0$	22.5	20
4	$140 + 20 + 5.6 + 0 =$	165.6	$<$	167.5 $=$	$160 + 7.5$	21.9	20
5	$140 + 20 + 4.2 + 0 =$	164.2	$<$	165.6 $=$	$160 + 5.6$	21.4	20
6	$140 + 20 + 3.2 + 0 =$	163.2	$<$	164.2 $=$	$160 + 4.2$	21.0	20
7	$140 + 20 + 2.4 + 0 =$	162.4	$<$	163.2 $=$	$160 + 3.2$	20.8	20
8	$140 + 20 + 1.8 + 0 =$	161.8	$<$	162.4 $=$	$160 + 2.4$	20.6	20
...	...	...		...	...	...	...
n	$140 + 20 + 0.0 + 0 =$	160.0	$=$	160.0 $=$	$160 + 0.0$	20.0	20
$n+1$	$140 + 20 + 0.0 + 0 =$	160.0	$=$	160.0 $=$	$160 + 0.0$	20.0	20
	$\quad\quad\quad 30.0\quad 10$				$\quad 40.0$		

than aggregate output or, what is the same thing, planned investment either greater than or less than realized investment.

We find disequilibrium through all these periods, despite the fact that the cause of disequilibrium, the rise in investment demand, is limited to Period 2 alone. This one-period rise in investment demand, however, produces the changing level of output in all these later periods by initiating a series of changes in consumption demand starting in Period 3. Thus, ΔC of 7.5 in Period 3 results from ΔY of 10 in Period 3, which results from ΔI of 10 in Period 2. Similarly, ΔC of 5.6 in Period 4 results from ΔY of 7.5 in Period 4, which results from ΔC of 7.5 in Period 3, which results from ΔY of 10 in Period 3, which results from ΔI of 10 in Period 2. In other words, the ΔI of Period 2 initiates a process in which ΔC in each period is 3/4 (the MPC) of ΔY in that period. Furthermore, given that ΔC is equal to 3/4 of ΔY of that period and that ΔY of each period is equal to $\Delta C + \Delta I$ of the preceding period, the fact that the increase in investment, ΔI, is limited to Period 2 alone means that ΔY and ΔC become smaller each period until eventually, in Period n, ΔC becomes zero.[2] Since ΔI is also zero in Period n, ΔY becomes zero, and the level of income and output is back to the equilibrium found in Period 1, or 160.

Although Table 8 1 shows that the equilibrium level of income established in Period n is the same as that of Period 1, it is important to note that the *cumulative* addition to income and output over the time interval in which the process works itself out is, in the present case, four times the size of the initiating increase in investment demand in Period 2. This cumulative addition to income and output is 40, as shown at the bottom of the column headed ΔY. It is composed of a cumulative addition to consumption of 30 and to investment of 10, as shown at the bottom of the columns headed ΔC and ΔI.[3] Thus, although the one-period injection of extra investment demand does not lift income and output to a permanently higher level, the *cumulative* effect in the present case is a flow of extra income and output four times the amount of that one-period injection of investment demand.

[2] For a one-period increase in investment spending of \$1, the *differences* between each period's aggregate spending and spending in the original period are given by the series

$$1, c, c^2, c^3, c^4, \ldots \ldots c^n$$

Since c is less than 1, the differences become smaller and smaller. After the passage of an infinite number of time periods represented by n, c^n becomes infinitely small, so that income returns to its original equilibrium level.

[3] Actually, the cumulative addition to investment demand does not occur in Period 2 as is suggested by the column headed ΔI. An increase in investment of 10 was planned for Period 2, but the realized increase in investment was zero. As shown by the next to last column, realized investment in Period 2 is 20, the same as in Period 1. The *realized* increases in investment may be identified in this column as the differences between the indicated values and 20—that is, 2.5 in Period 3, 1.9 in Period 4, and so forth. The sum of these changes will total 10, equal to the increase in planned investment of 10 shown in Period 2.

TABLE 8-2 A Permanent Increase in Investment Demand

Period	$C + I + \Delta C + \Delta I =$ Aggregate Demand	$\gtreqless$	Aggregate Output	$= Y + \Delta Y$	Investment Realized	Investment Planned
1	$140 + 20 + 0.0 + 0 = 160.0$	$=$	160.0	$= 160 + 0.0$	20.0	20
2	$140 + 20 + 0.0 + 10 = 170.0$	$>$	160.0	$= 160 + 0.0$	20.0	30
3	$140 + 20 + 7.5 + 10 = 177.5$	$>$	170.0	$= 160 + 10.0$	22.5	30
4	$140 + 20 + 13.1 + 10 = 183.1$	$>$	177.5	$= 160 + 17.5$	24.4	30
5	$140 + 20 + 17.4 + 10 = 187.4$	$>$	183.1	$= 160 + 23.1$	25.7	30
6	$140 + 20 + 20.5 + 10 = 190.5$	$>$	187.4	$= 160 + 27.4$	26.9	30
7	$140 + 20 + 22.9 + 10 = 192.9$	$>$	190.5	$= 160 + 30.5$	27.6	30
8	$140 + 20 + 24.7 + 10 = 194.7$	$>$	192.9	$= 160 + 32.9$	28.2	30
⋮	⋮		⋮	⋮	⋮	⋮
n	$140 + 20 + 30.0 + 10 = 200.0$	$=$	200.0	$= 160 + 40.0$	30.0	30
$n + 1$	$140 + 20 + 30.0 + 10 = 200.0$	$=$	200.0	$= 160 + 40.0$	30.0	30

A Permanent Shift in the Aggregate-Demand Function

If the aggregate-demand function shifts upward and remains at the new higher level period after period, the original equilibrium level of income and output will be replaced by a new, higher equilibrium level. This is the result shown in Figure 8–1 by the movement from Y of 160 to Y of 200.

To describe the process by which the system moves to a higher equilibrium level as a result of such a sustained increase in aggregate demand requires only that we extend the description of the process for a temporary increase in aggregate demand. In Table 8–1, ΔI of 10 in Period 2 called forth ΔY of 10 in Period 3, which in turn resulted in ΔC of 7.5 in Period 3. Because we then assumed that investment demand returned to its original level in Period 3, ΔY of Period 4, equal only to ΔC of 7.5 of Period 3, dropped below ΔY of Period 3, which was equal to ΔI of 10 of Period 2. In the present case, however, with a permanent rise in investment demand of 10, we have in Period 3 ΔI of 10 as well as ΔC of 7.5, so that ΔY of Period 4, equal now to ΔC of 7.5 plus ΔI of 10, is 17.5, greater than ΔY of 10 in Period 3. From ΔY of 17.5 in Period 4, we get ΔC of 13.1 in Period 4, so that ΔY in Period 5 is 23.1, the sum of ΔC of 13.1 plus the constant ΔI of 10. Thus, with investment sustained at the new higher level, ΔY in each period continues to rise above ΔY of the preceding period until a new equilibrium is established with ΔY of 40.

Table 8–2 records the period-by-period detail of this process. The column headings are the same as those in Table 8–1. The column headed ΔI starts out at zero in Period 1, becomes 10 in Period 2, and remains 10 in each succeeding period. As before, ΔY for any period is the sum of ΔI plus ΔC for the preceding period. In comparing the value of ΔY period by period, note that as ΔY becomes larger and larger, the change in ΔY becomes progressively smaller and in Period n becomes zero. In this period ΔY stabilizes at 40, and the sum of $Y + \Delta Y$ stabilizes at 200. With aggregate output at 200, income is 200, and with income at 200, the consumption function, $C = 20 + \frac{3}{4}Y$, indicates consumption demand of 170. Investment demand is given at 30, so aggregate demand is 200 and equal to aggregate output. Similarly, as shown in the last two columns of Table 8–2, in Period n realized investment reaches 30 and is equal to planned investment of 30. Viewed in either way, in Period n a new equilibrium is established.

THE MULTIPLIER—A SHIFT IN THE AGGREGATE DEMAND FUNCTION

As was pointed out in Figure 8–1 and Table 8–2, a permanent upward shift in the aggregate demand function results in a movement of income and output to a new equilibrium level that is higher than the original equilibrium level by some multiple of the upward shift in the aggregate demand function. The value of this multiple is known as the *multiplier* and represents the number by which the shift in the aggregate demand function must be multiplied to determine the change in the level of income and output required to establish a new equilibrium.[4] Under present assumptions, this multiple is 4.

Why do Figure 8–1 and Table 8–2 show a multiplier of 4 and not some other? The reason is that income receivers choose to spend on consumption 3/4 of any increase in income (MPC = 3/4) or that they choose to save, or not spend on consumption, 1/4 of any increase in income (MPS = 1/4). With MPS = 1/4, it is only when income and output have risen by 40 that income receivers will devote an additional 10 of their higher income to saving. Then $\Delta S = \Delta I$, 10 = 10, and a new equilibrium level of income and output is established.

Thus, with any given shift in the aggregate demand function, the change in income required to reestablish equilibrium is entirely dependent on the value of the MPC or the MPS. For example, still assuming that $\Delta I = 10$, we can simply determine the new equilibrium if MPC = 4/5 and MPS = 1/5. Instead of ΔY of 40 as before, we will now have ΔY of 50, for it is only when ΔY is 50 that ΔS will be 10 and therefore equal to ΔI of 10. Accordingly, until Y has risen by 50 (until ΔY equals 50), aggregate demand will exceed aggregate output and investment will exceed saving, forcing a further rise in income and output. By the same reasoning, if the MPC were 2/3 and the MPS 1/3, the rise in income would be 30.[5]

These and other possible combinations of MPC and MPS are all possible and plausible. Although many combinations are not plausible, there is a particular pair of these combinations that can help clarify the multiplier mechanism. One of these is MPC = 0 and MPS = 1. The rise in Y necessary to reestablish equilibrium in this case will be exactly equal to the permanent rise in I. If ΔI in Period 2 and in each subsequent period is 10, ΔY in Period 3 and in each subsequent period will be 10 also; for, if MPS = 1, ΔS will be 10 as soon as ΔY is 10. Therefore, $\Delta S = \Delta I$ in Period 3, and the new equilibrium level is immediately established at a level of income and output exactly 10 above the original level. The increase in investment does not lead to an increase in income larger than itself, for, with MPS = 1, the rise in income of 10 in Period 3 does not lead to a rise in consumption demand in Period 3. Instead, the income receivers choose

---

[4] Though made famous by the role it plays in Keynes's *General Theory*, the term itself was coined by another British economist, R. F. Kahn. Kahn's multiplier was an *employment* multiplier, measuring the ratio of the increment of total employment associated with a given increment of employment in the capital-goods industries. Keynes's multiplier is an *investment* multiplier, the ratio of the increment to total income associated with a given increment in investment. (See John Maynard Keynes, *The General Theory of Employment, Interest, and Money*, Harcourt, Brace & World, 1936, pp. 113–15.)

[5] While we may ask such questions and give such answers to illustrate the principle, it should be noted that if we were to assume some value other than 3/4 for the MPC (or 1/4 for the MPS) the original equilibrium would not have been 160. With an MPC of 4/5, the original equilibrium income and output would have been 200, equal to the aggregate-demand function, $20 + \frac{4}{5}Y + I$, in which I equals 20. From this original equilibrium, ΔI of 10 would result in ΔY of 50 before equilibrium was restored with ΔS of 10 equal to ΔI of 10; ΔY would be 50 as described above, but the rise in Y would have been from an original equilibrium with $Y = 200$ to a new equilibrium with $Y + \Delta Y = 250$.

to devote all the increase in income of Period 3 to saving (MPS = 1). There being no induced rise in consumption demand in Period 3, ΔY of Period 4 and each subsequent period is simply equal to ΔI of 10 for each such period. Unlike the situation in Table 8–2, in which only a part of the enlarged income stream of Period 3 was diverted into saving, here all of ΔY of Period 3 leaks out of the spending stream in Period 3, and the expansion process ends as quickly as it began. In a formal sense, the value of the multiplier is 1, but this is a far cry from the earlier results in which the multiplier was 4 (MPC = 3/4 and MPS = 1/4).

The other combination is MPC = 1 and MPS = 0. Starting off as before with ΔI of 10 in Period 2 and in each subsequent period, none of the additional income of 10 flowing to income receivers in Period 3 is diverted from the spending stream. Thus, the entire 10 of ΔY of Period 3 appears on the market as demand for consumption goods. In Period 3, $\Delta C = 10$, $\Delta I = 10$, and therefore in Period 4 $\Delta Y = 20$. In Period 4, all ΔY of that period appears as demand for consumption goods so that $\Delta C = 20$, $\Delta I = 10$, and therefore in Period 5, $\Delta Y = 30$. No new equilibrium would be possible in this case, and income would rise without limit. Equilibrium requires that $\Delta S = \Delta I$. But since all ΔY of any period is devoted to ΔC and none is diverted to ΔS, ΔS remains zero period after period and can never equal ΔI as required for equilibrium. Period after period, investment exceeds saving, and aggregate demand exceeds aggregate output. In this special situation, we would quickly have to drop our assumption that output expands proportionately with demand. This assumption is not too unreasonable for an economy with substantial unemployment of men and machines, but with demand growing without limit, unemployment would be quickly eliminated. As full employment was approached, output would cease expanding proportionately with demand; once all available resources were fully utilized, output would not expand at all. Demand would continue to rise, but the rising demand would mean only continuously rising prices paid for an amount of output temporarily at its physical maximum. Such is the situation on the assumption that MPC = 1 and MPS = 0.

In all the examples above, we have assumed that the aggregate-demand function shifts upward. Shifts in the opposite direction are equally possible. In such cases, the multiplier works against us instead of for us; it works to produce a multiple contraction of income and output instead of a multiple expansion. Thus, with a downward shift in the aggregate-demand function, the question to be answered is not how much income will rise before equilibrium is restored but how much it will fall before equilibrium is restored. With MPC = 3/4 and MPS = 1/4, if investment demand falls from 20 to 10 ($\Delta I = -10$), the *drop* in income and output necessary to restore equilibrium will be 40. The reasoning is the same as before. Income will drop until saving again equals investment. Since investment is reduced from 20 to 10, or by -10, saving must be reduced from 20 to 10, or by -10, to restore equilibrium. Given MPS $= 1/4$, only when income is reduced by 40 will saving be reduced by 10. As income receivers increase saving by 1/4 of any addition to income, so they decrease saving by 1/4 of any reduction in income. From the original equilibrium of 160, the system reaches a new equilibrium level with income and output reduced by 40 to 120.

The downward multiplier is 4 for the same reason that the upward multiplier is 4: because MPC = 3/4 and MPS = 1/4. If we assume different values for the MPC and the MPS, the results for a downward shift in the aggregate demand function parallel those just described, the only difference being the size of the multiplier. With MPC = 2/3 and MPS = 1/3, a downward shift in the aggregate demand function of 10 ($\Delta I = -10$) will produce a decline in income and output of 30.

Since the MPC or the MPS determines the multiplier and since the multiplier determines the size of the increase or decrease in income and output that will follow any given upward or downward shift in the aggregate-demand function, the practical importance of the MPC and the MPS is great. Given the variability of that portion of the aggregate-demand function made up of investment demand, the degree of instability of the entire economic system depends to some extent on the value of the MPC and the MPS. As business spending for plant and equipment goes up in one period and down in another, there is a direct impact on the level of income and output within each period. This in itself is a source of instability. Yet whatever the variability of investment demand, a relatively low MPC and a relatively high MPS will tend to produce less instability in the economy than will a relatively high MPC and a relatively low MPS. Of the two extreme cases we discussed earlier, that in which MPC = 1 and MPS = 0 will produce extreme instability in income and output, since any variability in investment spending from one period to the next will be greatly magnified by continuously rising induced consumption spending. At the other extreme, when MPC = 0 and MPS = 1, the instability in income and output will be far less, since the variability of investment spending from one period to the next will not be magnified at all by induced consumption spending.

Although any explanation of fluctuations in the level of income and output involves far more than just the variability of investment spending and the values of the MPC and the MPS, the values of the MPC and the MPS still play a vital role in explaining the amplitude of the upward and downward movements in income and output during business cycles. More will be said about this topic in Chapter 20, where the multiplier will be made a specific part of a multiplier-accelerator model of the business cycle.

THE MULTIPLIER—EQUATIONS

To determine the equilibrium level of income and output in the two-sector economy, we used the equation

$$Y = C + I \tag{1}$$

Once given the consumption function and the investment function, the equation could be readily solved.

$$Y = 20 + \tfrac{3}{4}Y + 20$$

$$160 = 140 + 20$$

If we retain this same consumption function but assume now an upward shift in the investment function, there will be an increase in the equilibrium level of income and output. Since any increase in Y, ΔY, must be equal to $\Delta C + \Delta I$, we have the following equation, the solution to which gives us the new equilibrium level of income and output. (This equation is the one from which the column headings in Tables 8–1 and 8–2 came.)

$$Y + \Delta Y = C + I + \Delta C + \Delta I$$
$$160 + \Delta Y = 140 + 20 + \Delta C + \Delta I \qquad [2]$$

Subtracting Equation [1], $Y = C + I$, from Equation [2], we have another equation, the solution to which indicates the *change* in the level of income necessary to produce the new equilibrium level of income.

$$\Delta Y = \Delta C + \Delta I \qquad [3]$$

The consumption function, $C = C_a + cY$, indicates that consumption spending, C, rises or falls by an amount equal to the MPC, or c (here 3/4) times the rise in income. That is, it says that $\Delta C = c\Delta Y$ or, in the present example, $\Delta C = \frac{3}{4}\Delta Y$. Substituting in Equation [3], we have the following:

$$\Delta Y = c\,\Delta Y + \Delta I$$
$$\Delta Y - c\,\Delta Y = \Delta I$$
$$\Delta Y(1 - c) = \Delta I$$
$$\Delta Y = \frac{1}{1 - c}\,\Delta I$$

and

$$\frac{\Delta Y}{\Delta I} = \frac{1}{1 - c}$$

or

$$\Delta Y = \tfrac{3}{4}\,\Delta Y + \Delta I$$
$$\Delta Y - \tfrac{3}{4}\,\Delta Y = \Delta I$$
$$\Delta Y(1 - 3/4) = \Delta I$$
$$\Delta Y = \frac{1}{1 - 3/4}\,\Delta I$$

and

$$\frac{\Delta Y}{\Delta I} = \frac{1}{1 - 3/4} = 4$$

If $\Delta I = 10$, $\Delta Y = 40$; the new equilibrium level of income and output will be 40 above the original level. Since $\Delta C = \frac{3}{4}\,\Delta Y$ and since $\Delta Y = 40$, $\Delta C = 30$. The rise in income and output is divided between a rise in consumption of 30 and a rise in investment of 10.

Given any change in investment, ΔI, the change in income and output necessary to reestablish equilibrium is known as soon as the multiplier is known. The multiplier, in turn, is known as soon as the MPC is known. Thus, as we have just seen, the general expression for the multiplier is

$$\frac{\Delta Y}{\Delta I} = \frac{1}{1 - \text{MPC}}$$

In other words, the multiplier is the reciprocal of 1 minus the MPC, so that the larger the value of the MPC, the larger will be the value of the multiplier. This is clearly in accord with our intuitive notion that the rise in income induced by a given rise in investment will be larger the larger the proportion of that investment outlay which is respent—that is, the larger the MPC. Thus, for any value of ΔI, the greater the size of the multiplier, the greater will be the increase in the equilibrium level of income.

There is a second approach to the determination of the multiplier. To determine the equilibrium level of income and output, we earlier used $Y = C + I$ and also

$$S = I \qquad\qquad [1]$$

Whereas $Y = C + I$ focuses on the equality between aggregate output and aggregate demand, $S = I$ focuses on the equality between saving and investment. Once given the saving function and the investment function, the equation could be readily solved for the equilibrium level of income and output as follows:

$$S = I$$
$$-20 + \tfrac{1}{4}Y = 20$$
$$\tfrac{1}{4}Y = 40$$
$$Y = 160$$

The further development of the approach in terms of saving and investment is exactly parallel with that above in terms of consumption and investment. Assuming an upward shift in the investment function, the new equilibrium level of income and output is that at which

$$S + \Delta S = I + \Delta I \qquad\qquad [2]$$

Since $S = I$ when $Y = 160$, we may subtract $S = I$ from Equation [2]. The solution to the remaining equation indicates the change in the level of income necessary to produce the new equilibrium level of income, given a specified change in the investment function.

$$\Delta S = \Delta I \qquad\qquad [3]$$

The saving function $S = S_a + sY$ indicates that saving rises or falls by an amount equal to the MPS, or s (here 1/4) times the rise or fall in income. That is, $\Delta S = s\Delta Y$. Substituting in Equation [3], we have:

$$s\Delta Y = \Delta I$$

$$\Delta Y = \frac{1}{s}\Delta I$$

$$\frac{\Delta Y}{\Delta I} = \frac{1}{s}$$

If, as before, $\Delta I = 10$, then $\Delta Y = 40$, or the new equilibrium level of income and output will be 40 above the original level. Given any change in investment, ΔI, the change in income and output necessary to restore equilibrium is known as soon as the multiplier is known. The multiplier, in turn, is known as soon as the MPS is known. Therefore, we have as a second general expression for the multiplier:

$$\frac{\Delta Y}{\Delta I} = \frac{1}{\text{MPS}}$$

Since MPS $= 1 -$ MPC, 1/MPS as here derived is exactly equal to our earlier equation for the multiplier, $1/(1 - \text{MPC})$. Thus, the multiplier is the reciprocal of 1 minus the MPC or the reciprocal of the MPS.

SIMPLE INCOME DETERMINATION—A CONCLUDING NOTE

In this chapter we have examined the theory of income determination under some highly simplifying assumptions—hence the use of the adjective, "simple." [6] Some of these assumptions will be dropped in later chapters. Naturally, the more of them that are dropped, the more complicated the theory becomes and the closer it comes to describing the infinitely complex process by which income and output change in the real world.

There is no doubt, however, that the simple theory outlined in this chapter sheds considerable light on the aggregate economic process in the world about us; it tells us things that are not immediately apparent. One may properly argue that it takes no high level of economic sophistication to recognize that output will be increased in an economy with idle men and idle machines if either businessmen or consumers or both step up their spending for goods and services. However, the completely unsophisticated will most likely expect output to increase by the amount of this initial increase in spending. But even the simple theory, merely by introducing the concepts of the consumption function, the marginal propensity to consume, and the multiplier, makes very clear the secondary consequences that produce an increase in income and output that is larger than the initial increase in business or consumer demand.

[6] For a very concise statement of the theory of this chapter (what Paul A. Samuelson calls the "heart of income analysis"), see his "The Simple Mathematics of Income Determination," in *Income, Employment, and Public Policy,* Norton, 1948, pp. 133–55.

Our simple theory not only shows the process by which an increase in autonomous spending will raise income and output by a multiple of that increase, but also indicates what determines the size of this multiple, admittedly under very restrictive assumptions. Although this simple theory cannot be applied directly to an explanation of the actual fluctuations in the level of income and output in the real world, it can explain an important truth, a truth necessary but not sufficient to an understanding of these fluctuations in the real world. To understand this is to understand the essence of what the simple theory has to tell us.

CHAPTER 9

INCOME AND CONSUMPTION

In the development of the simple theory of income determination in the preceding two chapters, we worked with a consumption function in which the MPC was constant, positive, and less than one and in which the APC exceeded the MPC at all levels of income. Although it was suggested that such a relationship between consumption and income appeared to be plausible, no real evidence was submitted in its support; the relationship was simply derived from a particular theory of consumer behavior that was described briefly in Chapter 7. The major tenets of this theory are that consumers devote a fraction of any increase in income to saving and that they save a larger fraction of a higher income than of a lower income. This specific theory of consumer spending, apart from some simplifications of a noncritical nature, is essentially the view that Keynes advanced in his *General Theory*.

Keynes's theory has been elaborated by others and has come to be known as the *absolute income hypothesis* or theory. Rival theories have also been developed, the major two being the *relative income* and *permanent income hypotheses* or theories. Each of these three theories of consumer spending involves a quite specific but different theory of consumer behavior—that is, each assigns a different role to income as an influence on consumer spending, or, otherwise expressed, each sees income as a determinant of consumption in a somewhat different way.

The primary purpose of this chapter is to investigate the relationship between consumption and income through an examination of these three major theories of consumer spending. The economists who have constructed these theories have all begun with a theory of individual consumer behavior and then generalized to cover aggregate behavior. In the testing of these theories, cross-section data provide empirical evidence on how spending varies at different levels of family income in any one year, and time-series data provide empirical evidence on how aggregate spending (or spending by all families combined) varies as aggregate income (or the income of all families combined) changes from one year or one quarter to the next. Our procedure in this chapter will follow a similar line. First, we will discuss the absolute income, relative income and permanent income theories as theories of individual consumer behavior and relate them to some simple cross-section data; and, second, we will discuss the same three theories in their generalized, or aggregative, form and relate the generalized theories to the aggregate, or time-series, data. This procedure divides our task into two parts that may be called cross-section analysis and time-series analysis.

CROSS–SECTION ANALYSIS

Cross-section data show for a given time period how much of family income was devoted to consumption spending, on the average, by a sample of families at various income levels. Relevant data from a budget study for the year 1950 are summarized in Table 9–1. Columns 2 and 3 give, in dollars, the average family disposable income and the average family consumption expenditures of the sample families in each income class given in Column 1. Column 4 was derived by

TABLE 9–1   Average Family Disposable Income and Consumption Expenditures by Income Class, 1950

(1) Family Income Class	(2) Family Disposable Income	(3) Family Consumption Expenditures	(4) apc	(5) mpc
Under $1,000	$ 614	$ 1,278	2.1	
				0.5
$1,000 to $2,000	1,532	1,768	1.2	
				.9
$2,000 to $3,000	2,534	2,718	1.1	
				.9
$3,000 to $4,000	3,487	3,570	1.0	
	.			.9
$4,000 to $5,000	4,462	4,450	1.0	
				.8
$5,000 to $6,000	5,449	5,257	1.0	
				.7
$6,000 to $7,500	6,618	6,043	0.9	
				.6
$7,500 to $10,000	8,434	7,108	0.8	
				0.5
$10,000 and over	15,914	10,773	0.7	

SOURCE: Table 1–1 in *Study of Consumer Expenditures, Incomes, and Savings*, Vol. 18, Wharton School of Finance and Commerce, University of Pennsylvania, 1957, p. 2. Columns 4 and 5 were derived from Columns 2 and 3 by the author.

dividing the dollar amounts in Column 3 by the dollar amounts in Column 2. The values in Column 4 may be related to our earlier concept of the average propensity to consume if we recognize, however, that these values relate to different levels of family income and not to different levels of aggregate income. The values in Column 4 show that as we move from lower to higher family incomes, the percentage of income devoted to consumption expenditures, the *apc*, decreases. (To differentiate the family from the aggregate average propensity to consume, *apc* is used for the former and, as before, APC for the latter.) Column 5 was also derived from the dollar amounts in Columns 2 and 3. Here the change in average consumption between each pair of income classes is divided by the change in average income between the corresponding pair of income classes. Again recognizing that the values relate to different levels of family income rather than to different levels of aggregate income, we may relate the values in Column 5 to our earlier concept of the marginal propensity to consume. These values show that as we move from lower- to higher-income classes consumption expenditures increase, but by less than the increase in income. With minor variations, other family budget studies made at different times reflect the same properties: The *apc* decreases with higher levels of family income, and the *mpc* (here using *mpc* for the family marginal propensity to consume) is positive but less than one.

The data given in Columns 2 and 3 of Table 9–1 have been plotted in Figure 9–1. The broken vertical lines represent the income classes of Table 9–1; the dot between each pair of broken lines indicates the average income (from Column 2) and average consumption expenditures (from Column 3) for the sample of families within each income class so delineated. These dots have been connected by a smooth line that may be called the *family consumption function*.

The familiar 45° line has been inserted in Figure 9–1 as a guide. Since the family consumption function crosses the 45° line at a family income level of about $4,400, we may deduce that in 1950, on the average, a family income level of about this amount represented the break-even income, or the income level at which consumption expenditures were equal to income so that there was neither family saving nor family dissaving. As we drop down to lower family income levels, there was increasing dissaving by the average family. Conversely, as we move up to higher family income levels, there was increasing saving by the average family.[1] Apart from some curvature of the family consumption function of Figure 9–1, which indicates that the *mpc* was not constant, there is a general similarity between the position and shape of this function and of those in the preceding chapters. They reflect the same properties: decreasing dissaving

[1] Figure 9–1 also shows that, on the average, families with incomes about $1,000 above $4,400 spent slightly less than their incomes, and families with incomes $1,000 below $4,400 spent slightly more than their incomes. In Column 4 of Table 9–1, the rounded figures fail to show these small differences, the *apc* being given as 1.0 for each of the three income classes covering family incomes from $3,000 to $6,000.

It should also be noted that, whereas $4,400 appears to be approximately the break-even income, many individual families with this income undoubtedly saved larger or smaller amounts, while many others undoubtedly dissaved larger or smaller amounts. It is only the "average" family at this income level that may be classified as being roughly at what was the break-even level of income in 1950.

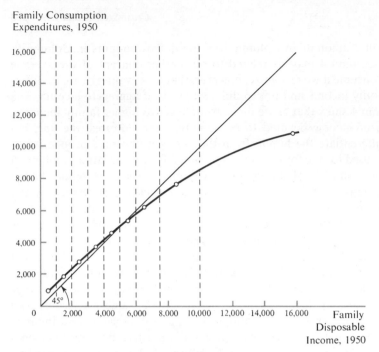

Family Consumption
Expenditures, 1950

Family
Disposable
Income, 1950

FIGURE 9–1   Family Consumption Function

as we move from very low income to the break-even income and then increasing saving as we move up to higher income.

Having demonstrated that, apart from some curvature, the properties of the empirically derived family consumption function are the same as those of the aggregate consumption function earlier assumed, one is tempted to conclude that the latter is a reasonably accurate description of the way that aggregate consumption expenditures actually do vary as the level of aggregate income varies. This easy conclusion is ruled out, however, as soon as we recall that we are talking about two completely different types of consumption function. One shows for a given time period how families at different income levels divide their respective incomes between consumption and saving. The other shows how all families combined would divide different *alternative* levels of aggregate income between consumption and saving. Whether or not we may apply conclusions drawn from cross-section studies of *family* income differences to the case of *aggregate* income differences is a question that can be approached only by turning to the theory of individual consumer behavior and the various theories of consumer spending mentioned above.

The Absolute Income Theory

The basic tenet of the absolute income theory is that the individual consumer determines what fraction of his current income he will devote to consumption on the basis of the *absolute* level of that income. Other things being equal, a rise in his absolute income will lead to a decrease in the fraction of that income

154

devoted to consumption. As we have noted, the first statement of this hypothesis is probably that made by Keynes in the *General Theory*. Its subsequent development is primarily associated with James Tobin and Arthur Smithies.[2]

For a simple illustration, assume that we were able to take all families at three different levels of family income, specifically $2,000, $4,000, and $6,000, for a given year and to ascertain the average consumption expenditures of all families at each of these income levels. We would expect these average consumption figures when plotted to show up as points like *D*, *E*, and *G* on the curve labeled *C* in Figure 9–2. (Disregard the curve labeled *C'*.) A pattern such as this for the three points is clearly what cross-section data from actual budget studies typically show. Suppose next that all the families at these income levels, as well as all families at all other income levels, should somehow enjoy a doubling of their income between this initial year and a subsequent year. Assuming no changes other than the change in income, how do families at each income level, on the average, divide their doubled incomes between consumption and saving? The theory of behavior that underlies the absolute income theory suggests that families would, on the average, divide their now doubled incomes in the same way as did the average family that previously occupied the income position to which the previously lower income families have now moved. This would mean that the families at the three income levels mentioned above would move along the family consumption function in Figure 9–2 from *D* to *E*, from *E* to *J*, and from *G* to *L*, respectively. Families at other income levels would move along the function in a similar manner. Because it is the absolute level of the family's income that is held to control the allocation of income between consumption and saving, this theory gives us the result of a decline in the average propensity to consume of the average family when families move up to a higher income level.[3]

If consumers do, in fact, respond to changes in income in this way, it follows that, of the aggregate income received by all consumers, the fraction that is spent decreases as that aggregate income increases. This relationship between aggregate income and aggregate consumption is one of the properties of the aggregate consumption function we employed in Chapter 7. That function, it will be recalled, was drawn to correspond, in the main, with the theory of consumer behavior stated by Keynes. Since that theory was essentially what we now call the absolute income theory, the relationship noted here, in which the fraction of aggregate income consumed declines as aggregate income rises, is of course the one to be expected.

[2] See J. Tobin, "Relative Income, Absolute Income, and Saving," in *Money, Trade, and Economic Growth*, Macmillan, 1951, pp. 135–56, and A. Smithies, "Forecasting Postwar Demand: I," in *Econometrica*, Jan. 1945, pp. 1–14.

[3] Thus, the $2,000 family whose *apc* was, on the average, 1.2 (or $2,400/$2,000) now becomes a $4,000 family whose *apc* is, on the average, 1.0 (or $4,000/$4,000). The $4,000 family whose *apc* was, on the average, 1.0 ($4,000/$4,000) now becomes an $8,000 family whose *apc* is, on the average, 0.8 (or $6,400/$8,000). And the $6,000 family whose *apc* was, on the average, 0.9 (or $5,400/$6,000) now becomes a $12,000 family whose *apc* is, on the average, 0.6 (or $7,200/$12,000).

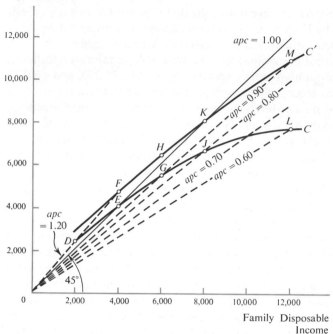

FIGURE 9–2 Family Consumption Function: Absolute and Relative Income

The absolute income theory seems to be a plausible theory of individual consumer behavior, and the noneconomist would probably accept it today without hesitation. If he were presented with the question before us, he would most likely say, in his plain language, that high-income families save a large fraction of their income for the obvious reason that these families are able to save a large fraction of a large income, whereas the very opposite is true of the low-income families for the same obvious reason. To him it would then be equally obvious that as families move up the income scale, they are able to save a larger fraction of their income and will obviously do so for the same reason that families previously at the levels others have now attained saved the larger fraction they did. In the first years following the appearance of the *General Theory*, economists also generally accepted the absolute income theory as basically correct, but the widespread acceptance enjoyed by this theory was short-lived. Although it still has some supporters, most economists lean toward one of the other theories, such as the relative income theory. Some reasons for this will become apparent as we continue.

The Relative Income Theory

The relative income theory, a theory closely associated with the name of James S. Duesenberry,[4] argues that the fraction of a family's income devoted to

[4] See J. S. Duesenberry, *Income, Saving, and the Theory of Consumer Behavior*, Harvard Univ. Press, 1949. See also D. S. Brady and R. Friedman, "Savings and the Income Distribution,"

consumption depends on the level of its income *relative* to the income of neigh-boring families or other families with which it identifies and not on the *absolute* level of the family's income. Thus, if a family's income rises but its *relative position* on the income scale remains unchanged because the incomes of other families with whom it identifies have risen at the same rate, its division of income between consumption and saving will remain unchanged. The family's absolute income has risen, so its absolute consumption and absolute saving will also rise, but the *fraction* of income devoted to consumption will be the same at the higher level of absolute income that it was at the lower level. To express the same argu-ment in a different way, if a family's income remains unchanged but the incomes of these other families rise, its income position relative to that of the other families has then changed. The relative income theory would argue that the deterioration in the relative position of this family would lead to a rise in the fraction of its income devoted to consumption, despite the fact that there has been no change in its absolute income.

In its focus on relative income, this theory emphasizes the imitative or emulative nature of consumption. A family with any given level of income will typically spend more on consumption if it lives in a community in which that income is a relatively low one than if it lives in a community in which that income is a relatively high one. This tendency to spend more in the one situation arises in part from the pressures on the family to "keep up with the Joneses" and in part from the fact that the family will observe in its everyday living what to it are the superior goods of other families and will be tempted to spend as a result of what Duesenberry calls the "demonstration" effect. Thus, studies have shown that Negro families with an income of $5,000 will, on the average, spend less than white families with an equal income, the reason being that the Negro family with this income will most likely live in a neighborhood in which $5,000 is a relatively high income for that neighborhood, whereas the white family will most likely live in a neighborhood in which this same income is further down the scale of incomes of families in that neighborhood.

If families behave in the way indicated by the relative income theory, the division of their income between spending and saving will clearly be different from the division suggested by the absolute-income theory. This basic differ-ence may be seen by turning back to Figure 9–2. Assume as before that the abso-lute income of all families doubles between an initial year and a subsequent year. There is then no change in the distribution of income. The top 1 percent of all families gets the same percentage of the aggregate income in both years, the bottom 1 percent gets the same percentage in both years, and similarly for every other percentile. Therefore, despite the doubling of each family's income, its relative position on the income scale is the same as it was before. The relative income theory then argues that there would be no reason, on the basis of the income change alone, to expect a change in the fraction of income consumed by

Studies in Income and Wealth, Vol. 10, National Bureau of Economic Research, Princeton Univ. Press, 1947, pp. 247–65, and F. Modigliani, "Fluctuations in the Saving-Income Ratio: A Problem in Economic Forecasting," same series, Vol. 11, 1949, pp. 371–443.

the average family. If there is no change in this ratio, with the doubling of its income each family would not move upward along the function labeled *C*, as suggested by the absolute income theory, since such a movement indicates a decrease in the ratio of income spent by each family. The relative income theory argues instead that each family moves in such a way as to create the new consumption function labeled *C'*. That is to say, the $2,000 family would move not from *D* to *E* but from *D* to *F*; the $4,000 family would move not from *E* to *J* but from *E* to *K*; and the $6,000 family would move not from *G* to *L* but from *G* to *M*. If the average family at each income level did respond to this doubling of income in the way indicated by the relative-income theory, its *apc* would be the same before and after the doubling of its income. Each family is on the same *apc* curve (depicted in Figure 9–2 by broken straight lines drawn from the origin) that it was on before the rise in its income.[5] According to the relative income theory, each family, in deciding on the fraction of its income to be spent, is uninfluenced by the fact that it is twice as well off in *absolute* terms and is influenced only by that fact that it is no better off at all in *relative* terms. Being no better off in this sense, its decision is to "live" as it did previously, devoting the same fraction of its income to consumption that it did before.

The relative income theory reaches this conclusion on the assumption that the distribution of income remains essentially unchanged as the level of aggregate income changes. However, if a redistribution occurs, those families whose incomes rise less rapidly than the average of those with whom they identify will tend to raise their *apc*, while those whose incomes rise more rapidly will tend to lower their *apc*. If increases in income are accompanied by a redistribution toward greater equality, the *apc* for all families (with the exception of those at the top of the income scale) will tend to be reduced. This again follows from the argument that the fraction of family income consumed is determined by the family's relative position on the income scale. The pressure of families at each level of the income scale to "keep up with the Joneses" is reduced as income differentials are reduced through redistribution toward greater equality.[6] Such redistribution brings the income of any one family and those families that it emulates or imitates closer together and tends, thereby, to reduce this family's *apc* by reducing the amount of its consumption that is imitative in origin.

The distribution of income in the United States has been altered in the direction of greater equality over the long run, but the experienced changes are so gradual that appreciable change is apparent only over a period of several decades or more.[7] On the other hand, the growth in real income itself is by comparison quite rapid, per capita GNP having doubled between 1939 and 1965. Thus, when changes in distribution are taken into account, we cannot expect the family consumption function to shift from *C* to *C'* in Figure 9–2 in the simple

[5] Thus, the $2,000 family whose *apc* was 1.2 (or $2,400/$2,000) is now a $4,000 family whose *apc* is still 1.2 (or $4,800/$4,000). The $4,000 family whose *apc* was 1.0 (or $4,000/$4,000) is now an $8,000 family whose *apc* is still 1.0 (or $8,000/$8,000). And the $6,000 family whose *apc* was 0.9 (or $5,400/$6,000) is now a $12,000 family whose *apc* is still 0.9 (or $10,800/$12,000).
[6] The influence of income distribution on consumption is examined further in Chapter 10.
[7] For some evidence, see footnote 14 on p. 189.

way described earlier. Still, the changes in income distribution actually experienced do not invalidate but only qualify the result that would be expected if the level of average family income increased with no change in income distribution.

The relative income theory, like the absolute income theory discussed above and the permanent income theory to be discussed below, is a theory of consumer behavior that relates the consumer's spending to his income on the assumption of no change in any of the other factors influencing consumption, of which the distribution of income is only one. Under this assumption, the relative income theory gives us the result described above: that the family consumption function shifts upward proportionately with changes in aggregate income received by all families. This result, therefore, turns out to be inconsistent with the result indicated by the absolute income theory. If relative income controls the fraction of income spent by the family, an equal percentage change in the incomes of all families will produce no change in the fraction of that enlarged aggregate income that is devoted to consumption. On the other hand, if absolute income controls, the fraction of aggregate income consumed declines as aggregate income increases. There will be a further comparison of the results reached by the absolute and relative income theories in the time-series analysis later in this chapter.

The Permanent Income Theory

Both the absolute and relative income theories focus on the individual family's "current" income as the income concept relevant to its spending. What is the meaning of current income in this context? Is the family's current income its measured income for a week, a month, a year, two years? Does the family adjust its consumption upward or downward from one week to the next in the face of a rise or fall in its measured income from one week to the next? Or does it do this on a monthly basis or a yearly basis? It seems fair to say that a family's spending in any one week is not closely related to its measured income during that specific week; we would not expect its consumption to be drastically affected in any one week even if its measured income for that one week alone should be zero. The same is true to a lesser degree if we take a time span of one month. Where is the line to be drawn? Most studies that take current income as the appropriate income concept take the current year, or sometimes the current and the preceding year, as the time span that is relevant.

A quite different approach to the role of income in the theory of consumer spending has been developed by Milton Friedman, and its point of departure is the rejection of this usual concept of "current" income and its replacement with what is called "permanent" income.[8] A family's permanent income in any

[8] See M. Friedman, *A Theory of the Consumption Function*, Princeton Univ. Press, 1957. A very similar theory, sometimes called the "life-cycle" hypothesis, was developed more or less independently by F. Modigliani and others. See A. Ando and F. Modigliani, "The 'Life Cycle' Hypothesis of Saving: Aggregate Implications and Tests," in *American Economic Review*, March 1963, pp. 55–84, and F. Modigliani and R. E. Brumberg, "Utility Analysis and the Consumption Function: An Interpretation of Cross-Section Data," in K. K. Kurihara,

one year is in no sense indicated by its current income for that year but is determined by the expected or anticipated income to be received over a long period of time, stretching out over a number of future years. In Friedman's words, permanent income "is to be interpreted as the mean income regarded as permanent by the consumer unit in question, which in turn depends on its horizon and farsightedness." [9] The time span that is relevant to permanent income is the minimum period of time over which income influences must be maintained in order to make the receiver of that income regard them as permanent.

Given this meaning of permanent income, a family's measured or observed income in any particular year may be larger or smaller than its permanent income. Friedman divides the family's measured income in the year into permanent and transitory components, so that its measured income is larger or smaller than its permanent income, depending on the sum of positive and negative transitory income components. For example, if a family wage earner receives an unexpected special bonus at work in one year and has no reason to expect the same bonus in following years, this income element is regarded as positive transitory income, and it raises his measured income above his permanent income. On the other hand, if the family wage earner suffers an unexpected loss of income due, say, to a plant shutdown as a result of fire, this income element is regarded as negative transitory income, and it reduces his measured income below his permanent income. These unforeseen additions to and subtractions from a family's income are expected to cancel out over the longer period relevant to permanent income, but they are present in any shorter period.

In the same way, Friedman divides measured consumption into permanent and transitory components.[10] A good purchased because of an attractive sale price or a normal purchase deferred due to unavailability of the good would be examples of positive and negative transitory consumption. As with measured income, a family's measured consumption in any particular period may be larger or smaller than its permanent consumption.

With these definitions at hand, we may turn to Friedman's basic argument that permanent consumption depends on permanent income. Specifically, the relationship he proposes is that permanent consumption is a constant proportion of permanent income in which the proportion depends only on the interest rate, on the ratio of "nonhuman" wealth to total (human plus nonhuman) wealth, and on tastes. Tastes are affected by factors such as age and family composition. The permanent consumption of different families with the same permanent income will thus vary with their tastes and other specified characteristics. However, the ratio of permanent consumption to permanent income is held to be independent of permanent income itself. If we visualize a group of

---

ed., *Post-Keynesian Economics*, Rutgers Univ. Press, 1954, pp. 388–436. Although the two hypotheses are very similar in principle, the Friedman version has gained wider attention, and discussion here will center on that version.

[9] Friedman, *op. cit.*, p. 93.

[10] It should also be noted that Friedman defines consumption as spending on services and nondurable goods plus the depreciation of consumer durable goods. A net addition to the family's stock of durable goods is treated as saving.

families identical in tastes and the other factors that determine this ratio, the hypothesis in its extreme form states that the fraction of each such family's permanent income devoted to consumption will be the same, whether that permanent income places the family near the bottom or near the top of the income scale. In other words, the *apc* of families at all levels of family income is held to be the same, when the *apc* is expressed as a ratio of permanent consumption to permanent income. This, of course, also means that the average propensity to save of families at all levels of family income is the same. The "rich" and the "poor" devote the same fraction of their incomes to saving!

This conclusion, which appears to conflict with what ordinary observation shows, follows from the argument of this theory that saving is primarily for the purpose of providing future consumption for the family. The family's intent is to even out consumption over a time period that is substantially longer than the single year but not necessarily as long as its remaining life span. Although this behavior is necessary if families at all income levels are to smooth out consumption, most economists question whether this is a correct description of actual behavior. It may be granted that most families make some attempt to even out consumption in this way, but it is questionable whether the preference for present over future goods is not greater for low-income families than it is for high-income families. However strong the desire of low-income families to avoid a level of consumption in later years that is even lower than the low level of the current year, it is difficult to believe that such families feel able to save the same fraction of their meager incomes that high-income families save of theirs. The pressures toward present consumption at the low-income levels are such that the preference for present goods over future goods would appear to be substantially stronger here than at the high-income levels. These pressures would be expected to operate to keep the consumption of low-income families high relative to their incomes and to keep the saving of high-income families high relative to their incomes.

Another basic argument of Friedman's permanent income theory is that the transitory component of consumption is uncorrelated with the transitory component of income. This amounts to saying that in a period in which a family's measured income contains a negative transitory component, it does not reduce its consumption in response, nor, under the opposite circumstance, does it raise its consumption in response. Unexpected increases or decreases in income thus result in equivalent increases or decreases in saving; consumption is unaffected by "windfall" gains or losses. Or, in other words, the marginal propensity to consume out of transitory, or "windfall," income is held to be zero. As they have questioned the argument that the fraction of family income saved is the same at all levels of family income, most economists have questioned whether this too is a correct description of actual consumer behavior. In the words of one critic, the hypothesis says, "The man who has a lucky day at the races does not buy his friends a drink, and the poor fellow whose wallet is stolen does not postpone the purchase of a new overcoat." [11] This critic argues,

[11] H. S. Houthakker, "The Permanent Income Hypothesis," in *American Economic Review*, June 1958, p. 398.

and submits some evidence to suggest, that "the lucky winner does not run to the savings bank but to the tavern, and the victim of theft does cut his coat according to his cloth." [12]

These basic arguments of the permanent income theory have raised considerable controversy and generated a sizable literature.[13] Empirical evidence has been presented on both sides, and the debate is far from resolved. Our purpose here is not to pursue this debate but merely to set forth some essentials of the permanent income theory and to relate these to the simple cross-section evidence provided by empirical family consumption functions.

Cross-section data such as those plotted in Figure 9–1 clearly do not form a pattern that would be expected on the basis of the permanent income theory. The data as given from the 1950 study, as well as data from similar studies made in other years, uniformly show the *apc* declining as we move from lower to higher levels of family income. However, data of this simple kind are in no way relevant to the permanent income theory, because, as we noted at the outset, that theory holds that current income is not the appropriate income concept in a theory that employs income as a determinant of consumption. These budget-study data present for different levels of family income the relationship between the "current" income and the "current" consumption of families. The permanent income theory does not deny the relationship shown by such studies; what it does deny is the appropriateness of the measured income and consumption variables employed in such studies. According to this theory, the use of current or measured income improperly mixes together permanent and transitory income, on the one hand, and permanent and transitory consumption, on the other. The fact that the *apc* out of current income declines with higher levels of current family income is held to be attributable to the influence of the transitory income and consumption components in current income and current consumption. A family consumption function that relates permanent consumption to permanent income would look quite different—according to the theory, it would be a straight line from the origin, thus showing a constant proportion of income consumed at all levels of family income. Only by turning to cross-section estimates of permanent income and permanent consumption could one test empirically whether the *apc* out of permanent income is the same at all levels of family income. The tests that have been made offer conflicting results.[14] Simple cross-

---

[12] *Ibid.*, p. 404.

[13] See, for example, I. Friend and I. B. Kravis, "Consumption Patterns and Permanent Income," in *American Economic Review*, May 1957, pp. 536–55; W. H. Watts, "Long-Run Income Expectations and Consumer Saving," in T. F. Dernberg, R. N. Rosett, and W. H. Watts, *Studies in Household Economic Behavior*, Yale Univ. Press, 1958, pp. 103–44; R. Bodkin, "Windfall Income and Consumption," in *American Economic Review*, Sept. 1959, pp. 602–14; and M. E. Kreinen, "Windfall Income and Consumption," in *American Economic Review*, June 1961, pp. 388–90.

[14] Permanent income is, of course, not directly measurable. However, various ways of approximating permanent income on a cross-section basis have been devised and provide the basis for testing the theory. Because the theory holds that transitory consumption is uncorrelated with transitory income, measured consumption may be said to depend on permanent income. For some cross-section tests relating measured consumption to permanent income, see I. Friend and I. B. Kravis, *op. cit.*

section data based on current income such as those given in Figure 9–1, however, do not directly shed light on this question.

Since the permanent income theory holds that the family consumption function relating permanent consumption to permanent income is a straight line from the origin, this theory leads directly to the conclusion that changes in aggregate permanent income give rise to proportional changes in aggregate permanent consumption. For, if the proportion of income saved is indeed the same at all levels of family income, changes in the permanent income of all families combined will have no effect on the proportion of aggregate income saved or consumed. This particular conclusion reached by the permanent income theory agrees with that reached by the relative income theory but disagrees with that reached by the absolute income theory—although it must be noted that the conclusions are not strictly comparable, since the absolute and relative income theories are not expressed in terms of the same income and consumption concepts used in the permanent income theory.

TIME-SERIES ANALYSIS

Prior to World War II, empirical evidence on the aggregate consumption-income relationship was limited to such evidence as could be drawn from cross-section data. During World War II, however, estimates of national totals for personal consumption expenditures and disposable personal income became available for the first time on a comprehensive basis. Unlike cross-section data, these data show specifically how aggregate consumption expenditures have varied with aggregate disposable personal income.

These data for the years 1929–68, in constant (1958) dollars, are listed in Columns 2 and 3 of Table 9–2. Column 4 shows the average propensity to consume, obtained by dividing the figures in Column 3 by the figures in Column 2. Column 5 shows the marginal propensity to consume, obtained by dividing the change in consumption from one year to the next by the change in disposable income for the same two years. Thus, in one simple table we have what appear to be all the data we need to discover how aggregate consumption has varied with aggregate income over the past forty years.

In Chapter 7 we assumed that this relationship has the following properties: (1) the MPC is positive but less than one; (2) the MPC is the same for all changes in income; and (3) the APC decreases as income increases. How do these properties check out against the actual data? For the first, Column 5 shows that in 13 of 39 cases the MPC is either negative, equal to, or greater than one. For the second, there is considerable variability in the magnitude of the MPC; far from being the same for all annual changes in income, it seems to be different for every annual change in income. The third property is far from fully satisfied. In 11 of 40 cases, the APC rises with a rise in income. In no case, however, does it fall with a decline in income. All but 2 of these 11 exceptions are found in

TABLE 9-2 Disposable Personal Income and Personal Consumption Expenditures, 1929–1968 (billions of 1958 dollars)

(1) Year	(2) Disposable Personal Income	(3) Personal Consumption Expenditures	(4) APC	(5) MPC
1929	$150.6	$139.6	0.927	—
1930	139.0	130.4	0.938	0.793
1931	133.7	126.1	0.943	0.811
1932	115.1	114.8	0.997	0.607
1933	112.2	112.8	1.005	0.690
1934	120.4	118.1	0.981	0.646
1935	131.8	125.5	0.952	0.649
1936	148.4	138.4	0.933	0.777
1937	153.1	143.1	0.935	1.000
1938	143.6	140.2	0.976	0.305
1939	155.9	148.2	0.951	0.650
1940	166.3	155.7	0.936	0.721
1941	190.3	165.4	0.869	0.404
1942	213.4	161.4	0.756	−0.173
1943	222.8	165.8	0.744	0.468
1944	231.6	171.4	0.740	0.636
1945	229.7	183.0	0.797	−6.105
1946	227.0	203.5	0.896	−7.593
1947	218.0	206.3	0.946	−0.311
1948	229.8	210.8	0.917	0.381
1949	230.8	216.5	0.938	5.700
1950	249.6	230.5	0.923	0.745
1951	255.7	232.8	0.910	0.377
1952	263.3	239.4	0.909	0.864
1953	275.4	250.8	0.911	0.942
1954	278.3	255.7	0.919	1.689
1955	296.7	274.2	0.924	1.005
1956	309.3	281.4	0.910	0.571
1957	315.8	288.2	0.913	1.046
1958	318.8	290.1	0.910	0.633
1959	333.0	307.3	0.923	1.211
1960	340.2	316.2	0.929	1.236
1961	350.7	322.6	0.920	0.609
1962	367.3	338.4	0.921	0.952
1963	381.3	353.3	0.927	1.064
1964	407.9	373.7	0.916	0.767
1965	435.0	397.7	0.914	0.886
1966	458.9	418.1	0.911	0.854
1967	477.7	430.3	0.901	0.649
1968	497.6	452.6	0.910	1.121

SOURCE: *The National Income and Product Accounts of the United States, 1929–1965, Statistical Tables*, U.S. Department of Commerce, 1966, and *Survey of Current Business*, U.S. Department of Commerce, July 1969. Columns 4 and 5 were computed from Columns 3 and 4 by the author.

the fifteen-year period 1949–63. Does not all this contrary evidence force us to reject the consumption-income relationship we earlier assumed, since it appears to be largely inconsistent with the way that consumers actually apportion their aggregate disposable income between consumption and saving?

These apparently pronounced differences, properly interpreted, do not necessarily lead to this conclusion. It was almost inevitable that there would be differences, even pronounced differences for some years, between the consumption-income relationship we adopted in developing the simple theory of income determination and the consumption-income relationship revealed by the aggregate data. The reason is that the former is a relationship between income and consumption drawn on the assumption that all the factors that influence consumption, other than the level of income, remain unchanged; the latter, on the other hand, is based on the measured year-to-year values for consumption, which are what they are as a result of all the factors that influence consumption. In other words, the changes in actual consumption are certainly influenced by the changes in income, but there are other factors at work such as the price level, interest rates, distribution of income, consumer asset holdings, and consumer credit terms. These factors also change and in so doing exert some influence on the level of consumption spending from year to year.

Ideally, what is needed is a way of isolating the portion of the actual changes in consumption that were due to changes in income from the portion of these actual changes that were due to the changes in all the other factors that influence consumption. Although advanced statistical techniques enable us to derive quantitative approximations of this kind, for present purposes a simpler approach will suffice.

The data from Columns 2 and 3 of Table 9–2 are plotted in Figure 9–3. Each dot on the chart indicates the combination of personal consumption expenditures and disposable personal income for a given year between 1929 and 1968. A glance at the scatter of the dots shows that consumption does not vary with income exactly in the way suggested in Chapter 7. To do so, a straight line with its intercept above zero on the vertical axis and with a positive slope of less than 1 would have to pass through every dot in the figure. Although no straight line will do this, there is one that comes close to doing this, if we ignore the six dots for the years 1941–46. Omitting these six years, the straight line drawn in the chart is the straight line fitted to the data for 1929–40 and 1947–68 by the method of least squares.[15] The equation for this empirical consumption function is $C = 8.3 + 0.89\,Y$.[16] The vertical differences between the dots and this straight

[15] This is the straight line of "best fit" in the sense that the sum of the squares of the deviations between actual consumption and consumption indicated by the line, known as a *regression line* or simply as a *regression*, will be less for this straight line than for any other that could be fitted to the data.

[16] This equation is the familiar one for the consumption function used in Chapter 7 $(C = C_a + cY)$, only now, instead of hypothetical figures for C_a and c, actual values computed from the data for the United States for 1929–40 and 1947–68 yield the empirical consumption function for this period. C_a, which is here $8.3 billion, indicates the height of the consumption function, or the point at which it intercepts the vertical axis. As earlier described, it is the amount of consumption spending at the zero level of income, recognizing that in reality the

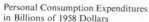

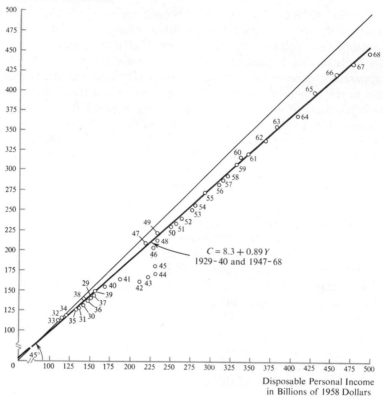

Personal Consumption Expenditures
in Billions of 1958 Dollars

$C = 8.3 + 0.89\,Y$
1929–40 and 1947–68

Disposable Personal Income
in Billions of 1958 Dollars

FIGURE 9–3 **Relationship Between Personal Consumption Expenditures and Disposable Personal Income, 1929–1968**

line are quite apparent. However, in view of the number of other factors that influence consumption spending, what is surprising is not that we find such differences but how small these differences actually are. The relationship between disposable income and consumption expenditures is remarkably close and seems to suggest that consumption is very largely explained by income. Since consumption so closely follows income, the many other factors that influence consumption spending, taken as a group, would seem to exert a far smaller influence on consumption spending than does the single factor of the level of disposable income.[17]

level of income could not fall to zero; c, which is here 0.89, is the MPC (or $\Delta C/\Delta Y$ with Y being disposable personal income), or the slope of the consumption function. If consumption were to change with every change in income as given by the equation, then for every change of $100 million in income, consumption would change by $89 million.

Actual empirical work on the consumption function involves much more complex functions than the simple equation in one variable here used. For an introduction to empirical estimates of the consumption function, see M. K. Evans, *Macroeconomic Activity*, Harper & Row, 1969, Ch. 3, and the references given there.

[17] Conclusions such as these, suggested by the single-equation, least-squares method used here, must be interpreted with great caution. This statistical method is acceptable for dealing with

A glaring exception to this conclusion is the period 1941–45, when the otherwise close relationship between consumption and disposable income seems to have broken completely.[18] The unusual distance of the dots for these years from the regression line is readily explained by the exceptional impact of certain nonincome factors in operation during World War II. Consumers spent much less than would have been expected solely on the basis of their incomes during these years because of the complete unavailability of certain durable goods like automobiles and the limited availability of other goods. To a lesser degree, consumers also spent less than would have been expected because of government pleas to save and purchase U.S. Savings Bonds. Less pronounced but still sizable departures from the regression line are found in the early postwar years. Although disposable income dropped to successively lower levels in 1945, 1946, and 1947, consumption expenditures rose sharply in 1945 and 1946 and moderately in 1947. As goods that had been unobtainable or obtainable only in limited quantities during the war years began to reappear on the market, the public went on a spending spree to meet long-unfulfilled needs. Although real disposable income showed virtually no overall change from 1944 to 1949, decreasing from 1944 to 1947 and increasing from 1947 to 1949, consumption expenditures rose in each of these years. The vast accumulation of wartime savings made the financing of these expenditures no problem. Thus, during the war years, and to a lesser extent during the early postwar years, consumption spending temporarily lost its close tie with income, as first it dropped far below (1941–45) and then rose above (1946–47) the amount that might have been expected solely on the basis of the level of disposable income.

---

variables that are independent, but the consumption and income variables are interdependent. Consumption depends on income, and income also depends on consumption. Therefore, we cannot conclude that the changes in income are the causes of changes in consumption from the fact that a line of regression shows a close relationship of consumption to income. The line of causation could run in the other direction, changes in income being caused by changes in consumption. What we have is a relationship of mutual interaction in which higher income means higher consumption and higher consumption means higher income. When we recall that consumption expenditures typically constitute almost two-thirds of gross national income, it is, furthermore, apparent that we would find a close relationship between income and consumption even if consumption were completely unrelated to income. Where interdependence exists between variables, the customary terminology of independent variable (income) and dependent variable (consumption) and the single-equation, least-squares method of deriving the relationship between the two is inappropriate. Each variable should have an equation of its own to explain the way it varies in a system of equations that are solved simultaneously. This is the method most frequently used today by econometricians in consumption-function estimation. For the introductory purpose of this chapter, we will limit ourselves to the simple one-equation, least-squares method, but it is essential to point out that this method is inherently defective in handling interdependent variables and that conclusions reached by this method cannot be taken at face value. For a discussion of this problem, see Evans, *op. cit.*, pp. 48–55.

[18] These years, 1941 to 1945, and also 1946 were omitted in computing the equation for the regression line. If included, they would have pulled the line down, thereby decreasing the differences between the line and the dots for these six years and increasing the differences between the line and the dots for the other years of the overall period. However, even if included, the dots for 1941–46 would still show the greatest departures from the regression line.

Since there is no doubt that the radical downward deviations of consumption spending from the regression line during the war years can be explained primarily by the consequences of the war itself, it is statistically proper to disregard these years in determining the "normal" consumption-income line that characterizes the relationship between income and consumption for a period of years other than those of major war. The year 1946, though a peacetime year, may also be disregarded as a year heavily influenced by the war.

The remaining years, 1929–40 and 1947–68, may be somewhat arbitrarily divided into three periods of approximately equal length: 1929–40, 1947–57, and 1958–68. A separate regression line fitted to the data for the prewar, earlier postwar, and later postwar periods should shed more light on the consumption-income relationship, for we can see how the fit of the line for each of these shorter periods compares with that for the overall period and how the shorter periods compare with one another.[19] The lines for the three shorter periods are shown in Figure 9–4, where the equation for the 1929–40 line is $C = 22.6 + 0.79\,Y$, for the 1947–57 line is $C = 15.2 + 0.86\,Y$, and for the 1958–68 line is $C = 15.5 + 0.88\,Y$.

In comparing each of these regression lines with that in Figure 9–3, which reflects the overall period, it is apparent that the regression lines for the shorter periods provide a better fit to the years on which each is based. It is, of course, still obvious that there are factors other than income influencing consumption during each of these three periods. In no year, however, did these factors produce a level of consumption spending that was widely different from that which would be expected on the basis of the regression line fitted to the data for each of these periods.

It is also apparent in Figure 9–4 that the regression line for the earlier postwar period has shifted noticeably upward relative to that for the prewar period. To show this more clearly, the line for the prewar period has been extended by a broken line to levels of income reached in the earlier postwar period. If consumers had chosen to allocate their income between consumption and saving in the same way in the earlier postwar period as they did in the prewar period, the dots for the earlier postwar years would have been scattered just above, just below, or right along this extended broken line. Instead, the dots all lie above this extended line. Apparently, in the earlier postwar period, consumers chose a permanently higher level of consumption relative to income than they chose in the prewar period.

The same relationship is found between the earlier and later postwar periods, but to a much less noticeable degree, as is evident from a comparison of the 1958–68 regression line with the broken line extended from the regression line for the earlier postwar period.[20] Although the congestion in the figure some-

---

[19] It would make for a more illuminating comparison if we could have each of the three periods begin with the economy at the upper or lower turning point in the business cycle and end similarly. However, the distortion introduced by the indicated choice of periods does not appear to be serious for the present purpose.

[20] There are no years omitted between these two periods as there are between the prewar and earlier postwar periods. We find that income in the first year of the later postwar period, 1958,

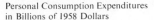

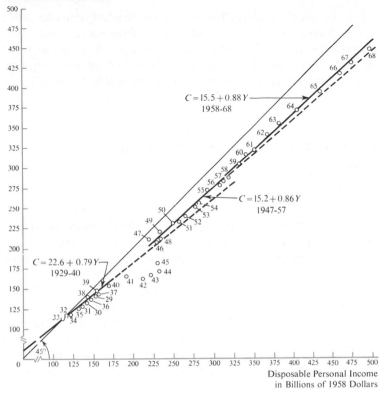

Personal Consumption Expenditures
in Billions of 1958 Dollars

$C = 15.5 + 0.88\,Y$
1958-68

$C = 15.2 + 0.86\,Y$
1947-57

$C = 22.6 + 0.79\,Y$
1929-40

$45°$

Disposable Personal Income
in Billions of 1958 Dollars

FIGURE 9-4   Relationship Between Personal Consumption Expenditures and Disposable Personal Income, 1929–1940, 1947–1957, and 1958–1968

what obscures the results, again the dots for all the years 1958–68 lie above the extended regression line for 1947–57. Here too consumers appear to have chosen a permanently higher level of consumption relative to income in the later years than they chose in the earlier postwar years.

The purpose of this examination of the time-series data has been to see what support, if any, the data give to the kind of theoretical consumption function we adopted in Chapter 7. When we look at the data on a year-to-year basis as a preliminary step, it is true that we find little support: The MPC varies considerably, at times even exceeding one or falling below zero, and the APC does not always fall with a rise in income. However, when we fit a linear regression line that "averages" the data for a number of years, we find that the line derived gives a good fit to the observations. If such a good fit is provided by a straight line with a positive slope less than one and an intercept with the vertical axis

is only $3 billion above the income of the last year of the earlier postwar period, 1957, whereas income of the first year of the earlier postwar period, 1947, is almost $50 billion above income of the last year of the prewar period, 1940. Other factors are involved, but this one in part accounts for the relatively smaller upward shift in the regression line for the later postwar period.

above zero, it follows, on the average for the period covered, that the APC decreases with rises in income and that the MPC is positive but less than one, the major assumptions made in the earlier theoretical consumption function. At this point at least, the empirical evidence seems to give substantial support to the type of theoretical consumption function we employed in Chapter 7.

CYCLICAL AND SECULAR CONSUMPTION-INCOME RELATIONSHIPS

The regression lines, or empirical consumption functions, derived from the time-series data for 1929–40, 1947–57, and 1958–68 may be described as *cyclical consumption functions*. Although each period covers more than a single business cycle, as that term is now most commonly understood, we may designate them as cyclical to distinguish between a period of such limited duration that the changes in consumption spending may be related to the cyclical ups and downs in disposable income and a much longer period, running over many decades, in which the changes in consumption spending may be related to the secular growth in disposable income. In such a long period, we may abstract from the cyclical fluctuations and derive what may be described as the *secular consumption function*. We may also describe the cyclical consumption function as the short-run consumption function and the secular as the long-run.

In the previous section, we saw that the theoretical consumption function adopted in Chapter 7 received support from the aggregate time-series data. It may be asked why this does not end the matter. Why now cyclical and secular consumption functions? In a formal sense, the answer is that the empirical consumption function revealed by the data for a long-run period is different from that revealed by the data for a short-run period. What is the basic relationship between disposable income and consumption if all factors that influence consumption—other than income—are absent? If the time-series data suggest a different relationship according to the time interval examined, our question remains unanswered until we explain this difference.

Figure 9–4 has already shown the nature of the problem. The regression line for 1929–40 gives a good fit to the data for that short-run period, and the regression lines for 1947–57 and 1958–68 give good fits to the data for those periods. In each case, the MPC is positive but less than 1 and is less than the APC—the properties we assumed in the theoretical consumption function of Chapter 7. Although this much is apparent, a problem arises from the fact that the line for each later period lies above the line we get by simply projecting the line for the preceding period. This suggests that the 1929–40 line may in turn have shifted upward from a regression line for a preceding short-run period, say 1919–28, and that a regression line to be computed for 1969–79 when that period is behind us will also have shifted upward from the 1958–68 line. If this indeed is what takes place over the long-run, the argument that the APC decreases with a rise in income is supported by the data *only* if we limit the application of that argument to a description of the short-run relationship between disposable income and consumption. Only then does the APC plainly decrease with increases in income. On the other hand, if from one short-run period to the next the entire function shifts upward, it does not necessarily follow that the APC will decrease with long-run increases in income. *The upward shift in the function could be such as to produce an APC that remains roughly unchanged in the long run.*

In fact, the data suggest that this is what actually does happen over the long run. To demonstrate this empirical long-run relationship, the data of Table 9–2 will not suffice. First, the period covered is not long enough. Second, annual data reflect changes within the short-run (intracycle) rather than changes between successive short-run periods (intercycle). Table 9–3 gives us the kind of

TABLE 9–3 **National Income and Personal Consumption Expenditures, 1869–1938 (billions of 1929 dollars)**

(1)	(2)	(3)	(4)
		Personal	
	National	*Consumption*	
Decade	*Income*	*Expenditures*	APC
1869–78	9.3	8.1	0.86
1874–83	13.6	11.6	.86
1879–88	17.9	15.3	.85
1884–93	21.0	17.7	.84
1889–98	24.2	20.2	.84
1894–1903	29.8	25.4	.85
1899–1908	37.3	32.3	.86
1904–13	45.0	39.1	.87
1909–18	50.6	44.0	.87
1914–23	57.3	50.7	.89
1919–28	69.0	62.0	.89
1924–33	73.3	68.9	.94
1929–38	72.0	71.0	0.99

SOURCE: Columns 2 and 3 are from Simon Kuznets, *National Product Since 1869*, National Bureau of Economic Research, Princeton Univ. Press, 1946, p. 119, and Column 4 is from Simon Kuznets, *National Income: A Summary of Findings*, National Bureau of Economic Research, Princeton Univ. Press, 1946, p. 53.

data we need for our purposes. The time span covered is seventy years, and the estimates for income in Column 2 and for consumption in Column 3 cover the full decades (here overlapping) that are shown in Column 1, so that the changes in the figures are changes between successive short-run periods.[21] The APC's

[21] Note that Table 9–3 shows national income rather than disposable personal income. For these early years, no satisfactory estimates of disposable personal income are available. Also, for the decades 1869–78 through 1914–23, estimates are for decades; and, for the decades 1919–28 through 1929–38, estimates are averages of annual estimates.

in Column 4 in this case represent the ratio of the estimated total of consumption expenditures for each ten-year period to the estimated total of national income for each corresponding ten-year period.

Table 9–3 shows us that although national income increased more than sevenfold from the 1869–78 period to the 1919–28 period, the APC varied only over the narrow range of 0.84 to 0.89. The last two periods, 1924–33 and 1929–38, both show an APC that is higher than the APC for any earlier period, the reason being that both these periods include the years of the Great Depression. Whether or not we include these last two periods, it is significant that the results listed in Column 4 are quite different from those given by the time-series data for the short-run periods examined earlier. In the short run, we found that as the level of income rose, the APC tended to decline; now we find that in the long run, as the level of income rises, the APC remains quite stable. Instead of finding that an ever smaller fraction of income was devoted to consumption as the level of income doubled and redoubled over the decades, we find that an approximately stable proportion of income was devoted to consumption decade after decade.[22]

The differences between the cyclical and secular relationships become more apparent when the data of Columns 2 and 3 in Table 9–3 are plotted, as in Figure 9–5. Apart from the dots for the 1924–33 and 1929–38 periods, both of which were pushed upward by the extraordinary severity of the Great Depression, a visually fitted straight-line consumption function drawn *from the origin* comes very close to passing through all the other dots in the figure. Unlike the general equation $C = C_a + cY$ for the *cyclical* straight-line consumption function that intersects the vertical axis above zero, the general equation for the *secular* straight-line consumption function is simply $C = bY$, in which the long-run MPC is designated by b to distinguish it from the short-run MPC, which is designated by c. The C_a constant becomes zero in the long-run function; the straight line intercepts the vertical axis at the origin. Since the APC equals the MPC at all levels of income for any straight-line consumption function that intersects the vertical axis at the origin, the long-run consumption function is one in which APC = MPC at all levels of income, in contrast to the short-run function in which APC > MPC at all levels of income. Another way of distinguishing the two functions is to describe the short-run, straight-line function as *nonproportional* and the long-run, straight-line function as *proportional*. This simply refers to the fact that, in the short run, consumption does not change proportionally with income; this proportion instead rises with falling income and falls with rising income. In the long run, consumption changes proportionally

[22] The findings of another study agree with those summarized in Table 9–3. See R. Goldsmith, *A Study of Saving in the United States*, Vol. 1, Princeton Univ. Press, 1955, pp. 393, 400.

Although the absolute magnitude of the ratio is different due to differences in definition, the ratio in the postwar period shows the same stability as the ratio in Table 9–3. For the overlapping periods, 1946–55, 1951–60, 1956–65, and 1961–68, the ratio of personal consumption expenditures to national income was 0.77, 0.77, 0.78, and 0.77, respectively. For these same periods, the ratio of personal consumption expenditures to disposable personal income in constant dollars was 0.92 in all four cases.

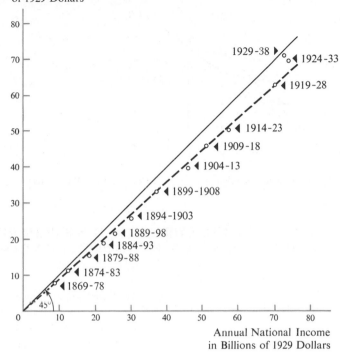

Annual Personal Consumption
Expenditures in Billions
of 1929 Dollars

FIGURE 9–5   Secular Consumption Function

with income; it remains roughly the same proportion of income as the level of income doubles and redoubles over the decades that make up the long run.

On the basis of the empirical consumption functions given in Figures 9–4 and 9–5, we may now construct Figure 9–6 to show in a general way the nature of the short-run and long-run functions suggested by the time-series data. Below the 45° line lies a line, labeled *LR*, that depicts the proportional relationship between disposable income and consumption suggested by the data for the long-run period. Each of the family of lines labeled *SR* represents the nonproportional relationship between disposable income and consumption suggested by the data for a short-run period. Figure 9–4 showed that the short-run consumption function shifted upward from the 1929–40 period to the 1947–57 period and again from the 1947–57 period to the 1958–68 period. Each successively higher *SR* line in Figure 9–6 represents such a shift in the function from one short-run period to the next. To understand the figure, it is essential to keep the time dimensions in mind. The *LR* curve relates to data covering an unbroken series of consecutive decades and designates the movement of consumption in relation to the movement of income decade by decade; each *SR* curve relates to only a segment of this long-run period and designates the movement of consumption in relation to the movement of income year by year over this segment of the long-run period.

173

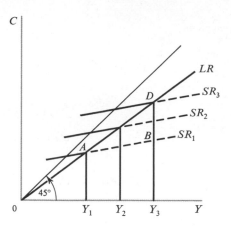

FIGURE 9–6 Secular and Cyclical Consumption Functions

RECONCILING THE CYCLICAL AND SECULAR RELATIONSHIPS: THE ABSOLUTE, RELATIVE, AND PERMANENT INCOME THEORIES

What is the "true" or underlying relationship between consumption and disposable personal income? If all other factors influencing consumption were absent, would consumption vary nonproportionally (along a curve such as *SR*) or proportionally (along a curve such as *LR*) as income changed? In other words, is the relationship basically nonproportional, as depicted by a consumption function such as *SR*, but with this function shifting upward over time at just the rate that produces a long-run proportional relationship? Or is the basic relationship one in which consumers as a group increase their consumption proportionally with the change in income, as shown by a consumption function like *LR*, with the nonproportional functions like *SR* indicating departures from the basic proportional relationship?

The absolute income theory takes the former position; the relative and permanent income theories take the latter position. We may see how the several theories lead to these positions as the theory of individual behavior of each is generalized to cover the aggregate behavior that lies behind the time-series data.

The Absolute Income Theory

The basic tenet of this theory is that the individual consumer's spending depends on the absolute level of his income. We saw earlier that this theory, when extended to aggregate behavior, indicates that increases in the aggregate income of all consumers should result in a decline in the APC, or the fraction of this aggregate income devoted to consumption. Since the actual level of aggregate income grows larger and larger in the long run, this theory leads to the conclusion that the APC should become smaller and smaller.[23] In terms of

[23] When the period under consideration stretches out over decades as it does here, it is essential to express the consumption and income variables in per capita form. If aggregate real income

174

Figure 9–6, as income increases in the long run, the theory would lead us to expect consumption to follow the path of an *SR* curve projected out to the right. However, the data for the long run show clearly that this is not what happens. One way of reconciling the position of the absolute-income theory that the basic relationship is nonproportional with the data that show the long-run relationship to be proportional is through an upward shift in the basic, nonproportional consumption function as a result of changes in factors other than income. There are a number of factors working in this direction: (1) With the increase in the accumulated wealth of households that has accompanied the long-run growth of income, households have tended to spend a larger fraction of any given level of income, thus contributing to an upward shift in the consumption function. (2) Over the present long-run period, there has been a continuing movement of population from the farms to the cities. Since the propensity of urban wage earners to consume is substantially higher than that of farm proprietors, this shift in population has contributed to an upward shift in the consumption function. (3) The percentage of older people in the population has increased over the long-run period. Since per capita consumption does not drop off as rapidly as does per capita income of this age group, the consumption function tends to shift upward as this age group becomes a larger part of the population. (4) New consumer goods have been introduced at a rapid rate over this long-run period. As more and more of these goods come to be regarded as "essentials" by the typical household, the consumption function tends to shift upward.

Factors like these, according to the absolute income theory, have caused the consumption function to shift upward by roughly the amount necessary to produce a proportional relationship between consumption and income over the long run and thus to prevent the appearance of what would otherwise be the nonproportional relationship that would be expected on the basis of the income factor alone.

The Relative Income Theory

Following the relative income theory, we reach the opposite position—that the basic relationship between consumption and income is proportional or is such that consumption in the long run tends to follow a path like that of the *LR* curve in Figure 9–6. The relative income theory must accordingly explain why the short-run relationship departs from the basic relationship that is held to be proportional.

When this theory, as earlier considered for individual consumer behavior, is extended to aggregate behavior, it is transformed into one that makes the ratio of consumption to income depend on the ratio of the *current income level* to the

---

grows no faster than total population, real income *per capita* remains unchanged, and there is no reason to expect a change in the APC on the basis of income alone. The situation that is relevant here is that in which real income per capita grows larger and larger, and in this situation the absolute-income theory holds that the ratio of real consumption per capita to real income per capita will become smaller and smaller.

peak income level previously attained. In the aggregate case, consumption in the current period thus depends on income in that period *relative* to the peak income level previously attained. In developing the peak income argument of the relative income theory, Duesenberry takes as his point of departure the known fact that income does not grow at an even pace over the long run but instead displays spurts and dips known as business cycles. These cyclical ups and downs in the level of income produce the nonproportional consumption-income relationship found in the short run. If there were no short-run income fluctuations of this sort, consumption would follow an uninterrupted path such as that traced out by the *LR* curve. However, there are such fluctuations in income that push the economy off the *LR* and onto the successive *SR* curves in an unbroken series over time.

To illustrate Duesenberry's theory in terms of Figure 9–6, let us suppose that a recession strikes when the economy is at income Y_1, which we will assume represents the highest level of income yet reached by the economy. As income falls over the course of the recession, consumers as a group will attempt to maintain the consumption level they enjoyed when income was at its peak. Consumers strongly resist any reduction in their standard of living but eventually find it necessary to cut back their expenditures gradually as their aggregate income falls. Thus, consumption falls but not proportionally with the fall in income. The economy moves down the SR_1 curve, and as it does, the APC rises and the APS falls. This reflects the fact that in an attempt to maintain the previously established higher standard of living, consumers will cut down their saving more than proportionally and consumption less than proportionally with the fall in income. Then, as recovery succeeds recession and the income level begins its move back toward its previous peak, consumption rises but less than proportionally with the rise in income. Consequently, the APC falls and the APS rises. The movement of consumption upward along the SR_1 curve is just the reverse of the earlier movement downward along this curve. Just as consumers cut down saving more than proportionally to defend the level of consumption on the downswing, so they increase saving more than proportionally on the upswing in order to restore saving to its previous level.

As the level of income rises to its previous peak and pushes on to higher ground, consumption does not follow the SR_1 line to the right past the previous peak income but instead shifts over to and follows the *LR* line. Since income is now rising to levels not previously attained, consumers no longer feel the increased urge to save that they felt during the period of recovery. They are now enjoying higher levels of income and feel better off and more certain of the future. They feel freer to consume a larger fraction of this income than the fraction of the below-peak income of the preceding recession. As income grows to ever higher peaks, the relationship between consumption and income is proportional; the APC and APS remain unchanged. If income should grow at a steady, uninterrupted rate over time, consumption would follow the proportional *LR* curve upward without varying. Since, however, it is the nature of the economy that a business downturn will succeed an upturn just as an upturn will succeed a downturn, instead of an uninterrupted movement along LR, the economy will slide into another recession after having established a new peak income of Y_2. The sequence is now a repetition of that just described but with the sequence traced out along the SR_2 curve from the peak income of Y_2. Recession will cause consumption to move down the SR_2 curve; recovery will cause it to move up the SR_2 curve until the previous peak at Y_2 is reattained. At this point consumption again will shift over to the LR curve, and the economy will move ahead to a new peak at Y_3.[24]

The aggregate behavior suggested by the relative-income theory may be expressed in a single consumption function that combines the properties of the long-run function, $C = bY$, and the short-run function, $C = C_a + cY$, as follows:

$$C = \overline{Y}(b - c) + cY$$

The peak level of income is indicated by $\overline{Y}$ and the current level of income by Y, so Y must for any time period be equal to or less than $\overline{Y}$. As long as income is steadily attaining new peaks during prosperity, peak income, $\overline{Y}$, will be equal to current income, Y, and the combined function reduces to the long-run consumption function $C = bY$.[25] The consumption-income relationship described by this function is the same as that described graphically by a movement along the LR line of Figure 9–6.

If a recession strikes and the current level of income drops below the peak attained earlier, $\overline{Y}$ is constant and greater than Y. With $\overline{Y}$ constant, $\overline{Y}(b - c)$ is also constant, so the constant C_a may be substituted for it. With current income below peak income, the combined function thus reduces to the short-run consumption function $C = C_a + cY$. As long as current income is below peak income, the consumption-income relationship described by this function is the same as that described graphically by a movement along an SR line of Figure 9–6.

---

[24]Although earlier we described such periods as 1929–40 and 1947–57 as cyclical periods, it was then noted that each such period is actually made up of more than one complete business cycle. Thus, in the period 1948–61, GNP in constant dollars moved from peak, P, to trough, T, to peak, P, as follows (Roman numerals indicate quarters): P–1948–IV, T–1949–IV, P–1953–II, T–1954–II, P–1957–II, T–1958–I, P–1960–II, and T–1961–I. Whether we measure from peak to peak or from trough to trough, each intervening period is a full business cycle, if we simply date the turning points of the cycle by the peaks and troughs in real GNP. It is to such cycles that the SR curves of Figure 9–6 most meaningfully apply. If one examines the consumption and disposable-income data quarter by quarter for each of the full cycles during 1948–61, he finds a marked tendency for the APC to rise and the APS to fall quarter by quarter during business-cycle contractions and vice versa during expansions, which is consistent with the nonproportional SR curves of Figure 9–6. Although a number of exceptions are found, most of these have a ready explanation. For example, the APC jumped up during 1950–III and 1951–I, despite the fact that these quarters are found in the expansion phase of the cycle. The reasons are the spending sprees following the outbreak of the Korean War (1950–II) and the entry of Communist China into that war (1950–IV).

[25]$C = b\overline{Y} - c\overline{Y} + cY$. As long as $\overline{Y} = Y$, $-c\overline{Y} + cY = 0$, and $C = b\overline{Y}$ or bY.

With recovery and the expansion of income beyond the peak attained previously, the combined function again reduces to the long-run function $C = bY$, and consumption again increases proportionally with income along the *LR* line.

The Permanent Income Theory

This theory, like the relative income theory, holds that the basic relationship between consumption and income is proportional, but the relationship here is between permanent consumption and permanent income. The estimates given in Table 9–3 show long-run proportionality between consumption and income with these quantities being measured quantities; discovering what the empirical long-run relationship between the corresponding permanent quantities may be requires estimates of these quantities. Professor Friedman has made such estimates going back to 1897, and the ratio of permanent consumption to permanent income revealed by his estimates for this long period is approximately constant. Thus, whether the ratio is derived from estimates of the kind in Table 9–3 or from estimates of permanent consumption and permanent income, a long-run relationship of proportionality is found.

The problem of reconciling the short-run nonproportional relationship with the long-run proportional relationship encountered in the cases of the absolute and relative income theories does not appear in the present case. As discussed earlier, the permanent income theory argues that the ratio of permanent consumption to permanent income is the same at all levels of family income, and this argument is directly translatable into a proportional relationship between aggregate permanent consumption and aggregate permanent income. A nonproportional short-run function such as *SR* in Figure 9–6 expresses a relationship between measured consumption and measured income. If our variables were permanent values instead of measured values, this function, it is argued, would be a proportional one. As aggregate permanent income increases to higher and higher levels in the long run, aggregate permanent consumption increases proportionally. Proportionality is found in both short run and long run, and there is no problem of reconciling different results as in the case of the other theories.

INCOME AND CONSUMPTION—A CONCLUDING NOTE

Empirical data covering well over a half-century tell us that the long-run relationship between consumption and income has been approximately proportional. We have seen that the relative and permanent income theories hold that this is the basic, underlying relationship between consumption and income, whereas the absolute income theory holds that the basic relationship is nonproportional. Which of the two is the "true" relationship is not a question of mere academic interest. If consumption is basically a nonproportional relationship, we may expect that an ever larger fraction of income will be saved as income grows over the long run, unless this tendency toward a rising APS (or declining APC) is offset by recurrent upward shifts in the consumption function itself, caused by such factors as the accumulating wealth of households, the growing urbanization of the population, the shifting age composition of the population, and the appearance of more and more new consumer goods that come to be regarded as "essentials" in the standard of living. Although some of these factors may continue to exert the same influence over the indefinite future, we cannot be certain that the influence of all such factors combined will be just enough to shift the consumption function upward at the rate necessary to give long-run proportionality between income and consumption.

The implications of such a development in terms of the simple theory of income determination are apparent. If the basic consumption function is nonproportional, then the higher the level of income grows, the greater the percentage of that income that will be devoted to saving. To maintain any given level of income, planned investment must equal planned saving. Therefore, to provide an ever growing level of income, an ever growing percentage of the economy's production would have to be channeled into investment in order to absorb the ever growing percentage of the economy's income that goes into saving. Whether businessmen will in fact find it profitable to carry planned investment to the required level will, in the absence of government intervention, decide the crucial question of whether or not the economy can continue to grow and generate ever higher levels of income and output.

If, on the other hand, the basic consumption function is proportional, this problem does not appear. Growth in income alone will not affect the fraction of income that is saved. Hence, the fraction of the economy's production that must be devoted to investment remains the same. Assuming that government's relative role remains unchanged, the economy faces the much less serious problem of expanding investment proportionally with the growth of income and output rather than more than proportionally. Whereas the whole complex of conditions that determine the amount of investment expenditures planned by businessmen might be sufficiently favorable to produce a growth of investment spending proportional with the growth of income, it is less likely that these conditions will be sufficiently favorable to produce a growth of investment spending that is more than proportional with the growth of income. This latter task is the one confronting us if the basic consumption function is nonproportional. In this situation, an inability to absorb such saving would stop the growth of income and output dead in its tracks.

Although this particular problem no longer carries the same forbidding implications that it did thirty years ago, we note it here to show that a practical question of great importance hinges in part on whether the basic consumption function is proportional or nonproportional. In the late thirties, before economists had the benefit of the data that later became available, the commonly held opinion followed Keynes in his belief that the basic consumption function was nonproportional. This contributed to another commonly held opinion, also suggested by Keynes, that the future would offer only more stagnation unless massive government deficits offset the volume of saving that was expected to grow more than proportionally with the growth of income. Of the several villains in this dismal picture, the belief in a nonproportional consumption function was one of no small importance.

The picture has changed over the years. More and more economists now feel that the basic consumption function is proportional, which amounts to a rejection of the major tenet of the absolute income theory. If this indeed is the "true" nature of the long-run consumption function, we may expect consumption to continue to absorb a relatively constant proportion of an ever-growing national output of goods and services over the years ahead. We will not have to depend for this result on uncertain special factors to shift a basically nonproportional long-run consumption function upward at the rate necessary to maintain consumption at a relatively constant proportion of output.

However, even though the basic relationship between consumption and income is one of proportionality, there is more to the explanation of consumption spending than the level of income. In the following chapter we will examine some other factors that influence consumption spending.

CHAPTER 10

OTHER FACTORS INFLUENCING CONSUMPTION

The empirical evidence on the consumption-income relationship examined in the preceding chapter certainly suggests that disposable income is by far the most important factor influencing consumption spending. More specifically, it suggests that disposable income is of far greater importance in explaining consumption on a decade-to-decade basis than it is on a year-to-year basis. By the same token, disposable income is of far greater importance in explaining consumption on a year-to-year basis than it is on a quarter-to-quarter basis. In other words, the shorter the time period under consideration, the more clearly do factors other than the level of income leave their mark on the level of consumption spending.

Even if we exclude the World War II and Korean War periods, *quarter-to-quarter* changes in income are not infrequently accompanied by changes in consumption in the opposite direction. In such cases, the effect of the change in income is more than offset by nonincome factors influencing consumption in the opposite direction. However, apart from 1942 and 1945–47, *year-to-year* changes in income are accompanied by year-to-year changes in consumption in the same direction. Here the effect of the change in income more than offsets any non-income factors influencing consumption in the opposite direction. Finally, not only have *decade-to-decade* changes in income since 1879 been accompanied by changes in consumption in the same direction, but, with the exception of the years of the Great Depression and World War II, the proportion of consumption to income in each decade has shown a remarkable stability. Thus, on a decade-to-decade basis, changes in income control almost completely.

What all this means is that changes in consumption spending, except perhaps from one decade to the next, cannot be explained solely on the basis of changes in disposable income. We cannot expect with any certainty that a change in income from one quarter to the next will be accompanied by a change in consumption in the same direction; the MPC is frequently negative. On the other hand, a change in income from one year to the next, if it is at all sizable, can with considerable certainty be expected to be accompanied by a change in consumption in the same direction. Even on a yearly basis, however, the change in consumption may be anywhere from a small to a large fraction of the change in income; the MPC is positive but highly variable.[1] In short, for the changes we are most interested in—annual and quarterly—we are forced to recognize that income alone is not the complete explanation of the changes in consumption we observe in the real world. Other factors are clearly at work.

Because these other factors exert varying influence on consumption in each year, we find that the straight-line, short-run consumption function for, say, 1958–68 does not pass through all the dots for these years in Figure 9–4.[2]

It is for this same reason that we find that the value for c, or 0.88, in the regression equation for this period, $C = 15.5 + 0.88\,Y$, does not tell us *for any particular pair of years* the amount of change in consumption that will accompany the indicated change in income from the first to the second of these two years. Instead, it tells us only the *average* relationship between changes in income and in consumption from year to year for the specific period of years in question.

From any perspective, the evidence clearly points to the presence of factors other than income that influence the amount that consumers spend in any year. While the income factor deserves and has received the major attention, the other factors are by no means of such little importance that they can be overlooked. In this chapter we will examine a few of them.

RATE OF INTEREST

While we may be reasonably certain that the rate of interest exerts some influence on the way in which any given level of aggregate disposable income is allocated between consumption and saving, we cannot say with equal certainty that a higher rate necessarily means that less of this income will be allocated to consumption and more to saving, or vice versa. The response to a change in the

---

[1] As was shown in Column 5 of Table 9–2, the MPC for year-to-year changes (omitting 1942–47) varied from a low of 0.305 in 1938 to a high of 5.7 in 1949. Large changes are found in adjoining years: from 1.236 in 1960 to 0.609 in 1961.

[2] This requires qualification. Even if a straight line fitted to the plotted values for any period passed exactly through each of the values, we could not unqualifiedly conclude that only income determined consumption. There could be any number of other factors, some working toward higher and some toward lower consumption spending, whose net influence in each and every year canceled out. The improbability of such a result is, however, apparent. Beyond this, even in the absence of any other such factors, we still could not conclude that income alone determined consumption from the fact that the straight line passed through each of the values. As noted in the preceding chapter, the two variables are actually interdependent, and the single-equation approach here employed ignores this interdependency and simply assumes that consumption is the dependent variable and income the independent variable.

rate of interest may be an increase *or* a decrease in the total amount saved out of the existing level of disposable income.

By first examining the saving behavior of the individual, we may see why the response, in the aggregate, may go in either direction. Apart from that portion of an individual's saving that is prompted by a desire to leave an estate, the individual's current saving, which amounts to currently foregone consumption, may be viewed as deferred consumption. Since the typical individual has a positive time preference (meaning that he prefers a dollar of present consumption to a dollar of future consumption), he is willing to abstain from a dollar of current consumption only in exchange for something more than a dollar of future consumption. Assuming a stable price level over time, the rate of interest a person can receive on saving indicates the amount of future consumption he can secure in exchange. For example, at a rate of 5 percent, he can exchange one dollar of current consumption for approximately one and a half dollars of consumption eight years later. The individual aiming at intertemporal utility maximization will, with a given interest rate, save the number of dollars out of his income such that the utility of the marginal dollar currently saved is just less than or just equal to the utility of the dollar sum to which that marginal dollar will have grown by a future date. He will, in other words, substitute future consumption for present consumption up to the point at which the marginal utility derived from the expenditure of the interest-augmented future dollar is just equal to or just greater than that derived from the expenditure of the current dollar.

Given the typical individual's schedule of preferences, it appears that the amount of saving out of his current income will therefore vary directly with the rate of interest. However, at the same time that a higher interest rate will tend to produce a substitution toward more future consumption and less present consumption, a higher interest rate also increases the individual's future income over what it would otherwise have been. Whatever the relationship between the individual's current income and expected future income had been, a higher interest rate raises his future income relative to his current income, which in turn may lead him to take part of this larger future income in the form of present consumption. Whether an individual with a given current income will save more on balance at a higher interest rate then depends on the relative strength of the *substitution effect*, which works toward more saving at higher interest rates, and the *income effect*, which works toward less saving at higher interest rates. For those lower-income individuals who will save only a relatively small part of their incomes even at high interest rates, the substitution effect will outweigh the income effect, and their saving will vary directly with the rate of interest. On the other hand, for individuals with large incomes who tend to save relatively large parts of these incomes, the opposite result may follow at high interest rates. The income effect may outweigh the substitution effect, with the result that higher interest rates will decrease the amount of current saving. For individuals in the former group, a supply curve relating the amount of saving to the rate of interest will slope upward to the right over any realistic range of interest rates. For individuals in the latter group, this supply curve may at some rate of interest display a backward bend, indicating that saving decreases with the interest rate for all rates above that at which this backward bend appears.[3]

There is a special case worth noting in which an individual's supply curve will be backward-sloping not only at high rates of interest but at all rates of interest. This is the case in which the saver's goal is simply the accumulation of a fixed dollar sum as of a particular future date and in which he saves whatever amount is needed to realize this goal. The higher the interest rate, the smaller then is the amount that he will find it necessary to save per time period in order to realize his goal.

Since individuals' supply curves may take on various shapes, the general shape of the aggregate supply curve, which is a summation of all these individual supply curves, can hardly be specified *a priori*. No simple, systematic relationship can be established between aggregate personal saving and the rate of interest. In view of this, many economists have taken an essentially agnostic position— they recognize that a change in the interest rate may change the amount of aggregate saving out of any given level of disposable income but that the direction of the change in saving, while most likely to be in the same direction as the change in the interest rate, may possibly be in the opposite direction.[4] This amounts to saying that interest-rate changes of the size found in actual experience do not, on balance, exert great influence on the amount of personal saving at any level of disposable income. There are forces working in both directions; these forces are in part offsetting and produce a net effect that is believed to be small.

The position that saving shows relatively little response to interest-rate changes has been widely held only since the thirties. It is quite different from that held by classical theory, in which the rate of interest was considered the most important factor influencing the amount of saving. Keynesian theory shifted the emphasis from the rate of interest to the level of income as the principal determinant of the amount the economy saves, regarding the former as of minor importance. As will be seen in Chapter 17, this is one of the essential differences between Keynesian and classical theory.

[3] For a detailed analysis in terms of indifference curves, see W. S. Vickrey, *Metastatics and Macroeconomics*, Harcourt, Brace & World, 1964, pp. 10–16.

[4] This contention should not be confused with an altogether different one—namely, that saving will tend to be placed in those institutions or in those forms that pay the highest rate of interest consistent with savers' other objectives. This says that persons, *once having saved*, will tend to seek the highest rate of interest for their savings; it does not say that a higher rate of interest will necessarily induce more saving at any given level of disposable income. Thus, the intense competition, including "price (interest-rate) competition," among savings institutions does not necessarily influence the amount of income saved but may affect only its allocation among the competing institutions.

PRICE LEVEL AND PRICE EXPECTATIONS

Another factor that influences aggregate consumption expenditures is the price level of consumer goods and services. If it rises, will aggregate consumption expenditures increase or decrease? If it falls, will these expenditures increase or decrease?

To answer these questions, several distinctions must initially be made. First, it is aggregate consumption expenditures and not expenditures on any particular good or service or group of goods and services with which we are concerned. A rise in the price of any single good or service for which there are good substitutes will lead to a transfer of expenditure to substitutes and a decrease in expenditures on the good that has risen in price, and vice versa. However, for a rise or fall in the *price level* of consumer goods and services (e.g., the Consumer Price Index), there can be no goods or services that are substitutes or to which expenditures may be diverted.[5] The only substitution now possible is one of personal saving for consumption expenditures or consumption expenditures for personal saving. Consumers may, in other words, react to any change in the price level, rise or fall, by spending either more or less of their incomes for goods and services.

How consumers as a group may react depends in the main on a second distinction, that between a change in the price level accompanied by a proportional change in aggregate current-dollar disposable income and a change accompanied by a more or less than proportional change in aggregate current-dollar disposable income.[6] If current-dollar disposable income rises or falls proportionally with the rise or fall in the consumer price level, constant-dollar or real disposable income remains unchanged. If it rises more or less than proportionally, real disposable income, of course, increases or decreases, respectively.

[5] Since a rise in the consumer price level does not involve proportional changes in the prices of all goods and services, some degree of substitution of goods that have risen relatively little or possibly even fallen in price for goods that have risen relatively sharply in price remains a possibility. However, it is also true that the cost to the average consumer of any likely assortment of goods and services, even after substitutions have been made wherever possible, will be higher after the rise in the price level than it was before. The greater the rise in the price level, the more certain this is to be true. This is all that is needed to qualify here as a rise in the price level as seen by the average consumer.

[6] There is no simple or unvarying relationship between a change in the consumer price level and a change in the level of current-dollar disposable income. It is possible for the two to change in opposite directions, although quarter-to-quarter data for recent years show, with few exceptions, changes in the same direction. Periods in which prices, not only of consumer goods and services but also of the other goods and services included in GNP, are rising are typically periods during which GNP in current dollars will be rising. Disposable income will rise along with GNP, but whether it rises more or less rapidly than GNP depends especially on how much of the enlarged gross income flow is diverted into tax receipts and retained corporate profits and how much the remaining gross income flow is supplemented by government transfer payments.

Now, given a rise in the price level of consumer goods and services, will aggregate consumption expenditures rise or fall? If a rise (fall) in the consumer price level is offset by a proportional rise (fall) in aggregate current-dollar disposable income, consumers as a group are, in terms of real income, no better or worse off than they were before and presumably will hold real consumption expenditures and saving unchanged.[7] This is the conclusion we reach on the basis of the Keynesian argument that real consumption is a function of real income.[8]

"Money Illusion"

Although there is no change in real income, a change may nonetheless occur in real consumption if consumers are subject to what economists call "money illusion."[9] Suppose, for example, that during a given time period the consumer price level rises 10 percent and the current-dollar disposable income of each family rises 10 percent. Those families that recognize that their money income is unchanged in real terms suffer no money illusion, and, other things being equal, will probably maintain their consumption and saving unchanged in real terms. They will increase both spending and saving in current dollars by 10 percent. Other families may be subject to a money illusion in either of two ways. Some may see only that the price level has risen and somehow overlook the fact that their current-dollar disposable income has risen proportionally. They will feel worse off and typically will increase the absolute amount of their consumption expenditures and increase the fraction of their disposable income devoted to consumption. Other families may see only the rise in their current-dollar disposable income and overlook the proportional rise in the price level. These families will feel better off and typically will increase the absolute amount of their consumption expenditures but decrease the fraction of their income devoted to consumption.

If we assume that no widespread money illusion exists among consumers, we may expect no appreciable change in the fraction of aggregate current-dollar disposable income devoted to consumption expenditures as a result of a change

[7] Among other difficulties passed over here is the possible redistribution of current-dollar income between the fixed income group and other groups that may result from a changing price level. Incomes of some groups may rise or fall faster than prices, of others slower than prices, and of still others not at all. To the extent that the marginal propensity of these groups to consume differs, an impact on real consumption expenditures would be expected. Income redistribution as a specific factor influencing real consumption expenditures will be considered in a later section.

[8] Although attention is limited here to the effect of price-level changes, aggregate consumer spending as well as spending on individual goods and services may be affected by *relative* price changes quite apart from changes in the price level. (See G. Ackley and D. B. Suits, "Relative Price Changes and Aggregate Consumer Demand," *American Economic Review*, Dec. 1950, pp. 785–804.)

[9] This term was coined by Irving Fisher, who used it to describe "a failure to perceive that the dollar or any other unit of money expands and shrinks in value." (See *The Money Illusion*, Adelphi, 1928, p. 4.)

in the consumer price level that is accompanied by a proportional change in current-dollar disposable income. In terms of the aggregate consumption function diagram, if we measure real income and real consumption on the two axes, the economy remains at the very same points on the income and consumption axes.

What about changes in the consumer price level that are not matched by compensating changes in current-dollar disposable income? Such changes mean changes in real disposable income, and a change in real disposable income should be expected to have a direct effect on real consumption expenditures. A rise in prices that leads to a fall in real disposable income should move consumers as a group back down the aggregate short-run consumption function. At this new point on the function, there is an absolute decrease in real consumption expenditures and an increase in the fraction of real disposable income devoted to consumption expenditures. Conversely, a fall in prices that leads to a rise in real disposable income moves consumers as a group up along the function with an absolute increase in real consumption expenditures and a decrease in the fraction of real disposable income devoted to consumption expenditures.

While these conclusions are valid, the changes in real consumption expenditures that result under these circumstances are not caused directly by the changes in the consumer price level but are brought about by the changes in real disposable income that accompany changes in the consumer price level. We already know from the empirical short-run consumption function that real consumption expenditures fluctuate with real income in this fashion. In short, we can say that a changing price level may affect real consumption expenditures to the extent that the changing price level is not offset by changes in current-dollar disposable income, provided that consumers are not subject to money illusion.

Price Expectations

In the preceding discussion, we were concerned with the relationship between *realized* changes in the consumer price level and *realized* changes in aggregate disposable income; we based our conclusion on the assumption that consumer spending behavior was determined *only* by the realized changes experienced by consumers in any time period. There are periods, however, in which the consumer price level is rising, current-dollar disposable income is rising to match prices, and real consumption expenditures are increasing. Note that we are now suggesting an increase in real consumption expenditures with no change in real disposable income. This result frequently occurs when the consumer price level has been rising fairly sharply for some time. It reflects the fact that consumers are devoting a larger fraction of real income to consumption expenditures "today" in *expectation* of still higher prices "tomorrow." Conversely, expectations of a lower price level in the future can lead to a postponement of real consumption expenditures currently, even though real disposable income has not fallen in the current period.

These changes in real consumption expenditures are the result not of the then current price level but of expectations as to what the future price level will be. Price-level expectations are but one of a number of types of expectation that may influence real consumption expenditures currently. For many families an important factor may be expectations as to the future level of their income. Consumption expenditures are influenced to some extent also by the general expectations concerning the short-run outlook for expansion or contraction in business activity. Finally, any developments that give rise to expectations of large-scale war will produce expectations of shortages and higher prices for goods. These expectations in turn will increase real consumption expenditures in the current period.[10]

Consumer expectations with respect to all kinds of changes—economic, social, and political—can each have their effect on real consumption expenditures in any period. While noted here in connection with the price level, expectations in this more general sense may properly be considered as a separate factor influencing real consumption expenditures. In this brief survey, however, space will not permit further discussion of expectations as a separate factor.[11]

DISTRIBUTION OF INCOME[12]

The level of aggregate disposable income is the most important factor that influences the level of aggregate consumption expenditures. However, with any given *level* of disposable income, the level of consumption expenditures resulting therefrom tends to be larger or smaller depending on the *distribution* of that income by income class. In general, the more equal that distribution is, the larger the fraction devoted to consumption tends to be. For example, an economy in which the 25 percent of the families with the highest incomes receive 30 percent

---

[10] See footnote 24 on p. 177. During the third quarter of 1950 and the first quarter of 1951, real consumption expenditures changed much more than would have been expected on the basis of the changes in real disposable income. Expectations, widely held by consumers, of shortages and higher prices clearly played a dominant role in the spending splurges of these two quarters.

[11] The major work on the influence of consumer expectations and attitudes on consumer spending has been done at the Survey Research Center of the University of Michigan. This work began in 1946 and continues to date. See, for example, E. Mueller, "Effects of Consumer Attitudes on Purchases," in *American Economic Review*, Dec. 1957, pp. 946–65, and "Consumer Attitudes: Their Significance and Forecasting Value," in *The Quality and Significance of Anticipations Data*, National Bureau of Economic Research, Princeton Univ. Press, 1960, pp. 149–81.

[12] Discussion here is limited to personal distribution or distribution by income group. For distribution by occupational group and functional share, see I. B. Kravis, "Relative Income Shares in Fact and Theory," in *American Economic Review*, Dec. 1959, pp. 917–49, and I. Friend and I. B. Kravis, "Entrepreneurial Income, Saving, and Investment," in *American Economic Review*, June 1957, pp. 269–301. At the same income levels, the marginal propensity of business owners and farmers to save is found to be greater than that of others. This suggests that shifts in the functional distribution of income over the business cycle may explain part of the short-run changes observed in consumption spending.

of total income and the 25 percent of the families with the lowest incomes receive 20 percent of total income is most likely to show a larger fraction of that total income devoted to consumption than if the top 25 percent of the families received 45 percent of the total income and the bottom 25 percent of the families received only 5 percent of the total income. This is suggested by the fact that the fraction of disposable income allocated to consumption is higher at low levels of family income and lower at higher levels of family income. The family budget data of Table 9-1 gave us in Figure 9-1 an empirical family consumption function that showed this relationship.

While we may say that the more equal the distribution of income, the higher the fraction of income devoted to consumption tends to be, it does not necessarily follow from this that, other things being equal, any change in the distribution of a given level of income against higher-income families and in favor of lower-income families will mean an increase in the fraction of that level of aggregate disposable income that is allocated to consumption.[13] Although a redistribution would appear offhand to work in this direction, a number of qualifications that limit the quantitative importance of such changes and even question the direction of such changes must be noted:

1. The first is the fact that changes in the distribution of income in any short period, even a period as long as a decade, are moderate.[14] Since the existing occupational wage differences, distribution of property ownership, differences in productive ability, and the whole complex of institutional factors that determine the distribution of income show little change from year to year, changes in the distribution of income from year to year are correspondingly small and can have only a small effect on the fraction of aggregate disposable income devoted to consumption from year to year. Apparently the effect becomes significant only over a period of a decade or several decades. Of course, a deliberate public policy designed to reduce income inequality rapidly, regardless of its consequences, could alter this conclusion. Based on our past experience, however, even with a progressive tax structure and other governmental measures that have contributed noticeably to less inequality, the year-to-year, or even decade-to-decade, changes in income distribution have not been a very important factor influencing the amount of consumption expenditures at any given level of income.

[13] Since the long-run trend in the distribution of income in the U.S. and other free economies has been toward less inequality, unless otherwise indicated all references to changes in distribution in the following pages will be to changes toward less inequality.

[14] The share of total personal income of all families received by the 20 percent of families with the lowest personal incomes changed from 4.8 percent in 1950 to 4.6 percent in 1960. For successively higher quintiles, the changes were from 10.9 percent to 11 percent, from 16.1 percent to 16.3 percent, from 22.1 percent to 22.6 percent, and, for the top quintile—the 20 percent of families with the highest personal incomes—from 46.1 percent to 45.5 percent. (Data for 1950 from *U.S. Income and Output*, 1958, Table II–13, p. 161; data for 1960 from *Survey of Current Business*, July 1962, Table 18, p. 16.) Thus, over a full decade, the largest change was the reduction in the share of the top quintile—of only 0.6 percent. (For an analysis of the factors affecting long-term changes in income inequality, see S. Kuznets, "Economic Growth and Income Inequality," in *American Economic Review*, March 1955, pp. 1–28.)

2. Given any change in income distribution, a second qualification arises from the fact that the increase in the fraction of income devoted to consumption may be much less than is suggested by a comparison of the way that families at different income levels divide their total incomes between consumption and saving. Redistribution of a *given* aggregate income involves compensating changes in family income, additions to the incomes of some families and reductions in the incomes of others. Families do not ordinarily allocate an addition to or a reduction in their incomes between consumption and saving in the same way as they allocate their total incomes between consumption and saving. The *mpc* describes the allocation of additions to or reductions in the family's disposable income; the *apc* describes the allocation of the family's total disposable income. This distinction is important because the differences in the *mpc* at various family income levels are much smaller than the differences in the *apc* between these same family income levels.[15] If it is true that the immediate effect of any redistribution of income on aggregate consumption expenditures depends on the *mpc* rather than the *apc* at various family income levels, it follows that the prospective expansionary effect on consumption of a change in distribution may be overestimated if this effect is gauged from differences in the *apc* rather than from differences in the *mpc*.

In fact, it is possible that the *mpc* may be virtually the same at each level of family income. In such a case, even though the *apc* at higher incomes may be much below what it is at lower incomes, a change in distribution would have virtually no effect on consumption expenditures. According to some findings, something approaching this result may be found in actual U.S. experience.[16] Without pushing the argument to this extreme, however, the absence of pronounced differences in the *mpc* at different levels of family income has been adopted as one support for the argument that income redistribution, at least of the order realized in recent years, is a factor that does not significantly increase the fraction of disposable income allocated to consumption expenditures.

3. The effect on consumption to be expected from a given redistribution of income differs according to whether we follow the absolute, relative, or perma-

---

[15] Reference here is to the evidence supplied by budget studies that relate measured consumption to measured income as in Figure 9–1. There the moderate curvature of the empirical family consumption function indicates moderate differences in the *mpc* at different family income levels. If the function were a straight line, the *mpc* would be the same at all levels of family income. The *apc* at different levels of family income could be shown in Figure 9–1 by the slopes of a set of straight lines from the origin to various points on the consumption function. (Such a set of *apc* lines is given in Figure 9–2.) For any two levels of family income, a comparison of the difference between the slopes of the two lines from the origin with the difference in the slope of the consumption function itself at these two income levels will show the difference in the *apc* to be greater than the difference in the *mpc*.

[16] See H. Lubell, "Effects of Redistribution of Income on Consumers' Expenditures," in *American Economic Review*, March 1947, pp. 157–70, and "Correction," in *American Economic Review*, Dec. 1947, p. 930. See also R. A. Musgrave and M. S. Painter, "The Impact of Alternative Tax Structures on Personal Consumption and Saving," in *Quarterly Journal of Economics*, Aug. 1948, pp. 475–99, and M. Bronfenbrenner, T. Yamane, and C. H. Lee, "A Study in Redistribution and Consumption," in *Review of Economics and Statistics*, May 1955, pp. 149–59.

nent income theory. As we will see, the relative income theory suggests that a decrease rather than an increase in consumption expenditures may be expected as a result of redistribution. The absolute income theory suggests just the opposite result, and the permanent income theory suggests that the amount of permanent consumption out of any given level of permanent income will be unaffected by a redistribution of that income.

Consider first the case in which spending and saving depend exclusively on absolute income. If a redistribution takes place with no change in the level of income, higher-income families will move down and lower-income families will move up the family consumption function in Figure 9–1. If each family regards its new position as permanent and immediately adjusts its spending to the amount that families at this income level customarily spend, we may expect an increase in the *apc* of the higher-income families after they move down and a decrease in the *apc* of the lower-income families after they move up. Since the *apc* of the lower-income families, though smaller after the redistribution than before, is still above the *apc* of the higher-income families, though this is larger after the redistribution than before, the net effect will be an increase in aggregate consumption expenditures at the given level of income.[17]

Consider next the case, in which relative income controls completely. The result is then quite different. With no change in aggregate disposable income, redistribution by definition means a change in relative incomes. All along the income scale, each family adjusts its spending to its new income level, not in accordance with the new, absolute level of that income, but in relation to the spending patterns of the families whose consumption standards it emulates. As the income of the higher-income families is reduced through redistribution, the pressure on families just below to "keep up with the Joneses" is reduced downward in accordance with their reduced incomes. This process will exert its influence all the way down the income scale. The lowest-income families may still have no choice but to spend all their higher incomes, since these incomes are just sufficient to cover basic necessities. Other families, however, may now find it possible to save a part of their income that was previously used to purchase the fancier automobile, the trip abroad, the backyard swimming pool, and other such goods and services that were largely emulative purchases. A redistribution, instead of leading to increased consumption, may actually decrease consumption, because the lessening of inequality wipes out some of society's emulative spending.

Finally, the case in which permanent consumption is related to permanent

[17] For example, as a result of redistribution a $21,000 family that had saved $6,300 (*aps* = 0.30) and spent $14,700 (*apc* = 0.70) becomes a $20,000 family that now saves $5,600 (*aps* = 0.28) and spends $14,400 (*apc* = 0.72). A $4,000 family that had saved nothing (*aps* = 0) and spent $4,000 (*apc* = 1) now becomes a $5,000 family that saves $200 (*aps* = 0.04) and spends $4,800 (*apc* = 0.96). The increase in saving of the low-income family will not be as great as the decrease in saving of the high-income family; the decrease in consumption of the high-income family will not be as great as the increase in consumption of the low-income family. Thus, the two families that showed total consumption of $18,700 and total saving of $6,300 before the redistribution show total consumption of $19,200 and total saving of $5,800 after the redistribution, although the combined income of the two families is $25,000 in both cases.

income in the way indicated by the permanent income theory gives yet a different result. Recall that this theory holds that the ratio of permanent consumption to permanent income is the same at all levels of family income and that there is zero correlation between transitory consumption and transitory income. A redistribution toward greater equality will provide increments of income to lower-income families and the opposite for higher-income families. These additions to and subtractions from income may at first be regarded by these families as positive and negative transitory-income components. In this case, the permanent income theory holds that neither the lower-income families nor the higher-income families will change the amount of their consumption, so that the redistribution is without effect on consumption. A program of redistribution that is maintained year after year will eventually cause the families gaining or losing income to regard these as permanent changes in income and will thus raise the permanent incomes of lower-income families above what they otherwise would have been. However, the aggregate of permanent consumption is unaffected to the extent that the ratio of permanent consumption to permanent income is, as the theory holds, the same for all otherwise similar families, regardless of the level of their permanent income. The result therefore appears to be the same in the short period, when the redistribution may be viewed by those who gain or lose from it as transitory changes in income, and in the longer period, when the redistribution is viewed by those who gain or lose from it as permanent changes in income.

Since each of the several theories suggests a quite different result, one cannot choose one result over another without first choosing one theory over another. And the relative merits of the competing theories continue to be sharply debated. Few economists so far have accepted the permanent-income theory in its extreme form, and therefore few economists would deny that redistribution has some effect on consumption. However, the importance of this effect is a matter on which there is little agreement. In contrast to the belief generally held thirty years ago, economists no longer believe that raising the level of aggregate consumption spending by redistribution is the simple matter they once thought it to be.

CONSUMER ASSETS

Some economists have attached considerable importance to the volume of assets, financial and nonfinancial, accumulated by consumers as a factor influencing consumption expenditures. Financial assets include cash, demand deposits, savings accounts with banks and with savings and loan associations, cash value of life-insurance policies, stocks and bonds—including U.S. Savings Bonds —and other types of financial claims held by consumers.[18] Nonfinancial or

---

[18] As a factor influencing consumption expenditures, economists usually count only "liquid assets," which exclude any financial assets, like conventional mortgages, that cannot be quickly

physical assets, in the broadest sense, include all valuable physical property owned by consumers, including land, buildings, automobiles, appliances, clothing, and even the food on the pantry shelf. For present purposes, that part of nonfinancial assets composed of durable consumer goods is particularly relevant, and reference to nonfinancial assets will mean these goods.

In recent decades, apart from several years during the Great Depression, consumers have saved a portion of their aggregate disposable income every year, and the larger part of this saving appears as an increase in their financial assets. The remaining part appears as an increase in one type of nonfinancial asset, residential structures purchased by consumers.[19] Each year consumers devote a portion of their aggregate consumption expenditures to the purchase of durable goods such as automobiles, refrigerators, and the like; the balance of consumption expenditures is for nondurable consumer goods and services. The amount spent on durable goods during the year less the depreciation on the total stock of these goods during the year appears as an increase in the stock of durable goods.

In terms of the national income accounts, the change in the volume of financial assets held by consumers in any year depends, first, on the collective decisions of consumers about the division of their disposable income between consumption and saving and, second, on how saving is apportioned between financial assets and the one nonfinancial asset—houses. The change in the stock of durable goods—total purchases less depreciation—depends on consumers' decisions about how that part of disposable income that is devoted to personal consumption expenditures shall be divided between spending for durable goods and spending for nondurable goods and services.

The effect of a change in the volume of financial assets held by consumers on the level of consumption expenditures is different from that of a change in the stock of durable consumer goods. We will consider separately the effects of changes in the amounts of these two types of assets.

---

converted into cash at fixed prices. Such assets are also usually considered without allowance for financial liabilities of consumers, the major part of which is debt outstanding as the result of purchases of houses and durable consumer goods.

[19]Apart from interest paid by consumers and personal transfer payments to foreigners, which are not regarded as expenditures by consumers for final product, all expenditures by consumers other than for newly constructed housing are treated in the national income accounts as personal consumption expenditures. Expenditures by consumers for such housing are part of gross private domestic investment on the product side; this is matched by an equal amount of gross saving on the income side. As persons devote funds to down payments on the purchase of houses or to the reduction of the principal of mortgage debt on houses previously purchased, such funds are treated as part of personal saving. As consumers devote funds to the reduction of the principal of any other indebtedness, such as installment debt on automobiles and other consumer durables, such funds too are part of personal saving, but the original purchase of these goods, unlike the purchase of houses, was treated as personal consumption expenditures, and not as investment expenditures.

Financial Assets

It is reasonable to expect that, on the average, the family with a higher disposable income will spend more than the family with a lower disposable income, other things being equal. It may also seem reasonable to expect that, on the average, the family with a larger accumulation of financial assets will spend more than will the family with a smaller accumulation of financial assets, other things (including the disposable income of each family) being equal. The rationale here is that a family's urge to add still more to its holdings of financial assets diminishes as its holdings of these assets increase. If most families reacted this way, as the total holdings of financial assets of all families increased over the years, a larger fraction of aggregate disposable income would be devoted to consumption and a smaller fraction to saving or to the accumulation of still more financial assets. In terms of the aggregate consumption function, this suggests that the entire curve would shift upward with the growth in the volume of financial assets, thereby producing a higher APC at each possible level of aggregate disposable income.

As a case in point, the upward shift in the aggregate consumption function in the earlier of the postwar periods shown in Figure 9-4 may be attributed to the huge amount of savings bonds, bank deposits, and other liquid assets accumulated by consumers during World War II. Recall that the upward shift in consumption was not limited just to consumption in the first few postwar years, which could be readily explained as spending to satisfy deferred demand. Instead, this shift characterizes later years as well. It may be argued that during the war years families built up a volume of liquid assets that they regarded as adequate or more than adequate to meet any future emergencies. With this accumulation of cash-equivalents to fall back on in case of need, families felt free in the postwar period to devote a larger fraction of their current disposable income to consumption. In contrast, a smaller fraction of disposable income had been devoted to consumption in the prewar period, for then only a small minority of the nation's families had an appreciable amount of such assets.

At first glance this explanation suggests a clear-cut connection between the volume of financial assets held by consumers and the fraction of their disposable income devoted to consumption. As before, however, qualifications appear as soon as we examine this theory a little more closely.

For one thing, the size of the consumption-inducing effect depends on the ownership distribution of these financial assets by income class.[20] An increase in the volume of these assets, if concentrated in the hands of upper-income families, may give little or no stimulus to consumption. Upper-income families save a large fraction of their incomes in any event, and it is doubtful whether the further growth in their holdings of financial assets would cause the fraction of their income that is saved to decrease.

---

[20] For a study of liquid-asset ownership by spending units grouped by income and also by occupation, education, and region, see M. E. Kreinen, "Analysis of Liquid Asset Ownership," in *Review of Economics and Statistics*, Feb. 1961, pp. 76–80.

A related qualification, which applies regardless of ownership distribution, is the possibility that for many families a taste of financial assets simply whets the appetite for more. Even families of moderate income may react this way. Their original preference for consumption over saving may, after the first taste of financial assets, change to a preference toward saving as the means of accelerating the accumulation of financial assets.[21] Although this may be far from common for many families, particularly for low-income families, it is still a factor to be considered. This in itself is sufficient to raise some doubt as to the direct connection posited above between the volume of financial assets held by consumers and the level of consumer expenditures at any given level of income.

Finally, the mere dollar volume of financial assets may suggest incorrect relationships; only the real value of the dollar volume held at any time is pertinent. A changing price level will cause the real value of a given volume of financial assets to rise or fall. Except for holdings of stocks, shares in mutual funds, or other such assets whose current-dollar valuation tends to rise and fall with the price level, all other financial assets are fixed-dollar assets. A family with $10,000 in fixed-dollar assets will, barring a money illusion, recognize a rise in the price level as a decrease in the real value of its fixed-dollar assets and a fall in the price level as an increase in the real value of these assets. For example, a doubling in the price level will be seen to cut in half the purchasing power of the $10,000. If a rise in the price level is matched by a proportional rise in the family's current-dollar disposable income so that its real income remains unchanged, it may nevertheless cause a reduction in its real consumption expenditures due to the depressing effect of the price-level change on the real value of its holdings of fixed-dollar assets. Conversely, if a fall in the price level is matched by a proportional fall in the family's current-dollar disposable income, it may increase its real consumption expenditures due to the expansionary effect exerted by the rise in the real value of its holdings of fixed-dollar assets.

The consumption-stimulating effect of an increase in the real value of financial assets brought about by a fall in the price level has been named the *Pigou Effect* after A. C. Pigou, the eminent British economist who first clearly set forth the relationships between consumption, financial assets, and the price level.[22] We will examine the Pigou Effect in more detail in Chapter 19 and find

[21] Note that a revision of preferences toward saving and away from consumption is also one toward income and away from consumption. Less consumption and more saving with the saving devoted to the acquisition of income-producing financial assets is a means of raising the level of family income and making possible still more saving.

[22] "The Classical Stationary State," in *Economic Journal*, Dec. 1943. See also his "Economic Progress in a Stable Environment," in *Economica*, Aug. 1947, reprinted in F. A. Lutz and L. W. Mints, eds., *Readings in Monetary Theory*, Irwin, 1951, pp. 241–51.

Less familiar than the Pigou Effect is a comparable effect on consumption following from the change in the real value of assets brought about by a change in the interest rate. A fall in the rate of interest increases the value of assets and may thereby cause asset-owners to raise consumption and reduce saving, although the income flow generated by their assets is unaffected by the fall in the interest rate. See B. P. Pesek and T. R. Saving, *Money, Wealth, and Economic Theory*, Macmillan, 1967, in which pp. 11–21 provide an introductory statement on the interest-induced wealth effect and the price-induced wealth effect, or Pigou Effect. See also M. J. Bailey, *National Income and the Price Level*, McGraw-Hill, 1962, Chapter 7.

that some writers have assigned it a highly important theoretical role that goes beyond that of a minor influence on consumption spending.

Despite these complications, which make the relationship between the volume of financial assets held by consumers and the fraction of their disposable income devoted to consumption a far from simple one, it seems that the level of real consumption expenditures generated at any level of real income does vary directly with the real value of the stock of financial assets held by consumers. However, although there seems to be a direct relationship here, the quantitative impact of this relationship is yet another question. All we can say with certainty is that changes in the real value of the volume of financial assets held by consumers do exert some direct effect on real consumption expenditures from any given level of real income.[23]

Nonfinancial Assets—The Stock of Durable Consumer Goods

Is there the same kind of direct relationship between the stock of durable consumer goods and real consumption expenditures? Once a family is equipped with automobile, refrigerator, washer and drier, range, television, and other durable goods that have come to be regarded as part of the "normal" standard of living, it is in a position to spend less of its income than it spent while acquiring these durable goods. If we can generalize for all families, a growing stock of consumer durables might be expected to dampen rather than stimulate aggregate consumption expenditures at any given level of aggregate disposable income. Not only will this stock yield services over a number of years, but it will eliminate the need for consumption expenditures on certain nondurable goods and services over these years. Thus, to some extent, television replaces the movies, and automobiles replace taxis and buses. Despite the sizable consumption outlay to acquire the durables, the reduction in consumption expenditures for nondurables and services made possible through the use of durables may outweigh the initial outlay over time. This suggests that the net effect of a growing stock of durables may be a decrease in the fraction of income spent.

This, however, neglects the fact that some expenditures for nondurables and services spring from the very ownership and use of durables—gasoline, oil, tires, repairs, parking fees, and insurance for the automobile and electricity, service calls, and parts for the television. In addition, there are some durables, such as home air conditioning units and cabin cruisers, for which, apart from the relatively large outlay for the durable itself and the current cost of its operation, there is no comparable decrease in expenditures on nondurables and services directly following from the possession of the durable good itself.

With such conflicting evidence, no conclusive answer can be made to the question of whether there is a direct relationship between the stock of consumer

---

[23] For an attempt to estimate statistically the importance of liquid-asset holdings of consumers on consumption expenditures, see A. Zellner, "The Short-Run Consumption Function," in *Econometrica*, October 1957, pp. 552–67, and "Further Analysis of the Short-Run Consumption Function with Emphasis on Liquid Assets," in *Econometrica*, July 1965, pp. 571–81.

durables and consumer expenditures. An approach to an answer would require that we somehow estimate (a) consumer expenditures for a given stock of durables plus all the expenditures on nondurables and services resulting from the ownership of these durables over their period in use and (b) the decrease in expenditures on other nondurables and services resulting from the use of these durables over the same period. If (a) exceeds (b), then growth in the stock of durables would suggest an increase in the percentage of disposable income devoted to consumer expenditures of all kinds. The difficulties in deciding which exceeds which are apparent.

One frequently noted factor that probably tends to raise (a) relative to (b) is the readiness with which many American consumers succumb to manufacturers' campaigns of "planned obsolescence." For some consumers, nothing short of "this year's model" will do when it comes to automobiles, high-fidelity components, movie cameras, and other durables. Easy consumer-credit terms assist in converting the consumer's urge to purchase into the purchase itself. Once acquired, the durable good's life in use is far short of its useful life. If enough consumers act in this manner, the share of disposable income that is spent could indeed be increased by a growth in the stock of durables. However, as a factor influencing the percentage of aggregate disposable income given over to consumption, this factor may be more interesting than important. It may well mean that a larger part of any level of disposable income goes to purchase durables, but this need not mean that there is not an offsetting decrease in the part of disposable income devoted to nondurables and services.

In the final analysis, economists are compelled to recognize that the specific relationship here in question may go in either direction. However, we should note an associated relationship whose direction is firmly established. Although the growth in the stock of durables may either increase or decrease the percentage of disposable income devoted to consumption, this growth does make the percentage less stable from year to year than it would otherwise be. Unlike consumer spending for certain nondurables and services that cannot be long postponed, spending for replacement of durables can be postponed for quite a while. In emergencies like World War II, the postponement can extend over a period of years. Postponement of replacement of durables that consumers regard as worn-out tends to occur in times of general business contraction and falling, stable, or slowly rising disposable income; early replacement of durables that consumers do not regard as worn-out tends to appear in times of general business expansions and rapidly rising disposable income.

Although this cyclical variability may be expected in any economy in which durable consumer goods are produced and purchased in any quantity, an economy in which 95 percent of all consumption expenditures is devoted to nondurables and services and only 5 percent to durables will show smaller variability in the percentage of income spent than an economy in which the respective percentages are 85 and 15. An increase in the percentage of disposable income saved is largely at the expense of the percentage of disposable income spent for durables. This seems to suggest that an economy in which consumers spend a large percentage of their disposable income for durables, and thereby build up an ever increasing stock of durables as real disposable income grows over time, will be one in which the percentage of income spent for durables, nondurables, and services combined will decline as the stock of durables grows. This does not follow, however. All it does say is that in such an economy the percentage of disposable income spent on consumer goods and services of all kinds may fluctuate more than in an economy in which the stock of durables is relatively small.

Disposable income tends to move more readily from expenditures on durables to saving than from expenditures on nondurables and services to saving, but a growing stock of durables is not necessarily a factor that will produce a systematic shift of disposable income into saving and away from expenditures on nondurables and services, or even away from expenditures on more durables. All we can add to our earlier conclusion that growth in the stock of consumer durable goods may increase or decrease the percentage of disposable income devoted to consumption is that growth in the stock of consumer durable goods makes the percentage of disposable income devoted to consumption fluctuate more than would otherwise be the case.

OTHER FACTORS, IN BRIEF

There are a number of other nonincome factors that affect consumption expenditures; a few of them will be mentioned here.

In any time period, relatively easy consumer-credit terms can stimulate consumer expenditures for durable goods, and relatively tight terms can do the opposite.[24] The explosion in consumer purchases of automobiles in 1955 is credited in large part to the unusually easy credit terms offered in that year. When we recall that an increase in expenditures for durables tends to be largely at the expense of a decrease in saving, we can understand how easy credit, which stimulates purchases of durables, can increase the fraction of aggregate disposable income that is spent in any time period.[25]

The difference between the rates of growth of aggregate disposable income and population over a period of years is another factor that influences the fraction of aggregate disposable income devoted to consumption. If the nation's population is growing faster than aggregate disposable income, disposable income per capita is decreasing, and this in turn tends to raise the fraction of aggregate disposable income that is consumed. Changes in certain characteristics

[24] Easier consumer credit is not the same as a lower rate of interest, although the latter may be one characteristic of easier consumer credit. Consumer installment credit may be said to be "easier," with no reduction in rates charged, if there is a lengthening of the repayment period on installment purchase contracts or if there is a relaxation of credit standards that makes credit available to applicants previously rejected.

[25] See P. W. McCracken, J. C. T. Mao, and C. Fricke, *Consumer Instalment Credit and Public Policy*, Bureau of Business Research, Univ. of Michigan, 1965. An appendix provides a case study of the role of installment credit in the 1955 auto sales year.

of the population, such as its age distribution, will also affect the fraction of aggregate income spent. For example, an increase in the percentage of the population that is made up of persons past working age or under working age will tend to increase the percentage of disposable income spent, since the average propensity to consume in these age groups is higher than the average for all age groups combined.[26]

Deferred demand, especially on the scale displayed in the years just following World War II, tends to push consumption expenditures above the level that would be expected on the basis of disposable income alone. But it is apparent that this factor, however important in this period, has little application in normal peacetime periods.

Over recent decades institutional changes have occurred that also affect the spending-saving patterns of consumers. For many families saving has become largely automatic with the popularization of long-term saving commitments through life insurance, private pension funds, and mortgage loans on homes, the repayment of which is amortized over a long period of years. Once families are committed, the amount of such quasi-compulsory saving is largely immune to changes in income. Since income does change, the stability of this portion of personal saving is another factor influencing the fraction of income that is devoted to consumption. For the portion of saving that remains a matter of current decision by the family each week or month, the diversity of forms in which personal saving may be placed is now so great that a saver may find an outlet for his saving that is virtually tailor-made to his requirements. To some degree this also affects the spending-saving patterns of consumers.

CONSUMPTION DEMAND—A CONCLUDING NOTE

In attempting to explain what determines the level of consumption spending, one is tempted, as were many economists in the early years following the appearance of Keynes's *General Theory*, to begin and end the explanation with the level of disposable income as *the* determinant. The time-series data that first became available for the U.S. economy during World War II gave empirical support to disposable income as the major factor in any explanation, but at the same time these data showed disposable income to be something less than a total explanation. Many other factors were found to have an influence on consumption spending, particularly in the short run, and these dispelled any notion of a stable relationship between changes in consumption and changes in disposable income on a quarter-to-quarter or even a year-to-year basis. However, despite the influence of these other factors, the data still clearly suggested that the level of disposable income dwarfs in importance any nonincome factors and, except for

[26] See J. Fisher, "Income, Spending, and Saving Patterns of Consumer Units in Different Age Groups," in *Studies in Income and Wealth*, Vol. 15, National Bureau of Economic Research, Princeton Univ. Press, 1952.

short-term changes in income and consumption, is more important than all these nonincome factors combined.

This dominance of the income factor permits economists to build meaningful theoretical models in which consumption is made a function of income alone. Such is the relationship given by the consumption function, $C = C_a + cY$, in which C and Y are variables and C_a and c are constants. We will employ this function repeatedly throughout the remainder of this book. Any change in consumption spending from one period to the next, ΔC, will be determined solely by the change in disposable income from one period to the next, ΔY. C_a and c are held unchanged. In other words, no further attention will be paid to changes in the various nonincome factors whose changes actually affect the height of the function, C_a, and its slope, c. By assuming that these nonincome factors remain unchanged, we have an unchanging consumption function whose height and slope is given, so that consumption can change only as a result of a change in disposable income. Thus, consumption is assumed to be entirely passive, responding to changes in income but not initiating them, as would be the case if the function were assumed to shift upward or downward with changes in nonincome factors.

One purpose served by the present chapter is to provide some understanding of what the nonincome variables are, of what their importance is, and of how each one may influence consumption spending. Such an understanding puts into perspective the simplified relationship in which consumption is assumed to be a function solely of the income variable. In an introductory treatment of macroeconomic theory, we must focus exclusively on the income variable to simplify what would otherwise be an exceedingly complex relationship. However, in the chapters ahead, it is important to keep in mind that, although income is certainly the all-important variable influencing consumption and the only variable that will appear explicitly in the models, consumption in practice depends also on a large number of nonincome variables.

CHAPTER 11

CAPITAL AND INVESTMENT

In a two-sector economy consisting only of consumers and businesses, aggregate demand for goods and services equals the sum of consumer demand and business demand, or the sum of personal consumption expenditures and private domestic investment expenditures. Since changes in consumption expenditures are usually the result rather than the cause of a change in income, the *initiating* force of a change in aggregate demand, and hence in income, is typically a change in investment expenditures. With changes in investment expenditures playing this strategic role, it follows that any explanation of the changes that occur in income requires that we first find an explanation for the frequent and sometimes drastic changes that take place in investment expenditures.

In seeking this explanation, economists have not been able to establish a relatively simple functional relationship between investment expenditures and any other single variable as they have done for consumption expenditures and disposable income. Although disposable income, we have seen, is not the total explanation of consumption, it is certainly the major factor in the explanation. However, there is no comparable single factor on which we can build a relatively simple explanation of investment spending. It would appear that we can safely argue that investment spending depends on the prospective profitability of such spending: Expenditures will be relatively large when the expected rate of profit is high and relatively small when the expected rate of profit is low. Even this apparently incontrovertible statement, however, would not pass without serious qualification by some economists.[1] And even if it were to pass, we would still be forced back to explain what determines the prospective rate of profit on investment projects. This, in turn, would force us to examine the many factors that

---

[1] For example, W. J. Baumol, *Business Behavior, Value and Growth*, rev. ed., Harcourt, Brace & World, 1967, Ch. 12.

affect businessmen's estimates of the profitability of such projects. We would be led to conclude that there are a number of factors of varying importance that determine investment expenditures, unlike the single factor of dominating importance found in the explanation of consumption expenditures.

To explain investment expenditures, we must identify the factors that affect businessmen's estimates of the profitability of investment projects and examine how changes in these factors will produce changes in the overall level of investment expenditures. This is done in the next two chapters. Before we can discuss these factors, however, we must first explain the meaning of the rate of return on capital goods and the relationships that exist between the stock of capital and the rate of investment spending.

THE MEANING OF CAPITAL AND INVESTMENT

Investment, a word with many meanings in popular usage, has only one meaning in national income analysis—the value of that part of the economy's output for any time period that takes the form of new structures, new producers' durable equipment, and change in inventories. In practice, apart from the change in inventories, the value of this output is measured by the amount of expenditure on these items. Investment so defined can be viewed, we recall, either in gross or net terms. If we deduct from gross investment expenditures an allowance for the amount of plant and durable equipment used up in turning out the period's output, we have net investment.

In any attempt to explain aggregate investment expenditures in any time period, one difficulty is the fact that different factors determine the different types of investment expenditure. No single investment theory can reasonably apply to all forms of investment expenditure. The amount of expenditures by persons for owner-occupied housing is not dominated by profit considerations as is the amount of expenditures by businessmen for commercial and industrial structures and for durable equipment. Similarly, the amount of expenditures by businessmen for new plant and equipment is affected by factors different from those that determine the amount they spend for additions to inventories, even though the profit motive dominates in both cases. Although some attention will be paid to other types of investment in Chapter 13, investment in this chapter will refer specifically to business expenditures for plant and equipment. In recent years these components have made up roughly two-thirds of gross private domestic investment.

Investment is a flow variable whose counterpart stock variable is capital. Capital, another word with many meanings, should here be understood to mean only the accumulated stock of plant and equipment held by business. If, for the economy as a whole, gross investment in any period equals the amount of capital used up during that period, there is neither net investment nor disinvestment and so no change in the stock of capital. If gross investment exceeds replacement requirements, the difference equals positive net investment, which represents an increase in the stock of capital. If gross investment is less than replacement requirements, the difference is negative net investment or disinvestment, which represents a decrease in the stock of capital.

Therefore, by definition, net investment is an addition to the stock of capital. Other things being equal, an addition to the stock of capital means an increase in the productive capacity of the economy. This must be the result when a larger physical stock of capital is available for use with an existing labor force, natural resources, and technology. In the same way, an increase in productive capacity must result when there is an increase in the labor force with no change in the stock of capital, natural resources, or technology or when there is an improvement in technology with no change in the stock of capital, labor force, or natural resources.[2]

The stock of capital for the economy as a whole tends to grow over time, and over time the labor force also tends to grow and productive techniques to improve. In practice, other things do not remain equal as the capital stock grows. However, for analytical purposes, it is necessary to isolate the growth in the capital stock from the growth in other factors in order to specify the increase in potential output associated with the growth in the capital stock. To assume an unchanged technology or a given "state of the arts" presents no serious conceptual difficulty; we are simply to understand that the same methods of production are employed. Net investment and the resultant growth in the stock of capital then means that more of the existing kinds of capital goods are employed in the same way as are existing capital goods. To assume an unchanged labor force does, however, present some conceptual difficulty. While the stock of capital might conceivably grow virtually without limit even in the absence of technological change, it is more difficult to imagine unlimited growth in the stock of capital without a growth in the labor force, because more workers would be needed to utilize the enlarged stock of capital.

If the stock of capital, the state of technology, and the labor force are all treated as variables, this conceptual difficulty disappears, and others appear. With all treated as variables, it is possible to have technological improvements that lead to a growth in the stock of capital without any corresponding increase in the amount of labor required for the efficient use of the now larger stock of capital. With the state of technology as a variable, we may also have a growth in the stock of capital that is intended not as a means of increasing capacity but rather as a means of reducing the cost of producing the level of output attained with existing capacity. "Modernization" of a firm's plant and equipment through net investment expenditures may amount to the adoption of technologically superior and therefore lower cost-per-unit methods of producing an unchanged level of output. Such net investment may be distinguished conceptually from net investment that is designed simply to expand the productive capacity of the firm's plant and equipment. However, for the economy as a whole, whether net

---

[2] As suggested by the "law of diminishing returns," the only plausible exception to this rule is the case in which the variable factor is so plentiful relative to the fixed factors that its marginal productivity falls to zero. This situation is very unusual.

investment is undertaken for "modernization" or for capacity expansion, all net investment increases the productive capacity of the economy as a whole. If a plant is "modernized" in order to permit a given level of output to be produced with less labor, the labor so released is potentially available to enlarge production elsewhere in the economy.

To avoid the complications inherent in simultaneously treating all these factors as variables, we will assume for the present that the state of technology, the size of the labor force, and the amount of the economy's natural resources are all given. As we develop the theory of net investment demand for the economy as a whole, we may simply identify the resultant expansion in the capital stock as an expansion in the productive capacity of the economy.

THE DECISION TO INVEST

Since most capital goods remain useful for many years, one can learn only after several years have passed whether the investment in these long-lived goods will turn out to be profitable or unprofitable. However, if a particular investment expenditure is made, for replacement as well as for expansion, it generally means that the businessman who invests has estimated that the investment will be profitable.[3]

Three Elements Involved

The businessman's estimate of the profit or loss that will accrue from any particular investment is based on the relationships among three elements: the expected income flow from the capital good in question, the purchase price of that good, and the market rate of interest. Because a forecast of what lies in the uncertain future is unavoidable, the crucial factor in the businessman's evaluation of the prospective profitability of any investment expenditure is his estimate of the income flow the capital good will yield over its life. Not only is the income stream it will yield over its life uncertain, but the life of the capital good itself is uncertain. Ignoring for the moment the question of uncertainty, suppose that management estimates that a particular machine can remain in use for a five-year period, at which time it will have only a negligible scrap value. Management will estimate its physical productivity—the increase in the number of units of final output made possible in each of the five years because of the addition of this machine to its stock of capital. This estimated physical productivity for each

[3] We make the standard assumption that the firm's objective is "profit maximization." Although it is well known that firms are influenced by other objectives, for simplicity "profit maximization" will be assumed here to be the exclusive objective. For a treatment of this subject, see N. W. Chamberlin, *The Firm: Micro-Economic Planning and Action*, McGraw-Hill, 1962, Chs. 4–5, and, at a more advanced level, F. Machlup, "Theories of the Firm: Marginalist, Behavioral, Managerial," in *American Economic Review*, March 1966, pp. 1–33.

year multiplied by the estimated price per unit (or more exactly the marginal revenue per unit) at which each year's additional output can be sold gives for each year the gross income flow expected from the machine. However, in producing and selling this additional output, extra raw materials, power, advertising, and labor will probably be required.[4] When the total cost of these extra inputs for each year is subtracted from the estimated gross income flow for each year, the remainder is the estimated net income produced by the machine in each year. In computing this figure, all costs that will be incurred in using the machine and in producing and selling its output are deducted, with two notable exceptions: (1) the annual depreciation expense, which on a straight-line basis would equal one-fifth of the purchase price of the machine, and (2) the annual interest cost, which would equal the undepreciated portion of the purchase price times the market rate of interest. Thus, if in the first year one-fifth of the original outlay is covered by setting aside in a depreciation reserve one-fifth of the purchase price of the capital good, the interest cost in the second year will equal the market rate of interest times four-fifths of the purchase price.[5] The five figures for the five years make up a series of estimated net income figures that may be designated as R_1, R_2, R_3, R_4, and R_5.

Suppose that the sum of R_1, R_2, R_3, R_4, and R_5 exceeds the purchase price of the capital good. Can this excess over the amount required to replace the machine be taken as the dollar amount of estimated profit from the machine over its five-year life? Can we divide this figure by five and call this amount the average profit per year? Can we divide this average amount by the purchase price of the machine and call this the rate of return on the investment? The answer to all these questions is no. Not all the excess of the income flow over the purchase price is profit. We made no allowance for the fact that the income flow from the capital good will trickle in over the next five years, while the outlay for the capital good is made in one lump sum at the time of purchase. To disregard the time difference between income and outlay would be to equate today's dollar with tomorrow's; as long as a positive rate of interest can be earned by any lender, a dollar to be received tomorrow will necessarily have less value than one received today. To compare properly the number of dollars paid out today in purchasing the capital good with the number of dollars of income that the capital good will earn over its life, we must compute the *present value* of those future dollars. This requires that we *discount* each of those future dollars for the number of years it is removed from the present; the present value depends on

---

[4] Although we have assumed that the labor force, natural resources, and technology are all unchanged, the individual firm can always get more labor and raw materials by competing them away from other firms. This is patently impossible for all firms together, but all firms may still redeploy the available labor force and the supply of raw materials so as to make optimum use of them in combination with a growing stock of capital. Of course, as all firms taken together increase the stock of capital, the additional output per additional unit of capital must eventually decrease, if the quantity of labor and other factors remains unchanged. Diminishing returns enter the picture.

[5] In the two-sector economy, there is no government and hence no taxes on business net income. If we recognize taxes, another deduction would, of course, have to be made to arrive at a figure for net income after taxes.

the rate at which the future dollars are to be discounted. Discounted at 4 percent, the sum of $100 to be received five years from today has a present value of $82.19; at 5 percent the same $100 has the smaller present value of $78.35; and at 6 percent the still smaller present value of $74.73. For $100 four years away discounted at 4, 5, and 6 percent, the present values would be $85.48, $82.27, and $79.21, respectively.

This discounting process—the process by which a future sum shrinks as it is translated into present value—is simply the reverse of the process by which a sum grows as it is carried into the future. If the present value of $100 to be received five years from today is $82.19 when discounted at 4 percent, $82.19 put out today at 4 percent interest will grow to $100 at the end of five years. Similarly, if the present value of $100 to be received four years from today is $79.21 when discounted at 6 percent, then $79.21 put out today at 6 percent interest will grow to $100 at the end of four years.

Let us assign specific dollar values to R_1, R_2, R_3, R_4, and R_5 and determine the present values of these amounts at 4, 5, and 6 percent discount rates. Suppose that for each of the five years the estimated income from the capital good is $100 after deduction of all expenses other than interest and depreciation. (To simplify, assume also that each year's income appears in one lump sum at the end of that year.) The results for each of the three discount rates are given in Table 11-1.

TABLE 11-1   **Present Value of an Income Stream at Various Rates of Discount**

		Discounted at	
Estimated Income	4%	5%	6%
R_1 $100 at end of 1st year	$ 96.15	$ 95.24	$ 94.34
R_2 $100 at end of 2nd year	92.46	90.70	89.00
R_3 $100 at end of 3rd year	88.90	86.38	83.96
R_4 $100 at end of 4th year	85.48	82.27	79.21
R_5 $100 at end of 5th year	82.19	78.35	74.73
Total of Present Values	$445.18	$432.94	$421.24

Under each discount rate, the present value of each $100 unit of income becomes smaller the further that $100 unit is removed from the present; for each given year, the higher the discount rate, the smaller the present value of that $100 unit of income.

The total given for the present values at the bottom of each column is the amount which, if put out today at the rate at the head of each column, would generate a stream of income of $100 at the end of each of the next five years and then nothing.[6] That is, this income stream provides a yield of 4 percent if it

---

[6] Thus, if one invests $445.18 at 4 percent for one year, he earns $17.81 in interest for that year, making his investment at the end of the first year $462.99. Withdrawing $100 from investment at the end of the first year, he invests $362.99 for the second year, on which he receives $14.52 of interest, making his investment at the end of the second year $377.51.

can be purchased for $445.18, a yield of 5 percent if it can be purchased for $432.94, and a yield of 6 percent if it can be purchased for $421.24.

Suppose that the machine that promises this income stream can actually be purchased for $432.94. Will it be a profitable investment? All we know so far is that if we buy the machine for $432.94 and if it produces net income of $100 per year for five years, we will have a 5 percent yield, or rate of return, on the funds invested in the machine over the five years. Is a prospective rate of return of 5 percent high enough to induce the businessman to make the investment expenditure? It is here that the market rate of interest enters the picture. If the firm must borrow the funds to purchase the machine and the rate it must pay for such funds exceeds 5 percent, the interest rate then exceeds the expected rate of return, and the investment would be unprofitable. If, on the other hand, the market rate of interest is below 5 percent, the investment would be profitable. If the firm need not borrow but has on hand its own funds, the comparison is between the rate of interest it could earn by simply lending these funds in the market at interest and the rate of return it expects from an investment of these funds in the machine. If the rate of interest it can secure by lending these funds exceeds 5 percent, the firm will be wiser to lend than to invest in the machine. If the rate at which it can lend funds in the market is less than 5 percent, it will be wiser to invest in the machine than to lend the funds. As a general rule, *it pays to invest in a capital good if the rate of return expected from that capital good over its life exceeds the current market rate of interest.* This "rule," however, is subject to a number of qualifications, some of which we will consider later.

Investment Equations

All this may also be expressed in terms of the general equation for the present value of a future income stream. To develop this equation, we start with the ordinary equation for the growth of a sum at compound interest. Suppose that the market rate of interest is 5 percent. If one lends $95.24 at 5 percent for one year, he will receive $100 at the end of the year.

$$\$95.24 + (0.05 \times \$95.24) = \$95.24(1 + 0.05) = \$100$$

In general, a lender will get back at the end of one year

$$P_1 = P_o(1 + i)$$

where i is the rate of interest and P_o is the amount lent. If he lends the amount

---

Withdrawing another $100 from investment, he invests $277.51 for the third year, on which he receives $11.10 in interest, making his investment at the end of the third year $288.61. Withdrawing another $100 from investment, he invests $188.61 for the fourth year, on which he receives $7.54 in interest, making his investment at the end of the fourth year $196.15. Withdrawing another $100 from investment, he invests $96.15 for the fifth year, on which he receives $3.85 in interest, making his investment at the end of the fifth year $100, which amount he withdraws to close out the investment.

P_1, which equals $P_o(1 + i)$, for the second year, he will get back at the end of the second year

$$P_2 = P_o(1 + i)(1 + i) = P_o(1 + i)^2$$

The rule is thus that a sum of P_o lent at interest rate i for t years will grow at the end of t years to

$$P_t = P_o(1 + i)^t$$

We have seen that the process of discounting a future sum to the present is the reverse of the process of accumulation. What is the present value of $100 receivable one year from today when the market rate of interest is 5 percent? We are given P_1 of $100 and i of 0.05 and wish to find P_o. Since $P_1 = P_o(1 + i)$, it follows that

$$P_o = \frac{P_1}{(1 + i)} = \frac{\$100}{(1 + 0.05)} = \$95.24$$

What is the present value of $100 receivable two years from today? Since $P_2 = P_o(1 + i)^2$, we have

$$P_o = \frac{P_2}{(1 + i)^2} = \frac{\$100}{(1 + 0.05)^2} = \$90.70$$

In general, we can find the present value of any series of future sums by discounting each portion of that series back to the present by the market rate of interest. Using V for present value and $R_1, R_2, \cdots, R_n$ for the series of sums, we have

$$V = \frac{R_1}{(1 + i)} + \frac{R_2}{(1 + i)^2} + \frac{R_3}{(1 + i)^3} + \cdots + \frac{R_n}{(1 + i)^n}$$

In the case of the machine that is expected to produce a stream of income of $100 at the end of each year for a period of five years, the present value of this income stream discounted at 5 percent is

$$V = \frac{\$100}{(1 + 0.05)} + \frac{\$100}{(1 + 0.05)^2} + \frac{\$100}{(1 + 0.05)^3} + \frac{\$100}{(1 + 0.05)^4} + \frac{\$100}{(1 + 0.05)^5}$$

$$= \$95.24 + \$90.70 + \$86.38 + \$82.27 + \$78.35$$

$$= \$432.94$$

These are the same results shown in the 5 percent column in Table 11–1.[7]

As can be seen in that table, a particular stream of income will have a different present value for every different discount rate used. What, then, is the appropriate discount rate? Since in practice the purchase price of a capital good is known, we are interested in determining the particular discount rate

[7] The present value of a dollar discounted at various rates and for various time periods may be found from tables provided in financial handbooks and finance textbooks. See H. Bierman, Jr., and S. Smidt, *The Capital Budgeting Decision*, rev. ed., Macmillan, 1967.

that will make the present value, V, of the expected income stream from that good equal to the purchase price of that good. Suppose, for example, that the purchase price of the capital good is $467.95 and the income stream is that given above. What we want to determine is the value of i that produces a V of $467.95. This we would find from the following equation:

$$\$467.95 = \frac{\$100}{(1 + i)} + \frac{\$100}{(1 + i)^2} + \frac{\$100}{(1 + i)^3} + \frac{\$100}{(1 + i)^4} + \frac{\$100}{(1 + i)^5}$$

The solution indicates that i is 2.25 percent. The present value of each $100 unit of the income stream when discounted at 2.25 percent is as follows:

$$\$467.95 = \$97.80 + \$95.65 + \$93.54 + \$91.49 + \$89.47$$

We could, of course, substitute any other possible price for the capital good and solve for i in the same way. With the income stream as given, the higher the price, the lower will be the value found for i; the lower the price, the higher will be the value found for i.

The Marginal Efficiency of Capital

In solving for i in this way, we have found the "rate of discount which would make the present value of . . . the returns expected from the capital-asset during its life just equal to its supply price." [8] This is Keynes's definition of the *marginal efficiency of capital*, a term that has become part of the language of the theory of capital and investment and one that we will use through the remainder of this book to indicate the rate of return expected from a capital asset.

In the manner described above, we may compute the marginal efficiency of capital, or MEC, for any capital good once we are given its supply price and the stream of income expected from that good. By comparing the MEC with the current market rate of interest, r, we can tell at once whether the contemplated investment promises to be profitable or unprofitable. Furthermore, simply by finding the difference between the MEC and r, we have the net rate of return expected on the capital asset after allowance for all costs, including the interest cost on the funds tied up in the capital good over its life and the depreciation cost of the asset itself. Thus, if the MEC is 6 percent and r is 4 percent, purchase of the capital good promises a net return of 2 percent over and above all costs.

Because the MEC and r are both percentages, they are sometimes confused, or, even worse, identified as the same thing. It is essential to see that the two percentages are distinctly different and that the businessman's estimate of the MEC for any capital good depends in no way on r. It is true that once the MEC has been estimated, the profitability of the capital good in question can be

[8] John Maynard Keynes, *The General Theory of Employment, Interest, and Money*, Harcourt, Brace & World, 1936, p. 135.

gauged only by comparing its MEC with *r*, but this is a step altogether distinct from that of estimating the MEC itself. The level of *r* determines whether a given capital good will be purchased, once its MEC is given, but *r* does not in any way determine the MEC of that good.

We may now note how all three elements—the income flow expected from a capital good, the supply price of that good, and the market rate of interest —fit together. An improvement in the business outlook that causes the businessman to revise upward his estimate of the expected income flow from a capital good will, given an unchanged price for the good, raise the MEC of that good. Alternatively, if there is no change in the income flow expected from the good, a drop in its price will raise its MEC. A fall in *r* will not affect the MEC of that good, but if *r* > MEC before the fall and if MEC > *r* after the fall, the purchase of the capital good, which previously appeared unprofitable, will now appear profitable. A downward revision in the expected income flow from the good, a rise in its price, or a rise in the market rate of interest will all work in the opposite direction—the direction of decreasing the expected profitability of the good or even turning it into expected loss.

The Factor of Uncertainty

Once the supply price of a capital good and the estimate of the income flow expected from that good are known, the calculation of its MEC would appear to be a simple matter of arithmetic. While in a way this is correct, it must be emphasized that the estimate of the income flow can be nothing more than an estimate of its future prospective returns and must therefore be an uncertain figure.

Clearly, the degree of uncertainty will vary with different capital projects. The rate of return on some projects can be estimated with considerable certainty. An electric utility that is expanding its generating facilities to satisfy an existing demand faces little uncertainty. Its monopoly position and publicly regulated rate structure, which is adjusted to give it a "fair return" ("fair MEC") on its capital stock, reduces uncertainty to a minimum. On the other hand, there is tremendous uncertainty as to the rate of return that a firm may expect from a project that involves the design and construction of special-purpose equipment or even of special-purpose buildings for the production of a radically different version of a product that is already available on the market in several satisfactory competing versions. If the project is carried out and if the new version of the product "clicks" and is adequately protected by patents, the gamble, great as it was, was in retrospect worth taking. However, before carrying out the project, the entrepreneur may have been able to see nothing more definite than an MEC ranging anywhere from 0 to 50 percent. In such circumstances he is hardly able to reach an easy decision by comparing the MEC with the rate of interest. The most careful evaluation of whatever objective criteria he has to work with may give him nothing but a wide range of possibilities. He may hold some of these possibilities to be more likely than others (e.g., a 1 percent chance that the MEC will be 50 percent, a 30 percent chance that it will be 10 percent, a 5 percent chance that it will be 0), but this is hardly the same as a single value for the MEC that may be compared with r as the basis for a straightforward decision.

The aggregate investment expenditures undertaken in any time period include capital projects in which the element of uncertainty ranges from a minimum to some unspecifiable maximum. Each of these projects is the result of a decision by the man or men in control of the firm or this branch of its operations, and different men will come up with different evaluations of the prospects for any capital project. The decision to invest would probably be affirmative in our example of the electric utility, no matter who the men in the decision-making position might be. In our other example, however, the decision would vary with the men to whom the project was presented for evaluation. Differences would crop up in their estimates of the possible range of outcomes, and even larger differences would arise in their estimates of the likelihood of each of these possible outcomes. Beyond this, even if two men were to come up with the same estimates, one might decide in favor of the project and the other against it; one man might have a "gambling spirit," while the other might be conservative.

Different decisions are to be expected from different men, because what all men face is, as Keynes put it, "the extreme precariousness of the basis of knowledge on which estimates of prospective yield have to be made." [9] Furthermore, the precariousness increases more than proportionately with the life of the asset whose yield is to be estimated. Although they must do it, businessmen show an understandable reluctance to stipulate the net income expected from a capital good five or more years from the time of purchase. They must estimate product prices, labor and other production costs, prices of capital goods, market demand, future tax rates, competitive conditions in the markets for their products, and all the other factors on which any given capital asset's net income will depend in that future year. In the face of such uncertainty, it would be surprising indeed to find one man's appraisal to be the same as that of another. The importance of the subjective element and its wide variation among different decision-makers is apparent.

In recent years, the businessman has been required to pay increasing attention to another aspect of uncertainty—obsolescence, or the prospect that the firm may have to discard capital equipment long before it has worn out or even paid for itself. In times of slower technological progress, this was a minor problem. But the rapid technological progress of recent years and the increasing threat of obsolescence cause businessmen now to speak of "payoff periods," which are shorter than the useful life of capital equipment, in which the capital outlay must be recovered. The greater the threat of obsolescence, the shorter management makes the pay-off period. [10]

[9] *Ibid.*, p. 149.
[10] For example, if the businessman estimates that technological improvements within the next five years will result in the appearance of equipment that will permit production of his product at lower cost per unit, other things being equal, he can hardly feel safe in buying the

Although there are many other aspects of the investment decision under conditions of uncertainty that could be considered here, it is sufficient for our purposes to have seen that the MEC, though readily defined, is less readily ascertained in a world of uncertainty. However, in what follows we will disregard the problem of uncertainty faced by the individual businessman in arriving at an estimate of the MEC for any capital good.[11] We will assume that he does come up with a "best" estimate of the MEC of a prospective project and that if the MEC so estimated exceeds r, the project is undertaken.

STOCK OF CAPITAL AND THE RATE OF INVESTMENT

At any point in time, a firm is confronted with a long list of possible investment projects. Apart from projects that arise as a result of changing technology, there are projects such as expansion of its existing factory building, construction of a new and larger building, purchase of more of the same equipment to expand production of existing lines, purchase of different equipment to produce a new line of goods, and purchase of trucks to handle its own deliveries. If the firm already has or can borrow the necessary funds, the investment expenditures for every possible project will or will not be made depending upon the MEC of each and the then current level of r. After estimating the MEC of each of the diverse investment projects it might undertake, the firm could prepare a schedule like Figure 11–1 to show the possibilities.

Figure 11–1 assumes that at a selected point in time the firm's stock of capital net of depreciation is valued at $500,000. If the market rate of interest is 6 percent, the first two projects in the schedule promise to be profitable. These projects require net investment expenditures of $125,000, and they will increase the firm's capital stock to $625,000. If the market rate of interest were

---

equipment available today unless he can recover his costs in five years or less. If he can, he will be in a position to purchase the technologically superior equipment five years hence and to maintain his competitive position in the market for his product. If he cannot, he must either take his loss in a lump sum by replacing equipment that has not yet paid for itself or else continue to operate this equipment and take his loss in the reduced profit margin that follows from his higher per unit cost as compared with the per unit cost of those competitors who are equipped with the superior equipment. (For some empirical evidence and analysis of payoff periods, see W. H. White, "The Changing Criteria in Investment Planning," in *Variability of Private Investment in Plant and Equipment*, Part 2, Joint Economic Committee, 1962.)

[11] We have considered here the economist's standard approach to the investment decision through time-discounted income flows. Because of the speculative element in any quantification of income flows that lie years ahead, actual business practice frequently differs from the economist's standard approach. See A. Merrett and A. Sykes, "Calculating the Rate of Return on Capital Projects," in *Journal of Industrial Economics*, Nov. 1960, pp. 98–115, and N. W. Chamberlin, *op. cit.*, pp. 270–78. The full range of problems involved in capital budgeting is treated in texts on managerial economics and the firm. See, for example, M. H. Spencer, *Managerial Economics*, 3rd ed., Irwin, 1968, and D. Vickers, *The Theory of the Firm: Production, Capital, and Finance*, McGraw-Hill, 1968.

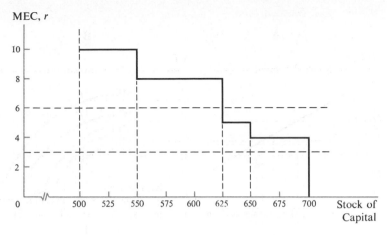

FIGURE 11–1 Schedule of the Marginal Efficiency of Capital for a Firm

3 percent, the third and fourth projects would also be profitable. Net invest-ment expenditures of another $75,000 would raise the firm's stock of capital to $700,000. Once the stock of capital has been expanded to the level at which the MEC of the last project has dropped to the level of r, the firm has that stock of capital which is for it the profit-maximizing stock. No further change is to be expected, barring the appearance of new projects with MEC above r and barring a fall in r itself. The firm's net investment in each succeeding period will be zero; its gross investment will be whatever is required for replacement purposes only.

What is true of one firm is true of others—management of every profit-conscious firm is continuously on the outlook for investment opportunities that promise to improve the appearance of the profit and loss statement over the years. If each firm in the economy were to prepare a schedule of the kind shown in Figure 11–1 and if all these schedules were added together, we would have an aggregate schedule of the MEC such as that shown in Part A of Figure 11–2.[12] The "lumpiness" of the investment projects available to the individual firm that produces the stair-like curve of Figure 11–1 evens out in aggregation to produce the smooth curve of Part A of Figure 11–2.

At any point in time, all firms combined have some existing aggregate stock of capital, say $800 billion. At the same point in time, there is some particular market rate of interest, say 6 percent (here assuming that a single rate prevails for all borrowers and for loans of all maturities and for all purposes). With the aggregate MEC schedule as given in Part A of Figure 11–2 and with

[12] In a strict sense, the aggregate schedule cannot be derived in so simple a manner. A drop in the rate of interest from 6 to 4.5 percent in Figure 11–1 may call forth more than $25,000 of net investment by the firm in question. Since the same drop in the interest rate will trigger investment by other firms, the resultant increase in aggregate demand may so improve the outlook of this firm as to raise the MEC of its other prospective projects above what they were before. In general, when we allow for this interdependence, the effect is to make the individual firm's schedule more elastic than otherwise. The determination of the aggregate schedule, however, becomes a problem in general equilibrium analysis, which allows for the interde-pendency between each firm's schedule and those of all other firms.

213

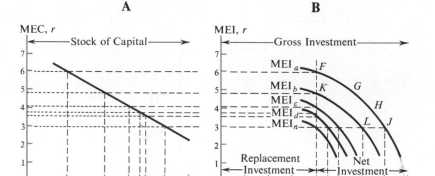

FIGURE 11–2 The Process of Capital Accumulation in Response to a Fall in the Rate of Interest

r at 6 percent, any expansion in the aggregate stock of capital beyond the existing $800 billion level promises a net return of less than 6 percent, or a return below the market rate of interest. Under these conditions, business as a whole may be said to have that stock of capital which maximizes profits; there is no reason to expand or contract the capital stock, and so there is no net investment or disinvestment. For some individual firms there may be net investment, but for others there will be an equal amount of disinvestment, making net investment zero for all firms combined. Under these conditions, there can be no net investment for all firms combined until there is either a drop in the rate of interest that produces a movement down the MEC schedule to a higher stock of capital, or a shift to the right of the MEC schedule that will, with an unchanged rate of interest, make the stock of capital consistent with profit maximization larger than it was. Let us examine in turn each of these changes.

A Fall in the Rate of Interest

In our example, we have assumed that with a capital stock of $800 billion, MEC is 6 percent. If r is also 6 percent, this would be the profit-maximizing stock of capital, and net investment spending would be zero. Assume now a drop in r from 6 to 3 percent.[13] At this lower rate, the profit-maximizing stock

[13] This drastic change is unrealistic, but it is chosen because it will show clearly in chart form the results that follow a fall in the interest rate.

of capital as given by the MEC schedule of Figure 11–2 is $880 billion. This means that $80 billion of net investment expenditures is needed to raise the capital stock to the higher, profit-maximizing level. How much will all firms combined actually invest per time period? And how long will it take these firms to build up the capital stock from the $800 billion to the $880 billion level?

In considering the individual firm, we were able to by-pass this kind of question. When a firm decides to increase its stock of capital, it can conceivably accomplish this virtually overnight. If the capital goods required are goods held in inventory by firms in the capital goods industries, the firm can move up to the higher capital stock desired as quickly as these goods can be delivered. If new construction is required, the firm can move up to the higher capital stock as quickly as this construction can be erected. Furthermore, it is unlikely that its investment expenditures would exert more than a negligible upward pressure on the supply prices of the capital goods in question.

For firms as a group, we cannot, however, by-pass this kind of question. To expand the aggregate stock of capital from $800 to $880 billion must take time. Although some firms may increase their stock of capital immediately by simply buying capital goods from other firms, there will be no increase in the stock of capital goods held by all firms combined unless more capital goods are produced, and the rate at which these goods can be produced is limited by the existing productive capacity of the capital goods industries.[14] Furthermore, as all firms combined step up their investment expenditures, the capital goods industries, in expanding output to meet this higher demand, will at some point experience rising marginal costs that may lead to higher prices for capital goods. These rising prices will in turn slow the rate of investment spending and thus lengthen the time period required to effect any given increase in the aggregate stock of capital.

Let us assume that the capacity output of the capital goods industries is $80 billion per time period, valuing capital goods at the prices in effect when their output is just the amount needed for replacement requirements.[15] With an existing capital stock of $800 billion, replacement requirements are $40 billion per time period, if we assume that 5 percent of these goods wear out in each time period. This means that the capital goods industries, operating at capacity output, can supply a net addition to the capital stock of $40 billion per time period. In other words, it will take two time periods *at capacity output* to raise the capital stock from $800 to $880 billion. Will the rate of

---

[14] Of course, the productive capacity of the capital goods industries may grow over time as these industries expand through net investment, but, for simplicity, we here assume no such change, or constant productive capacity in the capital goods industries.

[15] Since the MEC schedule will shift with every change in the supply price of capital goods, to produce the stable MEC schedule necessary to the following analysis requires that we assume that the MEC schedule is based on the fixed supply price for capital goods which is in effect when output of capital goods is, say, the amount necessary for replacement purposes only. This amount can reasonably be assumed to be stable in the short run.

net investment spending be sufficient to push the capital goods industries to capacity output? To find out what net investment expenditures will be per time period for all firms combined, turn to Figure 11–2.[16]

Part B of Figure 11–2 introduces the schedule of the *marginal efficiency of investment*, or the MEI schedule. This schedule indicates the rate of investment spending per time period at each possible market rate of interest. Separate MEI schedules are shown for a number of different levels of the stock of capital. With the MEC schedule as given in Part A, with r at 6 percent, and with the capital stock at $800 billion, the actual capital stock is the profit-maximizing stock, and net investment is zero. Therefore, we know that a schedule relating investment expenditures to the rate of interest must show zero net investment at an interest rate of 6 percent, which the MEI schedule labeled MEI_a does show (at point F). If, as we have assumed, r falls to 3 percent, net investment expenditures will appear. In the first time period after the drop in r, net investment will be $30 billion (or gross investment will be $70 billion), although the capacity of the capital goods industries permits $40 billion of net investment (or $80 billion of gross investment) per time period. Investment spending is, however, checked at a rate short of the capacity output of the capital goods industries by the rise in prices of these goods, which occurs as their rate of output is expanded in response to investment demand. *It is specifically the upward-sloping supply curve of capital goods that produces the downward-sloping MEI curve.* Furthermore, the more sharply the supply curve of capital goods slopes upward, the more sharply does the MEI curve slope downward.[17]

We can see more clearly why net investment in the first period following the fall in r will be exactly $30 billion by starting at point F on the MEI_a schedule and following this schedule down to point G. At G the MEI is 5 percent because the rise in net investment spending from a rate of zero to a rate of about $15 billion has so raised the prices of capital goods as to reduce to 5 percent the rate of return on investment in these goods. This, however, is still an MEI above r, which is 3 percent, so a higher rate of net investment spending is warranted. At point H the MEI has fallen to 4 percent because the still higher rate of net investment spending, now about $25 billion, has pushed the prices of capital goods to the still higher level at which the rate of return on investment in them is reduced to 4 percent. The MEI is still above r, so a still higher rate of net investment spending is warranted. At point J, the MEI is 3 percent, again for the reason that the still higher rate of net investment spending, now $30 billion, has pushed the prices of capital goods to the still higher level at

---

[16] This figure is adapted from G. Ackley, *Macroeconomic Theory*, Macmillan, 1961. See pp. 481–85. For alternative treatments, see A. P. Lerner, "On Some Recent Developments in Capital Theory," in *American Economic Review, Proceedings*, May 1965, pp. 284–95, *The Economics of Control*, Macmillan, 1944, pp. 330–38, and W. J. Fellner, *Trends and Cycles in Economic Activity*, Holt, 1956, pp. 203–06.

[17] Suppose the supply curve were perfectly elastic up to the capacity output. Then the MEI curve, MEI_a, instead of sloping downward, would be perfectly horizontal, or perfectly elastic, up to gross investment of $80 billion. The same would be true for the other MEI curves (to be explained on page 217).

which the rate of return on investment in them is reduced to 3 percent. It may now be seen that to push the rate of net investment spending beyond $30 billion would reduce the MEI still further, or below 3 percent and so below *r*. Accordingly, net investment will be at the $30 billion rate, no higher and no lower, in the first time period following the drop in *r*.

From the beginning to the end of this first time period, with net investment of $30 billion during the period, the capital stock will have risen to $830 billion from its beginning level of $800 billion. As shown in Part A, this increase in the capital stock of $30 billion reduces the MEC to about 5 percent (actually 4.87) from its previous level of 6. Since *r* is still 3 percent, a further growth in the capital stock is called for. What will be the amount by which it grows in the second period, or what will be the rate of net investment spending in the second period? This depends on the MEI schedule. With MEC now at 5 percent, we know that the new MEI schedule, relating investment expenditures to the rate of interest, must show zero net investment at an interest rate of 5 percent (point *K*). Thus, MEI_b, the new schedule, lies below MEI_a because of the increase in the stock of capital in the first time period; the whole MEI schedule must fall to a lower level with each movement to a lower point on the given MEC schedule. MEI_b slopes downward for the same reason that MEI_a sloped downward—the rising supply price of capital goods as the rate of output of these goods is expanded in response to investment demand.

The rate of net investment spending in the second period is determined in the same way as was the rate in the first period—net investment spending will be at that rate which reduces the MEI to equality with *r*. Schedule MEI_b shows that there will be net investment spending of $20 billion for the second period (point *L*). Note that this is below the $30 billion of net investment spending found in the first time period. Given that the prices of capital goods rise with their rate of output, as soon as net investment gets to the rate of $20 billion, the rise in prices of capital goods reduces the MEI from 5 to 3 percent, or to equality with *r*. In the first period, only when net investment reached the $30 billion rate was the rise in prices of capital goods sufficient to produce the greater drop in MEI from 6 to 3 percent, or to equality with *r*. In other words, the greater spread between MEI and *r* at the beginning of the first period permitted the higher rate of investment spending in that same period.

Net investment spending of $20 billion during the second period raises the stock of capital to $850 billion from its level of $830 at the beginning of the second period. The increase in the stock of capital reduces the MEC further to about 4 percent (actually 4.12), which produces the new, lower MEI schedule MEI_c. The rate of net investment spending in the third period as given by this schedule is $10 billion. This again raises the stock of capital, now from $850 to $860 billion. This in turn reduces the MEC, now below 4 percent, and creates the new, still lower MEI schedule MEI_d. The rate of net investment spending in the fourth period is then $5 billion. With no shift in the MEC schedule and with no further fall in *r*, net investment spending, lower in each succeeding period, eventually raises the stock of capital to $880 billion, at which level the MEC equals *r*. The actual stock of capital is now the profit-maximizing stock of capital for the interest rate of 3 percent. With the capital stock at $880 billion, the relevant MEI schedule is MEI_n, which shows net investment to be zero and gross investment equal to replacement investment per time period. We have reached a new equilibrium, which will be upset only by a shift in the MEC schedule or by a change in the market rate of interest.

To summarize: Given an unshifting MEC schedule, the appearance of a positive rate of net investment is seen to depend in the first instance on the size of the stock of capital and the rate of interest. Given the stock of capital we know MEC, and given r we know whether $MEC > r$, $MEC < r$, or $MEC = r$. A prerequisite to net investment is that $MEC > r$. If we have this situation, an increase in capital stock is called for, and this increase can come about only through net investment spending. The rate of net investment spending per time period depends on how steep the downward slope of the MEI schedule is (or more correctly its elasticity), and this in turn depends on how steep the upward slope (or the elasticity) of the supply curve of capital goods is. If the supply curve slopes sharply upward, the rate of investment spending will fall sharply downward with respect to the rate of interest. In any event, the capital stock will grow to the new profit-maximizing level, but its rate of growth will be slower the steeper the MEI schedule.

A Shift in the MEC Schedule[18]

Just as a drop in the rate of interest with no shift in the MEC schedule will raise the profit-maximizing stock of capital from its previous level, so an upward shift in the MEC schedule with no change in the rate of interest will have the same result. Schedule MEC_a of Figure 11–3 is identical with the MEC schedule shown in Figure 11–2. In both cases, assuming that r is 6 percent and the actual capital stock is $800 billion, the actual stock is the profit-maximizing stock, and net investment spending is zero. If the MEC schedule now shifts upward from MEC_a to MEC_b, the profit-maximizing stock of capital becomes $880 billion. Net investment now appears, because, with the capital stock at $800 billion, the MEC has risen from 6 to 9 percent. In other words, due to a rise in the expected income flow from capital goods, which is assumed here to be the cause of the upward shift in the MEC schedule, the rate of return expected from the first increment to the stock of capital over its existing level is 9 percent. Since r is still 6 percent, the MEC now exceeds r by 3 percent. Note that this is the same relationship between MEC and r as was given in Figure 11–2, the only difference being that here the 3 percent spread between MEC and r is brought about by a rise in MEC from 6 to 9

---

[18] Although the intent here is simply to distinguish between a change in the rate of interest and a shift in the MEC schedule, it should be noted that these two changes are not independent of each other. An increase in investment spending resulting from a fall in the rate of interest raises the level of income, which in turn (via the acceleration principle to be examined in Chapter 13) tends to cause a shift to the right in the MEC schedule. A movement along the schedule may, in other words, set into motion forces that cause a shift in the schedule.

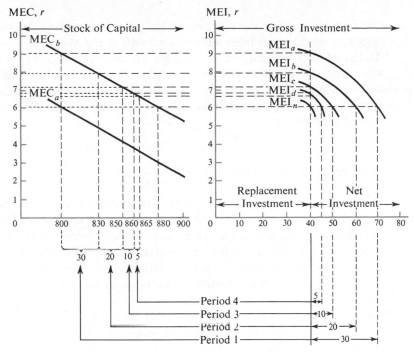

FIGURE 11-3 The Process of Capital Accumulation in Response to a Shift in the Schedule of the Marginal Efficiency of Capital

percent, whereas in Figure 11-2 the same spread was brought about by a drop in r from 6 to 3 percent.

As in the previous illustration, net investment expenditures of $80 billion are required to raise the capital stock to its new profit-maximizing level. The rate of net investment in each time period is the same in both illustrations as is the number of time periods required to increase the capital stock by $80 billion. Part B of Figure 11-3 differs from Part B of Figure 11-2 only in being higher above the horizontal axis. In Figure 11-2, investment in the first period after the fall in r was at the rate that reduced the MEI from 6 to 3 percent; in Figure 11-3, investment in the first period after the shift upward in the MEC schedule is at the rate that reduces the MEI from 9 to 6 percent. *The significant factor is the spread between MEI and r rather than the absolute level of either.* Since this spread is the same in both of our illustrations, the rate of net investment in each period will be the same.

It is, of course, quite possible that shifts in the MEC schedule could occur at the same time as changes in the market rate of interest. For example, the upward shift in the MEC schedule of Figure 11-3 could be accompanied by a fall in the interest rate like that shown in Figure 11-2. If this happened, the new profit-maximizing capital stock would be something greater than $880 billion. If there were a rise in the rate of interest, it might be sufficient to offset the rise in the profit-maximizing capital stock that otherwise would result from an upward shift in the MEC schedule. Conversely, a fall in the rate of interest

219

could be such as to offset the decrease in the profit-maximizing capital stock that otherwise would result from a downward shift in the MEC schedule.

Unless these combinations of changes are exactly offsetting, however, they will change the profit-maximizing capital stock. Given such a change, the net investment process as described is that by which the economy moves to the higher profit-maximizing capital stock, whatever it may be and whatever may have caused it to change.[19]

A Summary Formulation

The portion of aggregate demand that is accounted for by the business sector of the economy is measured by the investment expenditures of business for newly produced capital goods. To explain aggregate demand for any time period, we must concentrate on business investment expenditures for that time period rather than on the actual stock of capital held by business at any point within that time period. Net investment expenditures for any time period are the means by which a change in the capital stock is effected. In other words, net investment, which is zero when the actual capital stock equals the profit-maximizing capital stock, becomes positive when the profit-maximizing stock exceeds the actual stock. A prerequisite to the appearance of net investment expenditures is a rise in the profit-maximizing capital stock.

What produces such a change in the profit-maximizing capital stock? Once such a change occurs, the rate of net investment expenditures determines the time necessary to raise the capital stock to its profit-maximizing level. What determines this rate? In the preceding pages we have attempted to lay the conceptual groundwork for answering these two questions. Figure 11–4 presents in schematic form the various factors we have introduced so far. If the difference between the actual and profit-maximizing capital stock is zero, the rate of net investment expenditures will be zero. In this case, the portion of the chart lying below the vertical arrow is not really relevant; it becomes relevant only when there is a change somewhere above the arrow that produces a difference between the actual and the profit-maximizing capital stock. Whether such a difference will appear depends on the relationship between the MEC schedule and the

---

[19] Since, apart from several years during the Great Depression, the profit-maximizing capital stock has grown uninterruptedly over the years, we have not here specifically entered into the process by which the capital stock would be reduced over time below the actual capital stock at any point in time. In brief, if the movement were, say, from an actual capital stock of $880 billion to a desired capital stock of $800 billion, gross investment would drop all the way to zero, and net investment would accordingly become negative. The maximum possible rate of negative net investment, or of disinvestment, is set by the rate at which the capital stock is used up. If, as earlier assumed, this were simply 5 percent per time period, it would then take a little less than two time periods to reduce the actual stock from $880 billion to the desired stock of $800 billion. Since no capital goods are being purchased, the shape of the supply curve of capital goods and so the shape of the MEI schedule have nothing to do with the maximum disinvestment rate.

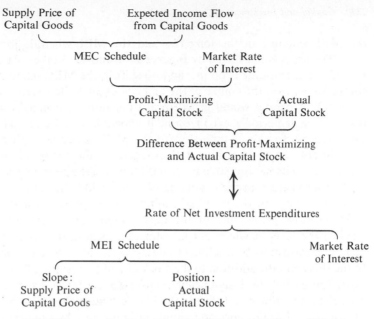

FIGURE 11–4 From the Stock of Capital to the Rate of Investment

market rate of interest. The MEC schedule in turn depends on the supply price of capital goods and the expected income flow from such goods.[20] If there is a change in any of these factors that is sufficient to produce a difference between the actual and the profit-maximizing capital stock, then the lower portion of the chart gives us the factors that determine the rate of net investment and thus the time required to raise the actual capital stock to the profit-maximizing level. Here we recall that the rate of net investment expenditures depends on the relationship between the rate of interest and the MEI schedule, that the overall slope of the MEI schedule depends in turn on the supply price of capital goods, and that its position vis-à-vis the axes depends on the actual stock of capital.

The MEI Schedule: Long Run and Short Run

So far we have discussed one factor that influences the rate of net investment spending—the growth in the stock of capital, represented graphically by a movement down the MEC schedule. This factor becomes important only in the long run; then the growth in the stock of capital is large enough, relative to the preexisting stock of capital, to cause an appreciable movement down the MEC schedule. For this reason, it is necessary that we now distinguish between

[20] As was noted earlier, in order to derive an MEC schedule, a particular price level of capital goods must be assumed. This means assuming the price level as one given at some point along the supply price schedule. For each different price level selected there will be a different MEC schedule, but for any one price level selected there will be a unique MEC schedule. To derive the MEI schedule, on the other hand, the complete supply price schedule is employed; it determines the overall slope of the MEI schedule.

the MEI schedule in the long run and the MEI schedule in the short run.

The process illustrated by Figures 11–2 and 11–3 takes place over the long run. Given a one-time drop in r and no shift in the MEC schedule, Figure 11–2 showed how, over the course of the first few of an endless series of time periods, the stock of capital would grow toward the new profit-maximizing stock as a result of each period's net investment expenditures. Figure 11–3 showed the same process for a one-time shift in the MEC schedule with no change in r.

In both cases we deliberately exaggerated the changes involved to clarify the process. The net investment expenditures of each period were sizable relative to the capital stock at the beginning of each period; this in turn meant that the resulting change in the stock of capital in each period would push down the MEI schedule perceptibly in the next period until that schedule eventually reached the level at which net investment expenditures became zero. This explanation must now be qualified to describe the MEI schedule in the short run. In the short run the addition to the stock of capital resulting from net investment expenditures will be insignificant relative to the large, existing capital stock. Therefore, the downward shift in the MEI schedule shown in Parts B of Figures 11–2 and 11–3 will be correspondingly insignificant. As a matter of fact, a short-run period in the present context is usually defined as a time interval of such length that the changes in capital stock, relative to the size of the capital stock before the changes, are too small to influence the level of net investment expenditures.

For short-run analysis, it is then possible, without appreciable error, to abstract from the effect of changes in the capital stock on the position of the MEI schedule. In terms of Figure 11–2, when r falls from 6 to 3 percent, the result is net investment of $30 billion in the first period following the fall in r. However, instead of the long-run results described by Figure 11–2, we may assume that the preexisting stock of capital is so large that the addition of $30 billion to that stock does not cause a perceptible movement down the MEC schedule. With no appreciable movement along the MEC schedule, the MEI schedule in the second period is virtually in the same position as in the first period. This means that the rate of investment expenditures in the second and in subsequent periods that make up the short run may remain virtually the same as that of the first period. This, it may be noted, is precisely what Keynes assumed in his *General Theory*.

In Chapter 22, on economic growth, we will be concerned with long-run analysis; we will have to look both ways in the manner originally described in connection with Figures 11–2 and 11–3. In the long run, net investment expenditures do move the economy along the MEC schedule. With the MEC schedule sloping downward, the result must be a downward shift of the MEI schedule and, assuming an unchanging supply curve for capital goods, a decrease in the rate of net investment expenditures. However, in this part of the book, we need look only one way—a difference between the actual and the profit-maximizing capital stock affects net investment expenditures, but these net investment expenditures *in the short run* do not appreciably affect the economy's position along the MEC schedule.

A CONCLUDING NOTE

Our concern in this chapter has been essentially with the meaning of capital and investment and with the mechanics of the relationships between the stock of capital and the rate of investment. If at any point in time the actual stock equals the profit-maximizing stock, an excess of the latter over the former will subsequently appear only if the market rate of interest falls or if the MEC schedule shifts upward. Either change will give rise to a positive rate of net investment spending. For short-run analysis, we may assume that the indicated rate of net investment spending may continue unchanged. However, in the long run the rise in the stock of capital resulting from net investment spending will depress the MEI schedule and with it the rate of net investment spending. This long-run result assumes that the growth in the stock of capital produces a movement along an unshifting MEC schedule, a schedule that necessarily slopes downward. In reality, however, it is possible that, long before net investment spending raises the actual stock of capital to the profit-maximizing level indicated by a given market rate of interest and a given MEC schedule, this schedule will have shifted and with its shift will follow a shift in the MEI schedule and so a change in the rate of net investment spending.

Now that we understand the mechanics by which changes in the profit-maximizing capital stock are translated into changes in the rate of investment, we are free to concentrate on the factors whose changes produce shifts in or movements along the MEC schedule and thereby produce changes in the profit-maximizing capital stock. In the following two chapters, we will examine some of the more important of these numerous factors.

CHAPTER 12

CHANGES IN INVESTMENT: I

The highly volatile nature of investment expenditures was brought out in Chapter 5 in our review of the composition of GNP from 1929 to 1968. Our purpose in this and the following chapter is to examine some of the major factors that cause these sometimes sharp and sudden fluctuations in investment expenditures. In terms of the apparatus developed in the preceding chapter, these factors, whatever they are, exert their influence on investment spending either by producing a movement along an existing MEC schedule or by producing a shift in the schedule itself. By the very construction of the MEC schedule, the only way to obtain a change in an existing profit-maximizing capital stock, given an unshifting MEC schedule, is through a change in the market rate of interest. How large the increase in the profit-maximizing stock will be for any given drop in the interest rate depends on the elasticity of the schedule. The more elastic it is, the more important are changes in the interest rate as an influence on the rate of investment expenditures. While there is some difference of opinion among economists as to the elasticity of the schedule, there is virtual unanimity of opinion that *shifts in the schedule* are much more important in explaining the observed changes in investment expenditures than are the *movements along a given schedule* that result from changes in the interest rate.

The first four items listed below are the major factors accounting for shifts in the schedule. The fifth factor is the one whose influence is reflected in movements along the schedule and whose importance depends on the elasticity of the schedule.

1. Expectations
2. Technological change and innovation
3. The level of income and output

4. Changes in the level of income and output
5. The rate of interest and the role of finance

Any list of this sort is a compromise. If one wanted the shortest possible list, the second and fourth factors would probably be selected by most economists as the two most important. For a longer list, two likely additions would be (1) the role of government in general and of taxation in particular and (2) the market position of firms, each firm's investment expenditures being influenced by whether it is part of a highly competitive or oligopolistic industry or whether it is a monopoly and thus the industry itself. A glaring omission from our list would appear to be the amount of business profits, but as we will see this factor is really covered by the third item in our list.[1]

The very idea of a list of factors is also nothing more than a convenience. There are differences of opinion among economists as to the relative importance of the numerous factors that influence investment spending, and, more seriously, little is known about the complex interactions that exist among these factors. In an effort to simplify, we will examine each of the factors separately in this and the following chapter. It must be remembered, however, that in the real world actual changes in investment spending are seldom attributable to any single factor. A change in any one factor may indeed affect investment spending, but the very change in one factor may directly or indirectly cause a change in another factor and so further stimulate or discourage investment spending.

Furthermore, this list of factors applies not to investment spending in the broader sense but more specifically to business investment spending for plant and equipment, the type of investment spending for which the concept of the MEC schedule was developed in Chapter 11. Gross private domestic investment is usually broken down into nonresidential structures and producers' durable equipment (roughly, "plant and equipment"), change in inventories, and residential structures. A list of causal factors for each of these three categories would not be identical, and the relative importance of those factors that would be found on all three lists would be different on each list. Since space does not permit detailed examination of all the factors influencing each different type of investment spending, we will concentrate on the principal factors influencing business plant and equipment expenditures, which is quantitatively the most important segment of gross private investment. This segment is especially significant for another reason: The major depressions experienced by the economy have been primarily the result of sharp declines in business spending for plant and equipment.

---

[1] In their empirical study, J. R. Meyer and E. Kuh limit themselves to three explanations, noting that "There is a plethora of theories to explain accumulation, in fact so many that selecting from among them the most worthwhile explanations has become most difficult." *The Investment Decision,* Harvard Univ. Press, 1957, p. 4.

EXPECTATIONS[2]

On the assumption that the basic objective of business enterprise is profit maximization, every investment expenditure by firms is made only if the firm expects that the expenditure will be profitable. However, the expectations held for any contemplated investment outlay change over time. As yesterday's less favorable expectations are replaced by today's more favorable expectations, some investment expenditures that were completely stalled yesterday may be enthusiastically carried forward today, and vice versa.

What causes an improvement in expectations? Although not always identifiable, the initial cause will ultimately be found in changes in the business situation that either have occurred already or seem certain to occur. The month just ended may have shown an increase in retail sales, an improvement of profit margins, or a spurt in stock prices. There may have been a rise in new orders or an announcement that government defense spending will soon be increased, both of which promise higher activity for the near future. Such developments, whatever may have caused them, typically cause businessmen to look more optimistically into the future. They may provide sufficient impetus to get a number of investment projects out of the planning stage and into the brick and mortar stage.[3]

Expectations as a Separate Factor

Some observers deny that changes in expectations are a separate factor affecting investment spending; they describe them as nothing more than a reflection of changes in the objective determinants of the business situation. However, they overlook a characteristic of investment spending long recognized by students of the business cycle.[4] For, though it is true that an improvement in expectations is based initially on one or more real changes, there is a tendency for the moderate optimism warranted by the facts to blossom into unwarranted

[2] The major theoretical work specifically on the role of expectations in investment has been done by G. L. S. Shackle. See *Expectation in Economics*, Cambridge Univ. Press, 1949, and *Uncertainty in Economics and Other Reflections*, Cambridge Univ. Press, 1955, which includes reprints of articles relevant here. See also G. Katona, "Psychological Analysis of Business Decisions and Expectations," in *American Economic Review*, March 1946, pp. 44–62.

[3] Clearly, these and any number of other generally favorable developments will not be sufficient to induce investment expenditures by a firm that is confronted at the same time with specific developments adverse to its future. For example, a firm whose output is almost entirely sold abroad can find little joy in generally favorable developments in the domestic economy, if at the same time import restrictions are clamped on its product in foreign markets. But, for all firms combined, such generally favorable developments must be conducive to some expansion in aggregate investment spending.

[4] For a review of the early literature on so-called psychological theories of the business cycle, see G. Haberler, *Prosperity and Depression*, Harvard Univ. Press, 1958, Ch. 6.

and unrestrained optimism. The speed with which optimistic or pessimistic expectations take hold seems at times to suggest that businessmen have lost sight of the meager factual basis from which they sprang. In this sense, expectations clearly are a factor deserving of separate consideration; once set off, changes in expectations take on, as it were, a life of their own.

As optimistic expectations replace pessimistic ones, they intensify whatever upward movement may have been set into motion by the changes in the real factors that initially produced the change in expectations. At first, the more cautious businessmen may find insufficient factual justification for investment expenditures today that could not be justified yesterday. The less cautious may be caught up sooner in the spreading exuberance. They will not be concerned with whether or not there is a solid basis for the swelling optimism; they will be concerned only with expanding their productive capacity in order to get their share of the expanded sales and enlarged profits expected from the coming, still higher level of business activity, a higher level that at some point in the upward movement is simply taken for granted. Even the more cautious may sooner or later be caught up in the wave of optimism, for as more and more firms expect improvement and act on these expectations, the resultant increased expenditures for new plant and equipment produce the very results expected. The possibility that an ensuing boom, based on little more than a wave of exaggeratedly optimistic expectations, may soon be followed by a collapse is considered by few. Once the downturn begins, excesses appear in the other direction. The facts of the now depressed situation justify some pessimism, but what appears is a wave of exaggeratedly pessimistic expectations that lose sight of the reality of conditions as did the preceding wave of optimism.

There is, in other words, an inherent tendency for expectations to lead to an overshooting of the mark called for by the reality of actual changes in the business situation. In the one direction, overly optimistic expectations may contribute to such an overexpansion in the stock of plant and equipment that the rate of return turns out to be, not only lower than that expected, but lower than it could have been if expectations had been somewhat less optimistic. In the other direction, overly pessimistic expectations may contribute to so great a contraction in business activity that the rate of return on plant and equipment turns out to be lower than it could have been if expectations had been less pessimistic.[5]

This description of events plainly assigns great importance to changes in expectations in investment determination. Although we cannot measure the extent to which the actual expansion or contraction of business investment spending in any period resulted from changes in expectations during that period or a preceding one, there is no doubt that changes in expectations have some influence. As will be explained later, the extent to which changes in expectations influence investment spending has probably diminished since World War II, but they certainly are still a factor to be included in any list one might set forth.

[5] See, for example, John Maynard Keynes, *The General Theory of Employment, Interest, and Money*, Harcourt, Brace & World, 1936, pp. 321–22.

Long-Term and Short-Term Expectations

The expectations described above are what Keynes called long-term expectations. Short-term expectations are those dealing with the prices firms expect to get for their output when they decide how much to produce with their existing plant and equipment. Long-term expectations are those dealing with the rate of return firms expect to earn if they expand their existing plant and equipment. Otherwise expressed, short-term expectations affect decisions of firms with regard to variations in the day-to-day level of output within their existing productive capacity; long-term expectations affect decisions of firms with regard to variations in the capacity level of output itself, that level varying with increases and decreases in the stock of fixed capital.

Short-term expectations affect investment in inventory; long-term expectations affect investment in plant and equipment. Long-term expectations are quantitatively the more important influence on aggregate investment spending, for overly optimistic or pessimistic long-term expectations can lead to much larger fluctuations in the stock of plant and equipment than the fluctuations in the stock of inventories that follow from overly optimistic or pessimistic short-term expectations. This is partially due to the fact that errors in short-term expectations are more quickly revealed and more quickly corrected. The failure of sales to come up to expectations is promptly disclosed by an unplanned increase in inventories, which can be corrected quickly by cutting production per time period below sales per time period. Similarly, the failure of sales to drop as far as expected will be promptly disclosed by a greater decrease in inventories than expected. Deficient inventories can also be corrected quickly, if productive capacity is available, by raising production per time period above sales per time period.

In contrast, errors in long-term expectations can contribute to an over-expansion of plant and equipment that is not quickly revealed and to a subsequent collapse of investment in plant and equipment that may require years to correct. The market will not promptly disclose the fact that the expansion of plant and equipment is excessive. The greater flow of final product that will result from an enlarged stock of plant and equipment must, of course, await the production of this plant and equipment; this may take several years. During this so-called gestation period, expectations are likely to improve as the increased income earned in the production of these capital goods comes into the market to purchase the relatively constant flow of consumer goods that existing plant and equipment are capable of turning out. Only when the expanded capital facilities finally begin to pour forth an increased flow of goods does the market reveal that productive capacity is excessive. Then, unless something occurs to bring about a recovery sooner, correction may be a long, drawn-out process in which the stock of capital is gradually worked down through normal wear and tear until replacement requirements finally call for a resumption of spending for plant and equipment.

Expectations and Investment Instability

Experience of the last twenty years suggests that changes in long-term expectations have become a less important factor in the explanation of the observed variations in plant and equipment expenditures than they were before World War II. One reason for this is a continuing tendency toward greater concentration in more and more industries. Huge errors of overexpansion or overcontraction are far more likely to occur in industries made up of hundreds of small firms than in industries dominated by a few big corporations. Where there are only a few, each is better equipped to study its market objectively and better able to discover what each of its few competitors is doing. Where there are hundreds of firms, each largely ignorant of what every other one is doing, there is a tendency for each to expand plant and equipment to meet an increase in demand that could be met by the expansion of only a few of their number. In addition, in an industry dominated by a few firms, it is likely that each firm will have carved out a secure position in the market and will therefore plan its expenditures for plant and equipment in accordance with the estimated long-run growth potential of the industry, which is largely uninfluenced by the recurrent waves of optimistic and pessimistic expectations that may sweep over the business community in general.

Another reason for the reduced influence of long-term expectations is that the postwar economy, despite a succession of brief and relatively mild downturns, has displayed a degree of stability that is in sharp contrast to prewar experience. In such a climate, expectations are not likely to reach an excess in either direction. Since the economy has not suffered a really severe downturn in recent years, there can hardly be expectations of any runaway expansion in output, employment, and general business activity. Such real changes can emerge only in an economy that has dropped to a very low level. Similarly, since the economy has not experienced wild security speculation, runaway rising prices, pronounced overexpansion of productive facilities in industry after industry, growing numbers of business bankruptcies, or any of the other symptoms that suggest an imminent economic collapse, businessmen have little cause to expect such a collapse. As unfavorable developments of a less serious nature do appear, expectations can and do turn pessimistic, but the degree of pessimism is restrained by the coincident expectation that the downturn, when it comes, will be mild and short.

In brief, given the degree of stability achieved by the economy over two decades, the excesses to which long-term expectations have previously been carried seem to be a thing of the past. They will undoubtedly remain an important factor in explaining variations in investment, but they probably will not again be the highly destabilizing factor they were at times in the past.

TECHNOLOGICAL CHANGE AND INNOVATION

An economy that year after year produces an unchanged variety of goods of unchanging quality in an unchanging way in firms with unchanging organization and finally sells these goods in unchanging markets is an economy in which there are no modifications in technology and no innovations. It is also an economy in which net investment is zero or is positive only to the extent necessary to meet the expansion generated by a growing population in what are otherwise unchanging markets.

No such economy has ever existed in this extreme form over any extended period of time, but reasonable approximations have been found in the most backward primitive societies, where production is almost entirely agricultural and is conducted by largely self-sufficient family units, and where technology is limited to primitive tools and methods that show little change over long periods of time.[6] At the other extreme are the economies of the heavily industrialized nations of the West, including in recent years Japan and Russia. In these countries every characteristic above assumed unchanged has undergone rapid and revolutionary change as the economies have driven toward maturity.

Although technological change and innovation have played roles of varying importance in different economies, one cannot underestimate their importance for the highly developed economies, whose very development is inseparable from them. It is especially for these economies that technological change and innovation have been and continue to be foremost among the factors affecting investment demand.

The Meaning of Technological Change and Innovation

A technological change is usually defined as a change that results in a shift in the production function.[7] The production function in its simplest form is nothing more than the relationship between physical quantities of inputs—in the form of land, labor, and capital—and physical quantities of output. The essence of the concept of the production function is that numerous alternative combinations can produce the same level of output. The only technological changes that are economically meaningful are those that permit either the production of a given output with less input or the production of more output with unchanged input.[8] Economists have traditionally emphasized shifts in the

[6] In terms of W. W. Rostow's five stages of economic growth, such a society resembles the "traditional" society. See *The Stages of Economic Growth*, Cambridge Univ. Press, 1961.
[7] For an introductory treatment of the way in which technological change may shift the production function, see E. Mansfield, *The Economics of Technological Change*, Norton, 1968, pp. 12–16.
[8] The production function in itself tells us neither the least-cost combination of inputs nor the level of output that will maximize the firm's profits. To determine this we need in addition

production function that permit a given level of output to be produced with less input as the result of the substitution of technologically improved capital equipment for labor. However, a shift in the production function may also be one in which a given level of output is produced with less input as a result of a combination of inputs altered in the other direction—less capital and more labor per unit of output, or even less capital and less labor per unit of output. These possibilities will be considered below as we examine the impact of technological change on investment expenditures in plant and equipment.

Although the terms are given different meanings by different writers, technological change is often defined somewhat narrowly as one type of the much broader field of change known as innovation. Thus, we find what is called "technological innovation"—technological change that involves a shift in the production function as described above. However, there are numerous other kinds of change that do not qualify as technological change in this narrow sense. The introduction of an altogether new good, the development of a new way of producing an existing good, a change in the quality of an existing good, even a new package for an existing good of unchanged quality are all innovations. Less closely tied to the properties of goods themselves are innovations such as the establishment of a new market for any good or the opening up of new sources of supply, improved methods of handling materials, the setting up of new types of business organization such as discount stores, or the introduction of time and motion studies. Some of these changes, such as a new way of producing an existing good, imply technological change; others, such as the establishment of a new market for an existing good, do not. There is no hard and fast distinction and no need here to attempt to draw one. However, in what follows it is important to keep in mind that we are using the term technological change in a narrow sense.

The broad meaning noted above is that given to the concept of innovation by Joseph A. Schumpeter, who found in innovation one of the driving forces in the capitalist process. Schumpeter developed innovation into the cornerstone of a theory of capitalist development and into an explanation of the recurring business cycles that a capitalist system characterized by innovation will pass through in the very course of its development.[9] What is of particular interest to us is the fact that, within the broad sweep of capitalist evolution, innovation has been and remains a factor that helps explain the changes in investment spending that the economy exhibits.

---

the prices of each input and the demand curve as seen by the firm for its output. Then, for profit maximization, the actual quantity of each input and the particular combination in which these inputs will be employed are those at which the marginal revenue product of each input is equal to its price. For a review of these concepts, see the theory of production in any introductory economics textbook—for example, P. A. Samuelson, *Economics*, 7th ed., McGraw-Hill, 1967, Ch. 27.

[9] See "The Analysis of Economic Change," in *Review of Economics and Statistics*, May 1935, pp. 2–10, reprinted in J. J. Clark and M. Cohen, eds., *Business Fluctuations, Growth, and Economic Stabilization*, Random House, 1963, pp. 46–59. For a fuller development, see Schumpeter's *The Theory of Economic Development*, Harvard Univ. Press, 1934, and *Business Cycles*, McGraw-Hill, 1939.

Technological Change and Investment Demand

Evidence exists that technological change shifts the MEC schedule upward, thereby enlarging the profit-maximizing capital stock, and thereby leading to a rise in the rate of investment spending. There is also evidence that technological change works in the opposite direction. Which result will occur is another of the many questions in economics for which there is no easy answer.

We have noted that an economically meaningful technological change is one that permits the production of a given output with less input or the production of more output with unchanged input. Such a technological change may increase capital input per unit of output and lower labor input per unit of output; if the reduction in outlay for labor input exceeds the increase in outlay for capital input per unit of output, the change is economically meaningful. A technological change may also lower capital input per unit of output and raise labor input per unit of output; again, if the reduction in outlay for capital input exceeds the increase in outlay for labor input per unit of output, we have an economically meaningful change. Lastly, a technological change may lower both labor input and capital input per unit of output, though not necessarily in the same proportion. If the reductions are in the same proportion, we have what is called "neutral technological change," according to one definition of this term. Thus we have the following three meaningful possibilities:

1. Capital-output ratio increases, and labor-output ratio decreases.
2. Capital-output ratio decreases, and labor-output ratio increases.
3. Capital-output ratio decreases, and labor-output ratio decreases.

We may also express these three possibilities in different terminology. A technological change that raises the capital-output ratio and reduces the labor-output ratio is capital using and labor-saving. Drawing similar parallels for the other two possibilities, we have the following list that matches the list above:[10]

1. Capital using and labor-saving.
2. Capital saving and labor using.
3. Capital saving and labor-saving.

Assuming at first an *unchanged* level of output, those technological changes that are capital using and labor-saving will tend to shift the MEC schedule upward and thereby raise the rate of investment spending. Those that are capital

---

[10] See G. Ackley, *Macroeconomic Theory*, Macmillan, 1961, p. 550, and W. S. Vickrey, *Metastatics and Macroeconomics*, Harcourt, Brace & World, 1964, pp. 35–42. Note that, in an absolute sense, the first case is capital using and labor-saving, the second case is capital saving and labor using, and the third case is both capital saving and labor-saving. But the third case, which is both absolutely capital saving and absolutely labor-saving, may be relatively capital saving or relatively capital using, or neutral. The second case, which is absolutely capital saving and absolutely labor using, is even more labor using in a relative sense. The first case, which is absolutely capital using and absolutely labor-saving, is even more capital using in a relative sense.

saving, whether they are also labor using (2 in the lists above) or labor-saving (3 in the lists above), will ordinarily have the opposite effect; they will tend to shift the MEC schedule downward and thereby reduce the rate of investment spending.[11]

Given our assumption that the level of output remains unchanged, these are the rather general effects on investment spending that may be expected from capital-using and capital-saving technological changes. Economists traditionally associated technological change primarily with one of these effects—namely, a rise in the rate of investment spending at any given level of output—because they looked on technological change as a force that leads to the use of more capital per unit of output and less labor per unit of output. They tended to neglect the less obvious possibility that technological change could lead to a reduction in capital input per unit of output and the still less obvious possibility that it could lead to a reduction in both capital input per unit of output and labor input per unit of output. For examples of such technological changes, there is the development of new construction materials and new techniques that have made possible "thin-walled" office buildings, which call for smaller capital input per unit of output (square foot of rentable floor space) with no apparent sacrifice in durability. Air travel, which has largely supplanted rail travel, also seems to call for smaller capital input per unit of output (passenger mile). The development of continuous casting in steel production by-passes several previously required stages in the steel-making process and thus eliminates the special capital facilities and the workers needed at these stages. Technological change of this last type leads to a reduction of both capital input and labor input per unit of output (ton of finished steel).

Nonetheless, the technological changes that economists have traditionally concentrated on do appear to be much more common; they increase the capital-output ratio, or they are capital using. A few modern examples are: the computerization of record keeping, previously performed by squads of clerks; the automation of assembly lines with hardly a laborer in sight; the system of direct long-distance dialing. To the extent that technological change is capital using, it tends to raise the rate of investment spending consistent with any given level of aggregate output.

[11] Under some conditions this may not be true. Consider the case of any nonmonopolized industry in which some firms in the ordinary course of events are ready to replace worn-out capital equipment with more efficient equipment based on new technology. This exerts pressure on their competitors to do the same, even though the capital equipment of these competitors may be far from worn out. Their equipment, though still useful, is rendered obsolete by the new technology; the maintenance of their competitive positions may require the premature abandonment of the old equipment. If such conditions generally prevailed through the economy, a steady stream of technological improvements, even though capital saving, could shift the MEC schedule upward and raise the rate of investment spending above what it would have been in the absence of any technological changes at all. This higher rate of investment spending could be consistent with a gradually diminishing stock of capital, since capital goods that have been rendered obsolete and taken out of use are no longer counted as part of the capital stock. See R. Eisner, "Technological Change, Obsolescence, and Aggregate Demand," in *American Economic Review*, March 1956, pp. 92–105.

The rather general conclusions indicated above follow from technological change on the assumption that aggregate output remains unchanged. But technological change takes place over time, and over time aggregate output expands. The relationship between technological change and the rate of investment spending as aggregate output grows is an exceedingly complex matter. Attempts have been made to identify the specific contributions to the long-run expansion of aggregate output made by the growth in the stock of capital, by the growth in the size and quality of the labor force, and by technological change.[12] If, as described above, a given level of aggregate output can as a result of technological change be produced with more capital and less labor, less capital and more labor, or even less of both inputs, then the rate of growth in output over the years could exceed the rate of growth of either of these inputs or of both of them combined. Output has indeed outpaced the growth of both labor and capital inputs. If it grew more rapidly than labor input but less rapidly than capital input, we could say that technological change over the years was labor-saving but capital using and therefore presumably stimulating to investment spending. If output grew more rapidly than capital input but less rapidly than labor input, we could say that technological change over the years was labor using but capital saving and therefore presumably discouraging to investment spending. Since it has grown more rapidly than either labor or capital input, it appears that technological change has in the long run reduced both the capital-output ratio and the labor-output ratio. In other words, technological change has been both capital saving and labor-saving. It is even more significant that technological change, rather than the capital stock or the labor force, emerges as the most important factor in the explanation of the actual rate of growth of output the American economy has experienced.

This brief digression into the question of growth of aggregate output may help us see that, in terms of the long-run growth of output, technological change is not so directly tied to or embodied in the stock of capital as was once thought to be the case. Specifically, industry by industry, an increase in capital stock is *not* the inevitable result of technological progress within each industry. One major study on the determinants of investment finds that "It is difficult to say anything worthwhile at the *a priori* level about the effect of a change in technology. Technological advance may be either labor-saving or capital saving and so, even though it may be expected to result in a diminution of cost and expansion of industry output, it is by no means certain that it must lead to an increase

---

[12] We will touch on this question in Chapter 21. The major studies on this subject include R. M. Solow, "Technical Change and the Aggregate Production Function," in *Review of Economics and Statistics*, Aug. 1957, pp. 312–20, reprinted in M. G. Mueller, ed., *Readings in Macroeconomics*, Holt, Rinehart and Winston, 1966, pp. 323–33; E. F. Denison, *The Sources of Economic Growth in the U.S. and the Alternatives Before Us*, Supplementary Paper No. 13, Committee for Economic Development, 1962; and S. Fabricant, *Basic Facts on Productivity Change*, Occasional Paper 63, National Bureau of Economic Research, Princeton Univ. Press, 1959. For a different type of approach to this question, see A. Carter, "The Economics of Technological Change," in *Scientific American*, April 1966.

in the amount of capital devoted to the industry." [13] The absence of any rigid or unvarying tie between technological progress and the stock of capital also rules out a fixed, direct tie between technological progress and the rate of investment.

Although we can conclude that, for any given level of output, capital-using technological change will tend to raise the rate of investment spending and capital-saving technological change will tend to do the opposite, we can only note at this point that the impact of technological change on the rate of investment spending under conditions of growing aggregate output may cause an increase *or* a decrease in the rate of investment spending. While technological change has clearly permitted a long-run expansion of output at a rate greater than that of the expansion of the capital input and labor input, whether this has also worked to produce a higher or lower rate of investment spending in the long run than would have been the case in the absence of technological change is a question to which there is no certain answer.

Innovation and Investment Demand

We have seen that technological change can be, and over the long run has been, of a capital-saving nature. For this reason, technological change itself may have a dampening effect on investment expenditures. This is not the case with innovation, however: "In the United States, innovations have been, are now, and probably will continue to be the most pervasive and dynamic of all stimulants to investment." [14] Despite the fact that engineering genius has over the years brought forth technological changes that permit the expansion of the output of goods and services with a less than proportional expansion of capital and labor, innovational genius has over these same years brought forth changes that require a growth in the capital stock and the number of persons employed, which capital-saving and labor-saving technological changes have not begun to offset.

Innovation in the form of a new product, even if accompanied by technological change that will in time permit a reduction in capital input per unit of output, may still lead to massive investment expenditures for the plant and equipment necessary for its production. Clearly, to produce this result, the reception of the new good by the public must be sufficiently favorable to require additional capital facilities. This assumes that existing plant and equipment are not adaptable to the production of this good or, if adaptable, are not available in the quantity needed to meet demand. For example, television sets could be produced at first by modifying the existing capital facilities and production techniques employed in the radio industry. However, television sets quickly

[13] R. Eisner and R. H. Strotz, "Determinants of Business Investment," in *Impacts of Monetary Policy*, Commission on Money and Credit, Prentice-Hall, 1963, p. 66.
[14] J. P. Lewis and R. C. Turner, *Business Conditions Analysis*, 2nd ed., McGraw-Hill, 1967, p. 202.

became overwhelmingly popular with the public, not in place of radio but in addition to it.[15] The value of the combined output of radio and television sets within a few years reached a level far beyond what the relatively mature radio industry would possibly have achieved on its own. Investment expenditures for plant and equipment jumped quickly from almost nothing in the forties to large figures in the fifties.

Historically, the growth in the nation's stock of capital is closely related to hundreds of such innovations, especially to a few of major importance. One such innovation was the spread of railroads across the continent during the last half of the nineteenth century. Apart from the huge sums required for rolling stock, roadbed, bridges, terminals, and other direct facilities, the web of tracks criss-crossing the nation made accessible new sources of raw materials and opened up new markets for finished goods, both of which were innovations that gave rise to further investment spending. At about the same time came the age of steel, which not only was a gigantic, investment-inducing innovation in itself but which supplied the vital ingredient without which hundreds of other innovations would not have appeared. With the turn of the century came the automobile, also an innovation that triggered many others, especially the growth of modern roads and highways and the rise of the petroleum industry. Another innovation that came with the turn of the century was electric power, which spawned the vast investment required for the electrification of the nation. The stream of innovations continues into the present with the introduction of the telephone, radio, commercial aviation, synthetic fibers and fabrics, pharmaceuticals, television, electronic data processing, and finally several with a still uncertain potential for the future, "automated" production equipment and nuclear energy.

None of these more recent innovations, at least so far, compares in its investment-generating impact with railroads in the nineteenth century or electric power and automobiles in the early twentieth. Because innovation is thought to exercise so important an influence on the rate of investment spending, the failure of recent decades to produce innovations with the impact of those of earlier times was a cause of some concern to economists, especially during the stagnant thirties. However, our experience since World War II indicates that innovation is at least as effective as before. But, instead of a handful of great innovations as in the preceding century and a half, hundreds of lesser innovations in the last twenty years have stimulated investment in a large number of products and processes throughout the economy. Their collective impact on investment demand, while not really measurable, probably compares favorably with that found during the earlier history of the economy. The source of the discoveries or inventions that lead to innovation has also changed; today inventions are more likely to come from systematic, large-scale, institutionalized research. The day is past when we could point with some degree of accuracy to such great

---

[15] For a study of "Consumer Response to Innovation: Television," see the article by this title in T. F. Dernburg, R. N. Rosett, and H. W. Watts, *Studies in Household Economic Behavior*, Yale Univ. Press, 1958.

"single-handed" achievements as Watt's steam engine, Bessemer's converter, or Edison's light bulb. Since innovations are now more often an end product of prolonged, expensive, and complex "multihanded" research, they also tend to appear at a more orderly pace.[16] Just as changes in businessmen's expectations are no longer as great a destabilizing force as they once were, so the more regular flow of innovations has probably reduced the destabilizing impact that came with the intermittent but massive innovations of the nineteenth and early twentieth centuries.[17]

Whatever the future may bring, whether a continuation of the orderly flow of lesser innovations that has characterized the past twenty years or the appearance of one or more major innovations like those of the more distant past, the maintenance of a high level of investment spending will still depend on a satisfactory rate of innovation of one kind or another. As in the past, technological progress will probably continue to give us ways to produce a unit of output with still less capital and labor input. Therefore, without innovation, the profit-maximizing capital stock will grow more slowly than would otherwise be the case. As a result, investment may languish; and without the necessary rate of investment, the private-enterprise economy will stagnate.

From the MEC Schedule to Income and Output

Each of the several factors examined so far in this chapter influences the rate of investment spending and thus influences the level of income and output. Before going on to still other factors, let us lay out step by step the mechanics of the process by which we get from factors such as technological changes, innovations, or changes in expectations to changes in the level of income and output.

Looking back to Part A of Figure 11–3, we may say that technological changes, innovations, or improved expectations that raise the rate of return expected from new capital goods push the MEC schedule upward. This in turn shifts the MEI schedule of Part B upward, resulting in a rise in investment spending. As a final step, Figure 8–1 shows how the increase in income that results from any given rise in investment spending may be determined graphically. This is all summarized in Figure 12–1. Parts A and B correspond with Parts A and B respectively of Figure 11–3; Part C corresponds with the saving-investment chart of Figure 8–1. To see how these several parts fit together, let us

[16] See J. A. Schumpeter, *Capitalism, Socialism, and Democracy*, 3rd ed., Harper, 1950, pp. 132–33, and J. K. Galbraith, *American Capitalism*, Houghton Mifflin, 1952, pp. 91–92. On the "clustering" of innovations, see J. Schmookler, "Invention, Innovation, and Business Cycles," in *Variability of Private Investment in Plant and Equipment*, Part 2, Joint Economic Committee, 1962, pp. 45–55.

[17] Apart from the rate at which innovations appear, the rate at which they spread from firm to firm (the so-called diffusion rate) may also affect investment in a destabilizing manner. On the diffusion rate, see F. Lynn, "An Investigation of the Rate of Development and Diffusion of Technology in Our Modern Industrial Society," *Report of the National Commission on Technology, Automation, and Economic Progress*, Washington, D.C., 1966, and E. Mansfield, *Industrial Research and Technological Innovation*, Norton, 1968, Ch. 7.

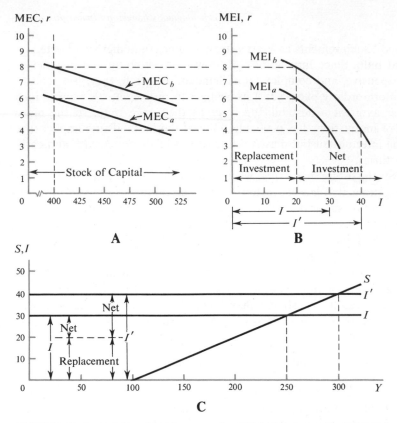

FIGURE 12–1 Relationship Between the MEC Schedule, the MEI Schedule, and the Level of Income and Output

trace the process set in motion by investment-inducing technological change, innovation, or improvement in expectations.

In Part A of Figure 12–1, the original MEC schedule is labeled MEC_a and the rate of interest is, say, 4 percent. The profit-maximizing capital stock is then $500 billion, but the actual stock is given as $400 billion. Thus, there is positive net investment per time period. The actual rate of net investment depends on the elasticity of the relevant MEI schedule in Part B; the schedule relevant to the existing capital stock is MEI_a. This schedule indicates that there is net investment spending of $10 billion; adding replacement investment of $20 billion makes gross investment $30 billion per time period. Barring a shift in the MEC schedule or in the rate of interest, this rate of investment spending will remain unchanged in the short run, for we may assume that net investment spending in the short run is not large enough to move us appreciably down the MEC schedule and so push the MEI schedule down below MEI_a. The indicated rate of gross investment spending, $30 billion, gives us the investment function, I, of Part C. The saving function of Part C intersects the investment function so derived at an income level of $250 billion.[18] This then is the equi-

[18] The saving function of Part C is $S = -20 + \frac{1}{5}Y$, and the investment function, derived as described above, is $I = 30$. The equilibrium level of income is given by $S = I$, here S and I being expressed in gross terms, or by $-20 + \frac{1}{5}Y = 30$, or $Y = 250$.

238

librium level of income consistent with the MEC_a schedule of Part A. With no change in any of these schedules, the indicated level of income will remain unchanged from one period to the next over the short run.

Now let us assume innovations in the form of various new products that require new plant and equipment for their production and that promise a rate of return on the new plant and equipment greater than the MEC on the existing capital stock. This shifts the MEC schedule upward from MEC_a to MEC_b, which in turn shifts the MEI schedule upward from MEI_a to MEI_b. This in turn raises the rate of gross investment spending from \$30 to \$40 billion and the rate of net investment spending from \$10 to \$20 billion. The indicated rate of gross investment spending of \$40 billion now gives us the higher investment function, I', of Part C. The saving function of Part C has an MPS equal to $1/5$, so the multiplier is $1/\frac{1}{5}$, or 5. The change in investment, ΔI, is \$10 billion. With $\Delta Y/\Delta I = 5$, $\Delta Y = \$50$ billion. The new level of income is \$300 billion, or \$50 billion above what it was before the shift in the investment function.

Any factor that shifts the MEC schedule upward will, other things being equal, set into motion a sequence such as that described. The result will be a rise in the rate of investment spending whose amount depends on the extent of the upward shift in the MEI schedule, which in turn depends on the extent of the upward shift in the MEC schedule. Given the increase in investment, or ΔI, the increase in the level of income, or ΔY, depends on the size of the multiplier.

LEVEL OF INCOME AND OUTPUT

Another important factor influencing the rate of investment spending is the level of income and output. One would hardly expect the amount spent by businessmen for new plant and equipment to be the same per time period when aggregate income is at the lower level reached during a recession as when income is at the higher level reached during prosperity. If there is such a direct relationship between the absolute level of income and investment spending, it means that the profit-maximizing capital stock depends, among other things, on the absolute level of income. As we have seen, a higher profit-maximizing capital stock is indicated by an MEC schedule positioned farther to the right, and vice versa; and, in the short run, the rate of investment spending will be greater, the farther to the right lies the MEC schedule, and vice versa. If the position of the MEC schedule depends in part on the absolute level of income, we find in this the connection between the income level and the rate of investment spending. However, in what follows, instead of working from the level of income to the position of the MEC schedule to the rate of investment spending, for simplicity we will go directly from the level of income to the rate of investment spending. We will first work through the mechanics of the model, which assumes that the rate of investment spending is a function of the absolute level of income, and then turn briefly to the reasons why the rate of investment spending may be expected to vary in this manner.

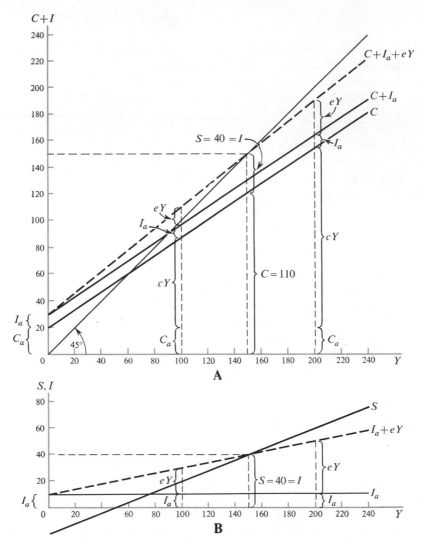

FIGURE 12–2   The Equilibrium Level of Income with Induced Investment

Investment—Autonomous and Induced

In the simple theory of income determination developed in Chapter 7, we treated investment as an amount uninfluenced by the level of income. In Figure 12–2 the solid-line consumption and investment functions correspond to those introduced in Chapter 7. Investment demand as given by the solid-line investment function of Figure 12–2 is 10 at all levels of income, which means that investment is unaffected by the level of income. Economists describe this situation as one in which investment is entirely *autonomous*.

If we now drop this assumption and agree that investment is somehow related to the level of income, we must specify this relationship. A plausible but very general statement is that the rate of investment will be higher with a higher level of income and lower with a lower level of income. This direct, functional relationship is shown in Figure 12–2 by the broken-line investment function. In Part A investment equals the distance between line *C* and the broken line. This distance becomes greater at higher levels of income, indicating a successively greater rate of investment spending at successively higher levels of income. Investment that is dependent on the level of income is described by economists as *induced* investment.

Accordingly, in terms of Figure 12–2, investment demand at any level of income may be shown as the sum of autonomous and induced investment. With income at 100, investment is 30 (the sum of autonomous investment of 10 and induced investment of 20); with income at 200, investment is 50 (the sum of autonomous investment of 10 and induced investment of 40).

Note that the investment function we are now describing has the same properties as the short-run consumption function developed in Chapter 7. The general equation for the short-run linear consumption function was there given as $C = C_a + cY$, in which C_a represented autonomous consumption, or the amount of consumption spending that is independent of the level of income, and cY represented induced consumption, or the amount of consumption spending that depends on the level of income. Similarly, the general equation for an investment function of the type given by the broken line of Part B of Figure 12–2 is $I = I_a + eY$, in which I_a represents autonomous investment, or the amount of investment spending that is independent of the level of income, and eY represents induced investment, or the amount of investment spending that depends on the level of income.[19]

In the consumption function, induced consumption equals cY, in which c indicates the marginal propensity to consume, or $\Delta C/\Delta Y$. In the investment function, we have in e an analogous concept known as the *marginal propensity to invest*, MPI, or $\Delta I/\Delta Y$.

The Equilibrium Level of Income and Output

To find the equilibrium level of income and output in a model that includes induced investment, the principle is the same as that elaborated earlier for models in which investment was assumed to be entirely autonomous. The equilibrium level of income and output is still that level at which aggregate demand equals aggregate output, or planned investment equals planned saving.[20] In Chapter 8 we had what amounted to the following:

$$Y = C + I$$
$$C = C_a + cY$$
$$I = I_a$$

[19] Since c has been used for the MPC and s for the MPS, this mnemonic approach suggests i for the MPI. But since this letter has already been used with other meaning, e will be used instead.
[20] We are still assuming that the price level remains unchanged, so that every change in income is matched by an equal change in output.

so that

$$Y = C_a + cY + I_a$$

With an investment function which assumes that investment, I, as well as consumption, C, depends on income, Y, we have the following:

$$Y = C + I$$
$$C = C_a + cY$$
$$I = I_a + eY$$

so that

$$Y = C_a + cY + I_a + eY$$

The consumption function in Figure 12–2 is $C = 20 + \frac{3}{5}Y$, and the new investment function is $I = 10 + \frac{1}{5}Y$. Therefore, the equilibrium level of income is readily determined as follows:

$$Y = 20 + \tfrac{3}{5}Y + 10 + \tfrac{1}{5}Y$$
$$Y - \tfrac{3}{5}Y - \tfrac{1}{5}Y = 30$$
$$\tfrac{1}{5}Y = 30$$
$$Y = 150$$

As shown in Part A of Figure 12–2, with Y of 150, C is 110 and I is 40. When output is 150, aggregate income is 150; and, when aggregate income is 150, consumer demand is $20 + \frac{3}{5}(150)$, or 110, and investment demand is $10 + \frac{1}{5}(150)$, or 40. Aggregate demand of $110 + 40$, or 150, exactly equals aggregate output of 150. This equality is one way of defining the equilibrium level of income and output.

We may also determine the equilibrium level of income by finding that level that equates planned saving and planned investment.

$$S = -20 + \tfrac{2}{5}Y$$
$$I = 10 + \tfrac{1}{5}Y$$
$$-20 + \tfrac{2}{5}Y = 10 + \tfrac{1}{5}Y$$
$$\tfrac{1}{5}Y = 30$$
$$Y = 150$$

Changes in the Equilibrium Level—The Super-Multiplier

Aggregate demand in the present model is the sum of consumption demand, $C = C_a + cY$, and investment demand, $I = I_a + eY$. If c, the MPC, is stable, a change in aggregate demand cannot originate with consumer spending unless there is a change in autonomous consumption, C_a—that is, unless the consumption function itself shifts. If e, the MPI, is stable, a change in aggregate demand cannot originate with investment spending unless there is a change in autonomous investment, I_a—that is, unless the investment function itself shifts.

Shift in the Investment Function. Since the original equilibrium level was derived from the aggregate demand function, $Y = C_a + cY + I_a + eY$, any change in the equilibrium level of income—that is, ΔY—must equal the sum of the changes in the components of the aggregate demand function—that is,

$$\Delta Y = \Delta C_a + c\,\Delta Y + \Delta I_a + e\,\Delta Y$$

This equation may be manipulated as follows:

$$\Delta Y - c\,\Delta Y - e\,\Delta Y = \Delta C_a + \Delta I_a$$
$$\Delta Y(1 - c - e) = \Delta C_a + \Delta I_a$$
$$\Delta Y = \frac{1}{1 - c - e}(\Delta C_a + \Delta I_a)$$

Assuming a rise in autonomous investment from 10 to 20, or ΔI_a of 10, and retaining the earlier adopted values for the MPC and MPI, we have

$$\Delta Y = \frac{1}{1 - 3/5 - 1/5}(0 + 10)$$
$$\Delta Y = 50$$

The previous equilibrium level was 150. With ΔY of 50, the new level is 200. A rise in autonomous investment of 10 has raised the equilibrium level of income by 50. These results are shown in Figure 12–3.

The introduction of induced investment, eY, into the model has modified the multiplier expression from $1/(1 - c)$ to $1/(1 - c - e)$, as shown above. Since the MPI is positive, the multiplier is larger than it would have been without induced investment. If investment did not respond to a rise in income, the multiplier would have been $1/(1 - 3/5)$, or 2.5, and the rise in income resulting from a rise in autonomous investment of 10 would have been only 25.

The multiplier that emerges from a model in which there is both induced consumption and induced investment has been labeled the super-multiplier.[21] As noted, it is necessarily greater than the simple multiplier, given a positive MPI, for if an initial rise in income, produced in our example by a rise in autonomous investment, leads not only to induced consumption spending but also to induced investment spending, the overall rise in income will be greater than if only consumption spending had responded to the rise in income.

Thus, in our example, instead of only induced consumption of 0.6 for every increase in income of 1, we now have induced consumption of 0.6 *plus* induced investment of 0.2, or a total of induced spending of 0.8, for every increase in income of 1. The MPC of 3/5 and the MPI of 1/5 may be combined

[21] This term was coined by J. R. Hicks. See *A Contribution to the Theory of the Trade Cycle*, Oxford Univ. Press, 1950, p. 62.

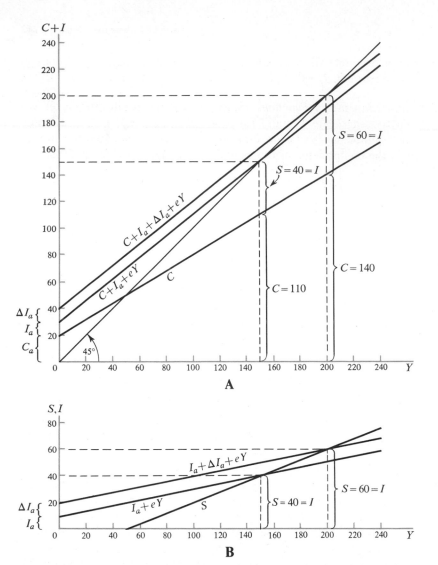

FIGURE 12–3   Effect of a Shift in the Investment Function on the Equilibrium Level of Income: The Super-Multiplier

to give what may be called the "marginal propensity to spend," here equal to 4/5. The super-multiplier may then be alternatively expressed as the reciprocal of 1 minus the marginal propensity to spend, and in our example this is 5. This means that to achieve equilibrium, with an MPC of 3/5 and an MPI of 1/5, or with a marginal propensity to spend of 4/5, income must rise by five times the increase in autonomous investment.[22]

[22] As in our previous models, the new equilibrium is reached at that income level at which planned saving equals planned investment. But, with induced investment supplementing autonomous investment, the rise in income must be greater to call forth additional saving equal to the sum of the increase in autonomous and induced investment. Thus, in our example, it is only after income has risen by 50 that planned saving will have been brought once again

Shift in the Consumption Function—"The Paradox of Thrift." An upward shift in the consumption function of $\Delta C_a = 10$ would yield the same results shown above for an upward shift in the investment function of $\Delta I_a = 10$. With MPC of 3/5 and MPI of 1/5, the super-multiplier is 5, and ΔC_a of 10 would lead to ΔY of 50. A downward shift in either the investment or the consumption function, say $\Delta I_a = -10$ or $\Delta C_a = -10$, will each give the same result— ΔY of -50. Although decreases in I_a or C_a produce results simply the reverse of those produced by increases, the case of a downward shift in the consumption function is worth further consideration, for it is this shift, combined with the present investment function, that is the source of the interesting result known as "the paradox of thrift."

Briefly stated, the paradox is this: If consumers seek to save a larger amount out of any given level of income, that attempt to save more may lead to an actual decrease in the amount they succeed in saving. This seemingly contradictory result was noted by Keynes in his *General Theory*, though someone else later gave it its present name.

The desire of consumers to save more at each level of income is, of course, the same as a desire to spend less at each level of income. We may refer to this change in plans as either a downward shift in the consumption function or an upward shift in the saving function. In Figure 12–4 we have the original saving function, $S = -20 + \frac{2}{5}Y$, and investment function, $I = 10 + \frac{1}{5}Y$, marked S and I, respectively. These functions give us the equilibrium level of income of 150. Now let us assume an increase in the thriftiness of consumers such that at each level of income they seek to save 10 more than previously; in other words, we assume an increase in autonomous saving of 10, or $\Delta S_a = 10$. The saving function shifts upward to $S = -10 + \frac{2}{5}Y$; this new saving function is marked $S + \Delta S_a$ in Figure 12–4. As a result of this shift in the saving function with no shift in the investment function, a new equilibrium is established at Y of 100. For only at Y of 100 is saving $[S = -10 + \frac{2}{5}(100) = 30]$ equal to investment $[I = 10 + \frac{1}{5}(100) = 30]$. Thus, from the original equilibrium level of income at which saving was 40, the attempt of consumers to increase saving to 50 leads not to an increase but to a decrease in saving to 30.

Why do we get this seemingly surprising result? An upward shift in the saving function is a downward shift in the consumption function. With no shift

---

into equality with planned investment. With ΔY of 50, ΔI is 20, made up of the rise in autonomous investment of 10 and in induced investment of $\frac{1}{5}(50)$, or 10. With ΔY of 50, ΔS is $\frac{2}{5}(50)$, or 20. Any smaller increase in income will show an excess of planned investment over planned saving and so a disequilibrium that leads to a further rise in income. Assuming ΔY of 40, we have ΔI of 18, made up of the increase in autonomous investment of 10 and induced investment of $\frac{1}{5}(40)$, or 8. With ΔY of 40, we have ΔS of $\frac{2}{5}(40)$, or 16. Therefore, $\Delta I > \Delta S$ (18 > 16), and income expands further. In terms of aggregate demand and aggregate output, with ΔY of 40, aggregate output is 190, and aggregate demand is 192, made up of $C = 20 + \frac{3}{5}(190)$, or 134, plus $I = 20 + \frac{1}{5}(190)$, or 58. With aggregate demand exceeding aggregate output, output and income expand further. With the increase of 10 in autonomous investment, aggregate demand will equal aggregate output, or planned saving will equal planned investment only with an increase in income and output of 50.

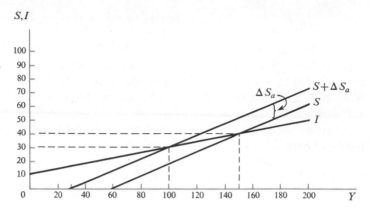

FIGURE 12–4   The Paradox of Thrift

in the investment function, aggregate demand is decreased, and this reduces income. The reduction in income causes not only an induced reduction in consumption but also an induced reduction in investment. To the extent that investment varies directly with the level of income, the new lower equilibrium level of income will find saving equated with investment at amounts below what they were before the upward shift in the saving function. If investment were entirely autonomous, no such paradox would appear. An upward shift in the saving function would still lead to a fall in income, but income would then fall only by the smaller amount necessary to bring planned saving into equality with the constant amount of planned investment.

Distinguishing Autonomous and Induced Investment in Practice.   The exact nature of the relationship between income and investment in the real economy is more complicated than in our simple model. For any series of time periods, the actual data for the economy do not permit us to say what part of each period's investment was induced by that period's income and what part was autonomous. Although we may believe that the higher investment found in periods of higher income was in part induced by the higher income, we cannot say what part of this higher investment was the result of an upward shift in the investment function, ΔI_a, and what part was induced by the higher level of income. For example, if we find from one period to the next a rise in income of $40 billion and a rise in investment of $10 billion, one possibility is that the whole $10 billion rise in investment was autonomous and the simple multiplier was 4. Another of the many possibilities is that $8 billion was autonomous and $2 billion induced and that the super-multiplier was accordingly 5.[23]

[23] In the first possibility, with $e = 0$, $\Delta I_a = 10$, and $\Delta Y = 40$, we have

$$\$40 \text{ billion} = \frac{1}{1 - c - 0} (\$10 \text{ billion})$$

indicating that c must be 3/4 and the simple multiplier, 4. In the other possibility, with $2 billion of investment induced by the $40 billion increase in income, $e = 1/20$. Therefore, with $e = 1/20$, $\Delta I_a = \$8$ billion, and $\Delta Y = \$40$ billion, we have

$$\$40 \text{ billion} = \frac{1}{1 - c - 1/20} (\$8 \text{ billion})$$

and c must be 3/4, or 15/20, to yield the required super-multiplier of 5.

246

Despite the fact that time-series data on GNP and gross private domestic investment show a direct, if not close, relationship, we cannot conclude from this what portion of each period's investment is induced. The problem is that even if investment were entirely autonomous, we would still expect to find a positive correlation between the level of investment and the level of income. Although advanced statistical methods enable economists to say something more definite about the relationship between investment spending and the level of income, we will limit ourselves in the next section to a nonstatistical appraisal of the plausibility of a direct relationship between the rate of investment and the level of income.

Investment as a Function of Income

We noted earlier that one could hardly expect the amount spent by businessmen for new plant and equipment to be the same when aggregate income is at a recession low as when it is at a prosperity peak. In other words, one would expect investment expenditures not to be entirely autonomous but to vary cyclically with the level of income. Let us look into some of the specific factors advanced in support of a direct relationship between income and investment.

The higher the level of aggregate income, the greater the aggregate profits earned by business tend to be, the profit share of aggregate income typically varying more than proportionately with changes in the level of income.[24] Since one guide to the probable future level of profits is simply the current level of profits, the higher aggregate profits that accompany a higher level of income today may create expectations of a continuation of the same level or even a rise in the level of aggregate profits tomorrow. Given such a higher level of profits, the favorable expectations that result may cause a rise in the desired capital stock, a shift in the MEC schedule to the right, and an increase in the rate of investment spending. To the extent that businessmen react in this fashion to the level of profits, we have one factor connecting investment spending to the absolute level of income.

The higher aggregate profits that accompany a higher level of income are conducive to an expansion of investment spending for a related reason. Higher profits not only improve expectations concerning the future level of profits but also make possible the internal financing of at least part of the investment expenditures that business may otherwise have wanted to undertake.[25] Even in the absence of improved expectations, the mere availability of such funds may lead to the investment of at least part of them in the expansion or modernization of plant and equipment, rather than to the commitment of all such funds to extra dividends or additions to cash, bank accounts, or short-term security holdings. To the extent that some investment projects that would not be undertaken if firms had to finance them through external funds may be undertaken

---

[24] See Table 5–3, pp. 84–87.
[25] The broad question of the cost and availability of investment funds will be examined in the following chapter.

if the funds are internally available, the availability of internal funds becomes another factor influencing investment. In the tie between the level of income, the amount of profits, and the volume of internally generated funds, we have another reason to expect greater investment spending at a higher level of income.[26]

An additional factor that is sometimes advanced in support of a direct relationship between the income level and investment spending is primarily a matter of the capital stock required to produce any given level of output. Assuming a stable price level, a higher level of income means a proportionately higher level of output. To produce a greater output with no change in technology frequently requires, among other things, an enlargement of the stock of plant and equipment. Since net investment is the only means by which the stock of plant and equipment may be enlarged, it seems to follow that the rate of net investment spending on plant and equipment is a direct function of the level of income and output.

It is here that one must make a subtle but crucial distinction between the level of income and output and *changes* in the level of income and output. If with income at a low level, business has plant and equipment in an amount just sufficient to produce the corresponding level of output, then it does follow that a higher rate of investment is necessary to accumulate the additional plant and equipment required to produce a higher level of output. However, note that the *increase* in investment undertaken for the purpose of enlarging productive capacity results from the *change* in the level of output and is independent of the *absolute level* of output, whether this be high or low. Thus, it is the process of moving from one level of output to another that calls for *additional* investment spending of the capacity-expanding kind; it does not matter here whether an increase in output of 10 is an increase from a level of 100 to a level of 110 or from a level of 200 to a level of 210.

Once the movement has been made to a new, higher level, assuming that this level remains unchanged, net investment spending generated by the need for additional productive capacity will again be zero, and gross investment spending will, for some time period, be what it was at the previous lower level of output. The more durable the newly acquired capital equipment is, the more distant will be the time when gross investment will be pushed upward by the need to replace this additional portion of the capital stock. If the new higher level of output remains unchanged over time, net investment spending undertaken to expand capacity will remain zero, even though gross investment spending will eventually be raised by the higher replacement requirement. Therefore,

[26] Profits receive primary emphasis in W. W. Heller, "The Anatomy of the Investment Decision," in *Harvard Business Review*, March 1951, pp. 95–103, and in Meyer and Kuh, *The Investment Decision*, Chs. 8 and 12. Professors Meyer and Kuh recognize that "while profits may be the proximate cause of investment, their dependence on the output level really means that output ultimately determines investment levels." However, this line of reasoning is qualified by the authors on pages 131–32. For an approach that emphasizes the level of income and output as a determinant of investment but minimizes the place of profits, see W. J. Baumol, *Business Behavior, Value and Growth*, rev. ed., Harcourt, Brace & World, 1967, Ch. 12.

if we limit ourselves to a time period not longer than the life of the newly acquired capital equipment, we find the same rate of gross investment after the rise to the new, higher level of income and output that we found before this rise in income and output took place. For a time period of this length, investment whose purpose is to alter productive capacity appears not to be linked in any close way with the absolute level of income and output. Thus, to the extent that the rate of investment spending is linked to the absolute level of income, it is investment undertaken primarily for modernization or cost-cutting purposes rather than for outright expansion of capacity.

In summary, of the several factors that suggest a direct relationship between the rate of investment and the level of income, we find the former tied to the latter to some extent through the aggregate profits of business. Since higher income usually means higher aggregate profits, higher investment may be expected to accompany higher income because higher current profits may lead to the expectation of continued high profits and because higher profits provide business with more internally generated funds whose availability may be a stimulus to investment spending of the modernization type. On the other hand, one does not find a clear-cut connection between the absolute level of income and the rate of investment spending undertaken primarily to alter productive capacity. To the extent that the rate of investment spending is technically associated with aggregate output, a change in the rate of investment spending is more plausibly ascribed to a change in the level of aggregate output than to any absolute level of output. This brings us to the fourth factor in our list, the *acceleration principle*, which specifically relates the rate of investment spending to changes in the level of output. This factor, which plays a prominent role in any explanation of investment spending, will be discussed in the next chapter.

CHAPTER 13

CHANGES IN INVESTMENT: II

An economy with a stable level of output and with the actual capital stock adjusted to the production of just this level of output will, in the absence of a shift in the MEC schedule or a change in the interest rate, show zero net investment and unchanging gross investment equal to replacement requirements. A change in investment spending will occur only if there is a shift in the MEC schedule or in the interest rate. As we saw in the preceding chapter, such a shift in the MEC schedule could be the result of technological changes, innovations, or changes in expectations.

CHANGES IN THE LEVEL OF INCOME AND OUTPUT

The MEC schedule may also shift as a result of a *change* in the level of income and output, produced by a rise in investment spending that results from technological changes, innovations, or changes in expectations. In other words, from an original equilibrium position in which the level of income and output and the rate of investment are both stable, there could be an increase in *autonomous* investment as the result, perhaps, of innovations that shift the MEC schedule upward The rise in autonomous investment spending will raise the level of income and output; this rise in income and output may itself lead to a further upward shift in the MEC schedule and so to a further rise in investment spending. It is specifically the relationship between changes in the level of income and output and investment spending that is our concern in this section.

250

Capital-Output Ratio

In the discussion of technological change, we saw that the capital-output ratio is not constant over time. Some technological changes involve an increase in capital per unit of output, others a decrease. To simplify, let us assume here that the capital-output ratio remains constant. This assumption enables us to specify the stock of capital necessary to the production of any level of output. Letting K represent the capital stock, Y the level of output, and w the capital-output ratio (or the number of dollars of capital required to produce one dollar of output per time period), we have

$$K = wY$$

If the constant capital-output ratio, w, is 3, then K of $300 is required to produce Y of $100, and to produce Y of $200 would require K of $600. If we assume an unchanging capital-output ratio, the required stock of capital will change over successive time periods *only* with changes in output. Designating some particular time period as t, preceding time periods as $t - 1$ and $t - 2$, and subsequent time periods as $t + 1$, and $t + 2$, let us suppose that in period t 1 precisely the required capital stock was on hand to produce the level of output of period $t - 1$. That is,

$$K_{t-1} = wY_{t-1}$$

If output then rises from Y_{t-1} to Y_t, the required capital stock would also rise from K_{t-1} to K_t, or,

$$K_t = wY_t$$

The needed increase in capital stock is $K_t - K_{t-1}$. To increase the capital stock, net investment expenditures are needed. To increase the capital stock during t from K_{t-1} to K_t, the net investment expenditures required equal the needed change in capital stock, or,

$$I_t = K_t - K_{t-1} \tag{1}$$

in which I_t is *net* investment for period t. By substituting wY_t for K_t and wY_{t-1} for K_{t-1}, we may also describe net investment expenditures required in period t as

$$I_t = wY_t - wY_{t-1} = w(Y_t - Y_{t-1}) \tag{2}$$

This equation simply says that net investment during t depends on the change in output from $t - 1$ to t multiplied by the capital-output ratio, w.[1] If $Y_t > Y_{t-1}$,

---

[1] It may be noted that Equations [1] and [2] represent our first encounter with so-called difference equations. By assuming that our variables have only a discrete set of possible values and that these values are available at certain uniformly spaced time intervals, we may date all the variables in our equations. Equations with variables so dated in this fashion are one type of difference equations. A set of such difference equations makes up a dynamic model— "dynamic" in that the value of a variable, say, for the time period t, is made dependent on

the equation indicates that there is positive net investment during period t; if $Y_t < Y_{t-1}$, there is negative net investment, or disinvestment, during period t. In short, for any assigned value of w and for any change in Y from $t - 1$ to t, the equation indicates the amount of net investment, positive or negative, for period t that is attributable to the change in the level of output.

The Acceleration Principle

The relationship between the change in the level of output and the volume of investment spending is known as the *acceleration principle*. The capital-output ratio, w, is known as the *accelerator*.

The acceleration principle as expressed in Equation [2] is straightforward. If the economy is already producing the capacity level of output that can be produced with the existing capital stock, and if there is a fixed ratio between output and capital, it is easy to see that any expansion of output must require an expansion of the capital stock. Furthermore, if the accelerator has a value greater than 1, the needed increase in capital stock must exceed the increase in output, so that the increase in investment spending will be greater than the increase in output that causes it. Otherwise expressed, to the extent that the demand for additional plant and equipment is derived from the demand for output, a change in the demand for output, given an accelerator greater than 1, leads to a magnification of the derived demand for the plant and equipment necessary to the production of additional output.[2]

To observe the acceleration principle in operation, let us trace changes in output and gross investment over a number of time periods. In Table 13–1, Column 1 simply indicates a series of time periods, and Column 2 gives the assumed level of income and output in each period. If we assume a constant capital-output ratio, w, of 3, the required stock of capital given in Column 3 is 3 times each period's output as given in Column 2. The average durability of capital goods is assumed to be ten time periods, so that in each time period there is replacement investment equal to 10 percent of the capital stock in existence in period t. This gives us in Column 4 an unvarying replacement investment of 30 per time period.[3] Net investment in any period, as shown in

---

the values of one or more other variables for time periods $t - 1$, $t - 2$, and so forth. For a discussion of the use of difference equations in economics, see W. J. Baumol, *Economic Dynamics*, 2nd ed., Macmillan, 1959, Part 4.

[2] Even if the accelerator is greater than 1, there are circumstances under which the amplitude of fluctuations in investment can be less than that of final demand. See W. J. Baumol, "Acceleration Without Magnification," in *American Economic Review*, June 1956, pp. 409–12.

[3] Replacement investment remains at 30 per time period despite the rise in capital stock in $t + 2$ and subsequent periods. The 30 added to capital stock in $t + 2$ does not need replacement until $t + 12$, the 45 added in $t + 3$ does not need replacement until $t + 13$, and so forth. These are all time periods beyond the table. Note also that the capital stock of 300 on hand in t must have been built up through net investment of 30 during each period, $t - 10$ through $t - 1$, in order to produce the constant 30 of replacement during each time period covered by the table.

TABLE 13–1   The Working of the Acceleration Principle

(1)	(2)	(3)	(4)	(5)	(6)
		Required	*Replacement*	*Net*	*Gross*
Period	*Output*	*Capital*	*Investment*	*Investment*	*Investment*
t	100	300	30	0	30
$t+1$	100	300	30	0	30
$t+2$	110	330	30	30	60
$t+3$	125	375	30	45	75
$t+4$	135	405	30	30	60
$t+5$	140	420	30	15	45
$t+6$	135	405	30	-15	15
$t+7$	125	375	30	-30	0
$t+8$	120	360	30	-15	15

Column 5, equals w times the change in Y between that period and the preceding period. Gross investment of Column 6 is the sum of replacement and net investment of Columns 4 and 5.

With output unchanged from t to $t+1$, firms need simply maintain the existing capital stock of 300. This is done by replacing the 30 that wear out during the period. However, when demand for output increases by 10 in $t+2$, new capital facilities of 30 are required. In terms of the equation in which I measures *net* investment only, we have $I_{t+2} = w(Y_{t+2} - Y_{t+1})$, or $30 = 3(110 - 100)$. Total demand for capital goods accordingly rises from 30 in $t+1$ to 60 in $t+2$, made up of 30 of replacement and 30 of net investment. With an accelerator of 3, the increase of 10 in demand for final output produces an increase of 30 in demand for capital goods. In percentage terms, a 10 percent increase in demand for final product calls for a 100 percent increase in demand for capital goods. In $t+3$, a further increase of 15 in demand for final output must be met. This requires additional capital goods of 45, which, when added to replacement requirements, makes gross investment 75 in $t+3$. The overall increase in demand for final output from t to $t+3$ is from 100 to 125, or 25 percent, but the increase in demand for capital goods is from 30 to 75, or 150 percent.

In $t+4$, despite the fact that the demand for final output rises still further, the demand for capital goods actually falls. This is the result of the decrease in the *absolute amount of increase* in demand for final output in $t+4$ as compared with $t+3$. Output in $t+4$ rises by only 10, which requires 30 of additional capital, whereas in $t+3$ output rose by 15, which required 45 of additional capital. A similar result is seen in $t+5$. In sum, a mere decrease in the absolute increase in demand for final output causes an absolute decrease in gross investment demand.

In $t+6$ there is an absolute decrease of 5 in demand for final output, which makes 15 of the existing capital stock redundant. This results in a further decrease in demand for capital goods. However, there is still investment demand of 15, because the 30 of capital goods used up in $t+6$ is 15 greater than the existing surplus of capital goods on hand at the beginning of the period. With the further fall of 10 in demand for final output in $t + 7$, the actual capital stock is 30 greater than required. By simply not replacing the 30 of capital goods that wear out during $t + 7$, this excess is worked off during the period. Therefore, gross investment is zero for the period.[4]

Finally, in $t + 8$ the result is the reverse of that noted in $t + 4$ and $t + 5$. Despite a further decrease in demand for final output, the demand for capital goods actually increases. This is the result of the decrease in the absolute amount of decrease in demand for final output. In $t + 7$ the decrease was 10, which decreased investment requirements by 30. In $t + 8$ the further decrease is only 5, which decreased investment requirements by 15, making gross investment 15 greater in $t + 8$ than it was in $t + 7$.

Although based on a number of questionable assumptions, the simple mechanics of the acceleration principle as described in terms of Table 13–1 suggest one possible reason for the relatively wider fluctuations in the demand for capital goods than in that for final goods in general, a real-world phenomenon that economists have long recognized. It also shows why, under certain circumstances, the peaks and troughs in demand for capital goods will occur earlier than the peaks and troughs in demand for final output, another real-world phenomenon observed in many business cycles.[5] But the acceleration principle can produce the results of Table 13–1 only by making certain assumptions, some of which may be unrealistic. It is clearly necessary to examine these assumptions in order to evaluate the practical significance of the principle.

Assumptions Underlying the Acceleration Principle

One assumption indispensable to the working of the acceleration principle is that the existing stock of plant and equipment is fully utilized. In Table 13–1, a rise in demand for output in $t + 2$ need not increase the demand for capital goods if firms already have excess capacity with which to meet this increase in demand. In this event, depending on the amount of excess capacity, net investment may remain zero (or even become negative) in the face of an increase

---

[4] If the fall in output in $t + 7$ had been greater than 10, the model would call for *negative gross investment*, which is impossible. In Ch. 20 we will consider how this "floor" to investment affects the operation of the acceleration principle.

[5] Decreases in investment spending often occur *before* the downturn in general business activity, and increases in investment spending often occur *before* the upturn in general business activity. In terms of Table 13–1, the peak in demand for final output is in $t + 5$, but the peak in demand for capital goods is in the earlier period, $t + 3$. The trough in demand for capital goods is in $t + 7$, but the trough in demand for final output is in some later period beyond the limits of the table. This downturn in capital spending while spending for final output is still rising and this upturn in capital spending while spending for final output is still falling follow from the assumption of Table 13–1 that the amount of increase in final output will decline period by period before there is an actual absolute fall in final output and that the amount of decrease in final output will decline period by period before there is an actual absolute increase in final output.

in demand.[6] Gross investment in $t + 2$ may remain the same as that of $t + 1$, or it may fall.

Although this assumption may be satisfied for particular firms or even industries, it will rarely be satisfied for the economy as a whole. It will come much closer to being satisfied during the later stages of the expansion phase of the business cycle, when demand is pressing against capacity, than in the early stages of expansion or at any stage of the contraction phase, when excess capacity blankets the economy.

A closely related assumption is that firms will increase capacity to meet every increase in demand. In effect, this means that businessmen act as automatons, responding to increased demand by increasing investment spending and to decreased demand by decreasing investment spending. In practice, however, even if their capital facilities are operating at capacity, businessmen will try somehow to squeeze additional output from existing plant and equipment unless and until they are convinced that the observed increase in demand is likely to be permanent.

Similarly, if and when an expansion of capital facilities appears warranted, the expansion may not be exactly that needed to meet the *current* increase in demand; it will probably be one sufficient to meet the increase in demand anticipated over a number of years in the future. Piecemeal expansion of facilities in response to short-run increases in demand may be uneconomical, or, depending on the industry, even technologically impossible. (One cannot add one-half of a blast furnace).

The assumption of a constant capital-output ratio or accelerator, w, is necessary to our simple mechanical model of the acceleration principle, but it is also rather unrealistic. Even if firms could and did automatically adjust their capital stock to each change in current demand, the capital-output ratio would not be constant. An increase in demand might be concentrated at one time on the output of industries whose technology calls for high capital-output ratios and at another time on the output of industries with low ratios. This means that, even in the absence of technological changes, the degree to which investment spending responds to any increase in demand for final output depends on the distribution of that increase in demand among the goods of different industries whose output is subject to different capital-output ratios.

This point suggests another qualification. When we disaggregate investment by industries, we may find that investment for the economy as a whole increases even without an increase in demand for final output. Thus, a redistribution of a given total demand among available goods may lead through the acceleration principle to more net investment in industries enjoying the

---

[6] Equation [2] on p. 251 may be rewritten as $I_t = w(Y_t - Y_{t-1}) - X_t$, in which X_t represents excess capacity at the beginning of Period t. Table 13–1 was prepared to show X equal to zero in all periods, but it need not and will not always be thus in reality. For example, if $w = 3$, $Y_t = 110$, $Y_{t-1} = 100$, and $X_t = 40$, I_t will be -10 rather than $+30$, as would be the case if there were no excess capacity. The issue of excess capacity in the working of the acceleration principle is considered in D. Streever, *Capacity Utilization and Business Investment*, Univ. of Illinois, Bureau of Economic and Business Research, Bulletin No. 86, 1960.

increased demand than disinvestment in those suffering the decreased demand—
since, at the limit, disinvestment in any industry cannot exceed the rate at which
capital facilities are used up.

In view of these qualifications, to what extent can the acceleration principle be accepted as an explanation of the level of investment spending? One
economist's answer is as follows: "In sum, there is an element of truth in the
acceleration principle, but it is an element that is so heavily overlaid by other
factors that the acceleration principle by itself is inadequate as a theory of
investment." [7] Others have reached much less negative answers to this question.
Any number have attempted to test the adequacy or inadequacy of the principle, and some of these have secured results regarded as favorable to the principle.[8] Although it says very little, at least this much is incontrovertible: The
decisions of businessmen with respect to spending for capital facilities are based
in part on changes in the quantities of their products sold. The acceleration
principle, however inadequate by itself, clearly emerges as one of a number of
major factors that are needed in combination to explain the fluctuations observed in the world of investment spending.[9]

THE RATE OF INTEREST AND THE ROLE OF FINANCE

The factors considered up to this point affect the rate of investment spending
by producing *shifts* in the MEC schedule. We come now to the final factor to
be considered, the rate of interest, changes in which affect investment by
producing a movement *along* an unshifting MEC schedule, thereby producing
a movement *along* an unshifting MEI schedule. The extent of the movement
along the MEC schedule that follows from any given change in the rate of
interest depends on the elasticity of the schedule. The more elastic the schedule,
the greater the increase or decrease in the profit-maximizing capital stock that
follows from any decrease or increase in the rate of interest. In order to specify

[7] A. D. Knox, "The Acceleration Principle and the Theory of Investment: A Survey," in
Economica, New Series, Aug. 1952, p. 297.

[8] For some early empirical work, see J. Tinbergen, "Statistical Evidence on the Acceleration
Principle," in *Economica*, New Series, May 1938, and S. Kuznets, "Relation Between Capital
Goods and Finished Products in the Business Cycle," in *Economic Essays in Honor of Wesley
Mitchell*, Columbia Univ. Press, 1934. Several more recent studies give considerable support
to the acceleration principle as an explanation of investment specifically in inventories. See
N. W. Robinson, "The Acceleration Principle: Department Store Inventories, 1920–1956,"
in *American Economic Review*, June 1959, pp. 348–58, and P. G. Darling, "Manufacturers'
Inventory Investment, 1947–1958: An Application of Acceleration Analysis," in *American
Economic Review*, Dec. 1959, pp. 950–62. For support of the principle as an explanation of
investment in fixed capital, see R. Eisner, "Investment: Fact and Fancy," in *American Economic Review*, May 1963, pp. 237–46.

[9] We will return to the acceleration principle in Chapter 20, where the interaction of the
principle and the multiplier analysis are examined in the broader context of business-cycle
theory.

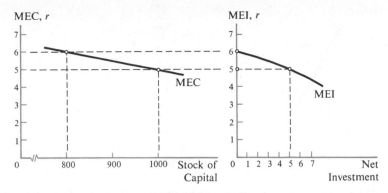

FIGURE 13-1   Net Investment with an Elastic Marginal Efficiency of Capital Schedule

the relationship between a change in the rate of interest and a change in the rate of investment spending, we must proceed from a change in the rate of interest through the resultant change in the profit-maximizing capital stock to the resultant change in the rate of investment.

Elasticity of the MEC Schedule and the Rate of Investment

As a first step, it will be helpful to review the relationships found in Chapter 11 between the rate of interest, the MEC schedule, and the MEI schedule. Figure 13-1 parallels Figure 11-2 except for changes in the numerical values and the omission of replacement investment. As in Figure 11-2, with the MEC schedule given in Part A, the actual capital stock given as $800 billion, and the interest rate given as 6 percent, we see that the actual capital stock is also the profit-maximizing capital stock. The rate of net investment as shown in Part B is accordingly zero. Now, if we assume a drop in the rate of interest from 6 to 5 percent, the profit-maximizing capital stock in Part A becomes $1,000 billion, and net investment in Part B becomes $5 billion for the first time period following the drop in the rate of interest. Since the addition of $5 billion to the stock of capital during the first period does not move the economy perceptibly down the MEC schedule, the MEI schedule does not shift downward appreciably, and the rate of investment remains virtually the same in the second and third periods and in as many periods as may properly be included in the short run.[10]

Figure 13-2 differs from Figure 13-1 only in the elasticity of its MEC schedule. In Figure 13-2 the MEC declines relatively more rapidly with increases in the stock of capital than in Figure 13-1. Assuming for Figure 13-2 the same initial equilibrium given in Figure 13-1, a drop in the rate of interest from 6 to 5 percent will increase the profit-maximizing capital stock only from $800 billion to $820 billion. Note, however, that, despite the inelasticity of the MEC schedule of Figure 13-2, the rate of investment in the first time period following the drop in the rate of interest is $5 billion in Figure 13-2, just as

[10] It will be recalled that the short run, as defined in Chapter 11, is a time interval in which the growth in the stock of capital is not great enough to depress the MEI schedule appreciably.

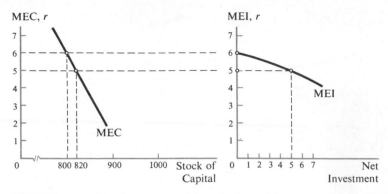

FIGURE 13–2   Net Investment with an Inelastic Marginal Efficiency of Capital Schedule

it is in Figure 13–1. Starting from a position in which the profit-maximizing capital stock equals the actual stock, the *initial* impact of a drop in the rate of interest on the rate of investment spending is independent of the elasticity of the MEC schedule. The reason is that the initial impact of such a drop depends only on the elasticity of the MEI schedule and the elasticity of this schedule is independent of the elasticity of the MEC schedule.[11]

Nonetheless, the elasticity of the MEC schedule must eventually exert an influence on the rate of investment spending. For, if the MEC schedule is relatively inelastic, additions to the stock of capital that result from each period's net investment will move the economy quickly down such a schedule. This we know will push down the MEI schedule and with it the rate of investment at the given market rate of interest. In short, other things being equal, the more inelastic the MEC schedule is, the sooner appreciable downward pressure on the MEI schedule will appear as a "feedback" from the growth in the stock of capital.

Although this analysis shows that the effect of a change in the rate of interest on the rate of investment spending in any time period depends on the elasticity of the MEC schedule, it does not tell us anything about what determines the elasticity of the schedule itself. We cannot appraise the significance of changes in the interest rate as one of the factors influencing the rate of investment unless we know something about what determines the elasticity of the MEC schedule itself.

Determinants of the Elasticity of the MEC Schedule

Assuming again that a firm buys capital goods only in the expectation that each purchase will turn out to be profitable, the elasticity of the MEC schedule for the economy as a whole may be said to depend on the significance of any given change in the interest rate as a factor altering the profit-maximizing capital stock for all firms combined. A fall in the interest rate may lead some firms to expand their stock of capital goods substantially, while the same fall in the interest rate may lead other firms to no expansion at all. The elasticity

[11] It will be recalled that the elasticity of the MEI schedule depends on the elasticity of the supply schedule of capital goods. The elasticity of the supply schedule of capital goods may be assumed to be the same in both cases, so the elasticity of the MEI schedule is the same in both figures. See pp. 216–18.

of the aggregate MEC schedule then depends on the combined responses of all firms to any change in the interest rate.

Our problem is then to investigate what determines whether any given change in the interest rate will lead to a larger or smaller change in the profit-maximizing capital stock. Although it is immediately apparent that a lower interest rate, other things being equal, is also a reduction in one cost of doing business, we find different responses by different businesses to such a drop. In seeking an explanation for this disparate reaction, we will get at the factors that determine the elasticity of the MEC schedule.

With all other things assumed to remain unchanged, especially the existing state of technology, one factor that determines how great an increase in the profit-maximizing capital stock will result from any given reduction in the interest rate is the extent to which firms find it technologically possible to substitute what is now the relatively cheaper capital input for what is now the relatively more expensive labor input. It must be seen here that, in terms of the cost of factor units, the comparison is between the rate of interest as the cost of capital and the wage rate as the cost of labor. Since we express the rate of return from or the productivity of an addition to the stock of capital as a percentage—namely, the MEC—we must for comparability express the cost of capital as another percentage—namely, the market rate of interest. A fall in the rate of interest is then a decrease in the cost of capital.[12] In contrast, since we express the return from or the productivity of an addition of a unit of a given type of labor as the dollar value of the output that will be produced because of the addition of a unit of that type of labor, the cost of labor is also expressed as a dollar value, the dollar cost of a unit of the given type of labor. A fall in the wage rate paid labor is then a decrease in the cost of labor.

With a fall in the interest rate and no change in the wage rate, there will be a tendency throughout the economy to substitute the cheaper input, capital, for the more expensive input, labor, in the production of any constant level of output. Although such a tendency will at least be present throughout the economy, the extent to which substitution of this sort actually takes place will vary widely from industry to industry and, to a lesser extent, from firm to firm within a particular industry.

For some firms the state of their technology may be such that, regardless of the fall in the cost of capital, substitution is severely limited or even impossi-

---

[12] If we express the productivity of a capital good by its MEC, which is a percentage, we must measure the "price" of that capital good not by the number of dollars paid for the good but by the rate of interest, explicit or implicit, paid for the funds used to purchase that good. The cost element represented by its supply price has already been allowed for in the computation of its MEC. The MEC, it will be recalled, is the percentage rate of return expected on the capital good after allowance for all costs other than interest cost. If the rate of interest is equal to the MEC of a capital good, we may say that the "price" we must pay for the good equals its expected rate of return and that there is no net rate of return on the good over and above all costs. A rate of interest below the MEC is a lower "price" for the good and a "price" that therefore leaves a net rate of return over and above all costs. Once given the MEC, the decision to buy or not to buy the capital good requires a comparison of its price, which is the rate of interest, with its return, which is its MEC.

ble. At the extreme, for firms whose technology is such that production requires a rigidly fixed combination of men and machines, a fall in the rate of interest will lead to no substitution of capital for labor.[13] For such firms, the amount of capital employed in the production of a given level of output is virtually independent of the interest rate. In this case, so far as substitution goes, a fall in the rate of interest will have no effect on the size of the profit-maximizing capital stock consistent with a constant level of output. This also means that the rate of investment spending will be unaffected by a drop in the rate of interest.

For other firms the amount of capital employed may be more or less sensitive to changes in the interest rate. Their technology may be such that, within limits, each drop in the interest rate can make further substitution of capital for labor profitable. To take a crude example that may readily be compared with the one above, suppose that the existing technology permits the firm a choice between a one man-one machine, one man-two machine, or one man-three machine combination. However, to switch to the one man-two machine combination requires purchase of an "Adapter A," which links two of the original machines in such a way that one worker may operate both, and to switch to a one man-three machine combination requires a second "Adapter A" plus one "Adapter B" to link three of the original machines in such a way that one worker may operate all three simultaneously. Each of the original machines will turn out the same number of units of output after the linkage as before. Before the fall in the rate of interest, the then current costs of capital and labor made the one man-one machine combination the least-cost combination. But with an initial fall in the interest rate, capital becomes relatively cheaper, so one "Adapter A" may be purchased for each two machines; one-half of the labor force employed in operating the machines may be replaced by capital. With some further fall in the interest rate, the least-cost combination may call for the purchase of another "Adapter A" and one "Adapter B" for each three original machines; one-third of the remaining labor force employed in operating the machines may be replaced by capital. The firm's output remains the same in all cases.

Our first factor is seen to be essentially technological in nature. With a given state of technology but with some opportunity for firms to vary factor combinations within this given state of technology, one way in which a drop in the rate of interest is translated into an increase in the profit-maximizing capital stock is through a substitution of capital for labor in the production of any level of output. The greater the possibilities available within the existing state of technology, the more elastic the MEC schedule will be.

---

[13] Even here, however, there is some opportunity for substitution. For example, if a firm has 100 machines and must have 100 workers to operate the machines and if the machines are subject to intermittent breakdown, the fall in the price of capital may lead to the purchase of one or more additional machines to be pressed into use when any of the 100 at any time in use breaks down. With the fall in the price of capital, this increase in the capital stock may be cost saving, for the relatively more expensive input, labor, will not remain idle while the relatively less expensive input, capital, is being repaired. It is true that one or more machines will always be idle or in repair, but this "idleness" may, with the lower interest rate, be less costly than the otherwise idle labor.

Closely related to this factor is the cost saving represented by a switch toward greater use of capital as a result of a drop in the rate of interest. Even though the existing technology may permit variation in the capital-labor combination, the extent to which such variation will occur in response to a change in the rate of interest depends on the cost advantage offered by such variation. Two illustrations may be traced through to show in a rough way the operation of this factor. In the first, a fall in the rate of interest leads to a cost advantage through the substitution of capital for labor in the production of a given level of output; in the second, a fall in the rate of interest leads to no reduction in the quantity of labor employed but to the use of more durable capital goods in combination with an unchanged quantity of labor.

In the first illustration, suppose that there are two firms, each with an output of identical value and each with identical costs of $1,000 per year. As shown in the table below, Firm A's method of production emphasizes labor, and Firm B's method emphasizes capital. Firm A's method may be described as more labor intensive and less capital intensive than Firm B's, and vice versa. The first part of the illustration assumes a market rate of interest of 6 percent, and the second part, one of 4 percent. In both parts, straight-line depreciation with a ten-year life for capital goods is assumed, making annual depreciation cost 10 percent of the value of the capital stock. Annual interest cost is simply the market rate times the capital stock. A drop in the interest rate from 6 to 4 percent reduces Firm A's total costs for the given output from $1,000 to $990, a reduction of 1 percent, and reduces Firm B's total costs for output of the same value from $1,000 to $920, a reduction of 8 percent. Since both firms are assumed to have output per period of equal value, the drop in the interest rate produces a 1 percent reduction in cost per unit of Firm A's output and an 8 percent reduction in cost per unit of Firm B's output.

		Capital Stock	Annual Depreciation	Annual Interest Cost	Annual Labor and Other Costs	Total Costs
Market Rate of Interest 6 Percent	Firm A	$ 500	$ 50	$ 30	$920	$1,000
	Firm B	4,000	400	240	360	1,000
Market Rate of Interest 4 Percent	Firm A	$ 500	$ 50	$ 20	$920	$ 990
	Firm B	4,000	400	160	360	920

With the rate of interest at 6 percent, Firm A's method of production, on a strict cost basis, is as good as Firm B's.[14] But with a drop in the rate of interest,

[14] Considerations other than total cost per unit would, of course, be relevant in choosing which is the "better" method. For example, the percentage of costs that are fixed is much lower for Firm A than for Firm B. This puts Firm A in a much better position to meet a decrease in demand, since it can reduce total costs almost proportionately with a reduction in output. On the other hand, if wage rates are subject to constant upward pressure, Firm B may be in a better position, since Firm A's costs for any level of output will rise much more sharply. These and other considerations would enter into determining which is the "better" method.

Firm B's more capital-intensive method of production has a significant cost advantage over Firm A's more labor-intensive method. Insofar as we can generalize from this illustration for the economy as a whole, the fall in the rate of interest will produce some tendency toward greater use of capital and less use of labor in the production of any given level of aggregate output.

In this first illustration, the methods of production of the two firms are essentially different: Firm A uses up $50 of capital goods and $920 of labor services in producing its output per year, and Firm B uses up $400 of capital goods and $360 of labor services in producing output of the same value in the same time period. In our second illustration, let us assume two firms whose methods of production are identical in that each uses up the same amount of labor services in the production of output of the same value but whose methods of production differ in terms of the *durability* of the capital goods they employ in combination with the same quantity of labor services.

In the second table, Firm Y has capital stock of $1,000 made up of capital goods with an average life of two years, and Firm Z has capital stock of $3,500 with an average life of ten years. Since both firms produce output of the same value and incur labor costs of the same amount, the capital stocks of the two firms make an equal contribution to output. At first glance, one may object that it is then better to invest $1,000 than $3,500 in capital, if both investments provide capital goods with equal capacity to produce. Is not interest cost at 6 percent on $1,000 only $60, whereas on $3,500 it is $210? This, however, overlooks the fact that the more expensive capital goods, though no more productive per year than the less expensive, are more expensive only because they are more durable and will make the same contribution to production over a greater number of years. Our figures are deliberately selected to show that they are not proportionately more expensive. The purchase price of the more durable capital goods is only 3.5 times that of the less durable, but their life is 5 times that of the less durable. This in turn means that the cost of the more durable capital goods, as measured by annual depreciation, $350, is less than the depreciation cost of the less durable goods, $500, the output from both collections of capital goods being the same for each year.

		Capital Stock	Annual Depre-ciation	Annual Interest Cost	Annual Labor and Other Costs	Total Costs
Market Rate	Firm Y	$1,000	$500	$ 60	$440	$1,000
of Interest	Firm Z	3,500	350	210	440	1,000
6 Percent						
Market Rate	Firm Y	$1,000	$500	$ 40	$440	$ 980
of Interest	Firm Z	3,500	350	140	440	930
4 Percent						

As in the previous illustration, we may say that, on a strict cost basis, Firm

Y's method of production is as good as Firm Z's when the interest rate is 6 percent.[15] Each has output of the same value produced at the same total cost. However, with a drop in the rate of interest from 6 to 4 percent, the second part of the illustration shows a decrease in total cost from $1,000 to $980, or 2 percent, for Firm Y and from $1,000 to $930, or 7 percent, for Firm Z. Since the value of output is the same for both firms, Firm Y has a 2 percent and Firm Z a 7 percent reduction in cost per unit of output. With a drop in the rate of interest, there is clearly a cost advantage in Firm Z's method, which employs more durable capital goods, or a cost disadvantage in Firm Y's method, which employs less durable capital goods. Insofar as we can generalize from this illustration for the economy as a whole, the fall in the interest rate will produce some tendency toward production of any given level of aggregate output with more durable capital goods. In other words, there will be a tendency to produce any given level of output with a larger stock of capital goods.

In both illustrations, a fall in the interest rate results in a tendency toward more capital-intensive production. In the first illustration, this was due to a substitution of capital for labor; in the second, it was due to the use of more durable capital goods with no reduction in the quantity of labor used. A fall in the rate of interest would, of course, tend to encourage substitution of capital for labor *and* the use of more durable capital goods simultaneously. Both tend to increase the profit-maximizing capital stock consistent with any given level of output, and, therefore, both work toward a higher rate of investment spending.

These then are the factors through which a change in the interest rate will affect the profit-maximizing capital stock. Whether the change in the profit-maximizing capital stock will be large enough to produce an MEC schedule that is elastic with respect to any given interest-rate change depends on the combined responses of all firms to that interest-rate change. It is one thing to indicate the factors that determine the responses of firms and quite another to conclude that the combined responses of all firms for any time period and for any change in the interest rate will produce an aggregate MEC schedule that is elastic or inelastic.

Elasticity of the MEC Schedule—Structures, Producers' Durable Equipment, and Business Inventories

Since the thirties, most economists have argued that the rate of investment spending for an industrially advanced economy such as that of the United States is interest-inelastic. Although this appears to be the consensus, this general conclusion is not equally applicable to all forms of investment spending.

To the extent that investment does respond to changes in the interest rate, the most pronounced response seems to occur in the field of investment spending for residential and business structures. The reasons for this are implicit in the illustrations above. For example, an additional one million square feet of living

---

[15] This is subject to other considerations of a type noted in the preceding footnote. Especially relevant would be Firm Z's greater exposure to the dangers of obsolescence.

space or office or factory space per year can be provided only by the construction of the required quantity of houses, apartments, office buildings, or factories.[16] Since the product yielded by construction as such is measured in square feet of floor space available per year, production of this product is technologically very capital intensive.[17] The sum of depreciation cost and interest cost per unit of output looms large as a fraction of total cost per unit of output of this kind. Furthermore, not only is production very capital intensive, but it is carried out with capital goods that are durable. To provide another one million square feet of floor space this year requires the construction of buildings that will provide this same output for many years. Since the interest cost on durable capital goods goes on for many years, even small changes in the interest rate can mean a substantial difference in the cost per unit of output (square foot of floor space per year). In other words, where the technology makes for capital-intensive production and where the nature of the capital employed is very durable, a change in the interest rate can make a great difference in cost per unit of output, and this will markedly affect the rate of investment expenditures in this type of capital goods.

The responsiveness in inventory investment to changes in the interest rate is of a different nature. Just as there is a profit-maximizing stock of plant and equipment, so there is a profit-maximizing stock of inventories. However, unlike the case of structures, the profit-maximizing stock of inventories is not likely to be very responsive to interest-rate changes. A lower rate of interest reduces the carrying cost of any given amount of inventories, of course, and therefore may be expected to increase the profit-maximizing stock of inventories, other things being equal. However, as we saw above, a fall in the rate of interest affects primarily the profit-maximizing capital stock consistent with any level of output by inducing substitutions of capital for labor or by inducing the use of more durable capital equipment. Neither of these factors has any real applicability to the determination of the profit-maximizing stock of inventories, this being determined primarily by the firm's sales, interest cost, and other carrying costs, rather than by its method of production.[18] However, the rate of interest will play some role in the determination of the firm's profit-maximizing inventory. Other things being equal, in the face of a rise in interest rates, firms will attempt to maintain their rate of production and sales with smaller stocks of inventories and a necessarily higher rate of turnover of these smaller stocks, particularly if interest rates rise sharply or if they rise to unusually high levels. The response will vary with different firms, depending in part on how large the interest cost of carrying

[16] An existing amount of floor space cannot be substantially "enlarged" by altering factor proportions. More labor applied to an unchanged quantity of floor space can make for more rapid repairs and redecoration and thus for higher utilization of the existing quantity, but possibilities in this direction are very limited.

[17] This is not to be confused with the capital-intensity in the production of the buildings that in turn produce the output in the form of a number of square feet of floor space per year. The production method employed in constructing the buildings is an altogether different question.

[18] For a simple model of the determination of the firm's optimal inventory, see W. J. Baumol, *Economic Theory and Operations Analysis*, 2nd ed., Prentice-Hall, 1965, Ch. 1.

inventories is as a percentage of the firm's total costs for any level of output.

Thus, we may expect the response to changes in the rate of interest for the economy as a whole to have the greatest impact on the stock of structures, less on the stock of producers' durable equipment, and least on the stock of business inventories. In view of the fact that different types of investment spending show different responses to changes in interest rates, it is obviously difficult to generalize with respect to the elasticity of investment spending in the aggregate. This is further complicated by other considerations not examined above. Among these is the likelihood of less inelasticity at high levels of the interest rate than at low, so that a change in the rate from 10 to 9 percent will probably lead to a greater increase in the profit-maximizing capital stock than will a rate change from 5 to 4.5 percent. In other words, whatever may be the elasticity of the overall schedule, we may expect it to be more inelastic at low rates of interest than at high.[19] Its actual elasticity, however, remains an unsettled question.

In summary, we can only repeat a generally accepted conclusion. In the words of Kuh and Meyer,

> It is difficult to say how sensitive the investment-interest rate relationship is likely to be in the short run, other than presuming it is something greater than zero. Available evidence, none of which is terribly satisfactory, suggests that the interest elasticity of demand is not large, at least in the historically relevant range of roughly 3 to 10 percent *per annum* charged for long term capital.[20]

The Role of Finance—Beyond the Rate of Interest

The question of financing investment spending has been developed to this point on the assumption that there is only one element in finance—the cost of money as expressed by the rate of interest. However, the role played by finance involves more than just the rate of interest. Some increase in the profit-maximizing capital stock and in the rate of investment spending may follow from a fall in the interest rate, but an increase may also follow from favorable changes in other elements on the side of finance, independent of any change in the rate of

[19] See A. H. Hansen, *Business Cycles and National Income*, Norton, 1964, pp. 133–38.

[20] E. Kuh and J. R. Meyer, "Investment, Liquidity and Monetary Policy," in *Impacts of Monetary Policy*, Commission on Money and Credit, Prentice-Hall, 1963, pp. 340–41. See also L. Tarshis, "The Elasticity of the Marginal Efficiency Function," in *American Economic Review*, Dec. 1961, pp. 958–85, and W. H. White, "Interest Elasticity of Investment Demand," in *American Economic Review*, Sept. 1956, pp. 565–87, and references cited there. An econometric study that finds a significant relationship between investment and interest rates, but with a one-year lag, is that of F. Gehrels and S. Wiggins, "Interest Rates and Manufacturers' Fixed Investment," in *American Economic Review*, March 1957, pp. 79–92. For an empirical study that examines the importance of the interest rate for aggregate investment in construction, machinery, and inventories in the United States from 1869 to 1929, see A. Spiro, "Empirical Research and the Rate of Interest," in *Review of Economics and Statistics*, Feb. 1958, pp. 52–58. For the results of a survey study covering the "tight money" episode of 1966, see J. Crockett, I. Friend, and H. Shavell, "The Impact of Monetary Stringency on Business Investment," in *Survey of Current Business*, Aug. 1967, pp. 10–26.

interest. In fact, it is not at all unlikely that favorable changes in other elements of a financial nature would lead to an expansion in the profit-maximizing capital stock even in the face of a rise in the interest rate.

As a preliminary point, we should note that the treatment of the rate of interest in the preceding pages is an oversimplification. It was assumed that funds were available without restriction to all borrowers at the market rate of interest. In reality, of course, there is no such thing as *the* market rate of interest; rather there is a whole complex of rates. The rate paid by any particular borrower depends on such variables as the term of the loan, the size of the loan, the collateral offered, and especially the creditworthiness of the borrower.[21] Although these differences do exist and must be recognized, the assumption of a single interest rate is convenient and permissible for the broad conclusions that economists seek to draw between the rate of interest and aggregate investment spending.

A closely related qualification has to do with the availability of funds at any given interest rate. It is not customary for banks to raise the interest rates charged to different classes of borrowers every time loan demand exceeds the lending capacity of the banks. There is in practice some stickiness of interest-rate movements in an upward as well as a downward direction. When loan demand exceeds the amount of funds available, banks tend, at least at first, to ration the available funds so that the loan applications of preferred borrowers are met in whole or in part, while those of less desirable borrowers are denied. If we include the availability as well as the cost of funds in our model, we make allowance for the fact that in times of tightening credit, investment spending may be restrained not by a higher rate of interest, but by the inability of some to borrow the full amount desired at going interest rates.[22] In effect, however, this is not substantially different from the situation in which supply and demand are brought into balance by changes in interest rates. What it means on the side of finance is that a rise in the interest rate is not the only factor that may restrain investment spending; the same restraint may be present in the form of an availability of a smaller amount of funds than borrowers seek at an interest rate held by the banks below the rate that would clear the market.[23]

---

[21] Beyond this, there is not necessarily some single rate paid by a single borrower, but a scale of rates that rises with each addition to the borrower's indebtedness. See A. G. Hart, *Anticipations, Uncertainty, and Dynamic Planning*, Augustus M. Kelley, Inc., 1951, pp. 39–50, and N. J. Cunningham, "Business Investment and the Marginal Cost of Funds," in *Metroeconomica*, Part I, Aug. 1958, pp. 60–73, and Part II, Dec. 1958, pp. 155–81.

[22] See G. L. Bach and C. J. Huizenga, "The Differential Effects of Tight Money," in *American Economic Review*, March 1961, pp. 52–80.

[23] This last sentence completely neglects the so-called availability doctrine, which argues that a small change in the interest rate can substantially affect investment spending through its influence on willingness of lenders to lend. This conclusion is reached in part on the basis of the "pinning-in effect"—that is, the reluctance of lenders to take capital losses on the sale of bonds in order to get the funds to make loans. (The relationship between a rise in the interest rate and a fall in bond prices will be discussed in Chapter 18.) So viewed, the effect of even a small rise in the interest rate is not so much in the cost of funds as in what it means to the availability of funds. Whatever applicability the doctrine has had seems limited to the period of transition from the pegged markets of the forties to the free markets of the fifties. In recent

Another simplification we introduced earlier was to treat the cost of funds borrowed by the firm as little different from the cost of funds that the firm generates internally. For the former there is an explicit interest rate, or the rate paid to lenders, and for the latter there is an implicit interest rate, or the rate the firm could have earned on its own funds had it loaned them out rather than invested them. It was recognized that the explicit rate would typically be higher than the implicit rate, since firms that are not in the lending business will usually have to pay a higher rate as borrowers than they can receive as lenders. In any case, we concluded that the interest rate, explicit or implicit, was to be compared with the expected rate of return on the prospective investment project in deciding whether or not to undertake the project. If for some firm the explicit rate was 6 percent at some point in time and the implicit rate 4 percent, any project that promised less than a 6 percent return would not be undertaken if the firm had to raise the funds externally, and any project that promised less than 4 percent would not be undertaken even if the firm had internally generated funds available.

Although this kind of test provides a handy rule of thumb, it is important to see that the difference between financing investment expenditures with external funds as against financing them with internal funds involves much more than the mere difference between the explicit interest rate and the implicit interest rate. For one thing, an investment project promising a firm a 10 or 15 percent return may be blocked, even if the explicit rate of interest on the required funds is only 6 percent. This is the situation where the firm encounters credit rationing of the sort noted above. The banker may say that if he had the funds, which he does not, they would be available at a 6 percent interest rate. If, however, the firm has its own funds available in the required amount, the project can be undertaken regardless of the implicit rate on the funds.

Even if a firm can earn, say, 6 percent by lending out its own funds, it may choose to invest these funds in a project promising only a 5 percent rate of return. Although management appears to be sacrificing profits by so doing, there is in the world of business a bias not only toward profits but also toward a growing enterprise and an expanding sales volume, even if gained at the expense of immediate profits. For firms with solidly established positions in their markets, investment under such conditions would be most likely for that portion of internally generated funds arising from depreciation charges; investment under such conditions would perhaps be less likely for the remaining internally generated funds arising from undistributed profits. However, no firm would be likely to go into debt to secure funds for investment purposes when the prospective

years, lenders have shown little reluctance to sell bonds in the face of rising interest rates. An extreme case of this came during 1966, when commercial banks' sales of state and local securities reached huge proportions in the face of rapidly rising yields on these securities. For the original statement of the "availability doctrine," see R. V. Roosa, "Interest Rates and the Central Bank," in *Money, Trade, and Economic Growth*, Macmillan, 1951, pp. 370–95. See also I. O. Scott, Jr., "The Availability Doctrine: Development and Implications," in *Canadian Journal of Economics and Political Science*, Nov. 1957, pp. 532–39.

rate of return on such investments was anything less than the rate paid for borrowed funds.[24]

In other words, there are really two implicit rates: the rate the firm could charge on loans to others and the rate the firm will charge on "loans" to itself. In practice, the difference between the explicit rate and the implicit rate that firms charge themselves is greater than the difference between the explicit rate and the implicit rate that firms could charge to others. Since the implicit rate that firms charge themselves is well below the explicit rate, prospective returns on investment projects must fall very low before firms will choose to lend their internally generated funds, rather than to invest them.[25]

Finally, there are other factors considered by firms in financing investment that are not closely related to how high or low the interest rate, explicit or implicit, may happen to be. One such factor is the internal availability of the necessary funds, rather than the cost of these funds. There is a definite preference among businessmen for internal over external financing, the interest rate apart, because of the reluctance to take on debt with the fixed interest charges and repayment schedule that such debt carries. To avoid fixed charges by recourse to external financing through new stock issues also has undesirable features. The issuance of new stock may mean the loss or at least a dilution of the control exercised previously by a group of stockholders. In addition, any type of external financing, whether it be bond or stock issues (avenues that, incidentally, are open at reasonable cost only to large firms) or bank borrowing, requires disclosure of detailed financial information that firms, for competitive reasons, may prefer to keep confidential, if possible.

The upshot of all this is that the traditional emphasis on the rate of interest has been modified by the fact that there is more involved on the side of finance than the cost of funds. In the investment decisions of many firms, the *source* of funds becomes a factor as important or even more important than the *cost* of funds. A drop in the rate of interest, other things being equal, leads to some increase in the profit-maximizing capital stock and so to some increase in the rate of investment spending, but an increase in the flow of internally generated funds may be expected to do the same. From a public policy point of view, this means that a policy designed to stimulate investment spending may operate by reducing interest rates or cutting corporate profits taxes, or both.[26] The former stimulates investment by reducing the cost of funds from both external and

[24] See E. M. Hoover, "Some Institutional Factors in Business Investment Decisions," in *American Economic Review*, May 1954, pp. 201–13.

[25] This is not inconsistent with the practice followed by large nonfinancial corporations of lending on short-term whatever funds are not immediately required to finance investment expenditures. Such funds are usually put into money-market instruments like treasury bills, other government securities near maturity, and commercial paper or into time deposits withdrawable on short notice. This practice is not necessarily evidence of a preference for lending over investment; usually it is simply a way of earning money with funds temporarily idle as they await expenditure for investment purposes.

[26] Fiscal devices other than the tax rate on corporate profits may, of course, be employed to the same end—for example, the introduction in 1962 of a tax credit on investment expenditures and revised guidelines for depreciation purposes.

internal sources; the latter stimulates investment by enlarging the dollar flow of funds from internal sources.

In later chapters, we will again find it necessary to return to the simplifications of earlier chapters. The whole complex of interest rates will again be reduced to *the* interest rate, and the role of finance will again be reduced to the cost of funds as measured by *the* interest rate. This becomes necessary if we are to use relatively simple models in our analysis. However, the reader should remember the other elements that are part of the financial side of investment spending, the elements identified in the last few pages, as necessary qualifications to the conclusions suggested by the simple models.

A CONCLUDING NOTE

In the last two chapters we have examined in some detail the more important factors that determine changes in investment expenditures. We have not attempted the more ambitious task of evaluating the relative importance of these factors and tracing the interactions among them. Actually, economists have a great deal more to learn about how these many factors interact. But the difficulties in acquiring such knowledge are formidable. For one thing, many more factors are involved than our highly aggregated list suggests; the factors in our list may be disaggregated into any number of subfactors. Furthermore, no single factor is of overriding importance, although some economists in recent years have attached great explanatory importance to the acceleration principle. Finally, the relative importance of each of the many factors is not constant over time; each change in aggregate investment spending is the result of changes in more than one factor, but each factor does not have an unvarying relative importance in every change in aggregate investment spending. The very instability of the factors themselves means that what is of relatively great importance at one time may be of little importance at another.

Nonetheless, the examination of the principal determinants of investment expenditures is not without great value in itself. It is the first step in an organized approach to one of the most difficult and important questions in economics. Through this step we have seen how each of the factors examined fits into the capital-investment phase of the economic process.

Although later chapters will have more to say about investment spending in other contexts, our analysis of the determinants of such spending will not be developed further. In constructing models later, we will simply assume changes in the rate of investment spending, without considering in detail the determinants of such changes. This is what was done in the first models developed in Chapter 7, where all investment was simply assumed to be autonomous, with no explanation offered for assumed changes in the rate of autonomous investment spending. With what we now know about the factors affecting investment spending, similar simplifying assumptions adopted in our later model-building will not be misleading.

CHAPTER 14

GOVERNMENT DEMAND

In this chapter we turn to the effects of government expenditures and taxation on the level of income and output. We will be dealing with aggregate demand composed of personal consumption, domestic investment, and government expenditures for final product, and an aggregate flow of income that is allocated not only to consumption expenditures and private saving but now also, in part, to taxes.

In general, government can expand aggregate demand in any time period by increasing the amount it adds to the stream of private spending through its purchases of goods and services or by decreasing the amount it diverts from the stream of private spending through its net tax collections. By the same token it can contract aggregate demand in any time period by decreasing the amount it adds to the stream of private spending through its purchases of goods and services or by increasing the amount it diverts from the stream of private spending through its net tax collections. The effect of government spending and taxation on aggregate demand thus depends, in the first instance, on how much government injects into the spending stream through its purchases and on how much it withdraws through net tax collections. Since the level of income depends on aggregate demand, government can clearly raise or lower the level of income through its policy with respect to spending and taxing.

FISCAL POLICY

This most important of government economic policies is known as its fiscal policy. In the years since the Great Depression, it has become generally accepted that the fiscal policy of the federal government should contribute to the attainment of certain economic goals. If the economy is operating at a level of income and output below that at which there is reasonably full utilization of the economy's resources, the appropriate fiscal policy is an expansionary one. If, on the other hand, the economy is at a level of income and output at which there is not only full utilization of resources but also strong upward pressure on prices, the appropriate fiscal policy is a contractionary one. In other words, fiscal policy should operate in a countercyclical fashion, promoting the stabilization of economic activity at high levels of output and employment. Other goals of fiscal policy include rapid economic growth, greater equality in the distribution of income, and maximum economic "well-being." These goals overlap to a degree; some compete with each other, and some complement each other. In order to avoid the complexities of dealing with a diversity of goals, we will simply take the goal of fiscal policy to be the stabilization of economic activity at its full-employment level. Taking full employment to mean full utilization of all of the economy's resources, we may refer to the corresponding output as the economy's full-employment output.

Accepting this as the goal of fiscal policy, we would next want to devise the set of fiscal policy actions that would best enable us to achieve this objective under the conditions with which the economy is confronted at a particular time. There are two sets of basic fiscal-policy alternatives. If the need is for an expansion of income, the fiscal-policy alternatives are to increase government spending, decrease taxes, or both. If, on the other hand, due to inflationary pressures, there is a need to contract income, the fiscal-policy alternatives are to decrease government spending, increase taxes, or both.

How does the government select the most effective alternative in any given situation? If there is a need for an expansion of income, what is the difference between increasing government purchases by a given dollar amount and decreasing tax collections by an equal amount? Can government produce any expansion in income by increasing its purchases by a given dollar amount if at the same time it increases its tax collections by an equal amount? Is there any difference between the expansionary effect of a given dollar increase in government purchases of goods and services and an equal increase in government transfer payments? To answer questions of this sort requires some understanding of the essential mechanics of fiscal policy.

To explain the mechanics of fiscal policy we will construct a series of three models, each of which is built on the models developed earlier for the two-sector economy. In the first, only tax receipts, T, and government purchases, G, are added to the two-sector model; government transfer payments are in effect assumed to be zero. In the second model, government transfer payments are added. Both of these models assume that tax receipts are independent of the level of income—that they are "autonomous," to use the term adopted earlier to describe consumption and investment expenditures that are independent of the level of income. In the third model, the breakdown of government expenditures into purchases of goods and services and transfer payments is retained, but tax receipts are recognized as being, in part, dependent on the level of income. Since increases and decreases in government expenditures have expansionary or contractionary effects on the level of income, it is found in this model, as is true in practice, that tax receipts depend in part on the level of government expenditures.[1]

Although, as we mentioned earlier, one accepted goal of fiscal policy is to promote full employment of the economy's resources, we will not attempt to show specifically in these three models how the level of government spending and taxation might be varied in order to accomplish this particular objective. The models simply assume certain amounts of government spending and taxation and indicate the expansionary or contractionary effect of each. The emphasis in this chapter will be on the pure mechanics of the relationships between government spending, taxation, and the level of income. However, we will note briefly in a final section of the chapter in terms of a fiscal model how the level of government spending and taxation might be adjusted to raise the level of output to the full-employment position. In addition, the final chapter of the book will be devoted in part to the question of economic stabilization, and more will be said about full-employment fiscal policy at that point.

FIRST FISCAL MODEL—INCLUDING NET TAXES AND GOVERNMENT PURCHASES

One version of the fundamental accounting identity for income and output in the three-sector economy developed in Chapter 3 was expressed as

$$C + S + T \equiv Y \equiv C + I + G$$

where Y is net national product and S and I are net private saving and net private domestic investment, respectively. This gave us the following identity for saving and investment:

$$S + (T - G) \equiv I$$

where $(T - G)$ equals public saving.

In the two-sector economy in which we assumed there were no undistributed corporate profits, disposable personal income was found to be equal to net national product. In the three-sector economy, however, with taxes taking a portion of the income flow generated by expenditures on net national product, disposable personal income is less than net national product by the amount of taxes. Letting Y represent net national product and Y_d disposable personal income, we now have

$$Y_d \equiv Y - T$$

[1] For a more detailed development of these same models, see N. F. Keiser, *Macroeconomics, Fiscal Policy, and Economic Growth*, Wiley, 1964, Ch. 8, especially pp. 135–47. A more advanced and highly theoretical treatment is found in B. Hansen, *The Economic Theory of Fiscal Policy*, Harvard Univ. Press, 1958.

or

$$Y \equiv Y_d + T$$

The consumption function for the two-sector economy, in which Y_d equaled Y, was $C = C_a + cY$. Now, with Y_d less than Y, the consumption function becomes $C = C_a + c(Y - T)$, or $C = C_a + cY_d$. With this consumption function, with investment assumed to be entirely autonomous, $I = I_a$, and with fixed amounts of government purchases and tax receipts assumed per time period, the equilibrium level of income is given by

$$Y = C_a + c(Y - T) + I + G$$

Expressed in terms of saving and investment, equilibrium will be found at that level of income and output at which planned saving plus taxes equals planned investment plus government purchases:

$$S + T = I + G$$

For example, assume that $c = 3/4$, $C_a = 20$, $I = 20$ and, for the moment, that T and G are both zero (which amounts to a two-sector economy). These are precisely the values assumed in the very first model of simple income determination in a two-sector economy, as illustrated in Figure 7–2. There we saw that the equilibrium level of income for the values given was 160. Now let us superimpose first a given level of government purchases and second a given level of taxes, and then let us trace the effects of each on the equilibrium level of income and output.

In Figure 14–1, C and $C + I$ in Part A and S and I in Part B correspond exactly to Parts A and B of Figure 7–2. The equation for C is $C = C_a + c(Y - T)$ in which $C_a = 20$, $c = 3/4$, and, for the moment, $T = 0$. The equation for I is simply $I = I_a$, in which $I_a = 20$. The equation for the saving function in Part B follows from the consumption function: $S = S_a + s(Y - T)$, in which $S_a = -C_a = -20$, and $s = 1 - c = 1/4$. The equilibrium level of income for these assumed values is, of course, 160 in Figure 14–1 as it was in Figure 7–2. Now we insert G of 25 per time period and assume that this amount is entirely deficit-financed so that taxes remain at zero. This is shown in Part A of Figure 14–1 by simply adding the "autonomous" public demand, G of 25, to private demand, $C + I$, to produce the aggregate demand function $C + I + G$ and, in Part B, by simply adding it again to investment demand, I, to produce the function labeled $I + G$. The new equilibrium level of income is now 260, 100 above what it was before aggregate demand was increased by the 25 of public demand.

Why did the equilibrium level of income rise by 100 with the addition of government expenditures of only 25? With government now in the picture the new equilibrium level of income must be that at which the amount of the income stream diverted from consumption into planned saving and tax payments is just equal to the amount added to the income stream in the form of investment and government expenditures. Since taxes are for the moment assumed to be zero,

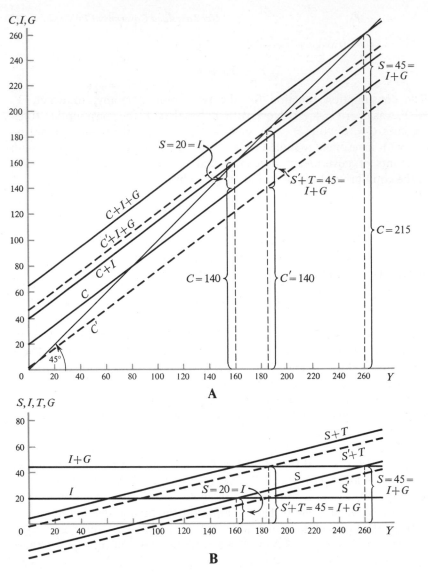

FIGURE 14-1 Equilibrium Level of Income, Including Government Expenditures and Taxation

to restore equilibrium following the injection of 25 in government spending, income must rise to the level at which planned saving alone is equal to the sum of planned investment and government expenditures. Given an MPC of 3/4 and an MPS of 1/4, it is clear that only when income has risen by 100 will there be additional saving of 25 leaking out of the income stream per period to match the 25 injected into the income stream per period by government spending. Thus, in Figure 14–1, we see that $S = 45 = I + G$ at Y of 260. Once income has risen by 100, aggregate demand is stabilized, and a new equilibrium is established.

The effect of adding a given amount of government expenditures, G, to the present model is essentially no different from the effect of an equal increase in

C_a or I_a. Like C_a or I_a, G is here a part of autonomous spending. With $c = 3/4$, the ordinary multiplier is 4, and any increase in autonomous spending (e.g., G of 25) will, other things being unchanged, raise income by four times the increase in autonomous spending to restore the system to equilibrium. The equation for the equilibrium level of income may be rewritten to show the multiplier explicitly. That is,

$$Y = C_a + c(Y - T) + I + G$$

may be rewritten as

$$Y = \frac{1}{1 - c}(C_a - cT + I + G)$$

Solving for the values we have assumed for c, C_a, I, G, and T, we have

$$260 = 4[20 - \tfrac{3}{4}(0) + 20 + 25]$$

Now let us suppose that government abandons its policy of deficit spending and that it collects in taxes 25 per time period to cover its expenditures of 25 per time period. With the imposition of this fixed amount of taxes, disposable income is 25 less than net national product at all levels of net national product. With an MPC of 3/4, it follows that taxes of 25 reduce consumption by 18.75 at each level of net national product. This is illustrated in Part A of Figure 14–1 by the new consumption function labeled C', which is positioned 18.75 below C. With an MPS of 1/4, taxes of 25 also reduce saving by 6.25 at each level of net national product. This is illustrated in Part B of Figure 14–1 by the new saving function labeled S', which lies 6.25 below S.

The new equilibrium level of income is now found in Part A by adding to C' the 20 of I and 25 of G to produce the new aggregate-demand function, $C' + I + G$. This function intersects the guideline at Y of 185. The equilibrium level may also be found in Part B by adding to S' the 25 of T to produce $S' + T$, which intersects $I + G$ at Y of 185. In Part A equilibrium is indicated at the level of Y at which aggregate demand equals aggregate output, or at which $Y = C' + I + G$; in Part B equilibrium is at the level of Y at which the aggregate diversions of income from consumption are offset by the aggregate of compensating expenditures, or the level of Y at which $S' + T = I + G$.

It is surprising at first glance to find that the injection by government of 25 into the income stream and the withdrawal in taxes of an exactly equal amount from the income stream still results in an expansion of the income stream from 160 to 185, an amount equal to the increase in the government budget. In the simplest terms, this result follows from the fact that the downward shift in the aggregate demand function due to T of 25 is less than the upward shift in that function due to G of 25. With the MPC of 3/4, T of 25 lowers the consumption function by 18.75 at each level of Y, or from C to C'. Since the upward shift of 25 resulting from G of 25 is 6.25 greater than the downward shift of 18.75 resulting from T of 25, the aggregate demand function with T and G both 25 is 6.25 above the aggregate demand function with T and G both zero. The net shift upward of 6.25 is subject to a multiplier of 4, which raises the equilibrium level of income by 25, from 160 to 185. As in previous models, this may also be explained in terms of saving and investment. Expressed in equation form, we have the following figures for the equilibrium positions, first with G and T both zero, and second with G and T both 25:

$$Y = C_a + c(Y - T) + I + G$$

$G = 0; T = 0$:

$$160 = 20 + \tfrac{3}{4}(160 - 0) + 20 + 0$$

$G = 25; T = 25$:

$$185 = 20 + \tfrac{3}{4}(185 - 25) + 20 + 25$$

$$S + T = I + G$$

$G = 0; T = 0$:

$$-20 + \tfrac{1}{4}(160 - 0) + 0 = 20 + 0$$

$G = 25; T = 25$:

$$-20 + \tfrac{1}{4}(185 - 25) + 25 = 20 + 25$$

Substitutions in either equation of larger or smaller amounts of G and T will, provided that G and T remain equal, result in a rise or fall in the equilibrium level of income equal to the amount of the increase or decrease in the size of the government budget. This result is known as the *balanced-budget theorem* or *unit-multiplier theorem*. We may see its meaning more clearly by again rewriting the aggregate demand equation to show the multiplier explicitly. That is,

$$Y = C_a + c(Y - T) + I + G$$

may be rewritten as

$$Y = \frac{1}{1 - c}(C_a - cT + I + G)$$

In this form, it may be seen that a change in any of the values within the parentheses will, assuming that the other values within the parentheses remain unchanged, produce a change in income equal to the change in that value times the ordinary multiplier, $1/(1 - c)$. Substituting the values from the previous example, we have

$$185 = \frac{1}{1 - 3/4}[20 - \tfrac{3}{4}(25) + 20 + 25]$$

If now, for example, we assume a change in I, the other values remaining unchanged, the new equilibrium level of Y is equal to the original level of Y plus the change in Y:

$$Y + \Delta Y = \frac{1}{1-c}(C_a - cT + I + G) + \frac{1}{1-c}\Delta I$$

Subtracting Y from both sides, there remains

$$\Delta Y = \frac{1}{1-c}\Delta I = \frac{\Delta I}{1-c}$$

A change in C_a or in G equal to the change in I will also produce a change in Y of equivalent amount, or

$$\Delta Y = \frac{\Delta I}{1-c} = \frac{\Delta C_a}{1-c} = \frac{\Delta G}{1-c}$$

where $\Delta I = \Delta C_a = \Delta G$. However, a change in T of the same amount as the change in I, C_a, or G will produce a smaller change in Y and one that is in the opposite direction, since

$$\Delta Y = \frac{-c\,\Delta T}{1-c}$$

We saw in the example above that the equilibrium level of income with $G = 0$ and $T = 0$ was 160. Then with $G = 25$ and $T = 0$, the equilibrium level rose from 160 to 260 or $\Delta Y = 100$. That is,

$$\Delta Y = \frac{\Delta G}{1-c} = \frac{25}{1 - 3/4} = 100$$

However, with both $T = 25$ and $G = 25$ in the model we found the new equilibrium level to be 185. The addition of $T = 25$ to the model pulled income down, since

$$\Delta Y = \frac{-c\,\Delta T}{1-c} = \frac{-\frac{3}{4}(25)}{1 - 3/4} = -75$$

Adding G of 25 raised the equilibrium level by 100 but adding T of 25 pulled the equilibrium level down by 75. Putting both together,

$$\Delta Y = \frac{\Delta G}{1-c} + \frac{-c\,\Delta T}{1-c} = 100 - 75 = 25$$

The change in Y is 25, as noted earlier.

The contractionary effect of an increase in taxes is thus less than the expansionary effect of an equal increase in government spending for goods and services. A rise in G is, in its entirety, an addition to aggregate demand, but a rise in T is not, in its entirety, a decrease in aggregate demand. Some part of the rise in T is absorbed by a decrease in S, and only the remainder by a decrease in C, or in aggregate demand.

The difference in the impact of ΔG and ΔT on the level of Y may also be seen by comparing the multipliers that apply to each. The government-purchases multiplier is the same as the multiplier applicable to a change in autonomous consumption or investment spending. Thus, for ΔG,

$$\Delta Y = \frac{\Delta G}{1 - c}$$

or

$$\frac{\Delta Y}{\Delta G} = \frac{1}{1 - c}$$

For ΔT, however, we derive what is called the *tax multiplier*, which is smaller than the government-purchases multiplier. A change in taxes leads to a change in autonomous demand that is only c times the change in taxes, whereas a change in government purchases leads to a change in autonomous demand that exactly equals the change in government purchases. Thus, for ΔT,

$$\Delta Y = \frac{-c \, \Delta T}{1 - c}$$

or

$$\frac{\Delta Y}{\Delta T} = \frac{-c}{1 - c}$$

If, as earlier, we assume c to be 3/4, a rise in government purchases is subject to a multiplier of 4, but a rise in taxes is subject to a multiplier of -3. In other words, an additional dollar of G will raise Y by \$4, and an additional dollar of T will reduce Y by \$3, leaving a \$1 rise in Y as the net effect of a rise of \$1 in both G and T.

Regardless of the value of c, the government purchases multiplier, $\Delta Y/\Delta G$, will always be one greater than the tax multiplier, $\Delta Y/\Delta T$. This may be shown by combining the separate multiplier expressions for ΔG and ΔT. Given

$$\frac{\Delta Y}{\Delta G} = \frac{1}{1 - c}$$

and

$$\frac{\Delta Y}{\Delta T} = \frac{-c}{1 - c}$$

by combining, we get

$$\frac{\Delta Y}{\Delta G} + \frac{\Delta Y}{\Delta T} = \frac{1}{1 - c} + \frac{-c}{1 - c} = \frac{1 - c}{1 - c} = 1$$

Since the former is always positive and the latter always negative, the sum of the two will always be unity, whatever the value of c.

A dramatic implication for fiscal policy seems to follow from the unit-multiplier theorem. If the level of the economy's output is below full employment, it would seem that government can raise the level to full employment by an appropriate expansion in the size of its budget, covering every dollar of additional expenditures with a dollar of additional taxes. The desired rise in income and output may thus be achieved by means of a fiscal policy that does not resort to deficit financing, with its real or alleged "evils." However, as we have noted a number of times before, these crude mechanical models are in each case subject to numerous qualifications that complicate the solution. The road to full employment is certainly not so simple as is suggested by the crude unit-multiplier theorem. Although it is not certain that a rise in the size of the budget, with taxes and expenditures both up by, say, $5 billion, will raise the level of income by $5 billion, it certainly will not be neutral in its effect on the level of income. To analyze the expansionary effects of a balanced budget properly involves more than the unit-multiplier theorem, but the mechanical model of that theorem as developed here at least dispels the notion that a balanced budget is fiscally neutral, as was once thought to be the case.[2]

SECOND FISCAL MODEL—INCLUDING GROSS TAXES, GOVERNMENT PURCHASES, AND TRANSFER PAYMENTS

The first model emphasized the effects on income of changes in the net tax receipts of government, T, and government purchases of goods and services, G. Now let us introduce a simple modification into the first model, which brings out the essential difference between the effects on income of changes in government purchases and changes in government transfer payments.

Net tax receipts, T, are equal to gross tax receipts minus government transfer payments and interest on debt, or $T_g - R$.[3] Expressing this as $T = T_g - R$ underscores the fact that R is really negative taxes, in effect an amount of gross tax receipts that is returned to individuals through government transfer and interest payments.[4] Substituting $T_g - R$ for T, the fundamental identity for net national product now becomes

$$C + S + T_g - R \equiv Y \equiv C + I + G$$

[2] The literature on the unit-multiplier theorem is summarized in W. J. Baumol and M. H. Peston, "More on the Multiplier Effects of a Balanced Budget," in *American Economic Review*, March 1955, pp. 140–48. The more important studies in this extensive literature are also listed in R. A. Musgrave, *The Theory of Public Finance*, McGraw-Hill, 1959, p. 430.

[3] To simplify the symbols, R will be used in this chapter to represent the sum of government transfer payments to persons, R_{gp}, and government interest payments, R_{gi}. Government transfer payments to foreigners, R_{gf}, do not enter into the three-sector models of this chapter.

[4] With a balanced budget, $G = T$ and $G + R = T_g$. By showing R as a deduction from gross tax receipts, we have $T_g - R = G$. If there is a deficit or surplus, $G > T$ or $G < T$; the size of the deficit or surplus, of course, remains unchanged in the equation as restated.

Disposable personal income, in turn, becomes

$$Y_d \equiv Y - T_g + R$$

The consumption function becomes

$$C = C_a + c(Y - T_g + R)$$

And the equilibrium level of income is given by

$$Y = C_a + c(Y - T_g + R) + I + G$$

which may be rewritten as

$$Y = \frac{1}{1 - c} (C_a - cT_g + cR + I + G)$$

This equation for the equilibrium level of income is identical to that for the first model, except that $T_g - R$ is now substituted for T. And the interpretation of this equation as rewritten is identical to that of its counterpart in the first model—a change in any of the values within the parentheses, on the assumption that all other values within the parentheses remain unchanged, will produce a change in income equal to the change in that value times the ordinary multiplier.

From the equation it is clear that the effect on Y of an increase in R will be less than the effect of an equal increase in G, as long as the MPC, or c, is less than 1. That is,

$$\frac{1}{1 - c} \Delta G > \frac{1}{1 - c} c \Delta R$$

where ΔG equals ΔR.

The reason for this difference is that, in the first instance, all of any increase in G is an addition to aggregate demand, whereas only part of any increase in R becomes an addition to aggregate demand. ΔG affects aggregate demand directly, but ΔR affects aggregate demand only indirectly through its effect on disposable income. Assuming that there is no change in tax receipts, ΔR increases disposable income directly by the full amount of ΔR. The consumption function indicates, however, that not all of any increase in disposable income will be devoted to consumer spending; some portion will be devoted to personal saving.[5] *In other words, at the first step, some portion of government transfer payments will fail to appear as demand for goods and services, but, at the first step, all government purchases appear as demand for goods and services.* Thus, in the case of government purchases, the full increase in government spending is subject to the ordinary multiplier, but in the case of government transfers only the part that is not diverted into saving is subject to the ordinary multiplier. These amounts may be designated ΔG and $c \Delta R$, respectively, as in the equation given above for the equilibrium level of income.

[5] The portion of disposable personal income made up of interest paid by consumers is, as in earlier models, assumed to be zero.

Instead of showing that all ΔG and only part of ΔR are subject to the ordinary multiplier, we may express the same thing differently in terms of the government-purchases multiplier and the government-transfers multiplier. For government purchases, we developed the following multiplier:

$$\Delta Y = \frac{1}{1-c} \Delta G$$

or

$$\frac{\Delta Y}{\Delta G} = \frac{1}{1-c}$$

For government transfers, we derive the multiplier to which the total of any change in transfers is subject as follows:

$$\Delta Y = \frac{1}{1-c} c \, \Delta R$$

or

$$\frac{\Delta Y}{\Delta R} = \frac{c}{1-c}$$

Regardless of the value of c, the government-transfers multiplier is one less than the government-purchases multiplier. Apart from the change in sign, it is the same as the tax multiplier. This equality between the tax multiplier and the government-transfers multiplier has several important implications that will be noted below.

First, for a numerical example, let us compare the effects of ΔG of 5 with ΔR of 5, assuming that c equals $3/4$:

$$\Delta Y = \frac{1}{1-c} \Delta G = 20$$

and

$$\Delta Y = \frac{1}{1-c} c \, \Delta R = 15$$

Expressed in terms of the government-purchases multiplier and the government-transfers multiplier, this means that ΔG is subject to a multiplier of 4 and ΔR to a multiplier of 3.

$$\frac{\Delta Y}{\Delta G} = \frac{1}{1-c} = 4$$

and

$$\frac{\Delta Y}{\Delta R} = \frac{c}{1-c} = 3$$

Since ΔG exerts a greater expansionary effect on Y than does ΔR when T_g

remains constant, one would also expect the expansionary effect of ΔG on Y to exceed that of ΔR when ΔT_g matches the increase in government expenditures. The balanced-budget theorem showed that an equal change in both G and T (for which we may now substitute T_g) would produce a change in Y equal to the change in the size of the budget. For example, with ΔG and ΔT_g both 5 and with c of $3/4$, we found the following:

$$\Delta Y = \frac{\Delta G}{1-c} + \frac{-c\,\Delta T_g}{1-c} = 20 - 15 = 5$$

Now, however, if the tax-financed increase in government expenditures is an increase in R rather than in G, we would have a different result.

$$\Delta Y = \frac{c\,\Delta R}{1-c} + \frac{-c\,\Delta T_g}{1-c} = 15 - 15 = 0$$

Unlike an increase in G, the expansionary effect of an increase in R is fully offset by the contractionary effect of an equal increase in T_g. In short, the expansionary effect suggested by the balanced-budget theorem applies, not to tax-financed changes in R, but only to tax-financed changes in G.

In practice, the differences between the expansionary effects of an increase in purchases as against those of an increase in transfer payments are not likely to be precisely those indicated by these crude models.[6] Despite the need for qualifications, the models still permit us to reach some tentative conclusions concerning the probable results of alternative fiscal policies. These conclusions may be summarized as follows. Assuming that government may, at its discretion, alter one or more of the variables according to plan, it may incur a deficit by (1) reducing tax receipts, (2) increasing purchases, (3) increasing transfer payments, or (4) any combination of these changes. In making a deficit of a given amount, an increase in purchases will have a greater expansionary effect than either a reduction in tax receipts or an increase in transfer payments. The expansionary effect of a deficit of given amount incurred by reducing tax receipts or raising transfer expenditures will be of the same order. Assuming that additional expenditures are to be covered by additional taxes, government can produce an expansionary effect only by increasing its purchases of goods and services. A reduction in its purchases accompanied by an equal reduction in tax receipts may be expected to be contractionary. In short, if government policy

---

[6] Just one of a number of reasons is that the crude models assume that the MPC is the same for all persons. However, the MPC of persons suffering a reduction in disposable income through additional tax payments may well be different from that of persons enjoying an increase in disposable income through receipt of transfer payments. The decrease in consumption of taxpayers will, therefore, not necessarily be the same as the increase in consumption of the beneficiaries of the transfer payments. The two sets of persons need not be the same. For example, unemployment compensation is financed through business taxes whose incidence may be on the owners or the customers of business or on both, but the beneficiaries of the compensation checks are the unemployed.

is to avoid a change in the size of the deficit or surplus, increasing or decreasing transfer payments and tax receipts in like amount will not directly affect the level of income.

THIRD FISCAL MODEL—INCLUDING GROSS TAX RECEIPTS AS A FUNCTION OF INCOME, GOVERNMENT PURCHASES, AND TRANSFER PAYMENTS

In the previous model, we developed the following equation for the equilibrium level of income, from which we may find, for any given value of c, the effect that a change in any one element within parentheses will have on Y if all the other elements remain constant:

$$Y = \frac{1}{1 - c}(C_a - cT_g + cR + I + G)$$

In reality, of course, a change in any one element is bound to affect the others through its effect on the level of income. A change in demand, whether directly through a change in autonomous consumption, C_a, investment, I, or government purchases, G, or indirectly through a change in government transfer payments, R, or tax receipts, T_g, will change the level of income; this change may call forth changes in other components of demand. The response of consumption spending to a change in income is already built into the model because consumption is assumed to be equal to $C_a + cY_d$. The response of investment spending could also be built into the model by substituting for the autonomous investment function, $I = I_a$, the investment function; $I = I_a + eY$, or, in a much more complicated model, some version of the accelerator investment function such as $I_t = I_a + w(Y_{t-1} - Y_{t-2})$. The response of government spending to changes in the level of income could also be built into the model, except that there is no simple, meaningful functional relationship between government spending, apart from transfer expenditures, and the level of income. To keep our discussion of this third model comparatively simple, we will continue to treat investment spending and government spending as completely autonomous.

There is one modification that may easily be made and will bring our third model closer to reality, and that is to allow for the fact that any change in income will typically affect tax receipts. In the previous model we assumed that tax receipts would remain constant in the face of a change in income. In practice this would happen only if government took just the offsetting action necessary to prevent the change in tax receipts that otherwise would follow automatically from a change in income. In recent years well over half the combined tax receipts of federal, state, and local governments have been from personal and corporate income taxes, and the revenue produced by these taxes, far from being independent of income, varies more than proportionately with changes in income.

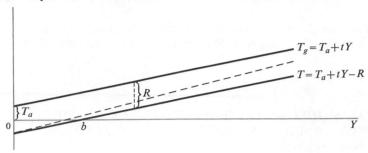

FIGURE 14–2   Gross and Net Tax Functions

Other mainstays in the tax structure, such as sales and excise tax receipts, are also related to income but less closely than income tax receipts. Given our present tax and rate structure, to prevent the changes in tax receipts that would automatically accompany a change in income would call for appropriate changes in tax and/or rate structure. Now, assuming as is found in practice that tax receipts are allowed to vary with changes in income, we may treat tax receipts roughly as a linear function of income. This gives us the following tax function:

$$T_g = T_a + tY$$

A tax function of this type is depicted by the T_g line in Figure 14–2. Notice that this function is of the same type as the consumption function, $C = C_a + cY$, and the investment function with induced investment, $I = I_a + eY$. Accordingly, it is interpreted in the same way. Just as c represents the MPC and e the MPI, so t stands for the MPT or the *marginal propensity to tax*. It indicates the marginal tax rate, $\Delta T_g / \Delta Y$, or the fraction of any change in income that will be diverted from income receivers to government with a given tax structure and tax rates. It is comparable to the single rate in a proportional income tax. Graphically, it is the slope of the T_g function, drawn in Figure 14–2 as 1/5. This tells us that for every change in Y of $5, there will be a change in T_g of $1. T_a, which is analogous to C_a and I_a, represents the amount of "autonomous" tax receipts, or the amount of tax receipts that is independent of the level of income. Although in practice income could not fall to zero, T_a indicates the amount of tax receipts at the theoretical zero level of income, which is depicted graphically by the intercept of the T_g function with the vertical axis.

The T_g function of Figure 14–2 shows T_a as a positive amount. Assuming that R remains the same at all levels of income and expressing the tax function in net terms, the net tax function, labeled T in the figure, would lie below the gross tax function by the amount of R. As before, R appears as negative tax receipts or as a subtraction from gross tax receipts. The net tax function, $T = T_a + tY - R$, crosses the vertical axis below zero, indicating that at very low levels of income, the amount of transfer payments would exceed the amount of gross tax receipts. Net tax receipts are shown to be negative at all income levels below $0b$. If we go a step further and recognize that transfer payments vary inversely with the level of income, the net tax function corresponding to the gross tax function given in Figure 14–2 would be one like the dashed line lying

284

above T. This reflects the fact that as income rises, unemployment compensation and other expenditures under general relief programs decrease. This results in a narrowing of the spread between the gross tax function and the net tax function as income rises and a widening of the spread as income falls. For the sake of simplicity, however, we will assume that R is independent of Y, so that $T_g = T_a + tY$ and $T = T_a + tY - R$.

Substituting the tax function, $T_g = T_a + tY$, for T_g, we now have

$$C + S + T_a + tY - R = Y = C + I + G$$

Disposable personal income becomes

$$Y_d = Y - (T_a + tY) + R$$

or

$$Y_d = Y - T_a - tY + R$$

The consumption function becomes

$$C = C_a + c(Y - T_a - tY + R)$$

Retaining our assumption that investment and government expenditures are entirely autonomous, the equilibrium level of income is given by

$$Y = C_a + c(Y - T_a - tY + R) + I + G$$

or

$$Y = C_a + cY - cT_a - ctY + cR + I + G$$

which may be rewritten as

$$Y = \frac{1}{1 - c(1 - t)}(C_a - cT_a + cR + I + G)$$

With tax receipts assumed to be independent of the level of income, the equation for the second model had a multiplier of $1/(1 - c)$. Recognizing that tax receipts are dependent on the level of income, the multiplier is reduced to $1/[1 - c(1 - t)]$. Assuming that $c = 3/4$ and that $t = 1/5$, we now have the smaller multiplier 2.5, instead of the previous multiplier 4. If the marginal propensity to tax, t, is greater than zero, the present model will always yield a smaller multiplier than the previous model. Thus, with $c = 3/4$ and $t = 1/5$, for a change in G of 10 we now have

$$\Delta Y = \frac{1}{1 - c(1 - t)} \Delta G = \frac{1}{1 - \frac{3}{4}(1 - 1/5)}(10) \doteq 25$$

instead of our earlier result,

$$Y = \frac{1}{1 - c} \Delta G = \frac{1}{1 - 3/4}(10) = 40$$

In the period in which G increases by 10, income increases by 10. If $t = 0$, disposable income also rises by 10, so that consumers have available to spend or save the full increase in income. If we now assume that $t = 1/5$, disposable income does not rise by the amount of the increase in income. Instead, 1/5 of the income increase of 10 is diverted to the government in the form of tax payments, leaving only 8 as the increase in disposable income. With $c = 3/4$, instead of induced consumption of 7.5, or 3/4 of 10, as in the previous model, we now have induced consumption of 6, or $3/4 \times 4/5 \times 10$. Thus, the marginal propensity to tax operates as a drag on consumption, reducing it to 6 from the 7.5 it would be if t equaled zero. In each of the subsequent periods required for the multiplier process to work itself out, 1/5 of the income generated in each period is also diverted to government in the form of tax payments. The final result is a new equilibrium level of income with ΔY of 25, made up of ΔG of 10 and ΔC of 15.

This process is described in detail in Table 14–1. Part A assumes $t = 1/5$

TABLE 14–1   Marginal Propensity to Tax and the Multiplier Process

		Part A $t = 1/5$, $c = 3/4$			
Period	ΔY	ΔG	ΔT_g	ΔY_d	ΔC
t	0	0	0	0	0
$t + 1$	10.0	10	2.0	8.0	0
$t + 2$	16.0	10	3.2	12.8	6.0
$t + 3$	19.6	10	3.9	15.7	9.6
$t + 4$	21.8	10	4.4	17.4	11.8
$t + 5$	23.0	10	4.6	18.4	13.0
$t + n$	25.0	10	5.0	20.0	15.0
		Part B $t = 0$, $c = 3/4$			
Period	ΔY	ΔG	ΔT_g	ΔY_d	ΔC
t	0	0	0	0	0
$t + 1$	10.0	10	0	10.0	0
$t + 2$	17.5	10	0	17.5	7.5
$t + 3$	23.1	10	0	23.1	13.1
$t + 4$	27.3	10	0	27.3	17.3
$t + 5$	30.5	10	0	30.5	20.5
$t + n$	40.0	10	0	40.0	30.0

NOTE: Figures are rounded to nearest tenth.

and traces the multiplier process given by the multiplier, $1/[1 - c(1 - t)]$. Part B assumes that tax receipts are independent of income, $t = 0$, and traces the familiar multiplier process given by the ordinary multiplier, $1/(1 - c)$. In both parts, there is an original equilibrium in Period t, which is upset in Period $t + 1$ by a permanent increase in government purchases of 10. For use in this model, a lagged consumption function is assumed so that a change in disposable income in any one period does not lead to a change in consumption spending until the following period.

In Part A, ΔG of 10 in Period $t + 1$ generates ΔY of 10 but ΔY_d of only 8, since 1/5 of ΔY is diverted to government as ΔT_g. In Period $t + 2$, ΔY is 16, which consists of ΔG of 10 and ΔC of 6, the latter being 3/4 of ΔY_d of Period $t + 1$. Of ΔY of 16, 1/5 (or 3.2) is diverted to government, leaving ΔY_d of 12.8. In Period $t + 3$, ΔY is then the sum of ΔG of 10 and ΔC of 9.6. Income gradually rises by Period $t + n$ to a new equilibrium 25 above the original equilibrium. In Part B, the process is the same, except that no portion of ΔY is diverted into tax payments. Without additional taxes to be paid on the additional income, disposable income is greater, consumption spending is greater, and the level of income rises faster and farther than in Part A. In this situation, income rises to a new equilibrium level 40 above the old. Similarly, since consumption is not subject to the drag of additional taxes, induced consumption rises by 30 in Part B as compared with only 15 in Part A.

Although it is clear that a positive marginal propensity to tax means a smaller expansion of income for any given increase in government spending than a zero marginal propensity to tax, it also means that the deficit created by any increase in government spending will be less than the amount of the increase in government spending. For example, in Part A the deficit created by ΔG of 10 is only 5 per time period, once the income equilibrium level has been reached— that is, $\Delta G - \Delta T_g = 5$ in Period $t + n$. In contrast, we see in Part B, with $t = 0$, that ΔG of 10 creates a deficit of 10 in each period. Part A is more relevant, since in the real world the MPT is positive. This suggests that normally an increase in government expenditures, with no change in tax rates or tax structure, will lead to a less than equal increase in the deficit. This point is sometimes missed by persons who overlook the expansion of the income flow produced by the increase in government spending. With a positive MPT, some part of the expanded income flow automatically becomes additional tax receipts of government and as such becomes a check to what otherwise would be a change in the deficit equal to the increase in government spending. As we can see in the present model, the greater the MPC, the greater will be this check to the size of the deficit accompanying any increase in government spending. If, for example, in Part A we substitute an MPC of 9/10 for the MPC of 3/4 and retain the same MPT of 1/5, the multiplier, $1/[1 - c(1 - t)]$ becomes 3.57. Then ΔG of 10 would produce a new equilibrium in Period $t + n$ with ΔY of 35.7. With ΔY of 35.7, ΔT_g would be 7.14 in Period $t + n$ and the deficit would be only 2.86 per period.

Without going into the complex mechanics that this model involves, one can still see how the deficit created by ΔG could be still smaller or could even be turned into a surplus if investment spending, here assumed to be entirely autonomous, $I = I_a$, were assumed to be responsive to the level of income, $I = I_a + eY$. If the initial rise in income generated by the increase in government spending should induce investment spending as well as consumption spending, then, depending on the value of the MPI and the MPC, the rise in the equilibrium level of income could conceivably be such that the additional tax receipts would match or exceed the increase in government spending. Thus, in the example, to produce a "balanced budget" there would have to be a rise in Y of 50, which would yield additional tax receipts of 10 equal to the increased government spending of 10 per period. To produce a "surplus," there would have to be a rise in Y that was larger than 50.

FISCAL MODELS AND THE FULL-EMPLOYMENT LEVEL OF INCOME

The several fiscal models developed to this point have shown how changes in G, R, and T_g, individually and in combination, affect the level of Y. We can summarize the implications of these simple fiscal models by demonstrating in terms of such a model how alternative fiscal policies may be used to lift an economy to its full-employment level of income and output.[7]

Let us begin with the most recently developed equation for the equilibrium level of income.

$$Y = C_a + c(Y - T_a - tY + R) + I + G$$

or

$$Y = \frac{1}{1 - c(1 - t)}(C_a - cT_a + cR + I + G)$$

We will assume that the following values apply:

$$C = 15 + \tfrac{3}{4}Y_d \qquad R = 10.66 \qquad T_g = 4 + \tfrac{1}{5}Y$$
$$I = 25 \qquad G = 35$$

Substituting in the equation for the equilibrium level of income, we have

$$Y = 15 + \tfrac{3}{4}(Y - 4 - \tfrac{1}{5}Y + 10.66) + 25 + 35$$
$$Y = 200$$

with $C = 140$, $I = 25$, and $G = 35$.

Let us further suppose that the full-employment level of Y is 225 at the existing price level and that expansion of output from 200 to the full-employment level will not raise the price level. The model suggests several possible routes to full employment. An increase in government expenditures for goods and services is one route. To determine the needed increase in government demand, we insert Y of 225 into the equation and solve for the necessary G,

$$225 = 15 + \tfrac{3}{4}[225 - 4 - \tfrac{1}{5}(225) + 10.66] + 25 + G$$
$$G = 45$$

---

[7] For a more detailed analysis of this use of fiscal policy expressed in terms of models, see N. F. Keiser, *op. cit.*, Ch. 9, and R. A. Musgrave, *op. cit.*, Ch. 18.

This could be found more simply and directly from the second equation given above, which shows the effective multiplier to be 2.5. To produce the required increase in Y of 25 would then call for an increase in G of 10 or from G of 35 to G of 45.

With Y at 200, T_g is 44 and $G + R$ is 45.66, indicating that there is a deficit of 1.66. If G rises by 10, resulting in a rise in Y of 25, T_g becomes 49, and the deficit rises to 6.66. Despite the increase in government expenditures of 10, the deficit rises by only 5; additional tax receipts of 5 are provided by the rise in income of 25.

A second route to full employment would be through tax reduction. Since tax receipts in the model depend on the level of income, tax reduction may take the form of a reduction in the marginal tax rate, t. To determine how far to reduce the tax rate, t, other things being equal, in order to produce aggregate demand of 225 and so income and output of 225, we insert Y of 225 into the equation and solve for the necessary value of t.

$$225 = 15 + \tfrac{3}{4}(225 - 4 - 225t + 10.66) + 25 + 35$$
$$t = 0.14$$

A reduction in the marginal tax rate from 0.20 to 0.14 will raise income by the required amount. Or, other things being equal, this is the tax rate that will produce the level of disposable income at which, given the marginal propensity to consume, consumption demand will, when added to investment and government demand, yield the required level of aggregate demand of 225 and so the required income level of 225.

As before, the required tax rate may be found more simply and directly from the alternative equation that originally showed the effective multiplier to be 2.5. That is,

$$\frac{200}{80} = \frac{1}{1 - \tfrac{3}{4}(1 - 1/5)} = 2.5$$

For Y of 225, the effective multiplier is thus 225/80 or 2.8125. To achieve this desired multiplier, t must be 0.14, as can be determined by solving the following for t:

$$\frac{225}{80} = \frac{1}{1 - \tfrac{3}{4}(1 - t)} = 2.8125$$

As we mentioned earlier, the expansionary effect of a deficit incurred by way of tax reduction is less than that of an equal deficit incurred by way of increased government purchases. The same result is found here, except that we must now compare the size of the deficit required to produce a specific expansion in income by way of increased government purchases and by way of decreased tax rate. Full employment was reached through increased purchases with an increase in the deficit from 1.66 to 6.66 per period. It is reached through a decreased tax rate with an increase in the deficit from 1.66 to 10.16 per period. In the present example, it takes an increase in the deficit of 8.5 per period via tax reduction to produce the expansion of income of 25 secured by a deficit of 5 per period via increased government purchases.

A third route to full employment would raise the income level by the required amount without any deficit financing. Since the expansionary effect of a dollar of government purchases is greater than the contractionary effect of a dollar of taxes, some amount of increase in government purchases and in taxes will raise income to the full-employment level and produce a balanced budget at the same time. To determine the level of G and T (net taxes) at which $G = T$ with $Y = 225$, we start off with:

$$225 = 15 + \tfrac{3}{4}(225 - 4 - 225t + 10.66) + 25 + G$$

Given that T (net taxes) at Y of 225 equals $4 + 225t - 10.66$, we substitute G for this expression and solve the equation for G:

$$225 = 15 + \tfrac{3}{4}(225 - G) + 25 + G$$
$$225 = 208.75 + \tfrac{1}{4}G$$
$$G = 65$$

Therefore, we know that T (net taxes) must equal 65 to produce a balanced budget with Y of 225. Corresponding to net tax receipts, T, of 65 are gross tax receipts, T_g, of 75.66. The required marginal tax rate, t, is therefore found from the tax function $75.66 = 4 + 225t$, or $t = 0.3185$. The final solution is then

$$225 = 15 + \tfrac{3}{4}[225 - 4 - 0.3185(225) + 10.66] + 25 + 65$$
$$225 = 135 + 25 + 65$$

in which $C = 140$, $I = 25$, and $G = 65$.

In comparison with the first route, this one calls for a much greater expansion in government purchases. In comparison with the second route, it calls for an increase in the marginal tax rate. Although it manages to raise the income level without deficit financing, it does so only by enlarging the share of the flow of goods and services and the share of the flow of income that is absorbed by government. A greater fraction of what is now a greater flow of final goods and services is made up of governmentally provided goods and services. A greater share of what is now a greater flow of income is diverted into taxes, and a smaller share is left for private consumption and saving.

The choice of which of these three fiscal policies to use in a given situation depends on what set of side-effects is regarded as the least harmful. Government must evaluate the relative merits and demerits of spending, taxing, and changing the size of the public debt. In practice, the first and second routes or some combination of the two have received the most attention. Although both involve deficits and therefore some growth in the public debt, the second does not enlarge the scope of government activities at all, and the other, while enlarging the scope of government activities, produces the desired effect on the income level without the relatively much greater enlargement of government activities necessitated by a fiscal policy with the budget-balancing restraint.

A CONCLUDING NOTE

No matter how elaborate fiscal models may be, they are all built essentially along the lines of the simple models discussed in this chapter. The chief purpose of all such models is to shed light on the way in which government taxing and spending affect aggregate demand and thus the level of income and output. However, as with previous models, it should be emphasized that the conclusions suggested by the succession of models in this chapter are based on the assumption of "other things being equal." Yet other things may change as a direct result of the government's taxing-borrowing-spending process, and to the extent that they do, the conclusions suggested by the models must be modified. Whatever these other changes may be, they may be examined through their effects on the consumption and investment functions.

In the case of the consumption function, the fiscal process may alter the slope or level (intercept with the vertical axis) of the function itself. The expansionary effect of a tax-financed increase in government purchases will be greater than is shown in the models if it leads to a rise in the MPC or in the level of the consumption function. Conversely, it will be smaller than is shown in the models if it leads to a fall in the MPC or in the level of the consumption function. One way the government's fiscal actions might produce such results is through their effect on the distribution of income. For example, to the extent that the MPC of the "poor" is greater than that of the "rich," government expenditures financed through a progressive income tax will raise the aggregate MPC and have a greater expansionary effect on the income level than if the aggregate MPC remains unchanged. If the same government expenditures were financed instead by sales taxation, they might conceivably lower the aggregate MPC and thus have a smaller expansionary effect on the income level than if the aggregate MPC had remained unchanged.

Even more important are the possible effects of the government taxing-spending process on the investment function. A tax-financed increase in government expenditures covered by higher corporate or progressive personal income tax rates might have an adverse effect on the MEC schedule and therefore an adverse effect on the investment function, which could offset the expansionary effect of the rise in government spending. Even the case in which the increased government expenditures are deficit financed is not necessarily without possible adverse effects on the investment function. The current increase in the national debt may generate fears of a coming rise in taxes or even of a deterioration in the credit of the government. The fact that fears of the possible financial collapse of government are entirely unfounded does not prevent them from arising, and it does not prevent them from adversely affecting the investment function. Furthermore, with a debt-financed increase in government expenditures, there is also a possibility of an adverse effect on investment through a rise in the rate of interest. If an increase in government borrowing is added to the existing private demand for loanable funds, the interest rate may be expected to rise. The central bank can expand the money supply to prevent this, but often the central bank, rightly or wrongly fearful of inflation, will not accommodate the increased demand for funds. If the MEC schedule is sufficiently elastic, the resulting decrease in investment spending may offset the otherwise expansionary effect of the increase in government spending. The increase in government expenditures, whether tax financed or debt financed, can also have an effect on investment expenditures for quite different reasons. Depending primarily on the nature of the expenditures—for example, whether they are for public power development or national defense—increased government activities may heighten the fear of socialism, and this fear will shift the MEC schedule downward.

These are simply a few of the numerous qualifications that must be recognized when one works with the simple models discussed in this chapter. The actual results of any change in the government's taxing-borrowing-spending program cannot be predicted with a high degree of accuracy. Yet, to the extent that a general statement is possible, most will agree that an increase in government spending or a reduction in taxes will encourage both consumption and investment spending and thus produce a rise in income and output that is greater in size than the initial reduction in taxes or increase in government spending. The models of the present chapter are intended simply to suggest in very general terms how this expansionary process may work itself out in practice.

CHAPTER 15

FOREIGN DEMAND

To this point, our analysis has assumed a "closed economy"—an economy considered in isolation from all others. In this chapter, we will relax this assumption and examine an "open economy"—a four-sector economy in which GNP by sector of demand is measured by the demand of the three domestic sectors plus that of the rest-of-the-world sector. Aggregate demand is now the sum of personal consumption expenditures, gross private domestic investment, government purchases, and net exports of goods and services, the last of which is a measure of the amount of aggregate demand for the domestic economy's output that arises from the domestic economy's transactions with the rest-of-the-world.

The purpose of this chapter is to describe how this foreign demand for the domestic economy's output affects the level of income and output in the domestic economy. We will confine our analysis in this chapter to fitting the simple mechanics of exports, imports, and the net export or import balance into an equilibrium model. Just as we omitted detailed analysis of the determinants of government spending and taxing in the preceding chapter, here we will omit a detailed analysis of the determinants of an economy's imports and exports. We will adopt a crude theory for the determination of each, and then concentrate on how the economy's exports and imports affect the level of income and output and how changes in exports and imports bring about fluctuations in the level of income and output.

ACCOUNTING IDENTITIES

In Chapter 4 we saw that it is an economy's net rather than gross exports that measure the amount of its final product secured by the rest-of-the-world and the amount of its gross national product accounted for by this sector of demand. Gross imports must be subtracted from gross exports in measuring GNP, since gross imports are already included in the measurement of the amount of final product secured by the domestic sectors of the economy. Since consumer, business, and government expenditures are for both domestic and foreign goods and services, $C + I_d + G$ no longer measures the amount of domestically produced final goods and services secured by these three sectors but this amount plus an amount equal to gross imports.[1] If somehow we could separate C into the amount spent for domestic and foreign output and do the same for I and G, then to the resulting total for consumption, investment, and government spending on domestic output could be added gross rather than net exports to yield aggregate expenditures by all four sectors of the economy for domestic output. Such a complete separation is, of course, impossible in practice. From the consumer's purchase of a ticket to see a foreign film to his purchase of a domestically produced automobile that consists in part of raw materials and parts that were produced abroad, he is purchasing simultaneously both domestic and foreign output combined in the same good or service. Similar cases also abound in domestic investment expenditures and in government purchases of goods and services.

As a consequence, we are forced in practice to measure aggregate expenditures of the three domestic sectors by their expenditures on final product, regardless of whether produced domestically or abroad. Such expenditures for any time period will include gross imports of goods and services for that time period. Because this overstates the amount of domestically produced output secured by the domestic sectors, gross imports are subtracted in a lump sum to yield in effect the amount of domestically produced output secured by domestic sectors. Expenditures by the rest-of-the-world for gross exports are then added to the expenditures by the domestic sectors net of gross imports to yield a sum that accurately represents aggregate expenditures, domestic and foreign, for the economy's final output. This gives us the GNP identity for the four-sector economy in the familiar form:[2]

[1] Here and in what follows, the amount of gross imports embodied in gross exports is assumed to be zero.

[2] If we could separate from each domestic sector's expenditures for final product the amount made up of foreign (f) goods and services, symbolically we would have for GNP in the four-sector economy

$$\text{GNP} \equiv (C - C_f) + (I_d - I_f) + (G - G_f) + X$$

in which X equals gross exports and $C_f + I_f + G_f$ equals gross imports, or M. Since this sepa-

$$\text{GNP} \equiv C + I_d + G + (X - M)$$

As always, corresponding to the flow of gross expenditures on the right is an equal flow of gross income on the left, which is split up as before into C, R_{pf}, S, and T. To show the breakdown on both the expenditures and income sides, we now have

$$C + R_{pf} + S + T \equiv \text{GNP} \equiv C + I_d + G + (X - M)$$

Since R_{pf}, personal transfer payments to foreigners, is negligible in terms of GNP, we may simplify the identity by assuming such transfer payments to be zero. This gives us a breakdown of the gross income flow into $C + S + T$, and the identity becomes

$$C + S + T \equiv \text{GNP} \equiv C + I_d + G + (X - M)$$

Although in so doing we no longer have a GNP identity, we may rewrite the preceding identity as

$$C + S + T + M \equiv C + I_d + G + X$$

The sum of expenditures on the right exceeds GNP by the amount of gross imports or M, as does the sum of income on the left. The expression is still an identity, however, and if C is dropped from both sides, we have an identity that is useful in the explanation of the determination of the equilibrium level of income in a four-sector economy.

EQUILIBRIUM LEVEL OF INCOME AND OUTPUT

A glance at the accounting identity for GNP indicates that, other things being equal, the domestic economy's income and output will rise from one period to the next as its gross exports rise or as its gross imports fall, since both these changes enlarge its net exports. It also follows that its income and output will fall from one period to the next as its gross exports fall or as its gross imports rise, since both these changes decrease its net exports. It follows in turn that the effect of imports and exports on the equilibrium level of the domestic economy's income and output must be found in the factors that determine the economy's imports and exports.

---

ration cannot be made in practice, we subtract gross imports in a lump sum from $C + I + G$ and add in gross exports:

$$\text{GNP} \equiv C + I_d + G - M + X$$

This may then be rewritten in the familiar form of the GNP identity.

In a very general way, the volume of gross exports of any economy depends on the prices of goods in the domestic economy relative to the prices of the same or substitute goods in other economies, on tariff and trade policies existing between the domestic and other economies, on the "shortage" or "surplus" of various currencies in foreign exchange markets, on the level of income in other countries, on the level of the domestic economy's imports, and on various other less significant factors. Some of the more important factors influencing an economy's exports are not directly related to conditions within that economy. For this reason, we may assume that gross exports of the domestic economy are wholly determined by external factors.[3] In other words, we may take gross exports as an autonomous variable, the value of which for any time period is wholly determined by forces outside the domestic economy.

The volume of imports of the domestic economy is determined by a similar list of factors. However, many of these factors are much more closely related to conditions within the economy than are those that determine exports. If, in the case of imports, we assume an unchanging system of international price differences, unchanging tariff, trade, and exchange restrictions, and all other factors unchanging except the level of domestic income, we may concentrate on one of the most important factors affecting gross imports—namely, the level of income within the domestic economy.

The Import Function

Other things being equal, as the level of income rises we expect an induced rise in consumption expenditures and perhaps also in investment expenditures. With a rise in expenditures we may also expect that some portion of these expenditures will be for imported goods and services. As a rough approximation, we will assume that there is a linear relationship between income and imports, which gives us the import function:

$$M = M_a + mY$$

in which M_a represents autonomous expenditures for imports and m is the *marginal propensity to import*, abbreviated as MPM. As in previous functions of this type, M_a is the amount of expenditures for imports at a theoretical zero level of income, or the amount of import expenditures that are independent of the level of income; m is simply the fraction of any change in income that will be devoted to expenditure on imports, or $m = \Delta M/\Delta Y$.

The upward-sloping line shown in Figure 15–1 depicts the import-income relationship described by the import function given above. Since exports are assumed to be externally determined, they are designated in the figure by a line parallel to the income axis. The level of the export line depends on the whole complex of external conditions. For the two functions as illustrated, we see that

[3] Later we will relax this assumption and examine how one factor, the imports of the domestic economy, may influence the exports of the domestic economy.

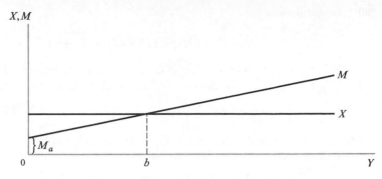

FIGURE 15–1 Import and Export Functions

at all income levels below $0b$ the economy has a net export balance and that at all income levels above $0b$ it has a net import (or negative net export) balance. Clearly, any change in the determinants of gross exports that shifts the export function upward will increase the net export balance or decrease the net import balance at each level of income. Similarly, any change that shifts the import function downward (decreases M_a) or reduces the slope of the import function (decreases m) will have the same effect.

The Equilibrium Level of Income—Equations

In the four-sector economy, the equilibrium level of income is that at which aggregate demand—the sum of consumption, investment, government, and net foreign expenditures—is equal to income. This gives us the following general equation for the equilibrium level of income:

$$Y = C + I + G + (X - M)$$

It could also be said that since $C + S + T = C + I + G + (X - M)$, the equilibrium level of income is also that at which $S + T = I + G + (X - M)$, or, when it is rearranged,

$$S + T + M = I + G + X$$

In this formulation, $S + T + M$ represents the portion of the economy's gross income flow that is diverted from consumption expenditure on domestically produced output. If the amount of compensating expenditures on domestically produced output, $I + G + X$, just equals these diversions or "leakages" from the income stream, then aggregate demand must equal aggregate income. The particular level of income at which this equality occurs is the equilibrium level.

If we now recognize that the economy's gross imports depend to some extent on the level of its income and assume that its gross exports are externally determined, the equilibrium equation is modified as follows:

$$Y = C + I + G + X - (M_a + mY)$$

We could also say that the equilibrium level of income is that at which

$$S + T + (M_a + mY) = I + G + X$$

Finally, assuming that I, T, and G are all autonomous, and that $C = C_a + c(Y - T)$, the equation for the equilibrium level of income becomes[4]

$$Y = C_a + c(Y - T) + I + G + X - (M_a + mY)$$

Since $S = -C_a + s(Y - T)$ and $-C_a = S_a$, we may also describe the equilibrium level of income as that level at which

$$S_a + s(Y - T) + T + (M_a + mY) = I + G + X$$

For a numerical example of the determination of the equilibrium level of income, assume the following values for the expenditure flows:

$$G = 26 \qquad\qquad T = 25$$
$$I = 20 \qquad\qquad M = M_a + mY = 2 + \tfrac{1}{10}Y$$
$$X = 17 \qquad\qquad C = C_a + c(Y - T) = 25 + \tfrac{8}{10}(Y - 25)$$

Substituting in the equation for the equilibrium level of income, we have

$$Y = C_a + c(Y - T) + I + G + X - (M_a + mY)$$
$$Y = 25 + \tfrac{8}{10}(Y - 25) + 20 + 26 + 17 - (2 + \tfrac{1}{10}Y)$$
$$Y = 220$$

or, in its alternative expression:

$$S_a + s(Y - T) + T + (M_a + mY) = I + G + X$$
$$-25 + \tfrac{2}{10}(Y - 25) + 25 + (2 + \tfrac{1}{10}Y) = 20 + 26 + 17$$
$$\tfrac{3}{10}Y = 63 + 3$$
$$Y = 220$$

The Equilibrium Level of Income—Graphs

Figure 15–2 illustrates the determination of the equilibrium level of income. Apart from the addition of net exports, the figure is identical in con-

---

[4] Apart from the addition of imports and exports, this equation is the same as that developed for the first fiscal model of Chapter 14. If the more complex third fiscal model, which included government transfer payments and the tax function, were expanded to allow for exports and the import function, we would have

$$Y = C_a + c(Y - T_a - tY + R) + I + G + X - (M_a + mY)$$

Alternatively, the equilibrium level of income would be that at which

$$S_a + s(Y - T_a - tY + R) + (T_a + tY - R) + (M_a + mY) = I + G + X$$

The analysis in this text will be limited throughout to the simpler model in which G and T are both autonomous and R is assumed to be zero.

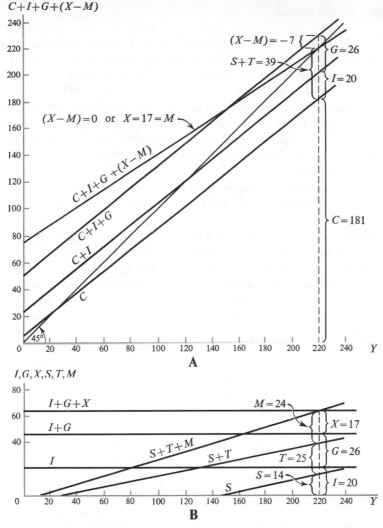

FIGURE 15–2 The Equilibrium Level of Income, Including Imports and Exports

struction to Figure 14–1. The consumption function is plotted from the equation $C = 25 + \frac{8}{10}(Y - 25)$. (The vertical intercept is therefore 5.) Autonomous investment of 20 is then superimposed on C to produce the $C + I$ function, and autonomous government purchases of 26 are superimposed on $C + I$ to yield the $C + I + G$ function. Finally, superimposed on the $C + I + G$ function is the last component of aggregate demand, net exports of $X - M$, and this gives the complete aggregate demand function $C + I + G + (X - M)$. Because gross exports are assumed to be independent of the level of domestic income and because gross imports are partially dependent on the level of domestic income, the excess of exports over imports of 15 (i.e., $17 - 2$) at the theoretical zero level of income gradually diminishes to zero at income of 150 (at which $X = 17$, and $M = 2 + \frac{1}{10}[150] = 17$). Therefore, up to Y of 150, foreign trade results in a net addition to aggregate demand—that is, $C + I + G +$

299

$(X - M) > C + I + G$. Above this level, however, imports exceed exports, and this excess grows larger at successively higher levels of income. Therefore, at income levels above 150, foreign trade results in a net reduction in aggregate demand—that is, $C + I + G > C + I + G + (X - M)$.

Because one component of aggregate demand, net exports, becomes negative at higher levels of income in our example, the aggregate demand function, which includes net foreign demand, lies below the demand function, which is composed of the demand of the three domestic sectors alone, at these higher levels of income.

The equilibrium income level is that level at which the aggregate demand function intersects the 45° guideline. In this case, when $Y = 220$, $C = 181$, $I = 20$, $G = 26$, and $X - M = -7$. When $Y = 220$, the four components of aggregate demand add up to 220, an amount equal to the income flow; therefore, only 220 can be the equilibrium income level. Following the argument of prevous analyses, Part A of Figure 15–2 shows that $C + I + G + (X - M) > Y$ at any level of Y below 220; this excess of demand over income leads to a rise in income. Part A shows that, at any level of Y above 220, $C + I + G + (X - M) < Y$. This deficiency of demand leads to a fall in income.

Given the values we have assumed for the various expenditure flows in our example, the inclusion of foreign trade means a lower equilibrium level than that which would be found in its absence. If $C + I + G$ were to remain the same in the absence of the availability of foreign-produced goods, the equilibrium level would occur at Y of 255, the income level at which the $C + I + G$ function cuts the 45° guideline.[5] The actual equilibrium in our example with foreign trade included is 220.

Part B of Figure 15–2 shows the alternative graphic approach to the determination of the equilibrium income level. Apart from the addition of gross imports and gross exports, the figure is identical in construction to Part B of Figure 14–1. Imports now appear as a third diversion from the amount of expenditure by consumers on domestically produced output; total diversions now equal $S + T + M$. Exports bring in a third expenditure, compensating for the diversions of income into $S + T + M$; total compensating expenditures now equal $I + G + X$. With these modifications for foreign trade, the equilibrium level of income is accordingly that at which $S + T + M = I + G + X$. As shown in Part B, this is at the income level of 220.

Part B of Figure 15–2 enables us to identify clearly each of these diversions from and the compensating injections into the spending stream. Putting them all together, at the income level of 220 we find that

$$S + T + M = I + G + X$$
$$14 + 25 + 24 = 20 + 26 + 17$$

It will be recalled from the analysis of the two-sector economy that if $I > S$,

---

[5] Without foreign-produced goods available, it is possible that C and perhaps also I might be lower at each level of Y. Consumers with strong preferences for imported goods might transfer part of what was spent on such goods to saving rather than all to domestically produced goods.

as here $20 > 14$, there would be a disequilibrium, and the level of income would rise. Similarly, in the three-sector economy, if $I + G > S + T$, as here $46 > 39$, there would be a disequilibrium and the level of income would rise. However, in this four-sector economy, the income-expansionary effect of $I + G > S + T$ is offset by the income-contractionary effect of $M > X$, or $24 > 17$. At the income level of 220, these forces offset each other precisely, the sum of the compensating injections matching the sum of income diversions, so income tends neither to expand nor to contract.

A Digression on "Balance of Payments" Equilibrium

The very concept of the equilibrium level of income raises special questions in the four-sector economy. Without entering into any of the complex questions of "balance of payments" equilibrium that are involved here, we can still show that the equilibrium income level determined in our example may be one that an economy cannot maintain over time.

Assume that with a given level of prices the equilibrium indicated in Figure 15–2 is consistent with full employment of the economy's resources. In a closed economy, a full employment equilibrium in which $I > S$ can presumably be maintained indefinitely as long as $T > G$ in each period by the amount that $I > S$. All that is required is that government run the necessary tax surplus period after period. In an open economy, however, if $I + G > S + T$ period after period, maintenance of the given equilibrium requires that $M > X$ in each period by the amount that $I + G > S + T$. In other words, what is required is a continuation of the given excess of imports over exports in each period. However, any downward shift in the import function or in the marginal propensity to import or any upward shift in the export function will reduce the net import balance and force an expansion in the equilibrium level of income. Since the original level of income was assumed to be consistent with full employment, this expansion of the income level will lead not to an expansion of output but to inflation of the price level of that output.

Maintenance of the required net import balance will sooner or later run into obstacles and cause inflation. If the domestic economy has substantial reserves of foreign exchange, the import excess can be financed from such reserves as long as they last. Or as long as the rest-of-the-world is willing to accumulate ever larger short-term balances in the domestic economy, the import excess may continue. Or as long as the rest-of-the-world is willing to put its surplus earnings of the domestic economy's currency into long-term investments in that economy, the import excess may continue. However, barring one or more of these conditions, the import surplus cannot be maintained over a long period of time. If, as part of its development program, the domestic economy persists in devoting the same amount of its output to domestic investment and government services, the only solution without outright inflation is to increase the amount of the income flow that is diverted into taxes and saving. As Figure 15–2 suggests, increases in either or both of these will reduce consumption, and the reduction in consumption will be in part a reduction in the consumption of foreign-produced goods. This will force imports down to the level of exports. In terms of $S + T + M = I + G + X$, the excess of M over X is eliminated in this case by increasing $S + T$ and decreasing M, without altering I, G, or X. If the net import balance cannot be maintained, correction could also be achieved through adjustment of other variables in the system.

The predicament we have just described is frequently faced by the underdeveloped economies of the world. Starting from a fully employed position, such economies try to achieve a faster rate of economic development than their real income and saving out of that income will permit. Their objective is to devote a large part of national output to domestic investment projects and government services, while still maintaining a tolerable level of real per capita consumption. A net import balance clearly helps in attaining these objectives. However, these countries are least of all in a position to do this on their own. They ordinarily have negligible foreign exchange reserves, rather than the large reserves necessary to finance a net import balance over a long period of time. They are countries in which the rest-of-the-world will not hold short-term balances and in which long-term private investment is avoided for reasons such as government instability and the fear of expropriation or nationalization of private property, especially foreign-owned private property. Since per capita real income is very low in the first place, it is virtually impossible to generate the volume of voluntary saving or to raise in taxes the amounts needed for ambitious private investment projects and expanding government services. Considerations such as these help explain why foreign aid, guaranties of long-term foreign investment, and other outside assistance have become so important in the acceleration of the development rate of underdeveloped nations.

THE FOREIGN-TRADE MULTIPLIER
AND CHANGES IN THE LEVEL OF INCOME

In an open economy, where imports depend, in part, on the level of income, the overall expansionary effect of any increase in autonomous demand will be dampened by the "leakage" of some part of any expansion of income into the purchase of imports. Assume that for some reason—say, rising prices in other countries—foreign importers find the domestic economy a more attractive place in which to buy. The result will be in an increase in the exports of the domestic economy, which will mean an equal initial increase in domestic income as additional production is turned out to meet increased foreign demand. The MPC indicates that this initial rise in income will induce an increase in consumption expenditures, but the MPM tells us that some of the additional consumption expenditures will be for imported goods.[6] Therefore, at the second

[6] It is assumed here and in what follows that the MPI is zero. If positive, there will be induced investment as well as induced consumption expenditures, and it may be expected that part of both will be for foreign-produced goods.

stage of the expansion process, domestic income rises, not by the full amount of induced consumption expenditures, but by this amount less the rise in induced consumption expenditures for imported goods. The restricted increase in income at the second stage leads to a smaller third-stage increase in domestic income than would otherwise be the case, for, again, part of the increased expenditures at the third stage is for imported goods. Thus, for any given increase in autonomous demand, the size of the multiplier is reduced when there is a positive marginal propensity to import.

To trace the effect of the marginal propensity to import on the multiplier in terms of our earlier equations, we may begin with the equation developed in this chapter for the equilibrium level of income in the four-sector economy.

$$Y = C_a + c(Y - T) + I + G + X - (M_a + mY)$$

This may be rewritten as

$$Y = \frac{1}{1 - c + m}(C_a - cT + I + G + X - M_a)$$

where $1/(1 - c + m)$ is the foreign-trade multiplier for a system in which consumption expenditures and import expenditures are linear functions of the level of domestic income.[7] As in other equations of the same type in preceding chapters, a change in any of the values within parentheses will result in a change in income equal to the change in that value times the multiplier. Let us suppose that there is a change in exports, ΔX.

$$Y + \Delta Y = \frac{1}{1 - c + m}(C_a - cT + I + G + X - M_a) + \frac{1}{1 - c + m}\Delta X$$

Subtracting Y from both sides leaves

$$\Delta Y = \frac{1}{1 - c + m}\Delta X$$

or

$$\frac{\Delta Y}{\Delta X} = \frac{1}{1 - c + m}$$

---

[7] A more complex foreign-trade multiplier would emerge from the equation that recognized taxes to be a function of the income level. Adding imports and exports to the equation developed for the third fiscal model of Chapter 14, we have the equation of footnote 4, p. 298.

$$Y = C_a + c(Y - T_a - tY + R) + I + G + X - (M_a + mY)$$

This may be rewritten as

$$Y = \frac{1}{1 - c + ct + m}(C_a - cT_a + cR + I + G + X - M_a)$$

in which the multiplier $1/(1 - c + ct + m)$ is that for the model in which consumption, imports, and taxes are all linear functions of the level of domestic income.

The same would be true for a change in C_a, I, or G and, with opposite sign, for a change in M_a.[8] Adopting the same values for the MPC and the MPM used earlier in the chapter and assuming ΔX of 18, we have

$$\Delta Y = \frac{1}{1 - \frac{8}{10} + \frac{1}{10}} (18) = 3.3(18) = 60$$

or

$$\frac{60}{18} = \frac{1}{1 - \frac{8}{10} + \frac{1}{10}} = 3.3$$

If there were no marginal propensity to import or if this propensity were zero, the multiplier would be the ordinary one, $1/(1 - c)$, or, in this example, 5. The rise in exports of 18 would raise the level of income by 90 instead of by 60. Whatever the value of the MPM, as long as it is positive it reduces the size of the effective multiplier. The MPM fits into the determination of the multiplier in the same way as the MPS.[9]

Another way of illustrating the effect of the MPM on the multiplier is to express the multiplier as $1/[1 - (c - m)]$, in which, as before, c is the marginal propensity to purchase both domestically produced goods and foreign-produced goods and m is the marginal propensity to purchase foreign-produced goods. The expression $c - m$ accordingly represents the marginal propensity to purchase domestically produced goods and is the propensity relevant to changes in the domestic level of income. If m were equal to c, the multiplier would be 1, for in this case any rise in autonomous demand would raise income only by the amount of that rise in autonomous demand. The full amount of the increase in income received at the first stage would be diverted to the purchase of foreign produced goods; there would be no induced increase in the purchase of domestically produced goods. As long as m is less than c, as is usual in practice, the multiplier will exceed 1. And finally if m were zero, c would become identical to the marginal propensity to purchase domestically produced goods, or the multiplier $1/[1 - (c - m)]$ would in effect be the ordinary multiplier $1/(1 - c)$.

Figure 15–3 depicts the method of determining the change in the equilibrium level of income that results from a change in autonomous demand.[10] In

---

[8] However, for a change in T in the present model, the multiplier becomes

$$\frac{\Delta Y}{\Delta T} = \frac{-c}{1 - c + m}$$

See pp. 275–77.

[9] In these terms, $1 - c$ is the MPS, or s. The greater $1 - c$, the greater is s, the greater is the "leakage" into saving from any change in income, and therefore the smaller is the expansion in income for any increase in autonomous demand. In turn, $s + m$ is the sum of the MPS and the MPM. The greater this sum, the greater is the "leakage" into saving and imports from any change in income, and therefore the smaller is the expansion in income for any increase in autonomous demand. Finally, for the multiplier including the MPT, ct is added to $s + m$ to produce $s + ct + m$. This then is the sum of MPS, MPC × MPT, and MPM. The greater this sum, the greater is the "leakage" of any change in income into saving, imports, and taxes, and the smaller is the expansion in income for any increase in autonomous demand.

[10] In order better to show the detail over the relevant range of income, note that this figure shows each function only over this narrower range of income

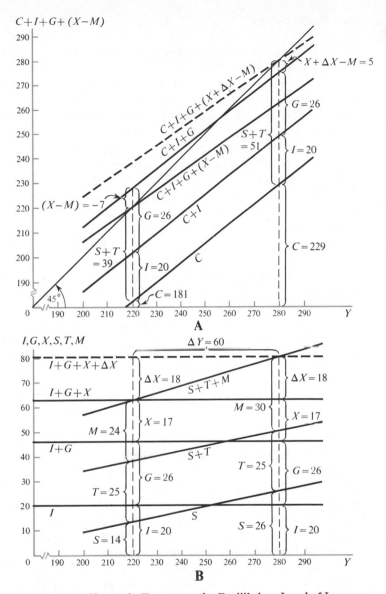

FIGURE 15–3   Effect of a Change in Exports on the Equilibrium Level of Income

Part A, for the income range shown, the solid-line schedules are the same as those in Figure 15–2. The aggregate demand function $C + I + G + (X - M)$ intersects the 45° line at the income level of 220 as in Figure 15–2. Now, suppose that there is an increase in exports of 18.[11] The resultant aggregate demand function, now labeled $C + I + G + (X + \Delta X - M)$, lies 18 above the previous aggregate demand function at each level of income and intersects the 45° line at income of 280, the new equilibrium income. With a rise in autonomous demand of 18 and a consequent rise in income of 60, the multiplier is $\Delta Y / \Delta X =$

[11] This unrealistically large increase is chosen to avoid "congestion" in the figure.

60/18, or 3.3, as was determined earlier in terms of the equation for the equilibrium level of income.

Before exports rose by 18, foreign trade exerted a net contractionary effect on the income level, for at the equilibrium level of 220, $X - M = 17 - 24 = -7$. The aggregate demand function lay below the demand function for the three domestic sectors alone. After the rise in exports of 18 and the establishment of the new equilibrium of 280, foreign trade exerts a net expansionary effect. At this new income level, $X + \Delta X - M = 17 + 18 - 30 = 5$. The new aggregate demand function now lies above the demand function for the three domestic sectors. Notice, however, that the expansionary effect following the rise in exports is checked to some extent by the induced expenditures for foreign produced output. The ordinary multiplier of 5, indicated by the MPC of 8/10, would produce a rise in income of 90 with ΔX of 18. But this greater rise in income is prevented by the MPM of 1/10, which reduces the effective multiplier to 3.3 and thus holds to 60 the rise in income from ΔX of 18. This income-restraining effect of the MPM is depicted graphically as the narrowing of the spread at successively higher levels of income between the demand function of the three domestic sectors and the new aggregate demand function.

Part B of Figure 15–3 shows these two equilibrium positions expressed in terms of the equality between $S + T + M$ and $I + G + X$. Again, apart from the narrower income range shown here, the solid-line functions are the same as those shown in Part B of Figure 15–2. There the initial equilibrium, $S + T + M = I + G + X$, occurred at income of 220. The increase in exports of 18 shifts the entire $I + G + X$ function, labeled $I + G + X + \Delta X$, upward by 18. The increase in exports, ΔX, sets the multiplier in operation and raises income to the new equilibrium level of 280. Since in the present model I, G, and T are assumed to remain unchanged despite changes in income, the new equilibrium must occur at that level of income where $\Delta X = \Delta S + \Delta M$. In other words, given the injection of ΔX, Y must rise to the level at which the diversions, $\Delta S + \Delta M$, from the income stream match the injection of ΔX into the income stream. Since the MPS $= 2/10$ and the MPM $= 1/10$, it is only when income rises by 60 that the sum of ΔS, which is $\frac{2}{10}(60)$, or 12, and ΔM, which is $\frac{1}{10}(60)$, or 6, will match ΔX. The rise in income must be 3.3 times the rise in exports, as we can see by expressing the multiplier in terms of the MPS, or s, and the MPM, or m: $\Delta Y / \Delta X = 1/(s + m)$. Thus, in the present example, $60/18 = 1/(2/10 + 1/10) = 3.3$.

If the rise in income generated by the rise in exports did not induce expenditures for foreign goods as well as for domestic goods, the net effect on income would be an increase of 90, or the increase in exports of 18 times the ordinary multiplier of 5 indicated by the MPS of 2/10. The income-restraining effect of the MPM is shown in Figure 15–3 as the widening spread at higher income levels between the schedule of "leakages" labeled $S + T$ and the schedule of "leakages" including imports, labeled $S + T + M$.

All this suggests that the greater the MPM, the greater is the reduction in the effective multiplier, and so the smaller is the expansion of income that follows any specific increase in autonomous demand. In practice, the MPM shows considerable variation among countries. It tends to be higher in countries, such as England, that are heavily engaged in foreign trade than in countries, such as the United States, that are not. This suggests further that, with allowance for any difference in the MPC, any increase in autonomous demand will have a smaller multiplier effect in a country such as England than in a country such as the United States. However, this conclusion is based on our assumption that a country's exports are entirely determined by external factors. If we drop this assumption and recognize that internal as well as external factors affect a country's exports, the probability that a country like England will have a smaller effective multiplier than a country like the United States does not necessarily follow. To see why this is so, let us consider one of the ways in which a nation's exports are tied to factors within that nation.

EXPORTS AS A FUNCTION OF IMPORTS

In any country, an increase in consumption, investment, or government demand will raise the level of income as long as there are no offsetting decreases in its net export balance or increases in its net import balance. With a positive marginal propensity to import, however, the rise in income leads to a rise in imports and, in the first instance, to a decrease in the net export balance or an increase in the net import balance. Such a rise in, say, U.S. gross imports is felt by all other countries combined as an equal increase in their gross exports. Since the rest-of-the-world experiences an increase in gross exports with no simultaneous increase in gross imports (U.S. exports did not increase in the first instance), one or more countries in the rest-of-the-world must show an increase in net exports or a decrease in net imports. This means that one or more countries will, other things being equal, show a rise in their domestic income levels. But these countries also have a positive marginal propensity to import, and some portion of the increase in their incomes will be diverted to the purchase of imported goods and services. There is reason to expect that the U.S. economy will secure some share of the increase in purchases made abroad by these foreign countries, and this will appear as a rise in U.S. gross exports. In this complicated fashion, changes in U.S. gross *exports* are indirectly influenced by changes in the income level in the United States.

If we recognize that changes in the level of income in the United States are a factor determining changes in U.S. exports, the earlier assumption that exports are determined entirely by external factors appears to be invalid. This assumption is nonetheless a valid approximation for small economies, in which even a large percentage change in income will be relatively small in absolute terms. Even with a high marginal propensity to import, the effect of such an increase in income on the country's gross imports will not be large enough to affect significantly the aggregate exports of other countries and thus the level of income in those countries. This being the case, the small country cannot expect an appreciable feedback in the form of increased exports to result from the increase in its imports. We must thus distinguish between countries that are large enough to influence perceptibly the income levels of other countries through changes in their imports and countries that are too small to do this. Size in this context is measured not merely by the real income level of the country; it is a compound of income level and marginal propensity to import. In terms of our earlier comparison, although the U.S. marginal propensity to import is smaller than that of England, the relatively high income level of the U.S. economy means that a moderate percentage change in its income may have a noticeable effect on the exports of the rest-of-the-world. (A 4 percent rise in GNP runs to more than $30 billion at annual rate; an MPM of 1/20 of GNP then means added imports of over $1.5 billion at annual rate.) On the other hand, although the income level of England is far smaller than that of the United States, the higher marginal propensity of the English economy to import means that even a moderate percentage change in its income level can have a noticeable impact on exports of the rest-of-the-world. (A 4 percent rise in GNP means over $3 billion at annual rate; an MPM of 1/5 of GNP means added imports of over $0.5 billion at annual rate.)

When there is a vigorous business expansion under way in a large country like the United States, the rising level of income induces an increased flow of imports into the United States, which is felt by some countries in the rest-of-the-world as a rise in their incomes. This induces a rise in imports in these countries, and, to the extent that the United States shares in these expanding foreign markets, U.S. exports increase. This further raises the income level in the United States and further enlarges U.S. imports from the rest-of-the-world. These repercussions continue to interact on both the income level of the United States and on that of countries in the rest-of-the-world. However, since the marginal propensities to import both here and abroad are less than 1, the amount of spending at each succeeding stage of this expansion process will decrease until income in the United States and in other countries tends to stabilize at new levels. In practice, of course, income changes of this sort are continually occurring as the result of changes in domestic demand in various countries. Therefore, before a series of international repercussions can work itself out, a new series is initiated by further changes in domestic demand in one or more important countries.

This crude description suggests why the income levels of different countries are interdependent. A rising level of income in a large country like the United States tends to raise income levels of some other countries. By the same process, a falling level of income here is felt by other countries as shrinkage in their exports and declining levels of income. As nations become more and more closely tied together through foreign trade, we encounter what economists have called the "international propagation of business cycles." Depression in one or more large countries tends to trigger depressions in other countries; prosperity in one or more large countries tends to promote prosperity in other countries.[12]

[12] What has been described here in a loose and informal way could as a next step be expressed in formal algebraic form. Because such algebraic formulations tend to become very cumbersome and complex, they are omitted from this introduction to the subject. However, they can

A CONCLUDING NOTE

As we mentioned at the outset, the purpose of this chapter has been to describe the way in which an economy's net export or import balance enters into the determination of that economy's equilibrium income level and the way in which changes in that balance can cause the economy's income level to fluctuate. The basic model was developed on the assumption that exports are externally determined and imports internally determined, and specific attention was paid to only one of the many internal factors that influence imports—namely, the level of income. Although we did not develop a formal model, we did note the way in which the exports of a large nation may depend indirectly on its level of income.

Many other factors also influence a nation's net export or import balance and thereby influence its income level. In a more thorough analysis, for example, we would drop the assumption of constant price levels in all countries, recognizing that differences in the relative prices of goods in different countries are the reason for international trade in such goods. If an economy finds its price level rising relative to the price levels of other economies, it may expect its imports to rise, even if its marginal propensity to import and its real income were to remain unchanged. (In terms of the import function, this would appear as an increase in M_a.) At the same time that its imports rise, its exports would decline as foreign importers (like domestic buyers) shifted purchases to other countries that offered the desired products at lower prices.

A more thorough analysis would also have to consider exchange-rate policies. The results of our analysis follow only if one assumes fixed exchange rates between currencies. Although most nations are today committed to maintaining a fixed value for their monetary units in terms of "key currencies," such as the U.S. dollar and the English pound, a country that permits its monetary unit to appreciate or depreciate substantially in terms of other currencies will find its net import or export balance fluctuating as a result of this, even though its marginal propensity to import and its real income remain unchanged.

Some other factors are changes in tariffs, quotas, foreign-exchange controls, and other controls imposed by each economy. The effects on the net import or export balance that might otherwise follow from changes in price levels or in foreign-exchange rates could, at least temporarily, be offset by appropriate manipulation of these devices.

A thorough analysis of these and other such factors may be found in basic texts on international economics. We mention these other factors here simply to emphasize the rigid assumptions on which the simple analysis in this chapter is based. Yet this analysis has enabled us to gain some insight into the question with which we started: In what way do an economy's foreign transactions affect the level of income and output within that economy?

---

be found in T. C. Schelling, *National Income Behavior*, McGraw-Hill, 1951, Chs. 14 and 15. See also C. P. Kindleberger, *International Economics*, 4th ed., 1968, Appendix G, pp. 578–87

CHAPTER 16

INCOME, OUTPUT, EMPLOYMENT, AND PRICES

A change in autonomous investment, consumption, government, or net foreign demand will cause the aggregate demand function to shift, and this shift will produce a change in the equilibrium level of income, a change greater than the shift in the aggregate demand function itself by an amount that varies with the size of the multiplier. In the preceding nine chapters we have examined in detail how changes in the various components of the aggregate demand function occur and how these changes are translated into changes in the income level. All through these chapters we emphasized that for any period aggregate expenditures—that is, the sum of autonomous and induced expenditures—simultaneously determine the value of final product and the level of money income for that period. This gave us the following basic equation:

$$Y = C + I + G + (X - M)$$

in which Y represents the equilibrium level of income as well as the value of final product, both of which equal expenditures on final product. Furthermore, by assuming that the prices of final product remain unchanged as aggregate expenditures on product rise and fall period by period, we were able to use changes in aggregate expenditures as a measure, not only of changes in the level of *money income* and the *value of output*, but also of changes in *real income* or the *physical volume of output*. In other words, we assumed that every change in the dollar value of Y was entirely a change in real income and output. If P represents the price level of total output and O represents the physical amount of that output, Y for any period necessarily equals $P \times O$. Expressed in these terms, our assumption was that any change in $C + I + G + (X - M)$ results only in a change in O with no change in P. Retaining the assumption of a stable price level, we found that Y and O changed proportionately with any change in aggregate expenditures.

This assumption of unchanging prices was made throughout the preceding chapters so that we could concentrate on the relationships between shifts in the aggregate demand function, varying values of the multiplier, and changes in the level of income without complicating the analysis by considering at the same time ways in which the volume of physical output might vary. Now, however, we must now drop the assumption of unchanging prices for a more realistic analysis. Shifts in the aggregate demand function will still lead to changes in the level of income and the value of output, but an increase in income, Y, may now be accompanied by higher P, greater O, or some combination of the two.

Another assumption we made was that the amount of employment varies proportionately with the level of output. Because the assumption of stable prices gave us a proportionate relationship between changes in the income level and physical output, the assumption of a proportionate relationship between employment and output indirectly gave us a proportionate relationship between income and employment. In this chapter, however, we will drop the assumption that employment varies proportionately with output, so shifts in the aggregate demand function will now lead to changes in income and the value of output that may be accompanied by a nonproportionate change in employment as well as in physical output.[1]

We will now confine our analysis to a set of relationships we previously excluded—namely, the relationships between money income, output, employment, and prices. The general discussion of these relationships will then be expanded as required, especially in Chapter 19, which adds money and interest to the analysis; Chapter 22, which concentrates on changes in output that are related to economic growth; and Chapter 23, which is concerned with inflationary changes in prices.

THE SUPPLY CURVE—FIRM AND INDUSTRY[2]

Any increase in aggregate expenditures for final product represents an equal increase in the sales receipts of those firms whose goods and services are being purchased.[3] How aggregate output, employment, and prices respond to such a

---

[1] In his *General Theory*, Keynes chose to relate aggregate demand directly to aggregate employment rather than to aggregate output, a practice that was not widely followed by other economists and will not be followed here. In so doing, Keynes faced the problem of converting employment into output, the equivalent of the problem here noted of converting output into employment. See John Maynard Keynes, *The General Theory of Employment, Interest, and Money*, Harcourt, Brace & World, 1936, Ch. 20.

[2] This section begins with a sketch of the relevant short-run micro theory. For a more thorough treatment, see K. E. Boulding, *Economic Analysis*, 4th ed., Harper, 1966, Chs. 18–20, or any other standard text on price theory.

[3] Not all expenditures for final product are for final product originating with firms. But, to simplify, we will assume that, although significant production also takes place in government and households, any change in aggregate expenditures is entirely for final goods and services produced in the business sector.

change in aggregate expenditures depends, of course, on how each of the thousands of firms affected reacts to an increased demand for its product. We will analyze first the response of the individual firm to a change in demand for its product, then the response of the individual industry, and finally the response of industry as a whole.[4]

The Firm's Supply Curve

A firm's response to changes in demand depends on, among other things, the time period in question. Economists generally define the short-run period as a length of time too short to allow firms to vary the amount of plant and equipment with which they operate. If we assume that technology, or the method of production, also remains constant over the short-run period, the only way a firm can change its output in response to a change in demand in the short run is to change the amount of labor it employs. Thus, in short-run analysis, the relationship between a firm's labor input and goods output is the first matter for consideration.

This input-output relationship is described by the firm's production function, or total product curve, shown in Figure 16–1A. The linear portion may be said to indicate "proportional returns" because it indicates that output varies proportionally with labor input up to output of O_1 or up to labor input of L_1. However, because more and more labor, the variable input, is being employed with a fixed amount of plant and equipment as we move along the labor axis, the proportional relationship between output of product and input of labor must eventually be succeeded by one that is less than proportional. Thus we see that, beyond labor input of L_1, the increment to total output that results from each increment of labor input becomes smaller and smaller. The nonlinear portion of the total product curve, starting at L_1, illustrates this stage of diminishing returns to further labor input. Finally, beyond labor input of L_2, further labor input will not increase total output at all; in fact, at some even higher level of labor input, output will begin to decrease as more workers are hired. In Figure 16–1 we see that, at labor input of L_2, diminishing returns that begin at L_1 have diminished all the way to zero. Given the production function shown, it should be clear that in the short run the firm would under no circumstances hire labor beyond the amount of L_2.[5]

---

[4] Except where we indicate otherwise, we will assume that all firms sell in purely competitive markets, that each firm attempts to maximize profits or minimize losses, that there is a constant money wage rate for each unit of labor provided by a perfectly homogeneous labor force whose services are sold in purely competitive markets, and that all firms are fully integrated. The last assumption means that, with the single exception of labor services, all variable inputs, including raw materials, necessary to the production of the firm's output are produced within the firm.

[5] Students familiar with the orthodox theory of the firm will recognize the modification of that theory in the present construction. Conventional theory shows the total product curve of Part A divided into three stages: more than proportional, proportional, and less than proportional (or diminishing) returns. The first stage does not appear in Figure 16–1, which assumes

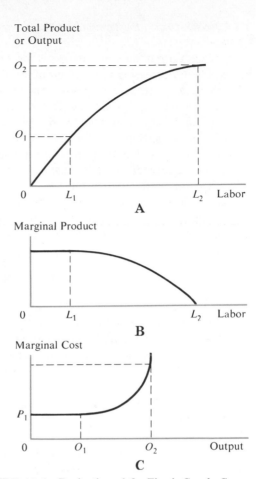

FIGURE 16–1 Derivation of the Firm's Supply Curve

The increment in total product that results from the addition of a unit of labor is termed the *marginal physical product* (MPP) of that unit of labor. Figure 16–1B shows the curve of the marginal physical product of labor derived from the total product curve of Part A.[6] Since the total product curve shows that the increment in output is the same for each increment of labor input over the linear portion of that curve (i.e., up to labor input L_1), the MPP of labor is constant over this range of labor input. Between L_1 and L_2, however, the total product curve shows that the increments in total output become smaller and smaller and finally become zero. Therefore, the MPP of labor diminishes as labor input increases from L_1 to L_2 and finally becomes zero when labor input reaches L_2.

---

proportional returns even at very low levels of the firm's output. There is, however, empirical evidence to support this form of total product curve and cost curves of the form that follows from it. See, for example, J. Dean, *Statistical Determination of Costs*, Univ. of Chicago Press, 1936, and *Cost Behavior and Price Policy*, National Bureau of Economic Research, Princeton Univ. Press, 1943, Ch. 5; and R. A. Lester, "Shortcomings of Marginal Analysis for Wage-Employment Problems," in *American Economic Review*, March 1946, pp. 67–72.

[6] The vertical scale of Part B is an expanded version of that scale in Part A.

313

Since output may be increased or decreased in the short run only by increasing or decreasing the amount of labor employed, the only cost that varies with changes in output is the amount the firm pays for labor. The costs associated with a fixed plant and equipment are constant in the short run because they will be incurred by the firm whether the plant and equipment are being used to capacity or are sitting idle. Since *marginal cost* (MC) is the cost of producing an additional unit of output, the marginal cost of a unit of output in our model is the additional labor cost incurred in its production. Figure 16–1C gives the firm's MC curve, showing the increase in total cost resulting from each additional unit of output. Since MC in this case is composed entirely of labor cost, it equals at any level of output the money wage rate of labor, W, divided by labor's marginal physical product, MPP, at that level of output.[7] Thus,

$$MC = \frac{W}{MPP}$$

Suppose, for example, that the total product curve shows that 10 man-days of labor can turn out 100 units of total product and that 11 man-days of labor can turn out 110 units. The MPP of the eleventh man-day of labor would thus be 10 units. If the increase in total cost resulting from the labor cost of one man-day of labor is $20, the marginal cost of a unit of output over the range from 100 to 110 is accordingly $2; that is, from the equation $MC = W/MPP$, $2 = $20/10$. If the total product curve shows that 12 man-days of labor can produce 120 units of output, the MPP of the twelfth man-day of labor would also be 10, and the marginal cost of a unit of output over the range of output from 110 to 120 is again $2 per unit. In terms of Figure 16–1, this indicates that labor input of 11 or 12 man-days must be below L_1, because only below L_1 does output vary proportionally with labor input. Since output varies proportionally with labor input up to L_1, the marginal cost of output must remain constant over the range of output that can be produced with labor input up to L_1. This range of output is zero to O_1, and the MC curve in Part C accordingly shows the same marginal cost for all levels of output up to O_1.

If the firm were to expand output beyond O_1, the MPP of labor would start to decline, and the MC of output would start to rise. Suppose, for example, that when labor input is increased from 15 to 16 man-days, total product rises from 145 to 150 units. The MPP of the sixteenth man-day of labor is only 5 units, but the cost of the sixteenth man-day of labor is, like all others, $20. This means that the marginal cost of a unit of output over this range of 145 to 150 is $20/5, or $4. In terms of Figure 16–1, the sixteenth man-day of labor must lie between L_1 and L_2, and the output from 145 to 150 must lie between O_1 and O_2. For this output, as we can see in Part C, marginal cost rises.

If, in its attempt to expand output, the firm should employ man-days of labor of L_2 or more, the MPP of labor would be zero. Marginal cost would accordingly become infinite at output O_2. With the given MPP curve, labor clearly would not be employed beyond L_2 in the short run, no matter how low

[7] For the case of several variable factors, see K. E. Boulding, *op. cit.*, Chs. 25–26.

the wage rate of labor and no matter how high the market price of output, as long as profit remained the guide to the firm's employment decision.

In a purely competitive market, the individual firm is only one of so large a number of producers of a homogeneous product that no one firm has any control over the price at which this product can be sold. This market price is determined by industry supply and demand, and the individual firm simply adjusts its output to the market-determined price in order to maximize profits. The firm's short-run profit-maximizing level of output is the point at which the marginal cost of output, MC, just equals the market price of output, P.[8] Because of this and because at each possible level of output MC $= W/$MPP, the profit-maximizing output can also be expressed as that output at which

$$P = \frac{W}{\text{MPP}}$$

or that output at which

$$W = P \times \text{MPP}$$

This identifies the output at which the additional receipts from the sale of the additional output produced by an additional unit of labor (i.e., $P \times$ MPP) just equals the wage rate of labor.

For example, if the market price were $2 per unit, output would be expanded to that level at which marginal cost was $2. If the fixed wage rate were $20 per man-day, this would occur at that level of output at which the MPP of labor was 10. At this output, the MPP of labor, 10, multiplied by the price per unit of output, $2, equals the wage rate of labor, $20. If the market price of output were $4, output would be carried to the higher level at which MC was $4. With the same fixed wage rate of $20 per man-day, this higher level of output would be that at which the MPP of labor had fallen to 5. (At this output the MPP of labor, 5, times P, the price per unit of output of $4, equals W, the wage rate.) Any level of output below that at which MC equals P—or, what is the same thing, at which receipts from the sale of the output produced by an additional unit of labor exceed the wage rate per unit of labor— would be a level of output whose expansion would increase profits. An expansion of output would add less to costs than to sales receipts. On the other hand, any level above the one at which MC equals P—or, what is the same thing, at which the receipts from the sale of the output produced by the last unit of labor are less than the wage rate per unit of labor—would be a level of output whose contraction would increase profits. A reduction in output would subtract more from costs than from sales receipts.

---

[8] Instead of MC $= P$, the more general expression is MC $=$ MR, in which MR is *marginal revenue*, the additional revenue from the sale of one more unit of output. Under our assumption of purely competitive markets, each individual firm in the industry can sell the amount of output it wishes to at the going market price, so that MR for it always equals P. Under imperfect competition the firm can sell more only by cutting P, so that MR is always less than P. For simplicity only, our analysis is limited to purely competitive markets, in which the individual firm finds MR always equal to P.

The marginal cost curve of Figure 16–1C, derived entirely from the marginal physical product of labor and the wage rate of labor, is also the firm's supply curve. It shows the various quantities of output (measured along the horizontal axis) that the firm will supply to the market at each price (measured along the vertical axis) in order to maximize its profits.[9]

Once the profit-maximizing level of output has been determined, the amount of labor that should be hired by the firm in order to achieve this level may be found directly from the total product curve given in Figure 16–1A. Given our other assumptions—as long as the money wage rate, the curve of the marginal product of labor, and the market price of output remain unchanged—the short-run equilibrium level of output and the amount of labor employed by the individual firm will remain unchanged. However, anything that reduces the money wage rate, alters the total-product curve in a way that raises the marginal product of labor, or raises the market price at which output can be sold will increase the level of output at which the firm maximizes profits. The amount of labor to be hired at this new level of output may, as before, be determined graphically from the appropriate point on the firm's total product curve.

The Industry's Supply Curve

The relationships we have just described for the individual firm apply to all firms in a purely competitive industry. The industry's supply curve is, then, simply the horizontal summation of the marginal cost curves of all firms in the industry. Since each firm in the industry operates in the short run with a fixed stock of plant and equipment and a fixed technology, the industry also operates with these fixed factors in the short run. For the same reason that the firm's supply curve eventually slopes upward, the industry's supply curve must eventually slope upward. Beyond a certain output, more output can be produced by the industry only at higher marginal cost and will therefore be supplied only at higher prices.

Curve S in Figure 16–2A is the supply curve for the entire industry.[10] To this supply curve is added a demand curve, D_1, for the product of this industry. (Disregard the other demand curves for the moment.[11]) Since the industry's

[9] Since MC is constant up to O_1, the firm's average variable cost is constant over this same range of output. If price is above P_1, the firm maximizing profits (or minimizing losses) will produce and sell something more than O_1. However, if price is below P_1, the firm will produce and sell no output, for this is a price that does not even cover its variable cost (here, labor cost) per unit of output. If price were exactly P_1, the firm would incur a loss equal to its fixed costs, whether it produced no output or output O_1.

[10] Although this curve is similar in shape to the individual firm's supply curve in Figure 16–1C, it must be recognized that the scale of the two figures differs on the horizontal but not on the vertical axis. A given interval along the horizontal axis of the industry graph represents a much larger number of units of output than the same interval along the axis of the individual firm's graph.

[11] In order to sidestep other complications at this point, the demand curves in Figure 16–2 show unitary elasticity throughout. Therefore, a change in the amount of expenditures on the

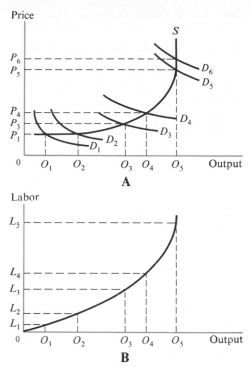

Price

A

Labor

B

FIGURE 16–2 Industry Supply Curve and Industry Employment

supply curve is the sum of the separate supply curves of all firms in the industry, the intersection of the supply and demand curves represents a price-output combination that will produce equilibrium for all firms in the industry. In Figure 16–2, O_1 is the amount all firms together will seek to sell at the established price P_1, and this is precisely the amount they can sell at this price.

Figure 16–2B enables us to identify the amount of employment the industry will provide at the indicated equilibrium output. Apart from the fact that it applies to the industry rather than to the firm, this curve is essentially the same as that in Figure 16–1A, with the axes reversed. The vertical axis shows the amount of labor required to produce industry output of any amount shown along the horizontal axis. Here, as before, we can see that as output expands beyond O_2 the labor input required per unit of output increases. O_5 is the maximum output that can be produced in the short run with any amount of labor.

In Figure 16–2 we can now begin to trace the effects of an increase in aggregate expenditures on output, employment, and prices. Let us first suppose that an increase in expenditures for the product of this particular industry results in a shift in the demand curve from D_1 to D_2. This increase in expenditures will be matched by a proportional increase in output from O_1 to O_2, so there is no

---

output of the industry will not be affected by any resultant change in the price of that industry's output. Any change in the amount that buyers choose to spend for the product of an industry is thus made to depend on variables other than a change in the price of the industry's product.

rise in price P_1. As the industry hires more workers at a constant wage rate in order to expand output to O_2, the MPP of labor does not decline, and, therefore, MC does not rise over this range of output. This constancy of marginal cost is reflected in the perfectly elastic supply curve that extends from the origin to O_2. Figure 16–2B shows that, for the specific increase in demand from D_1 to D_2, an increase in labor input from L_1 to L_2 is required by the industry in order to increase output from O_1 to O_2.

Now let us suppose that the initial equilibrium occurs at the intersection of S and D_3, at price P_3 and output O_3. An increase in expenditures equal in dollar amount to that which produces the shift from D_1 to D_2 will move the demand curve from D_3 to D_4 and raise the equilibrium price from P_3 to P_4. Unlike the preceding case, this increase in expenditures results in an increase in both price and output. The price increases in this case because the rise in demand occurs when the industry is already operating at an output level closer to capacity. Any attempt to expand output from this level will result in a fall in the MPP of labor. Between outputs O_3 and O_4, marginal cost must accordingly rise. Figure 16–2A shows marginal cost starting to rise as soon as output is pushed beyond O_2 and continuing to rise with each expansion of output beyond O_2. Figure 16–2B shows that for any expansion of output past O_2, the amount of labor needed per unit of additional output becomes larger and larger.

Finally, let us suppose that the initial equilibrium occurs at the intersection of S and D_5, at price P_5 and at output O_5. An increase in expenditures that is equal in dollar amount to the expenditures that result in a shift from D_1 to D_2 or from D_3 to D_4 will shift the demand curve from D_5 to D_6 and the equilibrium price from P_5 to P_6. In this case the increase in demand simply raises the price, leaving output unchanged at O_5. Prior to the increase in expenditures, the industry was already operating at its absolute maximum output for the short run; the marginal physical product of labor had declined to zero, and the marginal cost of output had become infinite. Since additional workers could add nothing to output, the firms in the industry would not, in the event of an increase in demand, hire labor beyond L_5. Here the quantity of labor is so great relative to the fixed stock of plant and equipment that the use of more labor is completely ruled out. The competition of buyers for what is now a nonexpanding amount of industry output would clear the market simply by pulling the price up by the amount that would absorb the increased expenditure on the industry's temporarily fixed capacity output. It is noteworthy that, since there is no accompanying rise in costs, the additional expenditure represented by the shift from D_5 to D_6 accrues in its entirety as additional profits to the firms in the industry.[12]

---

[12] The three price-output cases that we have just examined cover all three possible results of an increase in expenditures for an industry's product. If the situations are not already clear, consider the following arithmetic illustrations in which we assume that the increase in expenditures is in each case $1 million. If in the first case P_1 had been $10, the increase in expenditures would have meant additional output of 100,000 units secured by buyers at $10 per unit. If in the second case P_3 had been $15, the increase in expenditures would have meant a higher P

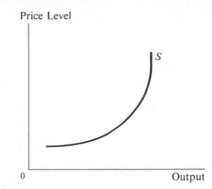

FIGURE 16–3 Aggregate Supply Function

THE AGGREGATE SUPPLY FUNCTION

Passing from the single industry to industry as a whole, the determination of price level, aggregate output, and employment is essentially an extension of the theory already developed. Keynes made this point with respect to the price level:

> In a single industry its particular price-level depends partly on the rate of re-numeration of the factors of production which enter into its marginal cost, and partly on the scale of output. There is no reason to modify this conclusion when we pass to industry as a whole. The general price-level depends partly on the rate of renumeration of the factors of production which enter into marginal cost and partly on the scale of output as a whole, i.e. (taking equipment and technique as given) on the volume of employment.[13]

If we assume that the "rate of remuneration of the factors of production which enter into marginal cost" and "equipment and technique" are given, we find between output as a whole and the general price level a relationship of the kind pictured in Figure 16–3. This is the *aggregate supply curve* or *function*. It is evident that it has properties similar to those of the supply curve of the single firm or the single industry, for just as the single firm or industry will, beyond some level of output, supply an ever larger output only at successively higher prices, so industry as a whole will, beyond some level of aggregate output,

---

and an increase in O. Two possibilities of this are P_4 of \$16.66 with an increase in O of 60,000 units and P_4 of \$20 with an increase in O of 50,000 units. The more inelastic the supply curve in the relevant range, the smaller will be the amount of the \$1 million increase in expenditures that is absorbed by an increase in output and the greater will be the amount that is absorbed by higher price. Finally, in the third case, if P_5 had been \$25 and O_5 250,000 units, the increase in expenditures would have meant a rise in price of \$4 per unit to P_6 of \$29, with no change in the number of units of output secured by buyers for this increase in their expenditures.
[13] *General Theory*, p. 294.

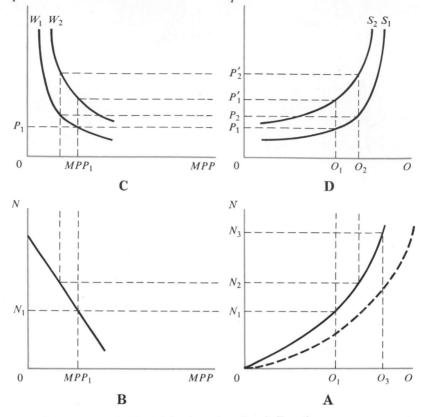

FIGURE 16–4 Derivation of the Aggregate Supply Function

supply an ever larger output of all kinds of final product only at successively higher prices. The aggregate supply function indicates the specific price level for each possible level of aggregate output up to the maximum output the economy is capable of producing with its existing labor force, plant and equipment, and technology.

Derivation of the Aggregate Supply Function

The basic determinants of the shape and position of the aggregate supply function are brought together in Figure 16–4. Part A is the *aggregate production function*, or total product curve, for the economy as a whole. Apart from the fact that the axes have been reversed for convenience, the curve has the same appearance and the same properties as the individual firm's production function, or total product curve, given in Figure 16–1A. If the composition of aggregate output is fairly stable, the aggregate production function will show a range of proportional returns followed by a range of diminishing returns for essentially the same reasons that the production function of the individual firm shows this. The attempt of a single firm or a single industry to expand its output further and further runs into the short-run barrier of fixed plant and equipment; the attempt of all firms and industries to expand aggregate output further and further runs into the same barrier.

Despite this apparent similarity, at least one important difference must be noted as we pass from the "part" to the "whole." If we assume that labor is reasonably mobile between industries and that no one industry employs more than a small fraction of the total labor force, the expansion of output by any single industry need not be checked by an inability to secure additional labor.[14] If it is willing and able to pay the price, one industry can compete workers away from other industries. But for industry as a whole, this option does not exist; there is some limit to the number of workers available in the economy as a whole and to the number of hours per week that they will work. Thus, to the short-run fixity of the economy's capital stock and given techniques of production must be added another restraint to the unlimited expansion of output—namely, the short-run limitation on the available supply of labor.

Figure 16–4A illustrates this limitation. Output could be expanded with the existing capital stock to a maximum level of O_3, but this is possible only if the amount of labor, N_3, required for this maximum output is available to industry as a whole. If the available labor force is less than N_3, the effective barrier to further expansion of output is a "shortage" of labor rather than a "shortage" of capital. On the occasions that the economy of a country like the United States approaches a full-capacity level of output (as it did during World War II), a shortage of labor is ordinarily the first effective barrier to further expansion of output. In other words, the expansion of output to meet an expanding aggregate demand is eventually checked not so much by a lack of plant and equipment as by a lack of labor to work what is for our economy a relatively abundant stock of plant and equipment.[15]

Figure 16–4B gives us the curve of the marginal physical product of labor. As in Figure 16–1B, this curve is derived directly from the production function in Part A. For the uses to be made of Figure 16–4, the axes of Parts A and B have been reversed from those in Figure 16–1, but the meaning of Part B is the same in both figures. The MPP schedule for the individual firm indicates the additional output that results from the addition of each unit of labor input. Similarly, the MPP schedule for industry as a whole indicates the addition to the economy's aggregate output that results from the addition of each unit of labor input.[16]

Figure 16–4C actually does nothing more than depict a relationship covered in earlier discussions of the theory of the firm and industry. Recall that,

---

[14] To the extent that an industry employs labor with a skill peculiar to that industry (e.g., photoengravers), a shortage of workers with this skill can check output expansion of such an industry regardless of the availability of workers with other skills.

[15] Professor Hansen has argued that, because of the slow rate of capital formation during the war years, plant and equipment were probably insufficient for the requirements of full, peacetime employment at the end of World War II. This appears to be an exception to the rule set forth. See A. H. Hansen, *Monetary Theory and Fiscal Policy*, McGraw-Hill, 1949, pp. 110–12.

[16] In practice, of course, we would be dealing in units of thousands of workers when estimating actual changes in the labor input for the economy as a whole, but the same principle applies in both cases.

in its attempt to maximize profits, the single firm will in the short run expand output to the level at which MC = P. Since MC = W/MPP, the profit-maximizing output is also that at which $P = W$/MPP. Thus, for any given money wage rate, W, the firm will hire labor up to the amount at which labor's MPP multiplied by P equals the given W. For the single firm and, by the same argument, for the single industry, once the profit-maximizing output has been determined for the given wage rate, more labor will be hired and more output produced only if forces within the market should produce a rise in P. The firm's employment of labor could then expand until the MPP of labor (which will decrease with the increase in the employment of labor) multiplied by the new, higher P is again equal to the unchanged W.

The same follows for industry as a whole. Curve W_1 in Figure 16–4C gives us nothing more than the various combinations of P and labor's MPP whose products equal the W that was assumed in drawing the W_1 curve. For example, if the level of employment N were such that the MPP of labor was 8, P would have to be 3 before producers would provide this level of employment at W equal to 24. If N were greater, so that MPP was smaller—for example 6—P would have to be 4 in order to make the employment of labor up to the amount at which its MPP fell to 6 consistent with the profit-maximization objective of producers. Although we have not yet explained the determination of the general price level P, it should be clear from this example that, with the given W, N would not be expanded to the level at which MPP fell to 6 unless at the same time P were to rise from its lower level to 4.

Figure 16–4D rounds out the apparatus by showing how the aggregate supply function is derived from the other parts of the figure. Thus, for any level N, Part A gives us the aggregate output, O, corresponding to that labor input; Part B gives us the MPP of labor corresponding to that labor input; and the W_1 curve of Part C gives us the price level, P, at which MPP $\times P$ equals the W that was assumed in drawing W_1. The P indicated in Part C and the O indicated in Part A combine to determine a specific point on the aggregate supply function of Part D. Suppose that aggregate employment is N_1. The production function shows that aggregate output is then O_1, and the MPP schedule shows that the MPP of labor at this level of N is MPP_1. With the W_1 curve based on the given wage rate, industry as a whole will find that the proceeds from the sale of output resulting from the final increment of labor employed will equal the wage cost of that labor only at price level P_1. At P_1, MC = P and profits are maximized. Therefore, output O_1 will be supplied at price level P_1, as shown in Part D. However, we clearly cannot say that O_1 will actually be the economy's aggregate output, N_1 its aggregate employment, and P_1 its price level. What these will be depends on the aggregate demand function as well as the aggregate supply function. All that the supply function itself can tell us is that *if* employment is to be N_1 and output is to be O_1, then the price level will have to be P_1; otherwise, employers will not find it in their interest to hire N_1 labor and produce O_1 output. Similarly, if we had started out with N of N_2, we would find that O_2 output would be supplied only at a price level of P_2.

Change in the Money Wage Rate

A rise in the money wage rate appears in Figure 16–4 as a shift to the right in the W curve, from W_1 to W_2. Given the same production function and therefore the same MPP of labor schedule, the effect of the rise in W with no change in the marginal productivity of labor is an upward shift in the aggregate supply function from S_1 to S_2. This shift shows that each level of output will now be supplied only at a price level higher than before or that at each price level a smaller output will be supplied than before. At the higher wage rate, O_1 will be supplied at P'_1, and O_2 will be supplied at P'_2, indicating that the price level at each level of output rises proportionately with the rise in the money wage rate $(P'_1/P_1 = W_2/W_1$, and $P'_2/P_2 = W_2/W_1)$.

If employers seek to maximize profits, they will equate the product of P and MPP with W. A rise in W accordingly means that there must be either an offsetting rise in P or an offsetting rise in MPP. An offsetting rise in the MPP of labor, given the diminishing marginal productivity of labor, is secured only by a reduction in N. In other words, the upward shift in the supply function may be viewed in either of two ways: For each possible level of P there is an O smaller by the amount necessary to raise the MPP of labor in the same proportion that W has risen. Or, for each possible level of O, there is a P higher in proportion to the rise in W.

Although a rise in the money wage rate that is unaccompanied by any change in the marginal productivity of labor must shift the aggregate supply function upward, as in Figure 16–4, O and N do not necessarily decline. The impact on P, O, and N of a rise in W depends also on what happens to aggregate demand. We must, therefore, examine how aggregate supply and aggregate demand combine to determine P, O, and N. We will then have the tools necessary for a preliminary analysis of the way in which a change in the wage rate affects P, O, and N through its effect on both aggregate supply and aggregate demand.

THE AGGREGATE SUPPLY AND
AGGREGATE DEMAND FUNCTIONS

The aggregate supply function as derived indicates the various levels of aggregate output that will be supplied at various price levels, given the money wage rate and the schedule of the marginal productivity of labor. The actual level of aggregate output and the actual price level for any time period then depend on the level of aggregate demand for that time period.[17] A series of aggregate

---

[17] Our analysis here disregards the interdependencies between the aggregate supply and demand functions. Although a detailed consideration of this topic is beyond the scope of this book, attention will be paid to the less involved interdependencies later in this chapter and in following chapters.

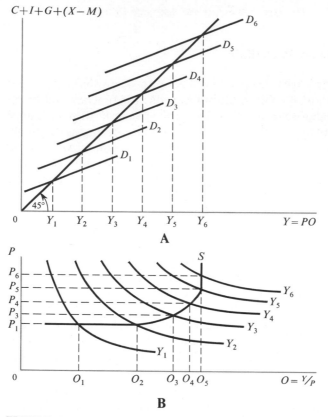

FIGURE 16–5 Aggregate Supply and Aggregate Demand Functions

demand functions labeled D_1, D_2, D_3, and so forth (only one of which, of course, would apply in any particular time period) is shown in Figure 16–5A. The point of intersection of any aggregate demand function with the 45° line indicates the equilibrium level of income, the level at which aggregate spending, $C + I + G + (X - M)$, is just equal to income, Y—or, what is the same thing, the level at which the diversions of income from consumption spending, $S + T$, are just equal to the compensating injections of spending, $I + G + (X - M)$. Since there is an equilibrium level of income for each aggregate demand function, there is for the series of these functions a series of equilibrium income levels, Y_1, Y_2, Y_3, and so forth, as shown on the horizontal axis in Part A. This much is nothing more than the analysis developed in the preceding chapters.

Unlike the preceding analysis, however, each of the aggregate demand functions is expressed here in money terms rather than real terms. In the earlier discussion, we described each aggregate demand function as showing how aggregate real expenditures would vary with real income, for there we assumed that the price level remained unchanged in the face of shifts in the aggregate demand function. Since we have now dropped that assumption, the aggregate demand function is expressed here in money terms and shows how aggregate money expenditures will vary with the money value of income. For example, a shift in the aggregate demand function from D_3 to D_4 would result in an increase in the equilibrium level of income from Y_3 to Y_4 as measured on the horizontal axis of Part A. On the assumption of a constant price level, all this increase would be an increase in real income or output. However, if, as in our present analysis, the price level may rise in response to an upward shift in the aggregate demand function, a shift from D_3 to D_4 will lead to the same increase in income as before—that is, from Y_3 to Y_4—but this increase in income will be partly an increase in real income or output and partly a rise in the price level. The greater the rise in the price level, the smaller will be the increase in real output corresponding to any given upward shift in the aggregate demand function.[18] What we now want to look into is how the change in the equilibrium level of income that results from any shift in the aggregate demand function is divided between a change in the price level and a change in output.

As noted above, each of the aggregate demand functions in Figure 16–5A determines an equilibrium level of money income shown on the horizontal axis. The different combinations of price level and real output consistent with any given equilibrium level of money income derived in Part A may be represented by a rectangular hyperbola in Part B.[19] We find in Part B a series of rectangular hyperbolas, labeled to correspond with each equilibrium level of money income found in Part A. The equilibrium price level and equilibrium output are then given for any equilibrium level of money income by the intersection with the aggregate supply function of the hyperbola representing that level of income. Thus, for the equilibrium income level Y_1, given by the aggregate demand curve D_1 in Part A, the hyperbola labeled Y_1 in Part B gives the various quantities of output, O, that can be purchased by expenditures equal to Y_1 at different price levels, P. The dollar amount of spending indicated by Y_1 can, of course, buy a relatively large O at a relatively low P, and vice versa. The particular

[18] This confronts us with the following problem. If an upward shift in the aggregate demand function results in a rise in the price level, the rise in the price level itself may feed back as an additional factor affecting shifts in the aggregate demand function. For example, a rise in autonomous investment that, under fixed prices, would have shifted the function from D_3 to D_4 may, as a result of the influence of a change in the price level on the function, result in a larger or smaller shift in the function than one from D_3 to D_4. How much the aggregate demand function will shift in response to any indicated change in autonomous investment or in any other type of autonomous spending cannot be determined within this model, for the model does not specify how a change in the price level will affect the extent of any shift in the aggregate demand function originating with a change in autonomous investment or other autonomous spending. In other words, within the model we can determine the change in the price level once we know the shift in the aggregate demand function, but we cannot determine the shift in this function until we know the change in the price level. Since this indeterminacy is not critical for the purposes of the present analysis, we may simply take as given the series of aggregate demand functions presented in Figure 16–5A, it being assumed that the particular shifts reflect the influence of price level changes as well as all other influences that give rise to shifts in the aggregate demand function.

[19] The general equation for a rectangular hyperbola is $xy = a$ in which $a > 0$. For the variables here, the specific equation becomes $PO = Y$. For any given level of Y, the function gives all possible combinations of P and O whose product is equal to Y. Or, graphically, all rectangles established by running perpendiculars from any point on the graph of the function to the axes will be equal in area.

combination of O and P that is the equilibrium combination is indicated by the intersection of the Y_1 curve with the S curve, or the combination is O_1 and P_1. In other words, from D_1, we have Y_1, and $Y_1 = O_1P_1$, given the aggregate supply function, S.

Turning to shifts in the aggregate demand function, we find that a rise from D_1 to D_2 leads to a proportionate expansion of output from O_1 to O_2 and no rise in the price level, since the S curve is perfectly elastic over the range of equilibrium income up to Y_2. A rise in aggregate demand from D_2 to D_3 will raise the equilibrium level of income to Y_3, which will mean a rise in output from O_2 to O_3 and a rise in the price level from P_1 to P_3, since the S curve is not perfectly elastic over the range of equilibrium income beyond Y_2. Similarly for a shift in aggregate demand from D_3 to D_4 or D_4 to D_5. Finally, a shift in aggregate demand from D_5 to D_6 will raise the equilibrium level of income from Y_5 to Y_6, which will mean a rise in the price level from P_5 to P_6 and no rise in O from its level of O_5, since it is assumed that the aggregate supply curve has become perfectly inelastic at O_5. The increase in the equilibrium level of income from Y_4 to Y_5 has pushed output up to its capacity level, and, on this assumption, further increases in the equilibrium level of income can be reflected only in proportionately higher price levels.

The results described above are based on the assumption that the composition of aggregate demand and hence aggregate output are fairly stable or that they vary in some systematic fashion. To the extent that this is not the case, it is possible that some rise in the price level will occur when demand shifts from D_1 to D_2 or that there will be a sharper rise in the price level and a smaller rise in output than those indicated as demand moves from D_2 to D_3 or from D_3 to D_4.

In practice, any change in aggregate demand may be distributed in an almost infinite number of ways among thousands of different commodities and services. Even though all industries may be operating with substantial excess capacity when aggregate demand is, for example, at D_2, the rise in aggregate demand from D_2 to D_3 may for some reason be concentrated on a few specific goods, and this may force the industries producing those goods up into the rapidly rising sections of their supply curves. Other industries that ordinarily enjoy some share of any increase in demand may be almost entirely by-passed. A case in point is the sudden surge in demand for consumers' durable goods that frequently accompanies a war scare. When this happens the rise in the general price level is greater and the rise in aggregate output smaller than if the increase in demand had been distributed more in line with the preexisting distribution of demand, a distribution that industry as a whole had adjusted to over the preceding years. If industry were in fact subject to pronounced and frequent shifts in the composition of demand for its aggregate output, we could not speak meaningfully of an aggregate supply function. In such circumstances, for any change in aggregate demand, the shape of this supply function would be steeper or flatter depending cn the unpredictable distribution of that change in demand and the ratio of actual output to capacity output in the particular industries that are suddenly hit by unexpected and sharp changes in the demand for their products. In practice, however, although sudden sharp changes in demand do appear at times and do upset the results suggested by the simple aggregate supply function, they are neither so frequent nor so pronounced as to be more than a qualification to the concept of the simple aggregate supply function previously described. Although subject to this and other qualifications, the simple aggregate supply function still provides an essentially valid description of the way aggregate output and the price level respond to short-run changes in aggregate demand.

AGGREGATE SUPPLY, AGGREGATE DEMAND, AND THE LEVEL OF EMPLOYMENT

Just as the supply and demand functions for the single industry define equilibrium price and output for its product, so the supply and demand functions for industry as a whole define its equilibrium price level and output. Corresponding to this aggregate output is a level of aggregate employment, shown by the aggregate production function for that level of output. In his *General Theory*, Keynes argued that this level of employment may be short of full employment. At the current money wage rate, the number of workers who seek employment may be greater than the number employed, and, what is more, the unemployment so defined can be an equilibrium situation. In a word, then, Keynesian theory argues that underemployment equilibrium is possible. As will be seen in Chapter 17, classical theory with its underlying assumptions did not recognize the possibility of equilibrium at less than full employment.

To illustrate how underemployment equilibrium might occur, let us suppose that at the current money wage rate the number of workers seeking employment is N_3 in Figure 16–6. Employment of N_3 then defines full employment of the labor force. But full employment clearly cannot be achieved with the supply function of S_1, unless the aggregate demand function (not shown here) is high enough to produce an equilibrium level of money income equal to Y_3. If income is at this level, the price level will be P_5 and output will be O_3, the output that provides employment of N_3. The lower level of demand that produces equilibrium income of Y_2 results in unemployment of N_2N_3. This unemployment can persist as long as income remains unchanged at Y_2 and the aggregate supply function remains unchanged at S_1. From the simple mechanics of the system, it would seem that if the going money wage rate were reduced far enough to shift the aggregate supply function from S_1 to S_2, unemployment could be wiped out, provided that the aggregate demand function remained at the level that provides the equilibrium income level of Y_2. This unchanged level of income would now be accompanied by the higher, full-employment level of output, O_3, and the lower price level, P_3. A deflation of money wage rates thus appears to be a means to full employment. This in part was the solution to unemployment advanced by classical economics. For reasons to be noted in the

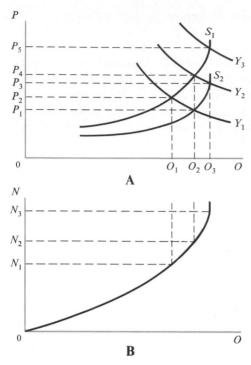

FIGURE 16-6　The Level of Employment

next section, Keynes and most economists since Keynes have ruled this out as a practical means of lifting an economy to its full-employment level of output.

　If unemployment cannot be wiped out through cuts in money wage rates that shift the aggregate supply function downward, the solution to the problem of unemployment must necessarily be found in an appropriate expansion of aggregate demand. In Figure 16-6, if aggregate demand is such as to produce the equilibrium level of income Y_2, output will be O_2 and employment N_2. An increase in aggregate demand that raises Y from Y_2 to Y_3 will raise output from O_2 to O_3, the output level that provides employment of N_3, which we are taking to be full employment.

　Even in this oversimplified approach, we can see why aggregate demand is the key determinant in the Keynesian theory of output and employment. Of course, much more is involved in the determination of output and employment than what appears in the crude apparatus employed here. One factor, for example, was mentioned earlier: An increase in aggregate demand concentrated in those industries already operating close to the capacity set by their fixed stock of plant and equipment will do little to increase aggregate output and employment, despite the fact that there may be idle workers and idle capacity throughout much of the remainder of the economy. Another factor that complicates analysis is that an increase in aggregate demand may fail to provide jobs for the unemployed if the types of workers needed to expand output are not the types unemployed at the time. This kind of "structural unemployment" has been much emphasized in recent years as the unskilled and the untrained fail to find employment while industry clamors for more workers with particular skills and training. Still another factor to be considered is that an increase in aggregate demand may fail to raise employment by the degree hoped for if the mobility of labor is low. Finally, to cite a factor mentioned earlier, full employment of the labor force may not be achieved in some economies, regardless of how high the level of aggregate demand, if the size of the labor force is so excessive relative to the stock of plant and equipment that further employment is checked by the shortage of capital. Labor cannot have very high productivity when it works with its "bare hands."

If, however, the actual level of aggregate demand is adequate for full employment, and if these and other obstacles are somehow overcome, we find the economy with a level of aggregate spending which, at the resultant price level, is just that required to call forth that level of output whose production provides full employment for the labor force. In terms of Figure 16–6, in which the aggregate supply function is S_1 and the aggregate demand function is such as to produce the income level of Y_3, we have Y_3, O_3, P_5, and N_3, where N_3 represents full employment for the labor force.

AGGREGATE SUPPLY, AGGREGATE DEMAND, AND THE MONEY WAGE RATE

A change in the money wage rate will produce a shift in the aggregate supply function, provided there is no offsetting change in the marginal productivity of labor. It is clear that, at any given level of aggregate demand, a downward shift in the supply function, say from S_1 to S_2 in Figure 16–6, will mean that a larger flow of output will be secured by buyers at the new, lower price level. Since the employment level depends on the level of output, this downward shift may raise the employment level if it is less than full. Since a reduction in the money wage rate is one way of shifting the aggregate supply function downward, it would seem that the employment level may be raised to its full-employment position by an appropriate cut in the money wage rate. This, as we mentioned earlier, is the solution for unemployment suggested by classical economists.

Notice, however, that this sequence—lower W, downward shift in S, higher O, greater N—can be expected only on the assumption that the aggregate demand function does not fall proportionately with the downward shift in the aggregate supply function. In Figure 16–6, full employment was represented by N_3; O_3 was therefore the level of output necessary for full employment. Assuming that the aggregate demand function is initially at a level that gives us the equilibrium level of income Y_2, output is O_2, price level is P_4, employment is N_2, and unemployment is N_2N_3, on the basis of the aggregate supply function, S_1. Now, if aggregate demand remains unchanged, a cut in W that shifts aggregate supply downward from S_1 to S_2 will result in the level of output O_3 that provides full employment N_3. But, if the cut in W that shifts supply from

S_1 to S_2 also causes a downward shift in demand that reduces the level of money income from Y_2 to Y_1, the price level will fall from P_4 to P_1, while output will remain unchanged at O_2 and the employment level will remain unchanged at N_2. In this case the lower money wage rate does nothing to put more men to work; it only causes a fall in the price level proportionate with the fall in the money wage rate. If, however, Y drops from its original position at Y_2 to some position *between* Y_1 and Y_2, the fall in the price level will be less, and there will be some expansion of output and an increase in the number of persons employed. Reduction in the wage rate would then appear to have some expansionary effect on output and employment.

The effects on price level, output, and employment of a rise in the money wage rate that shifts the aggregate supply function upward (e.g., from an original position at S_2 to a new position at S_1) may be traced in a similar manner.

All this, of course, does no more than present various possible effects of a change in the money wage rate on aggregate output, employment, and price level. That the aggregate supply function will shift upward or downward in response to a rise or fall in the wage rate is plausible enough. The critical factor influencing output and employment is then the extent of the shift in the aggregate demand function and the resultant change in the equilibrium level of money income that may be expected from a given rise or fall in the money wage rate. Modern analysis, following the position taken by Keynes, generally argues that a cut in the money wage rate is in itself unlikely to raise output and employment. The aggregate demand function will probably decrease proportionately with the downward shift in the aggregate supply function that results from the wage cut, and this in turn will result in a proportional fall in the equilibrium level of money income, as shown in Figure 16–6 by a downward shift in Y from Y_2 to Y_1 following the downward shift in the aggregate supply function from S_1 to S_2. Similarly, a rise in the money wage rate is unlikely to reduce output and employment, since the aggregate demand function will probably rise proportionately with the upward shift in the aggregate supply function that follows the wage rise, and this in turn will result in a proportionate increase in the level of money income, as shown by an upward shift in Y from Y_1 to Y_2 following an upward shift in the aggregate supply function from S_2 to S_1.

Why may these results be expected? Without entering into detail, the crux of the Keynesian conclusion is found in the argument that the change in demand will not be equal to the change in output that follows from a change in the money wage rate. In the case of a cut in the money wage rate, there is initially a rise in output and employment, because the most profitable level of output is now greater than it was before the cut in the money wage rate. Keynes argued, however, that the rise in demand will not be sufficient to buy the increase in output at the existing price level because the marginal propensity to consume is less than one. Some part of the additional income generated by the expansion of output is devoted to saving; otherwise expressed, only part of the additional income comes back into the market as additional consumption demand. Therefore, unless there is an increase in planned investment sufficient to absorb the amount of additional output not taken by consumers, the actual increase in investment that occurs is unplanned investment in the form of involuntary additions to inventories. Businessmen react by reducing output and employment and by cutting prices to work off the unwanted increase in inventories. This process will not be completed until output is back to its original level, for only at this level is there equilibrium in the sense that the sum of consumption demand and the unchanged amount of planned investment demand are just equal to the level of output. As output drops back to its original level, employment drops correspondingly. Since the original level of output and employment are those consistent with profit-maximization, it finally follows that the price level must have fallen proportionately with the money wage rate. We have the conclusion, noted earlier, that the result of a general cut in the money wage rate is a proportionate fall in the price level and no change in output and employment.

Analysis of the opposite case—of a rise in the money wage rate—involves the same kind of reasoning. The process now involves an initial decrease in output and employment. This is followed by a situation of excess demand because demand does not fall as much as output, given that the marginal propensity to consume is less than one. This excess demand brings a rise in the price level and an expansion of output and employment back to the level prevailing before the rise in the money wage rate. The new equilibrium is one in which the price level has risen proportionately with the wage rate and the level of output and employment are unchanged.

LABOR PRODUCTIVITY, THE WAGE RATE, AND THE PRICE LEVEL

The conclusion reached here on the relationship between changes in the wage rate and the price level is acceptable, even as a first approximation, only on the assumption that the curve of the marginal productivity of labor is fixed. In practice, however, the curve of the marginal productivity of labor is subject to gradual and persistent shifts over time.

If the quantity of capital increases or if the techniques of production improve, a greater flow of final output is possible at each level of employment. In terms of Figure 16–4, such changes would cause the production function to shift outward, as illustrated by the broken-line production function in Part A. After such a shift, at each level of N the MPP of labor is greater than it was when that labor input was combined with a smaller capital stock or with technologically inferior production methods.[20] With no change in W but with a higher

---

[20] There is, however, one exception. If the production function shifts outward but in a way that leaves it parallel with the original function throughout, the *average* product of labor will be changed while the *marginal* product will not. The marginal product is determined solely by the *slope* of the function and will therefore change only with a change in the slope. To simplify, we will assume that any outward shift in the function will be such that it will raise the marginal as well as the average product of labor at each level of employment.

MPP of labor, employers will find it profitable to increase the amount of output supplied at each price level or to supply each amount of output at a lower price level than was previously the case. In terms of Figure 16–4D, this is an outward shift in the supply function, say from S_2 to S_1. The extent of this shift in the supply function varies with the outward shift in the production function. For any given money wage rate, it thus appears that the aggregate supply function is uniquely determined by the aggregate production function and that a separate supply function will result from each possible shift in the production function.

This suggests in general terms why the conclusion drawn from the analysis in the previous section must be qualified. A rise in the money wage rate will not in itself cause an upward shift in the supply function, and thus a rise in the price level, if the percentage rise in the money wage rate is no greater than the percentage rise in the marginal productivity of labor. Given the rule for profit maximization, MPP $\times P = W$, if W rises by 5 percent in any year but the MPP of labor also rises by 5 percent, W/MPP (i.e., marginal cost) remains unchanged, and an unchanged P is still consistent with profit maximization. On the other hand, a percentage rise in W that exceeds the percentage rise in the MPP of labor indicates that a higher price level is necessary for profit maximization. In this case, W/MPP has increased, and, unless price rises to allow for the rise in cost, the rise in the wage rate occurs at the expense of the profit margin. The tendency in practice is for the price level to adjust by the amount necessary to cover any difference between the percentage changes in W and in the MPP of labor.

The data for the postwar years on labor productivity, compensation per employee man-hour, and price level attest to this tendency. Over these years, prices have moved approximately in proportion to the difference between the change in labor productivity and the change in compensation per employee man-hour. The productivity increase in 1949 was 2.8 percent, the increase in compensation per employee man-hour was 2.5 percent, and the price level decrease was 0.8 percent. The productivity increase in 1951 was 2.5 percent, the increase in compensation was 9.3 percent, and the price level increase was 7.9 percent. In 1964 the productivity increase of 3.1 percent was exceeded by an increase in compensation of 3.8 percent, and the price level rose 1.4 percent. In 1967 the much smaller productivity increase of 1.4 percent was exceeded by the much larger increase in compensation of 6.0 percent, and the price level rose 2.7 percent, twice the rate of increase of 1964.[21]

While there is more behind price-level movements than the relative changes in labor productivity and labor compensation, there is little doubt that the goal of reasonable stability in the price level cannot be attained in an economy in which the compensation of labor per man-hour is pushed up at a rate well in excess of the rate of increase in productivity per man-hour. This is why a money wage rate that rises at the same rate as "labor productivity" is now popularly described as "noninflationary," or consistent with price-level stability, and one

---

[21] *Annual Report of the Council of Economic Advisers*, Jan. 1965, Table 12, p. 109, and Feb. 1968, Table 15, p. 110.

that rises at a more rapid rate as "inflationary," or inconsistent with price-level stability.

Because this relationship is indicated by the theory and supported by the postwar data, the Council of Economic Advisers, in its January 1962 *Annual Report,* officially advanced for the first time the idea of general wage and price guideposts for price stability.[22] In its briefest form, the general wage guidepost for annual increases in total compensation per employee man-hour is that such increases in percentage terms should not exceed the trend of labor productivity.[23] If so limited, increases in labor compensation will be consistent with stable prices and an unchanged distribution of income between labor and others.

An arithmetic example will show how these results follow. Assume that a worker is paid $3.00 per hour, or $120.00 for a forty-hour week, and that output per worker per week is 200 units. Output per man-hour is 200 divided by 40, or 5 units, and labor cost per unit of output is $120 divided by 200, or $0.60, or, what is the same thing on an hourly basis, $3.00 divided by 5 equals $0.60. If as a result of a technological advance, better capital equipment, or any other reason, output rises by 3 percent to 206 units per week for the same 40 hours of labor, output per man-hour is also higher by 3 percent, or is now 5.15 units. If the worker receives an increase in compensation equal to the increase in productivity, he will get $3.09 per hour, or $123.60 for the forty-hour week. Labor cost per unit of output, however, remains unchanged at $0.60, or $3.09 divided by 5.15. If the price at which the product is sold remains unchanged, the difference between price per unit and labor cost per unit, which is the amount available for payment to others including stockholders, will also remain unchanged. However, with a 3 percent increase in the number of units produced and sold, the total amount remaining after labor cost is also higher by 3 percent. The wage guidepost thus indicates that a rise in the wage rate equal to the gain in productivity is consistent with a stable price for the product and a percentage increase in the earnings of the nonlabor factors equal to that received by labor.

Because productivity gains vary widely by industry and firms, the guidepost approach requires a price as well as a wage guidepost. The general price guidepost, in its simplest form, is that those firms that grant wage increases equal to the national trend productivity but experience a rise in productivity greater

---

[22] *Annual Report of the Council of Economic Advisers,* Jan. 1962, pp. 185–90. The genesis and principles of the guideposts are reviewed in the *Annual Report,* Jan. 1967, pp. 120–34. For subsequent statements, see the *Annual Report,* Feb. 1968, pp. 120–28, and Jan. 1969, pp. 118–21. The development of the guideposts as seen in the *Annual Reports* from 1962 to 1967 is examined in R. E. Slesinger, *National Economic Policy—The Presidential Reports,* Van Nostrand, 1968, pp. 100–27.

[23] Our model compared the "wage rate" with the "marginal physical product" of labor. Since, in practice, the cost of labor per hour includes all kinds of fringe benefits as well as the hourly wage rate, our use of the term "wage rate" must here be broadly interpreted as total compensation per employee man-hour. Secondly, since the productivity change in any one year can be influenced by short-run transitory factors, the Council has used the trend productivity, which is the annual average percentage change in output per man-hour during the latest five years.

than the national trend productivity should reduce prices by an amount to reflect this difference. Conversely, those firms that experience an increase in productivity less than the national trend productivity, but nonetheless grant wage increases equal to the national trend productivity, would appropriately raise prices to cover that portion of the compensation increase that is not matched by the productivity increase. While some prices would thus fall and others rise, the overall result should be approximate price stability.

If a guidepost program is to have any chance of success in providing price stability, labor in general must settle each year for an increase in compensation no greater than the wage-guidepost figure announced for that year, and firms in general must set prices that correspond to the price guidepost. The failure of firms to observe the price guidepost can lead to a rising price level in the same fashion as the failure of labor to limit its demands to the wage guidepost. The exercise of market power to raise prices to exploit what firms regard as favorable demand conditions for their output differs in kind but not in result from the exercise of bargaining power by organized labor to raise wage rates to exploit favorable demand conditions in the market for labor.

The original formulation of the guideposts in 1962 did not specify any particular trend productivity figure. Two recessions, 1957–58 and 1960–61, had occurred in the preceding five years, and it was difficult to identify the trend productivity for this period. Although no specific figure was stated in the next two *Reports*, in the 1964 *Report* the subsequently well-known figure of 3.2 percent appeared as the latest figure in a column labeled "trend productivity." In that year the 3.2 percent figure came to be the recognized general guidepost for wages. In following *Reports*, the Council gave increasingly clear indications of what it regarded as the trend of productivity. Thus in the January 1966 *Report*, the Council specifically recommended that the general wage guidepost be 3.2 percent for that year.

In the very same year there began a process that in effect marked the end, at least temporarily, of guideposts. Until mid-1966 the guideposts had been reasonably well observed by labor and business. On the part of labor, this to some degree may be attributed to a level of unemployment that averaged over 5 percent during 1962–65. With increases in labor compensation in most cases limited to the guidepost figure and with business pricing decisions generally in line with the price guidepost, the consumer price index rose less than 2 percent per year during 1962–65. Then the rapid upward surge in the economy in 1966 produced a fall in unemployment to 3.8 percent, and the resulting tightness in the labor market subjected the 3.2 percent wage guidepost to pressures unknown in the preceding years. More and more labor settlements were reached at figures in excess of the guidepost. Although it is more difficult to generalize on the side of prices, price decisions of firms with price discretion also appeared, more frequently than in preceding years, to be inconsistent with the decisions called for by the price guidepost. The consequence was that consumer prices rose by 3.3 percent during 1966, which meant that the Council was effectively barred from announcing in January 1967 a wage guidepost for 1967 equal to the trend productivity. A figure in the neighborhood of 3.2 percent would, on the average, have provided the worker with an increase in compensation no more than sufficient to cover the rise in living costs and therefore would have permitted no increase to reflect the rise in his productivity. This would be clearly unacceptable to the unions. For a case in point, a story in *Business Week* of November 26, 1966, was headlined, "Unions Call Five Percent a Minimum for 1967." For the Council to have officially announced a guidepost adjusted to recognize in some way the rise in living costs (e.g., 3.2 percent for productivity plus some percentage for cost of living, for a total well above productivity alone) would have served no useful purpose. With a further 3 percent increase in consumer prices in 1967, the Council reacted in its 1968 *Report* as in its 1967 *Report*: No guidepost figure was announced.

With the guidepost approach of the kind followed earlier at least temporarily inoperative, President Johnson in January 1968 established a Cabinet Committee on Price Stability, made up of heads of relevant government departments and coordinated by the Chairman of the Council of Economic Advisers. In addition to proposals designed to improve efficiency, remove bottlenecks, and improve technology in industries that are the source of persistent inflation, the committee in its report to the President in December 1968 also proposed a system of voluntary restraints that somewhat resembled the defunct guideposts. These restraints were in the form of standards whose acceptance by labor and business would hopefully carry the economy at least part way to the goal of price stability during the year 1969. Since average compensation per man-hour had risen by over 7 percent in 1968 and labor productivity by only about 3.2 percent during that year, wage settlements during 1969 that would bring the average increase in hourly compensation for the year to a little under 5 percent would be sufficient to bring the economy halfway back to the ultimate standard of productivity. Business was called on to show comparable restraint by absorbing a portion of unavoidable increases in costs through lower profit margins. The specific standard suggested for business was that it absorb increases of up to 1 percent in unit costs and accept as a guide in price decisions a profit target no higher than the average realized during 1967–68.

To some observers, the committee's report appeared as an attempt of the outgoing Administration to bring back to life the earlier wage-price guideposts. Like the guideposts that had died in 1967, the committee's proposed standards are "voluntary restraints." However, the committee also suggested that if the restraints fail, the government might set up machinery to "call to the public's attention flagrant departures from standards of responsible decision making." The committee's proposals that run along the lines of guideposts have not received much consideration from the Nixon Administration. Statements by highly placed persons during the first months of that Administration did not suggest that guideposts would be brought back in the near future.

Whatever the long-run future of guideposts in actual practice, it is likely that the Council of Economic Advisers of the Nixon Administration agrees fully with the emphasis placed by the previous Council on the principle underlying the wage guidepost: "The only valid and noninflationary standard for wage advances is the productivity principle. If price stability is eventually to be restored and maintained in a high-employment U.S. economy, wage settlements must once again conform to that standard." [24]

The theoretical underpinnings of this principle are found in the simple model developed in this chapter. Since the rationale of the wage guidepost in turn rests solidly on this principle, this brief look at the U.S. experience with guideposts over the years since 1962 has been inserted here as an illustration of the application of a principle, suggested by a theoretical model and supported by data, to the solution of a real-world problem. A full treatment of the problems involved in the application of this principle is found in the sizable literature on the guideposts that has developed since 1962. [25]

A CONCLUDING NOTE

Although some essential elements remain to be added in the chapters that follow, we now have the minimum ingredients of Keynesian theory necessary to reach meaningful, though still preliminary, answers to the critical questions of what determines an economy's aggregate income, output, employment, and price level. To express it as simply and briefly as possible, one may say that the answers to these questions depend on the relation between the aggregate supply and aggregate demand functions. In terms of the model developed in this chapter, the aggregate demand function determines the equilibrium level of money income, and the aggregate supply function indicates the output level and price level consistent with this level of money income. From the level of aggregate output we can determine the level of aggregate employment. But when we look behind these two functions we find that the answers actually depend on the behavior of all the factors in the economy that determine the position of and the shifts in these functions. In the preceding chapters, we have been concerned primarily with the factors that determine the aggregate demand function and its shifts. This chapter has finally provided the other blade of the scissors in the form of the aggregate supply function. [26]

We now have a basic model into which we can feed changes in any of these factors, and, *on the assumption that other factors remain constant,* we can

---

[24] *Annual Report*, Jan. 1967, p. 128, and repeated verbatim in *Annual Report*, Feb. 1968, p. 126. See also *Annual Report*, Jan. 1969, pp. 118–21.

[25] See "The Wage-Price Issue: The Need for Guideposts," *Hearing*, Joint Economic Committee, Jan. 1968; J. Sheahan, *The Wage-Price Guideposts*, Brookings Institution, 1968; G. L. Perry, "Wages and the Guideposts," in *American Economic Review*, Sept. 1967, pp. 897–904; M. Bronfenbrenner, "Guidepost-Mortem," in *Industrial and Labor Relations Review*, July 1967, pp. 637–49; and the various papers in G. P. Shultz and R. Z. Aliber, eds., *Guidelines, Informal Controls and the Market Place*, Univ. of Chicago Press, 1966.

[26] What may seem a disproportionate amount of attention paid to aggregate demand may be explained in Keynes's words: "The aggregate supply function . . . which depends in the main on the physical conditions of supply, involves few considerations which are not already familiar. The form may be unfamiliar but the underlying factors are not new. . . . But, in the main it is the part played by the aggregate demand function which has been overlooked." (*General Theory*, p. 89.)

trace out the results of such changes on income, output, employment, and the price level. The inevitable drawback, of course, is that other factors do not remain constant; the real complexities of analysis arise when one tries to trace the interaction and interdependencies of these factors.

Although a truly adequate analysis must investigate the way each relevant factor changes in response to a change in another, it is essential in a field as complicated as this that we emphasize the most important factors. Thus, Keynesian analysis stresses the factors that produce shifts in the aggregate demand function and, thereby, changes in the equilibrium level of income. The most basic conclusion of Keynesian analysis is that the aggregate demand function and the equilibrium level of income it establishes may at any time, with a given supply function, produce an equilibrium level of output below that which corresponds to full employment. This conclusion stands in sharp contrast to that generally held before Keynes's *General Theory* was published. Classical theory denied the possibility that the economy could be in equilibrium with less than full employment, for classical theory denied the possibility of the deficiency of aggregate demand that lies at the foundation of the most basic conclusion of the Keynesian theory. In the following chapter we will briefly consider the classical theory and contrast that theory with the Keynesian theory as developed so far in this and the preceding chapters.

CHAPTER 17

THE CLASSICAL THEORY

The Keynesian conclusion that the equilibrium output level may be below the level that provides full employment for the labor force appears to be quite plausible on the basis of the arguments developed in Chapter 16. The conclusion that an economy's equilibrium level of output would be *only* the level that provides full employment of its labor force appeared equally plausible to many generations of economists before the appearance of Keynes's *General Theory*.[1] There were, of course, dissenters who argued against this conclusion long before Keynes did, but, nonetheless, the theory that aggregate demand simply could not be deficient became widely accepted.

In this chapter we will examine an abbreviated model of the theory that denied the possibility of deficient aggregate demand and underemployment equilibrium, the theory that Keynes called the "classical" theory. Although our model is a classical one, the form in which we present it will nowhere be found in the writings of Ricardo, Mill, Marshall, or any of the other economists who were the creators and refiners of the classical theory. It was not until after the appearance of the *General Theory* that economists set to work to construct from the writings of the classical theorists complete models that might be placed side by side with the Keynesian model for comparison. Since, for simplicity, we will limit ourselves to the broad outlines of that classical model, we must note that our inattention to specific details amounts to inattention to the many qualifications that must be made to the conclusions we will draw. Nonetheless, the conclusions reached on this basis will at least suggest the directions in which the classical theory led.

The classical theory, whose broad outlines are described in this chapter,

[1] John Maynard Keynes, *The General Theory of Employment, Interest, and Money*, Harcourt, Brace & World, 1936.

is specifically classical theory as it was before Keynes's *General Theory*. As we will see below, the quantity theory of money is an essential part of classical theory, but today there is a "modern" version of quantity theory that differs markedly from the old version that was part of traditional classical theory. We will touch on the modern version in a later chapter; here our purpose is to cover the essentials of classical theory before Keynes, and so it is the "old" quantity theory that is examined as a part of that theory.

Our classical model is also limited to the classical explanations of the determination of employment, output, and price levels, for it was these explanations that came under attack by Keynes and others. The other basic questions of what is to be produced, how it is to be produced, and for whom it is to be produced provoked no disagreement. In Keynes's words:

> If we suppose the volume of output to be given, i.e. to be determined by forces outside the classical scheme of thought, then there is no objection to be raised against the classical analysis of the manner in which private self-interest will determine what in particular is produced, in what proportions the factors of production will be combined to produce it, and how the value of the final product will be distributed between them.[2]

Beyond this, not all classical theory relating to the determination of aggregate output and employment was disputed by Keynes. We have encountered parts of this generally accepted theory in the incomplete Keynesian model already developed. Here we will bring in the other elements of the classical theory and show how it led to the conclusion of automatic full employment.

THE LEVEL OF OUTPUT AND EMPLOYMENT IN CLASSICAL THEORY

The equilibrium levels of output and employment are determined in the classical system as soon as we are given (1) the economy's production function, from which is derived the demand curve for labor, and (2) the supply curve of labor. Parts A and B of Figure 17–1 are similar to Parts A and B of Figure 16–1. The MPP-of-labor curve, labeled D_L in Figure 17–1, is as before derived from the production function and shows that the MPP of labor decreases due to diminishing returns as the amount of labor employed increases. Since employers maximize profits by hiring labor up to the point at which $MPP \times P = W$, at

[2] *General Theory*, pp. 378–79. This is not to say, however, that the theory of distribution that was developed by classical economists is the last word. Although Keynes accepted this part of classical theory for his purposes, the very ground broken by Keynes in the theory of aggregate output and employment gave rise to a new interest in the macroeconomic aspects of income distribution. See, for example, S. Weintraub, *A General Theory of the Price Level, Output, Income, Distribution, and Economic Growth*, Chilton, 1959, and N. Kaldor, "Alternative Theories of Distribution," in *Review of Economic Studies*, Vol. 23, 1955–56.

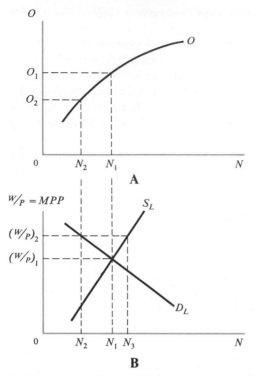

FIGURE 17–1   The Equilibrium Level of Employment and Output in Classical Theory

any given W more labor will be hired beyond an initial equilibrium only at a higher P, or at any given P more labor will be hired only at a lower W.[3] The level of employment consistent with profit maximization may alternatively be described as the level at which MPP $= W/P$ or the level at which MPP equals the real wage (which is the ratio of the money wage to the price level). Thus we may say that the amount of labor hired is an inverse function of the real wage. With a given production function and an initial equilibrium at which MPP $= W/P$, an increase in employment is not possible without a decrease in the real wage.

Keynes could find no fault with this postulate of classical theory, and in effect we adopted it in our Keynesian analysis of the determination of output and employment in Chapter 16. However, as we noted there, Keynes did argue that general cuts in money wage rates would ordinarily be incapable of eliminating unemployment, because, he held, such general cuts in money wage rates would lead to proportionate declines in the price level, P, and leave the real wage, W/P, unchanged. Thus, while Keynes agreed with classical theory that a reduction in the real wage was a prerequisite to an increase in employment, he did not agree that such a reduction could be secured through general cuts in money wage rates. As will be developed below, classical theory holds that cuts in money wage rates do not lead to proportionate declines in the price

[3] See pp. 313–15.

level, so, in that theory, cuts in money wage rates become a means of reducing the real wage and thereby a means of eliminating unemployment.

The curve S_L in Figure 17–1 shows that the labor supply is, like the demand for labor D_L, a function of the real wage W/P. But the labor supply is a direct rather than an inverse function of the real wage. This expresses the contention that a higher money wage rate will not call forth more labor if the price level rises proportionately, for in this event the real wage remains unchanged. For the same reason a lower money wage rate matched by a proportionate fall in the price level will not lead to a reduction in the quantity of labor supplied. The basis for this postulate of classical theory is the unpleasantness or irksomeness of more work; a larger *real* reward is necessary to induce labor to provide an ever larger supply of labor services.

Workers, as well as the firms that employ them, are maximizing units in this system. Firms will not hire more labor at a lower money wage rate if the prices at which they can sell their output falls proportionately with the money wage rate. Of relevance to the firm is the cost of a unit of labor relative to the price at which the firm's output sells—it is the real wage that counts. By the same token, workers will not supply more labor at a higher money wage rate if the prices of the goods purchased with their wages rise proportionately with the money wage rate. Of relevance to the worker is the money wage received per unit of labor supplied relative to the prices of the goods that can be purchased with that money wage—it is the real wage that counts. This maximizing behavior on either side of the market for labor gives us the demand curve for labor as an inverse function of the real wage and the supply curve as a direct function of the real wage.

The intersection of the supply and demand curves for labor determines the level of employment and the real wage and, one step removed, the level of aggregate output. With a real wage of $(W/P)_1$ in Figure 17–1, there is equilibrium between the supply of and demand for labor. At this real wage, employers choose to hire N_1 of labor and workers choose to provide N_1 of labor. With the aggregate production function of Part A, employment of N_1 indicates aggregate output of O_1.

In the classical scheme of things, any real wage other than $(W/P)_1$ in a system of competitive markets will generate forces causing the real wage to rise or fall by the amount necessary to establish equilibrium in the labor market. Assume, for example, that the real wage is $(W/P)_2$, at which real wage the quantity of labor supplied is N_3 and the quantity demanded is N_2. To achieve equilibrium there must be a fall in the real wage, and this may be accomplished by an appropriate decline in W, a rise in P, or some combination of the two.[4] A fall in W follows from the excess of supply over demand for labor, which leads to competition among workers for jobs. This causes workers to offer their services at a lower money wage, and a falling money wage, on the assumption

---

[4] We will later see that adjustment could be brought about entirely by a rising price level, but since we have not yet worked into the analysis the classical theory of the determination of the price level, it is best at this point to assume a constant price level.

of a constant price level, means a falling real wage. A falling real wage means that employers find it profitable to hire more labor (a movement down the demand curve) and that workers choose to supply less labor (a movement down the supply curve). Once the money wage has fallen by the amount necessary to reduce the real wage from $(W/P)_2$ to $(W/P)_1$, equilibrium is reached. Employment has risen from N_2 to N_1, and output has risen from O_2 to O_1. If we had assumed instead an initial real wage below the equilibrium real wage, the adjustment process would be similar. However, in this case there would be an excess demand for labor and competition among employers that would bid up the money wage by the amount necessary to raise the real wage to its equilibrium level.

The equilibrium level of employment so determined is also the full-employment level; that is, at this level all those who are able, willing, and seeking to work at prevailing wage rates are employed. Since any other level of employment is a disequilibrium level, a familiar proposition of classical theory is that *the equilibrium position in the market for labor is necessarily one of full employment*. Whatever unemployment, apart from frictional unemployment, persists in the face of this equilibrium must be voluntary unemployment. For example, with the equilibrium real wage established at $(W/P)_1$, any persons who are unemployed are considered to be voluntarily unemployed if they are seeking work but will accept work only at a money wage that, at the existing price level, means a real wage greater than $(W/P)_1$. They are seeking a real wage that is inconsistent with the marginal productivity of their labor, and in effect they are "pricing" themselves out of the market. Given our previous assumption of a constant price level, there is in the classical system no barrier to full employment or to the elimination of involuntary unemployment as long as labor is willing to reduce its money wage as required to produce that real wage at which all who wish to work will be hired.

SAY'S LAW

The equilibrium real wage defines full employment of the labor force, and full employment of the labor force (with a given production function) defines the full-employment level of output. Classical theory found no obstacle to the attainment of these positions as long as the money wage was flexible—that is, as long as it would fall in the face of unemployment. The possibility that this level of output once produced would not find a market was dismissed; Say's Law ruled out any deficiency of aggregate demand.

Say's Law, named for the French economist Jean Baptiste Say (1767–1832), most simply states that *supply creates its own demand*. More precisely, it states that whatever the level of output, the income created in the course of producing that output will necessarily lead to an equal amount of spending and thus an amount of spending sufficient to purchase the goods and services produced.

Thus, if output is below that which can be produced with a fully employed labor force, inadequate demand cannot stand in the way of an expansion of output. As long as there are idle resources that can be put to work, the very expansion of output resulting from the utilization of such resources will create a proportionate rise in income that will be used to purchase the expanded output. In this way, Say's Law denied that involuntary unemployment could be caused by a deficiency of aggregate demand.[5]

Say's Law is a theory that so closely resembles a familiar national income identity that there is some danger of finding the theory true because the identity is necessarily true. From the national income identities, it is clear that for every dollar of product there is a dollar of income. In whichever way we choose to define product, whether in gross (GNP) or net (NNP) terms, the product itself may be measured by the sum of incomes generated in producing it. This identity between product and income holds definitionally at any level of product, full-employment or anywhere below. The identity also says that any increase in product will be matched by an equal increase in income. But Say's Law says this plus something more that is not definitionally true: that any increase in income will be matched by an equal increase in spending. The heart of Keynesian theory is found in the argument that this last step, which is required to validate Say's Law, does not necessarily follow. The equal rise in spending may not appear.

What is the basis for this unvarying equality between income and spending presumed by Say's Law? In simplest terms, it is the argument that anyone (for example, a cobbler) who produces more product (shoes) than he needs for his personal use does so only to exchange this excess for the products of others. In the case of barter-exchange, and Say's Law was originally set forth for a barter economy, this is necessarily the case. To "supply" one good in barter is unavoidably to "demand" another. A long line of classical economists believed that the law was equally true in a money economy. Although one's excess production in a money economy is exchanged in the market for money and not for other goods, it may still be argued that the purpose of production is not to secure money as such but to secure money with which to buy the products of others. Though the interposition of money converts the direct or barter exchange of "goods for goods" into the indirect exchange of "goods for money for goods," the mere introduction of money was thought to make no difference. Money, it was thought, functions only as a "medium of exchange." Nobody other than a miser wants money for itself rather than for what it will buy. As soon as each person receives money for the sale of the goods or services he has supplied, he spends that money to buy goods and services supplied by others. This does not mean that every person spends whatever money he receives in a matter of minutes after receiving it. At any given time every person holds some

---

[5] For a concise summary of Say's Law, see W. S. Vickrey, *Metastatics and Macroeconomics*, Harcourt, Brace & World, 1964, pp. 168–70. A fuller exposition may be found in a textbook that was popular during the 1920s: F. M. Taylor, *Principles of Economics*, 9th ed., Ronald, 1921, pp. 196–205. For a detailed analysis, see J. A. Schumpeter, *History of Economic Analysis*, London: Oxford Univ. Press, 1954, pp. 615–25.

money because of the unevenness between his receipts and his expenditures. However, so long as people hold no more money than is required for this, money is being used only as a medium of exchange.

As soon as we recognize that people other than misers may at times have reasons to hold some money in idle cash balances—that is, to use money as a "store of value" and not only as a "medium of exchange"—a possible break appears in the chain between the receipt of aggregate income in the form of money and the spending of that money income for the aggregate output whose production generated it. Such a break in the chain invalidates Say's Law when applied to an economy using money. However, in order to proceed with the construction of the classical system, let us for the moment accept Say's Law as valid in a money-using economy. There is then no break between the receipt of money income and the spending thereof, and there is accordingly no such thing as a deficiency of aggregate demand.

THE QUANTITY THEORY OF MONEY

Classical theory relied on Say's Law to assure that aggregate demand would always be equal to aggregate supply; any increase in output automatically created an equal increase in spending that removed the increase in output from the market. Classical theory relied primarily on a flexible money wage to assure that the actual level of output at any time would be that produced by a fully employed labor force. Full employment, we remember, calls for a real wage that equates the supply of with the demand for labor; for any given price level, a flexible wage will adjust as required to produce the required real wage. All this leaves the price level unspecified, and to cover this classical theory relied on the quantity theory of money.

The Quantity Theory as a Theory of the Price Level

In the classical system money's function is essentially limited to that of a medium of exchange: Money is a device designed simply to overcome the difficulties unavoidable in barter exchange. But, even with money's role thus limited, a question remains: Does a bushel of wheat exchange for $2 and a ton of coal for $20, or does a bushel of wheat exchange for $5 and a ton of coal for $50? The answer given by classical theory is that the absolute level of prices, $2 or $5 for wheat and $20 or $50 for coal, depends on the quantity of money in the economy. This relationship in which the price level is made a function of the money supply is known as the *quantity theory of money*. Furthermore, the relationship between changes in the money supply and changes in the price level was held to be strictly proportional. This conclusion depended on several assumptions that may most simply be brought out by examining the identity $MV \equiv PO$, in which M is the supply of money, V is its velocity, or the number of times it turns over per time period in the purchase of final output O, and P is the price level of this output.[6]

It should be emphasized that $MV \equiv PO$ is nothing more than an identity and as such stands completely apart from the quantity theory or any other theory. It is analogous to the identity between product and income in the national income accounts, which stands completely apart from Say's Law. $MV \equiv PO$ says simply that the quantity of money multiplied by the number of times each unit of money on the average is spent for final output in any time period equals the quantity of final goods and services sold during that period multiplied by the price level of those goods and services. If O is the physical volume of goods and services represented by any period's GNP, P is the price level of these goods, and V is the number of times the money supply is used to purchase goods whose value is PO, the familiar GNP identity (neglecting net exports), GNP $\equiv C + I + G$, may be expanded to read $MV \equiv$ GNP $\equiv C + I + G \equiv PO$. Each part of this expression set off by an identity sign is identical in value to every other part; each part of this expression is merely a different way of describing the same dollar amount.

The $MV \equiv PO$ identity is converted into the quantity theory of money under the assumptions that O and V are constant or stable in the short run and that P is passive. With O and V constant, the assumption that P is passive means that P depends on changes in M rather than that changes in M depend on changes in P. Given these assumptions, any short-run increase (or decrease) in M must lead to a proportionate rise (or fall) in P.[7] Without these assumptions, however, it is just as inevitable that any increase (or decrease) in M will *not* lead to a proportionate rise (or fall) in P (barring the unlikely case in which changes in V and O are exactly offsetting).

The classical view that the level of output is stable in the short run is based on the argument that the normal level of output is that produced by a fully employed labor force working with a fixed stock of capital and given production techniques. In terms of Figure 17–1, the production function can shift upward with technological advances and growth in the capital stock, resulting in a rise in output with a given labor input, but these changes occur gradually over the long run. The labor supply curve can also shift to the right with a resultant increase in output, but this too is a change that occurs gradually with the growth in population over the long run. Short-run variations in output could appear as a result of departures from the normal position of a fully employed labor force, but such departures were regarded as infrequent and

[6] M is a stock variable and O a flow variable. If O is defined for one quarter, M is the average stock of money in the economy during that quarter, V is the number of times that average stock of money is used to purchase final output during that quarter, and P is the average price level of output for that quarter.

[7] For example, begin with $100 \times 4 = 2 \times 200$. Increase M by 10 percent to 110. On the assumptions of the constancy of V and O, we have $110 \times 4 = 2.2 \times 200$, or a 10 percent increase in P, a rise proportionate with the increase in M. Or, alternatively, rewrite the identity as $M(V/O) \equiv P$, in which the assumed constancy of V and O makes V/O a positive proportionality constant, here equal to $4/200$, or 0.02. Then, whatever the value for M, P is always 0.02 times that value.

subject to prompt correction in a system of competitive markets. Thus, given the assumption that full employment of the labor force is normal, the assumption of a stable level of output for any short-run period follows logically.

The classical view that the velocity or turnover rate of money is constant is based on the argument that the institutional, structural, and customary conditions that determine velocity usually change very gradually. Among these conditions are the frequency with which economic units receive and make payments, the regularity of these receipts and payments, and the portion of such receipts and payments that are on a money or barter basis.[8] Though these and all other conditions affecting the size of V are subject to change, quantity theory asserts the gradualness of such change in support of its conclusion that V is constant in the short run.[9]

The Quantity Theory as a Theory of Aggregate Demand

The quantity theory carries with it a crude theory of aggregate demand. If V is constant, the supply of money determines the total amount of spending for final output in any specified time period. Whatever the money supply may be, classical theory held that it was all in active circulation under normal conditions. There was no money in idle cash holdings. Here we encounter the same assumption that underlies Say's Law in its application to a money-using economy: People use money as nothing more than a medium of exchange. An absence of idle money is a necessary part of Say's Law when applied to a money-using economy, and it is an equally necessary part of the rigid quantity theory. Classical theory could see no reason why rational people would choose to hold any portion of their money receipts in idle cash form. As people came into the possession of money, there was in this view only one disposition for it: spending. Spending was either for consumption or capital goods. As we will see

---

[8] Even though no one may choose to hold idle cash, everyone holds some cash to even out the difference between receipts and payments. For example, if an employee is paid $200 every other Friday, he does not typically spend the whole $200 on payday (and end up "broke" for the next thirteen days). If he spends the $200 evenly over the two-week period, his average cash balance will turn out to be $100. Since his spending biweekly is $200, this $100 average balance has a V of 2 biweekly; since his spending annually is $5,200, this $100 average balance has a V of 52 annually. If he were instead paid $100 every Friday, by the same line of argument his average cash balance would be $50. This $50 average balance has a V of 4 biweekly and a V of 104 annually. Generalizing for the economy as a whole, with a given supply of money, a change in which everyone were paid half as much twice as often would mean the existing supply of money could handle a much greater volume of final purchases. This rise in V with constant M would mean a rise in PO proportionate with the rise in V.

This illustration covers frequency of receipts, only one of the many conditions that were believed to change very slowly and thus to make for stability in V. For a discussion of the determinants of V, see L. V. Chandler, *The Economics of Money and Banking*, 4th ed., Harper & Row, 1964, pp. 315–21.

[9] Even in its crude form, the quantity theory did not argue that short-run V and O were as stable or P as passive as is here assumed. We will retain these assumptions in the extreme form in which they have been given so that we may proceed with the construction of the simplified classical model.

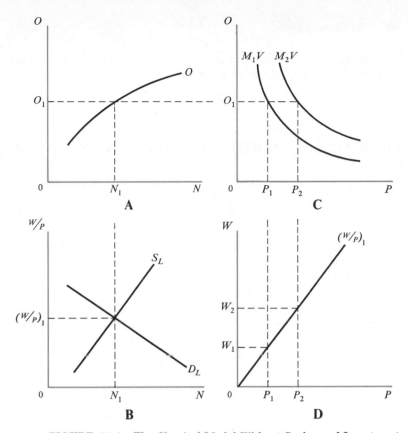

FIGURE 17–2   The Classical Model Without Saving and Investment

below, the act of saving, or not spending for consumption goods, was automatically transformed into an act of spending for capital goods. Money that was held back from consumption spending would be loaned to firms that would in turn spend the money, dollar for dollar, for capital goods. Thus, although persons do save, classical theory held that they would not hold any amounts saved in the form of cash and that therefore no money would escape from active circulation.

As long as money was used exclusively as a medium of exchange and thus remained completely in active circulation, any change in the supply of money would lead to a change in spending that was equal to the change in M times the constant multiple V. This brings us to Figure 17–2C.[10] Price level is measured along the horizontal axis and output along the vertical axis. The greater M is, the greater is MV; the greater MV is, the greater PO must be by the nature of the identity $MV \equiv PO$. If V is constant, changes in aggregate demand result only from changes in M, and any change in aggregate demand may be measured by the equal change in the product of $P \times O$ that accompanies the change in aggregate demand. If O_1 represents the full-employment output, meaning that O_1 is constant in the short run, the rise in P from P_1 to P_2 must be proportional to the increase in M, represented by the shift of the curve from M_1V to M_2V.

[10] Parts A and B merely repeat Figure 17–1; Part D will be discussed shortly.

Any increase in M shifts the curve to the right and, with O constant, raises P proportionately; any decrease in M shifts the curve to the left and, again with O constant, reduces P proportionately.

CLASSICAL MODEL WITHOUT SAVING AND INVESTMENT

Previously, the level of employment was shown to be determined by the supply of and demand for labor; the level of output (with a given production function) was shown to be determined by the level of employment; and the level of prices was shown to be determined by the supply of money. Figure 17–2 illustrates the interrelationships of the variables in this classical model.

In Part B, the intersection of the two curves defines the point of full employment, N_1, and the real wage, $(W/P)_1$, necessary to achieve full employment. With this real wage in effect, employment is N_1, which defines full-employment output, O_1, in Part A. The price level of output depends on M and V, and the curve M_1V specifies a particular money supply and some constant velocity of money. From $MV = PO$ (or from $P = MV/O$), once M, V, and O are known, the price level is also known.[11] In this case, given M_1V and O_1, the price level is P_1.

Part D of Figure 17–2 is new; it shows the money-wage adjustment necessary to establish equilibrium. In Part B $(W/P)_1$ is consistent with any number of pairs of values for W and P, and these possible pairs of values, when plotted, trace the upward-sloping straight line labeled $(W/P)_1$ in Part D. For a real wage higher than $(W/P)_1$, the slope of the line in Part D would be steeper and would thus combine a higher W with each P or a lower P with each W. For a real wage lower than $(W/P)_1$, the slope of the line in Part D would be flatter and would thus combine a lower W with each P or a higher P with each W. Only one money wage will produce the real wage $(W/P)_1$, indicated by the slope of the line in Part D, at the given price level. With the price level P_1 established in Part C, the required money wage is accordingly established in Part D as W_1. If the actual money wage in the market is higher than W_1—the money wage now identified as that required for full employment—then the resulting unemployment and competition among workers for jobs will force the money wage to drop until the system regains its full-employment equilibrium position.

The interconnected parts of Figure 17–2 thus enable us to identify the full set of equilibrium values for this simple classical system: employment N_1, output O_1, price level P_1, and money wage W_1. Barring any shift in the production function or the supply curve of labor or any change in the money supply or its velocity, the indicated set of equilibrium values will remain unchanged period after period. In practice, of course, these elements will change over time, but

---

[11] We may now change $MV \equiv PO$ to $MV = PO$, using the equality sign instead of the identity sign. We now have an equation that sets forth the condition for equilibrium. With MV and O given, equilibrium P is that P at which $P = MV/O$.

for each change, under classical assumptions, new equilibrium values will be established for the variables of the system. Tracing through several such changes will illustrate the mechanics of the system.

Effects of a Change in the Supply of Money

Consider first the case of an increase in the money supply as indicated by the shift of the MV curve from M_1V to M_2V in Figure 17–2C. The increase in M (with constant V) means an increase in total spending per time period of $V(M_2 - M_1)$ and a rise in the price level from P_1 to P_2 for the output level O_1. If the money wage does not rise proportionately with this rise in the price level, the real wage will fall, causing employers to try to expand output by hiring more workers, for a higher price for output without a higher money wage rate means greater profits with greater output. But a real wage below $(W/P)_1$ means that the quantity of labor available is too small to produce output O_1, let alone to expand output beyond this. Competition among employers for workers will then force the money wage up until it rises proportionately with the price level, leaving the equilibrium real wage unchanged at $(W/P)_1$ and the profit-maximizing output unchanged at O_1. The net result of the expansion of the money supply is a proportionate rise in the price level and in the money wage but no change in employment or output; the new equilibrium values are N_1, O_1, P_2, and W_2.

This, of course, is just what we should expect on quantity theory reasoning. The level of output is determined by the real factors of labor productivity and the quantity of labor employed; the money supply only sets the price level for this output. Increasing or decreasing the money supply will cause the price level of output to rise or fall proportionately, but the level of output itself will remain unchanged. Any change in the money supply that is accompanied by a change in the velocity of money will break the proportionate relationship between M and P but will still leave the level of output and employment unaffected by changes in either M or V.

Effects of a Change in the Supply of Labor

Now let us imagine an increase in the labor supply, as shown by the shift from S_L to S'_L in Figure 17–3. With no shift in the production function and so no shift in the curve of the MPP of labor, any increase in employment will lower the MPP of labor. The full-employment equilibrium previously was at N_1, with the MPP of labor or the real wage $(W/P)_1$. If there is to be full employment, the real wage must now fall from $(W/P)_1$ to $(W/P)_2$, for only at $(W/P)_2$ does the supply of labor equal the demand for labor. A fall in W/P is expected in classical theory under the pressure of unemployment now present at the real wage of $(W/P)_1$; competition among workers for jobs gradually forces down the money wage, and a drop in the money wage with no drop in the price level means a fall in the real wage.

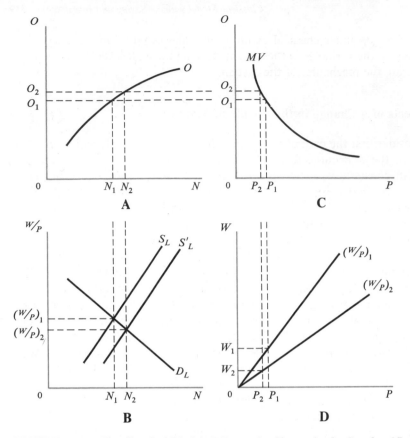

FIGURE 17–3 The Classical Model: Effects of a Change in the Supply of Labor

The present construction enables us to face a complication earlier side-stepped—the fact that a drop in the money wage must lead to a drop in the price level, with a given money supply and constant velocity. As the money wage falls below W_1, firms expand employment beyond N_1, which raises output beyond O_1. When MV is unchanged, aggregate demand is unchanged. To provide a market for enlarged output requires a fall in the price level. (From $MV = PO$, P must fall by the amount necessary to offset any rise in O.) But, though P must fall, P will not fall as far as W. If it did, the new real wage W/P would remain equal to $(W/P)_1$, and there would be no incentive for firms to hire more labor and expand output and therefore no reason for P to fall in the first place. Furthermore, if P fell as far as W, with no change in O, MV would exceed PO. This would mean that some part of the money supply was idle, a situation denied by classical theory. Thus, both P and W fall, but P falls less than W, and this provides both an incentive to firms to expand output and a market for that expanded output. This situation appears in Part D of Figure 17–3 as the fall in W from W_1 to W_2 and the fall in P from P_1 to P_2. This is the fall in the real wage that gives firms the incentive to expand N from N_1 to N_2 and so to expand O from O_1 to O_2. This also is the fall in P that makes it possible to sell the expanded output of O_2 with aggregate demand unchanged at MV in Part C.

A numerical "before" and "after" example may clarify the adjustments involved. The first row of the table below gives the equilibrium values for N, O, W, and P when labor demand is D_L, labor supply is S_L (Figure 17–3), the money supply is $75, and velocity is 4. The second row gives the new equilibrium values after the shift in S_L to S'_L. Full employment now calls for N of 150, at which level the MPP of labor is 1.66. If there is to be full employment, the real wage must fall from 2 to 1.66. Suppose that in the face of unemployment the money wage falls to $1.66. If P stayed at 1, this would reduce the real wage to $1.66/1$, or 1.66, the value required for full employment. At this real wage, N is 150 and O is 400. But output of 400 cannot be sold at a price level of 1, since aggregate demand is MV of $300. Therefore P must fall, but any fall in P raises the real wage and causes a contraction in N. Any unemployment must lead to a further fall in W, which in turn calls for a further fall in P. In this fashion, through successive adjustments, the process finally ends with the consistent set of values in the second row below.[12]

	N	O	W	P	MPP $= W/P$	M	V
Original equilibrium (subscripts 1)	100	300	$2.00	1.00	2.00	$75	4
New equilibrium (subscripts 2)	150	400	1.25	0.75	1.66	75	4

Given an increase in the labor supply, the crucial element of the process by which the system moves to its new equilibrium position is the adjustments that occur in the money wage and the price level. Whether unemployment threatens from an increase in the labor supply or for other reasons, flexibility of the money wage and price level is indispensable to the correction of unemployment. As long as the money wage responds to unemployment and as long as the price level responds to changes in output, full employment can always be regained according to this simple classical model.

[12] On the assumption of profit maximization, employers will not expand employment unless greater profits are expected from the sale of the higher level of output. In this case, there will be greater profits, as may be seen from the figures. At the original equilibrium, labor's share of the real output of 300 is $N \times$ MPP, or 100×2, or 200. The remainder, $O - (N \times$ MPP$)$, or 100, may be called the "profit share." At the new equilibrium, labor's share of the real output of 400 is 150×1.66, or 250, leaving 150 as the "profit share," an increase in profits of 50. In dollar terms, the flow of income at the original equilibrium is $300, or 300×1, divided into $200 for labor and $100 for profits. At the new equilibrium, it is the same $300, or 400×0.75, now divided into $187.50, or $150 \times $1.25 for labor and $112.50 for profits. Though labor's share is decreased in money terms from $200 to $187.50, the $187.50 adjusted for the fall in P from 1 to 0.75 is equal to $250 in "base period" prices. Similarly, the profits of $112.50 are equal to $150 in "base period" prices.

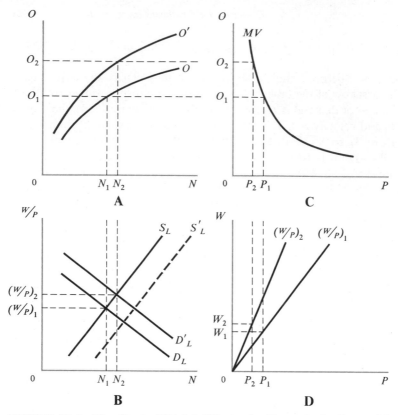

FIGURE 17–4 The Classical Model: Effects of a Change in the Demand for Labor

Effects of a Change in the Demand for Labor

Growth in the capital stock or technological advances will cause the production function to shift upward over time, as shown by the movement from O to O' in Figure 17–4A. At each possible level of employment, the MPP of labor is now greater than it was, since at each level of N the slope of O' exceeds the slope of O. This is reflected in Figure 17–4B as an upward or rightward shift in the demand curve for labor, indicating that it is now profitable for employers to hire more labor at each possible real wage. The equilibrium real wage rises from $(W/P)_1$ to $(W/P)_2$; employment rises from N_1 to N_2; and output rises from O_1 to O_2. With no change in the money supply, the greater output requires a fall in the price level from P_1 to P_2. At the new equilibrium real wage of $(W/P)_2$, price level P_2 calls for money wage W_2. In the present case, the rise in the real wage necessary to reestablish equilibrium is produced by a fall in P and a rise in W.

The first row of the following table repeats the set of figures previously used to describe the original equilibrium values; the second row gives a set of figures that describes the new equilibrium.

	N	O	W	P	MPP = W/P	M	V
Original equilibrium (subscripts 1)	100	300	$2.00	1.00	2.00	$75	4
New equilibrium (subscripts 2)	105	333	2.25	0.90	2.50	75	4

In passing, we may note several basic propositions in economics that are clearly brought out by the present analysis. For one, the gradual rise in the real wage, or "standard of living" of labor, is primarily the result of the gradual upward shift in the production function, which is largely attributable to technological progress and a growing stock of capital. If, over the same period in which these developments raised the schedule of marginal productivity of labor from D_L to D'_L, the supply curve of labor had also moved from S_L to S'_L, the number of workers employed would have risen, but the real wage would have remained the same. The actual gradual rise in the real wage experienced over the long run in Western economies has resulted primarily from the fact that the growth in capital and the rate of technological advance have exceeded the rate of growth in the labor force.

A second proposition brought out by this analysis is that the long-run growth of output (whether produced as here by an upward shift in the production function, or as in the previous case by a shift to the right in the labor supply curve, or as in practice by both) leads to a falling price level unless accompanied by an expansion in the money supply. Although an expansion of output with no rise in the money supply will in practice cause V to rise, V cannot rise without limit. Therefore, as output expands in the long run, M must expand to avoid what otherwise must be a gradually falling P. Although these propositions have been brought out by the classical model, they are accepted in principle by most economists today.

Effects of a Rigid Money Wage

From an initial equilibrium with given MV, an increase in the supply of labor calls for a fall in the money wage and a lesser fall in the price level to establish a new full-employment equilibrium at a lower real wage. Classical theory assumes perfectly competitive markets, and an excess supply of labor in such markets will automatically depress the money wage. If we now drop the assumption of perfect competition in the labor market, the results may be different. Consider, for example, the imperfection of competition that results when workers are organized into labor unions. There will be no barrier to a rise in the money wage when excess demand for labor appears, but there will now be a barrier to a fall in the money wage when excess supply appears.

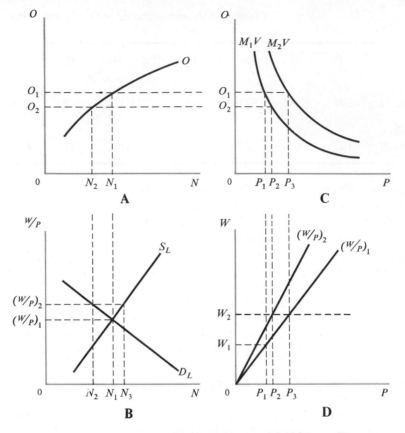

FIGURE 17-5   The Classical Model: Effects of a Rigid Money Wage

In other words, the money wage is flexible upward but may be rigid downward. Furthermore, in an imperfect market the money wage may be forced up even though there is no excess demand for labor. To illustrate, let us begin with a full-employment equilibrium position for the economy and observe the effect of a money wage that is arbitrarily pushed up, say by union pressure.

In Figure 17-5 there is full-employment equilibrium with a real wage of $(W/P)_1$ and values for other variables indicated by subscript 1. Suppose now that the money wage is forced up from W_1 to W_2. If the price level were to remain at P_1, a rise in the real wage would occur proportionate to the rise in the money wage. But, with the given M and V, the price level must rise; for in the absence of a rise in P there is a rise in the real wage, which means a decrease in O, and, with aggregate demand given by MV, a lower O means a higher P. While P must therefore rise, it cannot, however, rise as far as W, for if it did there would be no change in the real wage and so no change in output. The original output cannot all be sold with unchanged aggregate demand of MV at a higher P, so P must rise in proportion to the fall in O.

The process by which a new equilibrium is reached is one in which P, O, and N must all adjust to the rigidly fixed money wage W_2. The new equilibrium values for P, O, and N are designated by the subscript 2. As compared to the initial equilibrium there are now a higher real wage, a lower output level, and a higher price level. The higher real wage, which was artificially brought about by forcing up the money wage, forces employment down from N_1 to N_2. Since the amount of labor supplied is greater with a higher real wage, the amount of unemployment is not merely the difference between N_1 and N_2, but is the larger difference between N_3 and N_2. With the higher real wage, those workers fortunate enough to keep their jobs are, of course, better off than they were before the rise in the money wage.

To illustrate this situation, a numerical example follows similar to those given earlier. Since the new equilibrium is not one of full employment, the last three columns have been added to show the resulting unemployment. (S is labor supplied; D is labor demanded; U is labor unemployed.)

								Labor		
	N	O	W	P	MPP $= W/P$	M	V	S	D	U
Original equilibrium (subscripts 1)	100	300	$2.00	1.00	2.00	$75	4	100	100	0
New equilibrium (subscripts 2)	90	273	2.40	1.10	2.18	75	4	102	90	12

With full-employment equilibrium defined by a real wage of 2, we can see from the figures that unemployment must result from the arbitrary raising of the money wage from $2.00 to $2.40.

As long as the money wage is arbitrarily held above the level consistent with full employment, we have an *equilibrium situation with unemployment*. Although we have noted several times before that classical theory denied this possibility of equilibrium with unemployment, the denial was made only on the assumption that we were dealing with an economy in which the money wage was flexible. Underemployment equilibrium is therefore entirely consistent with classical theory when that theory is stripped of the assumption of flexible wage rates, an assumption indispensable to its full-employment conclusion.

In the *General Theory*, Keynes replaced the classical assumption of a flexible money wage with that of a rigid money wage, an assumption certainly more closely in agreement with the facts of observation. In so doing, Keynes could easily enough show that equilibrium with unemployment is possible. Though a great deal more is involved, what should be clear from analysis of the present case is that the corresponding change in assumption in the classical theory leads to the same possibility of underemployment equilibrium reached by Keynes in the *General Theory*.

Monetary Policy and Full Employment

In the classical scheme, if the money wage is held artificially above the level necessary for full employment, an appropriate expansion of the money supply may be an antidote. According to quantity theory, an increase in M

with V and O stable, will raise P proportionately. With a rigid money wage, the rise in P reduces the real wage and provides the profit incentive to employers to expand employment and output toward the full-employment level. There is, therefore, some appropriate expansion in the money supply that is sufficient first to raise P to the level that reduces the real wage, W/P, to the full-employment equilibrium level and second to purchase the full-employment output that results.

In terms of Figure 17–5D, to achieve the full-employment real wage of $(W/P)_1$ with the money wage inflexible at W_2 requires a price level of P_3, since at that level W_2/P_3 equals W_1/P_1, or $(W/P)_1$. With real wage of $(W/P)_1$, output is O_1. Therefore, in Part C, MV must be increased to equality with P_3O_1 to generate demand adequate to purchase full-employment output O_1 at price level P_3.[13]

The previous numerical example may be modified to show how an appropriately expansionary monetary policy may offset the effect of a rigid money wage. The first two rows of the following table are the same as before—the first describes the initial full-employment equilibrium, the second the under-employment equilibrium that results from a money wage artificially pushed up. The third row shows the return to a full-employment equilibrium that results from the appropriate expansion of M.

| | N | O | W | P | MPP $= W/P$ | M | V | Labor | | |
								S	D	U
Original equilibrium (subscripts 1)	100	300	$2.00	1.00	2.00	$75	4	100	100	0
Second equilibrium (subscripts 2)	90	273	2.40	1.10	2.18	75	4	102	90	12
Third equilibrium (N_1, O_1, W_2, P_3)	100	300	2.40	1.20	2.00	90	4	100	100	0

Note that the strict quantity theory does not hold because part of the additional demand created by the expansion of M is absorbed by the expansion of output that accompanies the fall in the real wage. M rises from \$75 to \$90, or by 20 percent; P rises from 1.10 to 1.20, or by less than 10 percent.

Thus, it would seem that monetary policy provides the solution to unemployment created by a rigid money wage. But it is equally apparent from the crude model before us that this method of securing full employment in the face of artificially high wage rate works only as long as the increase in M is not offset by a decrease in V. Aggregate demand must increase with the increase in M. Classical theory saw no "leakage" between an increase in M and an increase in aggregate demand. We can begin to see why monetary policy was *the* policy weapon of classical economists. When we return in the next chapter to Keynesian theory, we will see that this simple tie between changes in the money supply and

---

[13] With V constant, $\Delta M = M_2 V - M_1 V = P_3 O_1 - P_2 O_2$.

changes in aggregate demand disappears. In Keynesian theory, aggregate demand cannot be so simply increased or decreased by expansion or contraction of the money supply.

CLASSICAL MODEL WITH SAVING AND INVESTMENT

Although formally correct, the classical model we have been discussing is oversimplified because it fails to break aggregate demand down into demand for consumption goods and demand for capital goods. This means that it does not recognize the processes of saving and investment.

Saving and Investment

We must now recognize that not every dollar of income earned in the course of production is spent for consumption goods; some part of this income is withheld from consumption, or saved. Clearly, unless there is a dollar of planned investment spending for every dollar of income saved, Say's Law is invalidated. Another part of classical theory provides the mechanism that presumably assures that planned saving will not exceed planned investment.

This mechanism is the rate of interest. Classical theory treated saving as a direct function of the rate of interest and investment as an inverse function, as illustrated in Figure 17–6. The investment curve is simply the curve of the marginal efficiency of investment (MEI), whose derivation was explained in some detail in Chapter 11. There it was a part of our development of Keynesian theory; here we see that this was actually a part of the classical theory taken over by Keynes. It is important to note, however, that although both theories show investment as an inverse function of the rate of interest, this is not to say that both assign equal importance to the rate of interest as an influence on investment spending. The whole question of the elasticity of the investment demand schedule is involved, a topic we discussed at length in Chapter 13. Keynes and most economists since Keynes have argued that the curve is relatively inelastic. If it is elastic, a relatively small change in the rate of interest will be sufficient to call forth a relatively large change in investment; relatively small changes in the rate of interest will then be all that are required to keep planned saving and planned investment in balance as the saving and investment schedules shift. If it is inelastic, relatively large changes in the rate of interest will be required for this purpose.[14] The question then arises as to whether the

---

[14] It is also conceivable that both the investment and saving curves are so inelastic that a shift to the right in the saving curve or a shift to the left in the investment curve or a combination of the two may result in an intersection of the two curves only at a negative rate of interest. However low the rate of interest might fall, it assuredly could not fall below zero. The result is an impasse at which the rate of interest is completely powerless to equate saving and investment. See W. S. Vickrey, *op. cit.*, pp. 172–73.

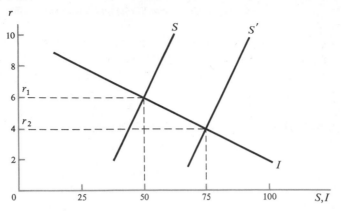

FIGURE 17–6 Classical Equilibria Between Saving and Investment

rate of interest will fluctuate freely over the wider range necessary to equate saving and investment. To simplify the exposition of the classical system, let us assume here that the curve is indeed elastic, so that investment is relatively responsive to changes in the rate of interest. Small changes will then keep saving and investment in balance.

The saving curve of Figure 17–6 is new. Here saving is made a direct function of the interest rate; in Keynesian theory, saving is a direct function of the level of income. The rate of interest may have an influence on saving, but it is of minor importance in the Keynesian scheme. In classical theory, the rate of interest is all important, and the level of income is of minor importance. Since the classical model argues that full employment is the normal state of affairs in the economy, the level of income is in effect ruled out as a variable in the short run, and so it is ruled out as an influence on the amount of saving. The problem in classical economics is to explain how saving will vary at the full-employment level of income, and the solution is provided by the rate of interest. The higher the rate of interest, the greater the amount of the full-employment income that is withheld from consumption or devoted to saving.

Given saving and investment curves such as S and I of Figure 17–6, competition between savers and investors would move the rate of interest to the level that equated saving and investment. If the rate were above r_1, there would be more funds supplied by savers than demanded by investors, and the competition among savers to find investors would force the rate down. If the rate were below r_1, competition would force the rate up. When the rate is at r_1, equilibrium is established, with every dollar saved or withheld from consumption spending matched by a dollar borrowed and devoted to investment spending.

It is important to see that this transfer of money from savers to investors also involves a transfer of resources. The decision to save part of current income is a decision by income recipients not to exercise their claims to the full amount of output that results from their productive services. This releases resources from the production of consumption goods and makes them available for the production of capital goods. These resources will be fully absorbed in the production of capital goods only if investors choose to purchase exactly the amount of capital goods that can be produced by the resources released as a result of saving. This means that if the rate of interest were above r_1 and somehow stayed above r_1, unemployed resources would appear, for the excess of S over I at an interest rate above r_1 reflects, in real terms, an excess of resources released from the production of consumption goods over the amount absorbed in the production of capital goods. One of these resources is, of course, labor, and the excess of S over I also means that there is an excess of labor available over labor employed. In a word, there is unemployment. Thus, in the classical system, if the rate of interest fails to equate saving and investment, it also fails in its assigned task of promptly reallocating the resources released from production of consumption goods to the production of capital goods, and unemployed resources are the result.

Changes in Saving and Investment

As long as the interest rate adjusts upward and downward to correct any disequilibrium, shifts in the saving and investment functions will lead to the establishment of new equilibrium positions. Suppose that income recipients become more thrifty; at each rate of interest they choose to save a larger part of their current income. This appears in Figure 17–6 as a shift to the right from S to S' in the saving curve and a decrease in the rate of interest from r_1 to the new equilibrium level r_2. A numerical example such as those presented earlier is given below to bring out the effects of an increase in thrift in the classical system. The first row indicates the values of the variables at the original full-employment equilibrium. Full employment of the labor force is N of 100, and full-employment output is O of 300. With the interest rate at r_1, say 6 percent, the real income of 300 was divided into 250 of consumption and 50 of saving; r of 6 percent also produced equilibrium with saving of 50 and investment of 50. If the saving curve now shifts to the right and the interest rate drops to r_2, say 4 percent, a new equilibrium is established at which saving of 75 (in real terms, O of 300 less C of 225) equals investment of 75. With no shift in the production function or the supply of labor, full-employment output remains at 300. The only change is in the distribution of output from 250 of consumption goods and 50 of capital goods to 225 of consumption goods and 75 of capital goods. Thus we see that the increased thriftiness of the public has produced a reallocation of resources—one away from the production of consumption goods and to the production of capital goods—but with the total production of goods unchanged at the full-employment level of 300.

	N	O	C	I	W	P	MPP $= W/P$	M	V
Original equilibrium (r = 6 percent)	100	300	250	50	$2.00	1.00	2.00	$75	4
New equilibrium (r = 4 percent)	100	300	225	75	2.00	1.00	2.00	75	4

If the saving function shifted in the opposite direction so that there was less saving at each rate of interest, we would have a higher rate of interest at which a smaller flow of saving would be equated with a smaller flow of investment but still with the flow of aggregate output unchanged from the full-employment level with which we started. The effects of shifts in the investment curve resulting from shifts in the MEC curve may be traced in the same way. Whatever the shifts in the saving and investment curves, however, the possibility of "oversaving" or "underconsumption" could not arise as long as the interest rate succeeded in balancing saving and investment.

Does the interest rate always promptly adjust as required to maintain equality between saving and investment? The Swedish economist Knut Wicksell (1851–1926) was one of the first to point out that there are conditions under which it would not. However, the full-employment conclusion would still result if prices and wages were sufficiently flexible. If the interest rate did not promptly adjust, there would be an excess of planned saving over planned investment or planned investment over planned saving. According to Keynesian theory, a fall or rise in income (output and employment) would be required at this point to bring saving and investment back into balance. This was not the case in classical theory, however. An excess of saving over investment would mean a deficiency of aggregate demand at the existing price level. This would lead to a deflation of prices and wages but would not interfere with the maintenance of the real wage consistent with full employment. Aggregate demand that had become deficient at the original price level would now be adequate to purchase the full-employment level of output at a lower price level. Conversely, an excess of planned investment over planned saving would mean an excess of aggregate demand at the existing price level. This would lead to an inflation of prices and wages but again would not interfere with the maintenance of the real wage consistent with full employment.

Summary Statement

The purpose of this chapter has been to show, in terms of a simple model, how classical theory answered the fundamental questions of macroeconomics. What determines the levels of employment, output, consumption, saving, investment, prices, and wages? Our discussion may now be summarized in a list of the basic propositions that make up classical theory. Each of these propositions will be related to the graphic apparatus of Figure 17–7, which adds nothing new but brings together the saving-investment branch of the classical system with its other branches, presented in two steps in the preceding pages.

1. As shown in Part B, the supply, S_L, and demand, D_L, for labor are both functions of the real wage, W/P. Because of diminishing returns, the demand curve slopes downward to the right (i.e., more labor is hired only at a lower real wage). Because of the essential disagreeableness of work, the supply curve slopes upward to the right (i.e., more labor is offered only at a higher real wage).

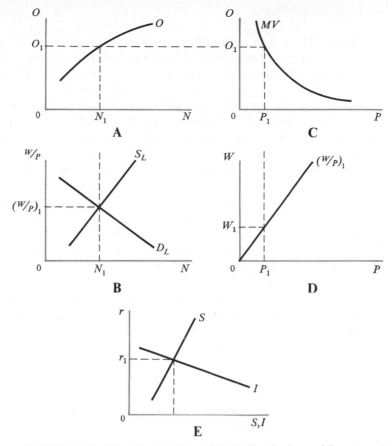

FIGURE 17–7 The Classical Model, Including Saving and Investment

The intersection of the supply and demand curves thus determines both the real wage $(W/P)_1$ and the level of employment N_1.

2. With fixed techniques of production and fixed capital stock, output in the short run becomes a function of employment, as shown by the production function in Part A. With employment determined in Part B as N_1, output is determined in Part A as O_1.

3. The price level, P, is determined by the supply of money, M, the curve MV in Part C defining a particular supply of money and a stable velocity of money. With output determined in Part A as O_1, the price level of that output is determined in Part C as P_1.

4. The money wage, W, adjusts to the price level to produce the real wage required for equilibrium. With the equilibrium real wage determined in Part B as $(W/P)_1$ and the price level determined in Part C as P_1, the required money wage is determined in Part D as W_1.

5. As shown in Part E, saving, S, is a direct function of the rate of interest; and investment, I, is an inverse function of the rate of interest. With the rate of interest as a measure of the reward for saving, the higher the rate of interest, the greater will be the volume of saving. With the interest rate as the "price" of capital goods, the lower the interest rate, the greater will be the volume of

investment. The rate of interest is determined by the intersection of the saving and investment functions, and it determines how real income is allocated between saving and consumption and how production (equal to real income) is allocated between consumption goods and capital goods.

These propositions are the basis for answers to the questions originally posed. But another equally important question lies behind the first and most critical one: Will the level of employment be that which equates the supply of and the demand for labor? Will it be the full-employment level? An affirmative answer to this question follows in classical theory as soon as we add a final proposition:

6. Both prices and wage are flexible, which simply means that the money wage will fall if unemployment appears, and the price level will fall if the existing level of output cannot be sold at going prices. If such flexibility does in fact exist, then the automatic full-employment conclusion follows logically. It also follows that output will be that which can be produced with a fully employed labor force, that the price level will be that at which the money supply with its given velocity will purchase this full-employment level of output, and that the money wage will be so related to the price level as to make it profitable for employers to produce the full-employment level of output.

The classical conclusion that the economy has an automatic tendency to move toward a full-employment equilibrium is not widely accepted today. But this and other conclusions of classical employment theory can be rejected only by rejecting the assumptions on which that theory rests, for the theory itself appears to be internally consistent. Once its assumptions are granted, the theory inevitably leads to the indicated conclusions.

We will not enter here into Keynes's specific attack on the assumptions that underlie classical theory, but most economists agree that his attack was successful. Not only did he offer persuasive arguments against these critical assumptions, but he replaced the rejected assumptions with others that appeared much more consistent with the facts of ordinary observation and statistical evidence. To the extent that the assumptions on which the classical theory was based could be shown to be unacceptable, the conclusions, including the automatic full-employment conclusion, reached by that theory also became unacceptable.

A CONCLUDING NOTE

If the classical analysis of the process by which the levels of employment, output, and prices are determined is unacceptable, at least in its application to the modern economy, it may appear that this lengthy chapter is basically unnecessary. To this there are a number of replies.

First, it is not altogether correct to label the classical theory of employment, output, and prices as unacceptable or in some sense "wrong." Since the aim of this chapter was to do no more than introduce the broad outlines of that theory, it could do no more than draw broad conclusions and compare these with the somewhat more detailed conclusions so far derived from our study of Keynesian theory. The omission of refinements that would give us a more accurate picture of classical theory leaves us with little choice but to categorize the basic propositions of classical theory as correct or incorrect, and such categorization is itself inherently incorrect. Alfred Marshall once said that every *short* statement about economics is misleading (with the possible exception of this one). Our statement here, relative to what is involved in a complete treatment, is such a short statement and unavoidably somewhat misleading.

Second, one's understanding of a new theory is surely enriched when that theory is contrasted with the old theory that it seeks to displace. The classical system was the accepted explanation of macroeconomic phenomena for well over a hundred years. A discussion of this theory, which is partially correct and a product of the not so distant past, helps us understand and appreciate the changes in macroeconomic theory that have occurred since the Great Depression.

Finally, it is important to note that, despite the dramatic success of Keynesian theory over the past three decades, classical theory is still the theory on which many men in positions of great responsibility, both in government and business, were raised. It is not even necessary for them to have received formal training in economics as young men—the stuff of which economics is made has a way of permeating men's minds and influencing their outlooks without any awareness on their part. At the very end of the *General Theory*, Keynes expressed this thought in what has come to be a much-quoted statement:

> . . . the ideas of economists and political philosophers, both when they are right and when they are wrong, are more powerful than is commonly understood. Indeed the world is ruled by little else. Practical men, who believe themselves to be quite exempt from any intellectual influences, are usually the slaves of some defunct economist. Madmen in authority, who hear voices in the air, are distilling their frenzy from some academic scribbler of a few years back.[15]

The defunct economists who continue to influence many of these men today are the economists who constructed the classical theory.

In a similar vein, we find the very last sentence in Alexander Gray's classic little handbook on economic thought:

> No point of view, once expressed, ever seems wholly to die; and in periods of transition like the present, our ears are full of the whisperings of dead men.[16]

For more than one reason, the teachings of the classical economists are of something more than historical interest today. The few reasons here given should be sufficient to make this point. The "Keynesian Revolution" did not so completely wipe out the "old order" that no sign of it remains today. So far at least, for both academic and practical reasons, a proper introduction to macroeconomic theory should include the fundamentals of the theory that held sway for more than a century before Keynes.

[15] *General Theory*, p. 383.
[16] *The Development of Economic Doctrine*, Longmans, Green, 1931, p. 370.

CHAPTER 18

MONEY AND INTEREST

Although Keynes's classic carries the title *The General Theory of Employment, Interest, and Money*, it is possible to work, as we have already done, part way through that theory without encountering money in a determinative role. Up to this point, money appears only as a common denominator or a convenient measuring stick in which to state values and measure flows. But at some point it must be recognized that money is a good deal more than this. This point is reached about halfway through the *General Theory*, where the following statement is found: "We have now introduced money into our causal nexus for the first time, and we are able to catch a first glimpse of the way in which changes in the quantity of money work their way into the economic system." [1] The "causal nexus" Keynes refers to is that between the supply of money and the rate of interest, the rate of interest, as we saw much earlier, being a factor that influences the rate of investment spending and so influences aggregate demand.

The primary purpose of the present chapter is to examine how the supply of and demand for money enter into the determination of the rate of interest. The theory to be discussed is a simplified version of the Keynesian liquidity-preference theory, which, as we shall see, differs sharply from the classical theory of the rate of interest discussed in Chapter 17. Although both the rate of interest and the supply of money are, of course, essential elements of classical theory, they are not tied together there as in Keynesian theory. The rate of interest in classical theory was seen to depend basically on the "real" factors of the supply of saving ("thrift") and the demand for investment ("productivity of capital"). The money supply entered the system primarily as the determinant of the absolute price level of output, whose amount was quite independent of the

[1] John Maynard Keynes, *The General Theory of Employment, Interest, and Money*, Harcourt, Brace & World, 1936, p. 173.

interest rate.[2] In Keynesian theory, however, changes in the money supply may affect the level of output and employment through their effect on the interest rate, which in turn affects aggregate demand and thus output and employment; the theory of money and interest thus becomes inseparable from the theory of output and employment. In this chapter we will concentrate on the theory of money and interest. Then, in Chapter 19, we will proceed to the general theory that incorporates output and employment with money and interest.

MONEY AND OTHER ASSETS

Money is ordinarily defined as anything that is generally accepted by the public in payment for goods, services, other valuable assets and in the discharge of debts. Strictly speaking, only currency, coin, and bank demand deposits qualify under this definition. Time and savings deposits, savings and loan shares, U.S. Savings Bonds, U.S. Treasury bills, and other federal government obligations near maturity come close to being money in this sense, for they may usually be converted into money quickly and with practically no loss of value. However, since these assets cannot generally be used to make payment until converted into coin, currency, or demand deposits, they do not fully qualify as money and are referred to instead as "near-money." If we choose to define money narrowly as anything that is generally acceptable as a means of payment, the total money supply at any point in time equals the sum of currency (which hereafter will be understood to include coin) and demand deposits held by the public.[3]

Any person may hold his wealth in any number of forms: money, as here defined; interest-bearing securities such as bonds; equity securities or stock shares; real estate or physical assets of other kinds. He may distribute his total wealth in various ways among these many forms. Two of these forms are of special relevance to this analysis: money and interest-bearing securities. A wealth-holder may at any time supply interest-bearing securities in the market and demand money, or he may supply money and demand interest-bearing securities. Although money is demanded for other reasons, the demand for money that is the opposite side of the supply of interest-bearing securities is

[2] In advanced literature the classical distinction between the "real" forces of supply and demand that establish relative prices and the supply of money that establishes the absolute price level has come to be called the "classical dichotomy," and the debate (at a very advanced level) that concerned the validity of this dichotomy has come to be called the "Patinkin controversy," after Don Patinkin, who played a leading role in the debate. For a brief summary of the controversy, see H. G. Johnson, "Monetary Theory and Policy," in *American Economic Review*, June 1962, pp. 337–40.

[3] The Board of Governors of the Federal Reserve System now shows currency and demand deposits under "money supply," but it also shows alongside these figures "related deposits," which include some of the near-monies mentioned above. See the tables under the heading "money supply" in the statistical section of any recent issue of the *Federal Reserve Bulletin*.

critical in the theory of interest. Once we have worked through the concept of the demand for money, we will have an explanation of why the interest rate is what it is at any time with the money supply as given at that time.

It should be noted that this approach is not the only currently acceptable approach to the explanation of the interest rate. An alternative known as the "loanable-funds theory" is expressed in terms of supply of and demand for *loanable funds* rather than *money*. Superficially the two appear to come to the same thing, the difference being that loanable-funds works with flows and liquidity-preference works with stocks; but beyond this difference, according to one expert, lies a question whose answer "is now so deeply embedded in mathematical argument that no one can be sure he has got it right." [4] The following discussion will be limited to the liquidity-preference theory.[5]

THE DEMAND FOR MONEY

One reason people demand money is that money is needed in any economy in which almost everyone, persons as well as firms, sells goods and services (including factor services) in the market for money and uses money in turn to buy the goods and services offered by others. Functionally this amounts to the use of money as a medium of exchange. Classical theory explained the demand for money as essentially a demand resulting from this need for money as a medium of exchange.

In Keynesian theory money becomes much more than a medium of exchange, much more than a device for mediating transactions in the marketplace. People also demand money for speculative purposes and as security against unforeseen needs for cash reserves. The breakdown of the demand for money into transactions and precautionary and speculative demands plays a vital part in the theory advanced by Keynes to explain the interest rate.

Transactions Demand

Everyone needs to hold some amount of money to carry on ordinary day-to-day dealings. How much money each person or firm will find a need to hold depends on factors such as the pattern of his or its receipts and expenditures. If one of two otherwise identical persons is paid $100 every week and the other is paid $200 biweekly, the former will require a smaller average cash balance for transactions purposes than will the latter, assuming that each spends his total income evenly over time. Or, take two firms with identical annual sales

---

[4] H. G. Johnson, "The *General Theory* after Twenty-Five Years," in *American Economic Review*, May 1961, p. 7.
[5] A compact exposition of the difference between the two theories is found in W. L. Smith's, "Monetary Theories of the Rate of Interest: A Dynamic Analysis," in *Review of Economics and Statistics*, Feb. 1958, pp. 15–21.

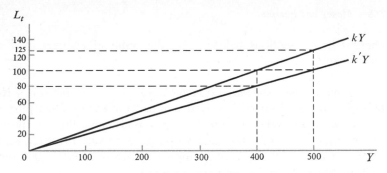

FIGURE 18–1   Transactions Demand for Money

and annual expenses; if the sales of one are concentrated during the summer months and its production is spread evenly over the year, while the other's sales and production are closely matched, the former will probably require a larger average cash balance for transactions purposes than will the latter. Other institutional, structural, and customary conditions also help determine the transactions demand for money, but for any short-run period these conditions are not subject to much change for the economy as a whole. If, therefore, we take these conditions as given, the total transactions demand of all persons and firms may be said to depend on the dollar volume of transactions.

Transactions Demand as a Function of Income.   Because the dollar volume of transactions for any period includes all kinds of transactions in intermediate product and purely financial transactions, it far exceeds that period's gross national product or gross national income. However, if we assume that the ratio of gross national income to the dollar volume of all transactions is reasonably stable, we may say as a first approximation that the transactions demand depends directly on the level of income. To further simplify, we will assume that the relationship is linear.

For example, if people need $1 to handle the transactions represented by $4 of income, required transactions balances will be $100 billion when income is at the $400 billion level and will be $125 billion when income is at the $500 billion level. This may be expressed in equation form as $L_t = kY$, in which L_t, the amount of transactions balances, depends on the level of income, with k assumed in this case to be $1/4$. This may be depicted by a line such as that labeled kY in Figure 18–1. If the institutional and structural conditions of the economy were different (if, for example, employees were paid lesser amounts more frequently), $1 of transactions balances might be sufficient for the transactions represented by $5 of income. This would reduce k to $1/5$ and produce line $k'Y$ in Figure 18–1. For income of $400 and $500 billion, transactions balances would be only $80 and $100 billion, respectively. Changes in the conditions determining k are, as noted above, minor over the period of a few years and may be ignored in short-run analysis. Thus we conclude that the chief determinant of changes in the actual amount of transactions balances held is changes in income. Changes in transactions balances are the result of movements along a line like kY rather than changes in the slope of the line. In the equation, changes in transactions balances are the result of changes in Y rather than changes in k.

Transactions Demand as a Function of the Rate of Interest. It is plausible to expect the amount of money demanded for transactions purposes to vary directly with the level of income. Perhaps it is also plausible to expect the amount of money demanded for transactions purposes to vary inversely with the rate of interest. Consider the case of an individual who is paid $1,000 on the first of each month and spends his total income evenly over each month. His saving per month and per year is zero. If every month had exactly four weeks, this individual's transactions demand for money at any point during the month could be determined from Figure 18–2A. In the middle of the first week, for example, it would be $875, and in the middle of the last week, $125. His trans-actions demand for money averages $500 for the month as a whole. If we split the month no finer than into four weeks, this individual holds for transactions purposes $750 of completely idle money during the first week, $500 during the second, and $250 during the third. Could he not convert this idle money into an interest-bearing asset? Parts B and C of the figure illustrate what he might do. On the first day of the first week (payday), $250 is retained to cover the first week's transactions (see Part B), and $750 is used to buy an earning asset (see Part C). On the first day of the second week, he cashes in $250 of his earning assets to obtain money to cover transactions of the second week, and so forth for the third and fourth weeks, after which the cycle repeats itself. In this fashion, the individual reduces his average transactions balance to $125 for the month (Part B) and makes his average earning-asset balance $375 for the month (Part C). These, of course, add up to the same $500 average balance shown in Part A.

Do people in general do this? Were banks to permit it, people might accomplish this by allocating their transactions balances between savings ac-counts and checking accounts. However, since most banks will not pay interest on funds left on deposit for less than a minimum period, this possibility is ruled out. In our example, the maximum period that any funds would be left in a savings account would be three weeks. Though larger amounts are required to enter this market, anyone may with safety put funds to work for a matter of days, weeks, or months in interest-bearing securities such as U.S. Treasury bills or commercial paper and other short-term money market instruments. The problem here is that there is a cost involved in buying and selling. One must weigh the financial cost and inconvenience of frequent entry to and exit from the market for securities against the apparent advantage of holding interest-bearing securities in place of idle transactions balances. Among other things, the cost per purchase and sale, the rate of interest, and the frequency of pur-chases and sales determine the profitability of switching from idle transactions balances to earning assets.[6] Nonetheless, with the cost per purchase and sale

---

[6] This point is examined in detail in J. Tobin, "The Interest-Elasticity of the Transactions Demand for Cash," in *Review of Economics and Statistics*, Aug. 1956, pp. 241–47, and in W. J. Baumol, "The Transactions Demand for Cash: An Inventory Theoretic Approach," in *Quarterly Journal of Economics*, Nov. 1952, pp. 545–56.

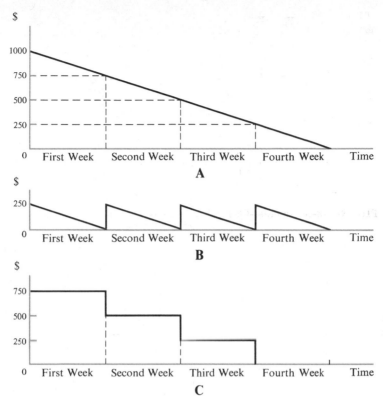

FIGURE 18–2 Hypothetical Allocation of an Individual's Transactions Balance Between Cash and Earning Assets

given, there is clearly some rate of interest at which it becomes profitable to switch what otherwise would be idle transaction balances into interest-bearing securities, even if the period for which these funds may be spared from transactions needs is measured only in weeks. The higher the interest rate, the larger will be the fraction of any given amount of transactions balances that can profitably be diverted into securities.

The relationships between the level of income, the rate of interest, and the transactions demand for money for the economy as a whole are depicted in Figure 18–3.[7] If $Y = \$400$ billion and $k = 1/4$, the transactions demand for money is $100 billion, as shown by the curve Y_1. This figure of $100 billion, however, holds only as long as the interest rate is not above 4 percent, for example. As the rate rises above 4 percent, the transactions demand for money becomes interest-elastic, indicating that, given the costs of switching into and out of securities, an interest rate above 4 percent is sufficiently high to attract some amount of transaction balances into securities. For still higher rates, the amount so diverted becomes larger, as indicated by the backward slope of the Y_1 curve. For a level of income of $500 billion, the transactions demand curve shifts to Y_2 but again slopes backward at an interest rate above 4 percent. The

[7] See A. H. Hansen, *Monetary Theory and Fiscal Policy*, McGraw-Hill, 1949, pp. 66–67.

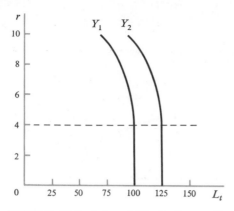

FIGURE 18–3 Interest-Elastic Transactions Demand for Money

curves Y_1 and Y_2 correspond to incomes of \$400 and \$500 billion on the kY curve of Figure 18–1.

It is difficult to generalize on the interest-elasticity of the transactions demand for money for the economy as a whole. A giant corporation that this month holds millions of dollars not needed for transactions until next month will not pass up the opportunity to put these funds in earning assets for a month or even less, if the rate of interest is high enough to permit a profit. An individual whose average transactions balance is moderate is less likely to be so interest-rate conscious. His transactions demand is apt to be completely interest-inelastic at other than irresistibly high interest rates not commonly found in actual experience.

Most economists agree there is in practice some rate of interest at which the transactions demand curve for money for the economy as a whole begins to slope backward (as in Figure 18–3). This means that our equation for transactions demand should become $L_t = f(Y, r)$ and that there is no longer a simple linear relationship between L_t and Y. To simplify our analysis, however, we will assume that this demand is perfectly inelastic with respect to the rate of interest and retain our simple equation for this demand: $L_t = kY$. In terms of Figure 18–3, the transactions demand for money becomes a function of the level of income alone. Changes in the level of income shift the demand curve, as from Y_1 to Y_2, but the curve is perfectly inelastic with respect to the rate of interest at high as well as low rates.

Precautionary Demand

Transactions demand for money stems largely from a lack of synchronization between receipts and expenditures; similarly, precautionary demand arises primarily because of the uncertainty of future receipts and expenditures. Precautionary balances enable persons to meet unanticipated increases in expenditures or unanticipated delays in receipts.

This type of demand for money may be expected to vary to some extent with one's income. Individuals need more money and are better able to set aside more money for this purpose at higher income levels. The precautionary demand

370

may also be expected to vary inversely with the interest rate. Unlike a transactions balance, which is something definitely scheduled for use in the near future, a precautionary balance is to secure one against a "rainy day" that may never come. At a high enough rate of interest one may be tempted to assume the greater risk of a smaller precautionary balance in exchange for the high interest rate that can be earned by converting part of this balance into interest-bearing assets.

Although precautionary demand may be formally distinguished from transactions demand, the total amount of money held to meet both demands is viewed primarily as a function of the level of income and, to some extent, of the rate of interest. As in the case of the transactions demand, we will assume, for the sake of simplicity, that precautionary demand is interest-inelastic and that it too depends solely on the level of income. If both transactions demand and precautionary demand are a function of income, the two may be combined so that our earlier equation, $L_t = kY$, may now be understood to include in L_t both transactions and precautionary balances.

Speculative Demand

The proposition that money is held for transactions and precautionary purposes does not conflict with the classical view. A transactions balance is nothing more than money in its function as a medium of exchange, and a precautionary balance can be added to the classical system without materially affecting its conclusions. But this is as far as the classical theory went. The speculative demand for money, a systematic part of the demand for money in Keynesian theory, represents a distinct break with classical theory.

Classical theory assumed that a person would hold no money in excess of the amount needed to meet his transactions (including precautionary) requirements. To do so would be to forgo the interest that could be earned by putting that money into a security. The reasoning was that, even if the rate of interest were very low, it is better to get some return than none at all. Keynes pointed out, however, that one who buys a bond is "speculating" that the interest rate will not rise appreciably during the period in which he intends to hold the bond. If he believes that it will rise, he would be wise to hold non-interest-bearing money. It is this uncertainty as to the future rate of interest that causes people to hold money for speculative purposes. If the future rate of interest were known with certainty, there would be no speculative demand for money, and there could be no objection to the classical concept of the demand for money.

Security Prices and the Rate of Interest.　To understand what is involved, we must examine the relationship between the interest rate and the market price of a debt security. Take, for example, a marketable U.S. government bond on which a purchaser faces no "credit risk"—that is, no risk that the interest and principal will not be paid as promised. There is no credit risk because the federal government can, if it so chooses, meet its obligations by merely creating the money needed for this purpose. Although credit risk is completely absent, there remains, however, what is called "market risk," the risk that the rate of interest may change.

If i represents the rate of return currently earned by security owners on bonds without credit risk and with a specified maturity, $R_1, R_2, \ldots R_n$ represent the number of dollars of interest to be paid on such bonds in years 1 through n, and A represents the principal amount to be paid at maturity in year n, then the current market value V of such a bond may be found from the equation:

$$V = \frac{R_1}{(1+i)} + \frac{R_2}{(1+i)^2} + \frac{R_3}{(1+i)^3} + \cdots \frac{R_n}{(1+i)^n} + \frac{A}{(1+i)^n}$$

Notice that apart from the last element this is the same equation used to determine the present value of a capital good when $R_1, R_2, \ldots R_n$ designated the stream of net income expected from that physical asset over its life, and i designated the rate at which this income stream was to be discounted.[8] Recall from that analysis that the higher the discount rate, the lower is the present value of that stream of income. The principle is the same here for a debt security. Instead of a stream of income that is produced by a capital good, we now have a stream of income that is produced by a bond. The rate at which this stream of interest income is to be discounted is the rate of interest currently earned in the market on bonds of this type with this maturity. The higher this interest rate, the lower will be the market value of the bond, and vice versa. Thus, once given the stream of interest payments and the principal amount to be paid at maturity, the present value of this bond can change for only one reason—a change in the interest rate. In contrast, corporate, state, and local bonds on which some credit risk exists can fluctuate in price as the market evaluation of credit risk varies. If we limit ourselves here to bonds of the federal government, we find that changes in the interest rate are the only cause of fluctuations in their prices.

The arithmetic relationship between the price of a bond and the rate of interest is most clearly brought out by the consol, a type of security issued by the British government. This security promises only to pay a specified number of dollars in interest per year. It has no redemption value or maturity date; an investor can convert it into money only by selling it in the market to another investor. If market conditions are such that 5 percent is the rate currently being earned on securities of this type, a consol will sell for $1,000 if it pays $50 in interest each year. A buyer who pays $1,000 will get a 5 percent return on his funds. In this special case of consols, the equation above reduces to:

$$V = \frac{R}{i}$$

or

$$\$1,000 = \frac{\$50}{0.05}$$

[8] See pp. 207–09. If a capital good had scrap value at the end of its life, this could be designated as A, and its present value would be computed as is the maturity value of a bond.

Yet, however attractive the 5 percent yield may appear, a prospective purchaser who believes that the interest rate will rise may be better off to hold his $1,000 completely idle, as a speculative balance, rather than buy this security. Suppose, for example, that he believes the interest rate one year from now will be 5.26 percent. The security must then sell at the lower price that yields 5.26 percent to its purchaser, or $V = \$50/0.0526 = \$950$. To buy the security today and hold it for one year promises interest income of $50 and capital loss of $50 or (apart from tax considerations) neither a net gain nor a net loss. In other words, a prospective purchaser who holds his $1,000 as idle cash for a full year and then buys the security will be as well off as one who buys it today, if the rate does in fact rise to 5.26 percent. If a prospective purchaser anticipated that the rate a year hence would be anything above 5.26 percent, it would clearly be to his advantage to hold cash rather than buy the security; if the expected rate were anything less than 5.26 percent, there would clearly be a gain in buying the security rather than in holding the cash.[9] With 5 percent as the original rate, an expected rate of 5.26 percent is the critical rate that marks the difference between an expected net gain and an expected net loss. If the anticipated changes were larger, the purchaser could expect a clear-cut net gain or loss. Thus, if the expected rate were 6 percent, the price of the bond would fall to $833.33, with a net loss to the purchaser of $116.66 for the year. On the other hand, if the expected rate were 4 percent, the price of the bond would rise to $1,250, with a net gain of $300 for the year. Including interest and capital gain or loss, a 1 percent rise in the rate results in a negative yield of 11.66 percent, a 1 percent fall in a positive yield of 30 percent for the year.

The same inverse relationship between the interest rate and price applies to conventional debt securities with specified maturity dates. However, as compared with a consol, the closer a conventional security is to its specified maturity date, the less sensitive its price will be to changes in the interest rate. A rise in the rate from 5 to 6 percent reduced the market value of the consol, which pays $50 interest per year, from $1,000 to $833.33. For a $1,000 bond paying $50 interest per year and maturing in ten years, the same rise in the interest rate would reduce market value from $1,000 to $926.39. If it were five years from maturity, the value would fall from $1,000 to $957.88, and if it were only one year from maturity it would fall from $1,000 to $990.57.[10] These results could be derived by inserting the appropriate figures into the first equation above and solving, but they are found very easily in published interest tables.

In sum, combining interest rate, maturity, and market value, we see that the market value of a debt security is inversely related to the rate of interest

---

[9] See *General Theory*, p. 202.

[10] This assumes that 5 percent was the original yield on the consol and on the three securities with varying maturities. Since yields customarily vary directly with maturity, a yield of 5 percent on the consol might be accompanied by yields of, say, 4, 3, and 2 percent, respectively, on the 10, 5, and 1 year maturities. If the consol sold for $1,000 to provide a yield of 5 percent, the other three securities, each of which promises $50 in interest per year, would probably have sold at successively greater premiums over $1,000. But it still follows that the fall in value that would result from an equal rise in the interest rate on each maturity will be less for the shorter maturity than for the longer.

and that any given change in the rate of interest will exert a greater effect on that market value the more distant the security is from maturity.[11]

Expectations and the Rate of Interest. Anyone who buys a bond or other debt security (other than one of very short maturity) is unavoidably speculating to some extent on future changes in the interest rate and facing the possibility of a financial gain or loss that comes with such changes. Although other considerations enter, persons who switch at any time from cash to bonds expect the interest rate to fall and bond prices to rise; they regard the present interest rate as "high" and present bond prices as "low." Those who switch from bonds to cash hold opposite expectations; they regard the present interest rate as low and bond prices as high. Clearly, anyone who views the current interest rate as high or low must have some "normal" rate in mind against which the current rate is being compared. This concept of a normal rate is itself a changing thing, there being, for example, some tendency in this country to expect a higher normal rate under a Republican than under a Democratic administration. But in one way or another, wealth-holders develop a concept of what is a normal interest rate and find the actual interest rate at times either high or low relative to their concept of normal.

Given the notion of a normal rate, if wealth-holders view the current rate as high, they then expect a drop in the rate as it returns to normal. At this high rate, wealth-holders will accordingly spurn cash and hold bonds. Not only do they thereby currently enjoy the high rate of return provided by bonds, but they can look forward to capital gains as bond prices rise with the anticipated fall of the interest rate to normal. If, on the other hand, wealth-holders view the current rate as low, they anticipate a rise in the rate as it returns to normal. They accordingly spurn bonds and hold cash. The penalty paid in interest forgone is relatively small when the interest rate is low; the prospective capital loss is relatively large if the rate should rise as expected from its low to its normal level. Holding idle cash becomes the financially prudent policy.

We have seen that the amount of speculative balances that people will want to hold varies inversely with the rate of interest. To accompany our equation $L_t = kY$ for the transactions and precautionary demand for money, we may now express the speculative demand for money in equation form as $L_s = l(r)$, noting that L_s is an inverse function of r and L_t is a direct function of Y.

This relationship is shown by the curve in Figure 18–4. The higher the rate of interest, the smaller the amount of assets that wealth-holders choose to hold in money form. At some high rate of interest, the curve indicates that they will hold no money in speculative balances. As drawn here, at a rate of 10 percent or higher the speculative demand curve in effect coincides with the vertical axis— the speculative demand for money is zero. This amounts to saying that all wealth-holders believe that the rate is so high that it can only fall or that even if it should creep still higher, the current high rate of interest will more than

[11] For a more thorough treatment of the relationship between interest rates and security prices, see C. R. Whittlesey, A. M. Freedman, and E. S. Herman, *Money and Banking*, 2nd ed., Macmillan, 1968, pp. 58–63.

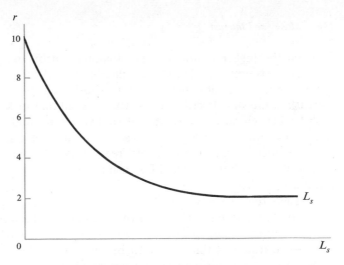

FIGURE 18–4   Speculative Demand for Money

offset any capital loss that may result. At this rate, no one prefers money to bonds; bonds become perfectly "safe." At the other end of the curve, speculative demand becomes perfectly elastic. In the present figure, this occurs at a rate of 2 percent, a rate so low that wealth-holders believe that it can go no lower. To hold bonds at this interest rate instead of money is to face almost certain capital loss as interest rates rise and to find little offset against this loss in the interest income that is provided when the interest rate is so low. This section of the curve, known as the "liquidity trap," will be discussed later in the chapter.[12]

The focus here has been on Keynes's theory of the speculative demand for money, a theory we will be working with in what lies ahead but a theory with a serious shortcoming that may be mentioned at this point. In that theory, Keynes gives the wealth-holder a choice between holding risky bonds and riskless cash. However, the wealth-holder in practice has the option of holding other debt forms that do not require that he incur risk in order to avoid the zero return on money holdings. He may, for example, hold wealth in time deposits, saving-and-loan shares, commercial paper, Treasury bills, and similar forms, all of which provide a rate of return, all of which in practice are immediately convertible into money, and all of which are either absolutely fixed in dollar value, regardless of changes in the market interest rate, or, in the case of a debt form like Treasury bills, are of such short term as to be virtually unaffected in value by changes in the market rate of interest.

Since the rate of interest received on holdings of short-term debt is typically lower than that on long-term debt, the wealth-holder is faced, not with the limited choice of risky long-term debt versus riskless cash, but with the choice

[12] Although we have here limited ourselves to Keynes's approach, which stresses the concept of a normal rate of interest in explaining a downward-sloping speculative demand curve, later writing has shown that the demand for money as an asset will be interest elastic without resorting to the concept of a normal rate of interest to arrive at this result. (See J. Tobin, "Liquidity Preference as Behavior Towards Risk," in *Review of Economic Studies*, Feb. 1958, pp. 65–86, reprinted in M. G. Mueller, ed., *Readings in Macroeconomics*, Holt, Rinehart & Winston, 1966, pp. 173–91.)

between the higher return on risky long-term debt and the lower return on riskless short-term debt. The very availability of such interest-bearing, short-term debts makes it difficult to believe that wealth-holders have a speculative demand for cash in the way described by Keynes. Recall that in Keynes's system this is cash held specifically because the alternative asset (bonds) carries the risk of a decline in value in the event of a rise in the market rate of interest. Since in practice other interest-bearing assets free of this risk are available to the wealth-holder, the speculative demand for cash as described by Keynes would seem to disappear.

There remains, however, the wealth-holder's choice between the lower rate of return that he can secure on short-term debt and the successively higher rates of return that he can secure on successively longer-term debt. The original Keynesian argument thus ceases to be relevant to the holding of speculative cash balances but instead becomes applicable to the explanation of the term structure or maturity structure of interest rates.[13] The question ceases to be one of how the wealth-holder allocates a portion of his wealth between riskless cash and risky bonds and becomes one of how he allocates a portion of his wealth over the spectrum from relatively low return but riskless short-term debt at the one extreme to relatively high return but risky long-term debt at the other extreme.

Although the availability of riskless, short-term, interest-bearing debt appears to rule out holdings of strictly speculative money balances, all persons and firms do, of course, hold transactions balances. As we noted earlier, the amount of transactions balances held at any level of income will become interest-elastic at some level of the interest rate, for people and firms will find ways of economizing on transaction balances in order to gain the rate of return available on riskless short-term debt when that rate becomes high enough to make such effort worthwhile. This behavior with respect to demand for transactions balances is in itself sufficient to produce a demand curve for money that slopes downward to the right. In what follows we could therefore discard completely the Keynesian speculative demand for money and work only with an interest-elastic transactions demand for money, and we would still reach results similar to those reached with a speculative demand for money included. However, in order to trace the theory as it was developed by Keynes, we will here follow the conventional procedure in which the transactions demand is treated as interest inelastic and in which an interest-elastic speculative demand for money is included. The transactions demand is thus $L_t = kY$, and the speculative demand is $L_s = l(r)$.

---

[13] For an introduction to this subject, see W. L. Smith, "The Maturity Structure of Interest Rates," in W. L. Smith and R. L. Teigen, eds., *Readings in Money, National Income and Stabilization Policy*, Irwin, 1965, pp. 400–06. See also F. A. Lutz, "The Structure of Interest Rates," in *Quarterly Journal of Economics*, Nov. 1940, pp. 36–63, reprinted in W. Fellner and B. Haley, eds., *Readings in the Theory of Income Distribution*, Irwin, 1946, pp. 499–529; J. M. Culbertson, "The Term Structure of Interest Rates," in *Quarterly Journal of Economics*, Nov. 1957, pp. 485–517; and D. Meiselman, *The Term Structure of Interest Rates*, Prentice-Hall, 1962.

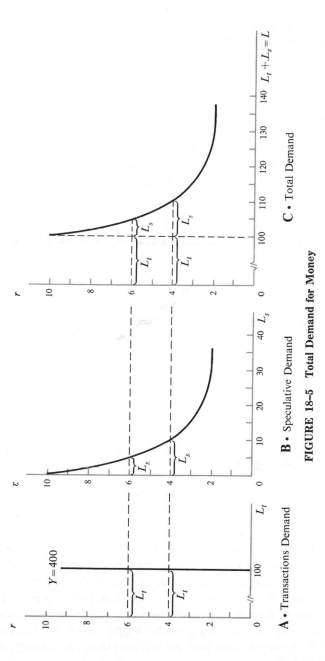

FIGURE 18-5 Total Demand for Money

Total Demand for Money

Combining the equation $L_t = kY$, which we understand to include precautionary demand, and the equation $L_s = l(r)$, we now have an equation for the total demand for money:

$$L_t + L_s = kY + l(r)$$

We know from k what L_t will be for each level of Y. We know from l what L_s will be for each level of r. We therefore know from k and l what the total demand for money will be for every possible combination of Y and r. This may be shown as in Figure 18–5.[14]

Part A of the figure shows the transactions demand for money as $100 billion when the level of income is $400 billion, assuming that k is 1/4. Part B shows the speculative demand for money as an inverse function of the interest rate. Part C shows the total demand curve for money, the sum of the separate demands of Parts A and B, or the sum of L_t and L_s. For example, at an income level of $400 billion and an interest rate of 4 percent, total money demanded is $110 billion; at the same income level but with an interest rate of 6 percent, total money demanded is $105 billion.

The Supply of and the Demand for Money

Regardless of the demand for money, the actual amount of money that people and firms hold at any time clearly cannot exceed the supply of money in the system at that time. Furthermore, the actual amount that people and firms hold at any time cannot be less than the supply of money in the system at that time. Someone must hold the total stock of money at all times.

Equilibrium in the market for money requires that the supply of money equal the demand for money. Thus, if M represents the supply of money, equilibrium requires that

$$M = L$$

where L is the sum of L_t and L_s.

The actual money supply, of course, changes over time in accordance with the policy decisions of the central bank that controls it. Later in this chapter we will discuss how and why the central bank may choose to increase or decrease the money supply. For the moment, let us assume that the supply of money is some fixed amount determined by central bank policy independently of the level of income or the rate of interest. The supply of money accordingly appears in Figure 18–6 as the perfectly inelastic supply curve M. The demand curve L ($= L_t + L_s$) is carried over, with the scale expanded but otherwise unchanged, from Figure 18–5C.

[14] An alternative graphic presentation is given by A. H. Hansen, *op. cit.*, pp. 68–69.

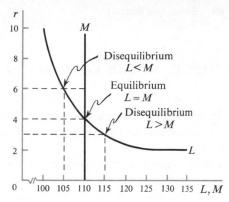

FIGURE 18–6   Equilibrium Between Supply of and Demand for Money

THE EQUILIBRIUM RATE OF INTEREST

Given the money supply and the income level, there is some particular rate of interest at which the sum of the transactions and speculative demands for money will just equal the actual supply of money. The rate of interest that equates the supply of and demand for money is the equilibrium rate of interest. When the supply of money is fixed at $110 billion, as in Figure 18–6, only at an interest rate of 4 percent is the amount of money demanded equal to the amount supplied. At a higher rate, say 6 percent, disequilibrium occurs, since money demanded is $105 billion and money supplied is still $110 billion. Because the total money supply must be held by someone, the public finds in such a situation that its actual holdings of money exceed the desired amount. After allowing for $100 billion required for transactions, people find that the $10 billion remaining is more than they choose to hold as idle cash at so high a rate of interest.

People will therefore enter the market to buy securities with the excess cash. The increased demand for securities will drive the prices of securities up and reduce their yield. This will continue until security prices have been pushed up by the amount necessary to reduce their yield to 4 percent, at which point people will be content to hold the $10 billion of speculative balances they actually do hold. Conversely, at any rate below the equilibrium rate, say at 3 percent, there is also a disequilibrium, but in this case one in which money demanded is $115 billion and money supplied is only $110 billion. At this low interest rate people would rather hold less in securities and more in cash. Therefore, people try to sell securities and get into cash. The increase in the supply of securities drives down their prices and raises their yield. This continues until security prices have fallen by the amount necessary to raise their yield to 4 percent, at which point people will be content to hold the $10 billion of speculative balances they actually do hold.

CHANGES IN THE EQUILIBRIUM RATE OF INTEREST

The interest rate, which is the price of money, will, like other prices, rise or fall in response to changes in supply and demand. Supply changes as government increases or decreases the stock of money. Total demand changes as the level of income or the speculative demand for money changes. As a first step we may, therefore, trace changes in the interest rate to changes in the money supply, the level of income, and the speculative demand for money. Changes in one of these variables may influence the value of another. For example, an increase in the money supply will reduce the rate of interest, stimulate investment spending, and raise the level of income, thereby increasing the transactions demand for money and raising the rate of interest above the level to which it fell as a result of the increase in the money supply. How all these interdependent variables fit together in a general model will be explained in Chapter 19. At this point, we will consider one change at a time, on the assumption that other things remain equal.

Changes in the Money Supply

The money supply, M, was defined earlier as the total currency and demand deposits held by the public. There are many factors that affect the size of this total; one of the most important of these is the change in Reserve Bank holdings of government securities. The Reserve authorities can raise or lower the money supply through "open-market operations," the popular name for transactions that alter Reserve Bank holdings of government securities.[15]

The Process of Monetary Expansion and Contraction. On any date, the balance sheets of the Federal Reserve Banks, the commercial banks, and all other firms and individuals collectively described as the public will reveal assets and liabilities measured in tens of billions of dollars. Our interest is only in the changes that occur in particular asset and liability items between two dates; such changes are indicated by $+$ and $-$ signs in the three balance sheets of Table 18–1.

Suppose that the Reserve authorities decide to increase the money supply by $10 billion. To do this the Reserve Banks purchase $2 billion of government securities in the open market. The sellers of these securities are assumed to be individuals and firms (excluding commercial banks) that are part of the public. The Reserve Banks issue checks drawn against themselves in order to pay the sellers. The sellers of the securities deposit these checks at their commercial

---

[15] The factors determining changes in the money supply are, of course, examined in detail in standard texts on money and banking. See, for example, E. Shapiro, E. Solomon, and W. L. White, *Money and Banking*, 5th ed., Holt, Rinehart and Winston, 1968, Ch. 10.

TABLE 18-1   An Expansion of the Money Supply

	FEDERAL RESERVE BANKS		COMMERCIAL BANKS		PUBLIC	
	Assets	*Liabilities*	*Assets*	*Liabilities*	*Assets*	*Liabilities*
Step 1	Securities $ + 2 —	Deposits $ + 2 —	Reserves $ + 2 —	Public's Deposits $ + 2 —	Securities $ − 2 Deposits + 2	— —
Step 2	— —	— —	Securities $ + 8 —	Public's Deposits $ + 8 —	Securities $ − 8 Deposits + 8	— —
Net effects	Securities $ + 2 —	Deposits $ + 2 —	Reserves $ + 2 Securities + 8	Public's Deposits $ + 10 —	Securities $ − 10 Deposits + 10	—

banks, thereby taking payment in the form of credit to their checking accounts; the commercial banks in turn send these checks to the Reserve Banks, taking payment in the form of a $2 billion increase in their deposit balances with the Reserve Banks. These transactions are summarized as Step 1 in the table. At this step, the public has increased its money holdings by $2 billion and decreased its security holdings by a like amount. The commercial banks, in turn, have increased their deposits with the Reserve Banks by $2 billion and their deposit liabilities to the public by a like amount. The Reserve Banks have increased their security holdings by $2 billion and, in payment, have created a like amount of deposit liabilities. These deposit liabilities amount to an addition to the legal reserves to the commercial banks.

Suppose that commercial banks are legally required to maintain a minimum reserve of, say, 20 percent of their demand deposit liabilities in the form of deposits at the Reserve Banks. If, prior to Step 1 above, the commercial banks had just the amount of reserves required to back up their existing deposit liabilities, they would now have excess reserves of $1.6 billion as a result of Step 1. Such reserves are nonearning assets, and the commercial banks proceed to put them to work—by buying securities, for example. The sellers of securities—that is, the public—receive in payment checks drawn by the various commercial banks against themselves as buyers; these checks are deposited at various commercial banks. Step 2 in Table 18-1 shows that commercial banks as a group acquired $8 billion in securities (assets) and created $8 billion of new demand deposits (liabilities) in the process. Step 2 also shows an increase of $8 billion in the public's demand deposits, or money holdings, and a decrease of the same amount in its security holdings.

The net effects of the original open-market purchase of $2 billion in securities by the Reserve Banks are as shown in the last part of the table. If we assume that there is a 20 percent reserve requirement and that banks expand deposits to the limit set by their reserves, commercial bank reserves are up by $2 billion, which, together with the $8 billion in securities, supports the $10 billion of new demand deposits held by the public. In exchange for this $10 billion of new deposits, the public has given up a similar amount of security holdings, $2 billion of which is held by the Reserve Banks. Demand deposits being money and securities not being money, there has been an increase in the money supply of $10 billion, or the banking system has "monetized" $10 billion worth of securities.

If, instead of buying $2 billion in securities, the Reserve Banks had sold to the public $2 billion from its portfolio, the effects would have been exactly reversed. In Table 18–1, each + sign would become a − sign, and vice versa. With the public now purchasers instead of sellers of securities, there would be a $10 billion decrease in the public's holdings of money and a $10 billion increase in its holdings of securities.

The results described here assume that the amount of the deposit liabilities of the banks are independent of the rate of interest that banks can earn on loans made or securities purchased. In other words, the banks are assumed to be fully "loaned up" at all times, so that any increase or decrease in their reserves will mean an expansion or contraction of their deposit liabilities by a fixed multiple of the change in reserves. Actually banks do carry some excess reserves, and an aspect of this behavior that is relevant here is the fact that the amount of excess reserves they hold tends to vary inversely with the interest rate. This is similar to the behavior of individual wealth-holders with respect to the amount of speculative balances they choose to hold at different interest rates. We thus find that, with no change in the total amount of reserves held by the banks, the amount of their deposit liabilities outstanding will vary directly with the rate of interest. Graphically, instead of a supply curve perfectly inelastic throughout as in Figure 18–6, the supply curve slopes upward to the right. If we allow for this aspect of bank behavior, we find that the supply of money as well as the demand for money depends on the rate of interest. However, since the supply elasticity is not crucial in what follows, we will for simplicity assume as earlier that the supply of money consistent with any given amount of bank reserves is interest-inelastic.[16]

Monetary Expansion and the Rate of Interest.   The *M* and *L* curves of Figure 18–7 are the same as those of Figure 18–6. As we saw there, with demand

[16] For an introduction to the relationship between the rate of interest and the supply of money, see J. J. Klein, *Money and the Economy*, Harcourt, Brace & World, 1965, pp. 262–65, and R. L. Teigen, "The Demand for and Supply of Money," in W. L. Smith and R. L. Teigen, eds., *Money, National Income and Stabilization Policy*, Irwin, 1965, pp. 60–63.

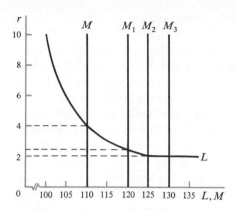

FIGURE 18–7 Changes in the Supply of Money and the Rate of Interest

as given, the money supply of $110 billion produces an equilibrium rate of interest of 4 percent. The M_1 curve shows the supply of money after the $10 billion increase that results from the expansion of bank credit. The increase in the supply of money forces the interest rate down to 2.5 percent. As long as there is no shift in the total demand curve for money, further increases in the supply of money will continue to lower the interest rate, and decreases will raise it. Although our model is highly simplified, it shows in general how the Reserve authorities can raise and lower the rate of interest by their ability to produce changes in the money supply, changes that are usually brought about by means of open-market operations as described above.

This ability rests in turn on the ability of the Reserve Banks to find sellers when it seeks to buy securities and to find buyers when it seeks to sell securities. As long as the Reserve Banks do not try to buy low and sell high in order to show a profit or avoid a loss in open-market transactions, there will be no shortage of buyers or sellers, whatever the scope of Federal Reserve operations in the open market. In Step 1 of our illustration, the Reserve Banks bought $2 billion in securities. Some rise in security prices may have been necessary to induce security-holders to swap interest-bearing securities for non-interest-bearing money. The rise in security prices would have been that needed to cause a sufficient number of security-holders to believe that security prices were high and likely to fall and that interest rates were low and likely to rise. When $8 billion more in securities was purchased by the commercial banks in Step 2, some further rise in security prices may have been necessary to induce the exchange of this amount of interest-bearing securities for money. In terms of Figure 18–7, for the complete sequence that involved an increase in the money supply of $10 billion, security prices had to rise enough to force the interest rate down from 4 to 2.5 percent. Only at this lower interest rate were people content to hold the additional $10 billion of money in place of an equal amount of securities.

The "Liquidity Trap." How much of a change in the rate of interest may be expected from any specific increase in the money supply depends, *ceteris paribus*, on the elasticity of the speculative demand curve. If it is more elastic over the range from 4 to 2.5 percent than the *L* curve of Figure 18–7, the decrease in the rate of interest effected by the $10 billion increase in the money supply would be less. If less elastic, it would be more.

There may be some relatively low rate (2 percent in Figure 18–7) at which the curve becomes perfectly elastic, indicating that the expectations of wealth-holders are virtually unanimous that the interest rate is so low that it can go no lower and that security prices are so high that they can go no higher. Although the Reserve authorities could, through open-market operations, expand the money supply past M_2 to M_3, they could not in so doing succeed in reducing the rate of interest below that set by the "liquidity trap." At this rate, the demand of wealth-holders for money is perfectly elastic, or the wealth-holders' supply of securities is perfectly elastic. The Reserve Banks could buy more and more securities in the open market, but the prices paid for them would stay the same. Monetary expansion is completely incapable of reducing the interest rate below the rate set by the liquidity trap.

Although it is an interesting and presumably possible phenomenon, the actual appearance of a liquidity trap is obviously a rarity. Seldom do interest rates reach the low level at which wealth-holders hold the expectations necessary to produce a liquidity trap. The closest approximation to a liquidity trap in recent U.S. experience was during the years immediately following the Great Depression, a period now thirty years behind us.[17] Although it is now viewed as an extreme case, the liquidity trap plays an important part in Keynes's *General Theory*, interestingly enough written at a time when the existence of a liquidity trap seemed more of a reality than a mere possibility. We will have more to say about the liquidity trap when we develop a general model of the economy in Chapter 19.

Changes in the Level of Income

If we take the money supply and speculative demand for money as given, the rate of interest will vary directly with the level of income. Handling the larger dollar volume of transactions associated with a higher level of income calls for larger transactions balances. Let us retain the assumption that $k = 1/4$; with income at the $400 billion level, the L curve of Figure 18–8 is the same as that in preceding figures. A rise in income from $400 to $420 billion raises trans-actions demand from $100 to $105 billion. As long as there is no change in speculative demand, the total demand curve shifts $5 billion to the right at each rate of interest to produce the new total demand curve L_1. With an increase in the demand for money and no change in supply, the rate of interest rises to a new equilibrium level of 6 percent.

The underlying process by which this rise in the interest rate takes place is

[17] The existence or nonexistence of the Keynesian liquidity trap has been investigated by J. Tobin in his study, "Liquidity Preference and Monetary Policy," in *Review of Economics and Statistics*, May 1947, pp. 124–31, and in a more sophisticated form by M. Bronfenbrenner and T. Mayer, "Liquidity Functions in the American Economy," in *Econometrica*, Oct. 1960, pp. 810–34. See also D. Laidler, "The Rate of Interest and the Demand for Money—Some Empirical Evidence," in *Journal of Political Economy*, Dec. 1966, pp. 543–55.

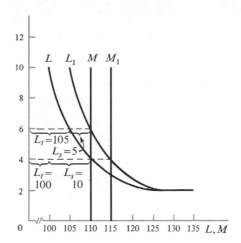

FIGURE 18–8   Changes in Income Level and the Rate of Interest

not revealed by Figure 18–8. Basically, the process involves the diversion of money from speculative to transactions balances. As people and firms find that more money is needed to handle the greater volume of transactions accompanying a rise in income, they sell some of their security holdings in the market in order to secure the additional transactions balances needed. Since we are assuming that there is no change in the total supply of money, the additional transactions balances can come only from speculative balances. This will occur as the prices of securities fall and their yields rise, the result of the increase in the supply of securities offered on the market. With the fall in prices and rise in yields, holders of speculative balances who were fearful of bonds at higher prices and lower yields will be tempted to switch to bonds at the more attractive price-yield combination now available. In our illustration, security prices must fall far enough to raise the interest rate from 4 to 6 percent in order to draw the required $5 billion out of speculative balances into transactions balances.

By the same reasoning, with the money supply fixed, a fall in the income level means a decline in the interest rate. When the income level falls, the public discovers that it is holding more in transactions balances than it needs. This excess money will seek a return in securities, thus pushing up the prices of securities and reducing their yields to the point at which the public willingly holds the larger, idle cash balances. The results of a decline in income from $420 to $400 billion are indicated in Figure 18–8 by a shift in the total demand curve from L_1 to L. The equilibrium interest rate falls from 6 to 4 percent.[18]

[18] Since changes in Y may result from changes in P, O, or both, a rise in P with no change in O will raise the interest rate as will a rise in O with no change in P. The amount of the change in the interest rate may vary, however, depending on whether the rise in Y is the result of a rise in P or in O. If it is the result of a rise in P, and if an initial rise in P is regarded as a forerunner of further rises in P—that is, if inflation is expected—a marked shift to the right in the speculative demand curve for money may well result. Fear of inflation will cause a flight out of bonds into cash and from cash into inflation hedges such as common stocks and goods, the prices of which will tend to keep pace with inflation. Thus, an income rise that is the result of a rise in the price level and that creates expectations of still further rises in the price level will mean a greater rise in the interest rate than will an equal rise in real income.

385

We are now in a position to tie together changes in the money supply and changes in the income level. If a rise in income is the result of an expanding real income in a growing economy, public policy may oppose a rise in the interest rate because of the adverse effect on investment spending and on the further expansion of real income. In the example given above of a $20 billion rise in income, open-market purchases of $1 billion of securities by the Reserve Banks would (on our earlier assumptions) provide the additional commercial bank reserves necessary for an overall increase of $5 billion in the money supply. This increase would provide the additional transactions balances called for by the $20 billion rise in income. There would be no rise in the interest rate and no danger of restraining the expansion of income through a restrictive monetary policy. This increase in the money supply is depicted in Figure 18–8 by the shift in the supply curve from M to M_1, and as a result the interest rate is held constant at 4 percent.

If income rises, an absence of expansionary action by the Reserve authorities may in effect become restrictive action as the Reserve authorities stand by and allow the market to "tighten" itself. Of course, if the rise in income is the result of rising prices and not rising output, and if further rises in prices are feared, we could not expect the Federal Reserve to take expansionary action to prevent a rise in the interest rate. On the contrary, a policy of "neutrality" whereby the market would be allowed to tighten itself or a policy of monetary contraction that would tighten the market even more would be in order. In short, if the rise in income is inflationary, the rise in the interest rate that will automatically occur in the absence of offsetting Federal Reserve action is called for to restrict investment demand and aggregate demand and reduce or eliminate the inflationary pressure.

Changes in the Speculative Demand for Money

In our earlier discussion of Keynes's speculative demand, we noted that wealth-holders develop a concept of what are "normal," "low," and "high" interest rates. This is not intended to mean that all wealth-holders have the same opinion as to what high, low, and normal rates may be at any particular time. There will be and must be diversity of judgment if the concept of a speculative demand function is to have any meaning.[19] Despite this diversity of

[19] If all wealth-holders held identical views as to the normal rate of interest at any particular time, and if each went "whole hog" into bonds at any rate above this rate and "whole hog" into cash at any rate below it, the speculative demand curve would be a perfectly elastic function at the level of this normal rate. Regardless of the size of the money supply, as long as it was greater than that needed for transactions purposes, the rate of interest would remain unchanged. With the actual rate equal to what wealth-holders regard as the normal rate, there would be no reason for this perfectly elastic function to shift upward or downward and therefore no way for the interest rate to change in response to any change in the money supply. Since the interest rate does actually change, it follows that the speculative demand curve must be less than perfectly elastic, if it is to have any meaning. This does not conflict with the possibility that a portion of the curve may be perfectly elastic. A liquidity trap may exist, but the whole curve cannot amount to a continuous liquidity trap.

judgment among individual wealth-holders, there will also be a consensus among wealth-holders as a group. References to high, low, and normal rates are to what average opinion holds these rates to be at any given time.

If for some reason the consensus is that the normal rate will rise from the neighborhood of 4 percent to the neighborhood of 6 percent, there will be a movement out of securities into cash, which will raise the interest rate to 6 percent. If there is no decrease in the money supply and no rise in the level of income, the interest rate will in fact rise if wealth-holders expect it to and if they act on their expectations. The same is true in the other direction. If there is no increase in the money supply and no fall in the level of income, the interest rate will fall from, say, the neighborhood of 4 percent to that of 3 percent, if wealth-holders expect it to fall and act on their expectations.

In Figure 18–8, with money supply given by M and demand for money given by L, the actual rate is 4 percent; we may assume this is regarded by wealth-holders as in the neighborhood of the normal rate. If now for some reason general opinion should come to hold that rates near 6 percent will be normal, rates above the neighborhood of 6 percent will come to be viewed as high and rates below the neighborhood of 6 percent will be viewed as low. This amounts to an upward shift in the whole demand curve from L to L_1. With no change in the money supply or in the level of income, a new equilibrium interest rate is established at 6 percent.

It is easy enough to trace the simple mechanics of the process by which a change in the equilibrium rate of interest will follow from a change in wealth-holders' opinions as to what the normal rate of interest will be. It is not at all easy to explain specifically what causes wealth-holders' opinions to change. To begin with, it seems clear that the particular opinions concerning normal interest rates at any time cannot be separated from the actual rates observed over the near and more distant past. In an economy that has never experienced a rate on high-grade long-term bonds above 8 percent, for example, wealth-holders are not likely to come to believe that a rate above 8 percent can be a normal rate. The same is true on the low side. But within a range so defined there still appears to be room for considerable variation in opinion as to what the normal rate will be from time to time. Though it is only part of an answer, one important determinant is wealth-holders' views concerning future Federal Reserve policy. If there were no offsetting Federal Reserve action, one would usually expect the interest rate to begin to rise at some point in a period of vigorous business expansion following a recession low. The increased transactions requirements, unless met by an expansion in the money supply, would tend to force the interest rate up, as in U.S. business cycles before World War II. But compare this, for example, with the experience during the first four years of the economic expansion that began early in 1961. GNP at annual rates in current dollars rose by over $150 billion from the first quarter of 1961 to the first quarter of 1965. However, the interest rate on long-term U.S. government bonds fluctuated over a range of less than 0.5 percent during this period. As a result of Federal Reserve action to prevent the long-term rate from rising sharply, this rate, which averaged 3.8 percent during the first quarter of 1961, averaged no higher than 4.1 percent during the first quarter of 1965, despite four continuous years of business expansion. What does experience like this mean to wealth-holders' views of the normal rate of interest? Changes in such views now become dependent on (1) the expected changes in all factors, domestic and international, that enter into the forecast of the coming business situation and (2) the expected response of the Reserve authorities to such changes, if changes actually come to pass as expected. Expected changes that would otherwise lead wealth-holders to anticipate a higher normal rate will not cause an upward shift in the speculative demand function if wealth-holders also expect that Federal Reserve policy will offset the rise in the rate that would otherwise occur.

An interesting result of this is the way the Reserve authorities may exploit wealth-holders' recognition of their power to maintain the interest rate unchanged or to raise or lower it. If, for example, a rise in the rate is deemed necessary by the Reserve authorities, instead of actually selling securities in the open market, they may achieve the desired rise through public statements by the Chairman of the Board of Governors and other high officials of the Federal Reserve, warning that inflation once again represents a dangerous threat to the stability of the economy. Wealth-holders will interpret this as tantamount to an announcement of a pending "tight money" policy. The higher rate that the Reserve authorities seek may then be produced simply as a result of the upward shift in the speculative demand for money; this shift will occur as wealth-holders act on their understanding of the real meaning of the statements made by the Reserve authorities. In this way, the Reserve authorities may accomplish, with nothing more than a few words, what could otherwise be accomplished only by positive open-market action.

To illustrate in terms of Figure 18–8, let us assume that the Reserve authorities have planned to bring about a desired tightening with the money supply unchanged at M. With the equilibrium rate at 4 percent, all that may be needed is to make wealth-holders believe that the Reserve authorities will raise the rate to 6 percent. This expectation can in itself produce a shift from L to L_1 in the demand function, which will yield the desired rise in the rate from 4 to 6 percent. The goal of Federal Reserve policy is thus achieved without actual intervention in the market by the Reserve authorities.

THE DEMAND FOR MONEY—FROM CLASSICAL TO POST-KEYNESIAN THEORY

The simple quantity theory of money carries with it a simple theory of the demand for money. People supply goods and services in the market and demand money rather than other goods in exchange, since only money has the unique characteristic of being generally acceptable in exchange for any and all other goods and services offered for sale in the market. As money is received, it is spent. The number of times per time period that the existing money supply appears in the market as demand for goods and services is its velocity, which, for reasons discussed earlier, the simple quantity theory regarded as stable in the short run. For a system whose output was at the full-employment level, output too was stable in the short run. This meant that the price level varied proportionately with the money supply. Any additional money flowing into the hands of the public through a money-creating expansion of bank credit would in turn flow into the market for goods and raise the price level of goods proportionately. Thus, it could be said that the price level equates the supply of and demand for money. Any rise in the supply of money will raise the price level by the amount necessary to create an increase in the demand for money equal to the increase in supply. The higher P is, the greater is PO; the greater PO is, the greater is the amount of M required to purchase PO with a stable V.

The concept of the demand for money does not emerge very clearly when the quantity theory is approached, as it was above, in terms of the $MV = PO$ equation. However, merely by substituting $1/k$ for V, we transform the $MV = PO$ equation into $M = kPO$. The former is known as the velocity formulation and the latter as the cash-balance formulation.[20] However, since $V = 1/k$ and $k = 1/V$, the two formulations come to the same thing algebraically. But there is a fundamental difference between the analyses that underlie each: "The central question in . . . velocity analysis was *how rapidly money is spent*. The central question in cash-balances analysis is why holders of cash *haven't spent it yet*." [21] D. H. Robertson expressed this distinction colorfully as money "on the wing" and money "sitting." [22] Money sitting leads one to ask why it is sitting and so, more specifically, why people demand money.

If $V = 4$, then $k = 1/4$. The former expression means that each dollar in the money supply is on the average used four times during the period for the purchase of final product. The latter means that people want to "keep by them" money equivalent in value to a certain stock of real goods and services, in this case an amount equal to 1/4 of the economy's output for the period.[23] To illustrate, let us take an initial equilibrium situation in which people's actual cash holdings are equal to desired cash holdings, and then let us assume an increase in the money supply. As a result of the increase, the public is holding more money than it wants to hold at the existing price level, and it attempts to rid itself of this excess cash by spending. On the assumption that output is at its full-employment level, the additional spending forces the price level up until the actual, larger cash holdings become desired cash holdings at the higher price level of output. To hold in cash an amount sufficient to command 1/4 of the

[20] The $MV = PO$ formulation is also known as the Fisher equation, after Irving Fisher. More correctly, it is an adaptation of the original Fisher equation, $MV = PT$, in which T included all monetary transactions and not only final product, or O. The $M = kPO$ formulation is known as the Marshallian equation, after Alfred Marshall. It is also popularly known as the Cambridge equation after the university at which Marshall, A. C. Pigou, D. H. Robertson, and Keynes (before the *General Theory*) developed this approach.

[21] A. G. Hart, P. B. Kenen, and A. D. Entine, *Money Debt and Economic Activity*, 4th ed., Prentice-Hall, 1969, p. 216.

[22] D. H. Robertson, *Money*, Univ. of Chicago Press, 1959, Ch. 2.

[23] See A. Marshall, *Money, Credit, and Commerce*, Macmillan, 1923, pp. 44–45.

period's output requires more money at a higher price level for output; thus the rise in P with given O equates the demand for M with the enlarged supply of M. A decrease in the money supply brings about a similar adjustment through a fall in the price level.

The basic assumption here is the same as in the velocity formulation of the simple quantity theory covered in the preceding chapter—people hold money for transaction purposes. Earlier in the chapter, the transactions demand for money was designated as L_t. Since $PO = Y$, we have

$$L_t = kPO = kY$$

If money is demanded only for transaction purposes, the total money supply, or M, is absorbed in L_t, and equilibrium between the supply of and demand for money, $M = L_t$, is given by $M = kY$.

Keynes introduced the speculative demand for money, L_s, to make $M = L_t + L_s$. Since $L_s = l(r)$, we have equilibrium between the supply of and demand for money when $M = kY + l(r)$. A rise in M may now be absorbed in part by speculative demand and in part by transactions demand. To show how an increase in M will be divided between the two demands requires the apparatus that will be developed in Chapter 20. However, we can see here that a rise in M will no longer mean a rise in Y equal to 4 times the rise in M, even though the public always wants to hold in transactions balances an amount equal to $\frac{1}{4}Y$. In Keynesian theory, an increase in M will affect Y only to the extent that the increase in M reduces r and to the extent that the reduction in r raises I (and possibly C). Given a less than perfectly elastic speculative demand function, the increase in M will lead to some fall in r, and, given a less than perfectly inelastic MEC schedule, the fall in r will lead to some rise in I and therefore in Y. But the ratio of the rise in Y to the rise in M may be 0.5, 1.2, 2.9, or any other figure less than 4. In short, changes in Y are no longer determinable from changes in M alone, as is true when transactions demand is the only demand for money.

Although Keynes treated the transactions (and precautionary) demand as interest-inelastic, we saw that this demand actually becomes interest-elastic at sufficiently high interest rates. Although Keynes made the speculative demand for money a function of the interest rate only, there are conditions under which this demand may also become a function of the level of income. If the transactions and precautionary and speculative demands all depend to some extent on both the level of income and the rate of interest, the separate demand functions for L_t and L_s may be combined into one and written as

$$L = f(Y, r)$$

This consolidated demand function avoids the artificiality of separating the demand for money into the three parts set forth by Keynes. People obviously do not divide their money holdings into three or more neat compartments to satisfy each of the three or more motives for holding cash. Statistically, for the economy as a whole, there is no way of separating the total money supply into active and idle balances without relying on very arbitrary assumptions. The consolidated equation, though general, has the advantage of showing that the demand for money for all purposes is a function of income level and interest rate.

Post-Keynesian developments in monetary theory emphasize another determinant of demand that was not explicitly allowed for by either the classical economists or Keynes—namely, the public's wealth. The amount of money the public chooses to hold will vary not only directly with income and inversely with the interest rate but also directly with the public's wealth. The greater the public's wealth, the greater will tend to be the amount of money the public wishes to hold, other things being equal. The argument is that wealth-holders will distribute any increase in wealth over the various forms in which wealth may be held, and one of these forms is, of course, money. With wealth included, our final equation for the demand for money becomes

$$L = f(Y, r, W)$$

in which W represents the economy's wealth. This equation explicitly mentions the three variables that are most important in the determination of the demand for money.[24]

It is not altogether correct to say that the recognition of wealth as a factor in the demand for money is a post-Keynesian development. Marshall and other economists in the classical tradition recognized wealth in this connection but did not pursue the point.[25] Keynes also recognized wealth as an influencing factor in the demand for money, but he felt it was a factor he could ignore in the short-run analysis in his *General Theory*. In the short run, the stock of capital, or more broadly the economy's real wealth, may be taken as given. Not being a variable, it could be excluded, he thought, as a factor explaining changes in the demand for money in an analysis limited to the short run.

Although Keynes's omission of wealth from the theory of the demand for money according to at least one critic "led him into analytical errors of far-reaching significance," [26] we will use in Chapter 19 the simpler Keynesian theory of the demand for money developed in the present chapter. We will, in other words, assume that the demand for money depends on only Y and r and that we can separate this total demand into two parts as in the earlier equation

[24] While there is quite general agreement that the variables that enter the demand function for money are to be selected from these three, there is little agreement as to whether the so-called "scale" variable is wealth, income, or some combination of both and whether the relevant interest rate is a short-term or long-term rate. For a statement of the nature of these and related problems in the specification of the demand function, see A. H. Meltzer, "The Demand for Money: The Evidence from the Time Series," in *Journal of Political Economy*, June 1963, pp. 219 22.

[25] Note the last phrase in the following sentence from Alfred Marshall, *op. cit.*, p. 44: "Let us suppose that the inhabitants of a country . . . find it just worth their while to keep by them on the average ready purchasing power to the extent of a tenth part of their annual income, together with a fiftieth part of their property."

[26] H. G. Johnson, *op. cit.*, p. 9.

$L = kY + l(r)$. Wealth as a factor in the demand for money will be ignored.

With this as our theory of the demand for money and with the liquidity-preference theory of the rate of interest that is derived from it, we can now proceed to combine the theory of money and interest developed in this chapter with the theory of income determination developed in earlier chapters. This will provide us with a general equilibrium model of income, output, money, and interest.

CHAPTER 19

INCOME, OUTPUT,
MONEY, AND INTEREST

In previous chapters we developed separately the theory of income determination and the theory of money and interest. Although this procedure provided an orderly introduction to the relevant theory, it must now be recognized for the simplification that it is—the two parts are actually so related that what happens in one depends on what happens in the other. In the theory of income determination developed in earlier chapters, we found that a rise in investment spending would raise the equilibrium level of income by an amount equal to the multiplier times the rise in investment spending. However, we implicitly assumed that the interest rate was given. If we now admit the interest rate as a variable in the system, the rise in investment spending will, by raising the level of income, also force up the rate of interest. This in turn will discourage investment, and the actual rise in the equilibrium level of income will be less than it would otherwise be. Similarly, in developing the theory of money and interest in Chapter 18, we saw that an increase in the money supply would reduce the interest rate, as shown by the movement down the given demand curve for money. However, this curve assumed a given level of income. If we now admit the income level as a variable in the system, the increase in the money supply will, by lowering the interest rate, stimulate investment spending and raise the level of income. This will increase the transactions demand for money, and the actual fall in the rate of interest will be less than it would otherwise be. Thus, it would seem that the rate of interest and the level of income are tied together in a rather complicated manner. In this chapter we will construct a general equilibrium model of the economy that can accommodate this and other complications.

THE GOODS MARKET AND THE MONEY MARKET

Our general model consists of two parts: The first draws together the determinants of equilibrium in the market for goods, and the second draws together the determinants of equilibrium in the market for money. Goods-market equilibrium is defined by an equality between saving and investment—the condition that gave us the equilibrium level of income. At the level of income at which $S = I$ (in a simple two-sector economy), the leakage from the income stream into saving is exactly matched by offsetting investment spending, or at this income level aggregate demand for goods just equals the aggregate supply of goods. There is, accordingly, goods-market equilibrium at this level of income. Money-market equilibrium is defined by an equality between the supply of and the demand for money—the condition that gave us the equilibrium rate of interest. At the rate of interest at which $M = L$, there is money-market equilibrium.[1]

The particular level of income at which $S = I$ depends in part on conditions in the market for money, and the particular interest rate at which $L = M$ depends in part on conditions in the market for goods. For a preliminary look at what is involved, let us review briefly the simplest possible Keynesian model as shown in Figure 19–1A. Given the S and I_1 curves, the equilibrium level of income is Y_1, at which level the supply of and demand for goods are equal. If investment depends at all on the interest rate, the I_1 curve must have been drawn on the assumption of some particular interest rate. A lower interest rate, *ceteris paribus*, would indicate a different position for the curve, say I_2 instead of I_1. This in turn would indicate a different equilibrium income level, Y_2 instead of Y_1. Part A of the figure, however, does not tell us what the rate of interest may be—it assumes some rate and proceeds from there.

Part B shows the determination of the equilibrium rate of interest. Given the M and L_1 curves, the equilibrium rate is r_1, at which rate the demand for and the supply of money are equal, or $L_{t_1} + L_{s_1} = L_1 = M$. But, since the demand for money is composed in part of the transactions demand, which depends on the level of income, the L_1 curve must have been drawn on the basis of some assumed income level that defined L_{t_1}. A higher income level,

[1] A complete general equilibrium model will also include a third market—namely, the market for factors of production, which, because of the short-run assumption of a fixed capital stock, becomes the market for labor. Equilibrium in this market requires equality between the supply of and the demand for labor. From a Keynesian viewpoint, disequilibrium in this market in the form of an excess supply of labor—that is, unemployment—can be corrected by policies designed to raise the level of output—that is, to shift the equilibrium in the goods market to a higher level of goods output whose production in turn calls for employment of more labor. From a classical viewpoint, the same disequilibrium would be removed automatically by falling wages and prices in a system characterized by such flexibility. Following the development of the basic model, which is limited to the goods and money markets, some attention will be given to these other questions in the last two sections of this chapter.

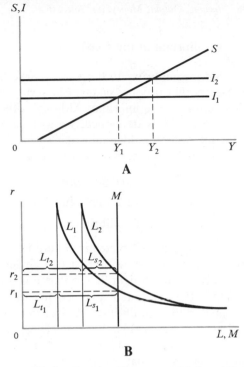

FIGURE 19–1 Equilibrium Levels of Income and Interest Rate

ceteris paribus, would indicate a different position for the curve, say L_2 instead of L_1. This would indicate a different equilibrium rate of interest at which $L_{t_2} + L_{s_2} = L_2 = M$. Part B, however, does not tell us what the level of income may be—it assumes some income level and proceeds from there.

It appears that we cannot determine the equilibrium income level without first knowing the interest rate and that we cannot determine the equilibrium interest rate without first knowing the income level. Somehow Y and r must be determined simultaneously. Although this cannot be done through Figure 19–1, there are nonetheless a particular income level and an interest rate that simultaneously provide equilibrium in the goods market behind Part A and in the money market behind Part B. The model to be developed in this chapter provides this simultaneous solution of the two equilibrium values and sheds light on some other important problems and policy questions.[2]

[2] This model was originally developed by J. R. Hicks in his article "Mr. Keynes and the 'Classics': A Suggested Interpretation," in *Econometrica*, April 1937, pp. 147–59, reprinted in W. Fellner and B. F. Haley, eds., *Readings in the Theory of Income Distribution*, Irwin, 1946, pp. 461–76. See also F. Modigliani, "Liquidity Preference and the Theory of Interest and Money," in F. A. Lutz and L. W. Mints, eds., *Readings in Monetary Theory*, Irwin, 1951, particularly pp. 190–206. For a detailed algebraic development of the basic model and extensions thereof, see W. L. Smith and R. L. Teigen, eds., *Readings in Money, National Income, and Stabilization Policy*, Irwin, 1965, pp. 1–29.

Equilibrium in the Goods Market

Since equilibrium in the goods market requires the equality of S and I, all the factors that produce changes in saving and investment influence the determination of this equilibrium. Although other factors may be introduced once the basic model is developed, we assume here that investment is a function of the interest rate alone and that saving is a function of income alone.[3] We then have three equations to cover the goods market.

Saving function: $S = S(Y)$

Investment function: $I = I(r)$

Equilibrium condition: $S(Y) = I(r)$

This system is depicted in Figure 19–2. Part A gives the MEI (investment demand) schedule, showing that investment spending varies inversely with the interest rate. The straight line in Part B is drawn at a 45° angle from the origin. Whatever the amount of planned investment measured along the horizontal axis of Part B, equilibrium requires that planned saving measured along the vertical axis of Part B be the same. Thus, all points along the 45° line in Part B indicate the equality of saving and investment. Part C brings in the saving function, showing that saving varies directly with income.

The *IS* curve in Part D is derived from the other parts of the figure. To illustrate, let us assume an interest rate of 3 percent in Part A, indicating that investment is $20 per time period.[4] In Part B, to satisfy the equality between S and I, saving must also be $20, as shown on the vertical axis. In Part C, we find that saving will be $20 only at an income level of $120.[5] Finally, bringing together Y of $120 from Part C and r of 3 percent from Part A, we have one combination of Y and r at which $S = I$, or at which there is equilibrium in the goods market. If we assume the lower interest rate of 2.5 percent, Part A indicates that investment will be $30, which gives us an income level of $140 in Part C. Therefore, Y of $140 and r of 2.5 percent is another combination of Y and r at which $S = I$. Other combinations could be found in the same way by starting with other assumed interest rates and finding the income level at which saving is equal to the amount of investment indicated by that interest rate. Connecting these combinations gives us the *IS* curve in Part D.

We find that there is no longer a single level of income at which $S = I$ but a different level for each different rate of interest. The lower the rate of interest, the higher is the level of income at which $S = I$. Viewed in one way, this follows from the fact that a high r means a low I, and a low I, through the multiplier, means a low Y. Viewed in another way, this follows from the fact that a low Y means a low S. Since equilibrium requires that $S = I$, a low S means a low I, and a low I is the result of a high r. Although the *IS* function indicates that equilibrium in the goods market will be found at a lower level

---

[3] All functions are stated in real terms or constant dollars.
[4] All dollar amounts are in billions.
[5] The saving function $S = S_a + sY$ is here $S = -40 + \frac{1}{2}Y$.

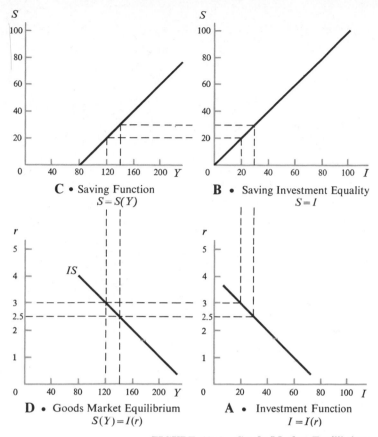

FIGURE 19–2   Goods-Market Equilibrium

of income for a higher rate of interest, it alone does not tell us what particular combination of Y and r will be found in any specific time period. All combinations on the IS function are equally possible equilibrium combinations of Y and r in the goods market.

Equilibrium in the Money Market

Equilibrium in the money market requires an equality between the supply of and the demand for money. The Keynesian theory of the demand for money makes the transactions demand for money (which includes precautionary demand) a direct function of the income level alone and the speculative demand for money an inverse function of the interest rate alone. This gives us three equations to cover the money market.

Transactions demand for money: $L_t = kY$

Speculative demand for money: $L_s = l(r)$

Equilibrium condition: $L_t + L_s = L = M$

The money supply, M, is determined independently by the monetary authority.

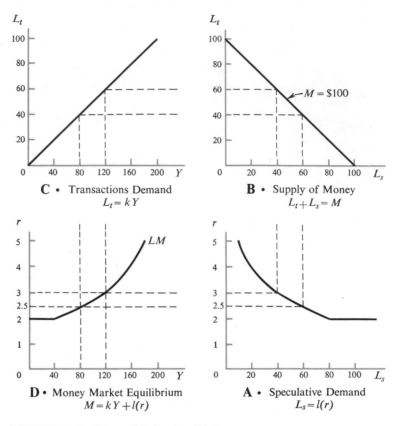

FIGURE 19–3   Money-Market Equilibrium

This system is depicted in Figure 19–3. Part A shows the speculative demand for money as a function of r. Part B is drawn to show a total money supply of $100, all of which must be held in either transactions balances or speculative balances. The points along the line indicate all the possible ways in which the given money supply may be divided between L_t and L_s. Part C shows the amount of money required for transactions purposes at each level of income on the assumption that $k = 1/2$. The LM curve of Part D is derived from the other parts as follows.

Assume in Part A an interest rate of 3 percent; at this interest rate the public will want to hold $40 in speculative balances. In Part B, subtracting the $40 of speculative balances from a total money supply of $100 leaves $60 of transactions balances, an amount consistent with an income level of $120 as shown in Part C. Finally, in Part D, bringing together Y of $120 from Part C and r of 3 percent from Part A, we have one combination of Y and r at which $L = M$, or at which there is equilibrium in the market for money. If we assume the lower rate of 2.5 percent, Part A indicates that speculative balances will be $60; Part B indicates that transactions balances will be $40; and Part C indicates the income level of $80 as that consistent with transactions balances of $40. This gives us another combination of Y and r—$80 and 2.5

398

percent—at which $L = M$. When other such combinations determined in this way are connected, the function in Part D labeled LM results.

Although particular characteristics of the LM function will call for attention later, in general it is seen that the function slopes upward to the right. With a given stock of money, money-market equilibrium is found at combinations of high interest rates and high income levels or low interest rates and low income levels. Viewed in one way, this can be seen to follow from the fact that a high level of income calls for relatively large transactions balances, which, with a given money supply, can be drawn out of speculative balances only by pushing up the interest rate. Viewed in another way, it can be seen to follow from the fact that a high interest rate is one at which speculative balances will be low; this releases more of the money supply for transactions balances that will be held in such balances only at a correspondingly high level of income. Although the LM function indicates in this fashion why equilibrium in the money market will occur at a higher interest rate for a higher level of income, it alone cannot tell us what particular combination of Y and r will be found in any given time period. All combinations on the LM function are equally possible equilibrium combinations in the money market.

GENERAL EQUILIBRIUM—THE GOODS AND MONEY MARKETS

Equilibrium between S and I is possible at various combinations of Y and r; similarly, equilibrium between L and M is possible at various combinations of Y and r. However, there is only one combination of Y and r at which both $S = I$ and $L = M$. This combination is defined by the intersection of the IS and LM functions, derived in Figures 19–2 and 19–3 and brought together in Figure 19–4. In this illustration, general equilibrium occurs with $Y = \$120$ and $r = 3$ percent. Every other combination of Y and r is a disequilibrium combination. Suppose that Y was $80 and r was 4 percent. With this Y, r combination, $S = I$ but $M > L$. After meeting the transactions demand that accompanies Y of $80, the balance of the money supply (which is necessarily held in speculative balances) is greater than the amount people want to hold at a 4 percent interest rate. (This amount would be held only at r of 2.5 percent.) The excess money then flows into the securities market, bids up security prices, and forces down the interest rate. The fall in the interest rate stimulates investment spending and moves the $S = I$ equilibrium down the IS curve to a combination of lower r and higher Y. This movement continues to the intersection at which $IS = LM$ and at which the rise in Y has so increased transactions demand and the fall in r has so increased speculative demand that $L = M$. An opposite disequilibrium in which again $S = I$ but now $L > M$— for example at $Y = \$160$ and $r = 2$ percent—would be corrected in a similar way.

These disequilibria were between L and M; S and I were in equilibrium

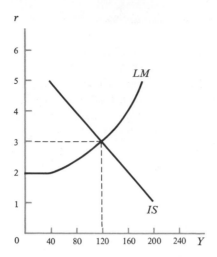

FIGURE 19–4   General Equilibrium in the Goods and Money Markets

throughout. Consider now a disequilibrium between S and I such as that at $Y = \$160$ and $r = 4$ percent. Here $L = M$ but $S > I$. The excess of S over I indicates a deficiency of demand, and Y falls. The fall in Y reduces the public's needs for transactions balances, and the funds so released spill over into speculative balances, thus reducing r. The $L = M$ equilibrium moves down the LM curve to a combination of lower r and lower Y. A falling r increases investment, and a falling Y decreases saving. Both of these changes help eliminate the excess of S over I. This movement continues to the intersection at which $IS = LM$. The fall in r has been that fall necessary to increase I, and the fall in Y has been that fall necessary to decrease S, by the amounts needed to produce equality between S and I at the Y, r combination at which $IS = LM$. An opposite disequilibrium in which $L = M$ but $I > S$, at Y of $\$80$ and r of 2.5 percent, for example, would be corrected in a similar way.

There are, of course, an infinite number of other disequilibrium positions at which S is greater than or less than I and L is greater than or less than M. A verbal description of the process by which disequilibria in both the goods market and the money market are simultaneously corrected is awkward. Suffice it to say that, assuming there are no shifts in any of the schedules underlying the IS and LM functions, the adjustment process will restore equilibrium at the intersection of the given IS and LM functions.

CHANGES IN GENERAL EQUILIBRIUM

The general equilibrium combination of Y and r identified by the intersection of the IS and LM functions will, of course, change in response to any shift in the IS or LM functions. Shifts in the IS function are caused by shifts in the investment function or the saving function (Figure 19–2A and C); shifts in the LM curve are caused by shifts in the money supply or transactions demand or speculative demand functions (Parts B, C, and A, respectively, of Figure 19–3). Finally, a shift in any of the functions on which the *IS* and *LM* curves are based may result from a change in any of the factors that determine the positions of these functions. We thus have a method of analysis by which we can trace the effects of a change in any of these many underlying factors through the system to its final effect on the income level and interest rate—assuming, of course, that all other factors remain unchanged.

An Increase in Investment

Suppose that innovations shift the investment demand schedule to the right, in the manner described in Chapter 12, so at each rate of interest the investment demand schedule now lies $20 to the right of the schedule shown in Figure 19–2. In terms of Figure 19–2, we find that the *IS* function has as a result shifted rightward by $40 at each rate of interest. With an increase in investment of $20, income must rise $40 to induce an increase in saving of $20 with an MPS of 1/2. This is nothing more than the simple multiplier, $\Delta Y = \Delta I/MPS$, which in the present case gives us $40 = $20/½. The original and the new *IS* functions are shown in Figure 19–5 as IS_1 and IS_2; they are combined with the original *LM* function derived in Figure 19–3.

The original equilibrium was at *Y* of $120 and *r* of 3 percent; the new equilibrium that results from the shift in the investment demand schedule is at *Y* of $140 and *r* of 3.5 percent. If the interest rate had not risen at all, income would have risen by $40, or from $120 to $160, as would be expected with the multiplier of 2. But we do not get the rise in income of 2 × $20. Instead, an increase in investment spending raises the income level, which in turn raises the interest rate, and this feeds back to make the increase in investment spending less than the $20 and the increase in income less than the $40 they

FIGURE 19–5 **Effect on General Equilibrium of an Increase in Investment**

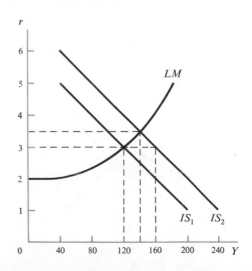

would have been with no rise in the interest rate. Thus, the actual rise in invest-ment is $10, which, with a multiplier of 2, gives us an increase in income of $20. In this fashion, the income-expansionary effect of an increase in aggregate demand is dampened by the rise in the interest rate brought about by an ex-pansion of income. As we shall later see, the extent of this dampening effect depends to some extent on how great the rise in the interest rate is, and the rise in the interest rate itself depends on the elasticity of the *LM* function.

An Increase in the Money Supply

Next take the case of a $20 increase in the money supply, which shifts the *M* curve in Figure 19–3B to the right by $20. With no change in the speculative demand function of Part A and no change in the transactions demand function of Part C, the increase in *M* of $20 will shift the *LM* function rightward by $40 at each rate of interest. Equilibrium between *L* and *M* requires a rise in *Y* sufficient to absorb the $20 increase in *M* in transactions balances, L_t. Since $L_t = kY$, we have $Y = L_t/k$ and $\Delta Y = \Delta L_t/k$. With k given as 1/2, ΔY must be $40 to produce a new equilibrium between *L* and *M* at each rate of interest. The original and the new *LM* functions, shown as LM_1 and LM_2 in Figure 19–6, are combined with the original *IS* function derived in Figure 19–2.

The original equilibrium was at *Y* of $120 and *r* of 3 percent; the new equilibrium that results from the increase in the money supply is at *Y* of approximately $140 and *r* of 2.5 percent. Although the increase in *M* of $20 will shift the *LM* curve $40 to the right at each rate of interest, it will not raise the equilibrium level of income by $40 because, with no shift in the *IS* curve, a rise in the equilibrium level of income can occur only if there is a fall in *r*. The new equilibrium is one in which approximately $10 of the increase in *M* is absorbed in speculative balances as *r* falls to about 2.5 percent. This is

FIGURE 19–6   Effect on General Equilibrium of an Increase in the Money Supply

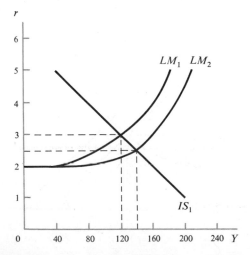

just the fall in *r* that is necessary to increase *I* by $10 and, through the multiplier, raise *Y* by $20, which absorbs the other $10 of the $20 increase of *M* in transactions balances.

Although the rise in the equilibrium level of income is less than $40, as long as there is no change other than the purely monetary one of an increase in the money supply, we still find that there is an increase in the level of real income. In short, monetary policy appears capable of influencing the economy's level of output. As will be explained below, the effect on the income level of an increase in the money supply depends on (1) how great the fall in the interest rate is, which in turn depends on the elasticity of the speculative demand function, and (2) how much investment spending rises as a result of any given drop in the interest rate, which in turn depends on the interest-elasticity of the investment demand function. If the interest rate falls with a rise in the money supply and if investment spending rises with a fall in the interest rate, some rise in the income level will result.

A Simultaneous Increase in Investment and the Money Supply

Now suppose that the two changes we have discussed separately occur simultaneously, so that the shift in the investment demand function moves the *IS* curve from IS_1 to IS_2, and the rise in the money supply moves the *LM* curve from LM_1 to LM_2, as shown in Figure 19–7. The result is a shift in the equilibrium position from *Y* of $120 and *r* of 3 percent to *Y* of $160 and *r* of 3 percent. A rise in investment spending, with no change in the money supply, produces a rise in income, but a rise that is dampened by the rise in the interest rate resulting from the income rise. If the money supply increases by just the amount necessary to prevent the rise in the interest rate that would otherwise

FIGURE 19–7   Effect on General Equilibrium of a Simultaneous Increase in Investment and the Money Supply

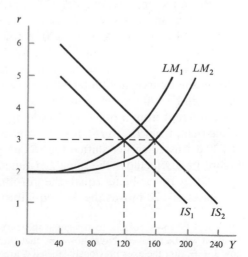

result from the rise in income, the full income-expansionary effect of the rise in investment will be realized. The increase in Y from \$120 to \$160, with an increase in investment of \$20 billion and a MPC of $1/2$, is just the result we found in the simple Keynesian model in Chapter 8. Now we see that this result will be realized only if an appropriately expansionary monetary policy, here an increase in M of \$20, is pursued to prevent what otherwise would be a rise in the rate of interest and so a smaller rise in the income level.

The effects of shifts in other functions may be traced in the same way. For example, an increase in "thrift," which appears as an upward shift in the saving function (Figure 19–2C), will shift the IS curve to the left and lower r and Y. An increase in the demand for money to be held in idle balances, which appears as a shift to the right in the speculative demand function (Figure 19–3A), will shift the LM curve to the left, raise r, and lower Y. A change in payments practices that makes it possible for each dollar of money to handle a larger volume of transactions per time period reduces k and appears as a less steeply inclined transactions demand function (Figure 19–3C). This will shift the LM curve to the right, lower r, and raise Y.

GOVERNMENT SPENDING, TAXATION, AND GENERAL EQUILIBRIUM

In now adding government spending and taxation to the general equilibrium model, the equilibrium condition $S = I$ in the goods market for a two-sector economy becomes $S + T = I + G$ for a three-sector economy. This simply means that the aggregate supply of and demand for goods will be equal when the sum of the diversions, $S + T$, from the real income stream is just matched by the sum of compensating injections, $I + G$, into the real income stream. The equilibrium condition in the money market is $L = M$ as before.

As in the first fiscal model of Chapter 14, government purchases of goods and services and net tax receipts are assumed to be independent of the level of income. Figure 19–8A shows \$20 of government purchases added to the same investment demand schedule in Figure 19–2. Since these purchases are also regarded as independent of the interest rate, the $I + G$ curve lies \$20 to the right of the I curve at all interest rates. Whatever the interest rate, the sum of I and G will be \$20 greater than I alone. In terms of its effect on Y, a dollar of G is no different from a dollar of I. Adding \$20 of G thus shifts the IS curve \$40 to the right, from IS_1 to IS_2, for the same reason that the increase in investment of \$20 discussed earlier shifted the IS curve to the right by \$40 in Figure 19–5.[6] Figure 19–8D includes the same LM function derived in Figure 19–3.

Other things being equal, the introduction of deficit-financed government purchases of \$20 moves the Y, r equilibrium from \$120 and 3 percent to \$140

---

[6] It would be more correct to designate the curve as *IG-ST* instead of *IS*, but the simpler notation will be retained. Note, however, that the axes in Parts A–C previously labeled *I* are now $I + G$, and the axes previously labeled *S* are now $S + T$.

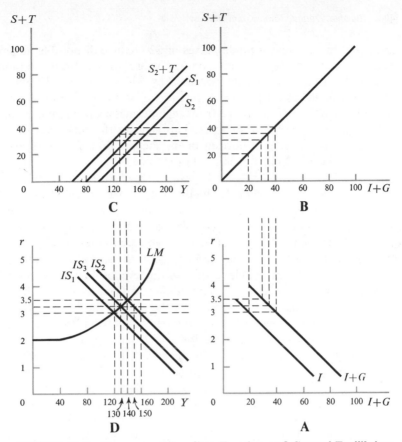

FIGURE 19–8   Government Spending, Taxation, and General Equilibrium

and 3.5 percent. Again the result shown is the same as that in Figure 19–5 for a $20 shift in the investment demand schedule. What otherwise would be an expansion in Y of $40, as indicated by the simple multiplier of 2, becomes the lesser expansion of $20 due to the effect of the rise in r that accompanies the rise in Y. Note, however, that there is this difference. G of $20 is unaffected by the rise in r it causes, but the rise in r reduces I by $10, which makes the net change in $I + G$ only $10 and the rise in income only $20. The full income-expansionary effect of G is not realized, because the resulting rise in r chokes off $10 of private investment spending. Thus, *a fiscal policy that is designed to raise the income level through a deficit-financed expansion of government spending may not produce the maximum possible rise of income unless that expansion in government spending is accompanied by an appropriately expansionary monetary policy.*[7]

Let us now suppose that there is a balanced budget and that the government collects taxes of $20 to match its spending of $20, thus avoiding deficit

---

[7] Because the government spending in this example is entirely deficit financed, we are concerned with the method of deficit financing employed. If entirely financed by the sale of government securities to the public, there will be no increase in the money supply; the results are as described above. If financed by the appropriate "mix" of sales to the public and to the banking system, there will be an increase in the money supply that permits the full $40 potential expansion in Y.

spending. In the present model, taxes of $20 reduce disposable income by $20. With the MPS of 1/2, the reduction in saving is one-half of this amount. Thus, at each level of Y, T of $20 reduces S by $10 and C by $10, which appears in Figure 19–8C as a downward shift of $10 in the saving function, or a shift from S_1 to S_2. To the leakage from income made up of saving must now be added the leakage of $20 for taxes. This gives us the curve $S_2 + T$, the sum of saving and taxes, or that portion of the income flow that does not appear as consumption spending at each level of income.[8]

I of Part A and S_1 of Part C gave us IS_1 of Part D; $I + G$ of Part A with T of zero gave us IS_2 of Part D; finally, $I + G$ of Part A with $S_2 + T$ of Part C gives us IS_3 of Part D. The new equilibrium position indicated by the intersection of IS_3 and LM in Part D is found at Y of $130 and r of 3.25 percent. In our illustration, adding G of $20 and an equal amount of T raises the equilibrium level of Y by one-half the increase in the size of the budget.[9]

With G and T both independent of the level of Y, we have a model similar to the one that gave us the unit multiplier in Chapter 14. In that model, the rise in Y was equal to the increase in the size of the budget. However, since the interest rate is now part of the model, we find that the actual multiplier is less than the balanced-budget multiplier of 1 that appears in the simpler model. An expansion in the size of the budget, with the budget balanced, will raise the income level, but the rise in income, which would otherwise be equal to the expansion in the size of the budget, will be dampened by the tendency for the interest rate to rise with the rise in income. In other words, *a fiscal policy designed to produce a rise in income while maintaining a balanced budget will produce the maximum possible income increase only if it is accompanied by an expansionary monetary policy that prevents what otherwise might be a rise in the interest rate and a consequent reduction in private investment spending.*

We have seen that a rise in the income level may be expected from an expansion in G with no change in T and even from an expansion in G that is matched by T. The third possibility, of course, is a reduction in T with no reduction in G, an example of which is the 1964 federal tax cut; Figure 19–8 may be used to illustrate a much-discussed aspect of this. Suppose the original equilibrium is that defined by the intersection of IS_3 and LM at Y of $130 and r of 3.25 percent; this is the equilibrium consistent with $I + G$ of Figure 19–8A and $S_2 + T$ of Figure 19–8C. With no change in G but a tax cut of $20, the $I + G$ curve remains as is, and the $S_2 + T$ curve shifts downward to S_1. This, in turn, causes the IS curve to shift from IS_3 to IS_2. But the full expansionary effect of the tax cut—a rise in Y from $130 to $150—is not realized because

[8] For example, with Y of $140 and T of zero, Y_d, or $Y - T$, would be $140; C would be $110, or $40 + \frac{1}{2}($140 - 0)$; and S would be $30, or $-$40 + \frac{1}{2}($140 - 0)$, the last figure as shown on the S_1 curve of Figure 19–8C at Y of $140. The imposition of T of $20 reduces Y_d to $120 when Y is $140. This reduces C to $100, or $40 + \frac{1}{2}($140 - $20)$, and S to $20, or $-$40 + \frac{1}{2}($140 - $20)$, the latter figure as shown on the S_2 curve at Y of $140. Finally, adding T of $20 makes total diversions from income $40 at Y of $140, as shown on the $S_2 + T$ curve.

[9] The original budget was one in which both G and T were zero.

the rate of interest rises. Hence, in judging the prospective effectiveness of the 1964 tax cut, one consideration was whether the increase in aggregate demand that would follow therefrom would be smaller than otherwise obtainable due to adverse monetary effects. In the President's words, "It would be self-defeating to cancel the stimulus of tax reduction by tightening money. Monetary and debt policy should be directed toward maintaining interest rates and credit conditions that encourage private investment." [10] The model in Figure 19–8 is far too simple to come to grips with the questions involved, but it suggests, in very general terms, that what is called for is an increase in the money supply sufficient to shift the *LM* curve to the right by the amount necessary to secure the greater rise in income—from $130 to $150—that will follow from the increase in aggregate demand to be expected at a stable interest rate.

Although we will not go beyond the simple model in which both *G* and *T* are assumed to be independent of *Y*, it should be noted that the *IS-LM* analysis of Figure 19–8 may be elaborated by introducing more realistic fiscal assumptions. In Part C, for example, *T* may be treated as a function of *Y*, and the effects of this more realistic fiscal assumption on the *Y*, *r* equilibrium combination may readily be traced. This model will show how the potential income-expansionary effect of, say, a rise in investment spending may be restrained by both a rise in the interest rate and a rise in tax receipts as income expands. Though it adds something to the simpler model of this section, like any other model of this kind it will again bring out the principal conclusion emphasized here: An increase in aggregate demand, whether the result of a shift in the investment function or the consumption function or of a change in government spending or taxation, will not produce the effect on income suggested by the crude multipliers in earlier chapters. When we recognize the role played by money and interest, we see how an otherwise greater expansion of income suggested by crude multipliers may be prevented by the rise in the interest rate that may accompany a rise in income.

THE *IS* AND *LM* ELASTICITIES
AND MONETARY-FISCAL POLICIES

So far we have intentionally avoided specific reference to the elasticities of the *IS* and *LM* functions so that we might concentrate on the general characteristics of the model and the general conclusions it suggests. In now taking account of the elasticities of these functions, we will find that some of these conclusions must be qualified and that some must even be abandoned in the extreme cases of perfectly elastic or inelastic functions. For example, it is possible, as we shall see in a moment, that an expansionary fiscal policy will raise only the interest rate and leave the income level unchanged or that it will raise only the income level and leave the interest rate unchanged. It is also possible that an expansion-

[10] *Economic Report of the President*, Jan. 1964 p. 11.

ary monetary policy will lower only the interest rate and leave the income level unchanged or that it will change neither the interest rate nor the level of income.

Elasticity of the *IS* and *LM* Functions

With a fixed money supply, the *LM* function as derived in Figure 19–3 slopes upward to the right. However, at one extreme the function may be expected to become perfectly elastic, and at the other extreme it may be expected to become perfectly inelastic, with a range of varying elasticities in between. In general, the higher the interest rate, the less elastic the corresponding point on the *LM* function will be. These three ranges are laid off in Figure 19–9, in which the perfectly elastic section is "the Keynesian range," the perfectly inelastic section is "the classical range," and the section between is "the intermediate range."

Why this particular shape with perfect elasticity at one extreme and perfect inelasticity at the other? Recall that at some very low rate of interest the speculative demand for money may become perfectly elastic, the result of a consensus by wealth-holders that the interest rate will fall no lower and that security prices will rise no higher. Wealth-holders accordingly stand ready to exchange securities for cash at existing security prices, which produces the liquidity trap on the speculative demand function. Here, on the *LM* function, it produces what is known as the Keynesian range. Recall that, at the other extreme, at some very high rate of interest, the speculative demand for money may become perfectly inelastic, the result of a consensus by wealth-holders that the interest rate will rise no higher and that security prices will fall no lower. At this or any higher rate, wealth-holders accordingly prefer to hold only securities and no idle cash. This perfectly inelastic section of the speculative demand function becomes what is known as the classical range on the *LM* function.

Why are the three sections into which the *LM* function has been divided labeled in this fashion? Recall that, in our simplified version of classical theory,

FIGURE 19–9   Elasticity of the *LM* Function

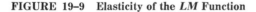
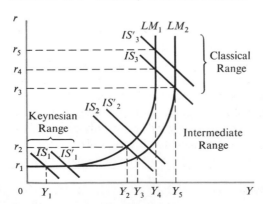

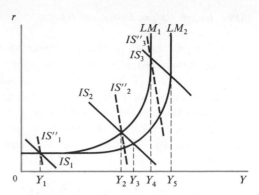

FIGURE 19–10   Elasticity of the IS Function

money is demanded only for transaction purposes. Thus, in Figure 19–3, classical theory assumes that the speculative demand for money is zero at each rate of interest. In effect, Part A of that figure vanishes. If the total money supply given in Part B is $100, that $100 will be held in transactions balances, or $M = L_t$ and $L_s = 0$. With k given in Part C as $1/2$, the LM curve of Part D becomes a perfectly vertical line at the income level of $200. If the public holds money only for transactions purposes and if it holds money balances equal to one-half of a period's income, money market equilibrium is found at an income level of $200 at all rates of interest.

With the exception of the perfectly inelastic section, or the so-called classical range, it would not be altogether incorrect to call the remainder of the *LM* function the Keynesian range. However, because of Keynes's emphasis on the ineffectiveness of monetary policy, the liquidity trap section alone has come to be identified as the Keynesian range. Within this range, monetary policy is completely ineffective; therefore, this range most closely fits Keynes's emphasis.

The *IS* function as derived in Figure 19–2 slopes downward to the right. Its elasticity depends on the responsiveness of investment spending to changes in the rate of interest and on the magnitude of the multiplier. If the investment demand schedule is perfectly inelastic, indicating that investment spending is completely insensitive to the interest rate, the *IS* curve derived in Part D will be perfectly inelastic, regardless of the magnitude of the multiplier. If, on the other hand, the investment demand schedule shows some elasticity, as seems to be the case, the *IS* curve will be more elastic the lower the MPS. The lower the MPS, the higher will be the multiplier and so the greater will be the change in income for any increase in investment resulting from a fall in the rate of interest. Figure 19–10 shows three pairs of *IS* curves, each made up of one highly inelastic and one elastic *IS* curve.

Monetary and Fiscal Policy

Monetary policy is the exercise of the central bank's control over the money supply as an instrument for achieving the objectives of general economic policy. Fiscal policy is the exercise of the government's control over public spending and tax collections as instruments for the same purpose. We will confine ourselves here to the single policy objective of raising the level of real income. The *IS-LM* framework then provides a basis for comparing the effect of the two types of policy on the income level and the interest rate and for comparing the conditions under which each type of policy will be effective or ineffective in producing the change in income that is the policy objective. For this purpose, the discussion is conveniently divided into three parts, each corresponding to a range of the *LM* function in Figure 19–9.

The Keynesian Range.   Consider first the Y_1, r_1 equilibrium in the Keynesian range. An increase in the money supply shifts the *LM* curve to the right, from LM_1 to LM_2, and means that *for each possible level of income M = L* only at a lower interest rate; the rate must fall by the amount necessary to make the public willing to hold larger idle cash balances. But this is not true in the "liquidity trap." Here the interest rate is already at what is for the time being an irreducible minimum. As the monetary authority purchases securities, security-holders are willing to exchange them for cash at the existing prices of securities. Therefore, expansion of the money supply cannot cause the interest rate to fall below the rate given by the trap. All that happens is that the public holds more in speculative balances and less in securities. Further increases in the money supply would be expected to shift the *LM* curve still farther to the right, but the lower end of the curve will remain anchored in the same liquidity trap. If the economy is already in the trap, it follows that monetary policy is powerless to raise the income level, since it cannot reduce the interest rate any further and thereby produce a movement down the IS_1 curve to a higher equilibrium income level. The belief that the economy was in the trap during the early thirties led Keynes to his then unorthodox fiscal policy prescriptions. Since government cannot raise the income level through monetary policy, whatever government is to do through monetary-fiscal policy it must then do through fiscal policy. If a rise in income cannot be achieved by producing a movement down the IS_1 curve through monetary expansion, a rise in income can be achieved by producing a shift in the IS_1 curve itself, say from IS_1 to IS'_1. Fiscal measures such as increased government spending or reduced taxes that could shift the *IS* curve became the order of the day.

It should be noted that, to the extent that monetary policy operates by raising investment spending through a reduction in the cost of money, the impasse of monetary policy for an economy caught in the trap means that the elasticity or inelasticity of the *IS* function is no longer relevant. In Figure 19–10, for example, it does not matter whether the *IS* function is the elastic IS_1 or the inelastic IS''_1.[11]

The liquidity trap is an extreme case that could occur only during a deep depression, if even then. A prosperous economy and a liquidity trap do not go hand in hand. Since the pure Keynesian range is the range of the liquidity trap, one can now appreciate what Professor Hicks meant by his observation,

---

[11] As we will see, the elasticity of the *IS* function does become relevant elsewhere, but not in the Keynesian range.

made shortly after the appearance of Keynes's book, that "the General Theory of Employment is the Economics of Depression." [12]

The Classical Range. Next let us examine the Y_4, r_4 equilibrium defined by the intersection of IS_3 and LM_1 in Figure 19–9. There is some increase in the money supply that will shift the LM_1 curve to LM_2. In contrast to the result in the Keynesian range, the result is now an increase in the income level from Y_4 to Y_5 and a fall in the interest rate from r_4 to r_3. In the classical range, the interest rate is so high that speculative balances are zero; money is held for transaction purposes only. If the monetary authority under these circumstances enters the market to purchase securities, security-holders can be induced to exchange securities for cash only at higher security prices. As security prices are bid up and the interest rate pushed down, investment is stimulated (and, in classical theory, saving is discouraged). Since nobody chooses to hold idle cash, expansion of the money supply will produce a new equilibrium only by reducing the interest rate by whatever amount is necessary to increase the income level sufficiently to absorb the full increase in the money supply in transactions balances. If in the present case we assume that $\Delta M = \$20$ and $k = 1/2$, equilibrium will be restored only when Y has risen by $\$40$, or, in general, when $\Delta Y = \Delta M / k$. In the classical range, the result follows the simple classical quantity theory of money as a theory of aggregate demand. Y rises proportionately with the increase in M. If $V = 2$ or $k = 1/2$, the rise in Y must be twice the rise in M in order to satisfy the equilibrium condition: $MV = Y$ or $M = kY$.

In contrast to the Keynesian range, in which monetary policy is completely ineffective, monetary policy appears to be completely effective in the classical range. No part of any increase in the money supply disappears into idle cash balances. The increase in the money supply means increased spending that produces that rise in the income level at which the total increase in the money supply is absorbed into transactions balances. Still assuming that all income changes are real changes, we find that the increase in the money supply that shifts LM_1 to LM_2 causes an increase from Y_4 to Y_5 in output as well as in income.

Again in contrast to the Keynesian range, in which fiscal policy alone can be effective, fiscal policy in the classical range is completely ineffective. An upward shift in the IS function from IS_3 to IS'_3 in Figure 19–9 can raise only the interest rate, from r_4 to r_5; the income level stays unchanged at Y_4. Given the increase in demand that lies behind the upward shift in the IS function, there will be a rise in the rate of interest sufficient to choke off enough demand to leave aggregate demand unchanged. Thus, if the rise in demand resulted from increased government spending, the rise in the interest rate will choke off an amount of private spending equal to the rise in government spending. The level of income is as high as the given money supply can support. In the classical range, an increase in income is thus impossible without an increase in the money

[12] J. R. Hicks, *op. cit.*, p. 472.

supply, and monetary policy becomes an all-powerful method of controlling the income level.

How does the elasticity of the *IS* function affect the equilibrium positions in the classical range? Let us compare the elastic IS_3 function and the inelastic IS''_3 function shown in Figure 19–10. Here we see that with the IS''_3 function no increase in the money supply and no reduction in the interest rate is capable of raising the income level from Y_4 to Y_5. Monetary policy will raise Y but not by the multiple of M given by $1/k$. Although this seems to upset the result suggested by classical theory, classical theorists would deny that the *IS* curve could be so inelastic. Recall that in both classical and Keynesian theory investment is a function of the interest rate, but in classical theory saving also is a function of the interest rate. Thus, it can be shown that only if both saving and investment are quite insensitive to the interest rate could there be an inelastic curve of the sort described by IS''_3 in Figure 19–10.[13] As long as one or the other is elastic, the resulting *IS* function will also be elastic, and with an elastic *IS* function the result of a change in the money supply is $\Delta Y = \Delta M/k$.

The Intermediate Range.   Finally, let us examine the equilibrium of Y_2, r_2, as defined by the intersection of IS_2 and LM_1 in Figure 19–9. Here again we see that there is some increase in the money supply that will shift the LM_1 function to LM_2. In the Keynesian range, this increase in M left both Y and r unchanged because the total increase in money supply was absorbed in speculative balances at the existing interest rate, which defines the liquidity trap. In the classical range, this increase in M raised Y by the amount necessary to absorb the full increase of M in transactions balances. This worked itself out through that reduction in the interest rate that raised spending by the amount needed to produce the required rise in income. In the intermediate range, however, the increase in M is absorbed partially in speculative balances and partially in transactions balances. The level of income rises but by an amount less than that which would require the full increase in M for transactions purposes.

To illustrate, let us suppose that ΔM is \$20 and k is $1/2$. The resultant shift in the *LM* function is \$40, but in this case the rise in income ($Y_3 - Y_2$) is only half that amount. In reducing the interest rate by the amount that produces the increase in spending needed to raise the income level by \$20, \$10 (one-half of the increase in the money supply) is absorbed in speculative balances. The remaining \$10 is just the additional amount of money needed for transactions purposes with the income level up by \$20.

Thus, in the intermediate range, monetary policy is found to have a degree of effectiveness but not the complete effectiveness it has in the classical range. In general, the closer the equilibrium intersection is to the classical range, the

---

[13] In terms of Figure 19–2C, we may show saving as a function of both Y and r by drawing in a similar fashion successively higher saving functions to correspond with successively higher interest rates. An inelastic investment function in Part A combined with this income-elastic and interest-elastic saving function in Part C will still produce an elastic *IS* function in Part D.

more effective monetary policy becomes, and the closer the intersection is to the Keynesian range, the less effective it becomes.

Within this range fiscal policy is also effective to some extent. Fiscal measures that shift the IS function from IS_2 to IS'_2, for example, will raise the level of income and the rate of interest to the new equilibrium defined by the intersection of IS'_2 and LM_1. If the shift in the IS function is the result of a deficit-financed increase in government spending, the interest rate must rise. We are assuming a fixed money supply described by LM_1, so the increased government spending is being financed by borrowing from the public. The sale of additional securities by the government depresses security prices, raises the interest rate, and chokes off some amount of private spending. The rise in the interest rate following any given increase in government spending will be greater the higher in the intermediate range the equilibrium happens to be. Conversely, it will be smaller the lower in the intermediate range the equilibrium happens to be. Although fiscal policy is found to have a degree of effectiveness anywhere in the intermediate range, in general it will be more effective the closer equilibrium is to the Keynesian range and less effective the closer equilibrium is to the classical range.

Although both monetary and fiscal policies have varying degrees of effectiveness in the intermediate range, the relative effectiveness of each depends in large part on the elasticity of the IS function. If the IS function is the inelastic IS''_2 in Figure 19–10, monetary policy can do very little to raise the level of income, even in the intermediate range; fiscal policy alone is effective in such a situation. Furthermore, an expansionary fiscal policy need not be concerned with adverse monetary effects in this case. A shift in an inelastic IS function will raise the interest rate, but the rise in the rate of interest will have little feedback on the amount of spending. Keynes maintained that the investment demand schedule (as well as the saving schedule) was interest-inelastic. If this is the case, the IS schedule must also be inelastic, and fiscal policy, which is completely effective in the Keynesian range, would be almost as effective in the intermediate range. If the IS schedule is indeed interest-inelastic, then the Keynesian range becomes, in effect, the complete LM curve, more applicable at the lower end than at the upper end but with some applicability throughout.

THE *IS* AND *LM* FUNCTIONS AND WAGE-PRICE FLEXIBILITY

The preceding analysis suggests that either fiscal or monetary policy or both may be employed in varying circumstances to shift the IS and LM functions to the right and raise the level of real income and output. In Chapter 16 we saw that the level of employment may be expressed as a function of the level of output and that there is accordingly some level of output that is sufficient to provide full employment for the labor force. If appropriate monetary and fiscal policies can raise output to this level, it may then be said that such policies are capable of providing the economy with full employment. But these policies, of course, refer to deliberate, planned actions taken by government to produce this result—actions justified by the apparent failure of automatic forces to accomplish the same objective. What about the argument of classical theory that an economy with flexible wages and prices automatically tends to be self-equilibrating at the full-employment income level? The preceding analysis in this chapter assumed that wages and prices were rigid and thus bypassed this question. In this section we assume instead that wages and prices are flexible, so that we can investigate what difference this assumption makes to the conclusions reached earlier in this chapter.

First, recall that the essence of the automatic full-employment mechanism of classical theory is that a cut in the money wage rate and the resultant reduction in costs will, under competitive conditions, lead to a fall in the price level, which, with no change in aggregate demand, will increase the amount of goods sold and raise production and employment. Accordingly, some appropriate cut in money wages and in prices will raise the level of real income to the level consistent with full employment of the labor force. Recall also that Keynes's basic objection to this part of classical theory was, in brief, that aggregate demand would fall proportionately with the fall in the money wage rate, leaving actual output and employment unchanged, while producing a lower price level for output and a lower money wage rate for labor. Keynes did recognize, however, that the classical corrective could be effective under certain circumstances that we were not prepared earlier to investigate. The analytical apparatus provided by the *IS* and *LM* functions may now be used to explain this and other aspects of the wage-price flexibility argument.

Wage-Price Flexibility and the Interest-Rate Effect

We have seen that the intersection of the *IS* and *LM* functions determines the equilibrium real income or output and the interest rate. An increase in real income can only occur when either the *IS* or the *LM* function shifts so as to produce a new equilibrium to the right of the previous one. Now let us assume that the original equilibrium level is Y_1, as defined by the intersection of IS_1 and LM_1 in Figure 19–11, and that there is some level of real income consistent with full employment, say at Y_f. Therefore, actual income of Y_1 falls short of full-employment income by the amount $Y_f - Y_1$. Unemployment leads to wage cuts, and wage cuts lead to falling prices. Assume a once-and-for-all decline in the money wage that leads to a proportional decline in the price level. In a simple two-sector economy, the deflation itself (with neither further decline nor rise in the price level expected by businessmen or by consumers) will leave real investment and real consumption expenditures unchanged. Although the prices of the goods that businessmen sell are now lower, the prices they pay for labor, capital goods, raw materials, and the like are lower to the same degree. Since the new lower wage and price levels are expected to continue unchanged, the schedules of the MEC and MEI are unaffected. At each possible rate of interest,

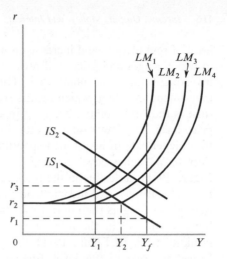

FIGURE 19–11   Wage-Price Flexibility and the Interest-Rate Effect

real investment spending is what it would have been before the deflation. In such a situation, we cannot expect the deflation to produce a shift to the right in the *IS* function through investment. Similarly, if consumption depends only on real income, the deflation will not shift the saving function downward or the *IS* function to the right, since the matching decline in wages and prices will mean a lower level of money income but an unchanged level of real income. For an economy with government and foreign trade, however, the *IS* function may shift as a result of deflation, as we shall see later. For a consumption function that makes real consumption depend on more than just the level of real income, the *IS* function may also shift as a result of deflation. We will ignore these complicating factors for the moment, however, to simplify our analysis. Thus, on the assumptions given, deflation leaves the investment and consumption functions unchanged and, accordingly, leaves the *IS* function unchanged.

What about the *LM* function? The wage-price deflation means that smaller transactions balances are now required at each level of real income. At the lower price level, the excess transactions balances spill over into speculative balances, bid up the prices of securities, and push down the interest rate at each possible level of real income. This amounts to a shift to the right in the *LM* function with each drop in the price level.[14] In Figure 19–11, the successive shifts in the *LM* function from LM_1 to LM_4 correspond to successively lower price levels. Each level of real income on the *Y* axis is associated with a lower interest rate up to the minimum interest rate set by the liquidity trap.

Thus, given a system of flexible wages and prices, deflation may raise the

[14] In Figure 19–3C, for example, the L_t function shows the relationship between transactions balances and money income on the assumption that $k = 1/2$. If the price level were to fall by 50 percent, instead of, for example, L_t of $60 for *Y* of $120, L_t would be reduced to $30. Only half as much money is needed to handle the transactions represented by a given real income when the prices at which these transactions take place are reduced by 50 percent. A new function could be drawn into Part C, and from it a new *LM* function could be derived (in Part D) that would lie to the right of the old *LM* function.

415

level of real income and increase employment, even though the deflation is one in which wages and prices fall proportionately, and leave the consumption and investment functions unaffected. This rise in income follows from a rise in investment spending, which results from the drop in the interest rate, which in turn is the result of the decrease in required transactions balances at a lower price level. The lower interest rate moves us down a given investment function to a higher rate of investment spending; this moves us down the given *IS* function to a higher level of real income at a lower interest rate. Thus, in Figure 19–11, a decline in the price level that shifts the *LM* function from LM_1 to LM_4 will raise real income from Y_1 to Y_2 by reducing the interest rate from r_3 to r_2. As long as the interest rate falls, real income rises. But there may be a limit to the fall in the interest rate at some positive rate established by the liquidity trap. In Figure 19–11 this limit is reached at r_2. Once deflation has forced the rate to this level, further deflation will continue to release money from transactions balances, but this money will be absorbed in speculative balances without further reducing the interest rate. As depicted in the illustration, no amount of deflation is able to raise the real income level to Y_f, which was defined above as that consistent with full employment.

As has been emphasized before, the Keynesian liquidity trap represents an extreme case. For a less extreme case, let us suppose that real income is somewhat below that which provides full employment and that the interest rate is well above the minimum rate that identifies the liquidity trap. An important question then arises: Is a policy of wage cuts the policy best designed to achieve a rise in real income? If we accept Keynes's position that whatever favorable income effect follows from wage cuts comes through the effect of deflation on the interest rate, then to achieve a reduction in the interest rate through the painful process of wage and price cuts is, as Professor Hansen once put it, "patently absurd." As we have seen, the shift in the *LM* function necessary to reduce the interest rate may be brought about much more simply through an expansion of the money supply. This can be done by the central bank without any direct interference with the wage and price structure. Working toward the same objective through wage and price cuts is to do it the "hard way." It was for this reason that Keynes identified wage cuts as "monetary management by the Trade Unions, aimed at full employment."[15]

Leaving monetary management to the banking system also avoids many difficult problems that arise in achieving the goal of a lower interest rate through wage and price reductions. In the first place, one must consider all the institutional barriers that stand in the way of a fall in wages and prices. One must also consider all the economic inequities and distress that inevitably result from wage and price cuts. For all wages and prices do not fall at the same rate; some groups benefit and others suffer as income is redistributed in the course of the deflation. Businesses that are saddled with heavy fixed debt may be unable to weather the storm; bankruptcies are bound to result. Most important of all, contrary to our simplifying assumption of a once-and-for-all cut in wages and

[15] John Maynard Keynes, *General Theory of Employment, Interest, and Money*, Harcourt, Brace & World, 1936, p. 267.

prices that would give rise to no expectations of further cuts, in practice one wage cut and one price cut often give rise to expectations of further cuts, and such "bearish" expectations will lead to a postponement of some investment and consumption (durable goods) expenditures. In this fashion, the favorable effect on income of the rise in spending that accompanies the fall in the interest rate could easily be swamped by the unfavorable effect on income of the fall in spending that results from expectations of further declines in wages and prices. For these and other reasons, most economists agree that if deflation affects income and employment through its effect on the interest rate, an expansionary monetary policy is assuredly to be preferred to deflation as the means of achieving the goal of a lower interest rate and higher income and employment levels.

Wage-Price Flexibility and the Pigou Effect

The argument that deflation raises the income level through a reduction in the interest rate is sometimes referred to as the Keynes Effect. As we saw, however, if the limit to the reduction in the rate of interest set by the liquidity trap is reached before real income can be raised to the full-employment level, wage and price flexibility working through the Keynes Effect is repudiated as a means of achieving full employment. An interesting attempt to counter the Keynesian argument and rehabilitate the classical theory's conclusion of automatic full employment through wage-price flexibility is found in the Pigou Effect, or the Real-Balance Effect, first advanced by Professor A. C. Pigou in the early forties and since then the source of a sizable literature.[16]

How does the Pigou Effect work? Suppose that investment falls off so that income and employment drop as in the ordinary Keynesian model. Unemployment causes money wages to fall, which means lower costs and lower prices. The prices of assets such as goods, buildings, land, and common-stock shares may be expected to fall as other prices do so that there will be no change in their real value. However, the fall in the price level means a rise in the real value of assets that are fixed in dollar terms, such as money, savings deposits, bonds, and mortgages. This increase in the real value of fixed-dollar assets makes the holders less anxious to build up further their asset holdings. They devote a smaller fraction of their current income to saving and a larger fraction to consumption, which amounts to a downward shift in the saving function or an upward shift in the consumption function. In terms of Figure 19-11, this appears as a shift to the right in the *IS* function. Thus, according to this argument, there is some decline in the price level that will raise the real value of a given stock of fixed-dollar assets sufficiently to shift the saving function

---

[16] A. C. Pigou, "The Classical Stationary State," in *Economic Journal*, Dec. 1943, pp. 345–51, and "Economic Progress in a Stable Environment," in *Economica*, Aug. 1947, pp. 180–88, reprinted in *Readings in Monetary Theory*, pp. 241–51, and D. Patinkin, "Price Flexibility and Full Employment," in *American Economic Review*, Sept. 1948, pp. 543–64, also reprinted in *Readings in Monetary Theory*, pp. 252–83. See also D. Patinkin, *Money, Interest, and Prices*, 2nd ed., Harper & Row, 1965, and B. P. Pesek and T. R. Saving, *Money, Wealth, and Economic Theory*, Macmillan, 1967.

downward by the amount necessary to shift the *IS* function to the position that produces that equilibrium level of real income consistent with full employment.

We mentioned the Pigou Effect in our discussion in Chapter 10 of factors influencing consumption expenditures. In terms of the consumption function, the Pigou Effect makes consumption depend not only on the level of real income (and other factors) but also on the real value of consumers' holdings of fixed-dollar assets. If wages and prices fall proportionately, as Keynes argued they do, real income remains unchanged and so, to the extent that consumption depends on real income, consumption remains unchanged. But if consumption also depends on the real value of consumer holdings of fixed-dollar assets, we may expect a higher average propensity to consume at each level of real income as a result of deflation. This means an upward shift in the consumption function and this in turn means a rightward shift of the *IS* function.[17] In terms of Figure 19–11, if we start with the *IS* function at IS_1, the argument is that there is some amount of deflation sufficient to raise the consumption function by the amount necessary to shift the *IS* function to IS_2. Given LM_4, this raises the level of real income from Y_2 to Y_f, or to full employment. We saw just above that, in terms of the Keynesian model, the income level of Y_f could not be attained through wage and price deflation. But that model did not allow for the Pigou Effect. If it is included, wage and price flexibility appear to convert the Keynesian model into one with equilibrium only at the full-employment income level.

To the extent that the Pigou Effect can raise the income level in this way, it may be said that Pigou met Keynes on the latter's own ground and there, at least in terms of pure theory, won a "triumph" for classical theory by showing that even the Keynesian model, if flexible wages and prices are incorporated, gives us the automatic full-employment conclusion of classical theory. This seems to invalidate the fundamental conclusion of the Keynesian model—namely, the possibility of underemployment equilibrium. But economists in general concede no such victory to Pigou and classical theory. They raise a number of criticisms of the Pigou Effect and of the attempt to rehabilitate classical theory through its use.

A first criticism is that the Pigovian argument cannot apply, in the simple form given above, to all fixed-dollar assets. Although the real value of all such assets held by a creditor increases as the price level falls, the real value of the corresponding debtor's obligations also increases. Conceivably the rise in the creditor's average propensity to consume could be just offset by the fall in the debtor's average propensity to consume, leaving the APC of the system as a whole unchanged. The Pigovian reply to this attack is to limit the argument to fixed-dollar obligations issued by the government, on the reasonable assumption that this debtor's expenditures will not be affected one way or the other by changes in the real burden of its debt resulting from changes in the price

---

[17] An upward shift in the consumption function is, of course, the same as a downward shift in the saving function. In Figure 19–2, a downward shift in the saving function of Part C with no shift in the investment function of Part A may be seen to shift the *IS* function of Part D upward or to the right.

level. In other words, deflation increases the real value of government debt holdings, the sum of currency and interest-bearing government securities, and thus stimulates consumption spending by those who hold these assets, without at the same time being offset by any decrease in spending by government. The net effect, as argued by Pigou, is an increase in aggregate spending.

But this assumes that the greater the real value of consumer holdings of fixed-dollar assets becomes, the greater consumption expenditures will be at any level of real income. The effect of consumer holdings of assets, both fixed-dollar and other, on consumption was discussed in Chapter 10, but no firm conclusion was reached. Despite this, let us give the benefit of the doubt to the Pigovian side and agree that a deflation-created rise in the real value of consumer holdings of currency and government securities will increase consumption spending at any given level of real income. The crucial question then becomes how great the rise in consumer spending will be for any given decrease in the price level. In the face of a certain amount of unemployment, it is one thing if a 10 percent decline in the price level and the accompanying increase in the real value of the stock of currency and government securities is sufficient to raise consumption spending by the amount needed to restore full employment; it is quite another if the Pigou Effect is so weak that the same result can only be achieved with an 80 percent decline in the price level. If a major deflation is required, this in itself effectively rules out reliance on the Pigou Effect as a practical means of restoring an economy to full employment.[18] A hyperdeflation may satisfy the purely theoretical requirements of the Pigou Effect, but in practice it might also produce economic distress leading to riots and even revolution.

If anything more than a minor deflation is required for the Pigou Effect to do its work—and this seems to be the case—we have the final and decisive objection to the Pigovian theory: its neglect of the role played by expectations. This is the same objection we noted earlier in discussing deflation as a means of reducing the interest rate. The instantaneous once-and-for-all deflation needed to give credibility to the Pigou Effect simply cannot be obtained in practice. Wages and prices cannot be substantially deflated without creating expectations of further deflation. An initial fall in wages and prices will often generate pessimistic forecasts and cause businessmen and consumers to reduce their expenditures. This being the case, the Pigovian argument appears impractical as an approach to the solution of the unemployment problem. In fact, Professor Pigou himself described certain aspects of his argument as "academic exercises, of some slight use for clarifying thought, but with very little chance of ever being posed on the chequer board of actual life." [19]

---

[18] Empirical testing to date has given mixed results. That the Pigou Effect is too weak to have any practical significance is suggested by T. Mayer's study, "The Empirical Significance of the Real Balance Effect," in *Quarterly Journal of Economics*, May 1959, pp. 275–91. A study that indicates a Pigou Effect of considerable strength is Ta-Chung Liu, "An Exploratory Quarterly Econometric Model of Effective Demand in the Postwar U.S. Economy," in *Econometrica*, July 1963, pp. 310–48, and especially pp. 331–32. See also D. Patinkin's discussion of some other investigations in *Money, Interest, and Prices, op. cit.*, pp. 651–64.

[19] *Readings in Monetary Theory*, p. 251.

Wage-Price Flexibility and Other Effects

The Keynes (interest-rate) Effect and the Pigou (real-balance) Effect have received the most attention in discussions of wage-price flexibility as a cure for unemployment, but there are several other effects that deserve mention.

Income-Redistribution Effects. Wage and price deflation involves some redistribution of real income in favor of fixed income groups. For any level of real income, the share of the total that goes to wage and profit recipients will decrease, and the share going to recipients of interest, rents, and pensions will increase. Some fixed income flows such as interest payments may go predominantly to upper-income groups, and others such as pensions may go predominantly to lower-income groups, but not much is really known about the income distribution of these total flows. To the extent that redistribution is in favor of lower-income groups, some rise in the consumption function is to be expected and therefore so is some shift to the right in the *IS* function. But the extent of this effect depends in turn on whether there is a sizable difference between upper- and lower-income groups in the marginal propensity to consume. Recall from our discussion in Chapter 10 of income distribution as a factor influencing consumption spending that the difference between the MPC at different levels of family income is not substantial. Since we cannot be sure whether redistribution is in favor of lower- or upper-income groups, and since the difference in the MPC is not appreciable in the first place, we can do no more than note the existence of fixed incomes as a factor to be considered in appraising the effects of wage-price deflation on consumption spending. However, this factor is probably of no great importance except during a drastic deflation.

Tax and Transfer-Payment Effects. Through its tax effects, wage-price deflation may be expected to have a favorable effect on consumption. With the progressive income tax the mainstay of the revenue system, deflation automatically shifts taxpayers into lower brackets and reduces the fraction of their real income that is paid in income taxes. There is then an increase in real disposable income and an increase in consumption. To some extent this favorable effect is offset by the existence of specific taxes (such as 10¢ per pack of cigarettes) the burden of which increases with deflation. The net effect is favorable, however, in a system whose overall tax structure is progressive. In those government programs that call for purchase of a fixed quantity of goods and services, expenditures on goods and services will tend to decline in line with the fall in price level. However, since transfer payments are at any time fixed in dollar terms, a fall in the price level means a rise in the real income represented by a given dollar flow of transfer payments. Therefore, we may expect an increase in real consumption by the beneficiaries of such payments.

Notice that government could provide the same stimulus to consumption spending with an unchanged price level by reducing taxes and raising transfer payments. The situation is comparable to that discussed earlier in connection with the Keynes Effect. Just as an expansionary monetary policy is an alternative to deflation as a means of reducing the interest rate, so an expansionary fiscal policy of cutting taxes and raising transfer payments is an alternative to deflation as a means of increasing after-tax incomes and thereby raising consumption expenditures. But, referring specifically to the wage-price flexibility argument, if there is deflation, tax and transfer-payment effects must be recognized as another stimulus to aggregate spending.

Foreign-Trade Effects. The final effect to consider is that on a nation's imports and exports. A decline in a nation's prices relative to the level of prices in other nations encourages exports and discourages imports, increasing the net export (or decreasing the net import) component of aggregate demand. In an open economy, aggregate demand is the sum of $C + I + G + (X - M)$, and a rise in $(X - M)$ will shift the IS function to the right, just as a rise in C, I, or G would. Because imports and exports play a much more important role in countries like England than in a country like the United States, the foreign-trade effect is more important there than here, but in an open economy some stimulus to demand and a shift in the IS function may be expected from a decline in its price level relative to the price level in other countries.

In summary, classical theory argued that an economy with flexible wages and prices would be self-equilibrating at the full-employment income level. We have examined this argument in terms of the various effects of wage-price flexibility: the Keynes Effect (or Interest-Rate Effect), the Pigou Effect (or Real-Balance Effect), and the effects of income redistribution, tax and transfer payments, and foreign trade, each of which covers one of a number of ways in which wage-price flexibility can produce changes in the level of real income. Keynes's position that deflation affects the real income level through a shift in the LM function and a reduction in the interest rate amounts to a repudiation of deflation as a sure road to the full-employment level of real income. This follows from the Keynesian liquidity trap, which sets a floor to the possible drop in the interest rate and is reinforced by the belief that the IS function is interest-inelastic. All the other effects operate not through shifts in the LM function but through shifts in the IS function. Income-expanding shifts in the IS function as a result of deflation are limited by no barrier such as the liquidity trap. A sufficient deflation of wages and prices might be capable of doing what classical theory said it would do—restore the economy to full employment—but not in the manner indicated by the crude quantity-theory reasoning examined in Chapter 17. Furthermore, the whole wage-price flexibility argument only holds up if the required deflation occurs without creating widespread expectations of further deflation during its course.

Although one can thus find some theoretical basis for the conclusion that an economy suffering general unemployment may find a cure through flexible wages and prices, it does not necessarily follow that this should be the medicine prescribed. While deflation may possibly bring the patient around, so too may other measures. Fiscal policy has been the most popular of these since the appearance of the *General Theory*. Beyond fiscal policy and, of course, monetary policy lie other measures, which reach an extreme with the outright socialization of investment. Whatever the appropriate policy for any set of circumstances, the classical policy of wage-price flexibility is a policy unlikely ever again to receive serious practical consideration, certainly not after the revolution in economic theory of the past three decades. It is now almost inconceivable that government would stand by passively in the face of deflation

> to test the proposition that if a deflating economy is left alone long enough, it will eventually, via a deflationary wage and price spiral, dig itself deeply enough into the mire to extricate itself. It is a political axiom of the mid-twentieth century that a government that conscientiously pursued this policy would not be around to observe the outcome.[20]

Today it is virtually certain that there will be some, even massive, intervention to check and reverse a rapid deflation that might automatically occur in a sharp and sudden business downturn. Although this would be the public policy pursued, it is important to note here that the *theoretical* support for reliance on the classical solution of flexible wages and prices was not so completely swept away as Keynes and his disciples believed it was in the early days following the appearance of the *General Theory*. This question is still disputed by Keynesian and anti-Keynesian theorists, but it has now become a question of pure theory removed from the province of applied economics. Few economists today, however anti-Keynesian, would prescribe the classical theory's medicine as a cure for general unemployment. However, the reason is, not that it will necessarily fail to effect a cure, but that it is less palatable and, most would agree, less effective than other medicines now available.

A CONCLUDING NOTE

This chapter concludes the analysis we began in Chapter 6. Although various related questions have been discussed along the way, our basic question has been the one posed at the very beginning of Chapter 6: What determines the economy's real income or output of final goods and services in any time period? This, as we have seen, is closely related to the question of what determines the level of employment. The further question of what determines the growth of output over the longer time period in which the supply of labor, quantity of capital, and technology may all change, as opposed to the shorter time period in which they may be treated as constant, will be discussed in Chapters 21 and 22.

Clearly, the answer to the basic question of short-run output determination is not a simple thing that can be packed into a summary formulation that is at

[20] J. P. Lewis and R. C. Turner, *Business Conditions Analysis*, 2nd ed., McGraw-Hill, 1967, p. 288.

once neat, brief, and comprehensive. Because our detailed analysis has repeatedly fallen back on simplifying expedients, any summary formulation necessarily compounds the simplification. Recognizing this serious limitation, let us turn to Figure 19–12, which provides a simplified formulation of the less simplified conceptual apparatus developed step by step over these past chapters.

Since our basic objective is the explanation of output determination, the figure is constructed to focus on output—all arrows point in this direction. We see that the immediate determinants of output are the aggregate supply and demand functions. Output and the price level are simultaneously determined by these functions. Since short-run analysis assumes a fixed capital stock, natural resources, and technology, the supply side is easily handled. These fixed factors define the production function. The money wage rate is determined by the bargains reached between employers and their employees. From the production function and the money wage rate so established, the aggregate supply function is determined. With a fixed production function in the short run, the aggregate supply function shifts upward or downward with any increase or decrease in the negotiated money wage rate.

Once the aggregate supply and demand functions are brought together, output and the price level are determined. Once output is determined, we may retrace our steps to find the employment level. With a given production function, actual employment will be whatever amount the production function shows is that needed to produce the indicated level of output. Backing up one more step, we see that the diagram shows unemployment (which may be zero) as the difference between the number in the labor force and the number employed.

In classical theory, unemployment may be eliminated by a reduction in the money wage rate. This will shift the aggregate supply function downward, which, with an unchanged aggregate demand function, will produce a new equilibrium at a higher output level and at a price level lower but lower less than in proportion to the reduction in the money wage rate. This reduction in the money wage rate relative to the reduction in the price level gives us a reduction in the real wage, which is prerequisite to an increase in output and employment with an unchanged production function. Recall that all these results depend on the classical argument that aggregate demand is independent of the money wage rate and is determined by the money supply (and a constant V or k). In its extreme form, the classical model would thus reduce the rather elaborate structure to the right of the aggregate demand function down to the single entry of money supply. It is also in this extreme version of the classical model that we find monetary policy completely effective. Instead of reducing the money wage rate in order to shift the aggregate supply function downward and thereby raise output and employment, the same result could be effected by an increase in the money supply, which would shift the aggregate demand function upward.

Figure 19–12 has been constructed to fit the Keynesian theory of the aggregate demand function, so we see here that aggregate demand depends on much more than the money supply, as shown by the complete structure

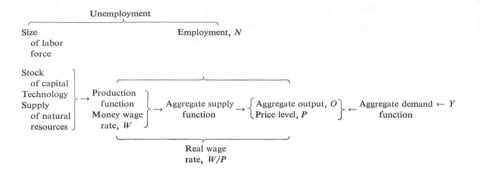

FIGURE 19–12 A Diagrammatic Summary of Income Theory

to the right of the aggregate demand function. Here, as a first step, enter all the direct determinants of the magnitudes of the four components into which aggregate demand is customarily divided. Apart from some rearranging, the long list of determinants includes all those mentioned or discussed at length in Chapters 7 through 15. That the list is still incomplete is acknowledged by the inclusion of "etc." at the appropriate places. The supply of and the demand for money appear in the structure not as direct determinants of aggregate demand but as determinants of the interest rate, which is one factor determining investment demand, which in turn is one component of aggregate demand. The supply of and the demand for money could also be shown as indirect determinants of consumption demand through the interest rate, but the interest rate is generally thought to exercise little influence on consumption.

Even though we limit ourselves only to the determinants specifically listed in the diagram, our list is still a long one. Shifts in the aggregate demand or aggregate supply functions (and so changes in output, the price level, and employment) may result from a rise or fall in the price level in other countries; technological advances; an expectation of rising or falling prices; changes in the distribution of income, propensity to consume, money supply, speculative demand for money, money wage rate, or consumer asset holdings; and many

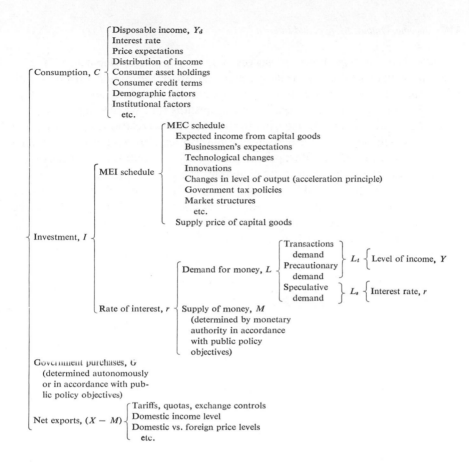

other such developments. To explain how the overall structure holds together, let us trace briefly just one of these possible changes through the system.

Suppose the money supply is increased. Unless the economy is so deep in depression that it is caught in a liquidity trap, there will be some decline in the interest rate. Unless the MEC schedule is perfectly inelastic, there will be some increase in the profit-maximizing capital stock as we move down the MEC schedule, as a result of a fall in the interest rate. Unless the MEI schedule is perfectly inelastic (investment already being at that rate at which the supply curve of capital goods is perfectly inelastic), there will be some rise in the rate of investment spending. Unless there is an offsetting decrease in some other component of aggregate spending, there will be an upward shift in the aggregate demand function. Unless the economy is at the perfectly elastic or perfectly inelastic portion of the aggregate supply function, there will be some rise in output, employment, and the price level. If aggregate supply is at the theoretical extreme of perfect inelasticity, the increase in the money supply will be purely inflationary; only the price level rises, with output and employment unchanged. If aggregate supply is perfectly elastic, only output and employment expand; the increase in the money supply will leave the price level unchanged.

Dozens of other sequences could be traced through this chart in similar fashion. The diagram, however, serves only as a point of departure. It does little more than lay out in neat but artificial order the major variables with which we must deal. It does not begin to show the complex interrelationships that exist among these variables, interrelationships that we also ignored in the verbal description above. If one tried to show these interrelationships in diagram form, he would soon have a bewildering maze of crisscrossing arrows running in all directions, which for most people would be more confusing than clarifying. Furthermore, the relationships are dynamic; the time sequence in which successive changes occur should be shown as well. The present diagram stops far short of all this. Nonetheless, recognizing its limitations, we may still find the diagram helpful at least in tying together the broad dimensions of the theoretical structure developed in Part II of this book.

PART III

CYCLES, GROWTH, AND STABILIZATION

CHAPTER 20

BUSINESS CYCLE THEORY

In Part II of this book we set as our primary task the development of the theory of the determination of aggregate income and output. This theory basically attempts to do no more than explain how investment, saving, and consumption interact to determine the income level and to explain how changes in these variables produce specific changes in income in a simple, comparative-statics framework. A more ambitious theory is one that attempts to analyze the dynamics of income movements, which in a capitalistic economy are seen to pass through alternating periods of expansion and contraction that we call business cycles. A theory capable of doing this goes beyond the theory of income determination—it must somehow answer a whole series of questions that arise specifically from the way the economy behaves during business cycles. Basic among these are questions like the following: Why does the expansion come to an end? Why does not the economy simply level off instead of moving downward into a recession? What determines how far down the economy will go during a slump? Why does the contraction sooner or later end and recovery begin?

Historically viewed, it is difficult to say when systematic study of these and other questions basic to the business cycle began. It certainly did not begin before recognition of the fact that economic activity does actually trace out wavelike movements or before recognition of the equally important fact that these movements are of a self-generating nature. Clement Juglar, one of the great names in the early study of business cycles, in his *Les Crises Commerciales* (published in 1862) may have been the first to put these features of the economy together.[1] The most commonly held view before this time was that of the

[1] See J. A. Schumpeter, *History of Economic Analysis*, Oxford Univ. Press, 1954, pp. 1123–24.

428

economy as a stable mechanism moving along on an even path that was occasionally disturbed by a "crisis." Economists had to progress beyond this kind of view before systematic study of business cycles could be said to have begun.

Wherever we choose to date the beginning of such study, any attempt to provide even the briefest discussion of the important contributions that have been made to business-cycle theory since that time would involve dozens of theorists and is the task of a book itself.[2] If we narrow our sights to the last few decades, most economists would include in their lists of important contributions the work of Schumpeter, Hansen, Metzler, Harrod, Kalecki, Samuelson, Kaldor, Hicks, Goodwin, and Duesenberry.[3] In this one chapter we can do no more than touch on the contributions made by a few of these modern economists. In the four sections that follow, we will be concerned specifically with Schumpeter's innovation theory, Kaldor's model, Samuelson's multiplier-accelerator interaction, and Hicks's model of the cycle.

In none of these analyses will we find it necessary to start completely from scratch. The variability of investment spending plays an important role in all modern business-cycle analyses, and certain theories of investment examined in Chapters 12 and 13 are carried over to this chapter and incorporated with modifications into the business-cycle analyses presented here. In Chapters 12 and 13 our purpose was simply to consider what determines the level of investment spending, with the question approached from the viewpoint of investment spending as one component of aggregate demand. Thus, in Chapter 12 innovation was recognized as one source of the type of investment spending that is classified as autonomous, or not geared to the level of income or to changes in the level of income. We designated autonomous investment as I_a, and in the first theory of investment discussed we assumed that all investment was autonomous. We merely mentioned in Chapter 12 that Schumpeter had built a theory

---

[2] The "classic" among the books of this kind is G. Haberler, *Prosperity and Depression*, Harvard Univ. Press, 1958. See also A. H. Hansen, *Business Cycles and National Income*, Norton, 1964; R. A. Gordon, *Business Fluctuations*, 2nd ed., Harper & Row, 1961; M. W. Lee, *Macroeconomics, Fluctuations, Growth and Stability*, 3rd ed., Irwin, 1963; and S. Bober, *The Economics of Cycles and Growth*, Wiley, 1968.

[3] Only a single work of each of these economists will here be noted: J. A. Schumpeter, *Business Cycles*, McGraw-Hill, 1939; A. H. Hansen, *Business Cycles and National Income*, Norton, 1964; L. A. Metzler, "Nature and Stability of Inventory Cycles," in *Review of Economics and Statistics*, Aug. 1941, pp. 113–29, reprinted in R. A. Gordon and L. R. Klein, eds., *Readings in Business Cycles*, Irwin, 1965, pp. 100–29; R. F. Harrod, *The Trade Cycle*, Clarendon, 1936; M. Kalecki, *Essays in the Theory of Economic Fluctuations*, Allen & Unwin, 1939; P. A. Samuelson, "Interaction Between the Multiplier Analysis and the Principle of Acceleration," in *Review of Economic Statistics*, May 1939, pp. 75–78, reprinted in G. Haberler, ed., *Readings in Business Cycle Theory*, Irwin, 1944, pp. 261–69; N. Kaldor, "A Model of the Trade Cycle," in *Economic Journal*, March 1940, pp. 78–92, reprinted in his *Essays on Economic Stability and Growth*, Free Press, 1960, pp. 177–92; J. R. Hicks, *A Contribution to the Theory of the Trade Cycle*, Oxford Univ. Press, 1940; R. M. Goodwin, "The Nonlinear Accelerator and Persistence of Business Cycles," in *Econometrica*, Jan. 1951, pp. 1–17; and J. S. Duesenberry, *Business Cycles and Economic Growth*, McGraw-Hill, 1958. For further references, see the bibliography in J. J. Clark and M. Cohen, eds., *Business Fluctuations, Growth, and Economic Stabilization*, Random House, 1963, pp. 623–69.

of the business cycle on the way that innovations influence the working of the economy; in this chapter we will look at innovations specifically from the viewpoint of the business cycle.

In the latter part of Chapter 12 we dropped the assumption that all investment was autonomous and examined the theory that the level of investment spending may depend in part on the absolute level of income. In place of $I = I_a$, we had the investment function: $I = I_a + eY$. We retained autonomous investment in the equation but treated it as a constant and focused on induced investment. Again, the purpose in Chapter 12 was to explain the level of investment spending, but the general idea that investment depends on the level of income will, with substantial modification, be found to be a cornerstone of Kaldor's theory of the cycle that we will consider in the second section of this chapter.

In Chapter 13 we introduced the acceleration principle as one of the leading relationships advanced by economists to explain the level of investment spending. There we had the investment equation: $I_t = I_a + w(Y_t - Y_{t-1})$. Samuelson combined the acceleration principle with the multiplier analysis, developed in Chapter 8 of this book, to show that the interaction of the two could trace out cyclical movements in the level of income. Samuelson's interaction is not really a business-cycle model, for it does not go much beyond the mere mechanics of the interaction. His analysis, however, has become a classic in business-cycle literature, for it showed how the interaction, once set into motion, is capable, in and of itself, of generating an endless series of successive expansions and contractions in the income level. Since continuous fluctuations in income are in fact characteristic of a free economy, it is not surprising that students of the business cycle soon thereafter seized on the interaction of the multiplier and accelerator as a factor that helps to explain the business cycle. The basic mechanics of the interaction will be traced in the third section of this chapter.

A number of business-cycle models came to be built on this interaction, but the one that has attracted the most attention is that developed by Hicks. The final section of this chapter will be devoted to a sketch of the major features of the Hicksian model of the business cycle.

SCHUMPETER'S INNOVATION THEORY

While there is no question of the major importance of innovations as an influence on investment spending, it is a far cry from this proposition to the one advanced by Schumpeter, which makes innovations the heart of the business cycle. In his view, the key to the explanation of the cycle is found in the recurrent bursts of innovational investment activity through which capitalistic economies pass.

If innovations do indeed tend to be bunched in time, the corresponding surge of investment expenditures required for their commercial adoption appears to be sufficient to explain why a boom in economic activity should result. This, however, is not only not a basis for a full theory of the cycle but not even acceptable as a basis for a theory of the expansion, or prosperity, phase, unless the argument that innovations do indeed tend to be clustered can be given support. As a first question, we may ask what basis there is for the argument that innovations are discontinuous over time.[4]

In the present context, an innovation is best viewed as the initial application of an invention,[5] and an invention is the discovery of a new process, product, or service by scientists and engineers. The discoveries that constitute inventions may be expected to appear on a more or less continuous basis over time. We do not find and would not expect to find a great burst of inventions over a period of several years and then practically none in the next few years and so forth in regular waves. The output flowing from the work of the scientists and engineers proceeds more evenly than this. The argument that innovations do show marked discontinuities does not then rest on the basis that inventions that are the source of innovations are similarly discontinuous. Rather, the argument rests essentially on what Schumpeter describes as the reluctance of the majority of businessmen to innovate at all under ordinary circumstances. The innovator, who by definition is the first to apply an invention, is also unavoidably the one who takes the risks involved in bringing forth a new and untried good or service or introducing a new process.[6] Despite cost studies, market testing, and all the other preliminary planning that is carried out, the success or failure of an innovation often can be resolved only by actual production and marketing. The majority of firms choose to avoid these risks; they follow a conservative policy and stick to the old and tried process, good, or service. The majority are anything but innovators.

Schumpeter distinguishes sharply between innovators and what may be called imitators. The former, those formally designated as "Entrepreneurs" by Schumpeter, are the leading actors in the whole drama of capitalistic evolution, not just in its business-cycle aspects that concern us here. They make up the small group of pioneering members of the business community who are constantly on the alert for the new and the different. It is they who, when the time seems propitious, proceed from inventions to innovations, trusting to their business acumen that the result will be success and not failure.

Where the entrepreneur is right and the innovation is successful, there is a reward in the form of extraordinary profits. But sooner or later these profits

---

[4] A brief statement on this is found in J. A. Schumpeter, *The Theory of Economic Development*, Harvard Univ. Press, 1934, pp. 228–30.

[5] See also p. 231.

[6] Here and elsewhere, in order to simplify the argument, we depart from Schumpeter's precise set of definitions—for example, that the innovator is not at all a risk-bearer, that being the function of the capitalist. The innovator may also be a capitalist, but he is a risk-bearer only in the latter role. (See *Business Cycles*, p. 104.) Also, Schumpeter's four-phase cycle (prosperity, recession, depression, recovery) is critical in his fully developed theory, but here we will speak loosely of expansion and contraction or upward and downward swings. (*Ibid.*, p. 149.)

will attract a swarm of imitators. The innovator's extraordinary profits may be due in part to an expanding market that results from the innovation itself, but they may also be due in part to a decrease in the market share held by his rivals. For the innovator's rivals, imitation may then become a matter of survival. The industry may accordingly display a flood of investment spending as more and more firms undertake the capital programs required to put their operations into a competitive position with those of the innovator.

We started off here with one innovation and one industry, but any number of other inventions are being applied throughout the economy at the same time. During a preceding downswing, innovations were at a standstill because they did not promise to be profitable, but inventions continued to accumulate. With the passage of time, the commercial possibilities of more and more of these inventions look better and better, until some of those farsighted, venturesome businessmen called innovators decide the prospects are sufficiently promising to take the plunge. With each successful innovator generating his following of imitators and with expanding business activity reinforcing the prospects for success of still other innovations, the economy rises into a period of expansion characterized by a bunching of innovations and the rapid growth in investment spending that accompanies the innovation process.

What brings the expansion to an end? In essence, it is the fact that the process of introducing innovations into the system comes to an end for the time being. The prosperity was fueled by the investment expenditures associated with innovations, but at some point the opportunity for investment in the new fields will begin to decline. For each innovation in the form of a new good, it is just a matter of time until the new factories required to produce the good are constructed. This innovation has then provided the investment expenditures to be expected from it. Thus, investment expenditures in general, whether incurred to produce new goods, reduce costs, open new markets, or develop new sources of supply, will eventually have been made and the desired capital goods acquired. All the innovations that entrepreneurs find worth adopting have now been adopted; the boom ends because the investment expenditures generated by innovations have now slowed to a trickle.

The upswing turns into a downswing as the impact of the maladjustments that were built into the system during the very process of innovational activity make themselves felt. In Schumpeter's words, such activity is "lopsided, discontinuous, disharmonious by nature. . . . the disharmony is inherent in the very *modus operandi* of the factors of progress." [7] The prosperity is then anything but a balanced development, and "depression is nothing more than the economic system's reaction to the boom or the adaptation to the situation into which the boom brings the system." [8]

As the process of innovation is the essence of the boom, the essence of the depression is the process of adjustment to the disturbance of existing structures,

---

[7] *Business Cycles*, p. 102.
[8] *The Theory of Economic Development*, p. 224.

techniques, and established ways of doing things that occurs during the boom. It is a painful process, which may be marked by bankruptcies of firms that failed to adjust to the innovational changes that occurred in their industries and also of firms that did adjust but found that their industries, under the stimulus of innovation, had expanded capacity far beyond the market demand. The process also includes a general deflation of credit and a decline in prices. Innovations during the upswing are financed in part by bank credit expansion, a development that tends to raise prices. This breeds overoptimism and speculation during the upswing. However, the slowdown of innovational activity comes, as was noted, with the completion of the new capital facilities; once these facilities start to pour forth into the market the new goods for whose production they were acquired, innovators secure the funds necessary to pay off bank loans. With this proceeding on a large scale, the downturn carries with it this general deflation of credit and a falling price level.

Following a period of readjustment to the altered economic circumstances brought on by the previous boom, the natural forces of recovery eventually begin to take hold, and at some point the more courageous entrepreneurs once again start to innovate. Others follow, investment spending surges, and a new boom is under way. This brings us back to the point at which we started.

We will not carry the discussion of Schumpeter's theory beyond the few essentials noted here. One economist has said that "The common practice amongst present day writers on business cycle theory is to devote a few respectful sentences to Schumpeter, without endeavoring to relate or compare his views with those of others, and then pass on and forget all about him." [9] This segregation of Schumpeter's theory from that of others is explained in part by the fact that his is so different from others. The difference may be brought out in terms of the distinction economists have long made between exogenous and endogenous theories of the business cycle. The exogenous theories find the root of the cycle in factors or forces *outside* the economic system. Included here are factors like wars, changes in rates of population growth, the weather, and innovations. The endogenous theories find the root of the cycle within the very mechanism of the economic system. These theories hold that the internal workings of the capitalist economy themselves give rise to self-generating cycles— an endless sequence of expansions and contractions. What is of special interest is that Schumpeter took a force that appears to be primarily outside the economic system (and one that is invariably so classified in textbook lists) and built a theory holding that this force produces self-generating cycles. To Schumpeter, the innovational process is thus made into an endogenous force *sui generis*. The contrast with the conventional type of endogenous theory will appear in following sections of this chapter as we examine Kaldor's and Hicks's models, which are clearly of this kind.

[9] R. C. O. Matthews, "Capital Stock Adjustment Theories of the Trade Cycle and the Problem of Policy," in K. K. Kurihara, ed., *Post-Keynesian Economics*, Rutgers Univ. Press, 1954, p. 172.

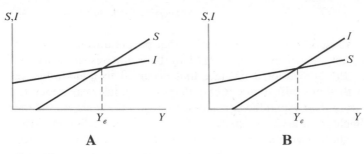

FIGURE 20–1 Stable and Unstable Equilibria

KALDOR'S MODEL OF THE CYCLE

This model of the cycle may be approached as a logical extension of a model of income determination presented in Chapter 12.[10] There we introduced the investment function $I = I_a + eY$. The saving function, as in the first model presented in Chapter 7, was $S = S_a + sY$. Graphically the model appeared as in Figure 20–1A. The equilibrium level of Y is Y_e, the only income level at which planned saving and planned investment are equal. With any given pair of linear saving and investment functions, there is a single equilibrium position, and any disturbance that results in a shift in either the saving or investment function or both would tend to be followed by a movement to a new equilibrium position. However, from the particular viewpoint of the business cycle, this model offers little, as it indicates more stability than the real world seems to show.

In Chapter 12 and now here, we implicitly assume that MPS > MPI, or $s > e$. Graphically, the assumption is that the slope of the saving function is greater than that of the investment function and that the investment function therefore cuts the saving function from above. Actually, the MPI may very well exceed the MPS. In this case, illustrated in Figure 20–1B, there is again a single equilibrium position, but it is now an unstable one. Any disturbance producing a movement above Y_e means that $I > S$ and that the income level would rise without limit, first to full employment and then beyond to hyper-inflation; any disturbance producing a movement below Y_e means that $S > I$ and that the income level would collapse to zero output and employment. In contrast to the case shown in Part A of the figure, the case shown in Part B gives us a greater instability than the real world shows. As an approach to an explanation of the business cycle, both cases are found wanting, one for too much stability and the other for too little.

Kaldor concludes from the preceding analysis that the saving and investment functions cannot both be linear, at least not over the full range of income change that occurs during the business cycle. Furthermore, some good reasons can be advanced to support the argument that neither of the two functions is indeed linear.

[10] See pp. 240–44.

If we think of the cycle as divided into phases of relatively high, relatively low, and "normal" income, we would not expect the MPI to be the same under all three conditions, which is the assumption of the linear investment function. A nonlinear function that appears to conform more closely with the behavior of investment during the course of the cycle is that shown in Figure 20–2A. Here, for both relatively high and relatively low levels of income, the curve is approximately flat—the MPI is approximately zero. The MPI may be expected to approach zero at relatively low income levels, for such income levels are accompanied by conditions of large excess capacity. Due to the presence of excess capacity, the rise in income from its low point will not at first induce investment spending. In other words, there is a range of income over which successive increments to income, ΔY, will be accompanied by small or zero increments to investment, ΔI, or $\Delta I/\Delta Y$ will be very small or zero over this range of Y. In the opposite case of relatively high levels of income, Kaldor argues that the MPI will be similarly small "because rising costs of construction, increasing costs and increasing difficulty of borrowing will dissuade entrepreneurs from expanding still faster—at a time when they already have large commitments." [11]

Similarly, in the case of the saving function we would not expect the MPS to be the same under the varying income conditions specified above. A nonlinear saving function that appears to conform more closely with the behavior of saving during the course of the cycle is shown in Figure 20–2B. At relatively high and relatively low income levels, the situation is the reverse of that shown for investment. Here the MPS is relatively large as compared with its magnitude at "normal" income levels. This may be explained along the following lines. As income falls to relatively low levels in recession, people cut saving drastically in the face of falling income in order to maintain something like their previous standard of living; then, in the early stages of recovery, they increase saving sharply in order to restore the depleted savings to their usual level. The MPS is thus relatively large, and the saving function is correspondingly steep. In the opposite case, at which income rises to relatively high levels, people tend to save not only a larger amount but also a larger proportion of their income.

[11] *Op. cit.*, p. 180.

FIGURE 20–2   Nonlinear Investment and Saving Functions

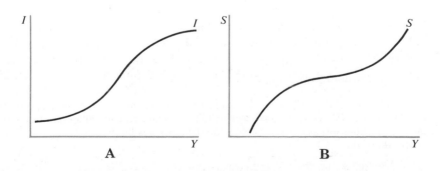

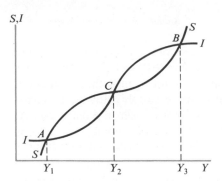

FIGURE 20–3 Multiple Equilibria

This tendency is reinforced by a shift in the distribution of income toward profits and against wages, given the fact that the MPS of profit recipients is higher than that of wage recipients. These forces are reflected in a steepening of the saving function at relatively high income levels in comparison with its slope over the range of "normal" income.

Figure 20–3 is derived by merely combining the nonlinear investment and saving functions of Figure 20–2.[12] This figure shows multiple equilibria, with both A and B as stable positions. At income levels below Y_1 or between Y_2 and Y_3, $I > S$, so the income level rises; at income levels between Y_1 and Y_2 or above Y_3, $S > I$, so the income level falls. C is an unstable position, so the income level Y_2 is not a possible equilibrium level. If Y is between Y_2 and Y_3, it will rise to Y_3; if it is between Y_1 and Y_2, it will fall to Y_1. It appears that the economy can reach stability only at some particular high level of income, Y_3, or at some particular low level of income, Y_1.

What we now have, however, is anything but a model of the business cycle, for the cycle is made up of alternating expansions and cont.actions, and Figure 20–3 simply shows two positions of stable equilibrium. For the answer to this, let us quote Kaldor: "The key to the explanation of the trade cycle is to be found in the fact that each of these two positions is stable only *in the short period:* that as activity continues at either one of these levels, forces gradually accumulate which sooner or later will render that particular position unstable." [13] If it can indeed be shown that the stable equilibrium at A becomes unstable over time and forces a movement to B, and similarly in the opposite case, we will have pushed ahead from what is shown by Figure 20–3 to a model of the business cycle.

Figure 20–3 shows how saving and investment may vary with the level of income over the course of the cycle. The level of income, however, is not the only major force affecting the amount of the economy's saving and investment. Kaldor introduces a second variable that plays a major role in cyclical changes in saving and investment—this is the economy's capital stock. Saving is a direct

[12] We follow Kaldor's model by assuming that the two functions are nonlinear as described by Figure 20–2. However, the analysis that follows would remain valid even if only one of the two functions was as described above and the other was linear.
[13] *Op. cit.*, p. 182.

function of the capital stock: For any level of income, the greater the capital stock, the larger is the amount of saving. Investment is an inverse function of the capital stock: For any level of income, the greater the capital stock, the smaller is the amount of investment. Our next step is to trace out how the changes in the capital stock that occur over time alter the equilibrium situations derived in Figure 20–3.

In Figure 20–4, the Stage I diagram corresponds to Figure 20–3. We start off in this diagram with the assumption that the economy is at the equilibrium position shown as B. This corresponds to a relatively high, or above "normal," income at which investment is correspondingly high. But the higher the rate of investment, the more rapid is the increase in the size of the capital stock. In terms of the analysis of Chapter 11, a growing capital stock means a movement down the MEC curve, which, unless somehow offset, in turn means a downward shift in the MEI curve, which appears here as a downward shift in the I curve. At the same time, the growth in the capital stock, which is a growth in the economy's wealth, will tend to push up the saving curve, S. This is a rise in the average propensity to save induced by an increase in the economy's wealth. As shown by the Stage II diagram, the downward movement of the I curve and the upward movement of the S curve result in a gradual shift to the left in the position of B and a gradual shift to the right in the position of C, so B and C are brought closer to each other. The critical point is reached when these gradual shifts of the I and S curves make the two curves tangential and bring B and C together as in the Stage III diagram. Now, at the position of $B + C$, $S > I$ in both directions, and the equilibrium is unstable in a downward

FIGURE 20–4   The Kaldor Model

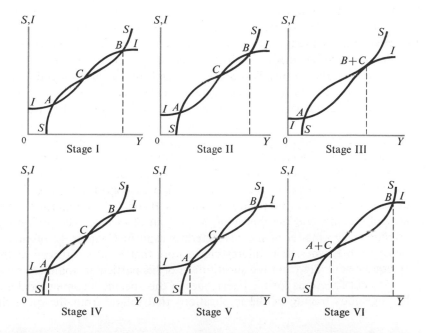

direction. The cyclical contraction, once started, reduces the income level until a new stable equilibrium is reached at the relatively low level that corresponds with A.

Again, A is a stable equilibrium only in the short period. Over time the S and I curves gradually shift; but now, with the system at a relatively low income level, the I curve shifts upward and the S curve shifts downward, as shown by the Stage IV diagram. If the level of investment corresponding to A is less than replacement requirements, some upward shift in the I curve will occur sooner or later for replacement reasons alone. Apart from or in addition to this, over time investment opportunities gradually accumulate. In terms of the analysis of Chapter 11, the MEC curve shifts to the right, pushing up the MEI curve, which here would mean an upward shift in the I curve. At the same time, any decline in the capital stock or in the economy's wealth that occurs during the period of relatively low income will tend to lower the average propensity to save, or push the S curve downward. These shifts cause the position of A to move to the right and that of C to move to the left, thus bringing A and C closer together, as is evident from the Stage IV and Stage V diagrams. Again, the critical point is reached when these gradual shifts of the I and S curves make the two curves tangential and bring A and C together, as in the Stage VI diagram. The $A + C$ position is unstable in an upward direction, since $I > S$ on both sides of the position. The cyclical expansion, once started, raises the income level until a new state of equilibrium is reached at the relatively high level that corresponds with B. The curves then gradually return to the positions shown in the Stage I diagram, from which positions another cycle begins.

The cyclical process described by Kaldor is thus self-generating. The very movement to relatively high income levels brings into play forces that, after a period of time, produce a downward movement to relatively low income levels, and vice versa. These forces, such as the changing size of the average propensity to save and the accumulation and decumulation of capital that occur over the cycle, are inherent in the economic process, or are endogenous forces in the full sense of that term. This stands in contrast to the innovational process, which is the force at the heart of Schumpeter's theory.

Kaldor's theory of the cycle appeared just four years after Keynes's book and is a relatively simple and very neat theory built directly on the saving-investment analysis of the *General Theory*. Although Keynes devoted a chapter of the *General Theory* to "Notes on the Trade Cycle" and offered further discussion of the subject at other points, he did not develop a theory of the cycle as such in the *General Theory*. His book was concerned basically with the development of what he regarded as a new theory of the determination of the *level* of income, and the theory of *fluctuations* of income received only passing attention. The model of income determination in Chapter 12 of this book is taken from Keynes. It is interesting to note that Kaldor's theory of the cycle emerges essentially from the substitution of his particular nonlinear saving and investment functions for the linear ones in this specific income model and from his ingenious tracing of the implications that follow from the quite different saving and investment relationships given by the nonlinear functions. If Keynes had gotten to the point of developing a formal model of the cycle in the *General Theory*, it might well have been one much like that examined in this section.

SAMUELSON'S MULTIPLIER-ACCELERATOR INTERACTION

In Chapter 13 we described the acceleration principle as a relationship in which any time period's net investment, I_t, is made dependent on the value of the accelerator, w, and the change in income between that and the preceding period, $Y_t - Y_{t-1}$.[14] Our interest in Chapter 13 was limited to an explanation of investment spending, and there the acceleration principle was considered solely from this point of view. In the present section we retain the acceleration principle as an explanation of investment spending and combine it with the familiar multiplier analysis. The interaction between the two produces the following general sequence of events.

Assuming initially a change in Y, the investment of any period, I_t, will differ from that of the preceding period, I_{t-1}, as indicated by the acceleration principle. However, a rise or fall in the level of investment will affect the level of Y in succeeding periods in a way determined by the multiplier analysis. But any change in the level of Y from one period to the next must, again via the acceleration principle, affect investment in each following period. Thus, as was shown by Samuelson in the article noted earlier, there is the possibility of an endless sequence of changes in income and output and in consumption and investment as a result of the way in which the multiplier and the acceleration principle interact. In what follows we will trace this interaction in detail through a multiplier-accelerator model.

A Multiplier-Accelerator Model

The accelerator investment function we used in Chapter 13 was $I_t = I_a + w(Y_t - Y_{t-1})$. Although not noted there, this function is but one of a group of possible investment functions incorporating the acceleration principle. Instead of making the accelerator apply to the change in total output, $Y_t - Y_{t-1}$, another function in this group makes the accelerator apply only to the change in the output of consumer goods, $C_t - C_{t-1}$. The resulting function, $I_t = I_a + w(C_t - C_{t-1})$, is used by Samuelson and will be used here.

Still other functions in this group result from employing a lagged form of the acceleration principle instead of the unlagged form used above. Thus, if we assume that the nonautonomous portion of investment spending in any period depends, not on the change in aggregate output between the current and the preceding period, but on the change in aggregate output between the preceding

[14] See pp. 251–54.

period and the period before that, we have as our investment function $I_t = I_a + w(Y_{t-1} - Y_{t-2})$. Or, if we use lagged consumption instead of lagged income, we have $I_t = I_a + w(C_{t-1} - C_{t-2})$. The lagged function appears to be the more plausible. A rise in the current period's spending over the preceding period's spending may indeed call forth business decisions to expand investment, but the actual investment spending cannot occur simultaneously with the appearance of the increase in spending that calls it forth. The lagged function allows for an interval of time between the decision to invest and the actual investment expenditures.

Similarly, in the case of the consumption function, we may work with lagged or unlagged relationships. The consumption function employed in earlier chapters, $C_t = C_a + cY_t$, assumes that consumption of each period depends on that period's autonomous consumption and that period's income level. It assumes that consumers adjust their spending to changes in income as fast as changes in income occur. One alternative to this function is the lagged function $C_t = C_a + cY_{t-1}$, which assumes that consumption in each period depends on that period's autonomous consumption and the preceding period's income level. It allows an interval of time between the receipt of income and the expenditure of that portion the recipient chooses to spend.

There are clearly many other possible investment and consumption functions, each of which is based on different assumptions concerning the timing and the way in which consumption and investment spending are influenced by changes in income and other variables. In what follows, since our immediate purpose is simply to illustrate the interaction between the multiplier and the acceleration principle, we will work with only one of the possible pairs of functions and will use the one that corresponds with that used by Samuelson in his original article:

$$C_t = C_a + cY_{t-1}$$
$$I_t = I_a + w(C_t - C_{t-1})$$

Since income and output of any period equals consumption plus investment demand during that period, or since $Y_t = C_t + I_t$, by substitution we derive the following general equation:[15]

$$Y_t = C_a + cY_{t-1} + I_a + w(C_t - C_{t-1})$$

This equation states that aggregate income and output in any period equals the

---

[15] In what follows we will work with the equation in this form. However, since $C_t = C_a + cY_{t-1}$ and $C_{t-1} = C_a + cY_{t-2}$, we may substitute these expressions for C_t and C_{t-1} in the equation above and write that equation in the alternative form

$$Y_t = C_a + cY_{t-1} + I_a + wcY_{t-1} - wcY_{t-2}$$

or

$$Y_t = C_a + I_a + c(1 + w)Y_{t-1} - wcY_{t-2}$$

Expressed in this way, investment is shown to depend on Y lagged plus the values of c and w instead of on C unlagged plus the value of w.

sum of autonomous consumption, C_a, and autonomous investment, I_a, plus an additional amount of consumption that depends on the marginal propensity to consume, c, times the income of the preceding period, and an additional amount of investment that depends on the capital-output ratio or the accelerator, w, times the change in consumption between the current and the preceding period. In other words, if we know C_a and I_a for any period and C for the current and preceding periods, we can, given the values of c and w, determine the income and output of any period by substituting in the equation for Y given above.

Table 20–1 shows the results that follow over twenty-two successive time periods from substituting in this equation. The column headings of the table are set up to match the order of the components given in the equation for Y. Total consumption for any period is the sum of Columns 2 and 3, total investment for any period is the sum of Columns 4 and 5, and the income for any period as given in Column 6 is therefore the sum of Columns 2 through 5. In this illustration, the MPC is assumed to be 0.6 (Column 3) and the accelerator to be 1.5 (Column 5). Column 8 shows the change in income from the table's first Period, $t - 2$. Note that in the first two periods, $t - 2$ and $t - 1$, the economy is in equilibrium with the level of income and output unchanged at 100.

If we now break into the table in Period t, induced consumption or cY_{t-1} is seen to be the same as in Period $t - 1$, since Y_{t-1} is the same as Y_{t-2} (both are 100). Induced investment in Period t, or $w(C_t - C_{t-1})$, is zero, since $C_t - C_{t-1}$ (or $70 - 70$) is zero.[16] Now suppose that in Period t, I_a rises from 30 to 40 and C_a remains unchanged at 10. How will the rise in I_a in Period t affect the level of income in Period t? Since induced consumption in t depends on income of $t - 1$, which is the same as income of $t - 2$, induced consumption remains at 60 in t as it was in $t - 1$. Since induced investment in t depends on the change in C between t and $t - 1$, which is zero, induced investment also remains unchanged at zero. The rise in income and output in t therefore equals the rise in autonomous investment spending of 10. We are assuming that this rise in autonomous investment spending is permanent, so I_a remains at 40 in $t + 1$ and subsequent periods. Induced consumption now rises from 60 in t to 66 in $t + 1$, since income of t has risen to 110 from its level of 100 in $t - 1$. Induced investment, 0 in t, rises in $t + 1$ to 9, for the change in C from t to $t + 1$ is 6. Thus, substituting in the equation for Y gives us the following:

$$Y_t = C_a + cY_{t-1} + I_a + w(C_t - C_{t-1})$$

---

[16] In Chapter 12 we used the term *induced* investment to describe investment that is dependent on the absolute level of a variable, there using income for that variable. Here we are concerned with investment that is dependent on the change in the level of the variable, with consumption used as that variable in the present illustration. Since investment that depends on a change in the size of a variable is quite different in meaning from investment that depends on the absolute size of a variable, separate terms would seem to be preferable. However, the general practice is to use "induced investment" to cover both cases, so the meaning in any case must be inferred from the context in which it is used.

TABLE 20–1 A Multiplier-Accelerator Model

(1) Period	(2) Autonomous Consumption C_a	(3) Induced Consumption $c(Y_{t-1})$ $c = 0.6$	(4) Autonomous Investment I_a	(5) Induced Investment $w(C_t - C_{t-1})$ $w = 1.5$	(6) Income and Output Y	(7) Change in Income and Output from Preceding Period	(8) Change in Income and Output from Period $t-2$
$t-2$	10	60.0	30	0	100.0		0
$t-1$	10	60.0	30	0	100.0	0	
t	10	60.0	40	0	110.0	10.0	10.0
$t+1$	10	66.0	40	9.0	125.0	15.0	25.0
$t+2$	10	75.0	40	13.5	138.5	13.5	38.5
$t+3$	10	83.1	40	12.2	145.3(P)	6.8	45.3
$t+4$	10	87.2	40	8.1	145.3	0	45.3
$t+5$	10	87.2	40	0	137.2	-8.1	37.2
$t+6$	10	82.3	40	-7.3	125.0	-12.2	25.0
$t+7$	10	75.0	40	-10.9	114.1	-10.9	14.1
$t+8$	10	68.4	40	-9.8	108.6(T)	-5.5	8.6
$t+9$	10	65.2	40	-4.9	110.2	1.6	10.2
$t+10$	10	66.1	40	1.5	117.6	7.4	17.6
$t+11$	10	70.6	40	6.6	127.2	9.6	27.2
$t+12$	10	76.3	40	8.6	135.0	7.8	35.0
$t+13$	10	81.0	40	7.0	138.0(P)	3.0	38.0
$t+14$	10	82.8	40	2.7	135.5	-2.5	35.5
$t+15$	10	81.3	40	-2.2	129.0	-6.5	29.0
$t+16$	10	77.4	40	-6.8	120.6	-8.4	20.6
$t+17$	10	72.4	40	-7.6	114.8	-5.8	14.8
$t+18$	10	68.9	40	-5.2	113.7(T)	-1.1	13.7
$t+19$	10	68.2	40	-1.0	117.2	3.5	17.2

NOTE: Figures have been rounded to the nearest tenth.

For Period t:

$$110 = 10 + 60 + 40 + 1.5(70 - 70)$$

For Period $t + 1$:

$$125 = 10 + 66 + 40 + 1.5(76 - 70)$$

For Period $t + 2$:

$$138.5 = 10 + 75 + 40 + 1.5(85 - 76)$$

All subsequent changes in induced consumption, induced investment, and the level of income may be traced through period by period in this same fashion.

The data given in Table 20–1 show that the level of income rises to a peak (P) in $t + 3$, then falls to a trough (T) in $t + 8$, rises to another peak in $t + 13$, and falls to another trough in $t + 18$. In short, the changing level of income and output reveals a series of cyclical fluctuations. It is interesting to note that this series of fluctuations is generated in this model by nothing more than one change—the rise in autonomous investment spending to a higher but constant rate in t, $t + 1$, and subsequent periods. Thus, by incorporating the accelerator in the investment function, a permanent increase in autonomous investment no longer necessarily means that the level of income and output will simply move up to a higher level and reestablish equilibrium there; instead it may, as we have seen, set the system off on a series of self-generating cyclical fluctuations without establishing a new equilibrium.

Variations on the Model

If the figures of Table 20–1 were continued to $t + 20$ and beyond, one would discover additional cycles, but cycles whose amplitude would become smaller over time. In the absence of any further disturbance, such as a change in C_a or I_a, these cycles would eventually die out, and the level of income would stabilize at 125, the equilibrium level indicated by the multiplier alone. This result, a series of "damped" cycles, follows from the specific values assumed for c and w in Table 20–1. Other values for c and w will give different results.

In his article, Samuelson set forth the various patterns of change that the level of income might display for different combinations of values of c and w, given a change in autonomous spending that upsets a previous equilibrium. All possible patterns fit into one of four cases, or into five if we include a special case: (A) Income moves upward or downward at a decreasing rate and asymptotically approaches a new equilibrium; (B) income fluctuates through a series of cycles of smaller and smaller amplitude until the cycles virtually disappear (as in Table 20–1); (C) income fluctuates through a series of cycles of wider and wider amplitude; (D) income moves upward or downward at an increasing rate; (E) income fluctuates through a series of cycles of constant amplitude (the special case). Cases A and B resemble each other in their stability—both tend to converge toward an equilibrium. Cases C and D resemble each other in their instability—both tend to diverge from equilibrium by increasing amounts. Case E is the in-between situation—movement is neither toward nor away from equilibrium. Otherwise classified, Cases B and C exhibit cyclical fluctuation; Cases A and D do not. The special case, E, goes with B and C in this classification. Each of these five income patterns is illustrated in Parts A through E of Figure 20–5.

FIGURE 20–5   Income Patterns for Various Values of *c* and *w*

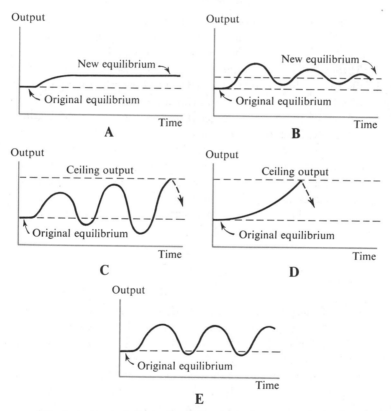

We have noted that the differences between these five income patterns result solely from different combinations of values for *c* and *w*. Every possible combination of *c* from zero to 1.2 and of *w* from zero to 5 may be located in Figure 20–6.[17] Those combinations of *c* and *w* that fall in the region of the quadrant labeled B will produce a series of damped cycles such as those shown in Part B of Figure 20–5 and in Table 20–1. Similarly, those combinations of *c* and *w* that fall in Regions *A, C,* and *D* will produce income movements such as those of Parts A, C, and D of Figure 20–5. Combinations of *c*

[17] This figure is adapted from Samuelson's on p. 268 of Haberler, *Readings in Business Cycle Theory.*

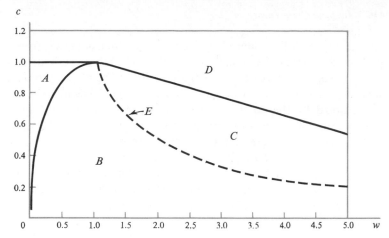

FIGURE 20–6 **Boundaries of Regions for Values of *c* and *w* Yielding Different Income Patterns**

and *w* that fall along the broken line marked *E* produce cycles of constant amplitude such as those of Part E of Figure 20–5.

Figure 20–6 also indicates that any particular income pattern, for example the explosive case of Region *D*, can result either from a relatively low multiplier and a relatively high accelerator (e.g., 2.5 and 5) or from a higher multiplier and a lower accelerator (e.g., 10 and 2.5).[18] Similarly, the damped-cycle case that results from a combination of *c* and *w* falling in Region *B* is possible with a relatively low multiplier and a relatively low accelerator (e.g., the values in Table 20–1, 2.5 and 1.5) or with a higher multiplier and a still lower accelerator (e.g., 5 and 0.5).[19]

In the development of the multiplier in Chapter 8, we saw that the size of the multiplier determines how much income will rise or fall in response to a given increase or decrease in autonomous investment or consumption spending. Beyond this, all that could be said at that point was that a high multiplier would, given the volatility of autonomous investment spending, produce a more unstable system than would a low multiplier. However, with the addition of the acceleration principle, we can say something more definite about the path of

[18] It may be noted that the same explosive case will follow even with an accelerator of zero, if the MPC is greater than 1. This is similar to one of the theoretical possibilities examined in the development of the multiplier. See pp. 144–45.

[19] It should be noted that the boundaries of regions shown in Figure 20–6 pertain specifically to the equation of the type above: $Y_t = C_a + cY_{t-1} + I_a + w(C_t - C_{t-1})$. Any other equation will give us a different set of boundaries. Thus, if we merely substitute $(C_{t-1} - C_{t-2})$ in the preceding equation—or, in other words, apply *w* to lagged rather than unlagged consumption—the instability of the model will be reduced. A figure like Figure 20–6 prepared for this equation would, among other differences, have the line *E* lying higher, indicating that higher values for *c* and *w* would be needed to produce antidamped, or explosive, cycles. For another case, if, instead of making the accelerator apply only to changes in consumption, we made it apply to changes in total output, we would make for a more unstable system. Thus, if we should substitute $(Y_{t-1} - Y_{t-2})$ in the equation above, the line *E* in Figure 20–6 would shift downward, actually to a vertical position at $w = 1$, so any value of the accelerator greater than 1 would lead to an antidamped or explosive cycle.

445

change that will be followed by income over time, ranging from the explosive path of Region *D* at one extreme to the equilibrium path of Region *A* at the other. Also, despite the fact that the volatility of aggregate investment spending springs in part from the volatility of autonomous investment spending, which is unexplained by the acceleration principle, we can say that some part of the overall volatility of investment spending is explained by the internal workings of the multiplier-accelerator interaction. As was illustrated in Table 20–1, all that is needed to set the interaction into motion is a change in autonomous investment (or autonomous consumption) spending. Given such a change, the system itself generates a greater or lesser volatility of induced investment as part of its own self-contained process of change.

The Multiplier-Accelerator Model and the Business Cycle

All students of the business cycle agree that movements in economic activity that are to be called business cycles take the form of recurrent alternations of expansion and contraction. A cumulative movement in one direction over time creates pressures that eventually cause a reversal and a movement in the opposite direction. The duration and amplitude of periods of expansion and contraction may vary substantially from cycle to cycle, and the duration of successive full cycles also shows wide variation. However, there remains as the essence of the cycle the recurrent alternations of upward and downward movements in economic activity that may be called oscillations.

From this point of view, the movements of economic activity (measured by aggregate output) shown in the various patterns of Figure 20–5 do not all display the oscillatory movements characteristic of the business cycle. In this connection, the noncyclic nature of Case A stands out most clearly. Given a disturbance, the system moves smoothly from an original equilibrium to a new equilibrium with no oscillation whatsoever. There is simply nothing cyclical here. Case B produces oscillations, but these are damped oscillations that tend to die out over time and thus conflict with the historical record that shows no tendency for cycles to disappear. However, the tendency for the cycle to disappear as portrayed by Case B follows from the assumption of only a single disturbance—for example, a one-time spurt in autonomous investment. In this event, the amplitude of the oscillations shrinks over time to zero. But in reality, further disturbances can be expected to occur quite frequently and at random intervals.[20] Technological advances, innovations, wars, natural disasters, can all produce jolts to the system. The inherent tendency of the system to react cyclically to a disturbance will result in an oscillatory movement, even though the disturbances occur at random over time. The resultant cyclical pattern will be quite irregular in terms of duration and amplitude of cycles, but the pattern in the real world is, of course, far from regular. Thus, with respect to Case B,

[20] This idea of erratic shocks was first brought forward by R. Frisch, "Propagation Problems and Impulse Problems in Dynamic Economics," in *Economic Essays in Honour of Gustav Cassel*, Allen & Unwin, 1933, pp. 171–205.

we may say that what otherwise shows up as a tendency for the cycle to disappear may be converted into an unending sequence of cycles by the addition of randomly distributed erratic shocks to the system.

Case C produces oscillations that increase in amplitude, or become explosive. This pattern at least produces the continuing oscillatory movement characteristic of business cycles, but it conflicts with the observed fact that actual movements are not explosive. However, a model with values for the multiplier and accelerator that puts the system into the region of Case C may be made consistent with the nonexplosive nature of observed business cycles if so-called *buffers* are added to the system. We will discuss these in more detail in the next section on Hicks's model; here it is sufficient to note that such buffers impose an upper limit, or "ceiling," on the expansion and a lower limit, or "floor," on the contraction and thus convert what otherwise would be the explosive upward or downward movements called for by the model into the limited oscillations characteristic of the actual business cycle.

What was said here about buffers in Case C applies also to Case D, except for the fact that in the latter case there is a directly explosive movement that is restrained instead of oscillations of increasing amplitude that must be eventually restrained. This may be seen in Cases C and D of Figure 20-5, where a ceiling is shown. Values for the multiplier and accelerator that put the system into the region of Case D can thus produce cycles, if again buffers are added to the model as in Case C and if reasons are given for the system to reverse direction after striking the buffers. Such reasons are found in Hicks's theory of the cycle that we turn to in the next section.

In the special situation of Case E, the cycle neither dies out nor explodes but goes on indefinitely at a constant amplitude. The problem here is the implausibility of this case—the result follows only in the very special situation in which the product of the accelerator and the marginal propensity to consume equals 1, a combination unlikely to be realized in practice. Any departure from this combination puts the system into the region of Case B or C, with the results that follow as discussed above.

The various types of movement that result from the multiplier-accelerator interaction have provided the basis for two groups of business-cycle theories. In one group are the theories of economists like Hicks and Goodwin, who have built theories on the assumption that the values of the multiplier and accelerator are such as to produce antidamped, or explosive, cycles. Hansen, the major name on the other side, has been the proponent of the *weak accelerator* theory. In his view, the interaction produces only damped cycles. The preponderance of opinion appears to support the antidamped cycle, and in the next section we turn to a discussion of the best known of the cycle models that proceed along these lines—the model developed by Hicks.

HICKS'S THEORY OF THE BUSINESS CYCLE

Business cycles, when viewed as fluctuations in the economy's real output of goods and services, have historically appeared as movements above and below a rising line of trend or growth. In this sense, it is a commonplace that the real output of the economy in a recession may be substantially larger than that same economy's output at the peak of the prosperity of a cycle a decade or so earlier. The mere growth of the economy makes this so.

Hicks begins by recognizing that since cycles have historically appeared against this background of growth, a theory of the cycle should similarly be constructed against a background that provides a theory of growth. Hicks defines a long-run equilibrium growth path for the economy that is determined by the growth rate of autonomous investment. The ratio of equilibrium income to autonomous investment depends on the magnitude of the accelerator and the multiplier, a result drawn from the Harrod-Domar theory of growth, which we will examine in Chapter 22. Hicks also assumes that autonomous investment tends to grow at a fairly constant percentage rate over the long run. With a fairly stable accelerator and multiplier, it then follows that there is an equilibrium growth path for income that exhibits the same constant percentage rate of growth as autonomous investment. The failure of actual output to move along this equilibrium growth path over time, its tendency instead to run now above it and then below it, identifies cycles. Hicks's theory then focuses on these movements that constitute cycles, but they are in this way kept in the perspective of a theory of the underlying growth path of the economy.

Hicks uses the term *autonomous* investment, in somewhat the same sense that we did in earlier chapters, to mean "public investment, investment that occurs in direct response to inventions, and much of the 'long-range' investment . . . which is only expected to pay for itself over a long period." [21] The remainder of all investment, and an amount that makes up a large proportion of the total of net investment in ordinary circumstances, is so-called *induced* investment, or investment that is called forth, directly or indirectly, by past changes in the level of output. Hicks recognizes that the distinction between autonomous and induced investment is not sharp in practice, but it is a distinction that is critical in developing his theory of the cycle.

We can begin to work our way into that theory through Figure 20–7. The line *AA* shows autonomous investment and the line *EE* the equilibrium growth path for income that is based on line *AA*. The vertical axis is in logarithmic scale, so that the straight lines given in the figure indicate a constant percentage rate of growth for the variables in question. Over time, equilibrium income given by line *EE* remains a constant multiple of autonomous investment, the size of

[21] *Op. cit.*, p. 59.

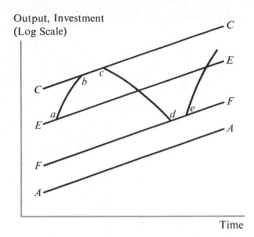

Output, Investment
(Log Scale)

Time

FIGURE 20–7   The Hicksian Cycle

the multiple depending on the magnitude of the accelerator and the multiplier, as noted above. The assumption that autonomous investment grows at anything like a constant rate is, of course, unrealistic, and Hicks's model permits occasional shifts in the rate of growth of autonomous investment. However, from the point of view of his model, variations in autonomous investment are exogenous changes (changes arising as a result of forces outside the model), whereas the basic purpose of the model itself is to investigate how the system it describes will behave in the absence of such exogenous changes.

The line *CC* shows the path of growth of ceiling output that can be produced with full employment of the economy's resources. It is not absolutely necessary that this line lie above *EE*, but this is one possibility and the one considered here. The remaining line, *FF*, describes the path of the lower limit, or floor, to which real income can fall during the contraction phase of the cycle. There will be more to say about this ceiling and floor in what follows, but first we must note why the income level does not follow the equilibrium growth path described by *EE*. Then, given a departure from this path, we will see why the lines *CC* and *FF* set the upper and lower boundaries within which the cycle moves.

The ordinary picture of the business cycle is, of course, one in which a period of expansion is followed by a period of contraction and this in turn by a period of expansion, and so forth. Although one also speaks of a long-run equilibrium growth path, the idea that the economy moves along in anything like a state of equilibrium is a denial of the existence of the cycle. However, to break into the apparatus described by Figure 20–7, we assume that over a period of time ending at Point *a* the economy has been in equilibrium or that the level of output has been expanding along the *EE* path and is at Point *a*. We assume next that an innovation or some other development produces a temporary spurt in autonomous investment, after which autonomous investment returns to its previous path described by line *AA*. This is the same technique we described in the Samuelson interaction to get the system out of

449

equilibrium, although we assumed there that the new higher level of autonomous investment was sustained. Once given this spurt in autonomous
investment, the path followed by the income level depends on the magnitude
of the accelerator and the multiplier. Hicks believes that in the standard business
cycle the magnitudes of these parameters are such as to fall in Regions *C* or *D*
of Figure 20–6, so any divergence of income from the *EE* path will take the form
of oscillations that either increase in amplitude (*C*) or simply produce an
explosive upward movement without oscillation (*D*). His study of the economic
history of the past century and a half leads him to the conclusion that the
movement of the economy over this long period cannot be explained as a
damped-cycle movement (Region *B* in Figure 20–6) that was kept going by a
series of random shocks. In his view, this long period is organized into a series
of seven- to ten-year cycles that display a regularity that cannot be accounted
for by such an erratic-shock, damped-cycle mechanism. Having thus taken the
position that the underlying structure is one that produces antidamped, or
explosive, cycles, Hicks then brings the ceiling to output (*CC*) into the model
to explain why explosions do not take place. Combining the floor (*FF*) with the
ceiling sets the limits within which cyclical movements occur.

Thus, starting at Point *a* and assuming a temporary burst of autonomous
investment spending, there is set into motion a cumulative movement upward
that is explained by the multiplier-accelerator interaction. The actual movement
of the economy's output is indicated by the path of the line from Point *a* to
Point *b*. The economy's ceiling output is also growing with time, but with the
rate of growth of actual output exceeding the rate of growth of ceiling output,
the rate at which actual output is growing must sooner or later be checked by
bumping against the ceiling. This brings into play a crucial element in the
analysis. In Hicks's words, "When the path has encountered the ceiling, it must
(after a little) bounce off from it, and begin to move in a downward direction.
This downward movement is inevitable." [22] In other words, the expansion must
end and a contraction must follow.

Simply stated, the inevitability of the contraction follows from the impossibility that output can continue to rise at a rate faster than that at which the
output ceiling itself is rising. Depending on the particular induced investment
equation one works with, induced investment in any one period is made to
depend in some specified way on the change in output over preceding periods.
However, the maximum change in output between periods once the ceiling has
been hit must be less than the change between periods during the time interval
that the economy is moving upward toward the ceiling. In other words, once
the system is at Point *b*, the growth of output per time period must be less than
it was per time period from Point *a* to Point *b*. In a related context, an examination of the multiplier-accelerator interaction in Table 20–1 shows that the mere
decrease in the amount of increase in output between periods is sufficient to
bring about a decrease in total output, or a downturn from the peak level of

[22] *Ibid.*, p. 98.

output attained. There is a lag between the time the ceiling is struck and the time the downturn begins, a lag assumed in Figure 20–7 to equal the time interval involved in moving from Point *b* to Point *c*, but sooner or later the downturn in output must begin. The inevitability of this downturn requires nothing more than the working of the acceleration principle combined with the assumption of a sufficiently strong accelerator to cause the system to hit the ceiling, once it departs from the equilibrium path of *EE*.

Once the downturn begins, the accelerator starts to work in the opposite direction. The change in income is now negative, so induced investment begins to decline. On the upswing, the limit to the expansion of real investment was set by the capacity of the system to produce, but on the downswing the limit to negative investment (disinvestment) in any period is set by that period's depreciation. For example, the decline in output may be such that the acceleration principle calls for disinvestment of $30 billion in a particular period, but if the wear and tear on the capital stock is only $10 billion for the period, then $10 billion is the maximum disinvestment for the period. Businessmen collectively have no way of disinvesting at the desired higher rate. Under conditions such as these, the acceleration principle becomes inoperative in the downward direction. What happens to the income level during the slump is then determined by the simple multiplier theory without any accelerator at work. The line *FF* is, in other words, set by autonomous investment times the multiplier.

Hicks holds that autonomous investment will typically decline during the course of a slump (the *AA* line shifts downward) but will remain positive and, over time, still maintain a more or less steady rate of growth. Thus, as shown by the movement from Point *d* to Point *e*, income may move upward along the floor as the growth of autonomous investment continues to support income but at a slump level. How long income may move along the floor depends in part on the redundancy of capital inherited from the splurge of induced investment in the earlier periods. Once this is worked off, new investment orders begin to appear for replacement purposes, and gross investment moves above the level accounted for by autonomous investment. We have a spurt in investment spending that pushes the income level upward from the *FF* line. Once this income movement begins, the accelerator again comes into play, induced investment appears, and a cumulative upward process is under way. The rise in income does not stop with the *EE* line, the income level consistent with the *AA* line for autonomous investment. Via the interaction of the multiplier and accelerator, income overshoots the *EE* line and goes on up until finally restrained by the ceiling, the *CC* line, from which, as before, it bounces off and starts the downward movement of another cycle.

The next cycle would follow the course of its predecessor, in line with the essentials of Hicks's theory covered in the preceding pages. We will not pursue this theory beyond these few essentials, nor will we go far into the criticisms of the theory, although there have been a good number of these. Different critics focus on what they regard as the major deficiencies of Hicks's theory, but they all pay some attention to the fact that at the foundation of the model is found the acceleration principle in a rigid form. For example, to Kaldor this is the major weakness of the model.[23] If the acceleration principle in rigid form is found to be unacceptable, then the multiplier-accelerator interaction that incorporates this principle in rigid form and is at the heart of the Hicksian model is also unacceptable. As Duesenberry has put it, "The basic concept of multiplier-accelerator interaction is an important one but we cannot really expect to explain observed cycles by a mechanical application of that concept," [24] and this is what Hicks's model appears to try to do.

Kaldor, whose cycle theory was discussed earlier, makes no use of the acceleration principle. In his model, investment is related directly to the *level* of income and inversely to the stock of capital. This approach, which is also associated with names like Kalecki and Goodwin, breaks the unrealistic, inflexible tie of investment to changes in output that is implied by the rigid acceleration principle, but it still retains the basic idea of the acceleration principle. Instead of the investment function incorporating the strict acceleration principle,

$$I_t = I_a + w(Y_{t-1} - Y_{t-2})$$

this approach gives us

$$I_t = I_a + hY_{t-1} - jK_t$$

where K is the stock of capital at the beginning of Period t and where h and j are constants. The new equation simply says that if output, Y, increases while the capital stock, K, remains constant, investment will rise to enlarge the capital stock, other things being equal. If, on the other hand, the capital stock increases while output remains constant, investment will fall as the desired stock of capital is reached. Thus, the new equation still includes the basic idea of the acceleration principle, for investment in any period will still aim to bring the actual capital stock into line with the amount desired for the production of the level of output that was recently turned out.[25] The difference is that this approach

---

[23] N. Kaldor, "Hicks on the Trade Cycle," in *Economic Journal*, Dec. 1951, pp. 833–47, reprinted in *Essays on Economic Stability and Growth*, Free Press, 1960, pp. 193–209.

[24] J. S. Duesenberry, "Hicks on the Trade Cycle," in *Quarterly Journal of Economics*, Aug. 1950, pp. 464–76, reprinted in J. J. Clark and M. Cohen, *op. cit.*, pp. 322–42.

[25] The new equation becomes identical with an earlier one in the special case in which h equals the capital-output ratio, w; and j equals unity. Adopting these values for the coefficients (and for simplicity setting I_a equal to zero),

$$I_t = wY_{t-1} - K_t$$

In the same way,

$$I_{t-1} = wY_{t-2} - K_{t-1}$$

$$wY_{t-2} = K_{t-1} + I_{t-1}$$

Since K_{t-1} equals the capital stock at the beginning of Period $t - 1$ and since I_{t-1} is the change in capital stock during Period $t - 1$, the capital stock at the beginning of Period t is the sum

does not contain any direct reference to the rate of change of income and output over successive periods. Although it retains a link between changes in output and the level of investment, it does this in such a way as to avoid some of the shortcomings of the rigid acceleration principle.[26]

Hicks's use of the acceleration principle in its rigid form is but one of a number of criticisms that have been made of his model, but we will not go into the others here. However, it may be noted that each of the economists who has written critical words on one aspect or another has also written words of high praise for this work of Hicks. For example, Kaldor refers to the "many brilliant and original pieces of analysis" found in Hicks's theory, and Duesenberry describes it as an "ingenious piece of work" and "the first coherent theory of the cycle to appear in some years." Despite the fact that the model has now been around for twenty years and despite the other work that has been done in business-cycle theory during this period, Hicks's model remains, in a sense, the last word in business-cycle theory.

---

of $K_{t-1} + I_{t-1}$, or K_t, or

$$wY_{t-2} = K_t$$

Substituting wY_{t-2} for K_t in the first equation above, we have

$$I_t = wY_{t-1} - wY_{t-2}$$

or

$$I_t = w(Y_{t-1} - Y_{t-2})$$

which is one of the expressions for the acceleration principle that was earlier noted.

[26] See R. C. O. Matthews, *Business Cycles*, Univ. of Chicago Press, 1959, Chs. 2 and 3, and J. S. Duesenberry, *Business Cycles and Economic Growth*, Ch. 3.

CHAPTER 21

THE NATURE
OF ECONOMIC GROWTH

The fluctuations in economic activity that we call business cycles historically take place around a rising line of trend or growth. It is an economic fact of life that cycles and growth go together in this way, and there is a mutual conditioning of each by the other over time. Nonetheless, we still find that few models are concerned with both cycles and growth. Since the builders of models are all aware of the interdependence between growth and cycles in the actual world, their separation in economic theory is, as might be guessed, due to the difficulty of devising a theoretical apparatus capable of handling both together. A model that does do this is appropriately described as a model of *cyclical growth*, and, as Professor Allen has said, "It does seem that, to get cyclical growth, we need a model of quite considerable complexity." [1] Such models are beyond the level of this book. Accordingly, we will limit ourselves to several models of economic growth that are essentially limited to a theory of growth. This parallels the treatment in the preceding chapter, in which the models were essentially limited to a theory of the business cycle. [2]

Growth models as such attempt to explain what determines the rate at which the economy's real output grows over a period of time that is long relative

[1] R. G. D. Allen, *Macro-Economic Theory*, St. Martin's Press, 1967, p. 385. A model of this kind manageable to the nonmathematical reader is that by R. M. Goodwin, "A Model of Cyclical Growth," in E. Lundberg, ed., *The Business Cycle in the Post-War World*, Macmillan, 1955, reprinted in R. A. Gordon and L. R. Klein, eds., *Readings in Business Cycles*, Irwin, 1965, pp. 6–22.

[2] Although Hicks's theory of the cycle is built on the foundation of a growth theory, there is not the formal integration of cycle and growth theory that is needed to constitute a theory of cyclical growth. Of the several theories considered in the preceding chapter, Schumpeter's innovation theory, in a unique way, genuinely fuses growth and cycle, although we did not develop that theory in sufficient detail to bring this out.

to the period of the business cycle, and beyond this they consider what is required in order that this growth rate be that rate at which the economy progresses along a path of steady, full employment. We will defer the analysis of growth models to the following chapter in order to devote this chapter to some background on the meaning and measurement of growth, the growth record of the U.S. economy, and estimates of the various sources that account for this record of growth.

THE MEANING AND MEASUREMENT OF ECONOMIC GROWTH

Economic growth can be most simply defined as the increase in the economy's output. Since business-cycle expansions are, in general, periods during which output increases and business-cycle contractions are periods during which output decreases, growth by this definition appears to be something we can observe from one quarter to the next during expansions, and the absence of growth appears to be what we observe during contractions. Viewed in this way, economic growth and business-cycle expansions become almost the same thing. This is essentially what the press means by growth when it reports the latest quarterly increase in real GNP as a measure of the economy's "growth" during that three-month period.

Most economists use a definition of growth like the above, but the time period regarded as relevant to the concept of growth is at the very minimum the length of a full business cycle. It then follows that if the level of the economy's output were to remain unchanged from one business-cycle peak to the next, the economist would find zero growth for the period of that full cycle measured from peak to peak. The expansion phase of the cycle, during which output increases, would not register growth but would, in this case, be the phase during which the economy did no more than regain the ground lost during the preceding contraction. In this view, the economy would show growth only to the extent that the later peak lies above the preceding peak.[3] This view is far more reasonable than the other, which would call any observed increase in output growth even though that increase still leaves aggregate output below the level reached at an earlier date.

We will use here the increase in the economy's output as the basic definition of growth, working with the version that makes the business cycle the minimum time period over which to measure growth. Our best measure of the economy's output is real GNP, or GNP in constant dollars. The reason for specifying constant dollars is, of course, that changes over the years in GNP in current dollars are the result of a mixture of price changes and output changes. Therefore, if growth is defined as the expansion of the economy's output and if we are

---

[3] For the actual record, Table 21–2, which occurs on p. 459, shows growth rates for each full cycle since 1910. In each cycle, it may be noted, output at the later peak was greater than at the earlier peak, as is indicated by the positive growth rate shown for each cycle.

to use GNP as a measure of growth, then price changes must be removed from GNP as in the constant-dollar series. Furthermore, if we are interested not merely in how much the economy's aggregate output expands over time but in how much the amount of output produced per person expands over time, real GNP must also be corrected for population increases. These two adjustments will give us what is for many purposes the most useful concept of economic growth—expansion in real GNP per capita.

From the basic concept of real GNP per capita, various related concepts of economic growth have been derived, each of which emphasizes a different facet of growth. One is "real consumption per capita," a concept that indicates the growth in consumer economic welfare. Such figures are derived initially from the deflated data for the personal consumption expenditures component of GNP converted to a per capita basis and sometimes adjusted for the changes in leisure that may be regarded as a part of real consumption. A further adjustment could be made by adding to personal consumption expenditures that portion of deflated government purchases of goods and services that is "clearly" in the nature of public consumption, such as public parks and recreation. The problem encountered in making this adjustment, is, of course, the fact that a large part of government purchases cannot be classified as "clearly" of a consumption or of an investment nature. A second and quite different growth concept is "real GNP per unit of labor input" or per combined unit of labor and capital input, a concept that stresses the changes in the economy's efficiency or productivity over time. These are but two of a number of growth concepts, each of which emphasizes a particular feature of the economy over time.

Aggregate real GNP or per capita real GNP is initially recorded as a time series of dollar amounts. In order to simplify comparisons between different time periods and to make comparisons between different economies, growth is usually expressed as an average annual rate between the beginning and terminal years of each period selected rather than in terms of the absolute dollar change over the period. Thus, for the U.S. economy real GNP per capita (in 1958 prices) increased from $1,670 in 1929 to $3,513 in 1968, an increase of 110.4 percent in a 39-year period. Expressed as an average annual rate of growth, real GNP per capita increased at a 1.9 percent rate over this period.[4] Notice, however, that

---

[4] The average annual growth rate may be determined from a compound-interest table by finding the interest rate required to produce the percentage change in the indicated time period. For the present example, the rate required for $1 to grow to $2.104 in thirty-nine years will be a rate between two of the rates given in the headings of such a table. In the ordinary compound-interest table, interpolation is then required to find the growth rate to the nearest tenth of a percent. This need for interpolation may be avoided by using a specially prepared growth-rate conversion table from which the growth rate to the nearest tenth of a percent may be read off directly. (See *Long Term Economic Growth*, Bureau of the Census, U.S. Dept. of Commerce, 1966, pp. 115–25.)

Alternatively, one can directly compute the growth rate by using the compound-interest formula:

$$\text{GNP}_t = \text{GNP}_b(1 + r)^n$$

where t designates the terminal year, b the beginning year of the period, n the number of

when measured from the depression level of $1,126 in 1933, the rise to $3,513 over the 35 years to 1968 represents an increase of 212 percent, or an average annual rate of growth of 3.3 percent, two-thirds greater than the growth rate found when 1929 was taken as the beginning year.

This illustration brings out the meaning of the average annual rate of growth and demonstrates how the choice of beginning and terminal years can markedly affect the rates derived. When a severely depressed year such as 1933 is used as the beginning year, the rate of growth to 1968 appears very impressive. When the prosperous year of 1929 is taken as the beginning year, which thereby also includes the depression years between 1929 and 1933, the result is somewhat greater than half of the other. To obtain the fairest representation of the actual growth rate over a period, the beginning and terminal years of the period should be similar in terms of business-cycle phase. For this purpose, the unemployment percentage is probably the best guide. Approached in this manner, the growth rate for the 1933–68 period is seen to be misleadingly high, because in 1933 the unemployment rate was at the all-time peak of 24.9 percent. In contrast, the unemployment rate in 1929 was only 3.2 percent, not much different from the 3.6 percent rate in 1968. Thus, for the 35-to-40-year period ending in 1968, the growth rate based on 1929 is clearly more realistic than that based on 1933 or any of the deeply depressed years between 1929 and 1933.

The misleading growth rates that can result from an economically inappropriate choice of beginning and terminal years and from the business-cycle fluctuations that may dominate any short period of years tend to be evened out when the period for which growth rates are computed is lengthened. In the following section we will examine growth rates for the U.S. economy over both long periods and shorter periods. The shorter periods have been selected to begin and end with the same phase of the business cycle.

GROWTH RECORD OF THE U.S. ECONOMY[5]

Table 21–1 summarizes the growth record of the U.S. economy for the period 1839–1959 and for three 40-year subperiods into which this long period has

---

years in the period, and r the average annual rate to be determined. Solve by converting the equation to logarithms:

$$\log (1 + r) = \frac{(\log \text{GNP}_t - \log \text{GNP}_b)}{n}$$

Substituting the data given in the text, r is found to be 1.9 percent. If our example had been in terms of real consumption per capita, the initial equation would have been

$$C_t = C_b(1 + r)^n$$

which may be solved in the same way.

[5] All references cited, other than *Long Term Economic Growth*, were published before the August 1965 release of the revised GNP figures by the Department of Commerce. Therefore,

TABLE 21–1   Growth Rates and Price Changes, 1839–1959

	Entire Period *1839–1959*	*Forty-Year Subperiods*		
		1839–1879	*1879–1919*	*1919–1959*
Aggregate real GNP	3.66%	4.31%	3.72%	2.97%
Price level	1.15	−0.16	1.91	1.40
Population	1.97	2.71	1.91	1.30
Real GNP per capita	1.64	1.55	1.76	1.64

SOURCE: R. W. Goldsmith, "Historical and Comparative Rates of Production, Productivity, and Prices," Joint Economic Committee, *Employment, Growth, and Price Levels, Hearings*, Part 2, 1959, p. 271. (All rates are average annual rates.)

been divided. The record is truly impressive for the overall period of 120 years. There is probably no other economy in history that has done as well during any period of equal length. Over this 120-year period, the aggregate output of the U.S. economy grew at a 3.66 percent average annual rate, which means that aggregate output doubled, on the average, every 19 years, or that there was a 32-fold expansion of output in five such intervals, or in less than a century. Allowing for population growth of almost 2 percent per year, per capita GNP grew at 1.64 percent over this long period, or per capita income doubled every 43 years.

When the long period is broken down into 40-year subperiods, we find that the growth rate of aggregate GNP declined in each successive subperiod—from 4.31 to 3.72 to 2.97 percent. Notice that the same decline does not appear in the per capita data because of variations in the rate of population increase. Of the three subperiods, aggregate GNP showed the most rapid growth during the 1839–79 period. Per capita GNP showed the slowest rate of growth during this period, however, because of the relatively rapid rate of population growth during this period—the rate was more than twice that of the most recent 40-year period. Though the rate of growth of aggregate output slowed during the 1879–1919 period from that preceding, the rate of population growth slowed even more to account for the highest of the three subperiod figures for per capita GNP. A still slower rate of population growth in the most recent subperiod resulted in a small decrease in the per capita GNP growth rate, even though the growth rate of aggregate GNP fell off sharply between these two subperiods.

Just as the rate of growth for this long period conceals variations in its subperiods, so each of these subperiods conceals even greater variations in the still shorter subperiods into which each may be divided. Table 21–2 divides the period 1910–60 into such shorter subperiods, each of which covers the span of a

the growth rates given in these references for the period since 1929 are based on prior estimates of GNP. However, the differences between the prior and revised estimates of constant-dollar GNP do not alter substantially the long-term trends. For example, the average annual growth rate of per capita GNP for 1929–64 has been raised from 1.6 to 1.7 percent by the revised estimates. See *Survey of Current Business*, U.S. Dept. of Commerce, Aug. 1965, p. 20.

TABLE 21–2   **Growth Rates and Price Changes During**
U.S. Business Cycles, 1910–1960

Business Cycle (Peak to Peak)	Average Annual Growth Rate of Real GNP	Average Annual Change in GNP Implicit Deflator
1910–13	4.4%	1.4%
1913–18	2.5	11.7
1918–20	1.8	6.8
1920–23	5.4	−6.4
1923–26	3.9	0.2
1926–29	2.8	−0.5
1929–37	0.1	−1.9
1937–44	7.1	4.7
1944–48	0.1	6.7
1948–53	4.4	2.1
1953–57	2.8	2.1
1957–60	2.7	1.5

SOURCE: J. W. Kendrick, "Concepts and Measures of Economic Growth," Table IV–1, pp. 268–69, in *Inflation, Growth, and Employment*, in the Commission on Money and Credit series, Prentice-Hall, 1964.

full business cycle measured from peak to peak.[6] The growth rate of aggregate real GNP (not per capita GNP) and the implicit price deflators are given for each of these business cycles.[7]

Over the dozen business cycles of this half-century period, the highest growth rate, 7.1 percent, occurs during the cycle that includes the years of World War II, and the highest peacetime growth rate, 5.4 percent, occurs during the cycle of the early twenties. The slowest growth rate, 0.1 percent, occurs during the cycles that include the Great Depression and the readjustment following World War II. The relatively high rate of 4.4 percent during the 1948–53 cycle reflects the impact of the Korean War and the still unsatisfied demand pent up from World War II. The next two cycles show a sharp drop in the growth rate relative to the preceding cycle. The poor growth performance of the U.S. economy over the years of these two cycles from 1953 to 1960 was the source of much heated discussion a few years ago. The 1953–60 period compared un-

---

[6] In contrast to the limitation of Table 21–2 to years of business-cycle peaks, detailed tables called growth-rate triangles, each including about 3,000 entries, have been prepared that show the growth rate of aggregate real GNP for every possible combination of initial and terminal years for the years from 1890 to 1965. (See *Long Term Economic Growth*, pp. 107–08.)

[7] The growth rates and the deflators given are actually those based on real GNP of the private domestic economy. This excludes GNP originating abroad and GNP originating with government (government employee wages, salaries, and supplements) and runs about 90 percent of aggregate real GNP over time. The difference between growth rates computed on the two bases becomes appreciable only during wartime and postwar adjustments because of the large rise and fall in federal government expenditures for national security during these periods. For example, including government GNP, the growth rate for the 1937–44 cycle is 8.5 instead of 7.1 percent and for the 1944–48 cycle is −2.4 instead of 0.1 percent.

favorably not only with the immediately preceding period of 1948–53 but also with the long period covered by all eighteen business cycles from 1910 to 1960. For these years the average annual rate of growth was 3.4 percent, well above the 2.7–2.8 percent rate for 1953–60.[8]

By the late sixties this experience of the fifties had passed into the background as the economy continued to enjoy a relatively rapid growth rate. The business cycle that began in 1960 had not ended as of the time of writing, but if we measure from the last peak which was in the first quarter of 1960 to the first quarter of 1969, we find a growth rate of 4.4 percent, equal to the highest rate achieved since the 1920–23 cycle, if we disregard the war-dominated cycle from 1937 to 1944.[9] The average annual change in the GNP implicit deflator for this nine-year period was 2.2 percent.

THE SOURCES OF PAST AND FUTURE ECONOMIC GROWTH IN THE UNITED STATES

If aggregate demand increases at the rate needed to absorb whatever expansion of output an increasing productive capacity can turn out, the economic growth rate in the years ahead may then be said to depend on the rate of growth in labor quantity and quality, in the stock of capital, and in the productivity of these factors, this productivity being primarily dependent on the pace of technological progress. These same sources that will determine the rate of growth in the future have determined the actual rate of growth achieved in the past. Historically, the more rapid has been the increase in the quantity and quality of labor, in the rate of capital accumulation, and in technological advance in any time period, the greater has been the growth rate recorded for that time period. Of course, where there has been serious underutilization of a growing capacity to produce in any period, the growth rate has been adversely affected in that period.

Economists have made a number of attempts in the past decade to allocate the realized rates of growth of specific time periods to these sources (and also to the subsources into which each may be divided) and to measure the relative importance of each in the growth actually realized by the economy. From these attempts to dissect the growth record of the past come clues to what the growth record of the future may be. If we accept, for example, the finding that in recent decades expansion in the size and improvement in the quality of the labor force

[8] Although a difference of only 0.70 percentage points may not appear very significant, its dimensions are readily appreciated when it is expressed in terms of real output. With 1968 GNP of $861 billion, an increase of only 0.70 percentage points in the rate means a GNP that is greater by more than $6 billion in the next year than what it would otherwise have been. At the end of a decade, it means a GNP greater by more than $67 billion than what it otherwise would have been.

[9] This relatively high rate indicated by the data for the 1960 I–1969 I period probably exceeds the true rate of growth. Although measured from 1960 I, which was a quarter of cycle peak, to the peak reached as of 1969 I, the initial and terminal years differ markedly in terms of unemployment percentage. This was 5.9 percent in 1960 I but only 3.3 percent in 1969 I.

accounted for about half the realized growth of output, increased productivity for about a third, and the enlarged stock of capital for the remainder, estimates of the changes expected in these sources in the future will at least give us some idea of what to expect.

Table 21–3 gives estimates of this kind based on Edward F. Denison's detailed quantitative study, *The Sources of Economic Growth in the United States.*[10] Three time periods are shown, the last of which is a projection for the 1960–80 period. For the 1909–29 period, we see that the growth rate of real national income is 2.82 percent and for the 1929–57 period, 2.93 percent.[11] The column of figures for each of these two realized growth rates shows the estimated portion of the total growth rate accounted for by each of a number of sources to which that actual growth rate can be attributed. In broad terms, we find that of the 2.93 percent growth rate for 1929–57, 2 percentage points are accounted for by the increase in total inputs, and the remaining 0.93 percentage points are accounted for by the increase in output per unit of input. Of the 2 percentage points, 1.57 are accounted for by the increase in the labor input (adjusted for quality change), and 0.43 percentage points are accounted for by the increase in the capital input. Further breakdowns are given for each of these input headings as well as for output per unit of input. The second set of columns converts the first set into percentages that give the percent of the growth rate (e.g., 2.93 = 100 percent) accounted for by each of the sources in the column.

In terms of percent of growth rates, the broadest conclusion that may be drawn for the 1929–57 period is that the increase in the quantity and quality of inputs was responsible for 68 percent of total growth and that the increase in output per unit of input (or the increase in productivity) for 32 percent.[12] Of

---

[10] Supplementary Paper No. 13, Committee for Economic Development, 1962. For an application of the viewpoint and methodology developed in Denison's original study to the postwar experience of the U.S. and eight European countries, see his *Why Growth Rates Differ*, Brookings Institution, 1967. A summary and criticism of Denison's original study is found in M. Abramovitz, "Economic Growth in the United States: A Review Article," in *American Economic Review*, Sept. 1962, pp. 762–82. For other studies on the sources of economic growth, see J. W. Kendrick, *Productivity Trends in the United States*, National Bureau of Economic Research, Princeton Univ. Press, 1961; M. Abramovitz, *Resource and Output Trends in the United States since 1870*, National Bureau of Economic Research, Princeton Univ. Press, 1959; R. M. Solow, "Technical Progress, Capital Formation, and Economic Growth," in *American Economic Review*, May 1962, pp. 76–86. The quantitative estimates on sources of economic growth contained in these studies are, as their authors make clear, based on shaky foundations. These foundations may be expected to be strengthened as research expands in this recently opened field.

[11] Note that the output measure here is real national income rather than the more familiar real GNP. (See E. F. Denison, *The Sources of Economic Growth*, pp. 24–25).

[12] It is important to note that these figures attribute a much larger proportion of economic growth to the growth of inputs and a much smaller proportion to output per unit of input than do other estimates. The difference is in classification, for Denison includes as part of labor input improvements in the quality of an hour's work; the alternative treatment combines these improvements with other sources into productivity or output per unit of input. If Denison's estimates are converted to this latter basis for the 1929–57 period, the 68 percent figure for inputs would be reduced to 42 percent, and the 32 percent figure for output per unit of input would be raised to 58 percent. (*Ibid.*, pp. 149–50.)

TABLE 21-3   Allocation of Growth Rate of Total Real National Income Among the Sources of Growth

	Percentage Points in Growth Rate			Percent of Growth Rate		
	1909–29	1929–57	1960–80	1909–29	1929–57	1960–80
Real national income	2.82	2.93	3.33	100	100	100
Increase in total inputs	2.26	2.00	2.19	80	68	66
Labor, adjusted for quality change	1.53	1.57	1.70	54	54	51
Employment and hours	1.11	0.80	0.98	39	27	29
Employment	1.11	1.00	1.33	39	34	40
Effect of shorter hours on quality of a man-year's work	0	−0.20	−0.35	0	−7	−11
Annual hours	−0.23	−0.53	−0.42	−8	−18	−13
Effect of shorter hours on quality of a man-hour's work	0.23	0.33	0.07	8	11	2
Education	0.35	0.67	0.64	12	23	19
Increased experience and better utilization of women workers	0.06	0.11	0.09	2	4	3
Changes in age-sex composition of labor force	0.01	−0.01	−0.01	0	0	0
Land	0	0	0	0	0	0
Capital	0.73	0.43	0.49	26	15	15
Nonfarm residential structures	0.13	0.05	na	5	2	na
Other structures and equipment	0.41	0.28	na	15	10	na
Inventories	0.16	0.08	na	6	3	na
U.S.-owned assets abroad	0.02	0.02	na	1	1	na
Foreign assets in U.S.	0.01	0	na	0	0	na
Increase in output per unit of input	0.56	0.93	1.14	20	32	34
Restrictions against optimum use of resources	na	−0.07	0	na	−2	0
Reduced waste of labor in agriculture	na	0.02	0.02	na	1	1
Industry shift from agriculture	na	0.05	0.01	na	2	0
Advance of knowledge	na	0.58	0.75	na	20	23
Change in lag in application of knowledge	na	0.01	0.03	na	0	1
Economies of scale—independent growth of local markets	na	0.07	0.05	na	2	2
Economies of scale—growth of national market	0.28	0.27	0.28	10	9	8

SOURCE: E. F. Denison, *The Sources of Economic Growth in the United States*, Supplementary Paper No. 13, Committee for Economic Development, 1962, p. 266. Contributions in percentage points are adjusted so that the sum of appropriate details equals totals. Percents of the growth rate have not been so adjusted. Na = not available.

the two inputs, the increase in labor was responsible for 54 percent of total growth and the increase in capital for only 15 percent. When the labor input is broken down, it is interesting to note that education was about two-thirds as important as employment (23 percent as against 34 percent). To express this differently, these data suggest that almost one-fourth of the total growth rate over the period may be ascribed to education. Not surprising but of considerable importance under labor input is the large negative figure that is the effect of shorter hours on annual hours.

In regard to the relative importance of the labor input in the two periods, it is striking that the percent is 54 in both periods. Notice, however, that within the breakdown under the labor input, education accounts for only 12 percent of the growth rate of the earlier period as against 23 percent in the later period, and the effect of shorter hours on annual hours accounted for only a −8 percent in the earlier period as against −18 percent in the later period.

If we now compare the relative importance of the capital input in the two periods, we find that the accumulation of capital was responsible for 26 percent of the economy's growth rate in the earlier period and only 15 percent in the later period. Whereas investment in "physical" capital thus became less important, investment in "human" capital, or in a better-educated labor force, became relatively more important, as we saw from the rise in the percent of the growth rate attributed to education.[13]

The estimate for the 1929–57 period is that increase in productivity, or output per unit of input, accounts for 32 percent of the period's growth. Most important here is the impact of the advance of knowledge and the economies of scale that have resulted from the growth of national markets. Advance in knowledge comes close to a narrow meaning of technological progress. Unfortunately, a breakdown under output per unit of input is not available for the earlier period, but the overall estimates for increase in output per unit of input do reflect the rising importance of this factor. It accounted for 20 percent of growth in the earlier period and 32 percent in the later period.[14]

Given the estimates of the contribution to the growth rates of past periods that have been made by the labor and capital inputs and by increases in productivity, or output per unit of input, one can estimate the future behavior of these determinants and from this arrive at an estimate of the future growth rate of the economy. Denison's estimates for the 1960–80 period are listed in

[13] The relationship between investment in people and economic growth is another facet of the broader problem of growth that has come under study in recent years. (See G. S. Becker, "Underinvestment in College Education?" in *American Economic Review*, May 1960, pp. 346–54, and *Human Capital*, Columbia Univ. Press, 1964; T. W. Schultz, "Investment in Human Capital," in *American Economic Review*, March 1961, pp. 1–17, and "The Rate of Return in Allocating Investment Resources to Education," in *Journal of Human Resource* Summer 1967, pp. 293–309).

[14] As we pointed out earlier, if changes in the quality of the labor input were treated not as changes in labor input but as changes in output per unit of input, the rise from the earlier to the later period in the percentage figure for output per unit of input would be substantially greater, and the rise in the labor input figure would be converted into a decline.

Table 21–3, both in percentage points of the estimated growth rate of 3.33 percent and in percent of the estimated growth rate (3.33 = 100 percent). If we could expect that the behavior of the principal determinants of growth would remain the same from the 1929–57 period to the 1960–80 period, arriving at the estimate for the future growth rate would be a simple matter of extrapolating from the earlier figures. But experience suggests that the factors of major importance in the past will not necessarily be of equal importance in the future. Examination of Table 21–3 shows the differences arrived at by Denison.

In such an examination, it must be recognized first and foremost that the 3.33 percent rate for 1960–80 is a *potential* rate and in this respect is dissimilar to the realized growth rates of the previous periods. It is a rate that, according to Denison's estimates, can be achieved with "high" employment, which he defines as 96 percent of the labor force employed. It also assumes that there will be no deep or prolonged depressions during the period. In other words, it amounts to the potential rate at which the economy will be able to expand its output of goods and services under conditions in which demand increases at the rate necessary to absorb the expansion in output.

Looking now at the breakdown of growth for 1960–80 into labor input, capital input, and output per unit of input, we find that, as compared with the 1929–57 period, labor input is expected to account for 66 rather than 68 percent of growth, capital input for the same 15 percent, and the increase in productivity for 34 rather than 32 percent. These figures are only slightly different from those for the 1929–57 period. The pronounced changes are found only when further breakdowns are made. For example, under labor input, education, which was very important as a source of economic growth in the past, will (according to Denison) be less important in the future because of the sizable gains that have already been made. For the same reason, the effect of shorter hours on the quality of a man-hour of work is expected to drop sharply from the 1929–57 period. Employment itself becomes more important as a factor of growth, since it is assumed that "high" employment will be maintained over the period as was not the case over parts of the 1929–57 period. Under changes in productivity we find that only advance in knowledge is expected to become more important than it was in the preceding period as a factor in growth. Denison argues that increases in output per unit of input resulting from economies of scale such as the growth of national markets or from the shift in industry from agriculture have already gone so far that the same contribution to growth made by these factors in the past cannot be expected in the future. Similar barriers do not stand in the way of advance of knowledge.

If an "acceptable" or "appropriate" growth rate for the U.S. economy in the years ahead is 4 to 5 percent (the range within which most economists and others put the figure), Denison's estimates suggest that it will not be attained even if the system is successful in maintaining high employment and avoiding serious downturns. However, his basic estimates assume that there will be no special new measures taken by government to influence the growth rate other than those necessary to establish high employment and prevent cyclical down-turns. The interesting question for the future then becomes: What steps could be taken to increase the growth rate above the 3.33 percent estimated by Denison? Denison gives a long list of possible actions and their estimated quantitative impact on the growth rate.[15] For example, to raise the growth rate by 1 percentage point through investment would require that the ratio of net investment to national income be more than tripled; this would involve an increase from about 6 percent to about 20 percent of national income.[16] To raise the growth rate by 0.1 percentage point, the economy would have to operate with a standard work week that is about one hour longer than it is at present.[17] However, with the single significant exception of increasing immigration, all the changes that would permanently raise the growth rate by a considerable amount impose costs of one kind or another. Considering the two possibilities mentioned above, for example, the diversion of resources to investment would impose a cost in the form of less consumption than otherwise, and a longer work week would impose a cost in the very direct form of more work and less leisure. Therefore, if we accept Denison's estimates, it appears that only drastic changes—some requiring radically different social and economic policies by government—would be capable of raising the long-run growth rate by more than the 1.5 percentage points needed to approach the 5 percent growth rate some people hope to achieve. However, given the growth rate of 3.33 projected in Denison's analysis, it seems possible to achieve the 4 percent others call for without any drastic changes in policy.

If we pursue this line of thought further, we encounter such questions as: Which growth-determining factors are subject to manipulation? To what extent may the growth rate be raised by manipulating various of these factors? How acceptable socially and economically are policies designed for this purpose? And what are the costs that must be charged against the faster growth achieved by these policies? These questions and many others like them have been and will continue to be much discussed. We can do no more than call attention to them here.

ECONOMIC GROWTH—DEVELOPED AND UNDERDEVELOPED ECONOMIES

A quantitative study of the sources of growth for any developed economy could proceed along much the same lines followed by Denison in his study of the U.S. economy. Although the relative quantitative importance of each of the primary sources of growth will not be the same in all developed economies, the primary sources themselves will be the same. Similarly, a theory of economic growth that attempts to explain the process by which growth takes

[15] E. F. Denison, *The Sources of Economic Growth*, pp. 276–79.
[16] *Ibid.*, p. 116.
[17] *Ibid.*, p. 278.

place in a developed economy will, in general, be applicable to any developed economy. It will not, however, be applicable in the same degree to an underdeveloped economy. Since the next chapter is devoted entirely to growth theory relevant to developed economies, it may be helpful at this point to mention the pertinent distinctions between growth in the two types of economies.

To begin with, the most serviceable and most commonly used criterion for classifying economies as developed or underdeveloped (or into three stages if we include "intermediate") is per capita real income.[18] Those with "low" per capita real income are considered underdeveloped; those with "high" per capita real income are developed. Income is judged to be high or low by comparing it to income in countries such as the United States, which is the "highest," or to the United Kingdom and Germany, which are relatively "high." It is the level of absolute per capita real income in one country relative to that in another that is relevant for this classification. On the other hand, the parallel criterion for classifying economies according to the speed of their growth rates for any particular period of years is the rate at which per capita real income grows. Notice that although underdeveloped countries are typically countries with low growth rates, it is possible for an underdeveloped country to show a high growth rate. If sustained, a high growth rate will clearly move the country out of the "underdeveloped" class.

If our purpose is only to compare how developed and underdeveloped economies have performed in terms of growth, we have a single problem whose solution could be provided by comparable data on per capita real income over time for both kinds of economies. However, if our purpose is to explain the process by which economic growth takes place in developed and underdeveloped economies, we are faced with two reasonably distinct problems. Because the two problems differ, economic growth theory has developed in the postwar period along two branches, one—called *development economics*— that attempts to explain the growth process in economies moving from the underdeveloped toward the developed stage, and another that attempts to explain the growth process in economies that are already developed. The two branches overlap to some extent, but there are still essential differences that make the separation analytically useful.

Underdeveloped economies are typically characterized by insufficient capital equipment, technological backwardness, structural unemployment, extreme income disparities, foreign indebtedness, low educational attainment, an unskilled labor force, and, in many cases, a deficiency of natural resources relative to the size of the population.[19] It is essentially these characteristics that make for the relatively low per capita real income that results in the designation "underdeveloped." Therefore, to explain the slow rate (or complete absence) of growth in such economies, we must start with the explanation of the social,

[18] For a discussion of this and other criteria, see B. Higgins, *Economic Development*, rev. ed., Norton, 1968, Ch. 1.
[19] See the list of characteristics suggested by K. K. Kurihara and the discussion thereof in his *The Keynesian Theory of Economic Development*, Columbia Univ. Press, 1959, Ch. 2.

cultural, and economic factors that gives rise to certain of these characteristics. The explanation of growth in developed economies, in contrast, takes *as given* the existence of a more or less adequate capital stock, a skilled labor force and an experienced managerial group, and technological progressiveness, and it seeks to explain the growth process in terms of the advances of output made possible by the expansion in the quantity of these basic determinants and the improvement of their quality.

What is thus taken as given for the developed economies is absent to a greater or lesser degree in the underdeveloped economies. To move up to the highroad of economic progress, underdeveloped economies must typically undergo an economic and social reorganization, and in some cases even a transformation of the whole system, involving the adoption of more advanced methods of production despite the cultural barriers to such steps, the development of efficient transportation and communications systems, the establishment of schools and facilities for public services (often termed *social capital*), and the development of modern monetary machinery that includes a capital market and other credit facilities. In some cases, these economies must first put an end to political instability and produce a climate conducive to the attraction of foreign capital. Broad changes are often needed in the economy's product "mix," and the increased mobility and relocation of labor needed to support such changes must be secured. Finally, there must be mass education and the provision of the necessary industrial skills to adapt labor to new types of work. These and many other developments must proceed more or less simultaneously. Included among these other developments are the accumulation of capital, the expansion of the quantity and quality of the labor force, and the achievement of the technological advances that are recognized as the basic determinants of growth in an already developed economy.

Since these and other developments are all typically involved in the problem of growth in an underdeveloped economy, much deeper "digging" is clearly called for in any attempt to explain the growth process in such economies. The theory of growth for a developed economy thus turns out to be the less complex of the two. Chapter 22 is devoted entirely to an introduction to growth theory of this simpler kind. Such thoery is not completely without relevance to the underdeveloped economies, but it is still essential to note that there are important underlying differences in the theory of economic growth in the two cases.

CHAPTER 22

ECONOMIC GROWTH
THEORY

Keynes's *General Theory* not only began a new chapter in the short-run theory of income and employment but produced as a by-product a revival of interest in long-run theory, or the theory of economic growth. In view of the impact made by the *General Theory*, it was only to be expected that economists would proceed to construct theories to dynamize and secularize the static, short-run theory presented by Keynes. Since the late thirties a huge body of growth theory has developed that not only has extended Keynesian theory to the long run but has gone far beyond this. Thus, Professors Hahn and Matthews, in presenting what is only a survey of the theory of economic growth for the period since the *General Theory*, require more than one hundred pages to complete the task.[1] In this chapter we will touch on only two, but probably the most basic two, of the growth theories that have been developed during this period. The theory that serves as the point of departure in the survey mentioned above and the one that invariably receives first consideration in any current discussion of modern growth theory is a theory that relates the growth rate of the economy's aggregate output to the growth rate of the economy's capital stock. In this approach, capital is the only factor of production explicitly considered, and it is assumed that labor is combined with capital in fixed proportions. This capital-accumulation growth theory is most commonly known as the *Harrod-Domar theory* and is the first of the two theories that will be examined in this chapter. Yet so rapid and so varied has been the growth of growth theory in the last few decades that this first theory may now be described as a relatively early and relatively simple approach to the growth question. Most of the growth theory that came later departed from this theory's assumption that labor and capital are combined in fixed proportions

---

[1] F. H. Hahn and R. C. O. Matthews, "The Theory of Economic Growth: A Survey," in *Economic Journal*, Dec. 1964, pp. 779–902.

and instead assumed substitutability between the capital and labor inputs, or variable proportions in the production process. The growth theory that is built on this basis is usually described as *neoclassical growth theory* and is the second theory we will look into in this chapter.

The restriction of our coverage to these particular theories neglects completely the body of growth theory that existed before the thirties. Although the last thirty years have been a period of unprecedentedly rapid development of growth theory, it must be noted that economists' concern with the question of economic growth goes back at least as far as 1776, to Adam Smith's *An Inquiry into the Nature and Causes of the Wealth of Nations*. The very title of this classic suggests the author's interest in the long-run question of the accumulation of wealth, one aspect of any study of the question of growth. In Smith's view of the process by which the economy's wealth expands, an important role is assigned to the "division of labor," or specialization. The idea of diminishing returns had not yet been "discovered," and Smith saw no obstacle to the increase of returns to labor through increased specialization. His conclusion was thus an optimistic one in which increased specialization would lead to a rising standard of living for a growing population. This optimistic conclusion was replaced a few decades later by a pessimistic one as a result of the work of Thomas Malthus and David Ricardo. The Malthusian population principle and the Ricardian diminishing returns and rent theory combine to force the great majority of the economy's population down to a subsistence standard of living—a case of zero growth per capita, or the case of a "stationary state." Between the writings of classical economists such as these and the writings of the economists of the past thirty years are such major contributions as the growth systems of Karl Marx and Joseph Schumpeter.[2] In short, growth theory is a product not of the past thirty years but rather of the past two hundred years.

HARROD-DOMAR GROWTH THEORY [3]

A basic principle emphasized by Harrod and Domar and incorporated in all modern growth theory is the dual effect of net investment: Net investment

---

[2] For an analysis of classical growth theory and the growth theory of Marx and Schumpeter, see, for example, B. Higgins, *Economic Development*, rev. ed., Norton, 1968, Chs. 3–5; W. J. Baumol, *Economic Dynamics*, 2nd ed., Macmillan, 1959, Chs. 2–3; and D. Hamberg, *Economic Growth and Instability*, Norton, 1956, Ch. 1.

[3] The basic elements of the Domar model are found in Evsey Domar, "Expansion and Employment," in *American Economic Review*, March 1947, pp. 34–55. See also his "Capital Expansion, Rate of Growth, and Employment," in *Econometrica*, April 1946, pp. 137–47, and "The Problem of Capital Accumulation," in *American Economic Review*, Dec. 1948, pp. 777–94. These and related essays by Domar are reprinted in his *Essays in the Theory of Economic Growth*, Oxford Univ. Press, 1957. For the Harrod model, see Roy F. Harrod, "An Essay in Dynamic Theory," in *Economic Journal*, March 1939, pp. 14–33, reprinted in A. H. Hansen

constitutes a demand for output, and it also increases the capacity of the economy to produce output. For example, constructing and equipping a new factory generates a demand for steel, brick, and machinery, and the factory once constructed and equipped increases the economy's productive capacity. The economy's net investment in any period thus has a *demand* and a *capacity* effect. If the amount of net investment in any period equals that period's net saving, it has the demand effect of removing from the market that portion of output not purchased by consumers, thereby making aggregate demand equal to aggregate output for the period and making that period's actual level of income and output the equilibrium level. This is nothing more than the familiar Keynesian principle that there must be equality between planned saving and planned investment if there is to be equilibrium in the level of income and output. What is not familiar from the Keynesian model is the fact that this period's net investment also has a capacity effect: It increases the economy's productive capacity in this period and thereby increases the next period's potential output. If this expanded capacity is to be fully utilized, aggregate demand in the next period will have to exceed that of this period. Thus, in general, as long as there is net investment in one period after another, aggregate demand must rise period after period if the expanding productive capacity resulting from net investment is to be fully utilized.

Increase in Capacity Output

The basic theory involves a simple production function that relates the generation of total output to the stock of capital via the capital-output ratio. Taking the techniques of production as given, some specified amount of capital goods is necessary to produce a given amount of output. If we let K represent the capital stock and Y the level of output, we may define the average capital-output ratio as K/Y.[4] Thus, if it takes $3 worth of capital goods to produce $1 worth of final output, a capital stock of $300 billion is required to produce aggregate final output of $100 billion, and the capital-output ratio is 3 to 1.[5]

---

and R. V. Clemence, eds., *Readings in Business Cycles and National Income*, Norton, 1953, pp. 200–19, and revised and expanded in Harrod's *Towards a Dynamic Economics*, St. Martin's, 1948 (see particularly pp. 63–100). The 1939 essay is refined but unchanged in essentials in Harrod's "Second Essay in Dynamic Theory," in *Economic Journal*, June 1960, pp. 277–93.

[4] Following more common practice, Y instead of O is used here to designate real income or output. Recall that $Y = PO$, but when a stable price level is assumed, $Y = O$; the growth model makes just this assumption.

[5] Note that the ratio depends on the time period chosen for the measurement of output. Capital stock of $300 billion will produce, say, $100 billion of output *per year*—that is, the 3 to 1 ratio. The same capital stock will produce $25 billion of output *per quarter*, a 12 to 1 ratio, and $8.3 billion *per month*, a 36 to 1 ratio. One year is the time period usually selected for measurement of flows. Note also that our analysis makes use of the average capital-output ratio for the economy as a whole; the capital-output ratio will, of course, vary among the different goods into which aggregate output may be broken down.

In contrast, the marginal capital-output ratio $\Delta K/\Delta Y$ tells us how much additional capital is necessary to produce a specified addition to that flow of output. The marginal ratio need not be equal to the average ratio as long as technology changes over time. It would rise with capital-using technological changes and fall with capital-saving technological changes. In the model, however, we assume a constant technology, so that $\Delta K/\Delta Y$ remains constant. To simplify the analysis still further, we assume that the constant $\Delta K/\Delta Y$ equals K/Y, so that K/Y is also constant.

The reciprocal of the average capital-output ratio, Y/K, represents the average productivity of capital. If \$3 of capital goods is required to produce \$1 of final output—that is, if $K/Y = 3$—the average productivity of capital, Y/K, will be 1/3, or 0.33. Given an increase in the capital stock, ΔK, then $\Delta Y/\Delta K$ indicates the ratio of the increase in capacity output to the increase in capital stock. Just as $\Delta K/\Delta Y$ need not be the same as K/Y, so $\Delta Y/\Delta K$ need not be the same as Y/K. The pace of technological advance will affect these ratios, but the simple model does not treat them as variables, so that $Y/K = \Delta Y/\Delta K$. This ratio of output to capital stock is designated by σ (sigma), which Domar calls the "potential social average productivity of capital." [6]

Since ΔK in any period equals that period's net investment, or I, $\Delta Y/\Delta K = \sigma$ may also be expressed as $\Delta Y/I = \sigma$ or $\Delta Y = \sigma I$. Thus, if $\sigma = 1/3$, \$1 of net investment will increase capacity output by 33.3¢. From this it follows that the cumulative net investment of any period increases capacity output by σI. This is the most important relationship in the model. By defining capacity output in terms of the capital stock, we find that the increase in capacity output for any period equals σI, or the average productivity of capital multiplied by that period's cumulated net investment. It must be noted that ΔY is not necessarily the *actual*, or *realized*, increase in output but rather is the *potential* increase possible with full utilization of the expanded productive capacity. Since these two figures may differ, let us now distinguish the potential from the actual, or realized, increase by appending subscripts: ΔY_p and ΔY_r.

Increase in Aggregate Demand

In a two-sector economy, aggregate demand equals the sum of consumption and investment expenditures. With a stable consumption function, consumption expenditures will rise only as a result of a rise in income, and therefore a rise in investment expenditures is necessary to initiate a rise in income. Consequently, we may determine the total rise in expenditures, or income, that will result from any given rise in investment by using the simple multiplier expression

$$\Delta Y - \frac{1}{s}\Delta I$$

[6] The full meaning of this lengthy term is explained by Domar in *Essays in the Theory of Economic Growth*, pp. 89–90.

in which *s* is the MPS.[7] This rise in income, or expenditures, is matched by an equal rise in actual output, since output responds proportionally with the rise in demand on our assumption of a stable price level. With subscript *r* designating realized, or actual, we have

$$\Delta Y_r = \frac{\Delta I}{s}$$

This brings us to a crucial asymmetry of the demand and capacity effects of investment. On the demand side, an increase in actual output, ΔY_r, is a function not of investment but of the *increment* to investment. (Recall from the basic Keynesian model that if net investment remains unchanged period after period, aggregate demand will remain unchanged and so will aggregate output.) But, on the supply side of the system, each period's net investment represents an addition to the capital stock and so an addition to the economy's productive capacity. If we assume constant net investment, potential output expands period by period, but actual output remains unchanged, so unused productive capacity must result. The assumed constant net investment will not be maintained by business period after period in the face of such excess capacity. This underscores the essential paradox of investment: To justify today's net investment, tomorrow's must exceed today's in order to provide the additional aggregate demand needed to purchase that part of the enlarged potential output that is not purchased by consumers. In other words, as long as there is positive net investment, net investment must increase to prevent a decrease in net investment. The economy cannot stand still period after period with a constant net investment; either it will move ahead (e.g., if autonomous consumption or government demand increases), or it will fall back. Only a stationary economy neither moves ahead nor falls back, but by definition there is zero net investment in a stationary economy. Zero net investment is not characteristic of any developed real-world economy. If then a real-world economy must be a growing economy, what is the rate at which it must move ahead to avoid falling back? In other words, what is its equilibrium rate of growth?

The Equilibrium Rate of Growth

There is some rate of growth at which the increase in actual output in each period, ΔY_r, will just equal that period's increase in capacity output, ΔY_p. This rate at which $\Delta Y_r = \Delta Y_p$ is called the *equilibrium rate of growth*. Of course, ΔY_r and ΔY_p are not rates as such but absolute amounts of change measured from one period to the next. However, by relating each such absolute amount

---

[7] In the long run, which we must use for growth analysis, it is reasonable to treat the marginal propensity to consume as equal to the average propensity to consume and, therefore, the marginal propensity to save as equal to the average propensity to save. As we saw in Chapter 9, the long-run empirical consumption function based on Kuznets' data showed this relationship between "average" and "marginal." In what follows, we may therefore refer only to the propensity to save, without distinguishing between marginal and average.

of change to the absolute actual amount of output and to the absolute capacity output of the preceding period, each may be expressed as a rate. Thus, from an original period in which there is equilibrium as given by $Y_r = Y_p$, it follows that if the rate $\Delta Y_r / Y_r$ remains equal to the rate $\Delta Y_p / Y_p$ period after period, Y_r will remain equal to Y_p period after period. In such a situation aggregate realized output grows as fast as aggregate potential output, thereby producing a path of equilibrium growth over time.

Since $\Delta Y_r = \Delta I / s$ and $\Delta Y_p = \sigma I$, the equilibrium rate is also that at which $\Delta I / s = \sigma I$. The left side shows the increment to aggregate realized output for the period; since this is equal to the increment of aggregate demand, it may be called the demand side. The right side shows the increment to productive capacity for the period and as such may be called the supply side. Note that investment appears on both sides of the equation, although not in the same form. On the left side we have the increment to net investment, or the difference between the net investment of any one period and that of the preceding. This absolute rate of increase of net investment times the multiplier determines the change in aggregate demand and therefore in aggregate output. On the right side of the equation, however, we find not the *change* in net investment for the period but the *total* net investment for the period. The reason, of course, is that total net investment for the period times the average productivity of capital determines the change in productive capacity.

We may solve this equation by multiplying both sides by s and then dividing both sides by I. Given that

$$\frac{\Delta I}{s} = \sigma I$$

Multiplying by s:

$$\Delta I = s\sigma I$$

Then, dividing by I:

$$\frac{\Delta I}{I} = s\sigma$$

In this form the left side of the equation now gives the required rate of growth of net investment. If actual output is to rise as fast as potential output, the growth rate of net investment must be $s\sigma$, or the propensity to save multiplied by the productivity of capital.

Although ΔI is subject to a multiplier that makes ΔY greater than ΔI, we can see that the growth rate of actual output, $\Delta Y_r / Y_r$, must be the same as the growth rate of investment, $\Delta I / I$. Since in equilibrium $\Delta Y_r = \Delta Y_p$ and since $\Delta Y_p = \sigma I$, it follows that $\Delta Y_r = \sigma I$. Furthermore, since $I = sY$ in equilibrium, then by substitution $\Delta Y = \sigma s Y$ and $\Delta Y / Y = s\sigma$. Therefore,

$$\frac{\Delta I}{I} = \frac{\Delta Y}{Y} = s\sigma$$

The rate at which actual output and investment must grow in order that actual output remain equal to potential output is determined by the propensity to save and the productivity of capital. The higher the propensity to save, the greater is the required growth rate, and conversely. The higher the productivity of capital, the greater is the required growth rate, and conversely. The meaning of these relationships may be brought out most clearly through the series of numerical illustrations that follow.

Numerical Illustrations of the Growth Process

Assume an economy in which for a given year aggregate demand equals the aggregate potential output that economy can produce with the capital stock existing at the beginning of the year. This defines an equilibrium for the year (say Year 1) in which $Y_r = Y_p$ and provides a take-off point from which we can trace the growth process over the next few years. Remembering that the equilibrium growth rate is given by $s\sigma$, we find in Table 22–1 the growth process for three different combinations of s and σ that yield growth rates of 5, 2.5, and 10 percent per year.

In Model 1 the productivity of capital is taken to be 0.25 and the propensity to save to be 0.20. The capital stock in place (Column 2) at the beginning of Year 1 is 400, or that necessary with σ of 0.25 for production of potential output, Y_p, of 100 (Column 3). Let us also assume that in Year 1 actual, or realized, output, Y_r (Column 4), was 100. Consumption (Column 5), equal to $(1 - s)Y_r$, was 80, so saving, equal to sY_r, was 20. Investment (Column 7) was also 20, yielding aggregate demand of 100, the amount necessary to make realized output equal to potential output. This much is the ordinary, short-run Keynesian model. Now allow for the fact that I of 20 in Year 1 increases by 20 the capital stock in existence at the beginning of Year 2. This increases capacity output of Year 2 by σI (or $\sigma \Delta K$)—that is, 5. This means that aggregate demand in Year 2 must also increase by σI to make use of the increase in capacity. But aggregate demand will increase only if investment increases. To secure the required increase in aggregate demand of 5 in Year 2, investment must rise from 20 to 21. Given the multiplier of 5 ($s = 1/5$), we then find an increase in demand of 5 composed of $\Delta C = 4$ (Column 6)[8] and $\Delta I = 1$. If investment in Year 2 does in fact rise at the required rate of 5 percent, or from 20 to 21, Y_r in Period 2 will equal Y_p in Period 2. Or, given that $\Delta I/I = s\sigma$, numerically for Period 2 we have $1/20 = 0.20 \times 0.25$. The growth rate of output, $\Delta Y/Y = s\sigma$, is then $(4 + 1)/100 = 0.20 \times 0.25$, where 4 represents the increase in consumption and 1 represents the increase in investment. With s and σ as given in Model 1 and as long as investment rises 5 percent per year, aggregate demand will rise as fast as potential output, and actual output will grow accordingly at the capacity rate of 5 percent. At this constant rate of growth, investment and consumption represent the same proportions of the expanding output, but the absolute increase in the amount of investment and of consumption grows larger each year. This means that the amount of investment in any given year must

[8] In Column 6, $\Delta C = (1 - s)\Delta I/s$. In equilibrium, this equals $\sigma I(1 - s)$.

TABLE 22–1 Illustrations of the Growth Process: Equilibrium Situations

(1) Year	(2) Capital Stock K	(3) Potential Output $Y_p = \sigma K$	(4) Realized Output $Y_r = C + I$	(5) Consumption $C = (1-s)Y_r$	(6) Change in Consumption $\Delta C = (1-s)\dfrac{\Delta I}{s}$	(7) Investment (autonomous) I	(8) Change in Investment (autonomous) ΔI
			[Model 1]	$s = 0.20,\ \sigma = 0.25,$ and $\Delta I/I = \Delta Y/Y = 0.05$			
1	400.00	100.00	100.00	80.00	—	20.00	—
2	420.00	105.00	105.00	84.00	4.00	21.00	1.00
3	441.00	110.25	110.25	88.20	4.20	22.05	1.05
4	463.05	115.76	115.76	92.61	4.41	23.14	1.09
			[Model 2]	$s = 0.10,\ \sigma = 0.25,$ and $\Delta I/I = \Delta Y/Y = 0.025$			
1	400.00	100.00	100.00	90.00	—	10.00	—
2	410.00	102.50	102.50	92.25	2.25	10.25	0.250
3	420.25	105.06	105.06	94.56	2.31	10.51	.256
4	430.76	107.69	107.69	96.62	2.36	10.77	.263
			[Model 3]	$s = 0.20,\ \sigma = 0.50,$ and $\Delta I/I = \Delta Y/Y = 0.10$			
1	200.0	100.0	100.0	80.0	—	20.0	—
2	220.0	110.0	110.0	88.0	8.0	22.0	2.0
3	242.0	121.0	121.0	96.8	8.8	24.2	2.2
4	266.2	133.1	133.1	106.5	9.7	26.6	2.4

always exceed the saving of the preceding year, if aggregate demand is to rise as fast as potential output.

Models 2 and 3 show how different values of σ and s affect the equilibrium growth rate.[9] The choice of the particular values of σ and s in these three models brings out the following points. First, the growth rate in Model 1 is twice that in Model 2 because the propensity to save is twice as large (0.20 instead of 0.10) with the same productivity of capital in both cases. An economy that can double the fraction of its resources that is diverted from the production of consumer goods can double the fraction of its resources that is devoted to capital accumulation. This means that if the productivity of capital remains unchanged, the economy can grow *potentially* at twice its previous rate with what amounts to a doubling of its propensity to save. Next, we find that the growth rate in Model 3 is twice that in Model 1 because the productivity of capital is twice as great (0.50 instead of 0.25) with the same propensity to save in both cases. This suggests that if the amount of output obtainable per unit of capital can somehow be doubled, an economy can double its *potential* rate of growth with the unchanged rate of capital accumulation set by its propensity to save. Finally, we note that the growth rate in Model 3 is four times the growth rate in Model 2 because both the productivity of capital and the propensity to save are twice what they are in Model 2.

Each of the models of Table 22–1 traces out an equilibrium growth path, the sole difference between them being in the values of σ and s, which determine the rate of equilibrium growth. In each model the economy follows an equilibrium growth path as a result of growth in aggregate demand equal to the growth in capacity output, a result that in turn depends on growth of investment at the required rate. Model 1–A of Table 22–2 repeats Model 1 of Table 22–1, in which investment grows at the required rate of 5 percent. Models 1–B and 1–C, however, show what happens to growth if investment fails to grow at the rate required to make full use of the growing capacity. In Model 1–B net investment remains constant, and in Model 1–C net investment grows but at less than the required rate.

The last two models describe disequilibrium situations. In Model 1–B, in which there is constant net investment of 20 per year, there is a constant addition to capacity of 5 each year. Since changes in aggregate demand depend on changes in net investment and not on the level of net investment, aggregate demand remains constant as long as net investment is constant. Since with each passing year 5 more is being added to excess capacity under these circumstances, it is not likely that net investment will be maintained even at 20 year after year. A decrease in net investment will follow, and this will cause aggregate demand to fall; depression and stagnation may follow. In Model 1–C investment does grow but at a rate too slow to absorb that part of growing capacity output that is not absorbed by consumption. This will also cause excess capacity to pile up year by year, which means that even the indicated lower-than-required growth rate probably cannot be maintained.

[9] Since output in Year 1 is set at 100 in all three models, the original capital stock in Model 3 is only 200 with productivity of capital assumed to be 0.50.

TABLE 22-2 Illustrations of the Growth Process: Disequilibrium Situations

(1) Year	(2) Capital Stock K	(3) Potential Output $Y_p = \sigma K$	(4) Realized Output $Y_r = C + I$	(5) Consumption $C = (1-s)Y_r$	(6) Change in Consumption $\Delta C = (1-s)\dfrac{\Delta I}{s}$	(7) Investment (autonomous) I	(8) Change in Investment (autonomous) ΔI
		[Model 1-A]	Investment grows at the required rate of 5 percent.				
1	400.00	100.00	100.00	80.00	—	20.00	—
2	420.00	105.00	105.00	84.00	4.00	21.00	1.00
3	441.00	110.25	110.25	88.20	4.20	22.05	1.05
4	463.05	115.76	115.76	92.61	4.41	23.14	1.09
		[Model 1-B]	Investment is constant.				
1	400	100	100	80	—	20	—
2	420	105	100	80	—	20	—
3	440	110	100	80	—	20	—
4	460	115	100	80	—	20	—
		[Model 1-C]	Investment grows at the too slow rate of 3 percent.				
1	400.00	100.00	100.00	80.00	—	20.00	—
2	420.00	105.00	103.00	82.40	2.40	20.60	0.60
3	440.60	110.15	106.09	84.87	2.47	21.22	.62
4	461.82	115.45	109.28	87.42	2.55	21.86	.64

A Graphic Representation of the Growth Process[10]

With a few modifications, the familiar Keynesian short-run saving-investment figure for the determination of the equilibrium level of output can be converted into a figure that illustrates the growth process described above in tabular form. In Figure 22–1, the intersection of S and I_1 defines an original equilibrium level of output at Y_1.[11] The short-run analysis suggested that the equilibrium level of output would remain at Y_1 as long as neither the saving nor the investment function shifted. With no such shift, investment would be just equal to the leakage into saving at the given level of income and output; whatever part of income was not spent for consumption would be offset by an equal (planned) amount spent for investment. With no change in total spending, there would be no change in the equilibrium level of income and output. As we now know, this is an unrealistic conclusion except for very short-run situations, because it neglects the capacity effect of that part of spending composed of net investment. Thus if we can incorporate this capacity effect into the figure, it can be used to illustrate the growth process in which capacity output does rise and in which full use of capacity is possible only if the amount of investment rises as required per time period.

Let us assume, as in Table 22–1, that $Y_r = Y_p$ at the output level Y_1 in Year 1. Net investment for the year is I_1, which raises the capital stock at the beginning of Year 2 by the same amount, so Y_p of Year 2 exceeds Y_p of Year 1. How large this increase in capacity output will be depends on I_1 and σ. The year's net investment is, of course, represented by the height of the I_1 function above the horizontal axis. The value of σ is represented by the slope of the E_1 function, which equals the reciprocal of σ. The higher the value of σ, the less will be the slope of the function. If $\sigma = 3/4$, the slope will be 1.33; if $\sigma = 1/4$, the slope will be 4, and in the special case in which $\sigma = 1$, the slope will be 1 (a 45° line), with the increase in capacity output just equal to net investment. With the slope of E_1 in Figure 22–1, I_1 raises productive capacity by Y_1Y_2. This is determined graphically by moving along the I_1 curve from S_1 to the intersection with the E_1 curve and dropping a vertical line to locate Y_2 on the output axis.

For Year 1 we assumed that $Y_r = Y_p$, but now Y_p of Year 2 exceeds Y_p of Year 1. If there is to be full utilization of the increased productive capacity in Year 2, Y_r must rise by an amount equal to the rise in Y_p. This in turn requires that aggregate demand rise by the same amount. With a stable saving function, the required rise in aggregate demand can occur only if investment rises in Year 2 by the amount necessary to offset the rise in saving at the higher level of output. In other words, if Y_r is to rise from Y_1 to Y_2, I_1 must rise to I_2 to offset the rise in saving from S_1 to S_2, which will accompany a rise in output to Y_2. If

[10] The figures in this section follow those developed by H. Pilvin in "A Geometric Analysis of Recent Growth Models," in *American Economic Review*, Sept. 1952, pp. 594–99.

[11] This portion of the figure differs from the familiar Keynesian figure only in that the short-run nonproportional saving function has been replaced by a long-run proportional function. As drawn, MPS = APS, in contrast to the short-run nonproportional function, in which MPS > APS.

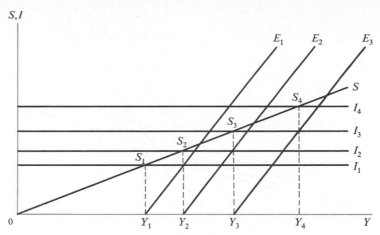

FIGURE 22–1 The Equilibrium Growth Process

such a rise in investment occurs, the economy will then operate at full capacity in Year 2; $Y_r = Y_p$ at the output level Y_2. The process then repeats itself. Investment of I_2 during Year 2 raises the capital stock at the beginning of Year 3 by the amount I_2. With an unchanged value for σ, this increase in capital stock raises the productive capacity of the economy in Year 3 from Y_2 to Y_3, as indicated by the E_2 line. Again, to make full use of the expanded productive capacity, investment will have to rise from I_2 to I_3 in Year 3.

As was brought out by Table 22–1, equilibrium growth requires that the absolute increase in investment in each period exceed the absolute increase in investment of the preceding period. In terms of Figure 22–1, $I_3I_2 > I_2I_1$ and $I_4I_3 > I_3I_2$. With a constant value for σ, the increase in capacity output in each period also exceeds that of the preceding period, or $Y_3Y_2 > Y_2Y_1$ and $Y_4Y_3 > Y_3Y_2$. If numerical values were inserted on the axes of Figure 22–1, the percentage changes from Y_1 to Y_2 and Y_2 to Y_3 and from I_1 to I_2 and I_2 to I_3 would prove to be equal to $s\sigma$, the slope of the S function multiplied by the reciprocal of the slope of the E function.

It should again be emphasized that the potential growth rate indicated by the slopes of the S and E functions will be realized only if net investment rises at the required rate. For, unless net investment rises fast enough from period to period, excess capacity will appear, causing a fall in net investment and a decline rather than a growth in actual output. This conclusion assumes that the slopes of the S and E functions, or the values for s and σ, do not change. However, if we assume a secularly declining average propensity to save or a secularly declining average productivity of capital, this conclusion does not follow. Growth then becomes possible period after period even though net investment remains constant; excess capacity does not appear to force a decline in net investment.

Figure 22–2, like Figure 22–1, indicates an original equilibrium between S_1 and I_1 at output Y_1 for Year 1. If, with the rise in productive capacity in Year 2 that results from I_1 of Year 1, the average propensity to save should so decrease as to generate the same amount of saving at Y_2 as at Y_1, aggregate demand will equal potential output Y_2 with no rise in investment demand.

479

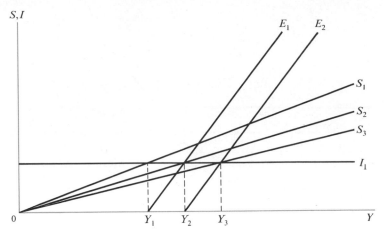

FIGURE 22-2 **The Growth Process with a Declining Propensity to Save**

Such is the result shown in Figure 22–2 by the shift in the saving function from S_1 to S_2. Net investment in Year 2 is then the same as in Year 1. Accordingly, at the next step the increase in capacity output from Year 2 to Year 3 is the same as from Year 1 to Year 2 ($Y_1Y_2 = Y_2Y_3$). If again in Year 3 the average propensity to save should fall by the appropriate amount (from S_2 to S_3), aggregate demand will be equal to capacity output in Year 3 with no rise in net investment over that of Year 2 (or Year 1). Year by year there is growth, for year by year the constant net investment adds to productive capacity. Year by year consumption demand rises by the amount needed to make use of this expanding capacity. Since the increments to capacity output and the increases in actual output are constant, the growth rate declines year by year—that is,

$$\frac{Y_2 - Y_1}{Y_1} > \frac{Y_3 - Y_2}{Y_2}$$

—but still there is growth.

The assumption of a secularly declining average propensity to save is not realistic. The statistical estimates we examined in Chapter 9 indicated that consumption and saving are stable proportions of income in the long run. The case is important, nonetheless, because it brings into focus the relationship between the magnitude of the propensity to save and the required growth of investment. If investment opportunities are such that investment does not rise fast enough to absorb the saving generated with the existing propensity to save, whatever policy actions can be taken to lower the propensity to save will make possible a higher rate of growth. In other words, where investment spending is sluggish, public policy aimed at discouraging saving and encouraging consumption is conducive to growth. If, on the other hand, investment opportunities are boundless, the opposite kind of policy is indicated. Fostering more rapid growth in such a situation calls for a rise in the long-run average propensity to save. Greater "thrift" means more rapid growth. This can be seen by reconstructing Figure 22–2 so that S_2 lies above S_1 and S_3 above S_2. In this situation, as long as investment rises to fill the gap, we find not only an absolute increase in

480

investment period by period but a rise in the percentage rate of growth of investment from period to period.

Just as changes in the propensity to save affect the growth rate, so will changes in the productivity of capital. A secular rise in the value of σ (a decreasing slope of the E function) with a stable s means that the required rate of growth rises. Therefore, it also means that investment must grow at an ever higher rate from one period to the next if actual output is to rise as fast as potential output. In an economy in which investment spending is sluggish, a rising productivity of capital makes more difficult the problem of expanding aggregate demand as fast as potential output. Under these conditions a secularly declining value for σ is conducive to growth. However, unlike the long-run propensity to save, which may be influenced to some extent by fiscal and other policy measures, the long-run value of the productivity of capital can be influenced little, if at all, by public policy measures. The changing ratio of Y to K over the long run is essentially a technological phenomenon. There is little chance that this ratio can be adjusted downward through policy measures as required to offset investment that fails to grow at the otherwise higher required rate.

The Addition of a Theory of Investment

The model, as developed so far, shows the rate at which investment *must* grow if aggregate demand is to grow at the rate needed to provide full utilization of a growing capital stock. Thus, Column 7 of Table 22–1 showed the dollar amounts of investment, and Figure 22–1 showed the successive positions of the autonomous investment curve, that must be attained if there is to be full utilization of productive capacity period after period. However, indicating what *must* happen in order to meet this objective tells us nothing about what *will* happen. There is nothing within the model itself to indicate what the actual value of investment will be period after period. We may now, if we like, expand the model by adding a theory of investment such as the acceleration theory so that the model will then contain a theory of what investment will be in each period. In combination with the theory of consumption already in the model, this addition will give us a model that contains a theory to cover both components of demand. It is specifically the inclusion of an acceleration theory of investment that, in a formal sense, is the major difference between the approach taken by Harrod and that taken by Domar. The full implications of Harrod's use of a theory of investment in his approach can be seen only by developing his approach in detail. However, we can gain some understanding of the effect of the addition of the acceleration investment equation to the model developed above merely by comparing Figure 22–1, which showed what investment must be if the system is to follow an equilibrium growth path, with Figure 22–3 below, which includes a theory of what investment will be.

One form of the acceleration theory of investment makes investment of any period equal to the accelerator times the change in the level of output

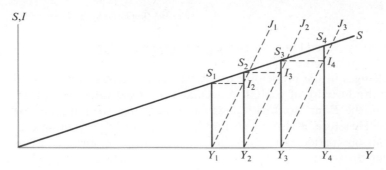

FIGURE 22-3   The Growth Process with an Acceleration Theory of Investment

between the current and the preceding period, or, as an equation, $I_t = w(Y_t - Y_{t-1})$.[12] This is the version presented in Chapter 13, the version used by Harrod, and the version on which Figure 22–3 is based. In this figure the change in output from Period 1 to Period 2 is given by the distance between Y_1 and Y_2 on the income or output axis. How much investment this induces in Period 2 depends on the size of the accelerator, and this is shown diagrammatically by the slope of the line labeled J_1. This and the other J lines are all drawn with a slope of 2 to conform with the assumption that the accelerator is 2. Thus, given a rise in output from Y_1 in Period 1 to Y_2 in Period 2, we find induced investment in Period 2 to be equal to the vertical distance I_2Y_2, or equal to twice the change in output, Y_1Y_2. The figure is so drawn that the rise in income, Y_1Y_2, is just sufficient to induce investment of I_2Y_2, which is just equal to the saving made available in Period 2. A lagged saving function is assumed in which each period's saving equals the propensity to save times the preceding period's income. Thus, saving made available in Period 2 is equal to S_1Y_1, which is matched in Period 2 by investment of I_2Y_2.

The rate of growth of income and output from Period 1 to Period 2 is equal to $(Y_2 - Y_1)/Y_1$. In Figure 22–3 the same rate of growth of income is maintained in succeeding periods, so that $(Y_2 - Y_1)/Y_1 = (Y_3 - Y_2)/Y_2$ and so forth. If income grows from period to period in the way described by the figure, the economy may be said to be moving along an equilibrium path. The only growth rate that will carry the system along such a path is the particular rate that is consistent with the values of the accelerator and propensity to save adopted in drawing the figure. Harrod calls this particular growth rate the

---

[12] It may be noted that algebraically the accelerator w, or K/Y, is the reciprocal of σ, or Y/K, the output-capital ratio or average productivity of capital, which appears above in the analysis that follows Domar's approach. If we rewrite $I_t = w(Y_t - Y_{t-1})$ in the simpler form, $I = w(\Delta Y)$, it will be seen that Domar's $\Delta Y = \sigma I$ may in turn be rewritten as $I = (1/\sigma)\Delta Y$— that is, in a form algebraically equal to Harrod's acceleration investment equation. However, although w and $1/\sigma$ are equal algebraically, their economic meanings are quite different. The rewritten Domar equation cannot be interpreted as is the Harrod equation, in which I is made a function of ΔY and w refers to the ratio that businessmen *desire* to establish between I and ΔY. No such intended or desired relationship between I and ΔY is present in the Domar approach. The equation from that model as originally given, $\Delta Y = \sigma I$, expresses the relationship that Domar employs—namely, a simple production function relationship in which the change in the period's capacity output is technologically equal to some fraction of the period's net investment.

warranted rate of growth, the term "warranted" suggesting that the given combination of accelerator and propensity to save "warrant" the rate of growth indicated. If the propensity to save were higher (a greater slope to the *S* curve), it could be seen that a higher rate of output growth would be required to keep the economy moving along an equilibrium growth path. A smaller accelerator (a lesser slope to the *J* curve) would have a similar effect. In the same way, a smaller propensity to save or a larger accelerator would each mean that a lower rate of output growth would be required to keep the economy moving along an equilibrium growth path.

This equilibrium growth path has been commonly described as a "razor's edge," for the slightest departure of the actual growth rate from the equilibrium, or warranted, rate throws the economy off the equilibrium growth path into either "stagnation" or "exhilaration." To illustrate, let us assume that income has risen by less than $Y_1 Y_2$ from Period 1 to Period 2. Induced investment in Period 2 would then be less than $I_2 Y_2$ and thus less than the amount of saving forthcoming in Period 2. This means a deficiency of demand, which means excess capacity, or a situation in which the existing capital stock is greater than that desired by business at the then current level of output. Paradoxically, this excess capacity results from the fact that business did not invest enough or acquire enough additional capacity. An appropriately higher level of investment would have prevented the deficiency of demand and the appearance of excess capacity. However, the fact is that excess capacity has appeared, and this causes a contraction of income and output, which in turn, via the accelerator, causes a further reduction in investment. But then saving again exceeds investment, and there is a still greater deficiency of aggregate demand. Thus, once given an initial divergence in which the actual growth rate falls below the equilibrium, or warranted, growth rate, the forces at work push the system, not back toward the equilibrium growth rate but farther and farther away from it. In the event of such a divergence, the result is deep, prolonged depression or stagnation.

In the case of the opposite divergence, let us suppose that output has risen by more than $Y_1 Y_2$ from Period 1 to Period 2. Induced investment in Period 2 would then be greater than $I_2 Y_2$ and thus more than the amount of saving made available in Period 2. This means an excess of demand, which in the present context means a capital shortage, or a situation in which the existing capital stock is less than that desired by business at the then current level of output. As in the case above, there is a paradox here: The capital shortage results from the fact that business invested too much. An appropriately lower level of investment would have prevented the excess demand that resulted in the capital shortage. However, once a capital shortage appears, investment rises as business tries to make up for the shortage. Investment again exceeds saving, and there is a still greater excess of demand. Once given the divergence in which the actual rate exceeds the equilibrium, or warranted, rate of growth, forces push the system farther and farther away from the equilibrium growth rate. Where the divergence is an actual rate above the equilibrium rate, the result is secular exhilaration.

Because the actual rate of growth is subject to all sorts of influences, it can be expected that it will depart from the equilibrium rate of growth that is dictated by the values of the propensity to save and the accelerator. The picture suggested by Harrod's formulation is thus one of an economy with an inherently unstable pattern of growth, marked by a tendency toward long periods of boom or stagnation. For, as we have seen, once the economy departs from the equilibrium growth path, it moves farther and farther away over time. It is a focus on this alleged tendency toward secular instability that is the most striking feature of Harrod's formulation of the basic capital-accumulation theory of economic growth known as the Harrod-Domar theory.

The Employment of Labor

The equilibrium, or warranted, rate of growth in the basic Harrod-Domar theory is the rate of growth that provides full utilization of a growing capital stock or the rate that results in neither shortage nor excess of capital. Although capital is the only factor of production that is explicitly considered, the model of course recognizes that labor too is needed in order to produce. Labor as a factor of production is, however, brought in through the assumption of fixed factor proportions, so it may be said that the amount of labor employed is indicated by the amount of capital in use. In other words, labor and capital are assumed to be perfectly *complementary* in the production process, but the focus of the model is on the stock of capital. The model also assumes constant returns to scale, so that, for example, a 1 percent increase in the amount of labor and capital will result in a 1 percent increase in the economy's capacity output.

If the economy grows at the equilibrium or warranted rate, the amount of labor employed will grow at the same rate, in view of the assumption of perfect complementarity. This suggests that there will be full employment of labor only if the warranted growth rate is equal to the growth rate of the labor force and only if the actual growth rate corresponds with the warranted growth rate. In the previous section we noted that the actual and the warranted rates may be expected to diverge, and here it is to be noted that the warranted growth rate and the labor force growth rate may also be expected to diverge, given the essentially demographic factors that determine the long-run growth of the labor force.

If the actual growth rate equals the warranted growth rate but the warranted growth rate exceeds the labor force growth rate, the result is accumulation of idle plant and equipment, for there would be more new capital added than new workers to operate it. Since businessmen quite plainly will not long continue to produce new plant and equipment that cannot be utilized for want of workers, the ceiling to the actual rate of growth in this case would appear to be a rate set by the growth of the labor force. The warranted rate might be 4 percent when the labor force growth rate is only 1 percent. Given the model's assumption of fixed proportions between labor and capital, the ceiling to the actual rate of growth of output would then be 1 percent.

The actual growth rate would not be limited to this 1 percent ceiling if we added to our illustration an allowance for the influence of technological advance. Technological advance of a labor-saving nature enables a smaller amount of labor and an unchanged amount of capital to produce an unchanged amount of output. In a growth context, this means that capital may now grow at a rate faster than the rate of growth of the labor force because technological advance is continuously releasing some labor from the existing capital stock, which *in effect* is equivalent to a rise in the rate of growth of the labor force. The process may be viewed as one in which the labor so released becomes available for employment with new capital goods that would not have been produced if this labor had not been made available by laborsaving technological advance. If this rate of technological advance is, say, 2 percent and the rate of growth of the labor force is 1 percent, the ceiling growth rate becomes 3 percent instead of the 1 percent rate set by the actual growth of the labor force alone. However, this ceiling is still below the 4 percent rate assumed as the warranted rate, so the actual rate must still fall below the warranted rate with the consequences of economic stagnation, as noted in the preceding section which deals with this situation.

In the opposite case, the labor force growth rate may be greater than the warranted growth rate. For example, if the propensity to save were relatively low and the investment of the amount of income saved permitted only a 2 percent growth rate for the capital stock, a labor force growth rate of more than 2 percent would mean insufficient plant and equipment to employ the full labor force. The ceiling to the actual rate of growth would then be imposed by the warranted rate. Again, the actual rate could fall below the warranted rate— with the consequences noted in the previous section—but if it were equal to the warranted rate, the result would be full utilization of the growing capital stock. However, with the labor force growth rate greater than this rate, the rate of growth of the capital stock would not be sufficient to provide full employment for the growing labor force. The dual objective of full utilization of both labor and capital cannot be satisfied under the conditions described, for labor and capital are employed in fixed proportions, and the labor force in this situation is simply growing faster than the capital stock. In short, full employment of labor becomes impossible.

These and other conclusions reached in the preceding discussion of the Harrod-Domar theory follow at least partially from the fact that a basic assumption of that theory is fixed factor proportions. If we were to drop the assumption that labor and capital are combined only in this way, it would no longer necessarily follow in the situation just described that full employment of the labor force would become impossible. If the labor force growth rate exceeds the warranted growth rate, the proportion of labor to capital in the production process might increase so as to permit full employment of the labor force. From a much broader point of view, if we drop the assumption of fixed factor proportions, it is no longer meaningful to say that we can explain the economy's growth rate in terms of the propensity to save and the productivity of capital.

With the possibility of variable proportions, the approach to an explanation of the growth rate must be one that brings the labor force explicitly into the analysis.

Once we introduce this possibility of variable factor proportions into the picture, we leave the world of Harrod-Domar. As noted in the introduction to this chapter, it is the adoption of the assumption of variable factor proportions that characterizes a body of more recent growth theory. The economists who returned to this neoclassical assumption of substitutability between factors built a new type of growth theory that differs basically from the Harrod-Domar type. In the next section we turn specifically to this neoclassical growth theory.

NEOCLASSICAL GROWTH THEORY [13]

In one sense, neoclassical growth theory stands at an opposite extreme from Harrod-Domar. In place of the Harrod-Domar assumption of a single production process that imposes a fixed ratio between capital and labor is the assumption of an indefinitely large number of production processes, one shading off from another in a way that permits any combination of labor and capital to be employed. Capital is thus regarded as a unique, abstract agent of production that can be adjusted at any time to absorb into employment a labor force of any size. With the combination of labor and capital capable of varying in this way, it follows that, instead of the fixed ratio between output and capital employed by Harrod-Domar, the output-capital ratio is also capable of varying continuously. Thus, the larger the labor force absorbed into employment with a given stock of capital, the greater will be the output-capital ratio, or the productivity of capital, and the smaller will be the output-labor ratio, or the productivity of labor. Similarly, the smaller the labor force absorbed into employment with a given stock of capital, the lower the productivity of capital and the higher the productivity of labor. These results follow simply as a matter of diminishing returns.

The neoclassical theory also differs from Harrod-Domar in the former's assumption of automatic full utilization of capital and labor. The question of whether or not the amount of saving generated by an economy with factors fully utilized will be matched by an equal amount of planned investment, a requisite to continued full utilization of factors, is answered in terms of classical theory:

---

[13] A sizable literature has developed since the mid-fifties. Among the major contributions are R. M. Solow, "A Contribution to the Theory of Economic Growth," in *Quarterly Journal of Economics*, Feb. 1956, pp. 65–94; "Technical Change and the Aggregate Production Function," in *Review of Economics and Statistics*, Aug. 1957, pp. 312–20; and E. S. Phelps, "The New View of Investment: A Neoclassical Analysis," in *Quarterly Journal of Economics*, Nov. 1962, pp. 548–67. For less technical and nonmathematical expositions of neoclassical growth theory, see H. G. Johnson, "The Neo-Classical One-Sector Growth Model: A Geometrical Exposition and Extension to a Monetary Economy," in *Economica*, Aug. 1966, pp. 265–87, and J. E. Meade, *A Neo-Classical Theory of Economic Growth*, Oxford Univ. Press, 1961.

All economic activity is carried out in conditions of perfect competition with flexible prices of inputs and outputs serving to balance supply and demand in all markets along the lines discussed in Chapter 17. Output then depends simply on the supply of inputs, for all inputs available will find employment. With the question of full utilization of inputs resolved in this way, the neoclassical theory's focus is on the growth path that will be followed by a system whose labor and capital resources remain fully utilized as the quantity of these resources grows over time. For this reason, there is no need to distinguish in this discussion between the growth rate of the economy's capacity, or potential, output and the growth rate of its actual, or realized, output, for the latter becomes the same as the former.

The Rate of Output Growth Without Technological Progress

The rate at which the output of the economy grows depends basically on the rate at which its capital stock, labor force, and technological know-how grow over time. The relationship for any particular period of time may be simply expressed in the form of the following production function:

$$Y = F(K, L, A)$$

in which K is the capital stock, L the labor force, and A an index of technological know-how whose magnitude will grow at some rate over time. As a first step, however, we will temporarily simplify the relationship by assuming that no technological progress takes place. The production function is then

$$Y = F(K, L)$$

In this simplest case, how does Y vary as K and L vary, other things being equal? In the Harrod-Domar theory, if both K and L increased by 1 percent, Y would increase by 1 percent. The neoclassical theory indicates the same result, for both theories assume a production function with constant returns to scale. However, in Harrod-Domar, a 1 percent increase in L with no increase in K (and with all the existing K already in full use) would mean no increase in Y because of the fixed proportion between L and K, whereas in neoclassical growth theory the same set of conditions would lead to some increase in Y because the enlarged L could be absorbed into employment with an unchanged K.

If the increase in L is not very great in the period in question, the increase in Y will be approximately equal to the increase in L times the marginal physical product of L, or $\Delta Y = \text{MPP}_L \cdot \Delta L$ in which MPP_L is the marginal physical product of labor, or the increase in Y that accompanies a unit increase in L with K held constant. If we had assumed an increase in K with no change in L, under the same assumptions we would have had $\Delta Y = \text{MPP}_K \cdot \Delta K$ in which MPP_K is the marginal physical product of capital, or the increase in Y that accompanies a unit increase in K with L held constant. Finally, for changes in both K and L in a given time period, we may write

$$\Delta Y = \text{MPP}_K \cdot \Delta K + \text{MPP}_L \cdot \Delta L$$

Dividing both sides by Y, we have

$$\frac{\Delta Y}{Y} = \left(\frac{\text{MPP}_K}{Y}\right) \Delta K + \left(\frac{\text{MPP}_L}{Y}\right) \Delta L$$

which may also be written as

$$\frac{\Delta Y}{Y} = \left(\frac{\text{MPP}_K \cdot K}{Y}\right) \frac{\Delta K}{K} + \left(\frac{\text{MPP}_L \cdot L}{Y}\right) \frac{\Delta L}{L} \qquad [1]$$

If we recall the assumption noted earlier of perfect competition in all markets and now adopt the marginal productivity theory of factor pricing, each unit of a factor will be paid its marginal product, and the total earnings of capital and labor will be equal to $\text{MPP}_K \cdot K$ and to $\text{MPP}_L \cdot L$, respectively. Given that factors are paid their marginal products, the total earnings of capital and labor will exactly absorb the total output in the case of the present production function with constant returns to scale. That is,

$$\text{MPP}_K \cdot K + \text{MPP}_L \cdot L = Y$$

Since

$$\frac{\text{MPP}_K \cdot K}{Y} + \frac{\text{MPP}_L \cdot L}{Y} = \frac{Y}{Y} = 1$$

we may substitute b for the first term on the left and $(1 - b)$ for the second term and rewrite Equation 1 in the following form:

$$\frac{\Delta Y}{Y} = b\left(\frac{\Delta K}{K}\right) + (1 - b)\frac{\Delta L}{L} \qquad [2]$$

The magnitude of b indicates the proportion of the total product or of total income that would be received as a return on capital, if capital were paid its marginal product. This is the same as saying that b measures the elasticity of output with respect to changes in the amount of capital used.[14] If $b = 0.25$, we can say either that the owners of capital would receive 0.25 percent of the economy's income if capital earned a return equal to its marginal product or that a 1.0 percent increase in the amount of capital in use would produce a 0.25 percent increase in output. These amount to two ways of saying the same

[14] The general concept of elasticity refers to a percentage change in one variable divided by the percentage change in another. If L is not changing, $b = \Delta Y/Y \div \Delta K/K$, or the percentage change in Y over the percentage change in K, or b is an elasticity.

thing. The same kind of statement may, of course, be made for labor by substituting $(1 - b)$, or 0.75, in the second preceding sentence.[15]

Assuming a value for b, say 0.25, we may read from Equation 2 the percentage change in output that will follow from a given percentage change in capital, labor, or both. If both K and L rise by 3 percent, output also rises by 3 percent, for the underlying production function is one with constant returns to scale. In this case, we have $\Delta Y/Y = 0.25 \times 3 + 0.75 \times 3 = 3$. However, note that capital and labor do not contribute equally to the growth in output, even though each factor grows at the same rate. In the illustration, 2.25 percentage points of the 3 percent growth rate are due to labor, and the remaining 0.75 percentage points are due to capital. Labor is given three times the weight of capital, for the weights correspond with their output elasticities, and these show that a 1 percent increase in labor will produce a percentage increase in output three times as large as a 1 percent increase in capital. Thus, a 3 percent increase in K and a 1 percent increase in L would indicate a 1.5 percent increase in output, but a 1 percent increase in K and a 3 percent increase in L would indicate a 2.5 percent increase in output.

The results derived here are very different from those indicated by the Harrod-Domar theory. In terms of the numerical example above, if we started from a position of full utilization of labor and capital, a 3 percent growth rate for K and a 1 percent growth rate for L, or vice versa, would in both cases mean a ceiling growth rate for Y of 1 percent. This again is the necessary result if we rule out the substitutability between factors that is not ruled out in neoclassical growth theory. In a more general way, we may bring out the basic difference between the Harrod-Domar and the neoclassical theories by rewriting Equation 2 in a way that incorporates the Harrod-Domar theory. Since $\Delta K = I = sY$ and since $Y/K = \sigma$ in which σ is the symbol used earlier for the output-capital ratio, or the productivity of capital, we may rewrite Equation 2 to read

$$\frac{\Delta Y}{Y} = b(s\sigma) + (1 - b)\frac{\Delta L}{L}$$

Recall that $s\sigma$ defined the equilibrium rate of growth in Harrod-Domar or the growth equation was simply $\Delta Y/Y = s\sigma$. In the neoclassical theory, with its allowance for substitutability between factors, the rate of growth of labor has its own influence on the rate of growth of output. The propensity to save, s, and the productivity of capital, σ, whose product equals the rate of growth of capital, are in themselves no longer sufficient to explain the rate of growth of output. Actually, the rate of growth of capital not only is insufficient in itself to

---

[15] That $(1 - b)$, or $\text{MPP}_L \cdot L/Y$, is equal to labor's share of total output follows the analysis of Chapter 16. We saw there that under competitive conditions employers will hire labor up to the point at which $\text{MPP}_L \cdot P = W$, or $\text{MPP}_L = W/P$. Substituting W/P for MPP_L in $\text{MPP}_L \cdot L/Y$ gives us WL/PY, or the total money wage income of labor as a fraction of the total money income for the economy. (Here Y is the same as O, the symbol used for output in Chapter 16.)

explain the rate of growth of output but may be of far less importance than the labor force in this regard. This follows from the fact that the influence of capital accumulation on the growth rate depends heavily on the size of b, and b may be relatively small. To trace through a numerical illustration, suppose that the economy's output is growing at 3 percent over a period when s is 0.10 and σ is 0.30, so $s\sigma$ equals 0.03, or 3 percent. If the economy became twice as thrifty and raised s to 0.20, would the rate of growth of output also double, rising to 6 percent? A doubling would result according to the Harrod-Domar theory, but here we find that it results only if b equals 1.[16] But b is actually in the neighborhood of 0.25 to 0.33, the range of the share of capital in total income. If b were 0.25, the doubling of the saving ratio would raise the growth rate of output only from 3.0 to 3.75 percent; if b were 0.33, such a doubling would raise the growth rate of output only from 3.0 to 4.0 percent. The fixed link between the rate of growth of capital and the rate of growth of output given by Harrod-Domar is replaced here by a link in which the rate of growth of output depends on both the rate of growth of capital and the rate of growth of the labor force and, further, on the output elasticities of capital and labor.

The Rate of Output Growth per Capita

Although there is obvious interest in how the rate of growth of aggregate output (or $\Delta Y/Y$) will vary with different rates of growth of labor and capital, of much greater interest is how the rate of growth of output per worker will vary under the same circumstances. If we subtract $\Delta L/L$ from $\Delta Y/Y$, we have the difference between the growth rate of aggregate output and the growth rate of the labor force, a difference that is approximately equal to the growth rate of output per worker. Therefore, we can convert Equation 2 into one that shows the growth rate of output per worker by subtracting $\Delta L/L$ from both sides. The same subtraction will show the growth rate of output *per capita*, if the rate of growth of population is the same as the rate of growth of the labor force. In what follows, if we assume these rates are equal, growth rates per worker may also be read as growth rates per capita. Making the indicated subtraction gives us

$$\frac{\Delta Y}{Y} - \frac{\Delta L}{L} = b\left(\frac{\Delta K}{K} - \frac{\Delta L}{L}\right)$$ [3]

The growth rate of output per worker ($\Delta Y/Y - \Delta L/L$) is equal to the growth rate of capital per worker ($\Delta K/K - \Delta L/L$) weighted by the elasticity of output with respect to capital. In order for the growth rate of output per worker to be above zero, the equation shows that there must be an increase in the stock of capital per worker—that is, a growth rate of capital greater than the growth

---

[16] If b were to equal 1, the neoclassical equation would reduce to $\Delta Y/Y = s\sigma$, or to the Harrod-Domar equation. However, for b to equal 1 requires that there be a surplus of labor that is not at all substitutable for capital in production, so output can grow only at the rate of growth of capital, or $\Delta Y/Y = \Delta K/K = s\sigma$.

rate of the labor force. For example, suppose that $\Delta Y/Y$ equals 2 percent and $\Delta L/L$ equals 1 percent, a combination that indicates a 1 percent rise in output per worker per period. The right-hand side of Equation 3 shows that, to secure this 1 percent rise in output per worker per period, the rate of growth of capital must be 5 percent, if we assume a value for b of 0.25, or 4 percent, if we assume a value for b of 0.33. Thus, given a value of b in this range, we find in the present case that a rate of growth of capital four to five times the rate of growth of the labor force is required to produce a 1 percent rate of growth in output per worker per period.[17]

Is it possible for the capital stock to grow at a higher rate than the rate of growth of the labor force period after period, which, according to Equation 3, is a prerequisite to a rising output per worker period after period? A rate of growth of the capital stock greater than the rate of growth of the labor force must result in a decline in the average productivity of capital, or in the output-capital ratio—diminishing returns makes this so. Correspondingly, there must result a rise in the average productivity of labor, or in the output-labor ratio. The decline in the average productivity of capital amounts to a fall in the rate of return on capital. This may be seen through a variation of Equation 3. The rate of growth of output per worker was expressed there as $\Delta Y/Y - \Delta L/L$, and we may in a similar way express the rate of growth of output per unit of capital as $\Delta Y/Y - \Delta K/K$. If we subtract $\Delta K/K$ from both sides of Equation 2, as we earlier subtracted $\Delta L/L$ from the same equation, we find

$$\frac{\Delta Y}{Y} - \frac{\Delta K}{K} = (1 - b)\left(\frac{\Delta L}{L} - \frac{\Delta K}{K}\right) \qquad [4]$$

If b is 0.25, a growth rate for capital of 5 percent and for labor of 1 percent produces a *decline* in the productivity of capital at a 3 percent rate per time period. Whatever the level from which the decline starts, if our periods are years, this means that in less than fifteen years the return on capital will have fallen to less than two-thirds of its previous level. As a matter of fact, Equation 4 indicates that for any value of b less than 1 and for any values of $\Delta K/K$ and $\Delta L/L$ in which $\Delta K/K > \Delta L/L$, the rate of growth of productivity of capital will be negative and the rate of return on capital will be a declining figure. Under these conditions, capital will not grow more rapidly than labor. The very-long-run adjustment in the present case will be one in which both capital and labor ultimately grow at the same rate.

However, we saw that growth in output per worker cannot be achieved unless there is growth in capital per worker, and here we see that the very-long-run tendency is for capital to grow at the same rate as labor. Since we know from the historical record both that capital has grown faster than labor and that there has been growth in output per worker, there appears to be something wrong with the formulation above. It is actually correct, given its assumptions,

[17] If we had assumed $\Delta Y/Y$ of 4 percent and $\Delta L/L$ of 3 percent, the growth rate of output would again be approximately 1 percent, but this would demand an even higher growth rate of capital: 7 percent for b of 0.25 and 6 percent for b of 0.33.

but one of the critical assumptions it makes is that no technological progress occurs. If this were indeed the case, the neoclassical model would lead to a so-called steady-state growth in which capital, labor, and output all grow at the same rate. It is only when allowance is made for technological progress that we find the real-world result of a rising output per worker, or a rising "standard of living."

Technological Progress and Output Growth

There is no question that technological progress contributes significantly to the growth rate of output, but there are difficult questions in establishing precisely how it works out its effect on the output growth rate. We will touch on this issue in the next section. As a first step, however, it is helpful to simplify things by viewing technological progress as a force that merely raises the growth rate of output above what it otherwise would be. It is thus viewed as a factor that is independent of the labor and capital factors with which it actually collaborates to some degree in production. With this simplification, we may refer to the rate of technological progress as a 2 percent rate if, in the course of the time period, such progress makes possible the production of an aggregate output 2 percent greater than would otherwise have been possible with an unchanged amount of labor and capital. Designating the rate of technological progress by $\Delta A/A$, we have in place of Equation 2 the following:

$$\frac{\Delta Y}{Y} = \frac{\Delta A}{A} + b\left(\frac{\Delta K}{K}\right) + (1 - b)\frac{\Delta L}{L} \qquad [5]$$

and in place of Equation 3 the following:

$$\frac{\Delta Y}{Y} - \frac{\Delta L}{L} = \frac{\Delta A}{A} + b\left(\frac{\Delta K}{K} - \frac{\Delta L}{L}\right) \qquad [6]$$

It is no longer true that growth of output per worker can occur only if there is growth in capital per worker. We now find that even if $\Delta K/K = \Delta L/L$, $\Delta Y/Y - \Delta L/L$ will be greater than zero by an amount equal to $\Delta A/A$. Indeed, the growth rate of output per worker will be still higher if $\Delta K/K > \Delta L/L$, but this is not a prerequisite to a positive growth rate in output per worker as it was before technological advance was brought into the equation.[18]

---

[18] In the same way that Equation 6 replaces Equation 3, we may replace Equation 4 with the following:

$$\frac{\Delta Y}{Y} - \frac{\Delta K}{K} = \frac{\Delta A}{A} + (1 - b)\left(\frac{\Delta L}{L} - \frac{\Delta K}{K}\right)$$

which indicates that the productivity of capital need not necessarily fall in the event the capital stock grows at a faster rate than the labor force. The innovations and technical changes that give $\Delta A/A$ its value may be sufficient to raise the productivity, or real return on new capital, more rapidly than it is reduced by a growing ratio of capital to labor—that is, by diminishing returns.

The rate of growth of output per worker thus depends on the capital stock per worker and the rate of technological advance. These two sources are all-inclusive if we view technological advance as a residual, or catchall, that includes all sources of growth other than the rise in capital per worker. Since the growth rate of output per worker is $\Delta Y/Y - \Delta L/L$ and since we know from Equation 3 that the growth rate of output per worker due to the growth in capital per worker is $b(\Delta K/K - \Delta L/L)$, the ratio of the latter to the former gives the proportion of the total growth rate of output per worker that is due to the growth in capital per worker. The proportion of the total growth rate of output per worker that is due to technological advance is then obtained as a residual, or the difference between this proportion and 1. The proportion due to growth in capital per worker, here designated by e, may be expressed as follows:

$$e = \frac{b\left(\dfrac{\Delta K}{K} - \dfrac{\Delta L}{L}\right)}{\dfrac{\Delta Y}{Y} - \dfrac{\Delta L}{L}}$$

If $\Delta K/K = \Delta Y/Y$, then $e = b$. We have seen that a realistic value for b is in the range from 0.25 to 0.33 so in this case e would be one-fourth to one-third. To the extent that $\Delta K/K$ is smaller than $\Delta Y/Y$—and this appears to have been the case for the last sixty years—the proportion e declines to less than one-fourth for b of 0.25 and to less than one-third for b of 0.33. Figures such as these have led economists working in this area to conclude that *less than one-third of the growth rate of output per worker over the years from the turn of the century can be attributed to the rise in capital per worker. Over two-thirds of the growth rate of output per worker has therefore to be attributed to all the other factors covered by the catchall called technological advance.* This same conclusion may be expressed alternatively by stating that *less than one-third of the growth rate of total output can be attributed to the growth rate of the labor and capital inputs, so over two-thirds of the growth rate of total output has to be attributed to increased output per unit of labor and capital inputs, or again to all the factors included under the catchall heading of technological advance.*[19]

These are rather startling conclusions, and it is worth looking briefly at some of the specific estimates that provide the basis for such conclusions. The first three columns of Table 22-3 give the historical record of growth rates of the capital and labor inputs and aggregate output for 1929–60 and for subperiods.[20] The figures in the last two columns are found as residuals by substi-

---

[19] These estimates differ markedly from those by Denison presented in Table 21–3. As noted in connection with that table, the much lower figure he gives for output per unit of input follows from differences in classification, the major one being his inclusion in the labor input of an allowance for the improvement in the quality of the labor force. This is similar to what we will refer to in the next section as the "embodiment of technological advance."

[20] GNP, the measure of output, and man-hours, the measure of labor input, are given here as *potential* rather than *actual* rates. To avoid the distortions that would result from different degrees of slack in the economy at the various terminal dates, the actual GNP and man-hour

TABLE 22–3   Selected Growth Rates 1929–60 and Subperiods (Average Annual Rates)

Period	Gross Capital Stock $\Delta K/K$	Potential Man-Hours $\Delta L/L$	Potential GNP $\Delta Y/Y$	Technological Advance $\Delta A/A$ with $b = 0.25$	Technological Advance $\Delta A/A$ with $b = 0.50$
1929–60	2.0	0.7	3.1	2.1	1.7
1929–47	1.0	0.5	2.5	1.9	1.7
1947–60	3.6	0.8	4.0	2.5	1.8
1947–54	4.0	0.7	4.4	2.9	2.1
1954–60	3.1	0.8	3.5	2.1	1.6

SOURCE: R. R. Nelson, "Aggregate Production Functions and Medium-Range Growth Projections," in *American Economic Review*, Sept. 1964, Tables 1 and 2, pp. 577 and 579.

tuting the figures from the first three columns in the following equation (which is the same as Equation 5 with the terms rearranged):

$$\frac{\Delta A}{A} = \frac{\Delta Y}{Y} - b\frac{\Delta K}{K} - (1 - b)\frac{\Delta L}{L}$$
$$2.1 = 3.1 - 0.25(2.0) - (0.75)0.7$$

Thus, on the assumption that *b* equals 0.25, for 1929–60 we find as shown a value for $\Delta A/A$ of 2.1 percent, or we have the conclusion noted above: Less than one-third of the growth rate of total output is attributable to the growth of the labor and capital inputs. The fraction of the total growth rate explained by the growth of labor and capital inputs is, of course, higher if *b* equals 0.50. However, even then this fraction remains below one-half for the 1929–60 period and for all the indicated subperiods.

    If we separate out the fraction of the growth rate of output that is attributable to the growth of the capital stock alone, we are down to less than one-sixth for the 1929–60 period, assuming that *b* equals 0.25. The output growth rate was 3.1 percent, of which 0.5 percentage points (0.25×2.0) are explained by the growth of the capital stock. If we look at the two major subperiods into which 1929–60 has been divided, the growth in the capital stock explains only 1/10 of the output growth rate for 1929–47 and about 1/4 of the output growth rate for 1947–60. To the earlier conclusion that labor and capital combined

figures are adjusted to what they would have been had the unemployment rate been 4.0 percent. The figures so adjusted give us what are designated as potential GNP and potential man-hours.

    This is one reason for the difference between the 3.1 percent growth-rate estimate given here and Denison's estimate of 2.93 percent given in Table 21–3. Other obvious reasons for a difference are the time periods covered and the aggregate in terms of which output is measured.

account for only about one-third of the growth rate of output, we may add the conclusion that capital accumulation by itself accounts for something like one-sixth of the growth rate of aggregate output during the 1929–60 period.

The Embodiment of Technological Progress

Technological progress was introduced into the preceding analysis in the simplest possible way—as a factor completely independent of the capital stock growth rate and the labor force growth rate. This way of bringing in technological progress amounts to viewing it as technical know-how falling like manna from heaven and somehow applying equally and impartially to all units of the economy's labor force and capital stock. Such technological progress is formally described as *disembodied*, for it yields its benefits without the necessity of embodiment in newly produced capital goods or newly trained or educated workers. As long as technological progress is disembodied, it is possible to assume in theory that the labor force is homogeneous, because the productivity of all workers, regardless of age, training, or education, will benefit proportionally from technological progress; and it is similarly possible to assume that all units of capital are homogeneous because all units of capital, regardless of age and design, will benefit proportionally from technological progress.

By contrast, *embodied* technological progress is a kind that must be physically incorporated in newly produced capital goods or newly trained or educated workers before it can contribute to the rate of growth of the economy's output. Capital can then no longer be assumed to be homogeneous. The capital stock becomes a mixed stock of different "vintages." Because they embody more technological progress, newer machines are more productive than older ones. Similarly, the labor force can no longer be assumed to be homogeneous. Like units of the capital stock, different individuals in the labor force are of different vintages, distinguished by age and training or education. Individuals of the current vintage are then more productive than individuals of earlier vintages.

Although embodied technological advances refer to those that are embodied in either the capital stock or the labor force—that is, in "physical capital" or "human capital"—we will in what follows limit attention to technological advance of a kind that either is or is not embodied in physical capital. Advances of this kind have been described as "design" or "organizational," the former requiring new capital goods and the latter requiring only new procedures or methods.

There is disagreement among economists working in this area as to what part of actual technological advance is design and what part is organizational. If it is true, as some argue, that the larger part is of a design nature and thus of a nature that must be embodied in new capital goods if its benefits are to be gained, then it also appears true that the real importance of the capital stock cannot be measured, as it was above, merely by the fraction of the growth rate of output that is directly explained by the growth rate of the physical stock of capital. We saw that for the period 1929–60 this fraction was a low one-sixth.

Its real importance is much greater than this fraction indicates, for the capital stock is the vehicle through which technological progress is worked into the production process and without which the growth rate of output would be only a fraction of what it actually is. From this point of view, the capital stock, which otherwise could be downgraded to a minor role as we saw above, re-assumes the position of primacy that most people always thought it occupied.

A numerical illustration will bring out the difference between the earlier approach, in which technological advance was assumed to be completely dis-embodied, and the present approach, in which it is in part embodied. We assume an economy whose capital stock is equally divided into one-year through twenty-year vintages. All capital goods last exactly twenty years, so at the end of each year the capital goods then of twenty-year vintage come up for replace-ment. This amount will be 5 percent of the capital stock. We also assume that gross investment is equal to replacement investment, or net investment is zero. This means that each year's gross investment is equal to 5 percent of the capital stock, which in turn is a physical stock that does not change in amount from year to year.

Some part of the economy's technological advance is embodied in newly produced capital goods. Let us assume that technological advance is such that the capital goods produced each year show a 3.5 percent quality improvement, or productivity increase, over the capital goods produced during the preceding year. Any variable that grows at a 3.5 percent compound rate per annum will double in size in twenty years. Therefore, a capital good newly produced in year t and embodying the improvements of year t and all preceding years will have twice the productivity of the capital good of year $t - 20$ that it replaces. The comparison is, of course, between capital goods of equal real cost; the physical makeup of the old and the new may be completely different.

Since gross investment is by assumption equal to replacement investment and since replacement is understood to be the amount of capital goods that must be produced during the period in order to keep the total capital stock unchanged, we appear to have a case of a zero growth rate in the capital stock. However, even though each unit of capital is replaced at the end of twenty years by another unit of equal real cost, the replacement unit is twice as productive as the replaced unit and thus in effect is equivalent in real terms to two of the replaced units. For example, if the total capital stock is thought of as 100 units, this year's gross investment of 5 units for replacement equals the 5 units that wear out during this year and keeps the total capital stock un-changed at 100 units; but, since the 5 replacement units are equivalent in productivity to 10 of the replaced units, in effect the capital stock has been enlarged from 100 to 105 units. In our simple case, this increase would not be revealed to the statistician who measured merely the number of units or the physical quantity of capital without regard for the fact that the units produced each year, even if alike in appearance to units produced in preceding years, incorporate quality improvements not present in units produced in preceding years. An increase in the capital stock is nonetheless there but not in explicit form. In the present example, this implicit, or effective, increase in the capital stock of 5, relative to the preexisting stock of 100, indicates what amounts to a 5 percent growth rate ($\Delta K/K = 5/100 = 5$ percent). Otherwise viewed, gross investment that is equal to replacement—that is, to 5 percent of the capital stock—is effectively gross investment equal to 10 percent of the capital stock, one half of which is 5 percent for replacement and the other half of which is, in effect, 5 percent for net investment.

On the basis of all the preceding assumptions and if we now add the final assumption that b equals 0.25, we find in this illustration that the part of technological advance that is embodied in the capital stock accounts for 0.25(5/100), or about 1.2 percentage points of the rate of output growth. This figure of 1.2 is derived from a whole series of assumptions, some quite arbitrary, and is likely to be far wide of the true figure which is unknown. Nonetheless, let us suppose for the moment that the true figure is at least one-half of the 1.2—that it is at least 0.6. What is relevant here is that whether we take 0.6 percentage points or a larger or even smaller figure, we still reach conclusions quite different from the conclusions reached in the previous section in which technological advance was completely disembodied.

There we presented some estimates for the 1929–60 period that showed that the output growth rate of 3.1 percent per year for this period was accounted for as follows: 0.5 by the growth rate of the labor force, 0.5 by the growth rate of the capital stock, and the residual of 2.1 by the catchall called technological advance. Some part of these 2.1 percentage points is undoubtedly made up of technological advance of a type that is embodied in the capital stock. On the assumption that the embodiment of technological advance in capital goods accounts for at least the 0.6 percentage points of the growth rate noted above, the 2.1 percentage point residual is reduced to around a 1.5 percentage point residual. This remains a catchall that includes disembodied technological advance, but it is now a conceptually narrower term that excludes the technological advance embodied in capital goods.

If 0.6 percentage points of the output growth rate could indeed be accounted for by the embodiment of technological advance in capital goods, the role of the capital stock in the growth process would be much more important than it appeared to be in the preceding section. Of the 3.1 percent growth rate of output for 1929–60, we saw that only 0.5 percentage points were accounted for by the growth in the quantity of capital goods. But suppose now that something like 0.6 percentage points of this growth rate are the result of embodied technological advance. This figure reflects the improvement in the quality of capital goods realized through modernization, and the improvement in the *quality* together with the growth in the *quantity* of capital goods may then account for over one-third of the growth rate of output. Again, the correct figure is not known, but if for the time period in question it was around 0.6 percentage points, it would mean that improvement in the quality of the capital stock was about as important as the growth in its quantity in explaining the rate of output growth.

As we have emphasized, this figure of 0.6 may understate or overstate the true importance of embodied technological advance and is submitted here for illustration only. Without knowing what the correct figure really is, many economists still feel, on the basis of available evidence, that the contribution of the capital stock to the rate of output growth comes in large part, if not in major part, from the role of capital as a vehicle for the embodiment of technological advance. There is, in sum, much more to the role of the capital stock in the growth process than the mere growth in the quantity of capital goods.

Although we chose to limit attention in this section to the question of the embodiment of technological advance in physical capital, it should be noted that the question of the embodiment of technological advance in "human capital" involves a parallel analysis. Just as the mere growth in the quantity of physical capital accounts for a part of the growth of output, so the mere growth in the quantity of human capital does the same. But, as in the case of the capital stock, over and above the mere growth in the amount of labor input is the question of the improvement in its quality as the result of the embodiment of education and training in people. Hard answers are not easy to come by, but it may well be that this is a more important factor in explaining the growth rate of output than is the embodiment of technological advance in the capital stock.[21]

A CONCLUDING NOTE

In contrast to the Harrod-Domar theory, which assumes fixed proportions between labor and capital, the basic neoclassical theory treats the capital stock as a unique, homogeneous resource that can be reshaped and adjusted to be used with any quantity of labor. However, once embodied technological progress is brought into the neoclassical theory, as was done in the preceding section, the capital stock can no longer be viewed as homogeneous; each vintage of capital goods differs from every other vintage in terms of the technological advance that it embodies, the current vintage embodying the latest. The fact that we recognize that units of the capital stock differ according to vintage logically suggests that we should also recognize that the amount of labor required for units of capital of each vintage may differ. For example, capital of the oldest vintage now in use typically requires more labor per unit than capital of more recent vintage, since the older capital was not designed to hold down the amount of required labor to the degree that is true of more recent capital designed in times of relatively higher labor costs.

In addition to these differences in labor requirements between capital of different vintages, in practice the labor requirement per unit of existing capital of each vintage is not variable over a wide range, so the total of existing capital will similarly have a fairly specific labor requirement. Instead of the neoclassical assumption that the whole of the capital stock can be combined with a larger

---

[21] Note that Denison's estimates for 1929–57 in Table 21–3 attribute 0.80 percentage points of the output growth rate to employment and hours and 0.78 to education and increased experience. The latter factors thus become about as important as mere growth in labor input.

or smaller quantity of labor, we find that this assumption is strictly applicable only to capital goods that are in the design stage. At this stage, it is possible to choose, within the existing technology, between alternative forms that have different labor requirements. However, once the capital goods are constructed, the labor requirement is pretty much fixed for these goods, which constitute the latest vintage, as they were earlier for the capital goods that make up the earlier vintages.

For capital goods of vintages other than the current one, the Harrod-Domar assumption of fixed proportions between labor and capital may thus be not too unrealistic. However, that the proportion is not a strictly fixed one follows from the fact that the proportion is subject to change in each year, for in each year there is the possibility of varying the labor-capital ratio via the labor requirement that designers have built into that year's capital goods. Although this cannot substantially change the average labor requirement per unit of the total capital stock in any one year, it can do so over a period of years, which is the time interval relevant to growth theory.

As is so often the case with rival theories that in their simple forms present opposite extremes, a type of growth theory that combines features of both the Harrod-Domar and the neoclassical theories may be a better one than either of the two taken separately. Such theories have been developed in which the existing capital stock has a fixed labor requirement and in which the capital goods about to be built may be built with any of a variety of labor requirements. This type of theory sacrifices the uniformity and relative simplicity of the Harrod-Domar and the neoclassical approaches, but, by providing a closer approximation to the complexity of the real world, it also helps improve our understanding of the process of growth in that extremely complicated real world.

CHAPTER 23

THE THEORY OF INFLATION

In the preceding chapters of Part III, we dealt with the relatively short-run theory of the business cycle and the relatively long-run theory of economic growth. The term "inflation" appeared at several points in these chapters, but no attention was paid to inflation as a phenomenon in itself. In this chapter we turn specifically to the phenomenon of inflation. The first section looks briefly at the problem of defining the term, and the remainder of the chapter examines the principal theories that economists have advanced to explain inflation.

INFLATION DEFINED

The obvious definition of inflation as a rising price level is far from unambiguous. One problem is that the presence or absence of inflation may depend in some periods on which of the available price indexes we use as a measuring stick of price change. For the years since 1964, there is no problem, for all three of the major price indexes given in Table 23–1 show comparable increases. However, for the period 1958–64, there was no inflation at all according to the Wholesale Price Index, but there was what may be called a mild, or "creeping," inflation according to the Consumer Price Index and an inflation a little stronger than this according to the GNP deflator.

In view of such differences, one cannot always say that there is or is not inflation or indicate the amount of it without reference to the price index on which one bases his conclusions. Because the GNP deflator has the broadest coverage and thus comes closest to the concept of the general price level of final

TABLE 23-1   Consumer Price Index, Wholesale Price Index, and
the GNP Deflator, 1945–1968

	CPI 1957–59 = 100	*WPI* 1957–59 = 100	GNP *Deflator* 1958 = 100
1945	62.7	57.9	59.7
1946	68.0	66.1	66.7
1947	77.8	81.2	74.6
1948	83.8	87.9	79.6
1949	83.0	83.5	79.1
1950	83.8	86.8	80.2
1951	90.5	96.7	85.6
1952	92.5	94.0	87.5
1953	93.2	92.7	88.3
1954	93.6	92.9	89.6
1955	93.3	93.2	90.9
1956	94.7	96.2	94.0
1957	98.0	99.0	97.5
1958	100.7	100.4	100.0
1959	101.5	100.6	101.6
1960	103.1	100.7	103.3
1961	104.2	100.3	104.6
1962	105.4	100.6	105.7
1963	106.7	100.3	107.1
1964	108.1	100.5	108.8
1965	109.9	102.5	110.9
1966	113.1	105.9	113.8
1967	116.3	106.1	117.3
1968	121.2	108.7	121.8

SOURCE: *Survey of Current Business*, U.S. Department of Commerce.

goods and services, economists in recent years have come to favor it as the best single guide to the measurement of inflation in the U.S. economy.[1]

Beyond this, whatever the price index chosen, there is a question of how much of a rise in that index is necessary in order to qualify that rise as inflation. For example, there is little argument but that the rise in the GNP deflator from 1965 to 1969 at an average annual rate of about 3.5 percent was of a magnitude that deserves to be called inflation, but does the rise in the GNP deflator from 1958 to 1964 at an average annual rate of about 1.5 percent qualify as inflation? Some people regard inflation as something bad but consider a price level

[1] Because the GNP deflator is available only on a quarterly basis and even then only with a considerable time lag, it is not very suitable for policy purposes. Month-by-month observations on the movement of prices rely on the two other principal indexes or others less familiar. For a description and criticism of each of the three indexes of Table 23-1, see J. Backman and M. R. Gainsbrugh,· *Inflation and the Price Indexes*, Subcommittee on Economic Statistics, Joint Economic Committee, July 1966.

rising at a rate of around 1.5 percent as something good, believing that such a gradually rising price level assists in achieving and maintaining full employment and a satisfactory rate of economic growth. Such persons would apply the term "inflation" only to what they regard as an "unhealthy" or "excessive" rise in the price level. Other people agree that inflation is something bad, but they go further and label any rise in the price level as inflation, even the rise during the 1958–64 period, slow as it was.

Unless we adopt this latter viewpoint and describe any rise in the price level as inflation, we are forced to admit the possibility of a noninflationary rise in the price level. If we accept this, it then appears that there is some rise in the price level per time period at which a price movement becomes inflationary. The problem is to determine how rapid the rise must be. Many writers tend to fall back on words such as "appreciable," "considerable," or "sizable," and some such question-begging is unavoidable. The only alternative is to resort to some fixed percentage rate, but the arbitrariness of any such figure would be worse than the ambiguous adjectives.

We encounter another definitional problem when we consider the time dimension. A 2 percent rise in the GNP deflator over any one quarter would, if sustained, amount to more than an 8 percent rise over a full year. An 8 percent rise in a year would be regarded by everyone as an appreciable and therefore an inflationary rise in the price level. But suppose the 2 percent rise in one quarter were to reverse itself in the following quarter. Shall we describe the first quarter as a period of inflation? Or must an upward price movement be not only appreciable but prolonged in order to qualify as an inflationary price movement? If so, we must again fall back on question-begging qualifications such as "continuing," "persistent," or "sustained" rises in the price level, but again this is unavoidable. The only alternative is to resort to some fixed calendar period, but the arbitrariness of the selection of any such period would be worse than the adjectives.

In short, as long as one defines inflation in terms of price level changes, no fully satisfactory definition is available. However, this is not too serious a problem, for what matters is not how fast and how long the price level must rise before the rise is called inflationary, but what causes the price level to rise in the first place and what are the consequences of different rates of price level change for the distribution of income, the level of output and employment, the growth rate, and other critical variables used to measure the economy's performance. Recognizing the ambiguities our words contain, we will define inflation simply as *a persistent and appreciable rise in the general level of prices.*[2]

---

[2] Mention should be made of at least one of a number of other developments that may be called inflation but are not covered by our definition. If an almost surely otherwise persistent and appreciable rise in the general price level is prevented during wartime by price controls and rationing, the underlying inflation is described as "suppressed" or "repressed." Although all may agree that there is some amount of suppressed or repressed inflation in such a period, the extent of such inflation is no more measurable than is anything else that is not observable. The conventional definition adopted here is limited to observable and so to measurable changes in prices.

We are now in a position to proceed to the major task of the chapter: an exposition of the principal theories advanced by economists to explain the occurrence of persistent and appreciable rises in the general price level. The theories are numerous; the subject is vast; the literature is voluminous; and, unfortunately, definitive conclusions are few. The diversity of theories results from the fact that there is no single theory capable of explaining all inflations that have occurred in various countries throughout history. This is not to say, however, that the different theories of the inflationary process are mutually exclusive; they overlap and are interrelated. To explain particular inflationary movements, economists often draw on a number of theories, for what appears to be a plausible theory or theories for one actual situation may be quite inappropriate for another. The sources of inflation at any one time may differ in developed and underdeveloped countries, in countries with strong labor organizations and those with weak ones, in countries with predominantly oligopolistic market structures and countries with more competitive structures, and in relatively closed economies and economies that are heavily involved in trade with other counties. Structural and institutional differences that exist between countries at any one time may be found in particular countries as they develop over time, so the sources of inflation will differ within a particular country over time. In introducing the subject, we will not become entangled in all the complexities raised by these differences. Instead we will center our attention on inflation theory relevant to an advanced economy such as that of the United States in the fifties and sixties.

Principal inflation theories may be classified as either demand or supply theories or, what is the same but in more familiar terminology, as either demand-pull or cost-push theories. After an analysis of these, we will consider certain relationships between demand-pull and cost-push theories and a form of "mixed" inflation theory that incorporates elements of both.

DEMAND-PULL INFLATION

One main branch of inflation theory runs in terms of generalized excess demand, sometimes loosely described as "too much money chasing too few goods." According to this theory, the general price level rises because the demand for goods and services exceeds the supply available at existing prices. This type of inflation theory was mentioned in Chapter 16, in which we developed the aggregate supply function and related it to the aggregate demand function as in Figure 16–5. In Figure 23–1B, as in Figure 16–5B, the S curve is the aggregate supply curve, and the family of Y curves are rectangular hyperbolas. The approach here, however, involves variables that were excluded in Chapter 16, for here the equilibrium level of money income, Y, is found in terms of the IS and LM curves of Figure 23–1A, while in Chapter 16 it was found simply by the intersection of the $C + I + G + (X - M)$ curve with the 45° line. Determination of the

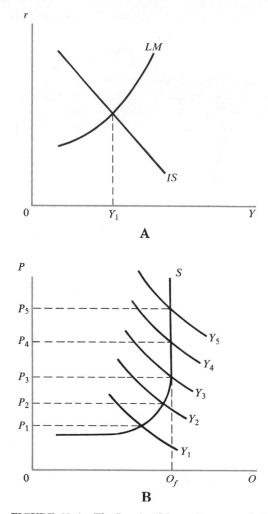

FIGURE 23–1   The Level of Money Income and the Price Level

equilibrium level of Y via the IS and LM curves allows for the influence of money and interest; determination of the equilibrium level of Y in Chapter 16 via the simple aggregate demand curve ignored the influence of money and interest.

Figure 23–1A indicates the determination of that particular equilibrium level of Y that is consistent with the IS and LM functions shown. Let us call this income level Y_1. If we visualize a succession of shifts to the right in either the IS or the LM functions or both, we are then describing successively higher levels of aggregate demand that trace out a series of successively higher equilibrium levels of Y on the horizontal axis of Part A. Each of these equilibrium levels of Y then appears in Part B as one of a series of rectangular hyperbolas labeled Y_1, Y_2, Y_3, and so forth.[3] Increases in Y from Y_1 to Y_3 are

[3] This particular construction is taken from H. G. Johnson, "Monetary Theory and Keynesian Economics," in the *Pakistan Economic Journal*, June 1958, pp. 56–70, reprinted in the author's

accompanied by higher output as well as higher prices.[4] Increases in Y beyond Y_3 involve no increase in output but only in prices. At Y_3 the economy encounters the output ceiling set by full employment, and increases in Y beyond this result in what Keynes described as "true inflation." [5] The more gradual rise in the price level expected from increases in demand that raise Y from Y_1 to Y_3 has sometimes been called "bottleneck inflation," because it results from shortages, imbalances, and rising marginal costs as full-employment output is approached. But, whether we find ourselves in the region at which true inflation appears or below it in the region at which bottleneck inflation appears, the cause of the inflation is found, *assuming a given aggregate supply function*, in the forces that produce successive shifts to the right in the *IS* and *LM* curves and thereby result in what turns out to be too rapid a rate of growth in the level of money income, Y. There are two principal theories that have been advanced to explain inflation of this type: the quantity theory and Keynesian-type theory. The first, in its simple form, emphasizes the quantity of money as the determinant of demand and the level of money income; the second finds the determinants of demand and the level of money income in a wide range of influences, which in effect amounts to a denial of the relationship between the money supply and the level of money income postulated by the simple quantity theory.

Simple Quantity Theory

In Chapter 17 we noted that the simple quantity theory of money may be viewed as a theory of the price level or a theory of aggregate demand. If the money supply turns over at a constant rate in the purchase of goods, increases in the money supply must mean proportionate increases in total spending. If the economy is at its full-employment level of output, increases in spending must mean proportionate rises in the price level. If the rise in the price level is persistent and appreciable, then by our definition we have inflation. Thus, given these conditions, inflation proceeds as long as and as fast as the money supply is expanding; it ceases when the money supply stops expanding.

We saw also that this type of quantity theory is a part of classical theory

---

Money, Trade and Economic Growth, Allen & Unwin, 1962, pp. 107–26. It is an admittedly oversimplified construction that, among other things, fails to show explicitly changes in P in Part B as a factor determining the position of the *LM* curve in Part A. Less simplified constructions are introduced later in the chapter.

[4] Recall that a given aggregate supply function assumes a fixed capital stock, technology, and money wage rate (as well as fixed prices for any other inputs entering into marginal cost and, in a world of imperfect competition, fixed money-profit margins). We will see later why the aggregate supply function tends to shift upward as a result of a rise in the price level produced by a rise in demand and in the level of money income; but, for the moment, so that we may concentrate on the demand side, the supply function is assumed to be independent of demand. In other words, changes in demand produce movements of the Y curve in Part B along an existing and unchanging supply function.

[5] John Maynard Keynes, *The General Theory of Employment, Interest, and Money*, Harcourt, Brace & World, 1936, p. 303.

and that classical theory is a theory of a fully employed economy. In terms of Figure 23–1, the normal output of the economy is then O_f, that consistent with full employment. With the aggregate supply function given by S, full employment output is achieved with that level of total spending that produces the money income level of Y_3. Increases in money income beyond Y_3 involve no increases in output but only higher prices, the situation Keynes described as true inflation. Successive rises in the price level from P_3 to P_4 and beyond are explained by the increases in the money supply that produce the shifts upward from Y_3.[6] Thus, if M rises at 5 percent per time period, Y rises at 5 percent per time period; and, with O at the full-employment level of O_f, P also rises at 5 percent per time period.

According to simple quantity theory reasoning, the inflationary process is halted when the money supply stops expanding. The monetary authority, through its control over the stock of money, is by this reasoning endowed with control over aggregate spending and so over the price level and so over inflation. Inflation occurs, nevertheless, because for one reason or another the money supply is allowed to increase while the economy's output is unchanged for the time being (or the money supply is allowed to increase faster than the economy's output grows). One reason for excessive increases in the money supply is the creation of new money by the central government to meet its obligations, a familiar experience in wartime and not unknown in peacetime. Whatever the reason for excessive increases in the money supply, if output is at the full-employment level (or if output is expanding more slowly than the money supply), there will be a rising price level according to simple quantity theory reasoning. If there is a prolonged and appreciable rise in the money supply (or an excess in the rate of creation of new money over the rate of expansion of output), the rising price level will, by the definition adopted, be described as inflation.

Modern Quantity Theory and Keynesian Theory

These are the conclusions suggested by the quantity theory in its extreme and rigid form. There is a modern statement of the quantity theory, associated primarily with Milton Friedman[7] of the University of Chicago, that departs from the extreme version advanced by some quantity theorists in the past.

---

[6] In terms of the simple quantity theory of Chapter 17, the LM curve of Figure 23–1A would appear as a vertical line whose position would shift rightward proportionally with increases in the money supply. This in turn would result in increases in Y proportionate with increases in the money supply.

[7] See his short (but difficult) essay, "The Quantity Theory of Money—A Restatement," in M. Friedman, ed., *Studies in the Quantity Theory of Money*, Univ. of Chicago Press, 1956, pp. 3–21. See also his "The Influence on Prices of Changes in the Effective Supply of Money," in Joint Economic Committee, *Employment, Growth and Price Levels, Hearings*, Part 4, 1959, pp. 605–69. In a nontechnical vein is his first lecture in *Inflation: Causes and Consequences*, Asia Publishing House, 1963, reprinted in his *Dollars and Deficits*, Prentice-Hall, 1968, pp. 21–39.

Contemporary quantity theorists no longer assume that full employment is the normal state of the economy or that the velocity of money is as stable as is required to yield the conclusions of the quantity theory in its extreme form. Modern quantity theory is thus similar to Keynesian theory in that it refers to income level rather than to price level. However, modern quantity theory continues to assign a very important role to money, whereas Keynesian theory, at least in its extreme form, argues that "money does not matter." Keynesian theory sees money as an essentially passive factor in economic change. The role it plays, to the extent that it is an active one, is limited to its effect on interest rates and, through interest rates, on investment. Because investment depends more importantly on factors other than interest rates, the quantity of money becomes a minor factor in explaining investment and so in explaining income. Thus, Keynesian theory argues that if the multiplier is relatively stable, we can predict changes in income from changes in investment, but it denies that we can predict changes in income from changes in the quantity of money because money has only an indirect and quite limited influence on investment.

In reply, modern quantity theorists argue that changes in income can be more accurately predicted from changes in the money supply than from changes in investment, because their empirical work suggests that the velocity of money exhibits a greater regularity of behavior than does the investment multiplier.[8] If the marginal propensity to save is quite unstable, the multiplier is correspondingly variable, and the stable relationship between investment changes and income changes postulated by the Keynesian model does not exist. On the other hand, if the velocity of money is more stable than the marginal propensity to save, a more stable relationship exists between changes in the quantity of money and changes in income than between changes in investment and changes in income. If this is indeed the relationship, money becomes very important, for it means that we can better explain changes in income from changes in the quantity of money than from changes in investment. The quantity of money then returns to the forefront, and the basic Keynesian system of autonomous expenditures and the multiplier is pushed into the background.

Although modern quantity theory assigns money this position of first importance in explaining income, it is a far cry from the conclusions of the crude quantity theory that changes in income will not only be proportionate to changes in the money supply but that these changes in income will be changes in the price level and not in output. The modern quantity theory does not assume that the economy is normally at full employment or that the velocity

[8] See M. Friedman and D. Meiselman, "The Relative Stability of Monetary Velocity and the Investment Multiplier in the United States, 1897–1958," in *Stabilization Policies*, Commission on Money and Credit Series, Prentice-Hall, 1963. For some critical articles, see A. Ando and F. Modigliani, "The Relative Stability of Monetary Velocity and the Investment Multiplier," and M. DePrano and T. Mayer, "Tests of the Relative Importance of Autonomous Expenditures and Money," both in *American Economic Review*, Sept. 1965. See also in this same issue the Reply by Friedman and Meiselman and Rejoinders by the four critics. For a very elementary statement of the thesis advanced by Friedman and Meiselman, see M. W. Keran, "Economic Theory and Forecasting," in *Review*, Federal Reserve Bank of St. Louis, March 1967, pp. 7–16.

of money is stable. Inflation is still found to be the result of excessive expansion of the money supply, but with velocity and output both recognized as variables, the relationship between prices and the quantity of money is not the simple one sometimes assumed by earlier quantity theorists.

Although the modern quantity theory has attracted a growing number of supporters, especially in the last few years, most economists still regard the approach of Keynesian theory as more fruitful in explaining income changes. As we have noted, in place of the emphasis on money and its velocity, Keynesian theory places emphasis on autonomous expenditures and the multiplier. If autonomous expenditures rise steadily, there will be a steady rise in income equal to a multiple of the rise in autonomous expenditures. In terms of Figure 23–1B, there will be continuous upward shifts in the Y curve. Once output is at full employment, inflation proceeds as long and as fast as these expenditures expand. This explanation of inflation appears to be much the same as the quantity theory explanation, but again the essential difference is that Keynesian theory argues that these upward shifts in the income curve cannot be explained in terms of changes in the money supply but can be understood only in terms of the whole complex of the determinants of the expenditure flows, of which the money supply is only one.

Wage-Price Flexibility—The Inflation Case

Whether we seek to explain demand-pull inflation along the lines of quantity theory or Keynesian theory, it is clear that once the economy is at the full-employment level of output, further increases in demand are purely inflationary. The question we now turn to is whether the inflation in prices and wages in itself tends to reduce real demand, which will thereby end or reduce the inflation. We have already examined the reverse question: whether a general deflation of prices and wages in times of unemployment could raise real demand and thereby raise aggregate output and employment. The extent to which inflation may be terminated or slowed may be analyzed in terms of the effects examined in Chapter 19—the Keynes (interest-rate) Effect, the Pigou (real-balance) Effect, and the income-redistribution, tax and transfer-payment, and foreign-trade effects.

The Interest-Rate Effect.   Inflation cannot continue endlessly if the money supply does not increase. As the price level rises, the transactions demand for money will increase about proportionately. With a fixed money supply, additional transaction balances can be secured only by drawing them from speculative balances. As more money is needed to handle the transactions represented by full-employment output at a higher price level, security owners obtain these balances by selling securities in the market. As a consequence, security prices fall and interest rates rise by the amount necessary to coax idle cash out of speculative balances.[9] Herein lies one possible restraint on inflation, for the rise in interest rates may initially reduce investment expenditures, which, through the fall in income, will also reduce consumption expenditures. The decrease in aggregate investment and consumption expenditure flows will decrease real demand.

In an inflationary boom, however, investment expenditures may remain virtually unaffected by the rise in interest rates, if the outlook for still higher prices and profits is so good that businessmen are willing to pay whatever rates the market asks in order to get the funds needed to expand their investment spending. To the extent that this occurs, rising interest rates will not check demand and so will not have an anti-inflationary effect. Inflation can then proceed still farther with a constant money supply. But at some point the required transaction balances, which have been growing with every jump in the price level, will absorb the total money supply. This will occur when interest rates have risen so far that speculative balances are reduced to zero. At this point, the lack of additional funds will put an end to the inflation of prices.[10]

In sum, when the money supply is fixed, a rising price level tends to bring about its own end, either through the contractionary effect on demand of the accompanying rise in interest rates or eventually by the sheer inability of the existing stock of money to support still higher levels of money income.

What the inflationary process will eventually do on its own the monetary authority may be able to do sooner with less inflation. Instead of waiting for pressure on the existing money supply to raise interest rates and check demand, the monetary authority may raise interest rates itself by reducing the money supply. Similarly, instead of waiting for inflation to be checked when the existing money supply can support no higher dollar volume of transactions, the monetary authority may check the inflation sooner, again by reducing the money supply. This argument plainly overlooks the practical difficulties inherent in an anti-inflationary monetary policy. For example, a restrictive monetary policy that brings an inflationary process to an abrupt end may also precipitate a reverse movement, a cure perhaps worse than the disease. Nonetheless, inasmuch as a continuing inflationary process must be fed by ever larger transaction balances, it is true that monetary policy may check the inflationary process by controlling the cost and availability of money.

The Pigou Effect.   A deflation of prices and wages increases the real value of the public's asset holdings that are fixed in dollar terms. This, according to the Pigou Effect, makes people less anxious to build up further their asset

[9] $M = M_t + M_s = kPO + l(r)$. With M fixed, M_t can rise only through a decrease in M_s. At full employment O and with constant k, required M_t varies proportionately with P. A rise in P will raise r by the amount needed to release from M_s into M_t an amount of M equal to $k\Delta PO$.

[10] It should be noted that inflation may continue even beyond this point to the extent that the velocity of M_t balances increases with rising prices, but the velocity of these balances eventually reaches an upper limit.

holdings and leads to the allocation of a larger part of current income to consumption and a smaller part to saving.[11] Thus, during deflation, the Pigou Effect may raise real consumption expenditures and, assuming an elastic supply function, raise the level of real income, output, and employment. During inflation, this process operates in reverse. Inflation reduces the real value of fixed-dollar assets, thereby damaging the wealth position of creditors and encouraging them to allocate more of their current income to saving and less to consumption, in an attempt to restore the real value of their asset holdings to preinflation dimensions. Thus, at any given level of money income, money consumption expenditures will be reduced, and to this extent there is a decrease in real demand and a decrease in the inflationary pressures originating with excess demand.

As we mentioned in our discussion of the Pigou Effect as it applies to deflation, the empirical significance of the effect is probably not great enough to qualify it as an important influence on aggregate demand. The same limitation holds in its application to inflation. Although it can be said that real consumption demand may be somewhat restrained by the depreciation in the real value of the public's holdings of fixed-dollar assets, it is unlikely that such restraint will be sufficiently large to put more than a small dent in a vigorous inflationary process.

Income-Redistribution Effect.   As deflation brings about some redistribution of income in favor of fixed-income groups, inflation brings about some redistribution against fixed-income groups. To the extent that the propensity to consume of these groups is higher than that of other income groups (primarily wage and profit recipients), some decrease in consumption out of a given level of income is to be expected as inflation redistributes income against the fixed-income groups. The downward shift in the consumption function that may result tends to reduce the inflationary pressures originating with excess demand.

Tax and Transfer-Payments Effects.   With a progressive tax structure and a system of transfer payments such as exists in the United States, tax and transfer payments will tend to reduce the fraction of gross income devoted to consumption as gross income rises with inflation. The reason is that the tax "bite" will rise more rapidly than gross income, thereby widening the spread between gross and disposable income as income rises. Furthermore, because government transfer payments per beneficiary are fixed in dollar terms, their total dollar amount will show little change once the economy has reached full employment.[12] The built-in stabilizing effects of the tax and transfer-payment

---

[11] Recall that the argument applies only to public holdings of assets issued by those debtors whose spending is not likely to be influenced by a change in the burden of their debt resulting from a changing price level. This, in effect, confines these fixed-dollar assets to public debt issues and currency.

[12] For example, old age and survivors' benefits will grow slowly with the growth in the eligible population. Unemployment compensation benefits will decrease as full employment is approached and will reach a minimum with the attainment of full employment, the position at which "true" inflation ensues.

structures reduce the fraction of gross money income devoted to consumption as gross money income rises and thereby tends to reduce the inflationary pressures originating with excess demand.

Foreign-Trade Effects.   If there is inflation in the domestic economy and price stability or a lesser rate of inflation in other economies, a dampening influence will be exerted on the domestic inflation by a decrease in the net export (or an increase in the net import) balance $(X - M)$ of the domestic economy. Depending on how significant foreign trade is to the domestic economy, there will be a larger or smaller downward shift in the aggregate demand function as a result of foreign-trade effects. Some dampening effect is to be expected, of course, in any but a completely closed economy. Thus we may conclude that there will be some reduction in the inflationary pressures as a result of foreign trade effects.

Taking all these effects into consideration, we find evidence that, even in the absence of anti-inflationary fiscal and monetary policies, an inflation that is left to itself will eventually burn itself out. Indispensable to this conclusion, however, is the assumption of a fixed money supply. With this restraint, an inflation will not be able to reach or even approach the extreme known as hyperinflation before the fixity of the money supply pulls it up short. However, if an inflation occurs at a time when there is still a great deal of monetary slack in the system, the previously redundant money supply may be ample to support an appreciable rise in the price level.

Monetary Expansion and the Inflationary Gap[13]

If we accept the proposition that a fixed money supply will eventually bring an end to an inflationary process, the question arises: Will an inflationary process also come to an end if the monetary authority permits the money supply to increase as rapidly as the price level rises? Under such circumstances, there is no interest rate effect, since money interest rates remain stable as the money supply rises by the amount needed to accommodate the rise in transactions requirements.[14] Will the combined impact of the real balance, income redistribution, tax and transfer-payments, foreign-trade effects, and other factors

---

[13] For the development of the models presented in this section, among the earliest contributions were those by T. C. Koopmans, "Dynamics of Inflation," in *Review of Economics and Statistics*, Feb. 1942, pp. 53–65, and A. Smithies, "The Behavior of Money National Income Under Inflationary Conditions," in *Quarterly Journal of Economics*, Nov. 1942, pp. 113–28. See also J. S. Duesenberry, "Mechanics of Inflation," in *Review of Economics and Statistics*, May 1950, pp. 144–49, and F. D. Holzman, "Income Determination in Open Inflation," *ibid.*, pp. 150–58.

[14] This also either assumes no upward shift in the speculative demand function for money as inflation proceeds or else assumes that there will be whatever further increase in the money supply is necessary to hold money interest rates unchanged as the speculative demand function does shift upward. On this assumption, real interest rates could reach or fall below zero to the extent that inflation proceeds faster than anticipated by holders of idle cash.

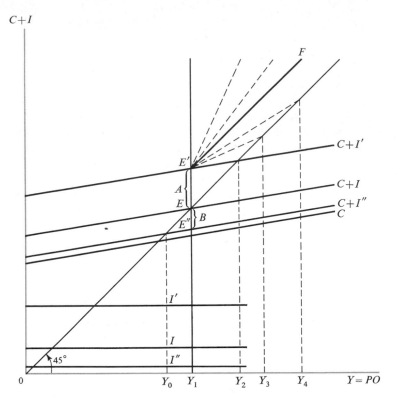

FIGURE 23–2 Inflationary and Deflationary Gaps

still to be discussed (such as "money illusion") eventually put an end to the inflation? Or does a money supply that expands as fast as prices rise necessarily mean an endless inflationary process?

To answer these questions, let us first turn to Figure 23–2. For simplicity, we have limited demand initially to the two sectors of investment and consumption spending. If we assume autonomous investment I, the equilibrium level of income is Y_1, given by the intersection of $C + I$ and the 45° line. At Y_1, planned saving equals planned investment, I. In all previous diagrams of this type, we assumed that every change in Y was matched by a proportionate change in O, giving us a stable P as Y varied. Now let us recognize that increases in Y beyond some point may result in higher P. Suppose that the aggregate supply function (not shown) is perfectly elastic up to the full-employment output and that it becomes perfectly inelastic at this output. With an underlying supply function of this "kinked" type, we may identify along the Y axis of Figure 23–2 the full-employment level at, say, Y_1. Up to this level of Y, all changes in Y are composed entirely of changes in O; beyond this point they are composed entirely of changes in P. At Y_1—the equilibrium income established by demand of $C + I$—the combined expenditures, E, of consumers and investors are exactly equal to the full-employment output of goods at current prices. What happens if there is then an increase in autonomous investment from I to I' that raises expenditures to E'? In this situation, desired expenditures exceed full-employment output, valued at current prices, by the amount A;

512

this may be called the *inflationary, or expansionary, gap*, for it must lead to a rise in *Y*. If, on the other hand, autonomous investment were to fall from *I* to *I″*, which reduces expenditures to *E″*, desired expenditures would fall short of full-employment output at current prices by the amount *B*; this may be called the *deflationary, or contractionary, gap*, for it must lead to a fall in *Y*.[15]

Starting from the full-employment equilibrium at Y_1, a decline in investment expenditures from *I* to *I″* produces a new equilibrium at Y_0. The fall in income from Y_1 to Y_0, equal to the deflationary gap, *B*, multiplied by the simple multiplier, $1/(1 - c)$, wipes out the deflationary gap and restores equilibrium, albeit an underemployment equilibrium. Because the aggregate supply function is perfectly elastic over the income range from 0 to Y_1, the decline in income is entirely a decline in real income, or 0. That is, real output at Y_0 equals Y_0/Y_1 of the full-employment output; the price level at Y_0 is the same as the price level at Y_1.

Starting again from the full-employment equilibrium at Y_1, one might jump to the conclusion that a rise in investment expenditures from *I* to *I′* will produce a new equilibrium at Y_2, indicated by the intersection of the *C* + *I′* function and the 45° line. The rise in income from Y_1 to Y_2, equal to the inflationary gap, *A*, times the simple multiplier, $1/(1 - c)$, would appear to wipe out the inflationary gap and restore equilibrium, though now at a higher price level. Since real output at Y_2 equals real output at Y_1, the rise in *P* must be proportionate to the rise in *Y* from Y_1 to Y_2. But will this (or any other) rise in the price level produce a new equilibrium? It will do so only if a rising price level causes *real* demand to decline because of the combined impact of the various effects discussed earlier or because of another factor that we will discuss later. With an initial rise from *E* to *E′* in total expenditures, a decline in real demand requires that money demand not rise as fast as money income. We know from the presence of the inflationary gap, *A*, that money income must rise. If money demand rises along a path such as either of the lines between *E′F* and the 45° line, real demand will decline with each rise in money income, and equilibrium will be restored at some money income level such as Y_2, Y_3, or Y_4. But can we expect aggregate money expenditures to move along such a path from *E′* when every such move means that either consumers or investors or both are getting less goods than they want? Will they not raise money expenditures as fast as money income rises in the effort to secure the larger quantities of goods desired? If this is the case, and their combined expenditures rise as fast as aggregate money income (the *E′F* path), or even faster (the paths lying above *E′F*), no equilibrium is possible, for the demand curve will never intersect the 45° line. Each increase in money income will lead to an equal or greater increase in money expenditures, and with output temporarily fixed at

[15] The concept of the inflationary gap and "gap analysis" in general was introduced in Keynes's booklet, *How to Pay for the War*, Harcourt, Brace & World, 1940. Although the inflationary gap in those days was seen to result from a rise in government wartime expenditures, against which there was no offsetting reduction in consumption expenditures, inflationary-gap analysis also includes the case of a rise in investment expenditures that is not offset by a fall in consumption expenditures. The illustration here and in what follows runs in the latter terms.

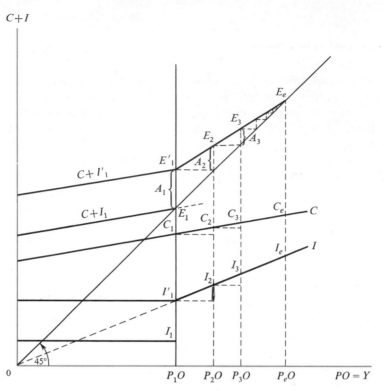

FIGURE 23–3   Convergent Inflationary Process

the full-employment level, prices will rise with each successively higher round of money income and money expenditures—inflation will proceed without limit.

A step-by-step analysis of these two cases, a *convergent inflationary process*, which terminates in a new equilibrium, and a *divergent inflationary process*, which involves continuous disequilibrium, will help clarify the essentials of the process of demand inflation.

A Convergent Inflationary Process.   Figure 23–3 shows the same initial full-employment equilibrium given in Figure 23–2. (In order to isolate price-level changes, PO is now shown on the income axis; at any point, PO is, of course, equal to Y.) Assume that inflationary gap, A_1, results from an increase in autonomous investment from I_1 to I'_1. Business seeks to secure more goods, and the indicated increase in investment spending is that necessary to purchase the additional goods at existing prices. The price level must rise, however, since the sum of consumption and investment expenditures, E'_1, now exceeds E_1, the value of full-employment output at preexisting prices.

Initially, the rise in investment expenditures will raise income by a like amount, from P_1O to P_2O. This rise in income consists entirely of higher prices, and the rise in P is proportional to the rise in expenditures. If E'_1 is 125 percent of E_1, P_2O will be 125 percent of P_1O, and P_2 will be 125 percent of P_1. Because of the rise in P, the indicated increase in I does not secure for business the desired amount of goods. A rise in prices of 25 percent means the physical

514

quantity of goods secured is only 80 percent of the amount planned. We will suppose, however, that business is determined to acquire per period the planned amount of goods and that it stands ready to raise investment expenditures as required to meet this goal. (Remember that we are assuming that the monetary authority will expand the money supply as required to prevent a rise in interest rates.) How much money business will spend per period in an attempt to achieve its goal depends, of course, on the price level. At price level P_1, expenditures of I'_1 would be required, but as we saw, I'_1 is inconsistent with P_1. Since every rise in the price level raises money income proportionately, business can secure the desired amount of goods only by raising investment expenditures so that at each income level they amount to the same proportion of money income that I'_1 is to P_1O. This proportion is indicated at each income level by the broken line projected from the origin through the intersection of I'_1 and the vertical at P_1O. Because P rises after income has exceeded P_1O, a kink appears in the investment curve at P_1O.

With income now at P_2O, the investment curve indicates that I will rise from I'_1 to I_2, which again produces an inflationary gap. The total gap, A_2, is greater than this rise in I, however. The rise in income from P_1O to P_2O will raise consumption expenditures by $c(P_2O - P_1O)$, where c is the marginal propensity to consume out of money income. At P_2O the inflationary gap is A_2, a gap smaller than A_1. This new gap raises money income to P_3O, at which, by the same reasoning, another but still smaller inflationary gap, A_3, appears. Thus, at each step, business comes closer to securing the amount of goods desired and so finds it necessary to raise its investment expenditures by ever smaller amounts. In this way, the inflationary gap is eventually closed when income has risen to P_eO, e designating an equilibrium price level. Barring further disturbances, the price level will then stabilize at P_e with an income level of P_eO.

This income level defines an equilibrium because investment expenditures of I_e secure for business the amount of goods it desires. Once this is accomplished, there is no further rise in investment expenditures, no further rise in the level of income, and, therefore, no further induced rise in consumption expenditures. It must be seen in this process that equilibrium is finally attained only because, for one or more reasons, *real* consumption expenditures fall below those at P_1O, even though the economy's real income remains unchanged as inflation carries money income up to P_2O, P_3O, and beyond. Before the rise in I from I_1 to I'_1, the full-employment real income or output was divided into I_1 of capital goods and C_1 of consumer goods. The rise in I triggered the inflationary process. When this process finally ends at P_eO, the share of the unchanged real output secured by consumers is lower ($C_1/P_1O > C_e/P_eO$), and the share secured by business is larger ($I_1/P_1O < I_e/P_eO$). This result could follow from the Pigou Effect and others discussed earlier, since these effects explain why money consumption expenditures might not rise as fast as the aggregate money income of the economy. This result could also follow from another factor— *money illusion*. Under money illusion consumers react to increases in money income as if they were increases in real income. They are aware only of the increase in money income, not of the proportionately higher prices. With the

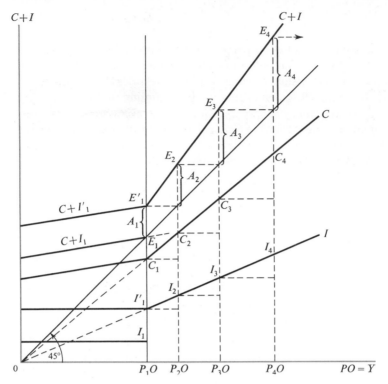

FIGURE 23–4 **Divergent Inflationary Process**

consumption function as shown, consumers save the same fraction of an increase in money income as they would of an increase in real income. Therefore, the higher that money income rises, the greater becomes the fraction of unchanged real income that is saved and the smaller becomes the fraction that is consumed. This decrease in real consumption releases the resources needed to satisfy the demands of business for investment goods. Money illusion thus becomes another possible explanation for a decrease in real consumption and release of resources to investment. Assuming that business is willing and able to raise its spending as required to secure the additional goods wanted, it is only through this release of resources to capital goods production that the inflation will end and an equilibrium level of income be at least temporarily reached.

A Divergent Inflationary Process. In the absence of money illusion or the Pigou Effect and other effects, consumers may be expected to try to maintain the real consumption they enjoyed at the full-employment income of P_1O as inflation carries money income to P_2O and above. This case is illustrated in Figure 23–4. As before, a rise from I_1 to I'_1 introduces the inflationary gap, A_1, and sets an inflationary process into motion. Now, however, consumers adjust money consumption expenditures upward with rising prices in an attempt to maintain the same real consumption enjoyed at P_1O. This results in a kink in the consumption function at P_1O. The slope of the consumption function beyond P_1O shows the same ratio of money consumption expenditures to money income that is found between consumption expenditures and income at the preinflation full-employment income level P_1O. As explained in the case of the investment function, this proportion is indicated at each income level beyond P_1O by the broken line projected from the origin through the intersection of C_1 and the vertical at P_1O.

Thus, when income rises from P_1O to P_2O as a result of the inflationary gap of A_1, consumption expenditures rise proportionately with income and so with the price level. If P_2 is 25 percent above P_1, C_2 will rise 25 percent above C_1. When income rises from P_1O to P_2O, the increase in consumption expenditures from C_1 to C_2 and the increase in investment expenditures from I'_1 to I_2 add up to the inflationary gap of A_2, a gap larger than A_1. This gap pushes income up to P_3O, at which level, by the same reasoning, a still greater gap, A_3, results. The widening of the gap suggests that inflation will proceed without limit. The gap will continue to widen as long as the combined real demands of consumers and business for output exceed the flow of output fixed at the full-employment level.

We have explained both divergent and convergent cases in terms of a two-sector economy. Expanding this to include government demand involves no change in the underlying analysis. The initial full-employment equilibrium at P_1O (which equals E_1) would require that $C_1 + I_1 + G_1 = P_1O$. A rise in the combined expenditures of the three sectors—whether it results, as before, from a rise in autonomous investment expenditures or, alternatively, from a rise in autonomous consumption or government expenditures—would create an inflationary gap at P_1O and force a rise in P. If each sector then persists in its attempt to satisfy its real demand by raising its money expenditures as fast as the price level rises, the inflationary gap will widen—inflation will proceed without limit. Only if the inflationary process leads in one way or another to a reduction of the real demand of one or more sectors will aggregate real demand be reduced to equality with the fixed level of aggregate real output, thereby ending the inflationary process.

Symbolically, we may express this as follows. Beginning with the initial full-employment equilibrium at P_1O, we have

$$C_1 + I_1 + G_1 = P_1O$$

At this point an increase in the expenditures of any sector will create an inflationary gap and raise the price level. The inflation will terminate only if

$$\frac{\Delta C}{\Delta PO} + \frac{\Delta I}{\Delta PO} + \frac{\Delta G}{\Delta PO} < 1$$

The three ratios represent the marginal propensity to spend out of money income for each of the three sectors. If the sum of additional spending by the three sectors is less than the rise in money income, there will be a decrease in real demand. The inflationary gap will narrow, and inflation will eventually end.

On the other hand, if

$$\frac{\Delta C}{\Delta PO} + \frac{\Delta I}{\Delta PO} + \frac{\Delta G}{\Delta PO} \geq 1$$

inflation will continue indefinitely. If the sum of additional spending of the three sectors is equal to or greater than the rise in money income, the inflationary gap will either remain constant or widen, and the inflation in both cases has no limit. Unless the combined marginal propensity to spend out of money income declines as money income rises, there will be no decrease in the combined real demands of the three sectors and hence no limit to the inflation.

Throughout this analysis we have assumed that the money supply expands at the rate necessary to prevent a rise in interest rates. In the convergent case, we found that inflation will come to an end despite the willingness of the monetary authority to finance still further inflation. The very rise in prices may lead to a decrease in aggregate real demand. In the divergent case, the inflation does not come to an end. However, if the money supply did not expand as assumed, this inflation would be checked sooner or later. The rise in interest rates would check investment spending (and possibly consumption spending); the real demand of business (and possibly of consumers) would be reduced. Even if spending were insensitive to higher interest rates, the inability of a nonexpanding money supply to finance ever higher levels of money income would, in the extreme case, bring an end to still higher levels of money income and so to inflation.

The models developed in this section bring out in a simple manner the essence of the Keynesian type of demand-inflation theory and the conditions under which demand inflation will terminate or continue.[16] As we emphasized at the outset, the approach here assumed away changes on the supply side of the market. In other words, the analysis assumed a given aggregate supply function that was independent of changes in the aggregate demand function. Inflation resulted from excess demand as the income curve shifted along a fixed supply function. As a next step, we turn to the inflation that may result from upward shifts in the aggregate supply function. Here again, to simplify the analysis, we will assume that shifts in aggregate supply are independent of changes in aggregate demand. This branch of inflation theory is called supply, or cost-push, inflation.

COST-PUSH INFLATION

For many years before the fifties, inflation theory ran predominantly in terms of generalized excess demand, explained either by quantity theory or Keynesian-

---

[16] A quite different and important demand-inflation model that space did not permit us to include is found in Bent Hansen, *A Study in the Theory of Inflation*, London: Allen & Unwin, 1951, especially Ch. 7. Unlike Keynes, who considered only excess demand in the goods market, Hansen disaggregates the system into a market for goods and a market for productive services (factors) and distinguishes a "goods gap" and a "factor gap." The inflationary process then is analyzed in terms of the relationships between these two possible gaps. For an introduction to Hansen's work, see B. N. Siegel, *Aggregate Economics and Public Policy*, rev. ed., Irwin, 1965, pp. 263–66.

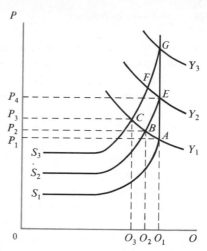

FIGURE 23–5   Shifts in the Aggregate Supply Function and Cost-Push Inflation

type theory. During the fifties there occurred a revival of supply, or cost, theories of inflation. Although sometimes referred to as the "New Inflation," [17] the general notion that price inflation can arise on the supply, or cost, side is far from new. In a survey of inflation theory, for example, M. Bronfenbrenner and F. D. Holzman note that

> Cost inflation has been the layman's instinctive explanation of general price increases since the dawn of the monetary system. We know of no inflationary movement that has not been blamed by some people on "profiteers," "speculators," "hoarders," or workers and peasants "living beyond their station." [18]

Of course we now know much that is "new" about the nature of cost-push inflation as a result of the research in recent years that recognizes the structural and institutional changes of these years, but the general notion that inflation can be caused by supply, or cost, is an old one.

This general notion may be illustrated by Figure 23–5, which is similar to Figure 23–1. However, instead of the single aggregate supply curve of the earlier figure, the present one shows a series of such supply curves. Suppose we break into Figure 23–5 with the economy at its full-employment output of O_1 and the price level at P_1. Then suppose that the supply function moves upward from S_1 to S_2. With no change in demand and no change in the money income level of Y_1, output will drop from O_1 to O_2, and the price level will rise from P_1 to P_2. Another upward movement of the supply function to S_3 will cut output still further to O_3 and raise the price level still higher to P_3. The process will continue for still further upward shifts in the supply function. To the extent that an inflationary rise in the price level occurs in this way, inflation may be described as pure supply, or pure cost-push, inflation.

There are two principal causes of inflationary shifts in the aggregate supply function, both of which represent the exercise of market power by specific

[17] See the book of this title by W. L. Thorp and R. E. Quandt, McGraw-Hill, 1959.
[18] "Survey of Inflation Theory," in *American Economic Review*, Sept. 1963, p. 613.

groups in the economy. One is higher money wages secured by labor unions, and the other is higher prices secured by business firms in monopolistic or oligopolistic industries. For purposes of classification, we may call these two principal causes of inflation on the supply side *wage-push* and *profit-push*.

Wage-push Inflation. If wage-rate increases outpace productivity increases, there will be an upward shift in the aggregate supply function. One cause of a rise in wage rates is an excess demand for labor. Once an economy has reached full employment, any increase in the level of money income will reflect only a rise in prices and no rise in output. Thus, from the initial equilibrium at O_1P_1 in Figure 23–5, a rise in money income from Y_1 to Y_2 is accompanied by a rise in the price level from P_1 to P_4. In this case, higher prices mean greater profits, and greater profits spur employers to expand output. Employers seek more labor for this purpose but it is not available. Their competition forces wage rates up and thereby forces the aggregate supply function up from S_1 to S_2. A new equilibrium, however temporary, may be identified by the intersection of S_2 and Y_2 with output at O_1 and the price level at P_4.

In this sequence, there has been a rise in wage rates with no rise in the productivity of labor, but notice that the rise in labor cost per unit of output is not the *cause* of the rise in the price level but the *result*. Wage rates rose as a result of an excess demand for labor; this would have occurred whether labor was organized or not. Although this is perhaps obvious, recognition of it is necessary if we are to see the fallacy in the argument of those who contend that any rise in wage rates in excess of the rise in labor productivity *causes* a rise in prices.

The concept of wage-push inflation must then be limited to increases in labor costs that are the cause and not the result of higher prices. Wage-push inflation can follow only from "spontaneous" or "autonomous" upward shifts in the supply function, as opposed to those that are "induced" by excess demand for labor. Induced shifts may occur with or without a strong labor movement, but spontaneous shifts require organized labor with sufficient strength to push up wage rates in the absence of any excess demand for labor. Where unions have this strength, there is the possibility of a rise in wage rates that may produce a spontaneous shift in the supply function from S_1 to S_2 even though there is no change in aggregate demand and in the level of money income from Y_1. As a first approximation, therefore, we can say that a rise in prices is the result of wage-push if the existing level of money income is not sufficient to support the rise in wage rates without a reduction in output and employment. This is illustrated by the reduction in output from O_1 to O_2 that results from the shift from S_1 to S_2. On the other hand, a shift from S_1 to S_2 will not reduce output if that shift is induced by excess demand for labor that follows from a rise in aggregate demand for goods and a rise in the money income level from Y_1 to Y_2.

Wage-push inflation is impossible in an economy in which wage rates are determined by purely competitive market forces. In such a situation wage rates will rise or fall only in response to variations in labor supply and demand, the latter in turn depending on variations in aggregate demand for final output. However, it is not necessary that the labor force be completely unionized for the conditions needed for wage-push to arise. It is sufficient that a substantial portion of the labor force be organized and that the strength of these organizations be great enough to force increases in money wages that exceed productivity increases. With a labor force partially organized and partially unorganized, as is the case in the U.S. and most other free economies, and to the extent that nonunion wages are closely tied (with established differentials) to union wages, it is possible for wage-push to originate in unionized industries and for the higher wages gained there to spread to other industries.

There are a number of reasons to expect this spread of higher wages to nonunion workers. Employers of nonunion labor may raise the wages of their employees in order to discourage unionization, prevent employee discontent, and avoid loss of valued employees. However, to the extent that nonunion wages are *not* adjusted to union wages in these and other ways, a wage-push process in unionized industries leads to an ever greater gap between union and nonunion wages. This gap will mean relatively higher prices on the goods produced by unionized industries, which may induce a shift of demand away from these goods in favor of the relatively lower-priced goods turned out by nonunionized industries. This gap also increases the possibility that new firms will enter the unionized industries and operate with nonunion labor. Developments such as these represent threats to the jobs and the higher wage rates of union employees and as such must act as a restraint on the push for higher wages in the unionized industries. Therefore, a wage-push inflationary process that creates a constantly widening gap between union and nonunion wage rates probably cannot be sustained. In sum, the initiation of an economy-wide wage-push inflation requires at least a partially organized labor force. The rate at which such an inflation will proceed and whether it can be sustained depends on, among other factors, the extent of unionization and the degree to which union-won gains spread to the balance of the labor force.

These results are based on the assumption that employers post higher prices for their products as rapidly as the forced increases in wage rates raise the cost of those products. Although the presence of labor unions on the supply side of the labor market is a prerequisite to wage-push inflation, the success of a union drive to force up wages depends in part on the demand conditions faced by the firms subjected to these wage demands. At one extreme is the individual firm, operating under competitive conditions, that cannot raise prices to offset higher wage rates without losing most of its sales, for under competitive conditions the demand curve for its output is highly elastic. Whether they are organized or not, workers cannot force such an individual firm to grant higher wages without eventually driving it out of business (unless the particular firm enjoys some special advantage that provides extraordinary profits). If, on the other hand, the same increase in wage rates is secured from all firms in a competitive industry, wage-push is at least possible. Despite the high elasticity of the demand curve facing each firm, no one firm need fear loss of sales to competitors by raising prices to cover higher wages, since all other firms in the industry may be expected to follow a similar policy. It still remains that the industry as a whole faces a less than perfectly inelastic demand curve. Therefore, if wage rates do not show similar rises in other industries, the industry in question may lose sales to others. Nonetheless, labor may still be able to force through a wage-push, albeit at the cost of some decrease in the output of this industry and in the employment it provides. Since the demand curves facing oligopolists are less elastic than those in more competitive markets, such firms present unions with the best opportunities for securing wage increases in excess of productivity increases with a minimum loss of jobs. Largely for this reason, wage-push, if it occurs, tends to be most pronounced in unionized oligopolistic industries. Although initiated in and offset by higher prices for the output of these industries, higher wages usually spread to other unionized industries as unions there seek to follow the "pattern" and to match the gains that have been won by other unions. The same increases may in turn spill over in large degree into nonunionized industries, as we mentioned earlier.

Thus, starting out with the existence of strong aggressive unions in the major oligopolistic industries, one can see how wage pressures originating there and wage gains won there can possibly spread through the system as a whole to produce some degree of wage-push inflation in the absence of any increase in current demand for output of the economy as a whole.[19]

Profit-Push Inflation

Profit-push is another variant of supply inflation. Just as labor unions may exercise their market power by forcing wage increases, so oligopolists and monopolists may, in their drive toward greater profits, raise prices more than enough to offset any cost increases. Again, just as labor unions are a prerequisite to a generalized wage-push inflation, so the existence of imperfectly competitive markets in the sale of goods and services is a prerequisite to profit-push inflation. Where prices of goods are set by the competition of buyers and sellers, as in agricultural commodities and raw materials, the seller cannot do very much about the price at which he sells. But many goods do not move through such markets, and the sellers of these goods "administer" prices. In an economy in which so-called administered prices abound, there is at least the possibility that these prices may be administered upward faster than costs in an attempt to earn greater profits. To the extent that such a process is widespread, profit-push inflation will result.

Although there is this similarity between the administered prices at which

---

[19] Of the extensive literature on wage-push, see, for example, S. H. Slichter, "Do Wage-Fixing Arrangements in the American Labor Market Have an Inflationary Bias?" in *American Economic Review*, May 1944, pp. 322–46; J. M. Clark, *The Wage-Price Problem*, American Bankers Association, 1960; W. A. Morton, "Trade Unionism, Full Employment, and Inflation," in *American Economic Review*, March 1950, pp. 13–39; and A. Kuhn, "Market Structures and Wage-Push Inflation," in *Industrial Labor Relations Review*, Jan. 1959, pp. 243–51.

labor unions supply labor to firms and the administered prices at which firms supply goods and services to their customers, the responsibility for supply inflation has still generally been placed with labor unions. One reason for this lies in the differences between the wage-setting process followed by unions and the price-setting process followed by business. It is argued that unions commonly press for higher wages with an objective that is little more specific than Samuel Gompers' classic goal of "more." This is either because unions regard the demand curve for labor as highly inelastic or because they are more concerned with higher wage rates than with the amount of unemployment that higher wage rates will produce with a given level of aggregate demand. In contrast to the officers of labor unions, those who administer prices of goods have a more or less definite objective in the form of profit maximization. Profits of a firm depend not only on prices but on sales and unit costs as well, and the latter depend in part on prices charged. Thus, although there is always the possibility of raising prices where prices are administered, the argument is that market realities enter more systematically into the setting of prices than into the setting of wage rates by labor unions. Firms with administered prices may generally respond promptly to wage increases by raising prices, but they are unlikely, when faced with unchanged demand and stable costs, to find cause to raise prices above those that are already "equilibrium" prices according to the profit maximization or other objectives of the firm.[20]

Inflation Control and the Phillips Curve

Restrictive monetary and fiscal policies are the standard weapons used to curb demand inflation. According to the quantity theory, demand inflation may be checked by a monetary policy that prevents expansion of the money supply, which is held to be its cause. According to Keynesian-type theories, apart from the possibility of an inflation being otherwise checked by tax and transfer-payment effects, "money illusion," and the like, restrictive fiscal and monetary policy measures carried to the degree necessary to check the expansion of aggregate money demand are clearly suggested as ways of ending inflation.

In a supply inflation, however, restrictive monetary and fiscal policies are not so clearly appropriate. Such measures have their immediate impact on aggregate demand, but supply inflation is not the result of aggregate demand pressing against the economy's full-employment output. As a matter of fact, in attempting to distinguish between demand and supply inflation, the most telling evidence of a supply inflation is a rising price level with output appreciably below that level indicated by full employment. Under these conditions, reliance on restrictive monetary and fiscal policies may, by reducing aggregate demand, actually aggravate the inflationary pressures rather than eliminate them—for

[20] On this see also the view of G. Haberler in P. D. Bradley, ed., *The Public Stake in Union Power*, Univ. of Virginia Press, 1959, pp. 63–85, and in International Economic Association, 1959 Conference, D. C. Hague, ed., *Inflation*, St. Martin's, 1962, pp. 27–31.

restrictive policy may restrain the rate of investment spending and thereby slow the rise in labor productivity that could otherwise offset, at least in part, a wage-push, which by definition is a more rapid rise in the money wage rate than in labor productivity. On the other hand, a restrictive policy may succeed in checking a wage-push inflation if it reduces aggregate demand and output by an amount sufficient to create enough unemployment to prevent wage increases in excess of productivity increases. The problem here is that the avoidance of wage-push inflation by maintaining whatever unemployment rate is necessary for that purpose may require an unemployment rate that is socially and economically unacceptable. In other words, we might be purchasing price stability only at the cost of considerable social distress and a slowed rate of economic growth. If sustained periods of 5 or 6 percent unemployment are necessary to achieve price stability, it would seem to many people the lesser of two evils to accept the presumably moderate inflation that accompanies a 4 or even 3 percent unemployment rate.

Since wage costs represent the backbone of the price structure, in recent years the interest of economists in supply inflation has understandably led them from an examination of the relationship between the rate of wage increase and the rate of price increase to an examination of the relationship between the rate of wage increase and the rate of unemployment of the labor force. The analysis of this relationship proceeds in terms of the "Phillips Curve," so named after A. W. Phillips, who pioneered in the investigation of this relationship for the United Kingdom.[21] In its simplest form, a Phillips Curve may be derived from an economy's data for a period of years by plotting for each year the percentage money wage increase (vertical axis) against the percentage of the labor force that is unemployed (horizontal axis). A curve fitted to the points so plotted will slope downward to the right as do curves A and B in Figure 23–6.[22]

Any curve of this general shape suggests that the rate of money wage increase is inversely related to the unemployment rate. It also seems to suggest that a sufficiently high unemployment rate will hold money wage increases down to a noninflationary rate, from which it might be concluded that a rising rate of unemployment can be depended on to eliminate price inflation of the wage-push variety.

Not every rate of money wage increase is, of course, inflationary. By drawing a horizontal line, say at level OW_1, we may indicate in Figure 23–6 the percentage increase in labor productivity and therefore the percentage increase in the money wage rate that, on the average, can be granted by employers without raising prices. An appropriate figure for the U.S. economy would be something like the 3.2 percent wage guidepost laid down a few years ago by

---

[21] See "The Relation between Unemployment and the Rate of Change in Money Wage Rates in the United Kingdom, 1862–1957," in *Economica*, Nov. 1958, pp. 283–99.

[22] Phillips found that the same relationship that fits the data for 1861–1913, with minor exceptions, fits the data for 1913–48 and 1948–57. This, of course, would not be expected in all economies or for every time period; the curve could shift over time either to the right or the left.

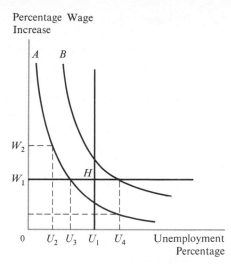

Percentage Wage Increase

FIGURE 23–6   Phillips Curves

the Council of Economic Advisers. Finally, by erecting a vertical line at OU_1, we may indicate the maximum "acceptable" percentage of unemployment, a figure that most U.S. economists would place between 3 and 4 percent.

The point of intersection, H, between the horizontal at OW_1 and the vertical at OU_1 is particularly significant. If the Phillips Curve intersects this horizontal line to the left of H, as the A curve does, it will suggest that supply inflation of the wage-push type may be avoided through monetary and fiscal policy without inflicting an unacceptably high unemployment rate on the economy. Thus, if the unemployment rate is as low as U_2, the wage increase rate is W_2, a rate in excess of the productivity rate of W_1 and so a rate of wage increase that indicates wage-push inflation. Resorting to restrictive monetary and fiscal policy in this case can end the wage-push inflation by reducing aggregate demand to a level at which the resulting unemployment rate rises to U_3. Since U_3 is still below U_1, it is still within the range of acceptability. Suppose, however, that the Phillips Curve is one like B, which cuts the horizontal line to the right of H. Only by forcing on the economy the unacceptably high unemployment rate of U_4 will wage demands be held in line with productivity and wage-push pressures against the price level be held in check. In such case, restrictive monetary and fiscal policy does not provide an acceptable solution.

Phillips concluded from his study for the United Kingdom that the money wage level would stabilize with 5 percent unemployment and that the rate of increase of money wages would be held down to the 2 to 3 percent rate of productivity increase with an unemployment rate of about 2.5 percent. In terms of Figure 23–6, this curve resembles A and thus intersects the horizontal productivity line to the left of H. Studies based on U.S. data indicate Phillips Curves that are more like B of Figure 23–6 and accordingly they lead to pessimistic conclusions. One study finds that a 5 to 6 percent unemployment rate would probably be required to hold wage increases to no more than the productivity growth of the U.S. economy. Furthermore, to satisfy the requirement of no

525

more than 3 percent unemployment (a commonly accepted definition of "full employment"), prices might have to rise by 4 to 5 percent per year, figures that spell something more than "creeping" inflation.[23]

If we succeed in achieving full employment, we must find some way other than the use of monetary and fiscal policy to prevent the supply inflation that these studies suggest may well result. One of the ways tried has been the use of wage and price guideposts, an approach discussed in Chapter 16. Other ways of combating the problem, quite different from the guidepost approach, include various forms of anti-union legislation, which at the extreme would abolish collective bargaining, or at least impose "right to work" laws or prohibit industry-wide bargaining. Our purpose here is only to note a few of these proposals and not to enter into the open question of their possible efficacy.[24] Although all such measures have implications that go far beyond their possible anti-inflationary applicability, it is sufficient here to note that some such measures may be needed if we are to develop a program designed to avoid supply inflation but still achieve the goals of full employment and rapid economic growth.

DEMAND-PULL VERSUS COST-PUSH INFLATION

Up to this point we have examined separately the two parts of what is now a well established dichotomy in inflation theory: demand-pull and cost-push. Although this dichotomy is now a part of the language of economics, some economists object to its implication that an inflation is *either* demand-pull *or* cost-push. They argue that any actual inflationary process contains some elements of both. Expressed in this fashion their argument can hardly be denied. However, if the dichotomy is accepted as nothing more than a convenient two-fold classification of types of causation, their objections do not apply: It is at least helpful in separating two distinct sets of forces that are usually simultaneously and interdependently at work in any actual inflationary process.

In terms of this dichotomy, it should be noted that there is a lack of symmetry between the demand-pull and cost-push theories. An inflationary process may begin with generalized excess demand and may be expected to persist as long as excess demand is present, even though no cost-push forces whatsoever

[23] See P. A. Samuelson and R. M. Solow, "Analytical Aspects of Anti-Inflation Policy," in *American Economic Review*, May 1960, p. 192. Another study of this sort draws even more pessimistic conclusions for the U.S. economy: See R. J. Bhatia, "Unemployment and the Rate of Change in Money Earnings in the United States, 1900–1958," in *Economica*, Aug. 1961, pp. 285–96. See also J. W. Barbarino, "Unionism and the General Wage Level," in *American Economic Review*, Dec. 1950, pp. 893–96.

[24] For a critical review of some proposals, see J. P. Lewis, "The Problem of Price Stabilization: A Progress Report," in *American Economic Review*, May 1959, pp. 309–32. For some specific proposals, see the statements of O. Eckstein in Joint Economic Committee, *Economic Report of the President, Hearings*, Jan. 1962, pp. 380–85, and of A. P. Lerner in Joint Economic Committee, *Employment, Growth, and Price Levels, Hearings*, Part 7, 1959, pp. 2262–66.

are at work. Excess demand will raise prices, which in turn will raise wage rates, but the rise in wage rates in this case is not the result of cost-push. Notice, however, that this does not rule out the possibility that cost-push forces may also be at work to produce an even greater rise in wage rates. On the other hand, an inflationary process may begin on the supply side, but it will not long persist unless there is an increase in demand. For example, an autonomous rise in wage rates will raise prices in the absence of any increase in demand. For a cost-push inflation so initiated to be sustained, however, one wage increase must be piled on top of another; but, in the absence of an increase in demand and in the level of money income, this would mean ever smaller production and ever greater unemployment. Sooner or later this must limit any inflationary process that depends on changes on the supply side alone.

This asymmetry can be illustrated by turning back to Figure 23–5. With output at O_1, increases in aggregate demand that raise the money income level from Y_1 to Y_2 to Y_3 and beyond can carry the price level ever higher, from A to E to G, and so forth, in a sustained inflationary process. With full employment, wage rates will rise along with prices as producers, encouraged to expand output by the enlarged profits that result from the rising level of money income, increase their demand for labor. As long as the forces feeding the demand for final output continue to raise the money income level ever higher, inflation will continue unchecked. In the extreme case, a runaway price level known as "hyperinflation" may result. However, starting again from O_1, a wage-push or a profit-push that shifts the aggregate supply function from S_1 to S_2 will, with the level of money income still at Y_1, produce an intersection at B and reduce output below the full-employment level. A further upward push on the supply side to S_3, unless accompanied by an increase in demand that raises money income above Y_1, will move the intersection to C and further reduce output and employment. The successive reductions in output and the growing unemployment that result under these conditions will bring the inflation to an end. Thus, unlike demand-pull, inflation may originate on the supply side, but it cannot be sustained unless demand and the level of money income increase.

The crucial question, of course, is the way that aggregate demand and the level of money income respond to the upward shift in supply. At one extreme we may find demand and income shifting upward proportionately with the upward shift in supply. If we take rising money wages as the cause of the upward shift in aggregate supply, such a result assumes that as firms raise prices in response to higher wage rates, the money income level rises proportionately to maintain output and employment unchanged at the higher prices. This is equivalent to no decrease in *real* demand, a result that can follow only if there is, for example, a sufficient expansion of the money supply and so no rise in interest rates that would reduce real investment demand. Or, combining the interest rate effect and the other effects earlier considered, this result can follow only if these effects do not produce a decrease in real demand or, to phrase it differently, if they do not prevent a rise in money demand and money income proportionate with the rise in the price and wage structure. But, because of these effects and for other reasons, it seems most likely that aggregate money demand will *not* rise in line with the rise in wages and that as a result there will be some decline in output and employment and a lesser rise in prices than would be the case on the assumptions above. To the extent that this is the economy's characteristic response to the cost-push, successive cost-pushes can indeed force up wages and prices, but only at the cost of reduced employment and output. Thus we reach the conclusion noted above: Pure cost-push cannot in itself produce a sustained inflationary process.

The Dilemma Model

If the conclusion just reached is correct, the prospects of an inflationary process being fed in a sustained way from the supply side alone seem quite limited. But this overlooks one crucial consideration: Although a cost-push will probably not produce a spontaneous rise in demand of the amount needed to prevent a reduction in output and employment, the required rise in demand may follow as the result of expansionary monetary and fiscal policies. Since cost-push left to itself can produce a reduction in output and aggravate any existing unemployment, it is likely that this very fact may lead the monetary and fiscal authorities to pursue policies designed to support output and employment even though the result of such policies is an inflationary process that cost-push forces alone could not bring about. This brings us face to face with a well-known dilemma: the apparent impossibility of simultaneously achieving full employment and avoiding some amount of inflation in an economy in which strong wage-push and/or profit-push forces are at work. Thus we are confronted with the apparent necessity of choosing between a sizable amount of unemployment and reasonable price stability or a smaller amount of unemployment and a rising price level.

Cost-push, viewed from this perspective, can thus mean a sustained inflationary process to the extent that "full employment at all costs" becomes the overriding economic objective of public policy. Such a policy requires the "validation" of an upward push of wages in order to prevent what otherwise would be an unacceptably high level of unemployment, but the validation of one wage-push is an open invitation to labor to bring off another wage-push. In terms of Figure 23–5, a "ratchet" is traced out by the movements from A to B to E to F to G as the price level moves up in a persistent inflationary process. This same process, it should be noted, can begin and proceed in an economy below full employment. Starting at B, a wage-push might shift us to C. An increase in demand that raises money income to Y_2 moves us to F, at which another wage-push (not shown) could shift the supply function upward yet another notch. As long as the policy is to validate each wage-push in the effort to prevent the worsening of an already existing unemployment problem, a sustained rise in the price level appears possible in an economy operating below full employment. This case of inflation in an underemployed economy is, as we saw earlier, possible with cost-push, but here we see that to be sustained such an inflation must be supported by a policy that validates the cost-push.

To validate or not to validate is to choose between the evil of inflation and the evil of unemployment. This dilemma between price stability and full employment has been the subject of much study in the years since World War II. It is, however, by no means as precisely delineated as the preceding discussion may suggest. Economists have differed sharply as to its seriousness. Some even feel that the dilemma hardly exists.[25] Were it not for a virtual government guarantee of full employment, a low percentage of unemployment would, in their judgment, be sufficient to prevent wage-push. In other words, for these economists it is the very assurance that government will not idly stand by in the face of worsening unemployment that gives rise to the cost-push in the first place. In terms of the earlier discussion of the Phillips Curve, these economists feel that the curve would lie far to the left if it were not for a public policy that guarantees full employment. At the other extreme are economists who believe that the position of the Phillips Curve, full-employment guarantee or not, lies so far to the right that price stability can be gained only at an unacceptably high unemployment rate.[26] Short of measures such as direct price and wage controls, these economists see little choice but to sanction some amount of inflation as the unavoidable price of maintaining tolerably low unemployment. In short, this group believes that the market power of organized labor and oligopolistic business is so great and their willingness to exploit it so unrestrained that the dilemma is both real and serious.

The Demand-Shift Model [27]

The dilemma model points out a basic difference between cost-push and demand-pull theory. Inflation may be caused by cost-push, but to be sustained it seems to need a public policy that will not countenance high unemployment and will pursue the expansionary fiscal and monetary policies necessary to avoid it. Now let us consider still another inflation model known as "sectoral" or "demand-shift," which argues that an inflation may be caused by neither cost-push nor demand-pull, although elements of cost-push and expanding demand come into play as the inflation takes hold.

Suppose that in an economy close to full employment but not subject to any overall excess of demand there is a rapid and sizable change in the *composition* of demand with no change in aggregate demand. The demand for the output of one or more industries expands sharply, and the demand for the output of all others combined drops by an equal amount. If not already at capacity,

[25] For a brief analysis and summary of the opposed views, see R. W. Spencer, "The Relation Between Prices and Employment: Two Views," in *Review*, Federal Reserve Bank of St. Louis, March 1969, pp. 15–21.

[26] See, for example, A. W. Phillips, "Employment, Inflation, Growth," in *Economica*, Feb. 1962, pp. 1–17.

[27] The demand-shift theory has been most fully developed by C. L. Schultze in his "Recent Inflation in the United States," Joint Economic Committee, *Employment, Growth, and Price Levels*, Study Paper No. 1, 1959. A summary of his study may be found in Joint Economic Committee, *Employment, Growth, and Price Levels*, Hearings, Part 7, 1959, pp. 2172–205.

the industries that enjoy the increase in demand will expand output to the limits of their capacity, but the demand pressures may still be expected to raise prices and profits, especially when capacity operations are attained. To expand output, the industries seek to hire more labor. If there is a tight labor market, a rise in wage rates may be necessary to attract the additional labor. Even if more workers are readily available, a rise in wages in these industries may still be expected as the employees demand a share of the much greater profits being earned by the firms. This does not constitute a wage-push in the earlier sense of that term; some rise in wage rates can easily be met out of the expanded profits. Firms may readily grant such increases to pacify labor and to promote the high morale necessary for maximum production. Under these conditions, we have good reason to expect at this point higher prices and higher wages in the industries subject to expanded demand.

Rising prices in a limited sector of the economy do not appreciably raise the general price level and do not amount to inflation. Actually, if prices and wages were as flexible downward in industries faced with decreasing demand as they are flexible upward in the industries faced with increasing demand, there would be no rise in the general price level at all and no semblance of inflation. However, not only are prices and wages not flexible downward in the face of decreasing demand, but experience indicates they may actually rise in the very face of such adverse market developments. The reason is that the workers in industries with contracting demand seek the same wage improvements that have been won by workers who are employed in the industries enjoying the expanded demand. In such situations, higher wage demands are "justified" by labor to keep wages in line with wages paid for similar work in other industries, specifically with the higher wages paid in the industries subject to increased demand. As we mentioned, the industries enjoying the expanded demand can absorb wage increases within limits out of expanded profits.[28] But other industries with no change in demand or actual decrease in demand cannot do this. Thus, to the extent that price-setting is tied more closely to costs than to demand, higher wages will lead directly to higher prices, even though demand is unchanged or in some industries even diminished. As the higher wages first won in the industries with expanded demand spread through the economy as a whole, the cost-push becomes generalized, and a conventional cost-push inflation emerges in the way described earlier.

The economic basis of the demand-shift model is the fact that in the U.S. economy, on an industry-by-industry basis, prices and wages tend to respond upward to increases in demand, at least to sharp increases, but rarely respond downward to decreases in demand. Clearly, demand-shift inflation would not occur in a different economy in which wages and prices were as flexible downward as they were upward and in which labor and other input factors were highly mobile. In such an economy there would be no rise in the absolute price

---

[28] This is not to say that they necessarily would. If the industries were "key" industries (e.g., the steel industry) whose prices and profits were much in the public eye, some absorption might be expected. At the same time, if these industries mark up prices with each rise in direct costs, the rise in prices would reflect both demand and wage-cost elements.

level but only a change in relative prices as a result of a shift in demand with no change in aggregate demand. But in our economy the ability of large groups of organized workers to match the gains won by others largely precludes such changes in relative wages. This in turn effectively precludes the changes in relative prices that are required to prevent the absolute rise in the general price level that otherwise can result from demand-shift. With this as the pattern, the result is the possibility that inflation can begin with demand-shift.

Although demand-shift may set the process into motion, generalized cost-push is clearly a necessary part of the process. And, as was explained previously in terms of the dilemma model, if cost-push is to result in a sustained inflationary movement, there must be an appropriate increase in aggregate demand, an increase secured to the extent that monetary and fiscal policies validate the higher prices and wages. This qualification does not detract from the importance of demand-shift in some inflationary processes; it merely notes that an inflation may begin in the absence of both demand-pull and cost-push, but that, once begun by demand-shift, it still depends on both cost-push and expanding demand for its continuation.

A CONCLUDING NOTE

The U.S. economy has experienced four sharp upward movements in prices since World War II: during the periods 1946–48, 1950–51, 1956–58, and 1965 to the time of writing in spring of 1969. These four inflations are revealed by the annual data for all three major indexes listed in Table 23–1. In terms of the Consumer Price Index (CPI), monthly data indicate that the four inflations may be somewhat more exactly dated from mid-1946 to late 1948, from mid-1950 (the outbreak of the Korean conflict) to mid-1951, from early 1956 to early 1958, and from late 1965 to a so far unknown ending date.

What were the causes of these particular inflations? In this chapter we have looked into the principal theories advanced by economists to explain inflations in advanced economies. It is yet another matter to identify which theory or theories are applicable to any specific inflationary process. The identification of causation presents perplexing, even impossible problems, but the closer economists can come to an understanding of the causal forces at work in any actual inflationary process, the more appropriate and effective can be the policy measures taken to control that inflation. We saw earlier that an inflation may burn itself out short of hyperinflation, if the inflationary process itself leads to a decrease in aggregate real demand. But to check an inflation before it has done the great damage that is characteristic of an inflation left on its own requires government intervention, and the types of intervention appropriate to a demand-pull inflation are not equally appropriate to cost-push or demand-shift. Restrictive monetary and fiscal policies are the standard remedies where the cause is clearly excess demand, but the same kind of policy cannot be so freely used where the cause is clearly cost-push or demand-shift. To curb cost-push inflation, measures such as stronger antitrust enforcement and anti-union legislation may be considered, but such measures are not relevant to demand-pull. Since the policy measures to be employed in an attack on an existing inflation depend on the nature of the particular inflationary forces at work, the need for identification of these particular forces is as important as the need for an understanding of the inflationary process in general.

CHAPTER 24

MACROECONOMIC POLICY

Since 1946 it has been the responsibility of the federal government to work toward the achievement and maintenance of full employment, price-level stability, and a high rate of economic growth. The Employment Act of that year called on the government for the first time to

> use all practicable means consistent with its needs and obligations and other essential considerations of national policy . . . to coordinate and utilize all its plans, functions, and resources for the purpose of creating and maintaining, in a manner calculated to foster and promote free competitive enterprise and the general welfare, conditions under which there will be afforded useful employment opportunities, including self-employment, for those able, willing, and seeking to work, and to promote maximum employment, production, and purchasing power.

The wording of the act, it will be noted, explicitly covers only what amounts to the single goal of full employment. However, as interpreted by numerous executive department statements and actions in which the Congress has concurred, the goals are generally understood to include price stability and rapid economic growth as well as the one directly stated.

Although the Employment Act is a landmark in economic legislation, its passage in 1946 does not mean that the federal government was not previously aware of a responsibility in the area to which the act refers. Still, there is a great difference between a mere awareness of a responsibility to work toward the goal of full employment and legislation which specifically directs that "all practicable means" be used to achieve this goal. The 1946 act does in this sense replace what at best was a vague and undefined sense of responsibility with a specific obligation that is defined as clearly as such things can be defined. In this regard, it is interesting to speculate on what differences there would have been in the actions taken by the federal government during the years of the Great Depression if the Employment Act of 1946 had appeared instead in 1926. Perhaps the Great Depression would have been much less great!

It may well be argued, however, that an act of this kind could not have come in 1926 and that it did come in 1946 only because, over the decade preceding 1946, the conviction had grown that the federal government not only had the responsibility to work toward the attainment of the specified goals but could make a truly significant contribution to the attainment of these goals. The power of the federal budget to eliminate unemployment had been revealed in dramatic fashion during the years of World War II. The conviction that the budget could and should be used as a means of helping to achieve and maintain full employment in peacetime had come to be generally held by 1946. This conviction stands in sharp contrast to one held by many before World War II, a conviction that underlies what one writer has described as the *moralistic economics* of those earlier years.[1] Those who accepted this moralistic economics adopted a "boom and bust" attitude toward business fluctuations. In a word, the causes of the bust were found in the excesses and maladjustments of the boom—in the speculation, unsound uses of credit, high living, and the like. The severity of the downturn also depended on the severity of the "economic sins" committed during the boom. Most importantly, because the moralistic economics did not recognize that government could, with the necessary tools in hand, contribute substantially to the stabilization of the economy, it could offer little help toward eliminating "boom and bust" except to preach an economic piety that might somehow reduce that instability. This kind of thinking appeared to reach a high point in the late twenties and early thirties, and to combat it was undoubtedly one of Keynes's purposes in writing the *General Theory*.

As we noted in the first chapter, Keynes's book was a success with few equals in the history of economics. Without it and its impact on the world of practical affairs, we would probably not have had the Employment Act of 1946. And had there been no Employment Act of 1946, it is doubtful that we would have had many of the federal government actions taken to attain high employment and promote economic growth during the twenty-five years since World War II. For with the act came the establishment of the Council of Economic Advisers in the executive branch and the Joint Economic Committee in the legislative branch. And through them and their research studies, committee hearings, and the annual Economic Report of the President came a new understanding on the part of the Congress, business, and the general public as to what federal government actions could do toward achieving these goals. A milestone among federal government actions undertaken to decrease unemployment and stimulate growth was the highly successful Revenue Act of 1964, but this action, in which Congress reduced tax rates at a time when the federal budget was already in sizable deficit and the economy was not in recession, could not have occurred in the absence of the Employment Act and the whole educational

---

[1] See J. M. Culbertson, *Macroeconomic Theory and Stabilization Policy*, McGraw-Hill, 1968, pp. 371–73.

process that came with it over the years after 1946. It seems safe to say that an action such as the 1964 tax measure would have been inconceivable if the economics of the time had been the moralistic economics of a few decades earlier.

Whether we speak of massive actions like the 1964 tax reduction or of lesser actions that do not make headlines, each represents the implementation, in whole or in part, of a particular policy—policy itself best being thought of as the specification of a prescribed course of action that is intended to achieve or contribute to the achievement of certain goals. Just as economists refer in the broadest of categories to three basic macroeconomic goals of full employment, price stability, and rapid economic growth (or four such goals, if we include balance-of-payments equilibrium), they similarly refer in equally broad categories to monetary policy and fiscal policy as the two basic types of policy that are employed in working toward the achievement of the specified goals. However, our macroeconomic goals, quite apart from the problem of what is really meant by such loose terms as "full employment," "price stability," and "rapid growth," cannot really be held within the confines of the three or four terms that make up the standard list. Similarly, our macroeconomic policies actually include some that are quite beyond what is covered by monetary policy and fiscal policy in the widest sense of those terms.

Under the heading of goals, at least two major goals in addition to those already mentioned should be identified. There is the goal of economic justice, the principal characteristic of which is an "equitable" distribution of income, and the goal of economic freedom, characterized by the right of every man to change jobs, join a labor union, enter a business, own property, purchase the goods he wants, and do endless other things. In a similar way, although monetary policy and fiscal policy are the policies we understandably hear the most about, we should note that policies such as labor, agricultural, antitrust, tariff, public housing, conservation, and others even less familiar, are all relevant in one way or another to the multiple macroeconomic goals we pursue in the real world.

A treatment of anything like a full list of macroeconomic goals and a full list of policies that might be relevant in the pursuit of these goals is clearly the task of an entire book or even of several books. In our restricted coverage, we will bypass such goals as economic justice and economic freedom, not because they are unimportant but because of space and because we have not developed in even the crudest form a theoretical framework needed for an analysis of policies appropriate to these goals. What we do have from earlier chapters is a theoretical framework adequate for an analysis of certain policies aimed at the specific goals of full employment, price stability, and economic growth, and it is to these three goals that we will limit our attention. On the side of policies, we will also limit ourselves to the two "giants of the industry"—monetary and fiscal.[2]

Each of these goals and policies has been met in various contexts in earlier

[2] For a discussion of the major goals and policies bypassed here, see K. E. Boulding, *Principles of Economic Policy*, Prentice-Hall, 1958.

chapters. Thus, in developing the short-run theory of income and employment in Part II, we occasionally mentioned specific monetary and fiscal policies designed to raise the level of real income and employment. Similarly, in the preceding chapters of Part III, we referred at several points to such policies as were relevant to the problems of the business cycle, economic growth, and inflation. However, all such references were incidental to the primary purpose of these chapters— namely, the development of the basic theory of income and employment and of certain theories of the cycle, growth, and inflation. Furthermore, what we covered earlier in no way got us into the practical problems of formulating policy in the real world. In the remainder of this chapter we will look at some of these practical problems. For example, we saw earlier through the *IS–LM* framework that in a depression, fiscal policy will be more effective than mone- tary policy in raising the income level. But to formulate specific fiscal policies to meet these conditions we need much more information than a theoretical framework like *IS–LM* can give us. Economic policies formulated for the actual economy must face the many practical problems that arise out of complex political, social, and economic institutions, procedures, and practices. While all these must be considered, it is also to be emphasized that the theoretical frame- work remains at the foundation of rational policy making and is absolutely indispensable to it. For without an underlying theory a policy-maker would have no notion of what consequences to expect from any proposed policy and thus no way of knowing whether the policy in question would be a help or a hindrance in achieving the goal which is the very reason for adopting the policy. In a word, there can be no intelligent policy in the absence of a well-reasoned theoretical framework on which to base policy. As we proceed in this chapter, it will become apparent both how the theoretical framework developed in earlier chapters lies at the bottom of policy formulation and why much more than just that theoretical framework is required for policy formulation.

Although nobody questions that monetary and fiscal policies must be coordinated if we are to get the best possible results, it is very convenient and also quite possible, up to a point, to discuss them in isolation from each other. The balance of this chapter is, therefore, divided into two parts, of which the first is concerned with monetary policy and the second with fiscal policy.

MONETARY POLICY

Monetary policy is policy that employs the central bank's control over the supply and cost of money as an instrument for achieving the objectives of economic policy. With respect to the objectives before us, the overall effective- ness of monetary policy thus depends on what contribution it can make to the attainment of full employment, price stability, and rapid economic growth.

Although a statement that is couched exclusively in terms of aggregate supply and demand is a crude oversimplification, it does provide a helpful initial overview of the general problem before us. We have seen that aggregate money demand may be expressed as the sum of $C + I + G + (X - M)$. If we are to achieve full employment, the basic requirement is clear: Policies must be aimed at raising the total of $C + I + G + (X - M)$ to the level required to call forth the aggregate supply that a fully employed economy is capable of producing. To what extent can monetary policy contribute to the achievement of this objective? To what extent, that is, can an expanding money supply and lower interest rates increase aggregate demand and raise output and employment? We know that if the economy is already at a position of reasonably full employment and if aggregate demand, $C + I + G + (X - M)$, is expanding faster than the productive capacity of the economy, rising prices will result. This gives rise to another question: To what extent can monetary policy be employed to control the level and composition of aggregate demand in such a way as to prevent inflation without at the same time causing a downturn in output and sacrificing full employment? In determining the economy's potential growth rate, one important factor is the rate at which the capital stock grows. The increment to the capital stock in each year depends essentially on what portion of that year's output consists of net investment. The greater the share of aggregate output devoted to investment, the more rapid will be the potential rate of growth, *ceteris paribus*. This leads us to a third and final question: To what extent can monetary policy be employed to vary the composition of aggregate demand and aggregate output in favor of investment and away from private and public consumption, while at the same time maintaining aggregate demand at the level needed for full employment and preventing it from rising above this to produce inflation? The same set of questions could be asked of fiscal policy.

To the extent that they can be found, definite answers to these questions require one to look behind as well as at the aggregates in terms of which the questions have been posed. But the questions when answered indicate the effectiveness of monetary and fiscal policy as a means of realizing the goals under consideration.

Instruments of Monetary Policy

The general instruments through which the central bank carries out its monetary policy are open-market operations, changes in legal reserve requirements, and changes in the central bank's discount rate. All these instruments operate directly or indirectly on the excess reserves of the commercial banks and thus influence the ability of the banks to extend credit. As the banks extend credit by making loans and buying securities, their assets increase; the opposite side of the increase in bank assets is an increase in deposit liabilities, primarily demand deposits. Since the banks are required to maintain among their assets an amount in legal reserves (for member banks, deposits with the Federal Reserve Banks and cash-in-vault) equal to specified percentages of their demand and time deposit liabilities, their ability to make more loans and buy more securities is limited by the amount of reserves they hold in excess of the amount required.

If at any time the banks have no more than the dollar volume of reserves necessary to meet the legal reserve requirements against the existing volume of deposits, further acquisition of earning assets is ruled out, for this would increase deposit liabilities, which, with no change in the volume of reserves, would create a deficiency of reserves. Since the deposit liabilities of the commercial banks comprise the bulk of the money supply (whether defined as currency and demand deposits only or as these plus time deposits at commercial banks), its rate of growth is subject to control by the central bank through control over the dollar volume of reserves held by the commercial banks and over the percentage reserve requirements against their deposits.

As was outlined in Chapter 18, the central bank can increase or decrease the dollar volume of these reserves through its open-market operations. This is the most effective instrument available to the central bank, because its flexibility enables the central bank to change course quickly, as conditions warrant, from a policy of increasing commercial bank reserves to decreasing them, and vice versa. The second instrument—changes in percentage reserve requirements—affects not the total dollar amount of reserves but the amount of excess reserves. Thus, the central bank may, in carrying out an expansionary policy, provide commercial banks with additional lending or deposit-creating power either by increasing the dollar amount of reserves through open-market purchases or, with no change in the existing dollar amount of reserves, by decreasing the percentage reserve requirements. The latter action reclassifies part of existing required reserves as excess reserves and, in terms of lending power of the banks, is similar in effect to an addition to excess reserves produced through open-market operations. However, because it is impractical to bring about frequent minor changes in excess reserves through changes in percentage reserve requirements, use of this instrument is reserved by the central bank for conditions in which relatively large additions to or subtractions from the excess reserves of the banks are deemed necessary. Lastly, changes in the discount rate do not in themselves affect reserves but rather alter the cost at which the commercial banks may secure additional reserves by borrowing from the central bank. In terms of controlling the banks' lending or deposit-creating power, this is the least important of the three general controls, because banks typically borrow from the central bank not for purposes of expanding their earning assets but to cover deficiencies in their reserves. There is a well-established tradition in this country, nurtured by the Federal Reserve itself, against borrowing from the central bank. Banks that do find it necessary to borrow typically seek to repay such loans promptly. Borrowing at the central bank thus serves essentially as a safety valve that banks can turn to in time of need. If the reserves needed to meet a bank's deficiency cannot be secured at lower cost by borrowing from other commercial banks that have excess reserves (so-called Federal funds) or by the sale of earning assets, they can be secured from the central bank at whatever the discount rate may be at the time.

As the central bank moves to restrain the ability of the commercial banks to make loans and buy securities, it simultaneously exerts upward pressure on the whole structure of interest rates. This is most apparent in the case of open-market operations. The sale of securities by the central bank, if on a large enough scale, can be carried out only at falling prices for the government securities offered by the central bank. This in itself raises the yields on these securities and tends to bring higher yields on other securities and higher interest rates and/or rationing of credit to loan applicants at the banks. The same results follow from an increase in percentage reserve requirements. Excess reserves are thereby reduced, and banks with reduced lending power but with unreduced loan demand may adjust by raising interest rates and/or by rationing their reduced lending power. The initial reaction to moderate tightening by the central bank will be credit rationing as the commercial banks altogether reject loan applications from other than regular customers and lend some regular customers less than the amounts requested. A more severe tightening by the central bank must at some point lead to rising interest rates on loans made by the banks. If restrictive action through open-market operations is carried far enough, the central bank will typically follow up by raising its discount rate. To some extent this is necessary in order to make the restrictive action effective. We noted that the commercial banks typically borrow from the central bank to meet reserve deficiencies. But, unless the central bank raises its lending rate as it restricts total reserves to the degree that forces higher interest rates at the commercial banks, there will be a danger of excessive borrowing at the central bank. Commercial banks might try to use the "discount window" to recover reserves lost through open-market sales by the central bank and then proceed to relend such funds at the higher rates then being earned on loans. A rise in the discount rate is one way of preventing such abuse of the central bank's discount window. When a rise in the discount rate occurs under these circumstances, it is clear that the rise is not so much a cause as an effect of credit tightening that was brought about by other central bank actions—typically, open-market sales. For example, the several rises that lifted the discount rate from 4.5 percent at the beginning of 1968 to 6.0 percent in the spring of 1969 were more a matter of bringing the discount rate more closely in line with market interest rates, which rose due to other Federal Reserve actions, than a means in itself of initiating a rise in interest rates and a tightening of credit conditions.

In addition to these general instruments, there are various selective instruments that Congress has authorized the Federal Reserve to employ from time to time. Unlike the general instruments, the selective instruments affect the types of credit extended by the commercial banks. The total volume of bank credit is not directly affected, but the composition of bank loan portfolios is. The immediate purpose of the selective controls is to regulate the amount of credit extended and the terms on which such credit is extended for selected purposes. For example, during World War II and the Korean War, the Federal Reserve was authorized to specify the terms—the minimum down payment and the maximum length of contract—on loans to purchasers of durable consumer goods. The maximum amount loaned by the bank (expressed as a fraction of the purchase price) and the maximum time period over which repayment could be spread were therefore specified. At present the major selective control, one that has been continuously in effect for the past thirty-five years, is that over purchase of securities on margin.[3] In this case the Federal Reserve specifies the fraction of the purchase price of securities that must be paid in cash. Effective in June 1968, this rate was raised to 80 percent from the 70 percent level at which it had been held for the preceding four and a half years.

Unlike general controls, selective controls make it possible for the central bank to restrain what is regarded as an unhealthy expansion of credit for specific purposes—say, for financing the purchase of securities or automobiles and other durable consumer goods—without at the same time imposing an undesired restraint on credit expansion in general. In this respect, selective controls may at times prove effective in meeting the goals of monetary policy in situations for which general controls are not suitable. In practice, however, the use of selective controls in this country has been limited for the most part to the special circumstances of wartime. We will confine ourselves in the analysis that follows to the implementation of monetary policy through general controls, which in present-day practice are significantly more important than selective controls.

Effectiveness of Monetary Policy in Recession

From the years of the Great Depression into the fifties, economists generally held that monetary policy was less effective in stimulating recovery from a depression than in controlling a boom and inflation. Their reference was to inflations of the demand-pull variety that were actually experienced during these years; monetary policy was recognized to be much less effective against inflations of the cost-push variety. Their reference was also to depression or severe contractions, such as those of 1929–33 and 1937–38, and not to such mild downturns as those suffered by the U.S. economy in the years since World War II; monetary policy was recognized to be of real assistance in such mild downturns but virtually powerless in the face of very sharp contractions. If we take the opposite combination of mild downturns and cost-push inflations, it then appears that monetary policy is the more effective against the downturns than against the inflations. Because our actual experience since the fifties has often involved just such a combination, it may be said that "the wheel has come full circle, and prevailing opinion has returned to the characteristic 1920's view that monetary policy is probably more effective in checking deflation than in checking inflation." [4]

Although our recent downturns have all been mild and, according to this argument, subject to treatment by monetary policy, what is the basis for the conclusion that monetary policy is ineffective in the face of a severe contraction? During such a downturn, the Federal Reserve can, of course, through open-

---

[3] The interest equalization tax on the purchase of foreign securities and longer-term commercial bank loans abroad, introduced in 1964–65 to restrain the outflow of capital, is a second but less familiar type of selective control now in effect, presumably on a temporary basis.

[4] H. G. Johnson, "Monetary Theory and Policy," in *American Economic Review*, July 1962, p. 366.

market operations pump more and more reserves into the banks and expand their ability to extend credit to all classes of borrowers. But the mere availability of abundant credit at highly favorable terms is not enough to induce borrowing by businessmen and consumers to finance additional spending, *if other conditions influencing spending decisions are so unfavorable as to offset the attractive credit terms.* When the economy is in a sharp downturn and the outlook is bleak, businessmen do not seek to borrow on short term to build up inventories. Instead they are anxious to reduce inventories and pay off any loans that were previously secured to finance these inventories. Neither do they seek to borrow on long term to finance expansion of plant and equipment; confronted with a business contraction and reduced sales, most find themselves with excess plant and equipment. In the same way, consumers fearful of unemployment or reduction in their incomes do not borrow to finance purchases of automobiles or other durables, expensive vacations, and the like; instead they seek to reduce whatever debts they have already incurred. There are two clichés commonly heard in this connection: "You can't push on a string" and "You can lead a horse to water, but you can't make him drink." In the face of a sharp downturn, there are very few thirsty horses.

This is not to say that an easy monetary policy in times of a severe contraction will be without beneficial effect; its effect will be largely that of preventing a bad situation from getting worse. A restrictive monetary policy combined with a business downturn would surely aggravate the downturn—the classic example of this was the monetary policy in 1931 that contributed to the deepening of the Great Depression. For contractions in general, a restrictive policy could convert an otherwise reasonably orderly liquidation of excessive inventories into a rout as banks called on businessmen to repay the loans that had been extended to finance inventories. Forced inventory liquidation of this sort leads to rapidly falling prices, business losses, and bankruptcies in a process that tends to spread ever more widely throughout the economy. If credit is readily available on favorable terms, it clearly has a stabilizing effect. By meeting the liquidity requirements of business, it can slow and perhaps reduce the extent of the downturn. In the case of a mild downturn, it may be sufficient in itself to reverse the direction of the downward movement.

Effectiveness of Monetary Policy in Boom and Inflation

Unlike the inflations of 1946–48 and 1950–51, the inflations of 1956–58 and the one that started in 1965 appeared to have cost-push elements at work. To the extent that cost-push predominates, both monetary and fiscal policies have quite limited effectiveness in checking the inflation and the boom of which it is a part. Whatever effectiveness monetary policy has against inflation, that effectiveness is at a maximum when the inflation is predominantly of a demand-pull type, and it is this type with which we will be concerned here. The problem in this case is one of an overly rapid expansion of aggregate demand, and the question is whether the central bank, through its control over the money supply and the cost of money, can check the overly rapid expansion of aggregate demand.

One way of approaching an answer to this very broad question is by analyzing the limitations on the effectiveness of a restrictive monetary policy. Even though the central bank holds the money supply unchanged or actually decreases it, an inflationary expansion of aggregate demand is still possible to the extent that the public finds ways of handling a rising dollar volume of spending with the same or even a diminished money supply. Thus, velocity changes appear as a first type of limitation. However, because there would appear to be a limit to the rise in the velocity of money, it seems that the central bank could pursue a policy as restrictive as necessary to offset any increase in the velocity of money. Thus, monetary policy should still be effective. This brings us to the limitations standing in the way of the pursuit of a monetary policy sufficiently restrictive to be effective. If there are such limitations that for various reasons cannot be overcome, the effectiveness of monetary policy is thereby equally limited.[5]

Velocity Changes as a Limitation on the Effectiveness of Restrictive Monetary Policy. By means of its general instruments of monetary management, the central bank can control expansion of the money supply and the cost of money. To support an increase in business activity, there must be either more money, a more rapid rate of turnover of the existing money supply, or some of both. When credit conditions are tightened and the creation of new money through the banking system is restrained, the policy objective of a slowdown in the rate of expansion of business activity will be realized, unless the public finds ways of thwarting this policy through more effective use of the existing money supply. To the extent that the public manages to do this, the restrictive effect of a tight monetary policy is reduced. The nature of our financial system is such that this indeed appears to be what happens, and it becomes an important limitation to the overall effectiveness of monetary policy.

For example, GNP in current dollars increased 43.5 percent from the fourth quarter of 1949 to the second quarter of 1953, while the money supply during the same period rose only 15.9 percent. Clearly, the indicated increase in economic activity, as measured by current-dollar GNP, could not have occurred without a rise in the velocity of money, taking as given the actual increase in the money supply. In fact, there was in this period a 23.6 percent rise in velocity. In absolute terms, GNP increased from $257 to $368.8 billion, and the money supply increased from $108.6 to $125.9 billion. The actual money supply increased by $17.3 billion; the indicated rise in velocity was the approximate monetary equivalent of another $25.6 billion increase in the money supply. By finding ways of mobilizing the existing money supply more effectively, the public *in effect* secured the additional money it needed to support the expanding level of activity. The data reveal similar results for other periods of expansion,

[5] This approach follows the one in Joint Economic Committee, *Employment, Growth, and Price Levels*, Staff Report, 1959, pp. 344–62.

such as from the second quarter of 1954 to the third quarter of 1957 and from the second quarter of 1958 to the second quarter of 1959.[6] Since under the present system of reserve requirements the Federal Reserve has practically no control over the velocity of money but only over the supply of money, sizable increases in velocity induced by restrictive monetary policy represent a serious limitation to the effectiveness of restrictive monetary policy.

What are some of the ways the public manages to make more effective use of an existing money supply, thereby thwarting the central bank's restrictive monetary policy? A brief examination of a few of the ways most discussed in the literature will at least convey the nature of the problem.[7]

1. Commercial Bank Portfolio Adjustments. Rising business activity brings more borrowers to the commercial banks. In carrying out its restrictive policy, the central bank takes the actions necessary to keep commercial bank excess reserves below the level that would permit the banks to accommodate fully this expanding demand for loans. Although banks may meet customer demand for loans by selling government securities and lending the proceeds to borrowers, this will not actually increase the total amount of credit extended. As the banks sell securities, their total deposits are drawn down as buyers make payment; an offsetting increase in loans simply restores deposits to their previous level. The total earning assets of banks and the total money supply are left unchanged. However, the replacement of government securities with loans in bank portfolios will, to some extent, represent a conversion of *idle deposits* into *active deposits*, even though there is no change in total deposits or in the money supply. Some part of the deposits given up by purchasers of government securities were probably idle deposits; in contrast, virtually all the deposits secured by borrowers will be active, since the purpose of business borrowing is to finance the purchase of goods, the payment of bills, and the like. The process is thus one in which idle deposits are activated and total spending is increased, even though the central bank has kept the total money supply unchanged.

There is an important interest rate effect in this process. If the central bank's actions prevent an increase in the money supply, the prices of securities will fall and their yields will rise as banks sell them in the market. The result is a general upward pressure on the structure of interest rates. This fall in security prices and rise in yields is usually necessary to persuade holders of deposits to switch from holding assets in the perfectly liquid form of deposits to holding

---

[6] The reverse occurs in periods of contraction. For example, the minor decline in GNP of 2.7 percent from the second quarter of 1953 to the second quarter of 1954 was accompanied by an increase in the money supply of 0.6 percent, but the decline in velocity was 3.1 percent. The absolute increase in the money supply was $0.7 billion, but the fall in velocity amounted to the monetary equivalent of a $3.9 billion decline in the money supply. *Ibid.*, Table 9–7, p. 345.

[7] For a fuller discussion, see the Joint Economic Committee, *ibid.*, pp. 344–59. See also H. S, Ellis, "Limitations of Monetary Policy," in N. H. Jacoby, ed., *United States Monetary Policy.* rev. ed., Praeger, 1964, pp. 195–214, and S. W. Rousseaus, "Velocity Changes and the Effectiveness of Monetary Policy, 1951–57," in *Review of Economics and Statistics*, Feb. 1960, pp. 27–36.

assets in the less liquid form of securities.[8] But falling security prices will mean capital losses to banks that sell securities to get funds to make loans. Will the reluctance of banks to take capital losses not rule out this process? The so-called locking-in effect of lower prices of securities would not appear to be controlling in most circumstances. It may be controlling if the rise in interest rates is expected to be short-lived, in which case banks may prefer to keep their government securities rather than sell at a capital loss, since the prospect of not only recouping such losses but showing a profit through higher interest rates on loans is not favorable in a short period of time. On the other hand, if banks expect interest rates to go on rising for some time, they will clearly have a profit incentive (and, what may be more important, the advantage of being able to satisfy loan requests of regular customers) in shifting out of government securities into loans. In such case, the capital loss on the sale of securities can be more than recouped through higher interest rates on loans. Furthermore, once loan demand begins to subside, it may be possible for the banks to switch back into government securities at prices below those at which they were sold, thus securing a financial gain in both directions. The shifting composition of bank portfolios over time shows that banks have indeed behaved in this manner in recent years, shifting out of securities into loans in times of restrictive Federal Reserve policy and building up holdings of government securities in times of easy Federal Reserve policy.

This process, by which the commercial banks in effect bring about some increase in the active money supply by moving into loans, raises the velocity of the total money supply. Hence, despite the tight control exercised by the monetary authority over the total quantity of money, the process described above emerges as one loophole in the effectiveness of general monetary controls.

2.   The Role of Financial Intermediaries. Some economists have argued that the rapid growth of financial intermediaries in the postwar period is another development that has seriously weakened the traditional monetary controls of the Federal Reserve.[9] These intermediaries, which include mutual savings banks, insurance companies, savings and loan associations, and mutual funds, receive savings from the public and in turn make loans and buy securities in much the same way that commercial banks do.[10] The essential difference, however, is their lack of money-creating ability. They are called "intermediaries" for the very reason that they do no more than channel savings into the hands of spenders. To the extent that the funds supplied by these intermediaries are derived from current saving by the public, they are acting, in a sense, strictly as "middlemen."

[8] This point was developed in detail in Chapter 18 in connection with the liquidity-preference theory of the interest rate.

[9] This was emphasized particularly by J. G. Gurley and E. S. Shaw. See their "Financial Aspects of Economic Development," in *American Economic Review*, Sept. 1955, pp. 515–38, and "Financial Intermediaries and the Saving-Investment Process," in *Journal of Finance*, May 1956, pp. 257–76. For a skeptical view of the extent to which intermediaries have weakened monetary controls, see W. L. Smith, "Financial Intermediaries and Monetary Controls," in *Quarterly Journal of Economics*, Nov. 1959, pp. 533–53.

[10] With respect to their operations in savings deposits, the commercial banks are also in the category of "intermediaries."

The types of loans they make and the securities they purchase affect the allocation of credit, but the credit provided would be matched dollar for dollar by current saving of the public. They could lend more only if the public saved more and placed these savings with them; they cannot create money for this purpose.

The argument, however, is that the operations of these intermediaries somehow weaken monetary policy. How is this supposed to happen? One way is through portfolio adjustments similar to those described above for commercial banks. In times of tightening credit, financial intermediaries may shift from government securities to loans with the same effects on the active money supply that follow equivalent commercial bank actions. A second way is unique to financial intermediaries: In times of tightening credit and rising interest rates, they may raise the interest rates they pay on funds placed with them. Attracted by these higher rates, some holders of idle demand deposits will convert these into interest-bearing obligations of the intermediaries. As the intermediaries extend credit on the basis of funds that have been attracted away from commercial banks, idle funds previously carried in demand deposits (or in cash hoards) are activated and velocity increases.

This process may occur in the way described because of the highly liquid nature of the obligations issued by some of these intermediaries. Persons who hold assets in the form of savings deposits or savings and loan shares regard them as approximately equivalent to demand deposits or cash in terms of liquidity. Although it is true that they cannot be used directly to make payment, they may in practice be converted quickly into checking accounts or cash, both of which, of course, can be used to make payment directly. In times of tightening credit, rising interest rates on the obligations of these intermediaries thus present the wealth-holder with increasing incentive to convert temporarily idle demand deposits into obligations of the financial intermediaries, for this involves practically no sacrifice of liquidity. Although economists describe such action as a conversion from money to near-money, those who convert their assets regard the difference in liquidity as negligible.

3. Other Factors. There are a number of other ways in which the private sector has managed to make more effective use of the available money supply. A few of these are the increased participation by banks in the Federal funds market as a means of economizing on reserves, the development by sales finance companies of improved methods of collecting funds and of borrowing funds from various sources all over the country, the use of repurchase agreements by government security dealers as a means of borrowing from sources otherwise unavailable, the development of a secondary market for FHA-insured as well as VA-guaranteed mortgages, and the easing of geographical restrictions on mortgage lending by savings and loan associations as a means of widening the market for mortgages and raising the mobility of mortgage funds. Under the pressure of tightening money, our highly complex financial system does manage in these various ways to obtain greater mileage from the available money supply. Success in this direction constitutes a significant "slippage" in the effectiveness of monetary policy.

Limitations on More Restrictive Monetary Policy as an Offset to Velocity Increases.   This brings us to the question of why the monetary authority cannot apply controls with sufficient severity to overcome the "slippage" that results from the rise in velocity brought about in the ways just discussed. After all, if a given decrease in the money supply fails to provide the desired restrictive effect simply because that decrease is offset by an increase in velocity, this appears to say only that a larger decrease in the money supply is required to do what a smaller decrease would do if velocity did not rise. Since the Federal Reserve at any time has the power to reduce the money supply by very large amounts, it would seem that the velocity changes do not matter very much.[11] The difficulty here is that there appears to be a limit to the restrictiveness of policy. A policy so restrictive as to overcome velocity changes not only may check an unhealthy expansion and inflation but also may bring about an undesirable contraction in business activity. There are several reasons why the degree of monetary restraint that would be required to overcome this velocity loophole may not be feasible in practice.

1.   Prevention of Instability in Financial Markets. To carry out a monetary policy that is sufficiently restrictive to control an inflationary expansion of aggregate demand may call for such extreme action by the central bank as to destabilize financial markets and invite a sharp decline in business activity. During August of 1966, the Federal Reserve nearly reached this point in its attempt to slow the economy. In the words of the Council of Economic Advisers, "Monetary policy was probably as tight as it could get without risking financial disorder. Any further increase in over-all demand could not have been effectively countered by general monetary policy." [12]

This destabilization of financial markets may come about through the effect that a highly restrictive Federal Reserve policy has on the portfolios of the commercial banks and other institutional investors. In order to raise funds to meet the demands of their business borrowers during the summer of 1966, the commercial banks dumped huge quantities of state and local government securities into the market in a relatively short period of time. Security prices fell, and interest rates rose to near record levels. Although the point of financial disorder was not quite reached in 1966, the point does exist at which the decline in security prices and the rise in interest rates can lead to widespread pessimism, deterioration of expectations, and wholesale cancellation of business investment projects and even of consumer durable goods purchases—developments that in themselves are sufficient to turn the system from inflation to contraction. To avoid such serious results, it would seem that the central bank must try to achieve the same total restraint through a more gradual and cautious policy. The problem

---

[11] It may even be argued that changes in velocity add to the effectiveness of monetary policy by providing a safety valve. If the Federal Reserve misjudges the situation and tightens too much, the rise in velocity will offset the tightening in part and give the authorities time to adjust their policy to less restriction before great damage is done. See L. S. Ritter, "Income-Velocity and Anti-Inflationary Monetary Policy," in *American Economic Review*, March 1959, pp. 120–29.

[12] *Annual Report of the Council of Economic Advisers*, January 1967, p. 60.

with this alternative is that such a policy, although free of the disequilibrating effects of the fast, vigorous policy, may take so long to accomplish what needs to be done that it becomes ineffective as a practical approach. Thus, a moderately restrictive policy may be all that is permissible if disorder is to be avoided, but a severely restrictive policy may be what is called for if an inflationary expansion is to be checked. The central bank must do whatever it can by pressing as hard as it dares without pressing as hard as it must.

2. Support of Treasury Debt-Management Operations. With a national debt of the present size and maturity distribution, the Treasury is frequently in the market selling new issues to raise funds to pay off maturing issues. In addition to such refunding operations on existing debt, the Treasury is also in the market in periods when the government is operating at a deficit in order to raise new money to finance these deficits. If the Federal Reserve should undertake a restrictive policy at the same time that the Treasury is faced with a large refunding or cash-borrowing operation, the Treasury may be unable to sell the securities at the prices and yields expected. Because the Federal Reserve has a special responsibility to the Treasury in connection with the latter's debt-management operations, it may therefore be compelled at times to sacrifice the tight policy it would otherwise pursue in order to enable the Treasury to carry out its financing operations successfully. This, at times, is another restraint on the Federal Reserve's ability to pursue the tight money policy that it feels is required in the interests of stability.[13]

3. Discriminatory Effect of a Tight Monetary Policy. A tight money policy effected through the general instruments of control is said to discriminate against particular sectors of the economy. In particular, it is thought to work against small businessmen, because they are poorer credit risks, and against residential construction and some types of state and local government spending, because they are the most sensitive to changes in credit cost.[14] At the same time,

[13] A related problem is the effect of a tight money policy on the interest cost of servicing a national debt that in gross terms in early 1969 exceeded $360 billion, of which about $225 billion was held by the public. With cash payments to the public for interest exceeding $10 billion per year, some argue against reliance on tight monetary policy because of its effect on the cost of debt service. This is really an argument more against the way monetary controls work than against their effectiveness. If tight policy is otherwise effective, higher interest cost on the debt may be the price to be paid if we are to achieve the stability such a policy helps provide. This differs from the argument in the text. The issue there is against tight money not because of its effect on the cost of debt servicing but because of the difficulties it could present to orderly debt management. The Federal Reserve cannot avoid this responsibility; and, though it limits the effectiveness of monetary policy, it is in the best interest of overall stabilization policy.

[14] See, for example, G. L. Bach and C. J. Huizenga, "The Differential Effects of Tight Money," in *American Economic Review*, March, 1961, pp. 52–80; F. Morris, "Impact of Monetary Policy on State and Local Governments: An Empirical Study," in *Journal of Finance*, May 1960, pp. 232–49; and J. R. Schlesinger, "Monetary Policy and Its Critics," in *Journal of Political Economy*, Dec. 1960, pp. 601–16. For a study of the 1966 tight money episode in specific connection with business investment spending, see J. Crockett, I. Friend, and H. Shavell, "The Impact of Monetary Stringency on Business Investment," in *Survey of Current Business*, U.S. Department of Commerce, Aug. 1967, pp. 10–27.

big corporations, with their excellent credit ratings and lesser sensitivity to the cost of credit, may find their requirements fully met.

A tight money policy is, of course, designed to restrain the total amount of credit extended in order to restrict aggregate demand. But the pressure resulting from tight money, if felt so unevenly in different sectors, will in itself limit recourse to tighter money as a means of restricting aggregate demand. It is impossible for policy-makers to ignore these differential impacts on various sectors, even if they choose to ignore them in the single-minded pursuit of their objective of restricting aggregate demand. The "injured," particularly those concerned with residential housing, a prime victim of tight money, make themselves heard. For example, the rise in the rate on FHA-insured and VA-guaranteed mortgage loans from 6.75 percent to 7.50 percent early in 1969 did not occur without strong protests from certain parties. However independent the monetary authority may be, it is not beyond the political influence of "injured" parties.

Uncertainty as a Limitation on the Effectiveness of Monetary Policy. So far we have been concerned with some of the limitations that prevent the central bank from carrying out the "appropriate" policy. The discussion assumed that the monetary authority knew what had to be done and that it could do what had to be done were it not for limitations of this kind. But, even in the complete absence of such limitations, there is what amounts to quite a different type of limitation—uncertainty at times as to what the policy should be, to effect no change or to ease or to tighten, and, beyond this, uncertainty as to the degree of easing or tightening that is called for in the face of the business outlook. In other words, in addition to limitations on the effectiveness of the policy actually adopted and executed, there is another limitation in the form of uncertainty as to exactly what the appropriate policy should be.

This uncertainty arises in large part from the uncertainty as to the length of the time lag between the execution of any particular policy and the impact of that policy on aggregate demand and income.[15] In order for policy to be effective, the monetary authority has to know how much time will pass before any given policy will produce its intended effect. Furthermore, the intended effect must be that needed to meet the business conditions forecasted for that future period. An error in the forecast of what conditions will be in that future period

---

[15] This is formally known as the "outside" lag. The full process of deciding on and carrying out policy involves three lags, the first of which is the "inside" lag, or the lapse of time between the moment at which there is a need for a change of policy and the moment at which the central bank acts. Inside lag is sometimes divided into "recognition" lag and "action" lag, but the time between recognition of the need for action and the taking of action is so short, relatively speaking, that the inside lag in effect becomes the recognition lag. The second lag is the "intermediate" lag, or the lapse of time between the moment at which action is taken and the moment at which the economy finds itself faced with changed money supply and interest rates. The third lag is the "outside" lag (noted in the text), or the lapse of time between a change in the cost and availability of credit and the effect thereof on aggregate spending, income, and output. (See T. Mayer, *Monetary Policy in the United States*, Random House, 1968, Ch. 6, and the references given there for further reading.)

or an error as to the future period in which today's policy will have its impact can make today's chosen policy the wrong policy. Nobody denies that these uncertainties exist, but some argue that, whatever the uncertainties, a policy in which the Federal Reserve at least "leans against the wind" is better than one in which its stands straight up whichever way the wind is blowing. In reply, Professor Milton Friedman, perhaps the foremost critic of the type of flexible monetary policy followed by the Federal Reserve, has written as follows:

> We seldom in fact know which way the economic wind is blowing until several months after the event, yet to be effective, we need to know which way the wind is going to be blowing when the measures we take now will be effective, itself a variable date that may be a half-year or a year or two years from now. Leaning against next year's wind is hardly an easy task in the present state of meteorology.[16]

Because of these uncertainties, Friedman would have the Federal Reserve expand the money supply at a fixed rate per year in line with the long-run growth rate of the economy, no matter which way the wind was blowing in any particular year. To do other than this, in his judgment, is more likely to contribute to instability than to help in achieving stability. The Federal Reserve has, of course, persistently done other than this over the years, its policy at times involving very rapid growth of the money supply and at other times involving actual decreases in the money supply. Friedman grants that the monetary authorities more frequently move in the right direction than in the wrong direction, but his major objection to their moves is brought out well by the following:

> Too late and too much has been the general practice. For example, in early 1966, it was the right policy for the Federal Reserve to move in a less expansionary direction—though it should have done so at least a year earlier. But when it moved, it went too far, producing the sharpest change in the rate of monetary growth of the post-war era. Again, having gone too far, it was the right policy for the Fed to reverse course at the end of 1966. But again it went too far, not only restoring but exceeding the earlier excessive rate of monetary growth. And this episode is no exception. Time and again this has been the course followed—as in 1919 and 1920, in 1937 and 1938, in 1953 and 1954, in 1959 and 1960.[17]

In recent years a rapidly growing number of monetary economists and professional groups have come to lean more and more toward Friedman's position. Various rules or guidelines less stringent than a straight percentage increase in the money stock per year have been proposed by some of these people, but all such proposals have in common the imposition of some restraint on the present virtually unrestrained power of the Federal Reserve to raise or

[16] *A Program for Monetary Stability*, Fordham Univ. Press, 1960, p. 93.
[17] M. Friedman, "The Role of Monetary Policy," in *American Economic Review*, March 1968, p. 16. The actual annual rates of growth of the money stock during the four-year period ending April 1969 were as follows: from April 1965 to April 1966, 6.0 percent; from April 1966 to January 1967, 0.0 percent; from January 1967 to December 1968, 6.8 percent; and from December 1968 to April 1969, 4.3 percent.

lower the rate of growth of the money supply in any period to whatever extent it thinks is called for in the interest of economic stabilization.[18]

One such guideline, which is of special interest because it originates with the Joint Economic Committee of the Congress and because it has been submitted to the Congress for possible action, reads as follows:

> To provide a first approximation to an economic posture that would manage to maintain price stability while encouraging maximum employment and rapid economic growth, the Congress should advise the Federal Reserve System that variations in the rate of increase of the money stock (currency plus demand deposits adjusted) ought to be too great or too sharp. In normal times, for the present, the desirable range of variation appears to be within the limits of 2 to 6 percent per annum, measured on a quarter-by-quarter basis—a range that centers on the rate of long-run increase in the potential gross national product in constant dollars, which is our sustainable real growth rate.[19]

It remains to be seen whether or not the Congress will impose on the Federal Reserve even the restraint of a guideline as broad as the 2 to 6 percent band proposed by the committee or any related type of restraint. If so, it will mark a distinct change from the purely discretionary monetary policy that the Federal Reserve has been permitted to follow over the past years. More important, of course, is whether it will mean a change for the better or not. This depends on whether Friedman's view, that monetary policy can contribute most to the goals before us by simply following the rule of a steady rate of growth of the money stock, is more correct or less incorrect than what is known as the eclectic view—the one that underlies the discretionary policy practiced by the Federal Reserve authorities. Our immediate concern in this section has been with monetary policy as a means of realizing certain goals. However, discussion of this issue in the years immediately ahead promises to center largely about the subsidiary matter just noted: the relative merits of the Friedman approach, which calls for guidelines, versus the major alternative approach, which permits the monetary authorities the wide discretion they now have.

[18] For the views of seventy-one academic, bank, and research monetary economists and of the Board of Governors, the Treasury, and the Council of Economic Advisers, on the question of guidelines for expanding the money supply, see *Compendium on Monetary Policy Guidelines and Federal Reserve Structure*, Committee on Banking and Currency, House of Representatives, Dec. 1968. A summary statement is provided on pp. 13–18, and on p. 18 a table is given showing that a substantial majority of the seventy-one economists favors a percent per annum growth of the money stock over alternative targets for monetary policy. For a survey of the arguments for and against rules, see R. Selden, "Stable Money Growth," in L. Yeager, ed., *In Search of a Monetary Constitution*, Harvard Univ. Press, 1962, pp. 322–55. See also M. Bronfenbrenner, "Monetary Rules: A New Look," in *Journal of Law and Economics*, Oct. 1965, pp. 173–94. Finally, it is interesting to note that this question of monetary rules, or guidelines, had aroused sufficient general interest by 1969 that the Council of Economic Advisers for the first time devoted space to the question in its January 1969 *Annual Report*. See pp. 89–93.

[19] Joint Economic Committee, *Standards for Guiding Monetary Action*, June 1968, p. 19. See also pp. 16–17 for similar views advanced by the Committee at earlier dates.

FISCAL POLICY

The deliberate use of fiscal policy to attain and maintain full employment and a stable price level is a development of the past thirty-five years. This use of fiscal policy began during the thirties, largely as the result of three developments: the apparent ineffectiveness of monetary policy as a means of overcoming the severe unemployment of the Great Depression, the "new economics" advanced by Keynes with its emphasis on aggregate demand, and the growing importance of government spending and taxation in relation to the economy's total income and output. From its relatively modest beginnings, fiscal policy has grown to become the major means by which public policy attempts to achieve full employment and to prevent inflation. As noted at the beginning of this chapter, the Employment Act of 1946 directed legislatively that fiscal policy be used toward the achievement of these ends.

In combating instability, whether in the form of recession or inflation, fiscal policy is carried out essentially through changes in government purchases, transfers, and tax collections. Such actions raise or lower the level of aggregate demand. In recession, the expansion of aggregate demand brought about by appropriate fiscal measures may lead to a rise in output and employment with little or no upward pressure on prices. In inflation, the contraction of aggregate demand brought about by appropriate fiscal measures may lead to a cessation of inflation with little or no adverse effect on output and employment. These, of course, are ideal results and have rarely been achieved in practice. They are results of a kind suggested by the simple fiscal models developed in detail in Chapter 14, where we examined under highly simplified assumptions the effects of changes in government purchases, transfer payments, and tax receipts on aggregate demand and income. Our concern in that chapter was only with the bare "mechanics" of fiscal policy, uncomplicated by the problems of formulating and implementing policies in a real-world setting. Our purpose now is to supplement the mechanics of the fiscal models with a discussion of just a few of the many real-world problems that complicate the planning and execution of fiscal policies and make it a far less certain process than these earlier models may have suggested.

A problem that, in a sense, underlies all other such problems is that of evaluating the impact of any overall fiscal program on the level of economic activity. Does a particular program of government expenditures and taxes have, on the whole, a stimulating or restraining influence, and what is the magnitude of that influence? To measure in a meaningful way the stimulating or restraining influence of any actual federal fiscal program or the federal budget as a whole for any time period requires recourse to what is called the *full-employment (or high-employment) budget surplus*, and it is to an examination of this concept that we will turn first. The full-employment budget surplus gives us a measure of the restraint or stimulus exerted by a particular fiscal program, but suppose that our objective is to provide more or less stimulus or more or less restraint than that indicated by a given fiscal program. The practical problem then faced is whether the fiscal program can be altered fairly promptly in a way that will yield the desired result in terms of stimulus or restraint. This is essentially the problem of flexibility in fiscal policy and is the second problem to be considered below. Any adjustment in the fiscal program to vary the restraint or stimulus exerted by that program calls for changes in the level and perhaps the composition of government purchases, transfer payments, and taxes or changes in various combinations of these. The third problem to be touched on concerns the practical difficulties involved in varying expenditures and taxes in the way that may be required if fiscal policy is to contribute to the stabilization of the economy. Finally, a fiscal policy of this kind during periods of recession is one that involves deficits, and deficits mean a growing national debt. The fourth, and last, problem we will look at is the problem, real or imaginary, of a growing national debt.

The Full-Employment Budget Surplus

It is an elementary but basic proposition that a rise in government purchases or transfer payments not matched by an equal rise in tax receipts will have an expansionary effect on the income level. Similarly, opposite combinations will have a contractionary effect on the income level. These statements are often expressed in shorthand form by saying that fiscal changes that involve a deficit are expansionary and fiscal changes that involve a surplus are contractionary. Accordingly, it would seem that all one need do to determine whether the impact of the government budget is expansionary or contractionary in any period is to note whether it shows a deficit or a surplus for that period. If it shows a deficit in this period but a smaller deficit than in the preceding period, the rule suggests that the budget is still expansionary but less so than it was in the preceding period. Similarly for other period-to-period changes in the size of the surplus or for changes from surplus to deficit and deficit to surplus.

Despite the convenience of having a rule that so easily answers the question of whether the influence of the budget is expansionary or contractionary, there are too many qualifications to the rule to permit it to be used as such. One such qualification follows from the unit-multiplier theorem examined in Chapter 14.[20] Here we will look into another qualification to this rule, one that shows, under certain circumstances, that a rise in the deficit from one period to the next is not indicative of a more expansionary budget, as suggested by the rule, but of the very opposite of this.[21]

---

[20] For example, a decline in tax receipts may be greater than the decline in government purchases, thus creating a deficit, but the overall effect of these changes on the income level may still be contractionary because the government-purchases multiplier is greater than the tax multiplier.

[21] A review of the third fiscal model presented in Chapter 14 will contribute to an understanding of the material that follows in this section.

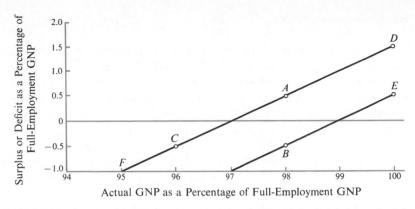

FIGURE 24–1   The Level of Economic Activity and the Federal Surplus or Deficit

The federal government has a budget program for each year that fixes both planned expenditures and tax rates. This program cannot, however, fix in advance the size of the deficit or surplus, because that will depend in part on the level of economic activity, which is unknown in advance. Given the possibility that economic activity may vary over a sizable range, an unchanged program of planned government expenditures and tax rates is accordingly consistent with a whole range of possible surpluses or deficits. The nature of this relationship is illustrated with hypothetical figures in Figure 24–1.

The horizontal axis of this figure shows actual GNP as a percentage of full-employment GNP, which is the estimate of the level of GNP that would be realized if the economy were operating at full employment. The vertical axis expresses the federal surplus or deficit as a percentage of full-employment GNP. Each of the two lines shown describes a different program of planned government expenditures and tax rates, the upper line involving a smaller amount of planned expenditures and/or higher tax rates than does the lower line. The upper line shows that the particular expenditure and tax program that determines the position of that line will result in a deficit equal to 0.5 percent of full-employment GNP if the actual level of economic activity is at 96 percent of the full employment level and a surplus equal to 0.5 percent of full-employment GNP if the actual level of economic activity is at 98 percent of full employment. These two situations are shown as *C* and *A*, respectively.

Now let us assume that the economy happens to be operating at the 98 percent level in the current period and that it is expected to remain at this level in the following period (assuming the absence of monetary and fiscal policy actions taken to move it to a higher level). In this event, with a budget program that gives us the upper line, a surplus equal to 0.5 percent of full-employment GNP is indicated at *A*.

Suppose, however, that the income level turns out to be only 96 rather than the 98 percent of the full-employment level that was expected. With an unchanged budget program, the budget has shifted from the surplus at *A* to the deficit at *C*. In this case, what must be seen is that the deficit is the result solely of unplanned, nondiscretionary, or automatic changes in tax receipts and expenditures. The deficit is passively induced by the slowdown in economic activity. Graphically what we find is simply a movement back down the upper line that designates the given unchanged budget program.

Consider next the opposite case of a discretionary change in the budget program, or a change that involves a shift in the line. Again we begin with the economy operating at the 98 percent level and with the budget program the one shown by the upper line. As before, this results in the surplus at *A*. Now, however, we assume a discretionary change in the budget program, such as a cut in tax rates or a planned increase in government expenditures. The height of the line reflects the basic budget program, and changes such as those noted would involve a downward shift of the line, say, to the position of the lower line. If the income level remained at 98 percent of the full-employment level, this new budget program would result in the deficit at *B* instead of the surplus at *A*.

Note that the deficit at *C* is equal to the deficit at *B*, but they nonetheless differ completely in what they say about the impact of the budget program. The movement from the surplus at *A* to the deficit at *C* is the result solely of the automatic decrease in tax receipts and the unplanned increase in expenditures for unemployment compensation that accompany the slowdown in economic activity. A deficit that originates in this way does not indicate any change in the impact of the existing budget program. On the other hand, the movement from the surplus at *A* to the deficit at *B* is the result solely of discretionary changes in the budget program that make the impact of that program more expansionary or less contractionary than it previously was.

In practice, a given change in the actual deficit or surplus from period to period may be the result of changes in both the budget program and the level of economic activity. Furthermore, a change in the level of economic activity may itself be the result of a change in the budget program—that is, a change in government demand—that is not offset by an opposite change in private demand. For a simple illustration, begin with the economy operating at the 98 percent level with a deficit at *B*, and assume a change in the budget program that shifts the line to the position of the upper line. If there were no change in the level of economic activity, there would be a movement from the deficit at *B* to the surplus at *A*, but the very increase in tax rates or decrease in expenditures that underlie the shift in the line are likely to cause a change in the level of economic activity.

Suppose the change in the budget program that produces this upward shift of the line were sufficiently restrictive, other things being given, to cause economic activity to fall all the way to the 95 percent level at which we find the deficit at *F*. In this event, we have a movement from the deficit at *B* not to the surplus at *A* but to the even larger deficit at *F*. If the impact of the budget is judged solely in terms of the size of the deficit or surplus, we would conclude incorrectly that we have a less restrictive or more expansionary budget program. On the other hand, if the impact of the budget is judged in terms of all the relevant information, we would conclude correctly that there has been a shift toward a more restrictive or less expansionary budget program. With all the relevant information at hand, we see in the present case that the rise in the deficit indicates not a more expansionary or less restrictive budget program but actually the very opposite of this.

This illustration resorts to an extreme case to emphasize the point, but the change in the size of the deficit or surplus is not a reliable guide to the change in the impact of the budget in the general case as well. One way to a more reliable guide is to remove the influence of changing levels of economic activity on the deficit or surplus consistent with any given budget program. It is in so doing that we derive what is called the full-employment budget surplus or deficit, a measure of the surplus or deficit that reflects only changes in the budget program and therefore a measure that indicates changes in the contractionary or expansionary impact of the budget program itself. This particular measure of budget surplus and deficit was introduced by the Council of Economic Advisers in 1962 and has been developed over the years since then.[22]

In formal terms, the full-employment budget surplus may be defined as the federal budget surplus, on a national income accounts basis, that would be generated by a given budget program if the economy were operating at full employment with stable prices throughout the year. Otherwise expressed, it is the difference between federal receipts and expenditures calculated for existing expenditure programs and tax rates but with expenditures for unemployment compensation adjusted to what they would be at full employment and with government receipts under existing tax rates adjusted to what they would be at full employment. Figure 24–1 shows at *D* and *E* the full-employment budget surplus (expressed there as a percent of full-employment GNP) that follows from the two budget programs represented by the two lines in that figure.

To estimate the size of the full-employment budget surplus or deficit for any quarter or year clearly calls for a series of other estimates of a kind suggested by the second definition above. First, we must have an estimate of what the GNP would be at full employment. The method used by the Council of Economic Advisers in arriving at this estimate is the growth rate extrapolation method, which is a simplification of what is popularly known as Okun's Law.[23] This method assumes that full-employment GNP in real terms grows at a fairly constant rate over extended periods of time. Once the rate is determined and a base year in which there was full employment is selected, the real full-employ-

---

[22] The concept actually originated in the mid-forties, but it received emphasis by the council starting in 1962. (See the *Annual Report of the Council of Economic Advisers*, Jan. 1962, pp. 78–84.) A more thorough discussion is found in M. E. Levy, *Fiscal Policy, Cycles and Growth*, National Industrial Conference Board, 1963, Ch. 6. See also R. Solomon, "A Note on the Full-Employment Budget Surplus," in *Review of Economics and Statistics*, Feb. 1964, pp. 105–08, and K. Carlson, "Estimates of the High-Employment Budget, 1947–1967," in *Review*, Federal Reserve Bank of St. Louis, June 1967, pp. 6–13.

[23] Okun's Law relates total output to labor-force utilization and productivity. For an analysis of this relationship, see A. M. Okun, "Potential GNP: Its Measurement and Significance," in *Papers and Proceedings of the Business and Economic Statistics Section of the American Statistical Association*, 1962, pp. 98–104. An adaptation of this article appears in A. M. Okun, ed., *The Battle Against Unemployment*, Norton, 1965, pp. 13–25. See also L. C. Thurow and L. D. Taylor, "The Interaction Between the Actual and the Potential Rates of Growth," in *Review of Economics and Statistics*, Nov. 1966, pp. 351–60.

ment GNP for other years can be calculated.[24] This real series is then converted into current dollar series by multiplying by the GNP implicit price deflator. Given the estimate for full-employment GNP, the second step is to estimate the amount of revenue that would be generated at this level of GNP under the existing tax structure and tax rates. This requires, among others, estimates of such variables as the proportions of full-employment GNP going to corporate profits and to personal income and then the application of an appropriate tax rate to each income component. As an example of one of the many difficulties that appear at this point, the appropriate tax rate under the personal income tax depends on the size of the tax base to which it is applied and the size of this base requires an estimate of how the distribution of income between personal income and corporate profits will change at full employment from what it is at a position below full employment. Last and least troublesome in this series of estimates is the estimation of government expenditures at full employment. This reduces to an estimate of what the amount of unemployment-compensation payments will be at the full-employment level of GNP, since other budget items are determined by administration proposals and congressional action and, with stable prices, may reasonably be treated as independent of the GNP level.

Figure 24–2 shows the actual and the full employment budget surplus or deficit for the 1956–68 period.[25] During most of these years, the actual budget was in deficit, but in the first ten of these thirteen years the full-employment budget was in surplus. In other words, given the legislated expenditure programs and the tax rates in effect in each year, the estimate is that the budget would have been in surplus by the amounts shown for each year from 1956 through 1965, if the economy had enjoyed full employment in each of these years. Unlike the series for the full-employment budget surplus or deficit, whose very computation has removed the effect of departures from full employment or the effects of the cyclical fluctuations that occur in GNP, the series for the actual budget surplus or deficit reflects these fluctuations and, for reasons earlier discussed, thereby obscures the extent to which the budget program itself is stimulative or restrictive. For example, the actual series shows a surplus of $2.1 billion in 1957 and a deficit of $10.2 billion in 1958, but one cannot conclude from these figures that the budget shifted from being moderately restrictive

[24] The base period selected by the Council of Economic Advisers is 1955. The growth rate of real GNP at full employment was estimated at 4.3 percent for 1947–53, at 3.5 percent for 1954–62, at 3.7 percent for 1962–65, and at 4.0 percent for 1966–68.

[25] An alternative form of presentation, which follows the lines of Figure 24–1, is to express the full-employment budget surplus or deficit for each period as a percentage of that period's full-employment GNP. This makes allowance for the changing scale of the economy. For example, the estimates of the Federal Reserve Bank of St. Louis show a full-employment budget surplus (at annual rate) of $6.8 billion in 1956 III and the same in 1964 IV. These appear at the same level in a presentation like Figure 24–2, but the latter would lie below the former in the alternative type of presentation that recognizes the growth in the full-employment GNP over time. However, this alternative presentation does not lend itself to showing the actual budget or deficit, for the ratio of the actual deficit or surplus to the full-employment GNP has no particular meaning. The presentation of Figure 24–2 does allow a comparison between a full-employment budget surplus or deficit and an actual budget surplus or deficit.

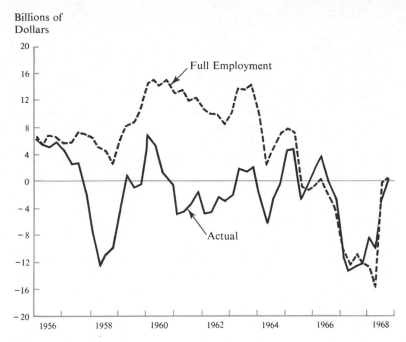

Billions of
Dollars

FIGURE 24–2   Full Employment and Actual Budget Surplus or Deficit, 1956–1968

in 1957 to being strongly stimulative in 1958. A sizable part of this $12.3 billion swing in the actual budget from 1957 to 1958 is due to the induced contraction in receipts and the induced expansion of expenditures that followed from the $5 billion decline in real GNP during the recession from 1957 to 1958. Expressed in terms of Figure 24–1, the indicated swing in the budget was due in part to a decrease in the percentage of full-employment GNP at which the economy was operating. Unlike these actual budget surplus and deficit figures, the estimates for the full-employment budget do not show a movement from surplus to deficit over the same period. The full-employment budget in 1957 is estimated at a $6.4 billion surplus and in 1958 at a $4.6 billion surplus, a swing of only $1.8 billion in contrast to the swing of $12.3 billion in the actual figures. The full-employment budget surplus is smaller in 1958 than in 1957, indicating a less restrictive budget in 1958 than in 1957 but still indicating a budget with a restrictive effect.

We may accept as a general rule that a full-employment budget surplus or deficit is, in and of itself, an indicator of a budget program that is restrictive or stimulative and that the size of this surplus or deficit is indicative of the degree of restraint or stimulus. Of course, in no sense does it follow from this that the goal of fiscal policy should be neither a full-employment budget surplus nor deficit but a budget program that is, in a sense, neutral. The very idea of employing fiscal policy for the purpose of attaining and maintaining full employment and preventing inflation calls at times for a budget program that is stimulative and at other times for a budget program that is restrictive. For example, given a budget program that produces some specific full-employment budget surplus, it follows that planned private investment expenditures must exceed

557

planned private saving by the amount of this surplus in order that full employment be realized. If the evidence suggests that private investment will exceed
private saving by a lesser amount, a correspondingly lower full-employment
budget surplus is the appropriate policy, assuming that full employment is the
objective of that policy. This in turn calls for discretionary increases in government expenditures or cuts in tax rates. In the opposite case, suppose that the
fiscal program is such as to produce some specific full-employment budget
deficit. It then follows that planned private investment must be less than planned
private saving at full employment by the amount of this deficit, if demand-pull
inflationary pressures are not to come into play. If the evidence suggests that
private investment will not be this much less than private saving, a correspondingly smaller full-employment budget deficit is suggested, assuming that now
the policy is aimed at the prevention of inflation.

In this way, the full-employment budget surplus appears as a tool of
analysis for planning appropriate fiscal actions designed to offset an excess or
deficiency of planned private investment relative to planned private saving at
the full-employment level. Such fiscal actions should thereby help the economy
to reach full employment if it is not already there or, if it is already there, to
prevent inflation. There are, of course, serious problems in using the tool. The
very calculation of the full-employment budget surplus is itself fairly crude,
and small changes in this surplus or deficit are probably not significant as more
than indicators of whether the fiscal program is moving toward more or less
restraint or stimulus from one quarter to the next. More serious is the problem,
found in an economy below full employment, of estimating what private saving
and private investment would be at full employment in order to know what the
appropriate full-employment budget surplus or deficit should be. Among still
other difficulties is that of securing the necessary discretionary flexibility in
expenditures and/or taxes, a question we will turn to in the following section.

Before turning to this, mention should be made of a concept closely related to that of the full-employment budget surplus—the concept of *fiscal drag*.
Underlying this notion is the fact that federal revenue rises more than proportionately with increases in GNP, especially for short-run increases in GNP, due
mainly to the progressive nature of the personal income tax and the high
responsiveness of corporate profits to changes in GNP. If federal expenditures
increase at the same rate as GNP, the result is a budget program whose revenue
side increases more than its expenditure side and a budget that therefore exerts
a drag on the growth of GNP. If the economy is already at full employment,
a budget program such as this will show a smaller deficit or larger surplus each
year. Since there is no reason to expect that this will be just offset by an equal
change in the difference between private saving and private investment, this
shrinking deficit or expanding surplus will eventually force the economy below
full employment. If it already is below full employment, this same budget
program will prevent the attainment of full employment. The best illustration
of the latter situation was found in the federal expenditure program and tax
structure as they were before 1964. An expansion of GNP toward the full-
employment level would automatically increase tax receipts by more than the

increase in expenditures and thus enlarge what was already a full-employment budget surplus. As we have seen, unless there was to be a corresponding excess of planned private investment over planned private saving at the full-employment level to offset such a full-employment budget surplus, this surplus itself would prevent the attainment of full employment. It is in this sense a "drag" on the very expansion of output and employment.

As shown by Figure 24–2, the full-employment budget was in fact highly restrictive until 1964, the year in which Congress approved the massive tax cut that had been called for by the administration in 1962. The reduction in taxes, combined with the expenditure program as it was then, wiped out the full-employment budget surplus in 1965 and also, given the magnitudes of private saving and investment, enabled the economy to achieve a full-employment level of output in 1966 for the first time since 1953. The reasonable balance that had been attained in 1965–66 was then upset by the large rise in federal spending for the Vietnam War. This pushed the full-employment budget into a deficit and led to the passage of the 10 percent income surtax in 1968, which was designed to offset what had become a budget with a substantial stimulative influence at a time when no such influence was desired.

When the surtax is removed, federal income tax rates will return, at least temporarily, to the levels set by the Revenue Act of 1964. However, even with these lower tax rates, we may face once again the problem of fiscal drag. For if federal expenditures expand no more than proportionately with GNP, while revenue, by the nature of the tax structure, automatically expands more than proportionately with GNP, there will follow a full-employment budget surplus that will impose an ever greater restrictive impact as time passes. If the economy is to avoid recession and unemployment, either federal expenditures must rise in a relative sense so that they come to constitute an ever larger fraction of the GNP or periodic reductions in tax rates must be arranged. Whether the solution should be in the form of a relatively larger federal expenditure program, especially for such pressing needs as education, hospitals, slum clearance, and control of air and water pollution, or reduced tax rates or some of both involves questions that go far beyond the concept of the fiscal drag itself. What is to be emphasized here is that the federal tax structure is such that our economy at full employment cannot continue to enjoy full employment unless the federal government either continuously expands its expenditures as a fraction of the GNP or cuts tax rates. To do neither is to permit the creation of a fiscal drag, which at some point will mean recession and unemployment.

Flexibility of Fiscal Policy

Planned private saving may exceed private investment at full employment so that a full-employment budget deficit is required if full employment is to be realized. If the actual situation happens to be one of a full-employment budget surplus and thus the actual level of income is one below full employment, the need seems clear: Discretionary changes in government expenditures and/or tax rates of the order required to produce the full-employment budget deficit that is consistent with the full-employment level of income. Meeting the need is another matter. Here we look briefly into the particular problem of whether we can secure the required degree of flexibility in government expenditures and/or tax rates to produce now a deficit and then a surplus as may be required to meet the needs of the situation. This same question was raised in connection with monetary policy in the first part of this chapter.

If we start off with a comparison of the relative flexibility of the two types of policy, it is generally conceded that monetary policy has the advantage here. Although this is due in part to the inherent flexibility of certain tools of monetary management like open-market operations, the greater flexibility of monetary policy is also due in part to the fact that the decision-making authority lies in an independent agency whose political aims are limited to its own perpetuation and the preservation of its customary role and whose power is concentrated in the hands of a few men. It is the seven-man Board of Governors of the Federal Reserve System or the twelve-man Federal Open Market Committee (which includes the same seven men plus the presidents of five of the Federal Reserve Banks) that makes the decisions on monetary policy in the United States. The presidents of the other Federal Reserve Banks, the Secretary of the Treasury, the Council of Economic Advisers, and others influence these decisions, but the power is nonetheless concentrated in these few hands. As we noted earlier, the last few years have seen growing strength in the movement toward limiting the almost complete discretionary authority the Board of Governors now possesses, but the board so far has kept this authority and with it the power to vary policy as promptly and to whatever degree the changes in business conditions seem, in its judgment, to warrant. The board's performance record is, of course, another matter; here we simply note the flexibility with which discretionary changes can be made in the area of monetary policy.

In contrast, the decision-making process in the area of fiscal policy involves, in a sense, the whole of the executive and legislative branches of the federal government. The political motivation here is also obviously of an altogether different kind, and decisions in the fiscal policy area, especially decisions involving higher tax rates, are not made without allowance for their effect on the electorate in the election that follows. Apart from this political bias, which is perhaps unavoidable in a system like ours, a certain lack of maneuverability follows simply from the fact that the decision-making power in the fiscal area rests in the hands of no small group. To get flexibility of a degree at all comparable with that found in the area of monetary policy would require that the President or some small group be given limited but discretionary power to vary certain tax rates and perhaps also some expenditure programs. President Kennedy's request for such authority in 1962 met with practically no success.[26]

---

[26] Specifically, the request was for standby authority to reduce individual income tax rates as much as 5 percentage points for a period of six months, to initiate up to $2 billion of capital improvements expenditures, and to extend the benefit period for unemployment compensation; the last two proposals were tied to the unemployment rate by a formula, a device to be discussed below. (See the *Economic Report of the President*, January 1962, pp. 17–20 and 72–76).

In his final budget message in January 1969, President Johnson recommended that the chief executive be granted limited discretionary power to vary tax rates. With respect to the 10 percent surcharge, he suggested that the President be given the authority to remove it entirely or partially as warranted by developments, with such presidential discretion to be subject to congressional veto within a limited time period. He further suggested that, "For the longer run, consideration should be given to establishing as a permanent part of our tax system an element of flexibility under which the President, again subject to congressional veto, would have discretion to raise or lower personal and corporation income tax rates within specified limits—such as 5% in either direction." [27]

Congress traditionally has closely guarded its power over the tax structure, tax rates, and expenditure programs, and it is unlikely that it will agree to relinquish the limited amount of power called for by Johnson's recommendations. So long as Congress retains almost complete power to make major discretionary changes, discretionary fiscal policy will remain anything but flexible, for it will continue to depend on legislative action, and legislative action will continue to be preceded by time-consuming congressional hearings and debate. Thus, in the field of changes in tax rates, the last two experiences (of 1964 and 1968) each required a one- to two-year period between the recommendation for change and the legislation providing for a change.

At present, what flexibility there is in fiscal policy is that provided by the so-called built-in, or automatic, stabilizers. It is these, we will see, that underlie the discussion in the preceding section of surpluses and deficits that automatically arise as the level of income increases and decreases. Beyond automatic flexibility is formula flexibility, a type of flexibility that would not require Congress to give the President the amount of power he would acquire with even limited discretionary authority. In the balance of this section we will take a brief look at the way fiscal policy now operates, with some flexibility provided by built-in stabilizers, and consider how this flexibility might be increased through the formula approach.

Built-in Flexibility. Built-in flexibility is achieved when changes in tax collections and government spending vary automatically, promptly, and in the right direction to produce a stabilizing effect on aggregate demand. Automaticity means that no specific action need be taken; promptness means that there is little lag between changes in aggregate demand and changes in government spending and tax collections; right direction means that decreases in aggregate demand call forth additional government spending and reduced tax collections, while increases in aggregate demand call forth the opposite. In

---

Though Congress took limited action on a capital improvements program, the President's request for a standby authority to cut tax rates received hardly any serious consideration.
[27] *The Budget of the United States Government*, Fiscal Year 1970, U.S. Government Printing Office, 1969, p. 12.

general, when aggregate demand and income are rising, automatic and prompt increases in tax receipts and decreases in transfer payments tend to dampen the expansion; when aggregate demand and income are falling, automatic and prompt decreases in tax receipts and increases in transfer payments tend to dampen the contraction.

These tendencies follow from the way in which total tax collections and government transfer payments automatically vary to prevent disposable personal income from rising or falling as much as GNP. In the case of a recession and falling GNP, for example, disposable personal income is protected somewhat because tax collections automatically fall and transfer payments automatically rise. Disposable personal income, therefore, falls less than it would if these stabilizers were not in operation. With disposable personal income so protected, personal consumption expenditures will fall less than they would if these stabilizers were not in operation. Finally, by avoiding what would otherwise be a sharper decline in consumption expenditures, the cumulative fall in GNP itself is less than it would be if these automatic stabilizers were not in operation. In simplest terms, this is the way built-in stabilizers produce a smaller fluctuation in GNP than would be the case in their absence.

This dampening of income movements is not an unmixed blessing. Whereas the resistance the built-in stabilizers provide to a downward movement is desirable in an underemployed economy, the resistance they provide to an upward movement in the same economy is undesirable. This, as we saw in the preceding section, is what is called fiscal drag and calls for appropriate offsetting actions in the form of discretionary changes in government expenditures or tax rates. In an economy at full employment, the built-in stabilizers would tend to have a stabilizing effect in both directions. They would offer resistance to the worsening of any downturn brought on by a sharp decline in demand and resistance to a worsening of any inflationary movement brought on by a sharp expansion in demand. In an economy operating at full employment, they provide a limited but helpful buffer against cumulative movements in either direction.

Economists quite generally favor the greatest possible use and strengthening of built-in stabilizers where possible. If one could ignore other public policy objectives, any number of changes could be adopted that would strengthen existing stabilizers. In the case of personal income tax, for example, a reduction in the size of the personal exemption and a tightening of deduction provisions would put a larger part of personal income into the base on which personal income taxes are computed, thereby increasing the cyclical variability of the revenue from this tax. A more progressive rate structure might contribute somewhat to the same end. In the case of indirect taxes, an *ad valorem* tax would increase the effectiveness of these stabilizers, since the revenue yield would vary more over the cycle under *ad valorem* than under *specific* taxes. In the case of government transfer payments, unemployment compensation payments could be made a more effective stabilizer by enlarging weekly benefits, lengthening the period over which these benefits may be received, and increasing the number of workers covered. Although each of these and a number of other changes could be made for the purpose of improving the effectiveness of an automatic program of stabilization, many such changes are ruled out because they conflict with and are judged subordinate to other aims of public policy.[28]

Partly because there are limits to how much automatic stabilization can be built into the system without causing conflict with other aims of public policy, most economists and many businessmen today are unwilling to limit the use of stabilizing fiscal policy to what can be accomplished through its passive role in an automatic program alone.[29] Instead, they generally favor an active role in which taxes and government spending (purchases of goods and services as well as transfer payments) are made to vary according to formula or executive discretionary action. The argument for a more active role for fiscal policy is substantially strengthened when we take into account a sometimes overlooked limitation of the most complete system of built-in stabilizers—namely, that the stabilizers in themselves cannot prevent a downturn from occurring because they do not come into effect until there already is some downturn in spending and income. True, they can help prevent a downturn from growing cumulatively worse, but they cannot in *themselves* reverse a downturn and initiate an expansion. On the other hand, although subject to other limitations, nonautomatic programs in which expansionary fiscal measures are initiated in the expectation of a downturn may in themselves (assuming correct forecasting) prevent downturns. Formula flexibility is like the built-in stabilizers in the sense that it is essentially automatic. However, it may be designed to allow a greater scope for stabilizing action than is provided by the built-in stabilizers, and, unlike the built-in stabilizers, may be able to reverse a downturn once begun.

[28] For an analysis of the quantitative impact of specific built-in stabilizers over a series of business cycles, see M. O. Clements, "The Quantitative Impact of Automatic Stabilizers," in *Review of Economics and Statistics*, Feb. 1960, pp. 56–61. Based on the business cycle contractions during 1947–57, the estimate in this study is that the combined effect of changes in personal income taxes withheld, corporate income tax accruals, excise tax collections, unemployment taxes, OASI benefit payments, and unemployment benefit payments produced, on the average, a fall in disposable personal income equal to only 48.6 percent of the fall in national income. For business cycle expansions during the 1947–57 period, the same stabilizers had, on the average, the combined effect of limiting the rise in disposable personal income to 72.2 percent of the rise in national income. Note that the fiscal stabilizers exercise a stronger effect on the downward side than on the upward side. See also W. Lewis, Jr., *Federal Fiscal Policy in the Postwar Recessions*, Brookings Institution, 1962. The second chapter of this study provides an analysis of the actual behavior of each of the major built-in stabilizers.

[29] The most influential group that long favored the restriction of stabilizing fiscal measures to those of a purely automatic nature is the Committee for Economic Development. The CED took this position in its first statement on the subject in 1947 in *Taxes and the Budget: A Program for Prosperity in a Free Economy*. Through a long series of national policy statements, the CED by 1958 had recognized the need for some discretionary action in its *Anti-Recession Policy for 1958*. Still, fiscal measures were assigned the inherently passive role provided by built-in stabilizers, the active role to be played by monetary measures. In a January 1969 statement called *Fiscal and Monetary Policies for Steady Economic Growth*, the CED took a large step toward discretionary fiscal policy and toward providing flexibility in this policy by recommending that Congress give the President power to vary personal and corporate income tax rates by up to 10 percent. With a few additional safeguards, the CED proposal was similar to that made by President Johnson in his final budget message.

Formula Flexibility.   Formula flexibility relies on changes in selected indexes such as the unemployment rate or the consumer price index as indicators of need for specific changes in income tax rates, transfer payments, or even public works expenditures. As in the case of built-in stabilizers, action takes place in response to realized changes in the business situation and in this sense is automatic rather than discretionary. For example, in oversimplified form, the formula could require a specified reduction in personal income tax rates when the unemployment percentage equaled or exceeded 5 percent for two consecutive months, or it might call for an increase in those tax rates when the consumer price index rose 5 percent in a specified time interval. Similarly, a formula could call for liberalizing unemployment compensation and other kinds of government transfer payments in response to increases in the unemployment rate. A number of small-scale public works projects could also be kept "on the shelf" until there were specific changes in the unemployment rate or in other indexes of business conditions. By relying on a formula in this fashion, changes in tax rates and expenditure programs would go into effect with minimum administrative delay and without forecasts of future business conditions—forecasts that, as is well known, may often be wrong.

Yet, despite the automaticity of action associated with rigid adherence to a formula, the action so triggered may be wrong just as often as action that is based on forecasts. If an unemployment rate that is above some specified level for a period of a few months is the signal for action, for example, corrective action may come just at the time when the forces that caused the high unemployment are dying out. There is no way of knowing such things in advance with certainty, but detailed study of the situation may provide, at the minimum, some understanding of the cause or causes of the business downturn and the high unemployment and hence some clue as to whether a turnabout may be near at hand. For example, if study suggests that the downturn resulted primarily from an inventory liquidation, an end to the downturn may not be many months off. If, on the other hand, study shows that decreasing plant and equipment expenditures are the cause, the situation may be more serious, and the action indicated by the formula or even more vigorous action may be in order. Without in any way detracting from the advantages of the formula device, action triggered by formula alone, without study of the total business situation, would receive the support of few economists. Actually, some economists support formula flexibility more for political than for economic reasons. They would favor granting the President limited authority to take discretionary action, but they are aware that Congress is probably not yet ready to delegate to him the authority for such action.

In sum, the present role of fiscal policy in limiting short-run fluctuations in economic activity is restricted essentially to the automatic, or built-in, stabilizers. Though action is taken from time to time by Congress itself, such action, by the nature of the legislative process, is not sufficiently flexible to be useful against truly short-run fluctuations in economic activity. For example, the massive tax cut approved by Congress in early 1964 (after almost two years of consideration) is widely recognized as one of the most important factors in sustaining the economic expansion that began in 1961. But if that tax cut had stimulated the economy enough to result in inflation, as many feared would be the case, could Congress have "promptly" reversed itself by raising tax rates? This would, of course, have been within its power, but such a degree of flexibility in the legislative process is ordinarily unattainable. The time required to put through the 10 percent surtax in 1968 attests to this. Unless greater flexibility is provided through either the formula approach with limited discretion or through an outright grant of some discretion to the President, it is fair to conclude that fiscal policy will remain far less effective as a means of achieving short-run stabilization than it might be.

Variations in Government Purchases, Transfer Payments, and Taxes

We noted earlier that to a limited extent built-in flexibility provides appropriately timed helpful fiscal response to recessionary and inflationary developments. In order to secure larger fiscal response, flexibility by formula or discretionary action is required. This brings us to the question of whether federal expenditures and tax receipts, even with discretionary action, can in practice be varied by the large amounts that may at times be necessary for successful stabilization policy.

The answer to this question is certainly quite different today from what it would have been in the twenties, if it had been asked in those days before fiscal policy had become a generally accepted means of achieving stabilization. For example, federal government purchases made up a little over 1 percent of GNP in 1929—$1.3 billion out of GNP of $103.1 billion. This percentage rose during the Great Depression, and, except for 1946–50, it has exceeded 10 percent of GNP in every year during and since World War II. Thus, to the extent that purchases of the federal government can be promptly reduced by, say, 10 percent as an anti-inflationary measure or raised 10 percent as an antirecessionary measure, the impact on the economy will be far greater today than a similar percentage change would have been in the days of relatively smaller federal budgets. Together with the growing importance of federal purchases relative to GNP has come a growing importance of federal transfer payments. These rose from less than $1 billion in 1929 to $55 billion in 1968, although GNP in the meantime had increased only eightfold. Roughly paralleling the growth of both types of federal spending has come, of course, a growing importance of federal tax receipts.

In developing the fiscal models of Chapter 14, we saw that variations in government purchases, transfer payments, and tax receipts could be used in various combinations to produce the desired expansionary or contractionary effects on aggregate demand and the level of income. Now let us take a look at some of the practical limitations on the use of such variations as tools of fiscal policy.

Purchases of Goods and Services. One way of reducing inflationary pressures is to reduce the level of government purchases, thereby reducing government demand for goods and services and releasing resources to meet private demands. In practice, however, the federal government has comparatively little freedom of action in this direction. Around 80 percent of federal purchases are currently for defense purposes. Whatever one's feelings about the appropriate level for such outlays, they are outlays of a type that cannot be varied to any appreciable degree simply on the basis of stabilization requirements. Thus, under present conditions, variation is essentially limited to the 20 percent of federal purchases that are of a nondefense nature, but there are also problems here. For example, sharp slashes in these expenditures are plainly not administratively feasible in the short run. Beyond this is the injustice of placing the major burden of fiscal adjustment on the nonmilitary public sector. While it may be possible to reduce or stretch out some kinds of nondefense spending, those kinds that are aimed at meeting the urgent problems of poverty and urban blight should be beyond cutting or stretching out. In times of inflationary pressures, it therefore does not seem that any large effect can be realized via cuts in nondefense expenditures except at a very high social cost. Inflation has to be attacked primarily through increases in tax rates, which places the major burden of the stabilization policy on the 80 percent of GNP that represents private uses of output rather than on the 3 percent of GNP that represents federal nondefense uses of output.

One way of combating a recession is to increase the level of government purchases, thereby increasing government demand for goods and services and absorbing idle resources in their production. Unless there are to be more government purchases just for the sake of purchases (i.e., disregarding the usefulness of what is purchased), the major part of expanded purchases to meet the problem of recession will have to be for public works such as roads, dams, public buildings, and the like. This brings us to the problem of the limited flexibility of public works projects.[30] Some lag is unavoidable, even with preplanning, between the decision to undertake a project and the actual initiation of expenditures on it. Furthermore, few public works projects are of a type that can be completed in a matter of months or even a year. Consequently, there is the possibility that the economy will recover and even enter a vigorous expansion, just when many antirecessionary public works projects are half completed. To abandon them at this point would be wasteful; to complete them would accelerate the expansionary movement at a time when this would be undesirable. This lack of flexibility is not a serious problem in the face of a

---

[30] See, for example, S. Maisel, "Varying Public Construction and Housing to Promote Economic Stability," in Joint Economic Committee, *Federal Expenditure Policy for Economic Growth and Stability*, Papers, 1957, pp. 382–97. See also his "Timing and Flexibility of a Public Works Program," in *Review of Economics and Statistics*, May 1949, pp. 147–52; J. Margolis, "Public Works and Economic Stability," in *Journal of Political Economy*, Aug. 1949, pp. 293–303; and R. L. Teigen, "The Effectiveness of Public Works as a Stabilization Device," in W. L. Smith and R. L. Teigen, eds., *Readings in Money, National Income and Stabilization Policy*, Irwin, 1965, pp. 302–08.

prolonged depression such as the one during the thirties, but it does mean that public works projects are of limited value in coping with short, cyclical downturns of the type the economy has suffered in the postwar period.

Transfer Payments.   Transfer payments by the federal government would appear to allow greater maneuverability than purchases, because they can be more quickly expanded or contracted as conditions require. But we encounter problems here too. To achieve a substantial reduction in transfer payments as a part of an anti-inflationary program would mean cutting benefit provisions under old age, survivors, and disability insurance, unemployment insurance, and retirement programs (which account for almost all federal government transfer payments apart from Medicare and Medicaid). Some of these payments are contractual obligations of government and cannot be touched; others, such as old age benefits, although subject to change by congressional action, occupy a place in the social fabric of this country that effectively rules out reductions. Thus, on inspection, sizable cutbacks in transfer payments as a means of reducing aggregate demand appear to be unattainable in practice.[31]

On the other hand, expansion of transfer payments as a means of stimulating the economy appears to be subject to no such limitation. What is more, because a large part of such funds are received by low-income persons, the likelihood is that most of such funds will be used promptly to finance an increase in consumption spending. Although transfer payments have this significant advantage on the side of stimulation, any increases in transfer payments are likely to be permanent, presenting a problem if restrictive action is subsequently indicated. This is the problem referred to in the preceding paragraph, a problem that limits the usefulness of transfer payments for short-run stabilization purposes that at times require expansionary action to be followed before long by action in the opposite direction.

Tax Receipts.   Fiscal policy may be used to attack the problem of excessive or deficient aggregate demand from the tax side as well as from the side of government purchases and transfer payments. For example, an overheated economy may be cooled by an appropriate rise in tax rates with no change in government spending. The only limitation to the use of tax rates for this purpose is the willingness of Congress to impose higher rates, a willingness often absent except in cases of extreme emergency, such as wartime. But, even if this reluctance to raise taxes is overcome, there is the complex problem of deciding which rates are to be raised and the amount by which each is to be raised. Just as an overly restrictive monetary policy may not only bring an inflationary expansion to an end but precipitate a decline, so an overly restrictive tax policy may have the same effect. In short, it may not only cool an overheated economy but may "freeze" it.

[31] We refer, of course, to discretionary reductions. Aggregate unemployment benefits will be reduced automatically as unemployment falls during the expansion phase of the business cycle. As we saw, this results from the operation of the unemployment insurance program as a built-in stabilizer.

To the extent that excessive aggregate demand can be attributed to developments in particular sectors of the economy, it may be possible to direct tax policy toward this sector without putting the brakes on the system as a whole. For example, if a boom in investment spending is under way, a rise in corporate income tax rates with unchanged personal income tax rates may be in order. In such a case, the dampening effect will fall, at least initially, on the sector that needs dampening.[32] If, on the other hand, the excess is primarily the result of a surge in consumption spending, the personal income tax would probably be a better vehicle through which to effect the required degree of restraint.

When the economy faces deficient aggregate demand and recession, the appropriate fiscal policy may, of course, be to cut tax rates. Here again, the question arises of how any given cut should be allocated over various types of taxes in order to get the maximum stimulative effect. In simplified form, the question is often approached as a choice between, or a combination of, tax cuts designed directly to stimulate consumption spending or investment spending. Because the cyclical fluctuations in investment spending are relatively greater than those in consumption spending, investment spending will usually be the more depressed of the two in times of recession. For this reason, some people argue that tax cuts should be aimed at encouraging investment, since the principal need is to raise the rate of investment spending in order to move the industries that are engaged in producing capital goods closer to their prosperity levels of output. Increased activity will mean rising income for consumers, from which, by way of the multiplier, will come the rise in consumption necessary to keep the upward movement rolling. Viewed from this perspective, tax cuts aimed directly at raising consumption spending will not, except after an unacceptably long lag, raise activity in the capital goods industries. This means that the immediate stimulus is not being applied where it is most needed. Others argue, however, that there is no better stimulus to investment spending than that provided by increased consumption spending. These economists claim that unless and until businessmen see an increase in the rate at which goods are moving into the hands of consumers, they will be little influenced in their investment decisions by tax inducements. Consequently, for these men the maximum stimulative effect of a given amount of tax reduction will be secured through tax changes that leave more after-tax income in the hands of consumers than in the hands of corporations. The specific arguments on both sides could be examined in detail and in more precise form, but our purpose is simply to point out that this is one of the basic questions to be answered in selecting the

---

[32] The decrease in after-tax profits of corporations may not, however, restrict the funds available to corporations to finance an expanding rate of investment spending. For example, if the outlook for growing corporate profits remains sufficiently favorable, corporations, despite the fact that government is now taking a larger share of this total, may offset the restraint of higher taxes by reducing the share of after-tax profits paid out in dividends. In addition, they may resort to borrowing as another source of additional investment funds. However, when the boom is being fed by investment spending, a restrictive monetary policy can play an important role by reducing the availability and raising the cost of funds being borrowed to finance the splurge of investment spending.

most effective expansionary tax policy. It should also be noted that the answer need not be the same in every situation; investment-stimulating tax changes may look more promising in one recession, consumption-stimulating tax changes in another.

Whether an expansionary tax policy is to be aimed primarily at consumption or investment spending, there are a number of techniques that may be employed for either purpose. To stimulate consumption spending, the principal reliance will be on cuts in the personal income tax, but cuts in excise tax rates may also help. To the extent that prices of taxed goods fall with lower excises, unchanged money expenditures will mean an increase in the total amount of goods that can be purchased, and this will stimulate an increase in the production of goods and an expansion of employment. Within the personal income tax structure, a stimulative effect may be gained either through cuts in rates or by such changes as increases in the size of personal exemptions or larger standard deductions. Within the rate structure, the cut may be limited to the first bracket (the "basic rate"), or it may be an across-the-board cut, or it may be still another variant. If the sole objective is to obtain the maximum stimulative effect on consumption for a given reduction in tax revenue, the most effective technique will probably be a reduction in the first bracket rate of the personal income tax. This is the only rate paid by taxpayers with the smallest taxable incomes, and these taxpayers are those most likely to devote any increase in take-home pay to additional consumption spending.

Investment spending may also be stimulated through a number of tax-related techniques. The most familiar are reductions in corporate income tax rates, liberalization of depreciation regulations, and tax credits on purchases of capital goods. Which technique is likely to give the maximum stimulus to investment for a given sacrifice of revenue, however, is much less certain in the field of business taxation than it is in personal income taxation.

Today it is generally accepted by economists and businessmen alike that changes in tax rates can and should be employed in the interest of greater economic stability. The specific tax changes that are to be made in pursuit of this goal, however, give rise to many difficult and controversial questions. In addition to the difficulties associated with determining which tax policies are best designed for stabilization purposes, there are also the difficulties of reconciling these policies with the goal of equity. What may appear at first glance to be the policies best designed for stabilization purposes may be policies that many people feel result in unfair distribution of the tax burden among different income classes or different types of income. This is an example of the conflict that can arise between economic stability and economic justice.

The compromise solution generally recommended for this problem is the one adopted in 1968 in connection with that year's tax increase. Under the 1968 surtax, the basic personal and corporate income tax rates were left unchanged, while taxpayers added 10 percent (on a full-year basis) to their income tax bills computed under those basic rates. This means that everybody's income tax bill went up by 10 percent, and the distribution of the burden imposed by the income tax remained essentially unchanged. Use of this relatively simple device thus bypasses some difficult and controversial questions that would otherwise make it even more difficult than it now is to secure discretionary changes in tax rates for stabilization purposes. The question of reforms in the tax structure and the rate schedules to provide a more equitable tax system can and should be approached as a problem apart from short-run tax decisions based on stabilization considerations.

Deficits and the Burden of the National Debt

In addition to the underlying problem of measuring the restrictive or stimulative impact of the federal budget, we have so far discussed two broad problems that are encountered in using fiscal policy to help achieve full employment and price stability: the problem of securing the degree of flexibility needed to meet short-run changes in the business situation and the problem of selecting the instruments (changes in government purchases, transfers, taxes, or combinations thereof) that are best suited to meet the needs of any particular situation. We now turn briefly to a third problem: the increase in the national debt that results from the budget deficits incurred through countercyclical fiscal policy in periods of recession.

To begin with, we can say that if the business cycle were perfectly symmetrical, this problem would not appear. In such a case the deficits incurred by the government during recession could be neatly balanced by the surpluses raised during prosperity. The budget would then be balanced over the business cycle, and countercyclical policy would involve only temporary increases in the national debt. But the economy does not behave in this idealized fashion. Fluctuations are not balanced departures above and below a long-run trend of full-employment growth, for the underlying secular tendency in any economy may be toward either stagnation or exhilaration. In a stagnant economy, short-run fluctuations will be characterized by relatively short and weak expansions and relatively long and severe contractions. Countercyclical fiscal policy operating against a weak underlying growth base may show surpluses in some years, but the deficits of other years will be greater, and the number of deficit years will exceed the number of surplus years. In this environment, fiscal policy is, in a sense, being employed as more than a countercyclical tool; it is being employed to counter an underlying stagnation of the economy as well. Immediately relevant is the fact that fiscal policy employed in such circumstances will not yield a budget that is balanced over the business cycle. The infrequent small surpluses will not be equal to the more frequent large deficits, and as a consequence the national debt will rise. An underlying secular tendency of exhilaration would, by the same reasoning, show the opposite results. The national debt will fall in the long run. Our concern here is with the former situation, in which the use of fiscal policy for stabilization purposes means a rising national debt.

If a rising national debt will at some point mean "national impoverishment" and "national bankruptcy," then it is clear that the use of fiscal policy is severely limited. We will see that arguments such as these, at least in their crude form, may be easily disposed of; they present no real barrier to the use of fiscal policy involving a rising debt. But may there not be real dangers in a rising debt? May not a rising debt, in some sense, impose a rising real burden on the economy, so that whatever debt-financed government expenditures may contribute through higher output and employment is offset, or more than offset, by a loss in another direction?

Traditional and New Views of National Debt.   According to the traditional view, national debt is not essentially different from private debt. The federal government as a debtor can end up completely impoverished and bankrupt if its indebtedness grows too large. Although government may exercise sufficient restraint to avoid these ultimate consequences, any growth in its debt is still held to have the following consequences: a shifting to future generations of the burden of today's government expenditures that are debt-financed; a rising interest charge and so the need for increased taxation; a redistribution of income toward greater inequality over time as taxes are collected to pay interest to bondholders, the effect of which is deflationary; and an inherent inflationary effect resulting from the borrowing itself.[33]

According to the more modern view of national debt, some of these arguments are held to be totally without merit, and others are considered trivial. Here, in summary form, are the answers offered to the traditional arguments.

The argument of national bankruptcy is held to be groundless. The federal government can meet its obligations to pay off maturing debt (and even interest on outstanding debt) by selling new debt. In an extreme case, it can always meet its obligations by printing paper money in the necessary amount. It is possible that a massive conversion of interest-bearing debt into money would lead to inflation, and the inflation so generated would amount to a partial repudiation of the national debt. However, the obligation of the government, even under these conditions, would have been legally met. In short, the national government cannot go bankrupt.

In the new view, the real burden of today's government borrowing cannot be shifted to the future; it is actually measured by the resources that are shifted away from private use to public use *today*. The labor services and other resources secured by the national government today cannot be borrowed from the future. What is more, if there is less than full utilization of existing resources, even this burden vanishes, for the resources used by government would otherwise have gone unused.

It is true that national debt incurred by, but not retired by, the present generation will be passed on to the next generation. But the financial claims

---

[33] These are what A. P. Lerner describes as *imaginary* as opposed to *real* effects of national debt. (See his "The Burden of the National Debt," in *Income, Employment, and Public Policy*, Norton, 1948, pp. 255–75.) Lerner, through his "functional finance," is the foremost objector to the traditional and foremost proponent of the new view. (See his "Functional Finance and the Federal Debt," in A. Smithies and J. K. Butters, eds., *Readings in Fiscal Policy*, Irwin, 1955, pp. 468–78.) For more on the traditional view, see J. Burkhead, "The Balanced Budget," *op. cit.*, pp. 3–27.

that comprise the national debt are then owned by and owed to the very same generation; in other words, although they inherit the obligation to pay interest on the bonds, they also inherit the bonds themselves. Even though a rising debt means a rising interest charge, the taxes raised to pay interest are collected from the nation's citizens, and these citizens are also the recipients of the interest paid. There is, of course, an important difference between an internally and an externally financed debt in this respect. The argument given above applies only to an internally financed debt such as that of the U.S. government. A debt that is incurred today by borrowing abroad *will* mean a burden on future generations, since an actual export of goods and services will in effect be required to make interest payments and repayments of principal. This means that less of what future generations produce will be available for their use as a result of the debt incurred by the present generation through borrowing abroad.

A related argument is that debt service on a national debt that is entirely internally held may involve some redistribution of income. For the most part, however, those who pay the taxes to pay the interest on national debt will be the same persons who, directly or indirectly through financial institutions, receive the interest. Some slight redistribution of income from lower- to upper-income groups may result, but the redistribution involved will be too mild to have a significant deflationary effect. Even if it did, in the extreme case, whatever deflationary effect might result could be avoided by borrowing rather than by taxing to pay the interest on the debt.

Finally, the possible inflationary effect of debt creation is, in the new view, no objection to an expanding debt. Fiscal policy relies on debt financing as a means of producing an expansion of output and employment, and such a policy is undertaken only when the economy is operating below full utilization of its resources. Under such circumstances there is little reason to be concerned about inflation. (Debt creation during wartime when the economy is operating at capacity is another story.) However, the danger of inflation in the future is increased by the growth in public holdings of liquid assets that results from debt creation today. In the new view of public debt, this threat, if and when it appears, may be met by a reverse policy of increased taxation and debt retirement.

Though the traditional view is subject to criticisms such as these, there remains some substance in its arguments.[34] There is, for example, no denying that some redistribution of income may result—most people would regard a redistribution that increases inequality as an undesirable effect. But, as we mentioned above, this is not likely to be quantitatively important. It is also true that future generations may suffer a real burden as a result of today's borrowing if that borrowing is to finance higher consumption for the present generation. Borrowing for this purpose may mean that scarce natural resources are depleted and the growth of the capital stock is reduced. But a moment's reflection suggests that this is not a result peculiar to borrowing. Increased tax-financed

[34] The principal defender of the traditional view is James M. Buchanan. See his *Public Principles of Public Debt*, Irwin, 1955.

government spending for consumption purposes could have the same results—the depletion of scarce resources in consumption in lieu of the use of such resources to build up the capital stock that will be passed on to the future.

With respect to the question of the shifting of the burden, it is clear that any meaningful analysis must take into account, among other things, the use made of borrowed funds. Since for the United States and other central governments national debts have risen to their present dimensions mainly from the financing of wars and their aftermath, the larger part of government expenditures financed by borrowing can hardly be called productive. But to the extent that debt increases as a result of fiscal policy employed for stabilization purposes, the debt incurred may be productive. Debt resulting from a reduction in corporate tax rates, which in turn stimulates private capital formation, may mean that future generations will inherit a larger capital stock than might otherwise be the case. Similarly, debt incurred to finance government expenditures devoted to building schools, roads, and other productive capital goods may have the same effect. Thus, it is at least possible that debt incurred for such purposes may benefit rather than burden future generations.

Economic Growth and Debt Burden.   From another point of view, regardless of the reasons for the growth of the debt, a growing debt need not mean that each successive generation will necessarily be required to shoulder an ever larger burden. The fundamental error made by those who still blindly reach this conclusion is their failure to recognize that the growth in the national debt may be matched, or more than matched, by the growth of the economy. The traditional view of public debt usually does not give this relationship the emphasis it deserves, but in recent years the emphasis has shifted in this direction. Today the burden of national debt is commonly expressed in terms of the fraction of the economy's income raised through taxes in order to make interest payments on the debt. This suggests that the burden of the debt depends not on its absolute size, but on its growth (and the rate of interest paid on it) relative to the growth in income that is the tax base from which the funds for interest payments on the debt are raised. Viewed in this manner, it is possible that a falling debt may impose a rising burden and a rising debt a falling burden.

Viewing the burden of the debt as the tax rate necessary for debt service, E. D. Domar, in what is now a classic article, laid out the conditions under which the burden of the debt may increase or decrease over time.[35]

If D is the amount of debt outstanding at the beginning of a year and i is the interest rate paid on the debt, the amount of taxes, T, necessary to cover the interest charge on the debt for the year is, of course, equal to Di. The fraction of national income, Y, that must be taken through taxation for debt service may be represented by t. Thus, the tax rate for debt service is

[35] See "The 'Burden of the Debt' and the National Income," in *American Economic Review*, Dec. 1944, pp. 798–827, reprinted in his *Essays in the Theory of Economic Growth*, Oxford Univ. Press, 1957, pp. 35–69.

$$t = \frac{T}{Y}$$

or

$$t = \frac{Di}{Y}$$

Dividing both numerator and denominator by Di, we have

$$t = \frac{1}{Y/Di}$$

or

$$t = \frac{1}{(1/i)(Y/D)}$$

From this it may be seen that the tax rate necessary for debt service depends on the ratio of income to the size of the debt multiplied by the rate of interest.[36] If the rate of interest is constant, the tax rate depends only on the ratio of income to debt.

If the debt grows continually over time and income does not, it is apparent that the tax rate for debt service will approach 100 percent. This will happen even if income grows by some absolute amount each year while each year's borrowing remains equal to some fixed percentage of income. However, if income grows at a constant percentage rate and borrowing remains equal to some fixed percentage of income, the required tax rate approaches

$$t = \frac{1}{(1/i)(G/b)}$$

in which G is the rate of growth of income and b is the ratio of deficit to income. This means that if i, G, and b are each 3 percent, taxes necessary for debt service will be 3 percent of income. If the rate of interest on the debt and the fraction of income borrowed remain at 3 percent each year, a doubling of the growth rate to 6 percent will reduce the tax rate for debt service to 1.5 percent and cut the debt burden in half; conversely, a halving of the growth rate to 1.5 percent per year will raise the tax rate for debt service to 6 percent and double the debt burden. Alternatively, if the deficit rises from 3 to 4 percent of income (with no

---

[36] This overstates the required tax rate somewhat, for the tax base actually includes interest paid by government as well as income in the sense of national income. To allow for this, we might write

$$t = \frac{Di}{Di + Y}$$

or

$$t = \frac{1}{1 + (Y/Di)}$$

or

$$t = \frac{1}{1 + (1/i)(Y/D)}$$

change in the interest rate on the debt), there will be no increase in the tax rate needed for debt service and no increase in debt burden if the growth rate rises from 3 to 4 percent.

How is all this related to our immediate problem of the use of fiscal policy for stabilization purposes? If fiscal policy can succeed in maintaining the system at full employment, even though it does so only at the cost of a rising national debt, the maintenance of full employment will be reflected over time in a more rapid rate of growth of income. Therefore, the tax rate required to service the constantly growing national debt need not rise; indeed, it may actually fall. In other words, the relationship between G and b becomes the crucial one. A rise in b does not mean a greater debt burden if the rise in b is matched by an equal rise in G. Thus, the problem of minimizing the burden of a growing debt is closely related to the problem of maintaining a rapid rate of growth of income. Fiscal policy may contribute to a more rapid rate of growth in one way by help-ing to maintain reasonably full employment. Thus, the objection to the use of fiscal policy to avoid or overcome recession on the grounds that such policy means a rise in the national debt and a rise in the interest charge may not be a valid objection.

Macroeconomic Policy and Economic Growth

To the extent that we noted specific goals in the course of discussing monetary and fiscal policy, those goals were full employment and price stability. In this final note we look briefly at the contribution that monetary and fiscal policy may make to the other major goal—that of economic growth.

At present, whatever contribution monetary policy makes to this goal is essentially made indirectly through its contribution to the goals of full employ-ment and price stability. This follows from the fact that monetary policy in the United States is carried out almost entirely through general instruments of con-trol that do not attempt to direct resources into particular uses, such as the production of capital goods instead of the production of consumer goods—an allocation that, other things being equal, would raise the potential growth rate of the economy. Instead, the general controls are used to stimulate or restrain aggregate demand, as the situation requires, in an attempt to provide full utilization of resources without inflation, leaving it to the free forces of the market to determine resource allocation. However, because of their differ-ential impact on various sectors of demand, monetary controls are not without their effects on the distribution of total spending between capital goods and consumer goods, tight money restraining the former more than the latter. Nonetheless, this is merely an incidental by-product of the exercise of general controls.

It might be possible, by using monetary controls specifically designed for the purpose, to shift the allocation of resources away from the production of consumer goods to that of capital goods and thus toward a potentially more rapid rate of growth. As we noted earlier, however, controls of this type have been little used in this country, and there are serious doubts as to whether they can be so used without conflicting with the objectives of full employment and price stability and, what in the long run could be more serious, without adversely affecting the functioning of the free enterprise system as we know it today. Since monetary policy as practiced in this country does not deliberately aim at raising the fraction of resources devoted to investment, it does not work directly on the growth rate; but, to the degree that it helps maintain the economy at full employment with stable prices, it thereby indirectly helps provide a more rapid growth rate.

Fiscal policy appears better designed than monetary policy to influence the way resources are allocated between the production of capital goods and other goods in an economy operating at full employment. Several approaches are possible. For example, suppose that government raises tax rates to generate a budget surplus. This surplus (assuming no equal decrease in private saving) means there will be some increase in the economy's total saving at the existing full-employment level of income. The government can then direct the surplus into investment either through appropriate public expenditures, public lending to private investors, or retirement of public debt. Whichever route is followed, there will be no decrease in aggregate demand but a reallocation of income away from consumption spending to saving and the allocation of the greater amount of saving to investment, which is greater by the same amount. The increase in the fraction of the economy's output devoted to public or private capital formation increases the productive capacity of the economy and makes possible higher levels of consumption in the future.

If the route chosen is that of higher government spending, the type of spending of course makes a difference. Since it is specified that spending shall be for investment, a rise in transfer payments is out of the question; the bulk of such funds simply result in increased consumption spending. The government spending must thus be for goods and services. Spending for what kinds of goods and services is best designed to raise the growth rate? Notice that the question here is not the same as that posed when government purchases are increased for stabilization purposes. In that case the purpose of expanded expenditures is primarily to provide jobs and to lift real income and output to the full-employment level. The focus is on useful job-providing and output-stimulating government purchases, which at the same time must be of a nature that meet the short-run flexibility required for stabilization purposes. In the case of growth, on the other hand, the main objective of expanded expenditures is to increase the productive capacity of the economy. Here the focus is on expenditures for education, worker retraining, health, highways, slum clearance, research and development, and other purposes that are likely to contribute most to the long-run increase in the productive capacity and therefore in the potential growth rate of the economy. The stabilization and growth objectives cannot be neatly separated in practice, for the shorter-run objective of achieving stability and the longer-run objective of achieving more rapid growth are interrelated in such a way that any substantial success in the latter demands success in the former. Despite the fact that the two are interdependent, it is worth separating them as we have done in order to see that the spending policies called for by each may differ.

The tax system used to raise the government surplus will also make a difference in the net effect the disposition of the surplus will have on the growth rate. Again, the question is not the same as that encountered in employing variations in tax receipts for stabilization purposes. As an anti-inflationary measure, tax increases could be designed to fall heavily on investment, if it appeared that the excessive demand was primarily the result of a surge of investment spending. When employed for growth purposes, however, the tax increases should be designed to reduce consumption, increase saving, and thereby release resources for investment. To produce a surplus by shifting a greater share of the tax burden to the returns from investment may decrease private investment expenditures at the same time that the surplus is devoted to public investment expenditures. Other things being equal, the net increase in investment or the net shift in resources from production of consumption goods to capital goods will be less than it would be if the surplus had been raised by an increase in taxes, the burden of which would fall mainly on consumption. Hence, in terms of the growth objective itself, the appropriate tax policy is one that reduces the burden on business income (especially corporate) relative to that on labor income. An increase in saving is the objective, and the fraction of after-tax corporate income that is saved is far larger than the fraction of disposable personal income that is saved.

The surplus can, of course, be produced with no rise in tax receipts but with a decrease in government expenditures. To be consistent with the objective of stimulating growth through fiscal policy, the expenditures reduced should be those of a public consumption nature or those such as transfer payments used to finance private consumption. However, the difficulties noted earlier in reducing transfers as part of a stabilizing fiscal policy also apply here. In this approach, the surplus would be devoted as before to lending to private investors or to retirement of public debt, either of which would lead to increased private investment, or would be devoted to increasing government expenditures of an investment nature.

It must be emphasized that this brief examination of the way in which monetary and fiscal policy may contribute to a more rapid rate of growth has been based on the assumption that the economy was operating at reasonably full employment with price stability. In practice, however, it should be evident that one will not be able to ignore the objectives of maintaining full employment and price stability tomorrow, even though they may be realized today, in order simply to concentrate attention on policies aimed at the goal of more rapid growth. Maintaining economic stability is a problem that must be faced day after day.

Furthermore, there are goals such as economic justice and economic freedom to which we have paid no attention in our concentration on several others, but these are goals that cannot be properly ignored. With the recognition of a number of goals, we also come to the conflicts that inevitably arise in concurrently chasing them all. Monetary and fiscal policies are at any time what they are as a result of compromises made in order to meet, as best they can be met, the conflicts encountered in the simultaneous pursuit of these multiple goals.

Finally, just as there are goals other than full employment, price stability, and growth, there are policies other than monetary and fiscal. Although our introduction to policy has attempted no more than to scratch the surface of monetary and fiscal policies, it should be noted again that other policies such as labor, agricultural, antitrust, and branches even more finely classified are all relevant in one way or another to the multiple goals before us in the real world. Thus, government is faced with the extremely complicated task of formulating and coordinating policies so that one policy does not defeat the purpose of another and so that the pursuit of one goal through various policies does not impose an unacceptable sacrifice of other goals. The contribution that such well-coordinated policies can make to the economic well-being of the nation's people can be as great as the problem of devising such policies is complex.

INDEX

(Italic page numbers indicate illustrations)